Major Problems in the Era of the
American Revolution 1760–1791

MAJOR PROBLEMS IN AMERICAN HISTORY SERIES

GENERAL EDITOR

THOMAS G. PATERSON

Major Problems in the Era of the American Revolution 1760–1791

DOCUMENTS AND ESSAYS

EDITED BY

RICHARD D. BROWN

UNIVERSITY OF CONNECTICUT

D. C. HEATH AND COMPANY
Lexington, Massachusetts   Toronto

Address editorial correspondence to:

D. C. Heath
125 Spring Street
Lexington, MA 02173

Cover: "Battle of Princeton" (detail) Historical Society of Pennsylvania. Photography: Bridgeman Art Library.

Published simultaneously in Canada.

Printed in the United States of America.

International Standard Book Number: 0-669-19755-6

Library of Congress Catalog Number: 91-70711

10 9 8 7 6 5 4 3 2 1

For my students

Preface

The Revolution and the formation of the Constitution rank as seminal events in the history of the United States—on this historians certainly agree. But when they explore the meaning of these events and their causes and consequences, agreement yields to controversy. Because the Revolution and Constitution stand at the foundation of the history of the United States and are central to establishing the legitimacy of American political and social viewpoints, Americans of all regions, classes, and origins have argued about their significance for generations. The events themselves are complex and multifaceted; moreover, they have been susceptible to diverse interpretations that are at once reasonable yet conflicting. For the student this may be a source of confusion, or worse, cynicism. If, after all, scholars cannot agree, and if the meaning of history itself changes from one decade to the next, why bother?

Why bother? This is a serious question that every teacher and student must confront. The first reason is that knowledge of the foundation of the United States is an essential part of being an educated citizen. To learn classic American historical texts such as the Declaration of Independence and the First Amendment is crucial for mastering the vocabulary of American culture.

A second, even more important reason to study the Revolution and Constitution is to position oneself to evaluate the public claims that politicians, journalists, lawyers, the clergy, educators, and others make regarding the meaning of these historical events. Anyone who listens to public discussion will find aspects of the Revolution and Constitution employed to justify a wide range of current domestic policies—whether abortion rights, affirmative action, gun control, school busing, tax support for private schools, censorship questions, or national programs for health insurance. In foreign policy, human rights, democracy, and freedom are regularly invoked to justify the giving or withholding of foreign aid and to support decisions of war and peace. Anyone who seeks to judge the legitimacy of these claims—or who wants to draw on the reservoir of principles expressed in the Revolution and Constitution to defend their own arguments—must possess a genuine familiarity with what happened.

A third, and more personal reason for studying the Revolutionary origins of the United States, is to locate oneself better in the moving stream of American history. Because the study of the Revolution and Constitution permits one to grasp some of the essential features of American politics, society, and culture, it enables us to make informed judgments about where we stand personally in relation to the past. As with all other historical study, it enables us to distinguish what is fundamental and durable from what is casual and transitory.

Like the other volumes in the series, *Major Problems in the Era of the American Revolution 1760–1791* approaches its subject in two ways: first, through primary sources; and second, through the interpretations of distinguished scholars. In both cases headnotes provide background information to enhance the reader's understanding of the selection. Enabling students to confront documents from the period directly is essential for grasping control of the subject. Nothing else is so empowering; for by reading the sources students can form their own opinions and measure the explanations of others against their own first-hand knowledge of the subject. The secondary essays supply interpretive possibilities. Because they are written by scholars who have read widely and deeply, they bring a sophistication to their topics that enables students to appreciate the complexity of events and to form discriminating judgments. Such active challenges between students, the primary sources, and the secondary texts encourage students to reach a lasting level of mastery of the Revolution and Constitution. When hour exams and finals have long faded from memory, knowledge of key texts like *Common Sense*, the *Declaration of Independence*, and the *Bill of Rights* endures, as does the understanding that the Revolution and the Constitution represent more than simple statements of democracy and freedom.

Assistance in preparing this volume has come from many historians, and I am grateful for their help. Several years ago, when I set about revising my own course on the Revolution and Constitution, I asked a number of scholars to share their syllabi with me. They are Fred Anderson, Lance Banning, Bernard Bailyn, Richard R. Beeman, Richard Buel, Richard L. Bushman, Robert M. Calhoon, Jere R. Daniell, Paul A. Gilje, Robert Gilmore, Robert A. Gross, Donald R. Hickey, Ronald Hoffman, Pauline Maier, Gary B. Nash, Thomas P. Slaughter, Alan Taylor, Gordon S. Wood, and Alfred F. Young. The course outlines and reading lists they so generously provided influenced my own course and have certainly affected the structure and selections in this book. In addition, I am grateful to Fred Anderson, Paul Bowers, Linda Grant De Pauw, Robert L. Ganyard, Richard R. Johnson, David W. Robson, and James Ronda, who read and criticized the manuscript for D. C. Heath. My colleague, Professor Thomas G. Paterson, the general editor of this series, made many valuable suggestions, and even took time to edit my prose. The D. C. Heath staff also deserves particular thanks. Developmental editor Sylvia Mallory, who supervised the overall design and editing process, was always cordial and constructive. Margaret Roll, the permissions editor, and Ron Hampton, the production editor, both contributed their professional skills unstintingly to this project. Overall, an author could not ask for a better team with which to work.

Finally, I am grateful to my students, undergraduate and graduate alike. Their questions and challenges, smiles and frowns, responsiveness and puzzlement—yes, and even yawns—have helped me learn about teaching as well as history.

R. D. B.

Contents

C H A P T E R   4

When Worlds Collide: From the Tea Act to the Declaration of Independence, 1773–1776

Page 130

C H A P T E R   5

Forging a National Army and Framing an International Alliance, 1776–1778

Page 189

CHAPTER 6

Struggling Toward Victory, 1779–1783

Page 222

CHAPTER 7

Casualties of Revolution: The Native Americans and the Loyalists- lose WAR

Page 259

C H A P T E R   8
Defining the Boundaries of Liberty for Women and African-Americans
Page 300

CHAPTER 9
The Challenge of Religious Freedom in a Christian Republic
Page 352

CHAPTER 10
The Articles of Confederation and the Achievements of National Union,
1781–1787
Page 389

CHAPTER 13
Ratification Politics and the Bill of Rights
Page 522

CHAPTER 14
Leadership and Heroism in the Revolutionary Era
Page 573

Interpreting the American Revolution

⚹

The meaning of the American Revolution, and even a precise definition of what it was, can never be established with absolute finality. The movement to independence and for the creation of the national republic—which lasted a full generation, from about 1763 to about 1789—was too rich in its variety of events, too intricate in its workings, and too heterogeneous in its participants and their motives to allow for a single incontestable and definitive interpretation. Moreover, because the Revolution was the crucial event for the formation of American nationality, our current sense of the United States must always influence the ways in which we see and understand the Revolution. Americans, who have most often and most thoroughly investigated the Revolution, cannot view it with complete detachment. We can and do learn more about what happened, but we cannot expect to fix the meaning of events permanently.

Yet certain coherent schools of general interpretation have been widely accepted during the past two centuries. A brief synopsis of them reveals the continuing vitality of some themes and helps us to place present-day interpretations in perspective. It is reasonable to begin with the ''Whig'' interpretation because it was the earliest, most durable viewpoint and has shaped debate over the Revolution from the era of its first appearance in the early republic.

The Whig view was initially articulated by victorious participants in the independence movement like David Ramsay, the South Carolina clergyman, and Mercy Otis Warren, the Massachusetts writer and a relative of patriot partisans. Their writings presented the Revolution as a movement for liberty in opposition to British tyranny. In the Whig interpretation's most full-blown, mid-nineteenth-century expression, the historian and Jacksonian Democrat George Bancroft explained the Revolution as a heroic struggle in which hardy yeoman farmers and idealistic merchants and planters took arms so as to defend their political liberty. In the process, they fashioned a democratic republic that became a model of free government for the rest of the world. This interpretation of the Revolution lay at the foundation of American nationalism and has been closely associated with patriotism. Until the beginning of the twentieth century, it was

1

the standard interpretation, favored by scholars, schoolteachers, journalists, and politicians alike.

Although the Whig view has never been wholly swept away from popular culture, it was effectively challenged at the turn of the twentieth century by university scholars such as George Louis Beer and Charles McLean Andrews, who, together with their students, most notably Lawrence Henry Gipson, formulated a new "imperial" interpretation based on British archival sources. They "discovered" that Britain had never intended to impose tyranny in the colonies, and they agreed with eighteenth-century British officials that in fact the colonists were a free people flourishing under imperial rule. Independence, these scholars explained, resulted from transatlantic misunderstandings and bureaucratic and parliamentary mismanagement. Although Britain was generally well intentioned, its system was haphazard, and its officials were clumsy. This interpretation did not erase notions of patriotic idealism or heroics, but it made them incidental. The key to understanding the Revolution, according to this school, lay in grasping British political culture on both sides of the Atlantic and the inadequacies of the imperial system for responding to changing issues and demands.

About the same time that the imperial school took root among American scholars, a new, critical viewpoint was articulated by political scientists, essayists, and historians, among them Charles A. Beard, Carl M. Becker, and Arthur M. Schlesinger. Their views, which came to be labeled "Progressive," focused on economic and political self-interest as the central motives propelling the Revolution. Indeed, the dynamic forces that shaped the movement for independence and the formation of state and national government were conflicts between merchants and farmers, easterners and westerners, city dwellers and country folk, aristocrats and democrats, creditors and debtors. Pulling patriotic icons like Washington, Hamilton, and Jefferson down from their pedestals, Progressive interpreters maintained that the same kinds of flesh-and-blood political contests characteristic of their own era were also operating at the nation's founding.

During the 1930s and 1940s this interpretation became widely established, in both academe through the writings of such scholars as Merrill M. Jensen and popular culture, where the novelist Kenneth Roberts used Progressive ideas in several best-selling novels about the Revolution. This interpretation made the Revolution relevant to contemporary political struggles. Like the older Whig interpretation, it has retained vitality and is particularly attractive to critics of national complacency and the status quo. But during the generation following World War II and in the 1950s especially, it was effectively challenged by scholars such as the political scientist Louis M. Hartz and the historian Richard E. Hofstadter.

Their works, influenced by a more global perspective and by a comparison of the American Revolution with the revolutions of France, Russia, and China, emphasized the broad republican consensus that the Revolutionaries shared, their commitment to pragmatic politics, and their affinity for practical compromises. Here there was no significant right-wing party that favored a hereditary system, just as there was no substantial support for social leveling and attacks on private property. American Revolutionaries might argue over tactics, but they were, it was said, generally united around the liberal, Lockean idea of a republic grounded on widespread property ownership and a state committed to fostering individual rights and opportunities. Because a mood of national unity prevailed during the postwar and cold war eras, this "consensus" interpretation had an appeal that made it popular far beyond the campus. As with the older Whig interpretation, it was popular among journalists, politicians, and schoolteachers.

of that fantastically successful political operator Robert Walpole. It was here, in the writings of the early-eighteenth-century opposition of both left and right—the left carrying forward with embellishments most of the radical notions of the seventeenth century, the right nourishing a nostalgia for a half-mythical rural world of stable hierarchical relations, but the two converging from these opposite poles to blast the bloated Leviathan of government they saw developing before them—it was in this populist cry against what appeared to be a swelling financial–governmental complex fat with corruption, complaisant and power-engrossing—in this shrill alarm of alienated intellectuals, outraged moralists, and frustrated politicians, that English radical thought took on the forms that would most specifically determine the outbreak and character of the American Revolution and that thereafter in vital respects would shape the course of American history.

These notions—derived, as I have suggested, from the early seventeenth century, fundamentally redeveloped in and immediately after the Exclusion Crisis, but now in the early eighteenth century given definitive shape by the political opposition—had great power; they carried great conviction; and they fitted neatly the peculiar circumstances of American social and political life. Bearing into the new, modern age of Walpole the traditional anti-statist convictions of seventeenth-century liberalism, the opposition's program was yet distinct in its insistence that all power—royal or plebiscitarian, autocratic or democratic—was evil: necessary, no doubt, for ordered life, but evil nevertheless in the threat it would always pose to the progress of liberty. The opposition's claims were distinct too in their insistence that the primary wielders of power must be kept apart, sealed off from collusive contact with each other in institutions defined by the principles of "mixed" government. And they were distinct, finally, in their heightened emphasis on the dangers of corruption—the corruption of massed wealth, the corruption of luxury, the corruption of indolence and moral obtuseness, all of which threatened to destroy the free British constitution and the rights it protected.

To Americans in distant provinces, faced with local governments that seemed at times to violate the basic precepts of political freedom; ultimately governed not by visible human beings they could acknowledge as natural leaders but by an unseen capricious, unmanageable, but fortunately quite benignly neglectful sovereign; and bred into a Protestant culture whose deeply-lying moralism was repeatedly stirred by waves of evangelical fervor—to such people, all of this made the most profound kind of sense, and it shaped their political awareness. Repeatedly through the middle years of the eighteenth century factional leaders responded to local crises by invoking these ideas—not testing their limits or probing their implications, not even applying them systematically, but drawing on them almost casually, and repeatedly, when it seemed appropriate in attacking the power of the state. Then, in the 1760s and 1770s, when the colonists believed themselves faced, not as heretofore with local threats but with an organized pan-Atlantic effort of highly placed autocrats to profit by reducing the free way of life the colonists had known—a "design" set on foot by manipulators of the colossus "at home"—they were led by the force of these ideas, reinforced by suddenly articulated views of the imperial constitution and by the latest formulations of the English radicals, into resistance and revolution.

The noble ideas of the Enlightenment and the abstracted principles of constitutional law were present in the responses of the colonists, but they do not form the immediate, instrumental grasp of their minds. They do not explain the triggering of the insurrection. That is explicable only in terms of that elaborate pattern of middle-level beliefs and ideas that formed for these colonial Britishers the map of social and political reality—a map, originally formed within early-seventeenth-century English libertarianism, fundamentally reshaped during and just after the Exclusion Crisis, modernized for the eighteenth century by the political opposition, the alienated intelligentsia, and the vigilant moralists of Walpole's time, and diffused by an intricate process of cultural dissemination through the political culture of the American colonies. No simpler genealogy can explain the derivation of America's Revolutionary ideology. There was no singular application of something scholars would later call "civic humanism" or "classical republicanism," nor were these ideas felt to be incompatible with what would later be described as "liberalism." The sanctity of private property and the benefits of commercial expansion, within customary boundaries, were simply assumed—the Revolution was fought in part to protect the individual's right to private property—nor were acquisitiveness, the preservation of private possessions, and reasonable economic development believed to be in necessary conflict with the civic rectitude that free, republican governments required to survive. Later, generations later, such a conflict might be seen to emerge in complex ways, but for the Revolutionary generation and its immediate successors these were harmonious values, implicit in a configuration of ideas that had evolved through critical passages of Anglo-American history.

But how, precisely, did these notions relate to political behavior? How simple and how unreal were the earlier assumptions either, on the one hand, that formal discourse and articulated belief bear directly on political processes or, on the other hand, that ideas are only epiphenomenal, superstructural, not the shapers of events but their rationalizations, and effectual only when wielded by propagandists whose professions are different from their true intent and whose aim is to manipulate the minds and so direct the actions of ignorant and suggestible masses. Both lead to confusion in interpreting an event like the Revolution. But both are resolvable into the concept of "ideology," which draws formal discourse into maps of reality—shifting patterns of values, attitudes, hopes, fears, and opinions through which people perceive the world and by which they are led to impose themselves upon it. Formal discourse can indeed be powerful in politics, but not because in some simple sense it constitutes motives or is a form of weaponry. Formal discourse becomes politically powerful when it articulates and fuses into effective formulations opinions and attitudes that are otherwise too scattered and vague to be acted upon; when it mobilizes a general mood; when it crystallizes otherwise inchoate social and political discontent and thereby directs it to attainable goals; when it clarifies, symbolizes, and elevates to structured consciousness the mingled urges that stir within us. But its power is not autonomous. It can only formulate, reshape, and direct forward moods, attitudes, ideas, and aspirations, rooted in social reality, that in some form, however crude or incomplete, already exist.

It is in these terms that ideas—not disembodied abstractions of the *philosophes*, or the formal arguments of constitutional lawyers, or the pure principles of "civic humanism" or of "classical republicanism," but the integrated set of values, beliefs, attitudes, and responses that had evolved through a century and a half of Anglo-American history—may be understood to have lain at the heart of the Revolutionary outbreak and to have shaped its outcome and consequences. The colonists—habituated to respond vigorously to acts of arbitrary rule; convinced that the existence of liberty was precarious even in the loosely governed provinces of the British-American world; more uncertain than ever of what the intricate shufflings in the distant corridors of power in England portended; and ever fearful that England's growing corruption would destroy its capacity to resist the aggressions of ruthless power seekers—saw behind the actions of the ministry not merely misgovernment and not merely insensitivity to the reality of life in the British overseas provinces but a deliberate design to destroy the constitutional safeguards of liberty. Only concerted resistance—violent resistance if necessary—could effectively oppose this threat. Within the ideological context of the time and in communities whose overall political structure was fragile and prone to conflict and in which direct, "mob" action against obnoxious authorities was familiar—in this situation forceful resistance became, for many, imperative, as did the effort that followed to build still stronger bastions against the inevitable aggressions of power.

The outbreak of the Revolution was not the result of social discontent, or of economic disturbances in the colonies, or of rising misery. Nor was there a transformation of mob behavior or of the lives of the inarticulate in the pre-Revolutionary years that accounts for the disruption of Anglo-American politics. The rebellion took place in a basically prosperous, if temporarily disordered economy and in communities whose effective social distances, for freemen, remained narrow enough and whose mobility, social and spatial, however it may have slowed from earlier days, was still high enough to absorb most group discontents. Nor was it the consequence simply of the inevitable growth of infant institutions and communities to the point where challenges to the parental authority became inescapable: neither institutions nor communities are doomed to grow through phases of oedipal conflict. There was good sense in the expectation occasionally heard in the eighteenth century that American institutions in time would gradually grow apart from Britain's, peacefully attenuating until the connection became mere friendly cooperation. American resistance in the 1760s and 1770s was a response to acts of imperial power deemed arbitrary, degrading, and uncontrollable—a response that was inflamed to the point of explosion by ideological currents generating fears everywhere in America that irresponsible and self-seeking adventurers—what the twentieth century would call political gangsters—had gained the power of the British government and were turning first to the colonies.

Inflamed sensibilities—exaggerated distrust and fear—surrounded the hard core of the Anglo-American constitutional conflict and gave it distinctive shape. These perceptions and anxieties made accommodation at first difficult and then impossible. By 1773 there was a widespread suspicion, primarily in New England but elsewhere as well, that the source of the conflict could be traced to actions taken by Governor Thomas Hutchinson of Massachusetts and a few of his colleagues in office. This long-respected scion of generations of enterprising New England leaders, it was believed, had deliberately misinformed the British ministry on the intentions and opinions of the colonists in order to advance his personal interests with the venal gang in Whitehall. Conversely, Hutchinson himself and most of the ministry believed that a clique of ruthless colonial demagogues headquartered in Boston was deliberately misinforming the American populace on the ministry's intentions in order to advance their own interests. Perhaps only Benjamin Franklin, who loved England, though somewhat despairingly, and who yet knew himself to be the embodiment to all the world of the hopes and possibilities of America, fully understood not only the substantive issues on both sides of the controversy but also the haze of misunderstandings that surrounded it. Believing that given sufficient time America's natural wealth and power would make its claims to British rights irresistible, he attempted, in one of the most revealing and consequential episodes of the early 1770s, to head off the approaching struggle by manipulating popular fears for what he took to be the general good. By arranging for the circulation of certain of Hutchinson's private letters of the late 1760s, he publicly documented the general suspicions of the governor's "deliberate misrepresentations" and, in thus pinning the blame for the conflict on Hutchinson, sought to exonerate the ministry and gain time for fresh approaches to reconciliation. But though Franklin's calculations were careful and sharp, he failed, in his long sojourn in England, to gauge correctly the intensity of the political and moral passions of the majority of his countrymen. The publication of Hutchinson's letters, bound, in the circumstance, to be considered incriminating, far from easing the conflict, intensified it. The "revelation" gave visible, human, and dramatic form to what previously had only been general, vague, and disputable surmises; it "proved" to an outraged public that purpose, not ignorance, neglect, or miscalculation, lay behind the actions of the British government and that reconciliation was therefore unlikely. Only Franklin, characteristically, landed on his feet. While the publication of Hutchinson's letters destroyed the Massachusetts governor and intensified the growing conflict, it helped transform the hitherto ambiguous Pennsylvanian into a popular Revolutionary hero.

All of which, as an explanation of the primary cause of the Revolution, is no more "intellectual" or "idealist" or "neo-Whig" than locating the origins of World War II in the fear and hatred of Nazism. It does not minimize the long-term background of the conflict but presumes it; it does not drain the Revolution of its internal social struggles, its sectional divisions, and its violence; it does not minimize the social and political changes that the Revolution created; it does not deny—indeed it alone explains—the upsurge of reformist zeal that is so central a part of the Revolution; nor does it rob the military struggle of its importance. It merely explains why at a particular time the colonists rebelled, and establishes the point of departure for the constructive efforts that followed.

II

Such, in my view, is the central theme of the origins of the Revolution. But this is, of course, only a beginning of an understanding of the meaning of the Revolution as a whole and of its role in shaping the course of American history. Yet seeing the origins of the Revolution this way makes it possible to come a bit closer to the stage of maturity in historical interpretation where partisanship is left behind, where historians, without abandoning their moral vision, can find an equal humanity in all the participants, the winners and the losers, where they can embrace the whole of the event, see it from all sides, mark out the latent limitations within which all the actors were obliged to act, and trace the influence of the event until it fades indistinguishably into the flow of history that succeeds it. It makes it possible, I believe, to understand the loyalists.

For a century and a half after the Revolution the loyalists' story was the subject of the fiercest and blindest partisanship that can be found anywhere in American historiography. The earliest patriotic chroniclers of the Revolution saw the loyalists as the worst of all enemies: traitors, betrayers of their own people and homeland. Just as they portrayed the Founding Fathers as flawless paragons commanding the almost universal allegiance of the population, so they saw the leading loyalists as craven sycophants of a vicious oligarchy, parasites of the worst corrupters of the *ancien régime,* and they simply blasted them into oblivion. Conversely, Tory historians in England, followed in a modified way in our own time by certain of the more scholarly "imperialist" historians, saw the loyalists much as the loyalists saw themselves, as sensible embodiments of law and order and of a benign rule against which a deluded and hysterical mass, led by demagogues, threw themselves in a frenzy. In recent years, it is true, the polemics have subsided, and the writing on the loyalists is more informative than it has been before, but this more objective writing is largely descriptive, often enumerative if not quantitative in its approach, and it fails to grasp the central interpretative problem that is posed by the lives of the loyalists. For if we are now able to see the peculiar patterns of fears, beliefs, attitudes, perceptions, and aspirations that underlay the Revolutionary movement, we have not yet made clear why any sensible and well-informed person could possibly have opposed the Revolution. And until that is done, until, that is, we also look deliberately from the point of view of the losers at what later would appear to have been the progressive development, we will not understand what that development was all about; we will not understand the human reality against which the victors struggled, and hence we will not have the story whole or entirely comprehensible.

There are no obvious external characteristics of the loyalist group, aside from the natural fact that it contained many Crown officeholders. A multitude of individual circumstances shaped the decisions that were made to remain loyal to Britain. Nor are the inner characteristics of this large group obvious. The loyalists were neither especially corrupt nor especially stupid nor especially closed to the possibilities of the future. Many of them, aside from the one point in their politics, are indistinguishable from the many obscure patriots whose involvement with events was superficial and who simply drifted marginally one way instead of the other in response to immediate pressures. Yet within the leadership of the loyalist group there appears to have been an essential if rather elusive characteristic, or set of characteristics, which, properly understood, illuminates the affirmative side of the Revolutionary movement that the loyalists resisted at such great cost.

Committed to the moral as well as the political integrity of the Anglo-American system as it existed, the loyalist leaders were insensitive to the moral basis of the protests that arose against it. Habituated for the most part to seek gains through an intricate and closely calibrated world of patronage and status, they did not respond to the aroused moral passion and the meliorative, optimistic, and idealist impulses that gripped the Revolutionaries' minds and that led them to condemn as corrupt and oppressive the whole system by which their world was governed. They did not sense the constrictions that the ruling order imposed on the naturally evolving currents of American life, or the frustration it engendered in those who failed to gain the privileges it could bestow. They could find only persistent irrationality in the arguments of the discontented and hence wrote off all of their efforts as politically pathological. And in a limited sense they were right. For the Revolutionary leaders, in their effort somehow to control a world whose political logic was a product of the system it explained, groped for conceptions that could not exist within the received framework of political ideas. They drew on convictions that ran deeper than logic and mobilized sources of political and social energy that burst the boundaries of received political and social wisdom. All of this is reflected in the loyalists' efforts to come to terms with the developing Revolution. They were outplayed, overtaken, bypassed.

Loyal officials who had risen within the narrow and complex passages of the old political system could not govern a morally aroused populace; they could not assimilate these new forces into the old world they knew so well. Thus Thomas Hutchinson, in refusing to approve a bill of 1771 prohibiting the slave trade in Massachusetts, said he could not believe that the motives of the supporters of the bill were what they said they were, namely, "a scruple . . . of the lawfulness in a merely moral respect of so great a restraint of liberty." After all, he wrote, technically in the eyes of Massachusetts law slaves were no worse off than servants bound "for a term of years exceeding the ordinary term of human life": they could not lawfully be executed by their masters, and it was even conceivable—though he admitted the point had never been determined—that they might own property.

Failing to carry the new, ideologically explosive politics with them by arguments and tactics that were familiar to them, failing often even to comprehend the nature of the forces that opposed them, and lacking both the means and the desire to control the turbulent communities by brute power, the loyalist leaders were forced to become devious simply to survive. Inevitably, therefore, they appeared hypocritical, ultimately conspiratorial, though in fact most of them were neither. As the pressure mounted, their responses narrowed. Their ideas became progressively more rigid, their imagination more limited, until in the end they could only plead for civil order as an absolute end in itself, which not only ignored the sources of the conflict but appeared unavoidably to be self-serving.

There is no better testimony to the newness of the forces that were shaping the Revolutionary movement than the failure of the loyalists to control them.

III

Some such understanding of the loyalists, or at least their leaders, must have a place in a general history of the Revolution consistent with what we now know of its origins. A further and perhaps more difficult challenge lies in interpreting within the same general theme the years that followed independence and that culminated in the permanent construction of the national government. For the developments of those years are of a different order from those of the years that preceded independence. The central and unifying themes shift; the approach that allowed one to understand the main events of the earlier years no longer serves for the later: a different kind of analysis and a different focus of attention are required.

The dominant fact of the earlier years had been the intensification of the ideological passions first ignited by the Stamp Act crisis and their final bursting into open insurrection. Thereafter the ideas, fears, and hopes that had first become decisive in the attacks on the British government were turned to positive uses in the framing of the first state constitutions, in the transforming of regressive social institutions that had been casually accepted in the ancien régime, and in directing Americans' efforts to new goals altogether: in education, in law, in religion, and in the distribution of land. But the Revolutionary spirit was changing as the original élan slowly filtered through the ordinary activities of life. The initial outburst, in which in some degree the majority of the colonists shared, could not be sustained, nor could the agreement on essentials that had brought together quite disparate groups. Passions cooled as ordinary life reasserted itself and cultural, sectional, and social differences, some of them newly created by the war and the displacement of the loyalists, became important. In the 1780s and 1790s the essential themes of American history became more complicated than they had been in the years before 1776. The creation of the American republic in the period between 1776 and the end of Washington's administration is the product of a complex interplay between the maturing of Revolutionary ideas and ideals and the involvements of everyday life—in politics, in business, and in a wide range of social activities.

A single characteristic of this later Revolutionary period predominates. Despite depressions, doubts, and fears for the future and despite the universal easing of ideological fervor, the general mood remained high through all of these years. There was a freshness and boldness in the tone of the eighties, a continuing belief that the world was still open, that young, energetic, daring, hopeful, imaginative men had taken charge and were drawing their power directly from the soil of the society they ruled and not from a distant, capricious, unmanageable sovereign. It was not simply that new liberty-protecting forms of government were being devised. A new civilization, it was felt, a civilization whose origins could now be seen to have lain in the earliest years of settlement, was being created, free from the weight of the past, free from the corruption and inflexibility of the tangled old-regime whose toils had so encumbered Americans in the late colonial period. Some sense of this had existed before independence, but unevenly, polemically, and without a generalized sanction. On a few rare occasions writers and preachers like Jonathan Mayhew had sketched a vision of future American grandeur; a sense of American separateness had begun to be felt and expressed and had been reinforced now and then from abroad; and in Congregational circles the sense of special mission that had gripped the minds of the Puritan settlers had in modified form persisted. But these had been scattered responses and expressions, constrained within the limits of a provincial culture whose metropolitan center had lain in the distant and ancient complexity of London.

If the colonists in the 1760s had been a "youthful" people, their mood had surely belied it. Nothing so clearly documents the transforming effect of the Revolution as the elevation of spirit, the sense of enterprise and experimentation, that suddenly emerged with independence and that may be found in every sphere of life in the earliest years of the new republic. This expectant stretching and spirited striving can be found in the systematic and ruthlessly aggressive provisions made for opening up new lands in the west and for settling new governments within them—provisions that ignored the welfare of the native population, already devastated by the Revolutionary War. The aggressive spirit of the age can be found, too, in the surge of people westward, hopefully risking security for new and quite unknown possibilities; in the vast outburst of domestic trade and commercial enterprise, spilling out across state boundaries and overseas, into the once restricted markets of the West Indies and Spanish America, into the continent of Europe, into Alaska, Russia, and even China; in experimental finance and path-breaking forms of banking; in bold if not always successful diplomacy; and above all in continuing experiments in government ranging from the recasting of public institutions and of the forms for recruiting leaders to the elimination or weakening of church establishments, the creation of federal relations among states, and a new concept of citizenship. Those years witnessed a release of American energies that swept forward into every corner of life. But in no simple way. The pattern is a complex one, in which ideological impulses move through the ordinary affairs of life, shape them, and are themselves reshaped by the pressures they meet.

In no area were these pressures more complex than in social organization. The background had been notably complex. For a century and a half conditions of life in these frontier communities had weakened the whole range of social reinforcements of traditional order. Yet, with complicated variations, a quasi-traditional order had existed, as had the sense that a proper social organization was hierarchical, with more or less clearly articulated levels of superiority and inferiority. The Revolution made changes in all of this, but not gross changes and not even immediately visible changes. There was no "leveling" of the social order and no outright destruction of familiar social institutions. "Democracy," in its modern form, was not created, in fact or theory, though the essential groundwork was laid. While the war, like so many wars before and since, transformed the economy and sped up mobility in significant ways, and while the displacement of the loyalists and the confiscation of much of their property created room at the top and sources of profit that had not existed before, no sweeping egalitarianism—in status, in wealth, or in power—was imposed. Newcomers to position and influence arrived more quickly and rose higher than they could have done earlier, but social distances remained much as before: narrow perhaps and rather easily bridgeable by European standards, but in local terms highly visible and palpable. And while the creation of new governments multiplied the available public offices and new men were everywhere seen in seats of power, and while the people as a whole were constitutionally involved in the processes of government as never before, socio-political elites whose origins went back a century persisted, apparently unaffected, in local communities, north and south.

And yet—everything was changing. The pressure of culturally sanctioned expectations had shifted to emphasize the status of free individuals as against the community and the integrity of their rights as against the powers of the state. The quasi-traditional society of the colonial period was not immediately destroyed, but the erosions that circumstance had made were not only multiplied, deepened, and broadened but ideologically reinforced as they had never been before. The effect upon a released society, developing economically, demographically, and institutionally at a remarkable rate, was transforming. The process of America's swift emergence as a distinctive society in the early nineteenth century we have scarcely begun to understand, but it is at least clear that the society Tocqueville found in America was the product of the gradually evolving interplay between a radical ideology and the circumstances of life in an expanding frontier world.

The convention at Philadelphia was a product of the same subtle interplay. The document it produced was neither a repudiation of '76, nor an instrument devised to protect aristocracies threatened in the states, nor an effort to preserve patrician rule, nor the product of a slaveholders' plot. It is a second-generation expression of the original ideological impulses of the Revolution applied to the everyday, practical problems of the late 1780s.

Young men, almost none of whom had played a major role in the struggle that had led to independence, took for granted what their predecessors had finally achieved and proceeded far beyond them, in circumstances that no one had foreseen. The old ideas and attitudes are there, but now they are viewed from different angles, in part reformulated, and applied to new problems. The fear of power is there, but so too is the inescapable need to create a government potentially more powerful than any yet known—a government complete with its own independent treasury based on the right to tax, a government equipped with all the apparatus of coercion that had proved so fearful a bane to the subjects of despotic regimes. New safeguards must be built; new possibilities explored in the balance of freedom and power. Consent of the governed and the idea of the actual representation of people are there as fundamental principles of government, but so too is the belief that the subjects of this government were not only people but states as well, whose sovereignty must be both preserved and dissolved in this newer and greater creation. The very concept of sovereignty must therefore be probed, and provision now deliberately made for just that inconceivable monster in politics—imperium in imperio, states within a state— that right-minded, liberal men had refused to consider barely a decade before. New, awkward, strange political, economic, and constitutional urgencies are everywhere there, impelling forward to an unknown terrain minds formed in an earlier Revolutionary world and loyal to its basic principles. The results were daring, too daring and too threatening for some, but they gave workable and hopeful solutions to inescapable problems, solutions devised by young minds using old notions in new experimental ways. In this sense the Constitution of 1787 was a typical creation of the age: hopeful, boldly experimental, realistic, and faithful to the urges and beliefs that had led to revolution.

IV

Such a view of the central themes of the Revolution helps one go beyond the immediate events of the Revolution itself and assess the most general meaning of the event in the broad sweep of eighteenth-century history and to isolate its impact on the overall course of American history.

There had been nothing inevitable in the outbreak of revolution. Deep flows of potentially revolutionary beliefs and apprehensions had moved through the delicate structure of mid-eighteenth-century American politics, but in the constitutional crisis of the 1770s there had been no necessity for these passionate concerns to break through the channels of civility. Even when an explosion in Anglo-American relations was generally expected, some knew ways to avoid it. Burke knew the way; so too, at least in the earlier years of crisis, did the preeminent victim of the Revolution, Thomas Hutchinson. But they, and others like them, lacked the power, and those who had the power lacked the concern and desire to avoid the confrontation. What was inevitable—what no one could have restrained—was America's emergence into the modern world as a liberal, more or less democratic, and capitalist society. That would have happened in any case. But that this emergence took place as it did—that it was impelled forward by a peculiar ideological explosion generated within a society less traditional than any then known in the Western world—this crucial fact has colored the whole of our subsequent history, and not only our own, but the world's.

How different elsewhere the process of modernization has been, and how important the differences are! In France, too, political modernization came through an eighteenth-century revolution, but there the prevailing ideas were radically egalitarian, directed to the destruction of a resistant, highly stratified social order dominated by a deeply entrenched nobility and capable of implementation only through a powerful, revolutionary state. The French Revolution created, at a cost of horrendous suffering and great bloodshed, a new state system more elaborate and more effective than the one it had overthrown, a state justified both by the dominant theories of revolution and by the belief that only such a power could dislodge the privileged world of the French ancien régime. In Germany two generations later an attempted liberal revolution failed altogether: its idealistic leaders lacked mass support, and could neither break through the protective barriers of the autocratic princely states nor free themselves from dependence on Prussian arms. Traditionalism thereafter deepened in Germany and produced in the end a dynamic industrial regime politically so paternalistic and socially so regressive that it constituted a threat to liberalism everywhere.

But it is the contrast with Britain that is ultimately most revealing. For Britain's was the parent political culture, and there too, as in America, well before the end of the eighteenth century, social and economic changes had eroded the traditional order and laid the groundwork for a modern liberal state. But the state that in fact resulted in nineteenth-century Britain was profoundly different from the American state; the two societies differed as much in politics as in social organization. The constitutional starting point had been the same: a balance of socio-constitutional forces in a theoretically "mixed" monarchical state. But Britain's political modernization, which eliminated the Crown and reduced the House of Lords as effective political forces while a slowly democratized and increasingly representative House of Commons rose to greater power, moved gradually, through decades of change. The reformers were the most pragmatic and the least theoretical of politicians; they were more Tory than Whig, and their goal was stability. Burke's and the Rockinghams' "economical reform" and Pitt's fiscal reorganization were pragmatic responses to political pressures and to the urgencies of war. Behind them lay no systematic effort to recast politics or the structure of the state, but they began the destruction of the system of "influence" through which the government for so long had been managed. And that was the merest beginning. Multiplying through the reigns of three weak and feckless kings, consolidated by threats from abroad and stresses at home, increments of change added bit by bit to the transforming of the eighteenth-century constitution. By the time of Peel's ministry of 1841 much was formally the same, but the essential structure had been rebuilt. All the powers of the state—executive, legislative, and administrative—had become concentrated in the majority leadership of the House of Commons, which was increasingly responsive to a broadening political world. The modern constitution, politics, and state had evolved slowly and had gradually re-shaped for modern use the system that Walpole had built. Somewhere deep within it there lay scattered elements of the ideas, fears, beliefs, and attitudes that had so engrossed the thoughts and so fired the imagination of opposition groups in eighteenth-century England and America; but they were now antique fragments, cemented haphazardly into the new radicalism of Bentham, the Chartists, and Mill.

In America, however, this earlier opposition ideology survived intact and fundamentally shaped the emerging state. The modernization of American politics and government during and after the Revolution took the form of a sudden realization of the program that had first been fully set forth by the opposition intelligentsia—the political moralists, the uncompromising republicans, the coffeehouse journalists, and the nostalgic Tories—in the reigns of the first two Georges. Where the English opposition of those years, forcing its way against a complacent social and political order, had only striven and dreamed, Americans, driven by the same aspirations but living in a society in many ways modern, and now released politically, could suddenly act. Where the English opposition had vainly agitated for partial reforms in the fierce debates that had raged over the duration of Parliaments, over restraints on the press, over standing armies, and over the force of wealth and patronage in corrupting popular rights, American leaders moved swiftly and with little social disruption to implement systematically the whole range of advanced ideas. In the process they not only built permanently into the modern American state system the specific constitutional and political reforms that had been vainly sought for so long in opposition circles, but also infused into American political culture two inner drives, two central spirits, that would distinguish it ever after.

The first is the belief that power is evil, a necessity perhaps but an evil necessity; that it is infinitely corrupting; and that it must be controlled, limited, restricted in every way compatible with a minimum of civil order. Written constitutions; the separation of powers; bills of rights; limitations on executives, on legislatures, and courts; restrictions on the right to coerce and to wage war—all express the profound distrust of power that lies at the ideological heart of the American Revolution and that has remained a permanent legacy. While in Britain the use of power became more concentrated in the passage to the modern state, and while in France and Germany it became more highly structured and more efficient, in America it became more diffused, more scattered, more open to suspicion, less likely ever to be unchallenged in the conduct of public life.

The distrust of power, generated deep within the ideological origins of the Revolution, runs through the entire course of American history and is a potent element in our national life today, when the instruments of power are so fearfully effective and the actuality of the state so overwhelming and inescapable.

Equally a part of our contemporary struggles is the second great theme that derives from the sources of Revolutionary ideology: the belief that through the ages it had been privilege—artificial, man-made and man-secured privilege, ascribed to some and denied to others mainly at birth—that, more than anything else except the misuse of power, had crushed men's hopes for fulfillment.

Not all of the early-eighteenth-century English opposition had been gripped by this belief. All elements had been concerned with corruption and with power, but this broad populist animus had drawn together quite different groups that shared only their common fear of the swollen politico-financial powers that, they believed, had created the Leviathan state. Some had been socially reactionary, or at least, like Bolingbroke, romantically nostalgic. They had sought not a broadening of the individual's self-determination but a return to a lost society of articulated statuses and elaborated hierarchies in which privilege counted for more rather than for less than it did in the modernizing world of eighteenth-century England. Americans had almost never shared these views, even in the proprietary and plantation colonies where the social reality might have seemed most congruous. When the Revolution moved from the negative, critical phase of the years before independence to the constructive era that followed, this reactionary strand of thought was simply ignored, to be taken up only occasionally thereafter by men who scarcely knew the context from which it was derived. The radical-libertarian impulse swept forward.

The dominant belief struck at the heart of the privileged world. Everywhere in America the principle prevailed that in a free community the purpose of institutions is to liberate people, not to confine them, and to give them the substance and the spirit to stand firm before the forces that would restrict them. To see in the Founders' failure to destroy chattel slavery the opposite belief, or some self-delusive hypocrisy that somehow condemns as false the liberal character of the Revolution—to see in the Declaration of Independence a statement of principles that was meant to apply only to whites and that was ignored even by its author in its application to slavery, and to believe that the purpose of the Constitution was to sustain aristocracy and perpetuate black bondage—is, I believe, to fundamentally misread the history of the time.

To condemn the founders of the Republic for having tolerated and perpetuated a society that rested on slavery is to expect them to have been able to transcend altogether the limitations of their own age. The eighteenth century was a brutal age. Human relations in British society were savage in a hundred different ways. In the placid countryside and sleepy market towns of eighteenth-century England, J. H. Plumb wrote,

> the starving poor were run down by the yeomanry, herded into jails, strung up on gibbets, transported to the colonies. No one cared. This was a part of life like the seasons, like the deep-drinking, meat-stuffing orgies of the good times and bumper harvests. The wheel turned, some were crushed, same favoured. Life was cheap enough. Boys were urged to fight. Dogs baited bulls and bears. Cocks slaughtered each other for trivial wagers. . . . Death came so easily. A stolen penknife and a boy of ten was strung up

at Norwich; a handkerchief, taken secretly by a girl of fourteen, brought her the noose. Every six weeks London gave itself to a raucous fete as men and women were dragged to Tyburn to meet their end at the hangman's hands. The same violence, the same cruelty, the same wild aggressive spirit infused all ranks of society. . . . Young aristocrats—the Macaronis—fantastically and extravagantly dressed, rip-roared through the town, tipping up night watchmen, beating up innocent men and women. Jails and workhouses resembled concentration camps; starvation and cruelty killed the sick, the poor and the guilty. . . . Vile slums in the overcrowded towns bred violent epidemics; typhoid, cholera, smallpox ravaged the land.

Chattel slavery was brutal and degrading, but as far as the colonists knew, slavery in one form or another had always existed, and if it was brutal and degrading, so too was much else of ordinary life at the lower levels of society. Only gradually were people coming to see that this was a peculiarly degrading and a uniquely brutalizing institution, and to this growing awareness the Revolution made a major contribution. To note only that certain leaders of the Revolution continued to enjoy the profits of so savage an institution and in their reforms failed to obliterate it inverts the proportions of the story. What is significant in the historical context of the time is not that the liberty-loving Revolutionaries allowed slavery to survive, but that they—even those who profited directly from the institution—went so far in condemning it, confining it, and setting in motion the forces that would ultimately destroy it. For they were practical and moderate men, though idealistic and hopeful of human progress. Their mingling of the ideal and the real, their reluctance to allow either element to absorb the other altogether, is one of the Revolution's distinctive features. And of this, as of so much else, Jefferson is the supreme exemplar. In him a ruthless practicality mingled so incongruously with a sublime idealism that his personality seemed to his enemies, as it has seemed to modern historians concentrating on his "darker side," to have been grossly lacking in integrity. All of the Founders hoped to create a free society in America; not all of them could, or would, recognize, as Jefferson did, that this could only end in the destruction of chattel slavery. And those who recognized this and who strove to break the hold of this vicious institution so long before its condemnation became a common moral stance acted within a system of priorities that limited what they could achieve.

The highest priority was reserved for whatever tended to guarantee the survival of the republican nation itself, for in its continuing existence lay all hopes for the future. Most of the Revolutionary leaders hated slavery—not one of them ever publicly praised it—but they valued the preservation of the Union more. A successful and liberty-loving republic might someday destroy the slavery that it had been obliged to tolerate at the start; a weak and fragmented nation would never be able to do so. The haters of slavery were also limited in what they could accomplish by their respect for property, which like personal liberty was also part of the liberal state they sought to create. And they were, finally, fearful of the unforeseeable consequences in race relations that would result if the slaves—to the colonists still mysteriously alien, politically backward, and at least latently hostile people—were suddenly set free. It took a vast leap of the imagination in the eighteenth century to consider integrating into the political community the existing slave population, whose very "nature" was the subject of puzzled inquiry and who had hitherto been politically nonexistent. But despite all of this, from the very earliest days of the Revolutionary movement the agonizing contradiction between chattel slavery and the freedom of a liberal state was seen, and the hope was formed that somehow, someday, the abhorrent practice of owning human beings would be destroyed. In the year of Jefferson's death slavery still existed, but it was destroyed in the North, forbidden in the Northwest, compressed deeper and deeper—and more and more explosively—into the South. An institution that had once been assumed and securely established had been challenged, confined, and transformed into an inescapable moral problem. If the Free Soilers of the 1850s, like the Republican platform writers of 1860, exaggerated the Founders' political commitment to the outright abolition of slavery, they correctly sensed the antislavery temper of the Revolutionary age. The ideological continuity between Jefferson and Lincoln is direct. However much their approach to the question of race may have differed, both deeply believed that slavery was wrong and ought to be restricted; both groped for ways of advancing that restriction; neither would destroy the Union to effect it.

The Founding Fathers were mortals, not gods; they could not overcome their own limitations and the complexities of life that kept them from realizing their ideals. But the destruction of privilege and the creation of a political system that demanded of its leaders the responsible and humane use of power were their highest aspirations. To note that the struggle to achieve these goals is still part of our lives—that it is indeed the very essence of the politics of our time—is only to say that the American Revolution, a unique product of the eighteenth century, is still in process. It will continue to be, so long as we seek to create a just and free society.

The Revolution's Roots in Urban Radicalism and Social Change

GARY B. NASH

Recent studies of the American Revolution have relied heavily on the role of ideas to explain the advent of the American rebellion against England. The gist of the ideological interpretation of the Revolution is that colonists, inheriting a tradition of protest against arbitrary rule, became convinced in the years after 1763 that the English government meant to impose in America "not merely misgovernment and not merely insensitivity to the reality of life in the British overseas provinces but a deliberate design to destroy the constitutional safeguards of liberty, which only concerted resistance—violent

Text by Gary B. Nash, "Social Change and the Growth of Prerevolutionary Urban Radicalism," from *The American Revolution: Explorations in the History of American Radicalism*, edited by Alfred F. Young, Copyright © 1976, pp. 5–32. Reprinted by permission of Northern Illinois University Press.

resistance if necessary—could effectively oppose." It was this conspiracy against liberty that "above all else . . . propelled [the colonists] into Revolution."*

An important corollary to this argument, which stresses the colonial defense of constitutional rights and liberties, is the notion that the material conditions of life in America were so generally favorable that social and economic factors deserve little consideration as a part of the impetus to revolution. "The outbreak of the Revolution," writes Bernard Bailyn, a leading proponent of the ideological school, "was not the result of social discontent, or of economic disturbances, or of rising misery, or of those mysterious social strains that seem to beguile the imaginations of historians straining to find peculiar predispositions to upheaval." Nor, asserts Bailyn, was there a "transformation of mob behavior or of the lives of the 'inarticulate' in the pre-Revolutionary years that accounts for the disruption of Anglo-American politics." Another historian, whose focus is economic change and not ideas, writes that "whatever it might have been, the American Revolution was not a rising of impoverished masses—or merchants—in search of their share of the wealth. The 'predicament of poverty,' in Hannah Arendt's phrase, was absent from the American scene"—so much so that even though the "secular trend in the concentration of wealth created an increasing gulf between the rich and the poor over the years separating 1607 and 1775, the fact remains that not only were the rich getting richer but the poor were also, albeit at a slower rate."

One of the purposes of this essay is to challenge these widely accepted notions that the "predicament of poverty" was unknown in colonial America, that the conditions of everyday life among "the inarticulate" had not changed in ways that led toward a revolutionary predisposition, and that "social discontent," "economic disturbances," and "social strains" can generally be ignored in searching for the roots of the Revolution. I do not suggest that we replace an ideological construction with a mechanistic economic interpretation, but argue that a popular ideology, affected by rapidly changing economic conditions in American cities, dynamically interacted with the more abstract Whig ideology borrowed from England. These two ideologies had their primary appeal within different parts of the social structure, were derived from different sensibilities concerning social equity, and thus had somewhat different goals. The Whig ideology, about which we know a great deal through recent studies, was drawn from English sources, had its main appeal within upper levels of colonial society, was limited to a defense of constitutional rights and political liberties, and had little to say about changing social and economic conditions in America or the need for change in the future. The popular ideology, about which we know very little, also had deep roots in English culture, but it resonated most strongly within the middle and lower strata of society and went far beyond constitutional rights

---

* Bailyn, "The Central Themes of the American Revolution: An Interpretation," in Stephen G. Kurtz and James H. Hutson, eds., *Essays on the American Revolution* (Chapel Hill: University of North Carolina Press, 1973), p. 12; this is an earlier version of the first essay in this volume, and includes the relevant footnote citations.

to a discussion of the proper distribution of wealth and power in the social system. It was this popular ideology that undergirded the politicization of the artisan and laboring classes in the cities and justified the dynamic role they assumed in the urban political process in the closing decades of the colonial period.

It is toward understanding this popular ideology and its role in the upsurge of revolutionary sentiment and action in the 1760s that this essay is devoted. Our focus will be on the three largest colonial cities—Boston, New York, and Philadelphia. Other areas, including the older, settled farming regions and backcountry, were also vitally important to the upwelling of revolutionary feeling in the fifteen years before 1776 and in the struggle that followed. But the northern cities were the first areas of revolutionary ferment, the communication centers where newspapers and pamphlets spread the revolutionary message, and the arenas of change in British North America where most of the trends overtaking colonial society in the eighteenth century were first and most intensely felt.

To understand how this popular ideology swelled into revolutionary commitment within the middle and lower ranks of colonial society, we must first comprehend how the material conditions of life were changing for city dwellers during the colonial period and how people at different levels of society were affected by these alterations. . . .

I

The most generally recognized alteration in eighteenth-century urban social structures is the long-range trend toward a less even distribution of wealth. Tax lists for Boston, Philadelphia, and New York, ranging over nearly a century prior to the Revolution, make this clear. By the early 1770s the top 5 percent of Boston's taxpayers controlled 49 percent of the taxable assets of the community, whereas they had held only 30 percent in 1687. In Philadelphia the top twentieth increased its share of wealth from 33 to 55 percent between 1693 and 1774. Those in the lower half of society, who in Boston in 1687 had commanded 9 percent of the taxable wealth, were left collectively with a mere 5 percent in 1771. In Philadelphia, those in the lower half of the wealth spectrum saw their share of wealth drop from 10.1 to 3.3 percent in the same period. It is now evident that the concentration of wealth had proceeded very far in the eighteenth-century cities.

Though city dwellers from the middle and lower ranks could not measure this redistribution of economic resources with statistical precision, they could readily discern the general trend. No one could doubt that upper-class merchants were amassing fortunes when four-wheeled coaches, manned by liveried Negro slaves, appeared in Boston's crooked streets, or when urban mansions, lavishly furnished in imitation of the English aristocracy, rose in Philadelphia and New York. . . . Wealth of this magnitude was not disguised in cities with populations ranging from about 16,000 in Boston to about 25,000 in New York and Philadelphia and with geographical expanses half as large as public university campuses today.

While urban growth produced a genuinely wealthy upper class, it simultaneously created a large class of impoverished city dwellers. All of the cities built almshouses in the 1730s in order to house under one roof as many of the growing number of poor as possible. . . . Beginning in Boston in the 1740s and in New York and Philadelphia somewhat later, poverty scarred the lives of a growing part of the urban populations. Among its causes were periodic unemployment, rising prices that outstripped wage increases, and war taxes which fell with unusual severity on the lower classes. In Boston, where the Overseers of the Poor had expended only £25–35 sterling per thousand inhabitants in the 1720s and 1730s, per capita expenditures for the poor more than doubled in the 1740s and 1750s, and then doubled again in the last fifteen years of the colonial period. Poor relief rose similarly in Philadelphia and New York after 1750. . . . The data on poor relief leave little room for doubt that the third quarter of the eighteenth century was an era of severe economic and social dislocation in the cities, and that by the end of the colonial period a large number of urban dwellers were without property, without opportunity, and, except for public aid, without the means of obtaining the necessities of life.

The economic changes that redistributed wealth, filled the almshouses to overflowing, and drove up poor rates also hit hard at the lower part of the middle class in the generation before the Revolution. These people— master artisans rather than laborers, skilled shipwrights rather than merchant seamen, shopkeepers rather than peddlers—were financially humbled in substantial numbers in Boston beginning in the 1740s and in Philadelphia and New York a dozen years later.

In Boston, this crumbling of middle-class economic security can be traced in individual cases through the probate records and in aggregate form in the declining number of "taxables." In that city, where the population remained nearly static, at about 15,500 from 1735 to the Revolution, the number of "rateable polls" declined from a high of more than 3,600 in 1785, when the city's economy was at its peak, to a low of about 2,500 around mid-century. By 1771, Boston's taxables still numbered less than 2,600. This decline of more than a thousand taxable adults was not caused by loss of population but by the sagging fortunes of more than 1,000 householders—almost one-third of the city's taxpaying population. . . . In Philadelphia, the decay of a substantial part of the "middling sort" similarly altered the urban scene, though the trend began later and did not proceed as far as in Boston. . . . Taxpayers dropped from the rolls because of poverty represented less than 3 percent of the taxables in the period before 1740, but they increased to about 6 to 7 percent in the two decades beginning in 1740, and then to one in every ten taxpayers in the fifteen years before the Revolution.

The probate records of Boston and Philadelphia tell a similar tale of economic insecurity hovering over the middle ranges of urban society. . . . Though many city dwellers had made spectacular individual ascents from the bottom, in the manner of Benjamin Franklin of Philadelphia or Isaac Sears of New York, the statistical chances of success for those beginning beneath the upper class were considerably less after the first quarter of the eighteenth century than before. The dominating fact of late colonial life for many middle-class as well as most lower-class city folk was not economic achievement but economic frustration.

II

Understanding that the cities were becoming centers of frustrated ambition, propertylessness, genuine distress for those in the lower strata, and stagnating fortunes for many in the middle class makes comprehensible much of the violence, protest, and impassioned rhetoric that occurred in the half-generation before the colonial challenge to British regulations began in 1764. Upper-class colonists typically condemned these verbal attacks and civil disorders as the work of the "rabble," the "mob," the "canaille," or individuals "of turbulent disposition." These labels were used to discredit crowd activity, and historians have only recently recognized that the "rabble" often included a broad range of city dwellers, from slaves and servants through laborers and seamen to artisans and shopkeepers—all of whom were directly or indirectly expressing grievances. Cutting across class lines, and often unified by economic conditions that struck at the welfare of both the lower and middle classes, these crowds began to play a larger role in a political process that grew more heated as the colonial period came to an end. This developing consciousness and political sophistication of ordinary city dwellers came rapidly to fruition in the early 1760s and thereafter played a major role in the advent of the Revolution.

Alienation and protest had been present in the northern cities, especially during periods of economic difficulty, since the early eighteenth century. In Boston, between 1709 and 1713, townspeople protested vigorously and then took extralegal action when Andrew Belcher, a wealthy merchant, refused to stop exporting grain during a bread shortage in the city. . . . Rank had no privileges, as even the lieutenant-governor was shot when he tried to intervene. Bostonians of meager means learned that through concerted action, the powerless could become powerful, if only for the moment. Wealthy merchants who would not listen to pleas from the community could be forced through collective action to subordinate profits to the public need. . . .

In Philadelphia, economic issues also set the mechanic and laborer against the rich as early as the 1720s. When a business recession brought unemployment and a severe shortage of specie (the only legal circulating medium), leading merchant-politicians argued that the problem was moral in nature. If the poor were unemployed or hungry, they had their own lack of industry and prudence to thank, wrote James Logan, a thriving merchant and land speculator. "The Sot, the Rambler, the Spendthrift, and the Slip Season," he charged, were at the heart of the slump. Schemes for reviving the economy with emissions of paper money were reckless attempts to cheat those who worked for their money instead of drinking their time away.

But, as in Boston, the majority of people were not fooled by such high-toned arguments. Angry tracts appeared on both sides of the debate concerning the causes and cure for recession. Those who favored paper money and called for restrictions on land speculators and monopolizers of the money market made an attack on wealth itself an important theme. Logan found bricks flying through his windows and a crowd threatening to level his house. . . . The "moral economy of the crowd," as E. P. Thompson has called it— the people's sense that basic rules of equity in social relations had been breached—had intervened when the rich would do nothing to relieve suffering in a period of economic decline. . . .

In Boston, resentment against the rich, focusing on specific economic grievances, continued to find voice in the middle third of the century. Moreover, since the forming of the caucus a generation before, well-coordinated street action channeled the wrath of townspeople against those who were thought to act against the interest of the commonality. In the 1730s an extended debate erupted on establishing a public market where prices and marketing conditions would be controlled. Many Bostonians in the lower and middle strata regarded a regulated public market as a device of merchants and fiscal conservatives to drive small retailers from the field and reap the profits of victualing Boston themselves. . . . The timbers of the public market which fell before the night raiders in 1737 showed how widely held was the conviction that only this kind of civil disobedience would "deliver the poor oppressed and distressed People out of the Hands of the Rich and Mighty." . . .

The growing sentiment in the cities against the wealthy was nourished by the Great Awakening—the outbreak of religious enthusiasm throughout the colonies beginning in the late 1730s. Although this eruption of evangelical fervor is primarily identified as a rural phenomenon, it also had powerful effects in the cities, where fiery preachers such as George Whitefield and Gilbert Tennant had their greatest successes. We have no study as yet of the Great Awakening in the cities, but clues abound that one important reason for its urban appeal was the fact that the evangelists took as one of their primary targets the growth of wealth and extravagance, accompanied by a dwindling of social concern in colonial America. Nowhere was this manifested more noticeably than in the cities.

The urban dwellers who thronged to hear George Whitefield in Philadelphia in 1739 and 1741 and those who crowded the Common in Boston to hear Whitefield and the vituperative James Davenport in the early 1740s were overwhelmingly from the "lower orders," so far as we can tell. What accounts for their "awakening" is the evangelists' presentation of a personal religion where humble folk might find succor from debt, daily toil, sickness, and want, and might express deeply felt emotions in an equality of fellowship. At the same time, the revivalist preachers spread a radical message concerning established authority. City dwellers were urged to partake in mass revivals, where the social distance between clergyman and parishioner and among worshippers themselves was obliterated. They were exhorted to be skeptical toward dogma and to participate in ecclesiastical affairs rather than bow passively to established hierarchy.

Through the Great Awakening, doctrinal controversy and attacks on religious leaders became widely accepted in the 1740s. In Boston the itinerant preacher James Davenport hotly indicted the rich and powerful and advised ordinary people to break through the crust of tradition in order to right the wrongs of a decaying society. It was the spectre of unlearned artisans and laborers assuming authority in this manner that frightened many upper-class city dwellers and led them to charge the revivalists with preaching levelism and anarchy. "It is . . . an exceedingly difficult, gloomy time with us . . . ," wrote one conservative clergyman from Boston. . . . Nor could the passing of the Awakening reverse the tide, for this new sense of power remained a part of the social outlook of ordinary people. In fact, the radical transformation of religious feeling overflowed into civil affairs. The new feeling of autonomy and importance was bred in the churches, but now it was carried into the streets. Laboring people in the city learned "to identify the millennium with the establishment of governments which derived their power from the people, and which were free from the great disparities of wealth which characterized the old world."

III

The crescendo of urban protest and extralegal activity in the pre-revolutionary decades cannot be separated from the condition of people's lives. Of course those who authored attacks on the growing concentration of wealth and power were rarely artisans or laborers; usually they were men who occupied the middle or upper echelons of society, and sometimes they were men who sought their own gain—installment in office, or the defeat of a competitor for government favors. But whatever their motives, their sharp criticisms of the changes in urban society were widely shared among humbler townspeople. . . . A rising tide of class antagonism and political consciousness, paralleling important economic changes, was a distinguishing feature of the cities at the end of the colonial period.

It is this organic link between the circumstances of people's lives and their political thought and action that has been overlooked by historians who concentrate on Whig ideology, which had its strongest appeal among the educated and well-to-do. The link had always been there, as detailed research into particular communities is beginning to show. But it became transparently clear in the late colonial period, even before England began demanding greater obedience and greater sacrifices in the colonies for the cause of the British Empire. The connection can be seen in New York in the 1760s, where the pleas of the impoverished against mercenary landlords were directly expressed in 1762, and where five years later the papers were pointing out that while the poor had vastly increased in recent years and while many families were selling their furniture at auction to pay their rent, carriage owners in the city had grown from five to seventy. The link can also be seen in Philadelphia, where growing restlessness at unemployment, bulging almshouses, rising poor taxes, and soaring prices for food and firewood helped to politicize the electorate and drew unprecedented numbers of people to the polls in the last decade of the colonial period.

However, it was in Boston, where poverty had struck first, cut deepest, and lasted longest, that the connection between changing urban conditions and rising political radicalism is most obvious. That it preceded the post-1763 imperial debate, rather than flowing from it, becomes apparent in a close examination of politics in that city between 1760 and 1765. . . .

The bitter Otis-Hutchinson fight of the early 1760s, carried on *before* English imperial policy became an issue in Massachusetts, revolved around a number of specific issues, including the replacement of William Bollan as provincial agent, the establishment of an Anglican mission in the shadow of Harvard College, the multiple offices held by Hutchinson and his relatives, the writs of assistance, and other problems. But more fundamentally, the struggle matched two incompatible conceptions of government and society. Developed during the controversies of preceding decades, these conceptions were spelled out in an outpouring of political rhetoric in the early 1760s and in the crystallization of two distinct factions.

James Otis, Samuel Adams, Royall Tyler, Oxenbridge Thacher, and a host of other Bostonians, linked to the artisans and laborers through a network of neighborhood taverns, fire companies, and the Caucus, espoused a vision of politics that gave credence to laboring-class views and regarded as entirely legitimate the participation of artisans and even laborers in the political process. This was not a new conception of the rightful political economy, but a very old one. The leaders of this movement were merely following in the footsteps of earlier popular leaders. . . . The town meeting, open to almost all property owners in the city and responsive to the propertyless as well, was the foundation of this system. By no means narrowly based, the "popular" party included many of the city's merchants, shopkeepers, lawyers, doctors, clergymen, and other well-to-do men. They provided leadership and filled the most important elective offices—overseers of the poor, tax assessors, town selectmen, and delegates to the House of Representatives. Lesser people filled minor offices and voiced their opinions at the town meetings where they were numerically dominant.

For the conservative merchants and lawyers, led and personified by Thomas Hutchinson, the old system spelled only chaos. "Reform" for these men meant paring back the responsibilities of the town meeting, substituting appointive for elective officeholders, restricting the freedom of the press, and breaking down the virulent anti-Anglican prejudice that still characterized the popular party. Like their opponents, members of the "prerogative" party had suffered as Boston's economy stagnated after 1740. But they saw the best hope for reviving the economy in handing over the management of town government to the wealthy and well-born exclusively. To see Otis address the crowd and to witness "the Rage of Patriotism . . . spread so violently . . . thro' town and country, that there is scarce a cobler or porter but has turn'd mountebank in politicks and erected his stage near the printing-press" was their vision of hell.

Between 1761 and 1764 proponents of the "popular" and "prerogative" conceptions of politics engaged in a furious battle of billingsgate that filled the columns of the *Gazette* and *Evening-Post*. It is easy to be diverted by the extreme forms which the scurrility took. Charges of "Racoon," "stinking

Skunk," "Pimp," "wild beast," "drunkard," and dozens of other choice titles were traded back and forth in verbal civil war. But more important than this stream of epithets was the deep-seated, class-tinged animosity which the polemical pieces exposed: hatred and suspicion of laboring people on the part of the Hutchinsonians; suspicion and hatred of the wealthy, Anglican, prerogative elite held by the common people. . . .

This reciprocal animosity and mistrust, suffusing the newspapers and pamphlets of the late colonial period, reveals the deeply-rooted social tensions that Bostonians would carry into the revolutionary era. These tensions shaped the ways in which different social groups began to think about *internal* political goals once the conflict against *external* authority began. In the end, the Hutchinson faction, looking not to the future but staring into the distant past, faced an impossible task—to convince a broad electorate that the very men who had accumulated fortunes in an era when most had suffered were alone qualified to govern in the interest of the whole community. Lower- and middle-class Bostonians had heard fiscal conservatives and political elitists pronounce the same platitudes for half a century. Even now, a generation before James Madison formally enunciated an interest-group theory of politics, they understood that each group had its particular interest to promote and that aristocratic politicians who claimed to work for the commonweal were not to be trusted. Such men employed the catchwords of the traditional system of politics—"public good," "community," "harmony," and "public virtue"—to cloak their own ambitions for aggrandizing wealth and power. The growing inequalities of wealth in Boston, which could be readily seen in the overcrowded almshouse and flocks of outreliefers in contrast to the urban splendor of men like Hutchinson and Oliver, were proof enough of that.

IV

Only by understanding the long animosity that the common people of Boston held for Thomas Hutchinson and his clique can sense be made of the extraordinary response to the Stamp Act in Boston in August 1765—the systematic destruction of the houses of Hutchinson and other wealthy and conservative Boston officials—and of the course of revolutionary politics in the city in the years that followed. It is possible, of course, to revert to the explanation of Peter Oliver, who, at the time, argued that "the People in general . . . were like the Mobility of all Countries, perfect Machines, wound up by any Hand who might first take the winch." In this view, the crowd was led by the nose by middle- and upper-class manipulators such as Otis and Samuel Adams, and used to further their own political ambitions. In this Newtonian formulation, the crowd could never be self-activating, for thought and planned action could have their source only in the minds of educated persons.

Such explanations, however, bear no relationship to the social realities in Boston at the time or to the long history of popular protest in the city. Again and again in the eighteenth century the Boston crowd had considered its interest, determined its enemies, and moved in a coordinated and discriminating way to gain its ends through street action. It was frequently supported in this by men higher up on the social scale—men who shielded the crowd leaders from subsequent attempts of the authorities to punish them. Thus, several socioeconomic groups, with interests that often coincided but sometimes diverged, found it profitable to coordinate their actions.

The attacks on Andrew Oliver's house on the evening of 14 August 1765, and on Hutchinson's house twelve days later, were entirely consistent with this pattern of politics. . . . [T]he crowd, led by the shoemaker Ebenezer MacIntosh, culminated a day of protest against the Stamp Act by reducing Oliver's mansion to a shambles. Accompanied by the sheriff, Hutchinson attempted to stop the property destruction. For his trouble, he was driven off with a hailstorm of stones. Less than two weeks later it was Hutchinson's turn. Forcing him and his family to flee, the crowd smashed in the doors with axes, reduced the furniture to splinters, stripped the walls bare, chopped through inner partitions until the house was a hollow shell, destroyed the formal gardens behind the house, drank the contents of the wine cellar, and carried off every moveable object of value except some of Hutchinson's books and papers, which were left to scatter in the wind. Not a person in Boston, neither private citizen nor officer of the law, attempted to stop the crowd. Its members worked through the night with almost military precision to raze the building, spending three hours alone "at the cupola before they could get it down," according to Governor Bernard.

Historians agree that in destroying the Boston mansions of Oliver and Hutchinson, the crowd was demonstrating against the Stamp Act. Oliver had been appointed Stamp Collector, and Hutchinson, though he publicly expressed his view that the act was unwise, had vowed to use his authority as lieutenant-governor to see it executed. But in conducting probably the most ferocious attack on private property in the history of the English colonies, the crowd was demonstrating against far more than Parliamentary policy. Stamp collectors were intimidated and handled roughly in many other cities. But nowhere else did the crowd choose to destroy property on such a grand scale and with such exacting thoroughness. The full meaning of these attacks can be extracted only by understanding the long-standing animus against the Oliver-Hutchinson circle. Beyond intimidating British officialdom, the crowd was giving vent to years of hostility at the accumulation of wealth and power by the aristocratic, Hutchinson-led prerogative faction. Behind every swing of the ax and every hurled stone, behind every shattered plate and splintered mahogany chair lay the fury of a Bostonian who had read or heard the repeated references to the people as "rabble," and who had suffered economic hardship while others grew rich. . . .

Seen in the context of three generations of social and economic change in Boston, and set against the drive for power of the Hutchinson-Oliver faction in Massachusetts, the Stamp Act riots provide a revealing example of the "moral economy of the crowd" in the early stages of the revolutionary movement. Members of the Boston "mob" needed no upper-class leaders to tell them about the economic stagnation of the late colonial period that had been affecting their lives and the structure of opportunity in the town. Nor did they need to destroy the homes of Oliver and Hutchinson in order to obtain the promise of these officeholders to hold the Stamp Act in abeyance. Instead, the crowd paid off some old debts and served notice on those whom it regarded as enemies of its interests. It was the culminating event of an era of protest against wealth and oligarchic power that had been growing in all the cities. In addition, it demonstrated the fragility of the union between protesting city dwellers of the laboring classes and their more bourgeois partners, for in the uninhibited August attacks on property, the Boston crowd went much farther than Caucus leaders such as James Otis and Samuel Adams had reckoned or wished to countenance.

V

In the other cities the growing resentment of wealth, the rejection of an elitist conception of politics, and the articulation of artisan- and laboring-class interests also gained momentum after 1765. These were vital developments in the revolutionary period. Indeed, it was the extraordinary new vigor of urban laboring people in defining and pursuing their goals that raised the frightening spectre of a radicalized form of politics and a radically changed society in the minds of many upper-class city dwellers, who later abandoned the resistance movement against England that they had initially supported and led.

That no full-fledged proletarian radical ideology emerged in the decade before the Revolution should not surprise us, for this was a preindustrial society in which no proletariat yet existed. Instead, we can best understand the long movement of protest against concentrated wealth and power, building powerfully as social and economic conditions changed in the cities, as a reflection of the disillusionment of laborers, artisans, and many middle-class city dwellers against a system that no longer delivered equitable rewards to the industrious. "Is it equitable that 99, rather 999, should suffer for the Extravagance or Grandeur of one," asked a New Yorker in 1765, "especially when it is considered that Men frequently owe their Wealth to the impoverishment of their Neighbors?" Such thoughts, cutting across class lines, were gaining force among large parts of the urban population in the late colonial period. They were directed squarely at outmoded notions that only the idle and profligate could fail in America and that only the educated and wealthy were entitled to manage political affairs.

But the absence of clearly identifiable class consciousness and of organized proletarian radicalism does not mean that a radical ideology, nurtured within the matrix of preindustrial values and modes of thought, failed to emerge during the Revolution. Though this chapter in the history of the Revolution is largely unwritten, current scholarship is making it clear that the radicalization of thought in the cities, set in motion by economic and social change, advanced very rapidly once the barriers of traditional thought were broken down. A storm of demands, often accompanied by crowd action to insure their implementation, rose from the urban "tradesmen" and "mechanicks": for the end of closed assembly debates and the erection of public galleries in the legislative houses; for published roll-call votes which would indicate how faithfully elected legislators followed the wishes of their constituents; for open-air meetings where laboring men could help devise and implement public policy; for more equitable laying of taxes; for price controls instituted by and for the laboring classes to shield them from avaricious men of wealth; and for the election of mechanics and other ordinary people at all levels of government.

How rapidly politics and political ideology could be transformed, as colonists debated the issue of rebellion, is well illustrated by the case of Philadelphia. In one brief decade preceding the Revolution the artisanry and laboring poor of the city moved from a position of clear political inferiority to a position of political control. They took over the political machinery of the city, pushed through the most radical state constitution of the period, and articulated concepts of society and political economy that would have stunned their predecessors. By mid-1776, laborers, artisans, and small tradesmen, employing extralegal measures when electoral politics failed, were in clear command in Philadelphia. Working with middle-class leaders such as James Cannon, Timothy Matlack, Thomas Young, and Thomas Paine, they launched a full-scale attack on wealth and even on the right to acquire unlimited private property. By the summer of 1776 the militant Privates Committee, which probably represented the poorest workers, became the foremost carrier of radical ideology in Pennsylvania. It urged the voters, in electing delegates for the constitutional convention, to shun "great and overgrown rich men [who] will be improper to be trusted, [for] they will be too apt to be framing distinctions in society, because they will reap the benefits of all such distinctions." Going even further, they drew up a bill of rights for consideration by the convention, which included the proposition that "an enormous proportion of property vested in a few individuals is dangerous to the rights, and destructive of the common happiness, of mankind; and therefore every free state hath a right by its laws to discourage the possession of such property." For four years, in an extremely fluid political scene, a radicalized artisanry shaped—and sometimes dominated—city and state politics, while setting forth the most fully articulated ideology of reform yet heard in America.

These calls for reform varied from city to city, depending on differing conditions, past politics, and the qualities of particular leaders. Not all the reforms were implemented, especially those that went to the heart of the structural problems in the economy. Pennsylvania, for example, did not adopt the radical limitation on property holding. But that we know from hindsight that the most radical challenges to the existing system were thwarted, or enjoyed only a short period of success, does not mean that they are not a vital part of the revolutionary story. At the time, the disaffected in the cities were questioning some of the most fundamental tenets of colonial thought. Ordinary people, in bold opposition to their superiors, to whom custom required that they defer, were creating power and suggesting solutions to problems affecting their daily lives. . . . How far these calls for radical reform extended and the success they achieved are matters that historians have begun to investigate only lately. But this much is clear: even though many reforms were defeated or instituted briefly and then abandoned, political thought and behavior would never again be the same in America.

Conflict and Consensus in the Revolution and Among Historians

EDMUND S. MORGAN

. . . [A] division has emerged among historians of the American Revolution, a division between those who emphasize the consensus achieved by the revolting colonists and those who emphasize conflicts among them. The division has excited attention and has perhaps been exaggerated because of the special position occupied by the revolution in our national consciousness. . . .

The alacrity with which the current division among scholars has been recognized, if not promoted, I believe, lies in this sanctifying power of the Revolution and its Founding Fathers. Those who contend that the Revolution bore few marks of social conflict or social upheaval seem to be denying the blessing of the Founding Fathers to present-day struggles against the establishment, while those who emphasize conflicts seem to be suggesting that conflicts, or at least conflicts against an upper class or established system, are sponsored by the Founding Fathers, consecrated in the fires at Valley Forge. . . . [T]o say that the Revolution did not achieve or aim at radical social change and lacked the conflicts that generally accompany such change is taken as a denial that radical social change is a good thing. Hence those who give the Founding Fathers failing grades as social revolutionaries are greeted, sometimes to their astonishment, as conservative. . . .

I

The type of internal conflict that historians have most eagerly searched for among Americans of the Revolutionary period is class conflict. The search is handicapped by a problem of identification. With the struggle of the colonies against the mother country dominating the scene, how does one distinguish a class conflict within that larger conflict?

Not by the side a man chose to support. Although the first historians of the loyalists did assume that they represented an upper if not a ruling class, subsequent investigations have revealed that loyalists, like patriots, were drawn from all classes. That a man sided with the mother country or against her tells us little about his social position. Although it seems altogether likely on the latest evidence that a larger percentage of the well-to-do could be found among the loyalists than among the revolutionists, the

---

Text by Edmund S. Morgan, "Conflict and Concensus," from *The Challenge of the American Revolution*, 1976, pp. 175–195; and "A Sense of Power" from *The Genius of George Washington*, 1980, pp. 3–25. Reprinted with permission of W. W. Norton Co.

Revolution cut sharply across nearly all previous divisions, whether regional, ethnic, religious, or class. It was not a conflict in which one side was predominantly upper class and the other predominantly lower class.

If, then, we look only at one side, at the Americans who supported the Revolution, or who did not oppose it, can we there find that lower-class rebels were bent on the overthrow or reduction of ruling-class rebels? A moment's reflection on the nature of the Revolutionary War may moderate our expectations. The Revolutionary effort against Great Britain tended to suppress or encompass social conflicts. Where it did not, where hostility between social groups rose to a level of intensity approximating that of the conflict with the mother country, one group or the other would be likely to join with the loyalists. Some merchants in New York City, for example, felt that the local Revolutionary leaders threatened their interests more than the mother country did; and similarly some tenant farmers of the Hudson Valley felt more bitter toward their patriot landlords than they did toward king and Parliament. But these men, whether merchants or tenants, by joining the loyalist side deprived themselves of a part in any contest about who should rule at home. Loyalism in this way tended to absorb social groups that felt endangered or oppressed by the Revolutionary party. It operated as a safety valve to remove from the American side men who felt a high degree of social discontent. Or to change the figure, it drew off men at either end of the political spectrum, reducing the range of disagreements. It removed from the scene the intransigents, of whatever persuasion, who might have prevented the achievement of consensus.

Disputes did occur, of course, among those who remained on the Revolutionary side, but the extraordinary social mobility characteristic of eighteenth-century American society usually prevented such disputes from hardening along class lines. Although recent statistical samplings point to a narrowing of economic opportunity in the latter half of the eighteenth century, Americans still enjoyed an upward mobility unknown in other societies. In a land of rising men a political group formed along lower-class lines had little prospect of endurance.

The Revolution probably increased social mobility temporarily both upward and downward, ruining the fortunes of many established families and opening opportunities for speedy ascent by daring upstarts. This very mobility engendered, as it always has, political disputes, but seldom along class lines. An American who had moved up from the lower ranks carried with him the expectation of sharing with those who had already arrived the offices of government traditionally exercised by the economically and socially successful. If he found himself excluded, he could call upon a wide electorate of his former equals but present inferiors to help him achieve the kind of office that they, no less than he, considered proper for successful men. But the fact that the lower ranks were involved in the contest should not obscure the fact that the contest itself was generally a struggle for office and power between members of an upper class: the new against the established. We must be wary of seeing such struggles, like Patrick Henry's successful bid for power in Virginia, as a rising of the oppressed against their masters.

I do not mean to argue that hostility between classes did not exist at all among those who supported the Revolution or that it cannot be discerned or recognized. In the anti-rent riots of 1766, for example, New York tenant farmers expressed a hostility to their landlords that was not entirely absorbed by loyalism after 1775. More than one scholar has found clear expressions of class conflict in the conduct of the war and of politics in Revolutionary New York. But in assessing class conflict as a Revolutionary force, we shall be hard pressed to find many instances outside New York in which antagonism rose to the level of actual fighting or even to openly expressed hostility of the kind that might be expected to lead to fighting.

American social structure was so fluid that to talk about social classes at all in most colonies or states requires the use of very loose economic categories such as rich, poor, and middle class, or contemporary designations like "the better sort" or "the poorer sort," or occupational categories like merchant, planter, lawyer, farmer, artisan, and seaman. Americans were no less skilled than other peoples in measuring the degree of deference due to each of their neighbors for the host of reasons and prejudices that confer honor or contempt on the members of any community. But such distinctions were local, seldom negotiable beyond the neighborhood where a man was known, and not always easy to discern even there.

Nevertheless, one absolute, clearly defined, and easily recognized division did exist, that between freeman and slave. Half a million Americans, perhaps a fifth of the total population, were slaves, and slavery is so direct an assault by one group of men on another that it can properly be considered as a form of class conflict in itself. In the American Revolution, however, slaves were unable to mount any serious uprising against their masters. Although the armies of both sides sooner or later made use of slaves and gave some of them freedom for their services, neither side provided the help necessary for large-scale insurrection. Both felt more need to woo masters than slaves. Perhaps the possibility of insurrection was even lessened by the few efforts of the British to promote it. When Lord Dunmore invited the slaves of Virginia to desert their masters and join his forces, he probably drew off many of the bolder individuals, leaving behind those who were less likely to rise in revolt later. Again loyalism tended to absorb men who might otherwise have directed their energies more radically against a local ruling class.

That the American Revolution did not produce an uprising of the group in colonial society that was most visibly and legally oppressed, and oppressed with the explicit or tacit approval of the rest of the society, is itself an instructive comment on the nature of social conflict and consensus during the Revolution. . . .

The development of slavery is perhaps the key to the consensus that prevailed in colonial America, for slavery meant the substitution of a helpless, closely guarded lower class for a dangerous, armed lower class that would fight if exploited too ruthlessly. The slave had more reason to revolt than the servant or the new freedman. But he was less able to. He had no hope, no rising expectations, and no arms. On top of that he was black.

His status in the community was proclaimed by his color and maintained by a tyranny in which white men of all ranks and regions consented and approved. The consensus on which colonial society rested was a racist consensus.

Had the southern plantations not shifted from free to slave labor, had the planters continued to import masses of indentured servants and continued to pour them into their own and other colonies a few years later as indigent freedmen, then the picture of social mobility in the colonial period and of class conflict in the Revolution might have been quite different. . . . It is perhaps the greatest irony of a Revolution fought in the name of freedom, a Revolution that indeed advanced the cause of freedom throughout the world, that the men who carried it out were able to unite against British oppression because they had so completely and successfully oppressed the largest segment of their own laboring population.

To be sure, there were those among the revolutionists who felt uncomfortable about rebelling against what they chose to call the threat of slavery, while they themselves held some 20 percent of their own population in slavery. But such feelings were translated into legal action only in states where slaves were few in number. Those were not the states where an enslaved labor force grew the country's principal exports. And if northerners freed their own slaves, they did not propose at this time to free their neighbors'. The racial consensus on which colonial society had rested was shaken a little but not broken by the Revolution. . . .

In sum, the evidence of Revolutionary class conflict is scanty, and for good reason. With a majority of laborers in chains and with the most discontented freemen venting their discontent in loyalism, the struggle over who should rule at home was unlikely to bear many of the marks of class conflict. Class conflict was indubitably present, but it did not surface with an effective intensity until a later day, after the Revolution had built a consensus that could both nourish and contain it, and after social, political, and economic change had produced greater provocations to it.

II

Let us turn now to another kind of conflict that was more intense and also, I believe, more significant for the Revolution. If we examine the occasions when Americans fought with one another or came very close to fighting between 1763 and 1789, excluding battles between loyalists and patriots, we find a number of episodes, all of them involving men who had moved from the older coastal regions into the interior: the march of the Paxton Boys against Philadelphia, the Regulator movement in the Carolinas with its Battle of Alamance, the activities of the Green Mountain Boys in Vermont, the skirmishes of Pennamite and Yankee in the Wyoming Valley of Pennsylvania, and Shays's Rebellion in Massachusetts. However diverse in immediate cause and attendant circumstances, these conflicts had one thing in common: they were all manifestations of the discontent of western settlers or settlers on new lands against governments dominated by or subservient to the interests of older or eastern regions.

Americans of the Revolutionary period were less successful in repressing sectional conflicts than conflicts arising from class or race. Though this fact is obvious and though the westward movement has received its full share of attention, historians considering the Revolution as a social movement have not always borne in mind two conspicuous conditions of life in eighteenth-century America, conditions that lay at the root of East-West conflict: first, the extraordinary rate of population growth and, second, the abundance of land, unoccupied or only thinly occupied by the native Indians.

Although the rate of population growth in the colonies varied a good deal from place to place and from year to year, the over-all long-range trend is clear. The total population of the thirteen colonies that participated in the Revolution more than doubled every twenty-five years during the eighteenth century. Beginning at about 250,000 in 1700, it rose to over 5,000,000 by 1800. As we learn more about the role of population growth in history, it may ultimately appear that the most significant social fact about America in the eighteenth century was this fearful growth, unlike anything that had been known in Europe in recorded history. . . .

The westward population explosion probably relieved the East from social conflicts that might have arisen from overcrowding; but it generated other conflicts potentially as dangerous. It set rival groups of speculators into contests for control of the richest western lands, contests that drew in and corrupted state governments and the national government. And it created a bloc of Americans who by moving west acquired different needs and interests from eastern Americans, but who by the same move lost their political ability to make their needs heard or attended to. People moved west so rapidly that even with the best of intentions a government could scarcely have kept up with them in furnishing the town or parish or county organization that formed the units of representation in the legislature. Because representation did not keep up with the expansion of population into new territory, governments remained under the domination of easterners and frequently neglected the needs of westerners. Even where representation was fairly proportioned, the location of the legislature subjected it to eastern influences that could bring it into serious conflict with the West. . . .

The Regulator movement represents another phase of the same East-West conflict: the eastern-dominated governments of South Carolina and North Carolina failed to extend the machinery of law enforcement into the West as rapidly as the needs of the settlers required, and so the West took the law in its own hands. In Shays's Rebellion the Shaysites, who also called themselves Regulators, hoped to gain by direct action what the government in Boston had denied them. The Pennamite-Yankee conflict and the activities of the Green Mountain Boys offer a variation on the theme. In these cases two colonial governments, representing different speculative interests, were engaged in a contest for western lands, and the actual settlers fought with each other. The significance of the frontier in early American history, if we may borrow that phrase, was that it kept Americans in conflict. Movement of the exploding population into new lands was continually generating new communities with interests differing from those of the older communities that retained, or at least claimed, control over them.

This kind of internal conflict among Americans was far more visible during the Revolutionary period than was class conflict. Although there were overtones of class conflict in any contest between established eastern interests and the interests of pioneer western farmers, the contest was primarily geographical, created by the problem of stretching the social and political apparatus that bound one group of people to another in the expanding American universe.

That this form of conflict produced more active hostility in the Revolutionary period will seem no more than natural if we view the Revolution itself from the same perspective. The English colonies in America stood to England in the way that the western parts of the colonies stood to the eastern parts, but with even stronger grievances and correspondingly stronger hostility. The institutions that England devised for her overseas emigrants in the wake of the Great Migration were even more inadequate by 1776 than the institutions that they had devised for themselves. While many colonial legislatures had too few representatives from their western areas, Parliament, which could legislate for all the colonies, had not a single representative from them. When the colonists cried out that Parliament without American representatives knew nothing about their needs and had no right to tax them, they spoke to England in the voice of westerners speaking to easterners. In the Declaration of Independence they announced that the social and political bonds that tied them to an eastern government were severed. The American Revolution was itself a revolt of settlers in a new land against a government that by its location and composition could not be properly acquainted with their needs and could not keep up with their growth. . . .

In sum, while class conflict tended to be muted during the Revolutionary period by social mobility among whites, by the enslavement of blacks, and by loyalism, sectional conflict was aggravated. The gravest form of sectional conflict was East-West, but it was not the only form. The greater North-South conflict had already cast its ominous shadow in congressional voting alignments, in the uneasiness of both northerners and southerners over the continuance of slavery, and in steps taken toward abolition of slavery in the North, but not in the South. The most farsighted Americans sensed already that North-South differences as well as East-West differences might one day lead to secession. Indeed in the late 1780s so many sectional disagreements were festering that men who had led their states to a united independence fifteen years earlier now predicted the breakup of the American nation.

III

We know that it did not break up. What, then, other than the superior wisdom of the Founding Fathers, prevented the breakup? What sort of consensus enabled Americans to contain not only the immediate threats to their union perceived in the 1780s but also the threats that grew with time from sectional and class conflict? The question in some measure answers itself. The Americans did achieve nationality during the Revolutionary period, and nationalism has proved to be the most powerful, if the least understood, social force of modern times. In the shrinking world of the twentieth century it has often been a sinister force, confining the vision of its devotees to a single country when they should be looking at the entire globe. But for Americans of the Revolutionary period the world was expanding instead of shrinking, and nationalism exerted a cohesive influence among the people of the several states, stretching instead of confining their political horizons. . . .

Nationalism was in itself the strongest force binding Americans of the Revolutionary generation together. Devotion to the nation helped to keep both sides in any conflict on speaking terms, helped to make disagreements negotiable within the framework of national politics, and even made possible the creation of a new and stronger framework in 1787 when the old one proved unsatisfactory. But nationalism was not the only force disposing Americans to bury their conflicts. The racial consensus of colonial times, though challenged and diminished, still prevailed and helped to keep the North-South conflict from coming to center stage. The revolutionists were not prepared to allow the issue of freedom for blacks to threaten the union of whites. By the consent of white Americans the American labor force, concentrated in the South, remained for the most part in slavery, outside the arena where American quarrels and conflicts were expected to take place. Contending factions, whether of class, region, or party, were agreed in not seeking or expecting the participation of men in chains.

The exclusion of most laborers meant that the participants on both sides of any conflict were men who possessed formidable powers, powers that were carefully withheld from slaves. Both sides could negotiate from strength and demand compromise. Although repression might be an effective mode of dealing with discontent or insubordination from slaves, it did not recommend itself as a way of handling men who had the means to fight back either politically or, if necessary, with force. Unlike the peasants of the Old World, Americans, or at least those Americans without black skin, possessed two palpable sources of power: most of them owned the land on which they lived, and a very large number of them owned guns. Land gave them economic and political power; and guns, we may as well admit, gave them firepower.

In the events that led up to the Revolution, England had failed to recognize the strength that these two kinds of power gave to her colonists. The colonists themselves knew at first hand that the ownership of land enabled a man to bid defiance to those who had traditionally controlled society through control of its lands. They had developed a society in which deference to birth and wealth was tempered by constant reminders to the rich and wellborn that their authority rested on the consent of ordinary property owners. Most adult male Americans owned property and could vote for the men who made the laws that affected their property. If they generally voted for a local bigwig, a man who held more property than they did, they did not hesitate to dump him if he neglected their interests. . . .

What alarmed Americans about taxation by Parliament was that they could not vote it down. The program that seemed so conventional and so reasonable from the standpoint of Whitehall appeared to the Americans as a threat to the power that enabled them to direct their own lives. If a legislature to which they elected no member could take their property in taxes, that legislature could ultimately take all their property and reduce them to the impotence of which they had such visible examples in the slaves at their feet. It was consensus on this point that enabled the colonies to unite so suddenly and so successfully against Parliamentary taxation. The American reaction to Parliamentary taxation seemed to England too hysterical and wicked to be genuine, and her statesmen failed to deal with it adequately, partly because they failed to recognize its existence. . . .

In order to maintain themselves as a single nation, Americans had to recognize the economic power and firepower that Britain ignored. By the time of the Revolution the proportion of the population owning land in the East may have been somewhat reduced from what it had been fifty or a hundred years earlier, but the westerner by definition was a man who had broken out of the limited acreage of the East. Whether or not he held a secure title, he knew how to make his living from the land and to make life uncomfortable for anyone who tried to stop him. And he was even more likely than the easterner to be armed. The westerner in our history has always been a man with a gun. Eastern-dominated governments simply did not have sufficient power of their own in the long run to impose on the West conditions that armed westerners would not agree to, any more than the Continental Congress could have imposed its edicts on the states, as some members proposed, by the use of military force. American nationalism was obliged to start with the assumption that the population was armed and that no group within it, slaves excepted, could be pushed very hard in any direction it did not want to go.

With a population already equalized to a large degree by firepower and economic power, the United States began its independence appropriately with the declaration that all men are created equal. The immediate purpose was to affirm the equality of England's transatlantic colonists with Englishmen in England, who were taxed only by their elected representatives. But the simplicity of the declaration of equality endowed it with a resonance that was momentous for the whole subsequent history of the nation whose existence it announced.

It could not have been predicted at the time that this would become a national creed. The men who adopted the declaration in 1776 would scarcely have been unanimous if they had been obliged to state precisely what they meant by "created equal." Many of them, including the author of the phrase, held slaves. If the preceding analysis is correct, the fact that they were able to unite at all depended in part on their denial of equality to black Americans. Even when applied only to white Americans, the meaning of equality was hardly as self-evident as Congress declared the proposition itself to be. The equality promulgated by the Congress at Philadelphia had no power to dissolve at once the conflicts and tensions in American society. Westerners were obliged for several years to flirt with Spain and England, while eastern speculators, many of them in Congress, quarreled over the profits they hoped to gain from western settlement if the West could be kept under eastern domination. James Madison tried in vain to secure a guarantee in the federal Constitution of the equality of western states. Instead the principle was precariously acknowledged only as a result of a shady bargain during the last weeks of the expiring Continental Congress.

But acknowledged it was in the end. The Northwest Ordinance, by stipulating that western states should be admitted to the union on equal terms with the existing states, saved the nation from future attempts to make subordinate colonists out of its western emigrants. As the revolutionists gradually became aware of the implications of the creed to which they had committed themselves, they also whittled down, albeit even more gradually, the inequities in their laws governing religion, representation, and inheritance. And as the social structure of the nation changed in subsequent generations, Americans probed further into the meaning of equality. . . .

Is it fair, then, to call this a point of consensus? Was it not mere rhetoric? Perhaps, if by rhetoric is meant the terms on which men can agree to speak together. An alternative rhetoric and an alternative social creed prevailed before the Revolution both in America and Europe and continued to prevail in most of Europe. That creed also offered a way to consensus, but of a quite different sort. It affirmed divine sanction for a social hierarchy in which every man knew his place and was expected to keep it. The old creed was designed to suppress the aspirations of lower classes, to make them content with their lot. Redress of grievances was not impossible, if superiors failed in their acknowledged obligations to inferiors; but the likelihood was much greater that oppression would go unchecked and that resentment would build into an explosive, revolutionary situation before redress could be obtained. The American Revolution itself was brought on by a British minister who had rejected what he called "the absurd opinion that all men are equal." That absurd opinion became the basis of the American consensus that grew out of the Revolution.

✕ *F U R T H E R   R E A D I N G*

Bernard Bailyn, *The Ideological Origins of the American Revolution* (1967)
Thomas C. Barrow, "The American Revolution Considered as a Colonial War for Independence," *William and Mary Quarterly*, 3d ser., 25 (1968), 452–464
Richard Buel, Jr., "Democracy and the American Revolution: A Frame of Reference," *William and Mary Quarterly*, 3d ser., 21 (1964), 165–190
Edwin G. Burrows and Michael Wallace, "The American Revolution: The Ideology and Practice of National Liberation," *Perspectives in American History* 6 (1972), 167–306

William M. Fowler, Jr., and Wallace Coyle, eds., *The American Revolution: Changing Perspectives* (1979)

Jack P. Greene, ed., *The American Revolution: Its Character and Limits* (1987)

J. Franklin Jameson, *The American Revolution Considered as a Social Movement* (1926)

Merrill Jensen, "The American People and the American Revolution," *Journal of American History* 57 (1970), 5–35

———, "Historians and the Nature of the American Revolution," in *The Reinterpretation of Early American History*, R. A. Billington, ed. (1966)

Stephen G. Kurtz and James H. Hutson, eds., *Essays on the American Revolution* (1973)

Jesse Lemisch, "The American Revolution Seen from the Bottom Up," in *Towards a New Past*, Barton Bernstein, ed. (1968)

Kenneth A. Lockridge, "Social Change and the Meaning of the American Revolution," *Journal of Social History* 4 (1973), 403–439

Edmund S. Morgan, *The Challenge of the American Revolution* (1976)

Richard B. Morris, *The American Revolution Reconsidered* (1967)

Robert R. Palmer, "The Revolution," in *The Comparative Approach to American History*, C. Vann Woodward, ed. (1968)

Frederick B. Tolles, "The American Revolution Considered as a Social Movement: A Re-Evaluation," *American Historical Review* 60 (1954–55), 1–12

Gordon S. Wood, "Rhetoric and Reality in the American Revolution," *William and Mary Quarterly*, 3d ser., 23 (1966), 3–32

Alfred F. Young, ed., *The American Revolution: Explorations in the History of American Radicalism* (1976)

CHAPTER
2

The British Empire
and the French and Indian War

✕

To understand the British imperial system and Britain's relationship to the colonies, it is important to recognize that the British government did not found any of the colonies. Indeed, the earliest colonies in the Chesapeake region and New England were settled and organized a generation or two before the British government made any attempt to develop a central policy on settlement or trade. Such efforts were begun intermittently in the 1650s and 1660s and thereafter, but domestic political instability prevented London authorities from establishing a comprehensive or consistent colonial policy. As a result, British imperial arrangements were never as logical, orderly, and coherent in practice as royal officials would have liked. Moreover, because most of the colonies had experienced generations of semiautonomous government under seventeenth-century charters, the goal of central control was a difficult, long-term challenge for eighteenth-century British administrators. In their domestic politics, military defense, and commercial activities, the colonies had operated largely on their own.

Europe's Seven Years' War (known in the colonies as the French and Indian War), which ended in 1763, marked a turning point in British imperial history. For the first time, Britain had concentrated its military resources in North America; with colonial help, the British conquered French Canada. In the process, cabinet-level British officials became concerned with the serious political and administrative defects of the imperial system they were supposed to rule. Britain meanwhile had run up a huge public debt by financing the war on the high seas and in Europe and America. After a century of operating an imperial policy sometimes described as ''salutary neglect,'' British leaders believed they had to find a better way to run the empire. But to colonial Americans, who shared in the glory of British victories and welcomed the expulsion of French power from North America, there was no better way. In their view, the empire had simply entered a new era of peace, prosperity, and growth; the imperial system wasn't broken and didn't need fixing.

During the reign of William and Mary in the 1690s, England laid the cornerstones of imperial policy. The Navigation Act, which created a tariff-protected trading system, and the commission of the Board of Trade, which established a general supervisory and policymaking agency, were two of these cornerstones; they would influence the shape of the empire for generations. In their actual execution, both measures, reproduced here as the first and second documents, permitted considerable discretion and flexibility. And over time, merchants and officials discovered profitable loopholes in these and other laws and regulations. As a result, British leaders would seek to maintain the basic imperial laws of the 1690s by closing the loopholes. A key effort in this direction is exemplified in the third document, the Order in Council on the customs service, which made a temporary wartime reform permanent.

Colonial unconcern regarding such administrative measures in the context of the victory over France is suggested by Massachusetts clergymen's celebratory sermons, an example of which is reprinted here as the fourth document. Jonathan Mayhew, whose British patriotism was expansive in 1759, was the same man who had made a stir in 1750 by using the anniversary of the execution of Charles I—a day that Anglicans held sacred to the late king's memory—as the occasion for a Lockean public attack on the idea of unlimited submission to a monarch. Mayhew would later emerge as a leading voice criticizing British measures. The final document, a sermon of 1763 by Reverend Thomas Barnard, brings a millennialist enthusiasm to the glorification of the British Empire. Later, Barnard too would passionately oppose British policy.

The Navigation Act, 1696

Whereas notwithstanding divers acts made for the encouragement of the navigation of this kingdom, . . . great abuses are daily committed to the prejudice of the English navigation, and the loss of a great part of the plantation trade to this kingdom, by the artifice and cunning of ill-disposed persons: for remedy whereof for the future. . . .

II. Be it enacted, . . . that after the five and twentieth day of March, one thousand six hundred and ninety-eight, no goods or merchandises whatsoever shall be imported into, or exported out of, any colony or plantation . . . or shall be laden in, or carried from any one port or place in the said colonies or plantations to any other port or place in the same, the kingdom of England, . . . in any ship or bottom but what is or shall be of the built of England, . . . or the said colonies or plantations, and wholly owned by the people thereof, or any of them, and navigated with the masters and three fourths of the mariners of the said places only, . . . under pain of forfeiture of ship and goods; one third part whereof to be to the use of his Majesty, . . . one third part to the governor of the said colonies or plantations, and the other third part to the person who shall inform and sue for the same. . . .

VI. And for the more effectual preventing of frauds, and regulating abuses in the plantation trade in America, be it further enacted . . . that all ships coming into, or going out of, any of the said plantations, and lading or unlading any goods or commodities, . . . and their ladings, shall be subject . . . to the same rules, visitations, searches, penalties, and forfeitures, . . . as ships and their ladings, and the commanders and masters of ships, are subject . . . unto in this kingdom, by virtue of an act of Parliament . . . entitled, An Act for preventing frauds, and regulating abuses in his Majesty's customs; and that the officers for collecting and managing his Majesty's revenue, and inspecting the plantation trade, in any of the said plantations, shall have the same powers and authorities, for visiting and searching of ships, and taking their entries, and for seizing . . . any of the goods prohibited to be imported or exported, . . . or for which any duties . . . ought to have been paid, . . . and also to enter houses or warehouses, to search for and seize any such goods; . . . and also that in case any officer or officers in the plantations shall be sued or molested for any thing done in the execution of their office, the officer . . . shall give this or other custom acts in evidence, and the judge to allow thereof, have and enjoy the like privileges and advantages, as are allowed by law to the officers of his Majesty's customs in England. . . .

IX. And it is further enacted . . . that all laws . . . at this time, or which hereafter shall be in practice, or endeavoured or pretended to be in force or practice, in any of the said plantations, which are in any wise repugnant to the before mentioned laws, . . . so far as they do relate to the said plantations, . . . or which are any ways repugnant to this present act, or to any other law hereafter to be made in this kingdom, so far as such law shall relate to . . . the said plantations, are illegal, null and void. . . .

XI. And for the better executing the several acts of Parliament relating to the plantation trade, be it enacted by the authority aforesaid, that the Lord Treasurer, Commissioners of the Treasury, and the Commissioners of the Customs in England . . . shall . . . appoint such . . . officers of the customs in any city, town, river, port, harbour or creek, . . . when and as often as to them shall seem needful; be it further also enacted, that upon any actions . . . that shall be brought . . . in the said plantations, upon any law . . . concerning his Majesty's duties, or ships or goods . . . by reason of any unlawful importations or exportations, there shall not be any jury, but of such only as are natives of England or Ireland, or are born in his Majesty's said plantations.

The Commission of the Board of Trade, 1696

His Majesty's Commission for promoting the trade of this kingdom and for inspecting and improving his plantations in America and elsewhere.

William the third, by the grace of God, king of England, Scotland, France, and Ireland, . . . Greeting:

Whereas we [the monarch] are extremely desirous that the trade of our kingdom of England, upon which the strength and riches thereof do in a great measure depend, should by all proper means be promoted and advanced; . . . we . . . appoint . . . you, to be our commissioners . . . for promoting the trade of our kingdom and for inspecting and improving our plantations in America and elsewhere. . . .

And we do . . . empower you . . . to take an account of the state and condition of the general trade of England, and also of the several particular trades in all foreign parts; . . . and to inquire into and examine what trades are or may prove hurtful, or are or may be made beneficial to our kingdom of England, and by what ways and means the profitable and advantageous trades may be more improved and extended, and such as are hurtful and prejudicial rectified or discouraged; and to inquire into the several obstructions of trade, and the means of removing the same. And also in what manner . . . the trade of our said kingdom may be most effectually protected and secured in all the parts thereof; and to consider by what means the several useful and profitable manufactures already settled in our said kingdom may be further improved, and how . . . new and profitable manufactures may be introduced.

And we do further . . . require you . . . to consider of some proper methods for setting on work and employing the poor of our said kingdom and making them useful to the public; . . . as also to consider of the best and most effectual means to regain, encourage, and establish the fishery of this kingdom.

And our further will . . . is that you, our said commissioners, or any five or more of you, do from time to time make representations . . . to us, or to our Privy Council, as the nature of the business shall require, which said representations are to be in writing, and to be signed by five or more of you.

And we do hereby further . . . require you . . . to inform yourselves of the present condition of our respective plantations, . . . the administration of the government and justice in those places [as well] as . . . the commerce . . . ; and also to inquire into the limits of soil and product of our several plantations, . . . and of the best means for . . . securing our colonies there, and how the same may be rendered most . . . beneficial to . . . England.

And we do . . . further . . . require you . . . to inform yourselves what naval stores may be furnished from our plantations and in what quantities and by what methods our royal purpose of having our kingdom supplied with naval stores from thence may be made practicable . . . ; and also to . . . inform yourselves of the best . . . methods of . . . improving in our plantations such other staples and . . . manufactures as our subjects of England are now obliged to fetch . . . from other princes and states; and also what staples and manufactures may be best encouraged there, and what trades are taken up and exercised there which . . . may prove prejudicial to England, . . . and whatsoever else may turn to the hurt of our kingdom of England.

And to examine . . . the usual instructions given to the governors of our plantations, and to see if anything may be . . . changed therein to advantage; . . . and as often as occasion shall require to consider of proper persons to be governors or deputy governors, or to be of our council or of

our council at law, or secretaries, in our . . . plantations in order to present
their names to us. . . .

And we do . . . empower you . . . to examine . . . such acts of the
assemblies of the plantations . . . as shall . . . be sent . . . hither for our
approbation; and to set down . . . the usefulness or mischief thereof to our
Crown and to . . . England, or to the plantations themselves; . . . and also
to consider what matters may be recommended . . . to be passed in the
assemblies there; to hear complaints of oppressions and maladministrations
in our plantations; . . . and also to require an account of all moneys given
for public uses by the assemblies in our plantations.

Order in Council on the Reform of the Customs Service, 1763

We, the Commissioners of your Majesty's Treasury beg leave humbly to
represent to your Majesty that having taken into consideration the present
state of the duties of customs imposed on your Majesty's subjects in America
and the West Indies, we find that the revenue arising therefrom is very small
and inconsiderable, having in no degree increased with the commerce of
those countries, and is not yet sufficient to defray a fourth part of the expense
necessary for collecting it. We observe with concern that through neglect,
connivance, and fraud, not only the revenue is impaired, but the commerce
of the colonies is diverted from its natural course and the . . . provisions of
many wise laws to secure it to the mother country are in great measure
defeated. Attention to objects of so great importance . . . is more indispensable when the military establishment necessary for maintaining these
colonies requires a large revenue to support it, and when their vast increase
in territory and population makes the proper regulation of their trade of
immediate necessity lest the continuance and extent of the dangerous evils
above-mentioned may render all attempts to remedy them hereafter . . .
utterly impracticable. We have endeavoured therefore to discover, and . . .
remove the causes, to which the deficiency of this revenue and the contraband
trade with other European nations are owing. For this purpose we have
ordered all the officers belonging to the customs in America and the West
Indies to be fully instructed in their duty to repair forthwith to their respective
stations and constantly to reside there for the future; and where we find
that a sufficient number of proper officers are not yet established, it is
intended to supply the deficiency by the appointment of others. We have
directed that all the officers of the revenue in your Majesty's plantations
should be furnished with new and ample instructions, enforcing in the strongest manner the strictest attention to their duty, and requiring that by regular
and constant correspondence they give an account, as well of their own
proceedings as of the conduct of the officers under them, and inform us
likewise of any obstructions they may meet. . . . We have ordered them to
transmit exact amounts of the imports and exports in their several districts,
of the state of the revenue, and of the illicit commerce with other European

states, . . . with such observations as may occur to them in regard either to the efficacy . . . of . . . regulations, or to such alterations as they may judge conducive to the . . . improvement of the revenue, to the prevention of those frauds by which it is impaired, and to the suppression of the contraband trade which has been . . . carried on with too much impunity; and we have directed the Commissioners of your Majesty's Customs immediately to dismiss every officer that shall fail to pay obedience to these instructions or be any way deficient in his duty. . . . We are further . . . of opinion that it will greatly contribute to the same salutary ends, and to the carrying of the several laws and regulations into execution with success, if all officers, both civil and military, are strictly commanded to give their assistance upon all proper occasions, and if the commanders-in-chief of your Majesty's ships and troops in America and the West Indies are directed to attend to this object with the utmost care, and to make such a disposition of the force under their respective commands as will be most serviceable in suppressing these dangerous practices, and in protecting the officers of the revenue from the violence of any desperate and lawless persons.

Jonathan Mayhew Celebrates British Valor, 1759

. . . [T]he British general was one of those rare military geniuses, which, like the Phoenix, appear but once an age, except perhaps in Great-Britain. He was one of those, whose courage nothing could abate; whose ardor, regulated by prudence, nothing could damp; whose resolution no difficulties, however great, could shake or alter, so long as a possibility remained of carrying his design into execution; and in fine, one of those, whose wisdom and address at a critical juncture, were not inferior to his other great military accomplishments. These great qualities, with which heaven had endow'd him, and to which heaven seldom fails of giving success, were now all called forth, and displayed at once, in drawing the numerous enemy from their inaccessible entrenchments, to a general battle, which he had long desired.

Behold him there, with his little body of British troops, himself the head to direct, and the soul to animate the whole, if such troops needed animation; the force of Canada moving towards him with slow and solemn steps, under a try'd, experienced and approv'd commander!—Unhappy *Montcalm!* courageous at least, if not prudent at this time! . . . What is it that induces thee to put the capital of Canada, and, with it, the whole country, upon so desperate a risque as the event of the ensuing battle? Perhaps thou reliest on thy superior numbers. But dost thou not know both British troops and French ones better, than to think the latter can stand before the former on even ground, tho' the disproportion of numbers be so great? Is there not something else of more consequence than numbers, when things are brought to such a crisis as the present? Dost thou not know, that God has given men different nerves, sinews, arms and hearts? Dost thou not know, that those who fight for a Tyrant, will not fight like free-born Britons? . . . Or, perhaps, thou thinkest thy relicks, thy crosses, and thy saints, either St. Peter, or thy great *Lady,* whom thou profanely stilest "The mother God," will now befriend, and make thee victorious. But remember, *that* little host now in array against thee, worship the God that made the heavens, earth, and seas, with all that they contain; the Lord of hosts is his name! His is the glory and the victory; and know, that the event of this battle shall be accordingly! Cross thyself speedily, if thou thinkest it will be of any advantage to thee! . . .

Behold! now the charge begins! Behold, now the enemy fall, they fly! Behold the horrid rout, the pursuit, the field covered with the slain! Behold, now the enemy regain their untimely-forsaken trenches! See, now they are stormed, and turned into canals running with a purple tide, till choaked with the dead and dying, fallen promiscuously on one another! Behold, there falls their valiant *Leader*! Behold now, the gates or ports of the capital open to receive the vanquished and flying; but hastily shut again, lest the victorious should enter with them, or before them!—In fine! behold this place, renowned for its strength, the power and pride of the enemy, against which so many fruitless attempts had been made, now surrender'd to his Britannic Majesty, whose colours, yonder, wave over the devoted city!

This, my brethren, is the Lord's doing; a great thing which he has performed for us, for our country and nation, whereof we are glad; and it may justly be wonderful in our eyes! That so small a force should obtain so great, compleat, and important a conquest, as it were in a moment, with so little loss of numbers on its own side, and so great a one on that of the enemy! Since the surrender of Quebec, we may, without much presumption, look on Canada as a conquered country.

Thomas Barnard Looks to Future Glories, 1763

Britain, favoured of God, has hitherto maintained her Liberty; Freedom has subsisted in Health and Vigour, overcome all Opposition; recovered of every Disorder: There may she ever flourish, and "under her Shadow we shall be safe." Not all the Vicissitudes of human Affairs have afforded Opportunity for the Destruction of the Freedom of our Nations. Intestine Frauds and Treasons, the Weakness and Wickedness of Princes, foreign Invasions, have all in Event ('tis wonderful!) but they have all, in Event, served to fix Liberty more firmly, to mark out her Path, determine her Bounds, extend her Influence.

Look back, my Hearers, to the most distant Times. . . . *England* was frequently in Jeopardy from Abroad; sometimes ready in Despair to subject herself to foreign Power, that she might free herself from domestic Tyranny, as in the Case of King *John*; once at the Brink of being swallowed up by an invincible *Armada* of *Spain*; once nigh remediless Confusion, thro' the infernal Arts of *Rome*, in the infamous Powder-Plot; and for a Century past, constantly endangered by the insidious Arts of *France*, the unceasing Enemy of her Tranquillity—an Enemy, at one Time tampering with her indolent, profuse, superstitious Princes; at another, abetting vagrant Pretenders to her Crown: At length, this aspiring Power rightly judged that her future Efforts of this Kind would be vain, if the *British* Plantations on the Continent of

America should flourish and extend, and derive Wealth and Strength for their Mother-Country: Her Ministry therefore, with Craft and Perfidy, laid a Plan for first stinting their Growth (as they found the inhuman stimulating the Savages to their Destruction, would not effect the Purpose) that they might by and by overwhelm them. This brought on the late bloody War, . . . to distress and weaken *Britain.* . . .

The Exaltation of *Great-Britain* to the Summit of earthly Grandeur and Glory, was reserved in the Counsels of God for the Age and Reign of GEORGE the *Third.* . . .

We see a King on the Throne (succeeding his royal Grandfather, of immortal Memory) rejoicing, that, to every other Motive, this of Birth is added, to endear his Subjects to him, to attach him to their Laws and Constitutions, and engage him to Vigilance and Zeal for their Protection. While the venerable Foundations of all we hold dear, are guarded with the strictest Care, while the lowest Subject is safe as the highest, in every Enjoyment he can desire; the most powerful Enemies, the most formidable Combination of them, have fallen into "the Pit which they themselves digged."

Auspicious Day! when Britain, the special Care of Heaven, blessed with a patriot-Sovereign, served by wise and faithful Councellors, brave Commanders, successful Fleets and Armies, seconded in her Efforts by all her Children, and by none more zealously than by those of *New-England,* . . . has it in her Power to demand Peace of the most powerful Enemies, on Terms, just and equal, safe, highly advantageous and glorious, beyond what were expected or even fought for, through a Deluge of Blood.

Happy Sovereign of such a People, generous Olive-Tree; whose Branches spread out, whose Fruit is dispersed for the Healing of the Nations! Happy Island of his Nativity; blessed the Womb that bare him! It is GEORGE the *Third,* who gives Peace to half the World. How can Faction but be dumb, contending Parties but melt into gentle Harmony.

In these Events, the Lord God hath spoken, who can but prophecy, "In his Days shall the Righteous flourish, and Abundance of Peace so long as the Moon endureth: He shall have Dominion from Sea to Sea: They that dwell in the Wilderness shall bow before him, and his Enemies shall lick the Dust. . . .

America, mayest well rejoice, the Children of *New-England* may be glad and triumph, in Reflection on Events past, and Prospect of the future. Encompassed with native Savages, our Fathers having escaped from Oppression, deepest felt by pious Minds, carried their Lives in their Hands, subjected to Captivities, to inhuman Cruelties and Massacres: Encompassed with crafty, faithless *Europeans,* who fought their Ruin, what Prospect could they have before them? The dearer and more valuable the Rights they had earned, the more gloomy the Fore-thought of losing them. And if we their Offspring, call to Mind the Ideas which possessed us in the Year 1756, with what Exultation must we sing, "The Snare is broken and we are escaped."

Now commences the Era of our quiet Enjoyment of those Liberties, which our Fathers purchased with the Toil of their whole Lives, their Treasure, their Blood. Safe from the Enemy of the Wilderness, safe from the griping Hand of arbitrary Sway and cruel Superstition; Here shall be the late founded Seat of Peace and Freedom. Here shall our indulgent Mother, who has most generously rescued and protected us, be served and honoured by growing Numbers, with all Duty, Love and Gratitude, till Time shall be no more. Here shall be a perennial Source of her Strength and Riches. Here shall Arts and Sciences, the Companions of Tranquility, flourish. Here shall her new Subjects and their Posterity, bless the Day, when their imagined Enemies Victories proved to them the Beginning of the most valuable Freedom. Here shall dwell uncorrupted Faith, the pure Worship of God in its primitive Simplicity, unawed, uninterrupted; here shall it extend itself and its benign Influences among those who have hitherto "sat in Darkness, in the Region and under the Shadow of Death." "Truth shall spring out of the Earth, and Righteousness shall look down from Heaven; yea the Lord shall give that which is good; Righteousness shall go before him, and shall set us in the Way of his Steps."

✸ *E S S A Y S*

Alan Rogers, a professor of history at Boston College, is the author of *Empire and Liberty: American Resistance to British Authority, 1755–1763* (1974), a key study of the internal friction that the French and Indian war generated within the empire. In the first essay, his discussion of the army reveals attitudes that could (and ultimately did) undermine the celebratory rhetoric of victory. In the second essay, Jack P. Greene of the Johns Hopkins University, one of the most eminent scholars of colonial America and the author of a major synthetic study of early America, *Pursuits of Happiness* (1988), describes deep and long-lasting tensions in the imperial system that underlay the surface harmony.

British-American Tensions During the War

ALAN ROGERS

The French were driven from North America by the combined strengths of the British and American armies. But, ironically, the relationship between Americans and Englishmen deteriorated during the Great War for Empire. At the same time, the war stimulated the growth of an American self-awareness, a sense of pride in being different from the British soldiers who came to fight the French. For these reasons, the victory over France did not mean the same thing to all members of the British Empire.

Until late 1756 colonial troops enjoyed a considerable degree of autonomy. In other words, there was not one British army led by a supreme commander, but two separate armies. The first three British commanders accepted this separate but equal arrangement of the military forces in America. Most American politicians preferred this command structure and, until Lord Loudoun assumed command in July 1756, no British general had either the power or the incentive to alter it. Loudoun was the first British general who tried to unify all of the troops under his command, a move that was passionately resisted by American military men and civilians. To colonial army officers, integration with regular troops meant loss of their rank; to soldiers in the ranks it meant subjection to a harsh code of military conduct, with swift, brutal punishment for infractions. Finally, many civilians regarded the policy that brought British regulars and colonial volunteers together in a single unit as a grave threat to the virtue of American soldiers. Therefore, when it came, or was threatened, integration brought about open conflict between British and American soldiers and stirred up resentment among the colonial populace at large.

Loudoun attempted to override colonial antagonism arising from this issue, while General Jeffery Amherst thought to reduce hostility by assigning colonial soldiers a subordinate role in the conduct of the war. Neither method successfully bridged the gulf separating Americans from Englishmen during the Great War for Empire.

To begin with, American soldiers and officers were vastly different from the Britons who were sent to fight in North America. There were important sociological differences separating the men who composed the two armies. The kind and degree of military skill possessed by American and British soldiers varied markedly. When these real differences were combined with other imagined and exaggerated differences, the result was that Englishmen and Americans came to have a poor opinion of one another.

All British officers who served in America during the Great War for Empire were not aristocrats, but the image of the officer corps was definitely aristocratic. Most officers had paid dearly for their commissions and even when they could not afford it, British officers were expected to live in a style commensurate with their rank. They were, above all, anxious to maintain the notion that a British officer was, *ipso facto,* a gentleman. . . .

Two additional points need to be made about the British officers who fought in the Great War for Empire. First, and almost without exception, British officers had been in the army for a long time. Better than 90 per cent of all the colonels of regiments during the period 1714–1763 had more than fifteen years of military service. Men who had reached the rank of general had served an average of twenty-five years in the army. As might be expected, most officers were not young men. Generals were about fifty-five years old in 1755, while the average age of a colonel was about fifty. In brief, British officers tended to be middle-aged gentlemen with decades of military experience.

American officers, on the other hand, tended to be young, middle-class men with very little, if any, military experience. To be sure, colonials believed just as the English did that the prerequisite for command was the status of a gentleman. . . . But the men whom colonials described as gentlemen were not regarded as social equals by British officers. For while most of the New England officers had had some education, nearly all of the high-ranking officers were also small businessmen or farmers or "pettifoggers"—certainly not gentlemen's callings by English standards. General John Forbes characterized the American officers he encountered as "an extreme bad collection of broken innkeepers, horse jockeys and Indian traders."

American officers were not only less genteel than the British, but they were younger as well. The average age for a general in the provincial army was forty-three, and Americans with the rank of colonel were on the average almost twenty-three years younger than British colonels. Finally, although these youngsters had virtually no military experience, they fully expected to be treated as equals by the older professionals who commanded the British army.

The differences between enlisted men were nearly as striking as those between officers. Colonial soldiers were much better off economically and far more pious than British redcoats. Although both armies had a relatively high proportion of lower-class men in their ranks, there were more skilled craftsmen and farmers in the provincial armies, young men who probably could make good use of the bounty money and wages offered to them for enlistment. It was probably these men who set the pious tone that characterized the provincial armies. There were strict regulations against profanity and cardplaying, and usually two religious services were held in camp each Sunday.

Thousands of colonial volunteers came face to face with redcoats for the first time during the Great War for Empire and by and large Americans came away from their encounter thinking the British were immoral. In a stroll around an encampment near Ticonderoga, for example, Private Joseph Nichols "observ'd but little profanity among our Provantials: But among the Regulars much profaneness." Unlike the pious Americans, British soldiers regarded the Lord's day as any other day. They sang bawdy songs and carried on business as usual. Ezra Stiles, Congregational minister and future president of Yale, was worried that continued contact with British soldiers would undermine American morality. . . . "The religion of the army is infidelity and gratification of the appetites . . . I look upon it that our officers are in danger of being corrupted with vicious principles. . . . " Colonial newspapers frequently printed stories about British regulars which supported the opinions of American soldiers in the field. Incidents of drunkenness, thievery, and murder involving redcoats were dutifully reported. . . .

Moreover, because most Americans assumed that morality and victory were closely linked, the string of British losses which extended through 1758 seemed to confirm their judgment of the regulars' character. At the same time, the conquest of Fort Frontenac by Colonel John Bradstreet's provincial army stimulated the growth of American pride. "Saying that provincials are worthless troops, wont go down now," Edward Shippen, a Pennsylvania merchant and politician, wrote his son in the wake of Bradstreet's victory. "Provincials," he rejoiced, "marched into the very heart of the enemy's country and took a fortress which is the very key to all the French settlements on the Lakes."

British officers firmly believed that American soldiers had nothing to be proud of. This belief was based in part on professional military judgment, but the wedge that was driven between Americans and British soldiers was composed chiefly of unsubstantiated opinions and prejudices. British professionals arrived in America with a jaundiced view of colonial soldiers which, despite a great deal of evidence to the contrary, they rarely changed. "The Americans are in general the dirtiest, the most contemptible, cowardly dogs that you can conceive," wrote Colonel James Wolfe from Louisbourg in 1758. "There is no depending upon them in action. They fall down dead in their own dirt and desert by battalions, officers and all." Many of Wolfe's brother officers shared his low opinion of American soldiers. General Braddock had hardly begun his ill-fated assault on Fort Duquesne when he concluded that American soldiers' "Slothfull and Languid Disposition renders them very unfit for Military Service." Lord Loudoun's estimation of the character of Americans was no better. Even the New Englanders who had gained a reputation as being America's best soldiers as a result of their capture of Louisbourg in 1745 were "frighten'd out of their senses at the Name of a Frenchman . . . ," according to Loudoun. Not surprisingly, this line of thought often led British officers to conclude that Americans were largely responsible for whatever defeats the French were able to inflict upon the British forces. General James Abercromby's bloody defeat at Ticonderoga in July 1758 was excused by many British observers simply because about 10,000 of his army of 16,000 men were provincials.

Moreover, to the dismay of British military leaders, the defects they saw in the American character were reflected and magnified by the peculiar political thought and practices of the colonists. British army officers assumed that unquestioned obedience and the subordination of personal freedom to military necessity were prerequisites to victory. To colonials long accustomed to a large measure of political freedom, such restrictions were unacceptable. They were willing to serve in an army, but they were unwilling to surrender all of their personal freedom as the British generals seemed to demand. In short, military service was defined differently by colonial volunteers than it was by British professionals.

Governor Robert Dinwiddie was one of the few imperial officers to recognize the dilemma inherent in the role of citizen-soldier. He warned the Board of Trade not to expect many Virginians to be willing to serve in the armed forces. Most of the people, he pointed out early in the war, were freeholders whose elected representatives "strenuously insist on their Privileges." Among other things, this meant the House of Burgesses refused to put Virginia troops completely under the control of the military. The governor had to approve all court martials, and the defendant had the right to appeal to the House of Burgesses. This arrangement exasperated Colonel George Washington. Civilian interference in military affairs, the young officer complained to Loudoun, is designed to make "Command Intricate and precarious; and to render it difficult to support Authority and not offend the Civil Powers, who tenacious of Liberty and prone to Censure, condemn all Proceedings that are not exactly Lawful, never considering what Cases may arise to make it necessary and excusable." Harassed by what he considered a lack of cooperation, Loudoun joined with Washington in condemning civilian interference in military matters. In fact, after only six weeks in America, Loudoun was convinced that colonial governments were more a hindrance than a help. "Till we have every thing necessary, for carrying on the War here, within ourselves, independent of Aid from this Country," he wrote the Duke of Cumberland, "we shall go on very slowly."

Above all, of course, Loudoun wanted to be free from any dependence upon colonial troops. According to professional military standards, American volunteers simply were not trained soldiers. By a trained soldier, British officers meant a highly disciplined career man; one who was able to execute the 184 movements in the manual of arms, while under fire if necessary; a man who would stand and face an enemy across an open field; a man who fought because he was ordered to.

American volunteers did not measure up to these professional standards. Indeed, it seems unlikely that many colonials would evaluate their military service by the yardstick of British standards. The standard for military behavior used by Americans was their experience with local militia units, and militiamen were required to make only a slight adjustment in their usual patterns of behavior. There was some drilling and some shooting at the periodic training sessions for militiamen, but the habits of command and obedience, which were prerequisites for a well-trained army, were not inculcated. Because militia officers were either elected by the men or selected by the legislature, their position of authority was ultimately subject to popular control, hardly an ideal military situation. In short, the colonial militia was an almost perfect reflection of American society.

This was not nearly so true of the provincial army units. While they did not compare favorably with the British army, they were a long way from casual militia units. Discipline was stricter, duty harder and longer, and the rewards were unlikely to be compensatory with the risks. Therefore, the New England colonies who supplied most of the provincial troops had to devise a variety of inducements and penalties in order to fill their quotas. To begin with, they offered high wages and a bounty upon enlistment. A Connecticut volunteer, for example, earned about 10d. sterling per day. (A British regular, by comparison, was paid less than half that amount.) There were other incentives designed to promote enlistments in the provincial forces: volunteers were often exempted from taxation; soldiers were allowed to keep their equipment after serving for one campaign; and they were paid subsistence money while they were en route to and from the battle area.

Still there were not enough volunteers to fill the quotas. Therefore, from time to time draft laws were reluctantly enacted by the New York, Massachusetts, and Connecticut legislatures. Generally, the laws required all able-bodied men between the ages of sixteen and fifty to report to their local militia unit. There, a predetermined number of men were impressed for service in the provincial army.

This was not a popular procedure with either the lawmakers, who much preferred to entice volunteers into the army, or with the citizens, who were loath to leave their families to fight on some distant battlefield. . . . For those men who enlisted or were unlucky enough to be drafted, life in a provincial regiment was often a grim experience. Death lurked everywhere—on the battlefield, along a wilderness trail, and especially in camps. Because they were not adequately equipped and trained to survive long encampments, colonial soldiers were disastrously vulnerable to disease. . . .

The number of American soldiers available for duty was further reduced by a high desertion rate. When conditions became intolerable, or when a battle was won or lost, or simply when the men "got home in their heads," they left the army in droves. According to the Mutiny Act, which after 1756 applied to all British soldiers, desertion was punishable by death. But with this, as with other matters of military discipline, officers in the colonial armies only rarely allowed the maximum penalty to be carried out. If they were caught, deserters were tried, convicted, and sentenced; but then a provincial officer almost always stepped in and spared the man's life. If he got beyond the confines of the camp, the deserter had clear sailing, for the laws against harboring such men were universally ignored. Therefore the customary method used in America to round up deserters was for the governor to issue a proclamation pardoning all men who voluntarily returned to the army.

This typically American remedy appalled British officers. It seemed to support their biased opinions about the character of Americans and it led them to the conclusion that provincials were too undependable to be used as fighting men. For this reason colonial troops were either assigned to unimportant posts or used as common laborers. . . . Or colonials could be strategically sacrificed. Americans were stationed at Fort William Henry in 1756 and Fort Cumberland in 1758 because British professionals believed these were not defensible positions. As the war progressed, American volunteers were employed increasingly in noncombat roles, or as James Otis later put it, as the "hewers of wood and drawers of water." "The Provincials," wrote Colonel James Robertson with disarming candor, are "sufficient to work out Boats, drive our Waggons, and fell our Trees, and do the Works that in inhabited Countrys are performed by Peasants." . . .

The mere fact that most Americans dutifully obeyed British orders and thus in some minor way participated in driving France from North America is certainly not in itself evidence of Anglo-American solidarity. Indeed, the discriminatory military structure that grew up during the war, based as it was on "national" differences, contributed to the widening chasm between Great Britain and the colonies. For, paradoxically, while Americans were cast in a subordinate role, they thought of themselves as superior to the British. The seeds of this belief were sown in the early years of the war and although its nourishment was sometimes reduced to a trickle, an American self-confidence flowered nevertheless. . . .

The real and imagined differences between American and British soldiers created a situation that put these two protagonists on a collision course. Especially during the early years of the war—before American troops had been relegated to second-class status—there were a number of serious clashes between British and American officers. The root of the problem, which first came to the surface in the summer of 1756, was that by royal order American officers of whatever rank were to be regarded as captains with the least seniority whenever the provincial troops they commanded were joined with regular troops. The order made it clear that the British government had no confidence in American officers, no understanding of the way in which a volunteer army was recruited in the colonies, and no concern for colonial legislative authority. . . .

The deep resentment felt by colonial officers who lost their rank when British officers assumed command of an operation manifested itself repeatedly during the Great War for Empire. William Williams, a young Massachusetts officer, complained bitterly that British officers treated the Americans like "Orderly Serjeants." "We must do what we are biden and if not, Threatened with this and the Other Thing," he wrote his cousin, Israel Williams. "If things are not put upon some other Footing," he concluded, "I am of the Mind tis not worth while to proceed." Thomas Hutchinson heard similar hostile opinions expressed by other Americans. "There are a thousand stories all over the Country" having to do with how shabbily provincials were treated by British officers, "which it's impossible to satisfy people about."

The low opinions that Americans and Englishmen formed about one another during the Great War for Empire were not quickly forgotten. In the sharp verbal exchanges prior to the American Revolution, these opinions became important factors in the decisions made on both sides of the Atlantic to wage war in 1776. British officers who had served in America prior to 1763 spoke contemptuously in the House of Commons about the military qualities of the colonists. The First Lord of the Admiralty asserted that the Americans were "raw, undisciplined, cowardly men. I wish instead of 40 to 50,000 of these brave fellows, they would produce in the field [against us] at least 200,000, the more the better . . . if they didn't run away, they would starve themselves into compliance. . . ." General James Grant, who had served with little distinction in Forbes's assault on Fort Duquesne in 1758, also publicly condemned American soldiers. According to Grant, Americans were neither as brave nor as devoted to the protection of women as were the British. And he boasted that during the Great War for Empire British officers such as himself had taken the measure of provincial soldiers and decided they should be treated simply as beasts of burden.

While he was in England, Benjamin Franklin assumed the task of replying to these slurs on American valor. In an anonymous letter to the *Public Advertiser* in February 1775, he pointed to instances of American bravery, including the battles at Louisbourg and Lake George, and praised colonial troops for "having covered the Retreat of the British Regulars and saved them from utter Destruction in the Expedition under Braddock." Turning to British failures in America, Franklin listed General Grant's rout by Indians in 1758, as well as several other "Campaigns of shameful Defeats or as shameful Inactivity."

Despite the efforts of Franklin and a few others, including General Thomas Gage, the British ministry remained absolutely confident that their professional army could crush America's amateur troops. In the spring of

1775, shortly before he left England, Franklin heard a British army officer who had once served in America boast that "with a thousand British grenadiers he would undertake to go from one end of America to the other, and geld all the males, partly by force and partly by a little coaxing." . . .

Large numbers of Americans and Englishmen came together for the first time during the Great War for Empire. They emerged from this experience thinking less of one another than they had before the war. To be sure, the images Americans had of themselves and of the Englishmen they encountered were not wholly accurate. On the one hand, when Americans thought of British soldiers they thought of Braddock's defeat, of Loudoun's ineptness, and, in general, of the redcoats' inability to fight in the American environment. On the other hand, as a result of their wartime experiences, Americans thought of themselves as men of the highest character, motivated to fight by the highest ideals, and especially able to fight in the wilderness. Although these myths did not determine the events that led to the breakup of the British Empire, they did make Americans less fearful of British threats after 1763.

The Preconditions of the American Revolution

JACK P. GREENE

I

To a question about "the temper of America towards Great-Britain before the year 1763," Benjamin Franklin, in his famous "examination" before the House of Commons during the debates over the repeal of the Stamp Act in early 1766, replied that it was the "best in the world." The colonies, he said,

> submitted willingly to the government of the Crown, and paid, in all their courts, obedience to acts of parliament. Numerous as the people are in the several old provinces, they cost you nothing in forts, citadels, garrisons or armies, to keep them in subjection. They were governed by this country at the expense only of a little pen, ink, and paper. They were led by a thread. They had not only a respect, but an affection, for Great Britain, for its laws, its customs and manners, and even a fondness for its fashions, that greatly increased the commerce. Natives of Britain were always treated with particular regard; to be an Old-England man was, of itself, a character of some respect, and gave a kind of rank among us.

That Franklin was correct in this assessment was widely seconded by his contemporaries and has been the . . . judgment of the most sophisticated students of the problem. . . .

So persuaded have modern historians been that the relationship between

"An Uneasy Connection: An Analysis of the Preconditions of the American Revolution," by Jack P. Greene from *Essays on the American Revolution* edited by Stephen G. Kurtz and James H. Hutson. Published for the Institute of Early American History and Culture, Williamsburg Virginia. Copyright © 1973 The University of North Carolina Press.

Britain and the colonies prior to the Stamp Act crisis was basically satisfactory to both parties that they have . . . organized their continuing search for an adequate explanation of the American Revolution around a single, overriding question: why in less than a dozen years after 1763 the colonists became so estranged from Britain as to take up arms against her and, a little more than a year later, to declare for independence. The focus of their inquiries has thus been primarily upon the colonial response to the pre-Revolutionary controversy and upon the many medium-range issues and conditions that contributed to the creation of a revolutionary situation in the colonies between 1764 and 1774 and the short-run developments that touched off armed conflict in 1775 and led to the colonial decision to seek independence in 1776.

A result of this preoccupation with the immediate origins of the Revolution has been the neglect of two other, interrelated questions also raised by Franklin's remarks: first, whether the relationship between Britain and the colonies actually was so satisfactory prior to 1763, and, second, if the existing imperial system worked as well for Britain as Franklin contended, why the British government would ever undertake—much less persist in—measures that would . . . impair such a . . . beneficial arrangement. . . . Neither of these questions is new. They were widely canvassed . . . on both sides of the Atlantic in the 1760s and 1770s, and they provided a focus for most of the early students of the causes of the Revolution. . . . But no recent historian has dealt with both of these questions systematically. . . . This essay seeks . . . to provide a comprehensive discussion of the preconditions—the long-term, underlying causes—of the Revolution. . . .

II

When one looks closely at the relationship between Britain and the colonies during the century from 1660 to 1760, one discovers . . . that it was in many respects an uneasy connection . . . through the middle decades of the eighteenth century as a result of several important structural changes taking place in both the colonies and Britain. Throughout these decades, contemporaries on both sides of the Atlantic conventionally described the imperial-colonial relationship in terms of the familiar parent-child metaphor with Britain as the mother country and the colonies as its infant offspring. The clear implication of this usage was, of course, that the colonies had by no means yet reached a state of competency. . . . However, by the middle of the eighteenth century in most of the colonies, the colonists themselves were already handling a substantial portion of their internal affairs with an impressive . . . efficiency: to an extraordinary degree, the several colonies had become . . . "pockets of approximate independence" within the transatlantic imperial polity. In all save the newest colonies of Georgia and Nova Scotia, they possessed by 1750 virtually all of the conditions necessary for self-governing states.

The first of these conditions was the emergence of stable, coherent, effective, and acknowledged local political and social elites. . . . By the middle of the century, there existed in virtually every colony authoritative ruling groups with great social and economic power, extensive political experience, confidence in their capacity to govern, and broad public support. Indeed, the direction of colonial political life throughout the middle of the eighteenth century was probably toward more and more public deference to these ruling elites; certainly, their willingness to mobilize various groups of marginal members of political society in the protests against the Stamp Act as well as at later stages of the pre-Revolutionary conflict strongly suggests not a fear of such groups but a confidence in their ability to control them. . . .

A second and complementary condition was the development of . . . centers and institutions in which authority was concentrated and from which it was dispersed outward through a settled network of local urban administrative centers and institutions to the outermost perimeters of colonial society. Whether merely small administrative centers such as Annapolis or Williamsburg or large, central trading places such as Philadelphia, Boston, New York, and Charleston, the colonial capitals supplied the colonists with internal foci to which they customarily looked for political leadership and models for social behavior.

Perhaps even more important was the emergence of a set of viable governing institutions . . . in the towns and the counties and, especially significant, at the colony level in the form of the elected lower houses of assembly. More than any other political institution . . . the lower houses were endowed with charismatic authority both because, as the representatives of the colonists, they were thought to hold in trusteeship all of the sacred rights and privileges of the public and to be the sole giver of internal public law and because of their presumed—and actively cultivated—equivalence to the British Parliament, that emporium of British freedom and embodiment of all that was most sacred to Englishmen everywhere. As powerful, independent, self-confident institutions . . . the lower houses were potentially effective mechanisms for crystallizing and expressing grievances against Great Britain. Together with the elites who spoke through them, the local centers and institutions, particularly the lower houses, . . . provided authoritative symbols for the colony at large and thereby served as a preexisting local alternative to imperial authority.

A third and closely related condition was the development of remarkably elastic political systems. . . . First, they were inclusivist rather than exclusivist. For analytic purposes, one may divide the potential participants in the political process, that is, the free adult male population, into three categories: the elite, including both colony-wide and local officeholders; a broader "politically relevant strata or mobilized population" that participated with some regularity in the political process; and a passive or underlying population that took little part in the political system, in some cases because they were legally excluded by racial or property qualifications and in others because they had no interest in doing so. . . . The first two groups were relatively large and the third group relatively small. The elite seems . . . to have taken in as much as 3 percent to 5 percent of the free adult males, while the second category may have included as many as 60 percent to 90 percent of the same group. This wide diffusion of offices and extensive participation in the political process meant that colonial Americans—leaders and followers alike—had very wide training in politics and self-government and were thoroughly socialized to a . . . tested political system.

A second sense in which the political systems of the colonies were elastic was in their capacity to permit the resolution of internal conflict. Indeed, they were early forced to develop that capacity. The expansive character of American life prevented any group from obtaining a long-standing monopoly of political power, economic opportunity, or social status; new groups were constantly springing up demanding parity with the old. . . . The capacity of the political systems of the colonies to absorb new and diverse groups was steadily expanding during the middle of the century as a result of severe pressures created by a combination of rapid demographic and economic growth and increasing social, cultural, and religious diversity.

The rising competence of the colonies in nonpolitical or semipolitical spheres during the eighteenth century was a fourth condition that had prepared them for self-government. This competence was made possible by the dramatic enlargement of internal and external trade, travel, and migration; the increasing availability of knowledge through a broad spectrum of educational, cultural, social, economic, and religious institutions and through a rising number of books, magazines, and newspapers of colonial, British, and European origin accessible to the colonists; the development of more efficient means and networks of communication within and among the colonies and between the colonies and Great Britain; and the emergence of relatively large numbers of men with the technical skills, especially in law, trade, and finance, requisite for the successful functioning of an autonomous society. These developments not only provided the colonists with some of the technical wherewithal—for example, lawyers and newspapers—that turned out to be of crucial importance in resisting Britain and creating a new nation; they also helped to free the colonies from total dependence upon Britain for certain kinds of essential skills, to raise levels of literacy and education within the colonies, to liberate them from their former isolation and rusticity, to widen their "range of perception and imagination," and to create a potential for cooperation, for overcoming the "inherent localism" and traditional disunity they had stubbornly . . . manifested. . . .

A fifth and final condition was the tremendous increase in the size and wealth of the colonies in terms of the number of people, the amount of productive land, labor, and skills, and the extent of settled territory. The wealth of the colonies had become sufficient to give them a potential for economic and military resistance, while the sheer vastness of all of the continental colonies, taken together, constituted a formidable obstacle to suppressing any large-scale or broadly diffused movement of resistance. Indeed, this condition may well have been the most important of all, because it is the only one of the five not shared to a large degree by the British West Indian colonies, which did not revolt.

It is thus clear in retrospect that the colonies had achieved a high degree of competency by the 1750s and 1760s. . . . By 1760 the colonies were thus not only able to meet most of the objective conditions necessary for self-government but even had to a significant degree been governing themselves, maintaining internal civil order, prospering, and building an ever more complex and closely integrated society for at least three-quarters of a century and in some cases much longer. Equally important, such a large measure of de facto autonomy at every level and in all sectors of colonial society—with all of the responsibilities it required—had prepared them psychologically for self-government and independence.

The corollary of this impressive increase in colonial competency was the continued weakness of British power in the colonies. The bureaucratic structures organized, for the most part during the Restoration, to . . . control . . . the colonies had never been adequate. . . . There was no central governing agency within Britain with effective authority to deal quickly and efficiently with colonial matters until 1768, on the very eve of the Revolution. The Board of Trade, which had primary responsibility for the colonies after 1696, had only advisory powers, and its history is essentially one of failure to obtain the ministerial and parliamentary support necessary for its many and repeated attempts to establish a more elaborate and effective system of colonial administration. Moreover, its staff was so small and the number of separate colonies . . . so great that it could not possibly keep abreast of the rapidly fluctuating political and economic circumstances of every colony. . . . Finally, like all of the agencies within the British government that had any colonial responsibilities, the Board was invariably more responsive to the demands of powerful interest groups within Britain than it was to those of the colonists. The result, therefore, was an administrative structure in Britain that . . . had insufficient influence or power either to obtain support for its policies at home or to enforce them in the colonies, a structure that was both poorly informed about what was happening in the colonies and only minimally responsive to colonial demands.

Within the colonies the situation was little, if any, better. Imperial administrative machinery was insufficient for the enforcement of imperial policy, and authorities in Britain had no effective controls over the machinery that did exist. The governors, the primary representatives of the imperial government in the colonies, had almost no coercive resources at their command. Prior to the . . . mid-1750s, there was no more than a handful of regular troops in any colony on more than a temporary basis. . . . Of course, most governors did have some utilitarian resources in the form of crown or proprietary lands or . . . other special privileges . . . that could be used to build up a solid base of support for their administration. But few had much patronage—in the Anglo-American political world of the eighteenth century, the most important utilitarian resource of all—at their disposal. Imperial authorities never sought to strengthen the ties between Britain and the colonies by systematically admitting "the leading members of the provincial aristocracies" into the metropolitan political establishment. Increasingly, in fact, they even excluded such men from the few royal offices available in the colonies, which, especially after 1720, were usually filled by the ministry at home with needy place seekers. After 1740, even the largely honorific seats on the governors' advisory councils, which had in earlier times usually been reserved for wealthy and well-affected colonists, came more and more to be filled in the same way.

With little prospect for solid backing from home, only a rudimentary bureaucracy on which they could count for assistance (and over which they frequently had little control), and little patronage through which they might have gained the support of strategically placed members of local elites, governors frequently allied themselves with the dominant political groups within the colonies and did little more than keep up the appearance of adherence to the policies of the home government. Far from being able to co-opt the provincial elites by binding them to the imperial order in the colonies with strong ties of interest and obligation, the governors were, rather, co-opted by those elites; and the local standing and influence of governors, which in many cases was by no means inconsiderable, came to depend at least as much upon local connections as upon their formal position as representatives of the imperial government. Gubernatorial influence was thus highly personal and did not automatically extend beyond an individual governor to his successor, much less to the imperial government in Britain. . . .

The counterpoint of this continuing weakness of British power in the colonies was the dramatic increase in the importance of the colonies to Britain's economy during the first seven decades of the eighteenth century. The population of the continental colonies soared from 257,060 in 1700 to 635,083 in 1730 and 1,593,625 in 1760. . . . As the population increased, the colonies not only supplied Britain at extremely favorable rates with a growing variety of raw materials, many of which were subsequently reexported at a considerable profit to British middlemen, but also provided a growing stimulus to British manufacturers by taking an ever-rising amount of British finished products. Indeed, during the eighteenth century, the colonial trade became "the most rapidly growing section"—and accounted for a significant proportion of the total volume—of British overseas trade. Imports from the colonies (including the West Indies) accounted for 20 percent of the total volume of English imports in 1700–1701 and 36 percent in 1772–1773, while exports to the colonies rose from 10 percent of the total volume of English exports during the former year to 37 percent during the latter. . . . The colonial trade thus constituted a large and critical segment of the British economy and was becoming more important every decade. . . . To a considerable degree, the growing awareness of how much the economic well-being of Britain actually did depend upon the colonies . . . accounts for Parliament's willingness to contribute substantial sums toward the expenses of settling Georgia beginning in the 1730s and Nova Scotia starting in 1749 and to make such enormous outlays of money and men in defense of them during the Seven Years' War. Such profitable possessions could never be permitted to fall into the hands of Britain's Continental rivals.

III

SUM -

In itself, no one of these structural features—not the growing competence of the colonies, the continued weakness of British power in the colonies, or the increasing importance of the colonies to Britain's economy—was productive of sufficient strain to make the possibility of revolution very great; in combination, however, they contributed to the development of two fundamental discrepancies within the imperial-colonial relationship, discrepancies that made the potential for dysfunction within the empire extremely high. The first was the obvious discrepancy between theory and fact, between what imperial authorities thought the colonies should be and what they actually were. The increasing competency of the colonies during the eighteenth century obviously called for some adjustment in imperial behavior and attitudes towards the colonies, and such an adjustment appeared to have been made during the long ministry of Sir Robert Walpole from 1721 to 1742. Under Walpole, an informal accommodation between imperial authorities and the colonies had been achieved that permitted the colonies a generous amount of de facto self-government and economic freedom. . . . This accommodation represented something of a return to the old contractual relationship between mother country and colonies that had obtained during the first half century of English colonization, a relationship that had permitted the colonists the widest possible latitude to pursue their own objectives with a minimum of reciprocal obligations to the imperial government at home. But the accommodation was entirely pragmatic: it required no intellectual adjustment on the part of the authorities in Britain. On the contrary, by helping to forestall any explicit colonial challenges to traditional imperial notions about the colonies, it actually reinforced them. Equally important, by contributing to keep imperial-colonial relations relatively placid, it also helped to foster the dangerous illusion within the British political nation that imperial authorities actually did have the colonies firmly in hand—or at least that they could bring them under strict control if it ever became necessary to do so.

There were, of course, still other foundations for this illusion. The one seemingly substantial basis for it was the remarkable success of the navigation system that had been worked out largely between 1651 and 1705. . . . subsequently designated mercantilism. . . .

By and large, this success was attributable far less to imperial coercion than to colonial compliance. . . . This is not to say, of course, that there were not significant pockets of dissatisfaction with the system . . . within the colonies . . . or that some specific aspects of the system, most notably the Molasses Act of 1733, would not have created major colonial discontent had they been enforced, or that the system was not more profitable for Britain than it was for the colonies. It is to say that the extent of colonial compliance suggests . . . a very high degree of accommodation to the system and that, however voluntary and selective in character that compliance may have been, it provided, along with the concomitant absence of much manifest colonial opposition to the system as a whole, the principal support for the imperial illusion of control over the colonies.

A far more compelling foundation for this illusion was the overpowering conviction . . . of the inherent superiority of Britain, of its political institutions and its culture. . . . Following the Glorious Revolution, it was widely believed within the British political nation that the British constitution as it ·1688 had been restored by the Revolutionary Settlement represented the ultimate political achievement of all time, permitting the enjoyment of so many liberties and at the same time preserving a high degree of political order. "Pride in the liberty-preserving constitution of Britain was universal," extending to all groups both in and out of power, and this pride was matched by an almost equally pervasive reverence for the king, Lords, and Commons assembled in Parliament, which was at once the chief guardian of the constitution and its omnipotent interpreter. . . . Parliament seemed to embody all that was most sacred to Englishmen everywhere—in the colonies as well as in Britain. . . . The power of Parliament knew no geographical bounds within the British dominions: it was limited only by its own obligation not to violate the essential principles of the constitution, an obligation that it alone had . . . the authority to judge.

Nor were Britain's superiority and glory limited to the political realm. The prose and poetry of Addison, Defoe, Gay, Pope, Steele, Swift, and a host of lesser writers during the first half of the eighteenth century were widely heralded as evidence that Britain had achieved its "Augustan Age" in literature. And, despite a number of temporary setbacks, the economic picture, especially as measured by a rising volume of foreign trade and a quickening pace in domestic economic activity, seemed to be especially bright, so bright, in fact, that it was thought in Britain and feared on the Continent that Britain would eventually outstrip all of its traditional Continental rivals in wealth and power.

Not everyone, of course, viewed the situation in Hanoverian Britain with approval. Implicit in the comparison of contemporary Britain with Augustan Rome was a "historically derived fatalism," a prediction that, like the Rome of Augustus, the Britain of George I and George II would sooner or later degenerate from its epitome of virtue and freedom into a corrupt state of vice and slavery. . . . Despite the obviously disquieting implications of the parallel between Rome and Britain, Britain's greatest days, the Cassandras to the contrary notwithstanding, still seemed—throughout the middle decades of the eighteenth century—to lie in the future rather than in the present.

In the face of such achievements, . . . who could doubt that Britain was in every respect superior to its colonies overseas? . . . As imperial usage of the parent-child metaphor so clearly revealed, the colonies were by definition thought to be subordinate and dependent, bound by their position within the imperial family order to yield obedience to their mother country and unable, like children, either to control their own passions—were they not forever squabbling among themselves?—or to protect themselves from external aggression. . . . Acknowledgment of colonial competency on the part of British authorities was virtually impossible, for competency carried with it the hint of an equivalence between the colonies and Britain. In view of . . . British convictions of superiority, such a hint would have been a . . . violation of the national self-image.

The second discrepancy within the imperial-colonial relationship was between two divergent conceptions of what the relationship actually was. This discrepancy may be discussed in terms of a question raised by much of the previous discussion: if British coercive power over the colonies was so weak and colonial competence so high, what was it that continued to bind the colonies to Britain? Part of the answer, as we have already suggested, is to be found in the very real utilitarian benefits they derived from the connection. Despite the limitations imposed upon them by the navigation system, perhaps in part because of them, the colonies had prospered during the first half of the eighteenth century and had a strong vested interest in maintaining their economic ties with Britain. Far more important than these utilitarian benefits, however, were, as Franklin underscored in his *Examination,* the vital and deeply rooted customary bonds of allegiance and affection that tied the colonies very tightly to their parent state, ties whose strength had increased enormously through the middle decades of the eighteenth century as a result of the growing involvement of the colonies with Britain, the emergence of colonial elites intent upon reproducing in the colonies a society that resembled that of Britain as closely as possible, and the increasing Anglicization of colonial life in both form and substance.

These bonds had powerful symbolic and psychological roots. For the colonists, Britain was the central source of not only political and cultural but moral authority. . . . So much weight did the authority of the metropolis carry in the colonies that, as Franklin also suggested in his *Examination,* those individuals in the colonies who were or were thought to be "closely and positively" connected through institutional or personal ties to Britain automatically enjoyed a "special status." Moreover, as the colonies came more and more into the ambit of British life during the eighteenth century, . . . the extent of their dependence increased because their closer proximity to the center made them feel their . . . position as outsiders far more compellingly than did their forebears.

Britain also served the colonies as a source of pride and self-esteem as well as of moral authority. To have a share, if often largely only a peripheral share, in the achievements of Britain during the eighteenth century . . . was an exhilarating experience that operated to heighten British patriotism in the colonies and to strengthen still further the psychological bonds between them and Britain. Thus, whatever the weaknesses of British coercive power and whatever the objectionable conditions attached to the utilitarian benefits offered the colonies by the connection with Britain, Britain had enormously powerful normative resources with which to bind the colonies to it.

But . . . strong as it was, the colonial attachment to Britain . . . was conditional. If it was true, as John Dickinson later remarked, that the "Dependence" of the colonists could not "be retained but by preserving their affections," it was also true, as he so strongly emphasized, that "their affections" could not "be preserved, but by treating them in such a manner, as they think consistent with Freedom and Justice." If to British authorities the parent-child metaphor meant that the colonies were to be dependent and subordinate, to the colonists it meant that Britain was to be nurturant and protective. . . . They expected Britain to provide a favorable political and economic climate in which they could pursue with a minimum amount of anxiety their own, specifically colonial and individual, ends, while it also continued to provide a praiseworthy example by which they could measure their own achievements.

To provide such a standard of measurement British authorities had to behave toward the colonies in accordance with . . . pervasive beliefs about the limits of legitimate political action that had become . . . sacred components of colonial political culture as it had gradually taken shape during the first century and a half of settlement. . . . Perhaps because they were so far removed from the center of power within the empire, the colonists . . . seem to have found the literature of opposition, the writings of those resident Britons who were also on the outside, especially attractive. . . . But there was a hard core of unchallenged beliefs that was common to all major variants of Anglo-American political and social thought and formed the central premises for an emerging colonial perceptual system. . . . Proceeding from the assumptions that all men were by nature imperfect creatures who could not withstand the temptations of power and luxury and that power and luxury were corrupting and aggressive forces whose natural victims were liberty and virtue, this system of ideas stressed the omnipresent dangers to society and the polity from corruption by luxury and power, respectively. It emphasized the necessity for virtue, personal independence, disinterestedness, and devotion to the public welfare by rulers and the importance of a balanced government by which the various constituent components of the polity would keep a constant check upon one another as the only device by which liberty could be preserved. . . . Because all societies were thought to be highly susceptible to internal decay through moral corruption, . . . any . . . sign of increasing luxury or vice was a source of grave concern, a harbinger of certain decline. This system of ideas thus taught people to explain any deviation from the existing political situation, especially those that seemed somehow to be inimical to one's fundamental interests or to the manifest principles of the constitution, as the probable result of a conspiracy of corrupt men in power to subvert liberty in behalf of their own selfish designs.

Plausible enough to people out of power in Britain itself, such an explanation was extraordinarily persuasive to the inhabitants of distant colonies who were not only far removed from the point at which decisions were made but did not participate . . . in the system that made them. The simple fact of distance between Britain and the colonies thus created an underlying propensity towards distortion within the imperial-colonial relationship that made it absolutely crucial that British authorities always act in accord with the traditional imperatives of Anglo-American political culture in their relations with the colonies. . . .

But the voluntary attachment of the colonies to Britain depended upon something far more fundamental than the careful observation by British authorities of these traditional imperatives: it depended as well upon their willingness not to violate a basic substructure of expectations among the colonists that those imperatives were thought to protect. . . . The most obvious and explicit element in this substructure of expectations was that the imperial government would not . . . violate the sanctity of the elected lower houses of assembly and other institutions and symbols of self-government in each colony, institutions and symbols that, as we remarked earlier, had come to assume such extensive authority within the colonies that they, rather than Parliament, had . . . come to be regarded by the colonists as the . . . primary guardians of their rights and property.

A second . . . component of this substructure of . . . assumptions was the expectation that the imperial government would place as few impediments as possible in the way of the colonists' free pursuit of their own social and economic interests. . . . What the actions of the colonists seemed to assume, in fact, is that political society was a human device not only . . . for the maintenance of orderly relations among the men who composed it . . . but also . . . for the protection of the individual's property in his land, goods, and person, in which one's property in person included the right . . . of pursuing . . . one's interests, of seeking to alter one's place on the scale of economic well-being, social status, or political power. . . .

This is not to suggest that colonial behavior was free from the usual imperatives . . . that placed very heavy emphasis upon the obligations of citizens to put the welfare of the community as a whole before any personal considerations. On the contrary, in the colonies, as in every other contemporary Western society, such imperatives dominated explicit thinking about social and political relations. As was the case in Britain and elsewhere, however, the power of such ideas derived primarily out of men's needs to legitimate their actions—to themselves as well as to others—by conceiving of and presenting them in certain time-honored and publicly sanctioned forms. . . .

In terms of the present discussion, however, the important points are that, however much . . . they disapproved of self-oriented behavior in a specifically colonial context, they found it fully acceptable in the larger arena of imperial affairs. For one thing, of course, what seemed to imperial officials to be patently self-interested behavior by colonists might very well have been in the best general interests of a particular colony and therefore have appeared to the colonists as a selfless example of community-mindedness. But more important, the wide latitude in the pursuit of their own colonial and individual ends enjoyed by the colonists during their first century and a half and especially during and immediately after Walpole's tenure conditioned them to think of their connection with Britain as an instrumentality through which they might profitably seek those ends.

A third, related . . . component of this . . . structure of expectations was the assumption that the imperial government would not interfere with the capacity of the colonists as individuals to maintain their personal autonomy. . . . The implicit expectation of the colonists was thus that the British government would continue to provide a stable external background that would not call into question their accustomed autonomy, their ability— so crucial to their self-esteem and their continuing capacity to function as successful individuals in colonial society—to act in accordance with the mandates of virtue and independence. . . .

The voluntary attachment of the colonists to Britain thus depended . . . upon . . . assumptions that it was the moral obligation of the *mother* country to provide nurturance and protection for the colonies. What nurturance and protection had come to mean for the colonists . . . were: first, that the imperial government would not undermine . . . the colonists' self-esteem as defined by their capacity as individuals to act . . . with a high degree of autonomy . . . in the colonial environment; second, that it would interfere as little as possible with their ability to pursue whatever . . . activity seemed to them to be in their best interests; third, that it would respect the sanctity of the local self-governing institutions on which they depended for the . . . protection of the property, in person as well as in goods, they had acquired; . . . and, fourth, that in its dealings with the colonies it would continue to manifest respect for all of those central imperatives of Anglo-American political culture that were thought by Englishmen everywhere to be essential for the preservation of liberty and property.

This cluster of . . . expectations on the part of the colonists suggested a conception of the imperial-colonial connection that was fundamentally different from that held by imperial authorities. The divergency is most clearly revealed in the different meanings attached to the parent-child metaphor in Britain and in the colonies, in the explicit British emphasis upon the disciplinary implications of the metaphor and the colonial stress upon the nurturant and facilitative. The British emphasis implied a relationship of perpetual dependency of the colonies upon the mother country, while the colonial suggested an eventual equivalence. . . .

The existence of these two related and overlapping discrepancies, the one between imperial theory and colonial reality and the other between imperial and colonial ideas about the nature of the imperial-colonial connection, . . . gave the British Empire a latent potential for revolution through the middle decades of the eighteenth century. I say *latent* potential because these discrepancies had first to be clearly defined and their implications fully explored before they could actually . . . cause the disruption . . . of the empire. So long as they were only dimly perceived and not explicitly confronted, these discrepancies actually functioned as an essential . . . component of stability with the empire, because they permitted the colonists to exercise a considerable amount of autonomy without requiring imperial officials explicitly to abandon their traditional notions about the character of the empire. So long as the imperial government did not attempt to remove these discrepancies by enforcing those notions or acting in a sustained or systematic way upon them, the potential for any large-scale revolt by the colonies was not extremely high.

This is not to say, of course, that these discrepancies were not in themselves productive of considerable strain and anxiety on both sides of the Atlantic. The intermittent attempts by imperial authorities to establish closer supervision over the colonies . . . had given rise to . . . repeated demands by colonists for some explicit arrangement that would have provided them with considerable autonomy in both the political and economic realms and afforded them full protection against the awesome might of the imperial government. For the British, there was always the fear that these irrepressible . . . little "commonwealths" in America would . . . acquire the wherewithal to become "independent" of their "Mother Kingdom." These fears were fed not merely by the facts of colonial behavior but by the very logic of the parent-child metaphor, for that logic suggested that the colonies, like children, would eventually reach their maturity and become independent. . . .

Given the potential for dysfunction produced by these two discrepancies in the imperial-colonial relationship, there was a strong possibility that some serious . . . transgression of the existing moral order as it was conceived by one party or the other would shatter it beyond repair. But . . . such a transgression was necessary before any of the preconditions we have been describing could become causes of revolution or imperial disintegration. Some structural conditions had pointed the colonists toward equivalence and independence and, in doing so, had undermined the traditional bonds between Britain and the colonies and made the relationship . . . fragile. But these preconditions did no more than make the creation of a dysfunctional situation possible. Whether . . . such a situation would be created would be determined by other kinds of intervening causes.

IV

What began the process by which the old British Empire acquired . . . a marked susceptibility to disintegration or revolution, what, in fact, was the salient precondition of the American Revolution, was the decision by colonial authorities in Britain to abandon Walpole's policy of accommodation and to attempt to bring the colonies under much more rigid controls. This decision was taken, not abruptly in 1763, . . . but gradually in the decade beginning in 1748. Neither this general decision nor the many specific policy decisions of which it was composed constituted any sharp ideological break with the past. On the contrary, they merely represented another attempt to implement the traditional goals of English colonial policy . . . in accord with the guiding assumptions behind the British conception of the meaning of the parent-child metaphor. But the situation differed markedly from the one that had obtained during the Restoration or in the decades immediately following the Glorious Revolution, the two periods during which similarly systematic attempts had been made. The differences arose out of the conjoint facts that the colonies were infinitely more competent and correspondingly less dependent upon Britain . . . and that the attempt followed a long period of over a quarter of a century during which the imperial government appeared to have abandoned most of the goals it suddenly once again seemed bent upon achieving. . . .

The explanation for this fundamental change in . . . British policy towards the colonies is to be found in three separate conditions, one long-run and two short-run. The long-run condition, which . . . was . . . the most important, was the extraordinary territorial, demographic, and economic growth of the colonies. . . . At least since the 1690s, British officials had intermittently expressed the fear that the colonies might one day seek to throw off their dependency on Britain, set up their own manufactures, and become economic rivals rather than subordinate and complementary partners with Britain, goals, they implied, that were probably the secret ambition of many colonials. . . . The extent to which such anxiety . . . underlay the redirection of British policy towards the colonies may be gauged by a significant rise in the frequency and urgency of explicit expressions of fears of colonial independence within imperial circles during the late 1740s and the 1750s. Much later, during the Stamp Act crisis, an anonymous American writer protested "the *jealous* and baseless supposition, formed on the other side of the water, that the colonists want only a favorable opportunity of setting up for themselves. This charge against us hath for many years been kept a going in *Britain,* with such diligence and management," he complained, "that the minds of the people there are almost universally embittered against us." Though this writer did not even sense the deep-seated anxiety that underlay these charges, he was correct in his perception that they were everywhere manifest: in official position papers prepared by the Board of Trade, in correspondence between imperial officials and royal governors, in speeches in the House of Commons, and in a proliferating number of tracts— both published and unpublished—on the state of the colonies and the need for reforms in their administration.

If the rapid growth of the colonies with the consequent increase in their value to Britain was the single most important precondition behind the shift in British policy beginning in the late 1740s, there were two short-run conditions that, in combination, accounted for its timing. The first was the end of the era of internal domestic political instability in Britain that had begun in 1739 and was intensified by the vigorous competition for power through the mid-1740s following the fall of Sir Robert Walpole in 1742. Having already won the confidence of George II and wooed many opposition leaders to the side of the government, Henry Pelham finally managed to restore "peace to the body politic" and establish his regime on "a sound parliamentary basis" as a result of the government's overwhelming victory in the elections of 1747. "For the next seven years . . . the stability characteristic of Walpole's ministry at its zenith was again the salient feature of English government," and this freedom from domestic distractions along with the conclusion of the War of the Austrian Succession in 1748 meant that British political leaders were freer than at any time since the mid-1730s to devote significant attention to the colonies.

An even more important short-run condition that helped to determine

the timing of this shift in policy and that itself contributed to intensify the
. . . heightened sense of urgency that lay behind it was the simultaneous
eruption of . . . severe political and social disturbances in many of the
colonies. During the late 1740s and early 1750s, there were so many problems
. . . in so many colonies that the empire seemed to authorities . . . in London
to be on the verge of disintegration. Violent factional disputes had thrown
New Jersey into civil war, put an end to all legislative activity in New
Hampshire and North Carolina, and seriously weakened the position of the
royal administration in Jamaica, Bermuda, and New York. From New York,
South Carolina, New Jersey, Bermuda, Jamaica, North Carolina, and New
Hampshire—from all of the royal colonies except Massachusetts, Virginia,
Barbados, and the Leeward Islands—governors complained that they were
powerless to carry out imperial directions against the opposition of local
interests and the exorbitant power of the local lower houses of assembly.
From Bermuda there came reports that the status of the king's governor
had sunk so low that one member of the assembly had even offered a reward
for his assassination. So desperate was the situation throughout all the colonies that it became exceedingly difficult for imperial authorities to maintain
their illusion of control over them. . . .

Under the guidance of Halifax, who continued in office until 1761, the
Board of Trade systematically set about the task of shoring up imperial
authority in the colonies. It presided over a major effort to strengthen the
defenses of the British colonies against French Canada by turning Nova
Scotia, hitherto only a nominal British colony inhabited almost entirely by
neutral and even hostile French, into a full-fledged British colony. Much
more important, it prepared a series of long reports on the difficulties in
most of the major trouble spots in the colonies, and the recommendations
in these reports clearly revealed that, despite the long era of accommodation
and easy administration since the advent of Walpole, the members of the
Board and other colonial officials had not altered their long-standing conceptions about the proper relationship between the mother country and the
colonies and that they were intent upon enforcing the traditional, but hitherto
largely unachieved, goals of British colonial policy. Except for the Nova
Scotia enterprise, which received strong backing from the administration and
large sums of money from Parliament, none of the Board's recommendations
received the necessary support from the administration, though colonial
affairs did receive far more attention from the Privy Council and administration than they had in the past few decades. However desperate the situation in the colonies might appear to those best informed about it, existing
procedures were too cumbersome and the preoccupation with domestic matters too great to permit effective action on most colonial problems. In part
to remedy this situation, Halifax pushed very hard to have himself appointed
a separate secretary of state with broad jurisdiction and full responsibility
for the colonies. Although he failed in this effort . . . he did succeed in
securing enlarged powers for the Board of Trade in April 1752.

Armed with its new powers, the Board embarked upon an even more
vigorous campaign to bring the colonies under closer imperial control. It

established a packet-boat system to provide more regular communications with the colonies, urged each of the royal governors to secure a comprehensive revisal of the laws of his colony and to send home copies of all public papers promptly, revived ancient demands for settling a permanent revenue in those colonies that had not already voted one, insisted upon the inclusion of suspending clauses in an ever-wider variety of colonial laws, vigorously denounced any efforts by the colonial lower houses that seemed in any way to threaten the prerogative of the crown, issued a number of restrictive royal instructions, and enjoined the governors "strictly to adhere to your instructions and not to deviate from them in any point but upon evident necessity justified by the particular Circumstances of the case."

Although the Board of Trade's programs were greeted in many places with enthusiasm by royal officeholders and others who had long been alarmed by the imbalance of the colonial constitutions in favor of the representative assemblies, they were, in general, adamantly opposed by the lower houses and other powerful local interest groups, whose members considered them a violation of the traditional relationship between mother country and colonies . . . and, in many instances, an attack upon the established constitutions of the colonies. Even with its enlarged authority and its new assertiveness, the Board could not effectively meet such opposition. The Board could and did intimidate the governors into a strict observance of their instructions, but that only reduced their room for maneuver when they needed all the latitude possible to accomplish the impossible tasks assigned to them. Thus, the Board succeeded in its objectives only in New Hampshire, where Gov. Benning Wentworth had put together a powerful political combination that monopolized all political power and stifled opposition, and in the new civil governments in Nova Scotia and Georgia, where the Board took extraordinary pains "to check all Irregularities and unnecessary Deviations from the Constitution of the Mother Country in their Infancy." By the time the outbreak of the Seven Years' War forced it to suspend its reform activities in 1756, the Board had realized that its general campaign was a failure. Especially in the older colonies on the continent, imperial control was not much greater in 1756 than it had been eight years earlier. Unable to accomplish its objectives with the prerogative powers at its command, the Board increasingly had been driven to threaten the intervention of Parliament, and in 1757, the House of Commons actually did intervene for the first time in the domestic affairs of a colony when it censured the Jamaica Assembly for making extravagant constitutional claims while resisting instructions from the Board.

Collectively, the efforts of Halifax and his colleagues between 1748 and 1756 represented a major reversal in the tone and quality of imperial behavior toward the colonies. . . . It amounted to a shift on the part of imperial authorities from a posture . . . that was essentially permissive to one that was basically restrictive . . . [and dependent] upon coercion. These years witnessed . . . the attempted imposition of a whole series of . . . policies that . . . threatened . . . the . . . structure of colonial expectations about the nature of the imperial-colonial relationship and the proper modes of imperial behavior. . . . The vast majority of those policies that colonials found so objectionable between 1759 and 1776 were, in fact, either worked out or proposed in one form or another during these years, and attempts were actually made to implement many of them.

Although the program of reform between 1748 and 1756 engendered among the colonists considerable . . . dissatisfaction, . . . it obviously did not create a general malaise that brought the colonists to the brink of rebellion. . . . The impact of most of its . . . components was too local to invite . . . general . . . opposition, and the program as a whole was sufficiently scattered and contingent as to conceal from those not at or near the center of colonial administration . . . its full depth and general character. The result was that most of the program could be interpreted by the colonists as simply additional episodes in the continuing efforts of the imperial administration, "except in some short and shining Periods, to establish," in John Dickinson's words, "a Prerogative in America quite different from that in Great Britain." Such efforts and the "invidious Distinction" they sought to create between Englishmen in the colonies and those at home had always been a source of "Uneasiness" among the colonists. But they could scarcely be regarded as new. . . .

In terms of the causal significance of this change in . . . policy for the American Revolution, the fact that it yielded only minimal results is . . . as important as the fact that it was undertaken in the first place and much more important than the isolated and transitory pockets of discontent it created among the colonists. For the abject failure of most of . . . this early effort at reform served both to heighten imperial fears that the colonies would sooner or later get completely out of hand and to increase—almost to the point of obsession—imperial determination to secure tighter control over the colonies and to channel the colonists' expansive energies into forms . . . more acceptable to Britain. More specifically, this general lack of success had two results of momentous implications for the future. First, it helped to persuade many powerful figures in the British political nation that the successful exertion of British control over the colonies would require much more than the . . . piecemeal solutions that had been attempted between 1748 and 1756. The . . . sentiment for a more comprehensive and sweeping program of reform was manifest in a number of new proposals by imperial officials and would-be imperial statesmen alike during and just after the war for, in the words of Malachy Postlethwayt in 1757, "a strict and speedy inquiry [by Parliament] . . . to remedy [colonial] disorders before they grow too obstinate, and to put the government and trade of all our colonies into so good and sound a state, that every one may have its due share of nutriment, and thereby be the better fitted and disposed for the uses and benefit of the whole body politic, *especially of Great-Britain, their head, mother, and protectress.*" The second result, as Postlethwayt's statement suggests, was to convince imperial officials that any such reconstruction would have to be undertaken by Parliament, because "no other Authority than that of the British Parliament," as a writer later suggested in 1763, would "be regarded in the colonys or be able to awe them into acquiescence."

V

It is thus primarily because of the conclusions drawn from the experience by the British political nation, rather than because of the many specific local and largely unconnected grievances they created among the colonists, that the reforms of the years 1748 to 1756 and the fundamental redirection of British policy that they represented must be given a central place in the causal pattern of the Revolution. This is not to suggest that a revolution was logically inevitable after 1748 or 1756 or that under different conditions imperial officials might not have subsequently changed their posture and policies toward the colonies. It is to say that the experience of imperial officials with the reform program between 1748 and 1756 made a severe disruption within the empire highly probable and that the empirical conditions that obtained thereafter only served to confirm the conclusions already drawn from the earlier experience and to keep imperial officials firmly on a reformist course.

Although the Seven Years' War forced the temporary abandonment of the reform program, the war experience only intensified the impulses that had lain behind it, as the weakness of British authority over the colonies was more fully exposed than ever before. Throughout the war, aggressive lower houses openly used the government's need for defense funds to pry still more authority away from the governors; many colonial traders flagrantly violated the navigation acts, in many cases with the implicit connivance of the colonial governments and even of imperial customs officials; and many of the colonial legislatures failed to comply with imperial requisitions for men and money for the war effort—even with the promise of reimbursement by Parliament. The war experience thus reinforced . . . imperial fears of loss of control over and potential rivalry from the colonies, deepened their suspicions that the colonists harbored secret desires for independence, and intensified their determination for reform. As soon as the British and colonial armies had defeated the French in Canada in 1759 and 1760 and colonial support for the war effort was no longer vital, imperial authorities . . . undertook a variety of new restrictive measures to bolster imperial authority over the colonies. . . . The new measures of 1759 to 1764 were merely a renewal and an extension of the earlier reform program.

But they were an extension within a significantly different—and far more fragile—context. The war had been a liberating and (psychologically) reinforcing experience for the colonists. That so much of the war was fought on American soil and that the British government made such an enormous effort to defend the colonies contributed to an expanded sense of colonial self-importance. Moreover, . . . the war . . . produced a surge of British patriotism among the colonists and . . . created among them heightened expectations for a larger role within the empire, a role that would raise the status of the colonies . . . to . . . a near equivalence with the mother country. By contrast, the war left many members of the British political nation with feelings of bitterness and resentment towards the colonists and a determination to restore them to a proper state of dependence. Having incurred an enormous debt and a heavy tax burden in defense of the colonies and having had exaggerated reports of American opulence and the low level of taxation in the colonies, they regarded colonial failures to comply with royal requisitions and . . . violations of imperial regulations as evidences of extreme ingratitude that could not go unremarked, lest such excessive behavior rob Britain of the large investment it had made in protecting and securing the colonies.

If the experience of the war caused the expectations of men on opposite sides of the Atlantic about the relationship between Britain and the colonies in the postwar world to veer off in such different directions, the war itself altered the very structure of that relationship. . . . The expulsion of the French and Spanish from eastern North America removed the need for the last absolutely essential nurturing element the British had to offer the mainland colonies—protection against the French and Spanish—and thereby presumably removed a major . . . remaining block that had helped to keep whatever fantasies the colonists may have had about equivalence and independence in an unconscious and unarticulated state. . . . More important, . . . by destroying their rivals and thus making it less necessary to pacify the colonies, the British victory left imperial authorities with a much freer hand to go ahead with their program of colonial reform. Moreover, for the first time during and after the war, the British had significant coercive resources in the colonies in the form of a large number of royal troops. By giving them an excessive confidence in their ability to suppress potential colonial opposition, the presence of these troops may well have made imperial officials less cautious in dealing with the colonies than they had been a decade earlier.

In combination, the psychological consequences and structural changes produced by the war made the relationship between Britain and the colonies much more volatile. . . . The colonists now had heightened expectations about their position in the empire and less need for Britain's protection, while British officials were bitter about colonial behavior during the war, more determined than ever to bring the colonies under closer control, persuaded that they would have to use the authority of Parliament to do so, and possessed of an army to back them up if it should be needed. Given this set of . . . conditions, it was highly predictable that British officials in the 1760s would take some action, probably even by bringing parliamentary authority to bear upon the colonies in new, unaccustomed, and hence, for the colonists, illegitimate ways, that could be interpreted . . . as a fundamental violation of the existing relationship between them and Great Britain.

The Grenville program . . . did precisely that. The Sugar Act and the associated reforms in the navigation system immediately followed by the Stamp Act seemed to the colonists to be . . . a sharp and deadly assault upon . . . sacred components of the customary moral order as the colonists had come to perceive it. This program, along with the severe crisis produced by the Stamp Act, did in fact alter the quality and character of imperial-colonial relations profoundly.

The first of the imperial reform measures to affect equally all of the colonies at once, the Stamp Act forced the colonists to identify more fully than ever before some of the major . . . sources of strain within the imperial-colonial connection and even to restructure their perceptions of that relationship. . . . From the new perspective supplied by the Grenville program, they began to redefine their situation in a way that permitted them to interpret as grievances things that had previously gone unremarked and to regard components of the earlier ad hoc imperial reform program as part of a comprehensive assault upon the existing moral order that had been in progress for some time. This new perspective not only made the colonists hypersensitive to any subsequent violations of that moral order but also . . . created a strong predisposition to distort as violations a variety of imperial behaviors that were not in fact violations with the result that . . . they became grievances anyway because they were regarded as such. Moreover, because the Stamp Act could be interpreted as at least a partial withdrawal of affection by the parent state, it permitted the colonists to raise to the level of consciousness . . . preexisting hostile wishes . . . toward Britain and thereby to legitimate aggressive actions against the imperial government.

For the British political nation, on the other hand, the intensity of colonial opposition during the Stamp Act crisis only confirmed their . . . suspicions that the colonists wanted . . . "to throw off all dependence and subjection." . . . The separation of the colonies would inevitably mean, many people thought, that Britain would "dwindle and decline every day in our trade, whilst they thrive and prosper exceedingly" so that Britons would "run away as fast as they can from this country to that, and Old England" would "become a poor, deserted, deplorable kingdom," reduced to impotence and robbed of its power by children of its own nurture. Clearly, imperial authorities had been right in the impulse that had animated them since 1748: the colonies had to be brought under tighter control.

. . . To dismiss colonial fears of conspiracy as they developed between 1763 and 1776 as simple paranoia arising out of a particular culturally conditioned mind set . . . is seriously deficient. Clearly, the kind of conspiracy many colonists thought existed did not: there was no secret combination of power-hungry ministers seeking to destroy liberty in America. Since 1748, however, there had been [a] . . . continuing effort by imperial authorities to bring the colonies under tighter regulation, an effort to implement—by various forms of coercion, if necessary—an older conception of what the colonies ought to be. . . . Given the colonists' customary expectations about the nature of the imperial-colonial relationship, this effort, and its many specific components, seemed to the colonists—and *was in fact*—a fundamental attack upon the . . . moral order within the empire as they conceived of that order. In view of the "utter neglect paid by the State or nation of Great Britain to these Settlements," of the relative laxity of imperial controls prior to 1748, Britain's subsequent efforts at reform, at the assertion of "an absolute Dominion over the Colonies," could only be interpreted by many colonists as oppressive and self-serving, as . . . evidence that Britain had never had much genuine affection for or interest in the colonies "until they grew into maturity and opulence," whereupon they finally attracted "not her love, but her avarice, and in consequence the imposition of her Maternal Authority." In this situation, the parent-child metaphor, "so long applyed to Great Britain and her Colonys," came to be seen by the colonists in the years after 1765, not as a reference of affection, but as a degrading . . . symbol of subjection.

VI

The assumption behind this essay has been that any satisfactory analysis of the causes of the American Revolution has to consider not only the nature and content of colonial opposition to Britain after 1763 but also the long-term conditions that made the imperial-colonial relationship, however satisfactory it may have seemed on the surface, so fragile; and we must also consider when and why British authorities altered their traditional posture towards the colonies. What I have tried to suggest is that the change in posture began in the late 1740s and that the explanation for it is to be found primarily in the dramatic rise of the economic importance of the colonies to Britain and the attendant fears within the British political nation that the colonies would shake off their dependence and leave Britain to sink slowly back into its former undifferentiated state among the nations of western Europe. Fed by developments in the 1750s and 1760s, these fears underlay British behavior throughout the years of controversy from 1763 to 1776. Ironically, . . . the measures taken by imperial authorities to prevent these fears from coming true helped to bring about the very thing they most wished to prevent.

FURTHER READING

Fred Anderson, *A People's Army: Massachusetts Soldiers and Society in the Seven Years' War* (1984)

George Louis Beer, *British Colonial Policy, 1754–1765* (1907)

Ian R. Christie, *Crisis of Empire: Great Britain and the American Colonies, 1754–1783* (1967)

Lawrence H. Gipson, "The American Revolution as an Aftermath of the Great War for the Empire, 1754–1763," *Political Science Quarterly* 65 (1950), 86–104

———, *The Great War for the Empire: The Years of Defeat, 1754–1757* (1946)

———, *The Great War for the Empire: The Victorious Years, 1758–1760* (1949)

———, *The Great War for the Empire: The Culmination, 1760–1763* (1953)

Edward P. Hamilton, *The French and Indian Wars: The Story of Battles and Forts in the Wilderness* (1962)

Michael Kammen, *Empire and Interest: The American Colonies and the Politics of Mercantilism* (1970)

Paul E. Kopperman, *Braddock at the Monongahela* (1977)

Leonard W. Labaree, "Benjamin Franklin and the Defense of Pennsylvania, 1754–1757," *Pennsylvania History* 29 (1962), 7–23

———, *Royal Government in America: A Study of the British Colonial System Before 1783* (1930)

Douglas Edward Leach, *Roots of Conflict: British Armed Forces and Colonial Americans, 1677–1763* (1986)

Jack D. Marietta, "Conscience, the Quaker Community, and the French and Indian War," *Pennsylvania Magazine of History and Biography* 95 (1971), 3–27

John M. Murrin, "The French and Indian War, the American Revolution, and the Counterfactual Hypotheses: Reflections on Lawrence Henry Gipson and John Shy," *Reviews in American History* 1 (1973), 307–318

Curtis P. Nettels, "British Mercantilism and the Economic Development of the Thirteen Colonies," *Journal of Economic History* 12 (1952), 105–114

Francis Parkman, *Montcalm and Wolfe* (1884)

William Pencak, *War, Politics and Revolution in Provincial Massachusetts* (1981)

G. A. Rawlyk, *Yankees at Louisbourg* (1967)

O. A. Sherrard, *Lord Chatham: Pitt and the Seven Years' War* (1955)

John Shy, *Toward Lexington: The Role of the British Army in the Coming of the American Revolution* (1965)

Jack M. Sosin, *Whitehall and the Wilderness: The Middle West in British Colonial Policy, 1760–1775* (1961)

C. P. Stacey, *Quebec, 1759: The Siege and the Battle* (1959)

CHAPTER

3

British Reforms
and Colonial Resistance,
1765–1770

✕

When, in the aftermath of the French and Indian War, Britain sought to reform its imperial system, it employed both administrative and legislative measures. Colonial administration was tightened by regulations such as the Orders
in Council, which ended absentee office-holding in the colonies and provided lucrative incentives for customs enforcement; in addition, the Royal Proclamation
of 1763 curtailed settlement west of the Appalachians. Even more important for
enlarging British political power, as well as crystallizing American resistance,
was new legislation: the Currency and Revenue (or Sugar) acts of 1764 and the
Stamp Act of March 22, 1765. While all these measures sparked colonial protest, it was the Stamp Act that set off a wave of resistance of unprecedented
breadth, intensity, and intercolonial coordination. This law extended to America
a broadly based form of direct taxation long used in Britain. It required the
colonists to pay a tax, in silver, on a long list of legal documents and printed
materials. Every paper filed in a legal proceeding, every deed and land survey,
every will, all licenses and diplomas, as well as all bonds written to secure loans
were included. Colonists in all walks of life were affected, because the Stamp Act
also taxed every indenture and apprenticeship paper, all newspapers and newspaper advertisements, pamphlets, almanacs, and even playing cards.

Protests, both verbal and violent, erupted all over the colonies. Some emphasized the absolute constitutional right to taxation by representatives; others
complained of the adverse economic effects of the Stamp Act; and some asserted
that while Parliament had the right to regulate colonial trade through legislation, it could not legally enact taxes for the colonies.

American opposition succeeded, but only in part. In 1766, Lord Rockingham, the new prime minister, persuaded Parliament to repeal the Stamp Act
as a matter of expedience, but at the same time, Parliament passed the Declaratory Act, asserting its full legislative powers. In the following year, 1767, it
would enact the Townshend Duties to raise revenues on the importation of

nearly all kinds of paper, on the widely used commodity tea, on window glass, painters' colors, and red and white lead (also used in paint). The new taxes provoked new protests, a nonimportation movement, and the further development of constitutional arguments. Finally, in 1770, the Townshend Acts were repealed except for the duty on tea, which Britain retained as a matter of principle.

✳ D O C U M E N T S

The first three documents—the Virginia Resolves of 1765 (proposed by Patrick Henry), Governor Francis Bernard's account of the Boston riot of August 14, 1765, and the Declarations of the Stamp Act Congress—show the ideas and actions of a politically awakened colonial population. The several following documents, comprising the "William Pym" newspaper essay, the interrogation of Benjamin Franklin on colonial affairs before the House of Commons, Lord Camden's speech, the Stamp Act repeal, and the Declaratory Act of 1766, afford insights into British interpretations of colonial views, as well as general British assumptions and expectations. The eighth document is an excerpt from John Dickinson's *Letters from a Farmer in Pennsylvania,* which first appeared serially in colonial newspapers in 1767–1768. *Letters,* the most widely read discussion of the constitutional issues in the colonies at the time, provided a theoretical foundation for colonial opposition, including nonimportation, as is illustrated by the final selection, Charleston merchants' agreement in 1769 on nonimportation.

Virginia Stamp Act Resolutions, 1765

Whereas, the honourable House of Commons in England, have of late draw[n] into question how far the General Assembly of this colony hath power to enact laws for laying of taxes and imposing duties payable by the people of this, his Majesty's most ancient colony: . . .

Resolved, that the first adventurers, settlers of this his Majesty's colony and dominion of Virginia, brought with them and transmitted to their posterity, and all other his Majesty's subjects since inhabiting in this his Majesty's colony, all the privileges and immunities that have at any time been held, enjoyed, and possessed by the people of Great Britain.

Resolved, that by two royal charters granted by King James the first, the colonists aforesaid are declared and entitled to all privileges and immunities of natural born subjects, to all intents and purposes as if they had been abiding and born within the realm of England.

Resolved, that the taxation of the people by themselves, or by persons chosen by themselves to represent them, who can only know what taxes the people are able to bear, or the easiest method of raising them, and must themselves be affected by every tax laid on the people, is the only security against a burdensome taxation, and the distinguishing characteristic of British freedom, without which the ancient constitution cannot exist.

Resolved, that his Majesty's liege people of this ancient colony have enjoyed the right of being thus governed by their own Assembly in the article of taxes and internal police, and that the same have never been forfeited, or any other way yielded up, but have been constantly recognized by the king and people of Great Britain. [The next three resolutions were not passed but circulated widely in colonial newspapers.]

Resolved, therefore, that the General Assembly of this colony, together with his Majesty or his substitutes, have in their representatives capacity, the only exclusive right and power to lay taxes and imposts upon the inhabitants of this colony; and that every attempt to vest such power in any other person or persons whatever than the General Assembly aforesaid, is illegal, unconstitutional, and unjust, and has a manifest tendency to destroy British as well as American liberty.

Resolved, that his Majesty's liege people, the inhabitants of this colony, are not bound to yield obedience to any law or ordinance whatever, designed to impose any taxation whatsoever upon them, other than the laws or ordinances of the General Assembly aforesaid.

Resolved, that any person who shall, by speaking or writing, assert or maintain that any person or persons other than the General Assembly of this colony, have any right or power to impose or lay any taxation on the people here, shall be deemed an enemy to his Majesty's colony.

Governor Francis Bernard Describes the Boston Riot, 1765

Castle William August 15, 1765

My Lords,

I am extremely concerned, that I am obliged to give your Lordships the Relation that is to follow; as it will reflect disgrace upon this Province, and bring the Town of Boston under great difficulties. Two or three months ago, I thought that this People would have submitted to the Stamp Act without actual Opposition. Murmurs indeed were continually heard, but they seemed to be such as would in time die away; But the publishing the Virginia Resolves proved an Alarm bell to the disaffected. From that time an infamous weekly Paper, which is printed here, has swarmed with libells of the most atrocious kind. These have been urged with so much Vehemence and so industriously repeated, that I have considered them as preludes to Action. But I did not think, that it would have commenced so early, or be carried to such Lengths, as it has been.

Yesterday Morning at break of day was discovered hanging upon a Tree in a Street of the Town an Effigy, with inscriptions, shewing that it was intended to represent Mr. Oliver, the Secretary, who had lately accepted the Office of Stamp Distributor. Some of the Neighbours offered to take it down, but they were given to know, that would not be permitted. Many Gentlemen, especially some of the Council, treated it as a boyish sport, that did not deserve the Notice of the Governor and Council. But I did not think so however I contented myself with the Lt. Governor, as Chief Justice, directing the Sheriff to order his Officers to take down the Effigy; and I appointed a Council to meet in the Afternoon to consider what should be done, if the Sheriff's Officers were obstructed in removing the Effigy.

Before the Council met, the Sheriff reported, that his Officers had endeavoured to take down the Effigy: but could not do it without imminent danger of their lives. The Council met I represented this Transaction to them as the beginning in my Opinion, of much greater Commotions. I desired their Advice, what I should do upon this Occasion. A Majority of the Council spoke in form against doing anything but upon very different Principles: some said, that it was trifling Business, which, if let alone, would subside of itself, but, if taken notice of would become a serious Affair. Others said, that it was a serious Affair already; that it was a preconcerted Business, in which the greatest Part of the Town was engaged; that we had no force to oppose to it, and making an Opposition to it, without a power to support the Opposition, would only inflame the People; and be a means of extending the mischief to persons not at present the Objects of it. Tho' the Council were allmost unanimous in advising, that nothing should be done, they were averse to having such advice entered upon the Council Book. But I insisted upon their giving me an Answer to my Question, and that it should be entered in the Book; when, after a long altercation, it was avoided by their advising me to order the Sheriff to assemble the Peace Officers and preserve the peace which I immediately ordered, being a matter of form rather than of real Significance.

It now grew dark when the Mob, which had been gathering all the Afternoon, came down to the Town House, bringing the Effigy with them, and knowing we were sitting in the Council Chamber, they gave three Huzzas by way of defiance, and passed on. From thence they went to a new Building, lately erected by Mr Oliver to let out for Shops, and not quite finished: this they called the Stamp Office, and pulled it down to the Ground in five minutes. From thence they went to Mr Oliver's House; before which they beheaded the Effigy; and broke all the Windows next the Street; then they carried the Effigy to Fort hill near Mr Oliver's House, where they burnt the Effigy in a Bonfire made of the Timber they had pulled down from the Building. Mr Oliver had removed his family from his House, and remained himself with a few friends, when the Mob returned to attack the House. Mr Oliver was prevailed upon to retire, and his friends kept Possession of the House. The Mob finding the Doors barricaded, broke down the whole fence of the Garden towards fort hill, and coming on beat in all the doors and Windows of the Garden front, and entered the House, the Gentlemen there retiring. As soon as they had got Possession, they searched about for Mr Oliver, declaring they would kill him; finding that he had left the House, a party set out to search two neighbouring Houses, in one of which Mr Oliver was, but happily they were diverted from this pursuit by a Gentleman telling them, that Mr Oliver was gone with the Governor to the Castle. Otherwise he would certainly have been murdered. After 11 o'clock the Mob seeming to grow quiet, the (Lt. Governor) Chief Justice and the Sheriff ventured to go to Mr Oliver's House to endeavour to perswade them to disperse. As soon as they began to speak, a Ringleader cried out, The Governor and the

Sheriff! to your Arms, my boys! Presently after a volley of Stones followed, and the two Gentlemen narrowly escaped thro' favour of the Night, not without some bruises. I should have mentioned before, that I sent a written order to the Colonel of the Regiment of Militia, to beat an Alarm; he answered, that it would signify nothing, for as soon as the drum was heard, the drummer would be knocked down, and the drum broke; he added, that probably all the drummers of the Regiment were in the Mob. Nothing more being to be done, The Mob were left to disperse at their own Time, which they did about 12 o'clock.

The Declarations of the Stamp Act Congress, 1765

The members of this congress, sincerely devoted, with the warmest sentiments of affection and duty to his Majesty's person and government; inviolably attached to the present happy establishment of the Protestant succession, and with minds deeply impressed by a sense of the present and impending misfortunes of the British colonies on this continent; . . . make the following declarations, of our humble opinion, respecting the most essential rights and liberties of the colonists, and of the grievances under which they labour, by reason of several late acts of Parliament.

I. That his Majesty's subjects in these colonies, owe the same allegiance to the Crown of Great Britain, that is owing from his subjects born within the realm, and all due subordination to that august body, the Parliament of Great Britain.

II. That his Majesty's liege subjects in these colonies are entitled to all the inherent rights and liberties of his natural born subjects within the kingdom of Great Britain.

III. That it is inseparably essential to the freedom of a people, and the undoubted right of Englishmen, that no taxes should be imposed on them, but with their own consent, given personally, or by their representatives.

IV. That the people of these colonies are not, and from their local circumstances, cannot be represented in the House of Commons in Great Britain.

V. That the only representatives of the people of these colonies, are persons chosen therein, by themselves; and that no taxes ever have been, or can be constitutionally imposed on them, but by their respective legislature.

VI. That all supplies to the Crown, being free gifts of the people, it is unreasonable and inconsistent with the principles and spirit of the British constitution, for the people of Great Britain to grant to his Majesty the property of the colonists.

VII. That trial by jury is the inherent and invaluable right of every British subject in these colonies.

VIII. That the late Act of Parliament, entitled, An Act for granting and applying certain Stamp Duties, . . . by imposing taxes on the inhabitants of these colonies, and the said Act, and several other Acts, by extending the jurisdiction of the courts of admiralty beyond its ancient limits, have a manifest tendency to subvert the rights and liberties of the colonists.

IX. That the duties imposed by several late Acts of Parliament, from the peculiar circumstances of these colonies, will be extremely burdensome and grievous, and from the scarcity of specie, the payment of them absolutely impracticable.

X. That as the profits of the trade of these colonies ultimately centre in Great Britain, to pay for the manufactures which they are obliged to take from thence, they eventually contribute very largely to all supplies granted there to the Crown.

XI. That the restrictions imposed by several late Acts of Parliament, on the trade of these colonies, will render them unable to purchase the manufactures of Great Britain.

XII. That the increase, prosperity and happiness of these colonies, depend on the full and free enjoyment of their rights and liberties, and an intercourse with Great Britain, mutually affectionate and advantageous.

XIII. That it is the right of the British subjects in these colonies, to petition the king or either house of Parliament.

Lastly, that it is the indispensable duty of these colonies to the best of sovereigns, to the mother country, and to themselves, to endeavour by a loyal and dutiful address to his Majesty, and humble applications to both houses of Parliament, to procure the repeal of the Act for granting and applying certain stamp duties, of all clauses of any other Acts of Parliament, whereby the jurisdiction of the admiralty is extended as aforesaid, and of the other late Acts for the restriction of American commerce.

"William Pym" Asserts Parliamentary Supremacy, 1765

The people in our American colonies lay a very great stress upon the importance of their charters, and imagine that the privileges granted to their ancestors, at the time of their original establishment, must infallibly exempt them from participating in the least inconvenience of the Mother country, though the Mother country must share in every inconvenience of theirs. This mode of reasoning is however no less new than it is extraordinary: and one would almost be tempted to imagine that the persons, who argue in this manner, were alike unacquainted with the nature of the colonies and the constitution of this kingdom.

I shall very readily grant, that the colonies at the time of their first settling might receive particular indulgences from the Crown, to encourage adventurers to go over; and I will also grant, that these charters should be as inviolably adhered to as the nature of public contingencies will admit. But at the same time let me inform my fellow subjects of America, that a resolution of the British parliament can at any time set aside all the charters that have ever been granted by our monarchs; and that consequently nothing can be more idle than this pompous exclamation about their charter exemptions, whenever such a resolution has actually passed.

The great business of the British Legislative power is, to consult upon what new laws may be necessary for the general good of the British dominions, and to remove any casual inconveniences which may arise from the existence of their former acts. In the prosecution of this important end, they cannot expect but what the most salutary laws will prove oppressive to some part of the people. However no injury, which may be sustained by individuals, is to prevent them from promoting the welfare of the community; for if they debated till they framed an ordinance agreeable to the wishes of every body, 'twould be utterly impossible for them ever to frame any ordinance at all.

If then the Legislative power of this country have a right to alter or annul those public acts which were solemnly passed by former princes and former parliaments; it must be a necessary consequence that they have an equal right to annul the private charters of former princes also; and that these charters, which are by no means to be set in the same degree of importance with our laws, are at least every whit as subject to their jurisdiction and authority. This is a circumstance which the assembly of Virginia in particular should have attended to before their late unaccountable resolutions; and 'tis what I hope the assemblies of our other settlements will judiciously attend to, if they find the least propensity to follow the extraordinary example of their Sister-colony.

The people of Ireland, though they have a parliament of their own (and a parliament, I will take the liberty of saying, composed of people to the full as eminent for their fortune and abilities, as any of our American assemblies) are nevertheless under the immediate subjection of the British Legislature. The vote of an English Senate can in an instant abrogate all the laws of that kingdom; and surely none of the plantations can possibly plead a greater share either of merit or privileges than our Irish fellow subjects; who nevertheless behave with an uncommon degree of respect to our decisions; and never presume to blame the hand which increases their burdens, however they may groan beneath the heaviness of the load.

I am very well aware that the present impatience, which the whole kingdom feels at the least increase of taxes, will naturally create a number of friends for the colonies: but at the same time let us consider that the propriety of the tax, which has excited such a ferment among our American fellow-subjects, is not now the foundation of dispute. The question now is, Whether those American subjects are, or are not, bound by the resolutions of a British parliament? If they are *not,* they are entirely a separate people from us, and the mere reception of officers appointed in this kingdom, is nothing but an idle farce of government, which it is by no means our interest to keep up, if it is to produce us no benefit but the honour of protecting them whenever they are attacked by their enemies. On the other hand, if the people of America *are* bound by the proceedings of the English legislature, what excuse can the Virginians possibly make for the late indecent vote (to give it no harsher appellation) of their assembly. The present crisis, Sir, is really an alarming one; and after all the blood and treasure which we have expended in defence of the colonies, it is now questioned, whether we have any interest in those colonies at all.

If the people of Virginia were offended either with the tax itself, or with the mode of taxation, the proper method of proceeding would have been to petition the parliament, to point out the grievances arising from it, and to solicit the necessary redress. This is the invariable manner in which all the rest of their fellow-subjects (at least the European part of their fellow subjects) have acted in cases of a like nature. But to think of bullying their King, and the august Council of the Mother country, into an acquiescence with their sentiments, by a rash and hot headed vote; not only must expose them to the ridicule, but to the resentment of every considerate man who wishes well either to their interest or to the prosperity of this kingdom.

The people of the colonies know very well that the taxes of the Mother country are every day increasing; and can they expect that no addition whatsoever will be made to theirs? They know very well that a great part of our national debt was contracted in establishing them on a firm foundation, and protecting them from the arbitrary attempts of their implacable ene- mies.—Can anything then be so unreasonable, as a refusal of their assistance to wipe a little of it off? For my own part I am as much astonished at their want of justice, as I am surprized at their want of gratitude; and cannot help declaring it as my opinion, that we ought to shew but a very small share of sensibility for the circumstances of those people who are so utterly regardless of ours. To be sure, Sir, in assisting the colonies we had an eye to our own interest. It would be ridiculous otherwise to squander away our blood and our treasure in their defence. But certainly the benefit was mutual; and consequently the disadvantage should be mutual too. If we reap emo- luments from the existence of the colonies, the colonies owe every thing to our encouragement and protection. As therefore we share in the same pros- perity, we ought to participate of the same distress; and nothing can be more inequitable, than the least disinclination to bear a regular portion of those disbursements, which were applied to support the general interest both of the mother-country and themselves.

Examination of Benjamin Franklin Before the House of Commons, 1766

Q. What is your name, and place of abode?
A. Franklin, of Philadelphia.
Q. Do the Americans pay any considerable taxes among themselves?
A. Certainly many, and very heavy taxes.
Q. What are the present taxes in Pennsylvania, laid by the laws of the colony?
A. There are taxes on all estates real and personal, a poll tax, a tax on all offices, professions, trades and businesses, according to their profits; an excise on all wine, rum, and other spirits; and a duty of Ten Pounds per head on all Negroes imported, with some other duties.

Q. For what purposes are those taxes laid?

A. For the support of the civil and military establishments of the country, and to discharge the heavy debt contracted in the last war.

Q. How long are those taxes to continue?

A. Those for discharging the debt are to continue till 1772, and longer, if the debt should not be then all discharged. The others must always continue. . . .

Q. Are not the Colonies, from their circumstances, very able to pay the stamp duty?

A. In my opinion, there is not gold and silver enough in the Colonies to pay the stamp duty for one year.

Q. Don't you know that the money arising from the stamps was all to be laid out in America?

A. I know it is appropriated by the act to the American service; but it will be spent in the conquered Colonies, where the soldiers are, not in the Colonies that pay it.

Q. Is there not a ballance of trade due from the Colonies where the troops are posted, that will bring back the money to the old colonies?

A. I think not. I believe very little would come back. I know of no trade likely to bring it back. I think it would come from the Colonies where it was spent directly to England; for I have always observed, that in every Colony the more plenty the means of remittance to England, the more goods are sent for, and the more trade with England carried on. . . .

Q. Do you think it right that America should be protected by this country, and pay no part of the expence?

A. That is not the case. The Colonies raised, cloathed and paid, during the last war, near 25000 men, and spent many millions.

Q. Were you not reimbursed by parliament?

A. We were only reimbursed what, in your opinion, we had advanced beyond our proportion, or beyond what might reasonably be expected from us; and it was a very small part of what we spent. Pennsylvania, in particular, disbursed about 500,000 Pounds, and the reimbursements, in the whole, did not exceed 60,000 Pounds.

Q. You have said that you pay heavy taxes in Pennsylvania; what do they amount to in the Pound?

A. The tax on all estates, real and personal, is Eighteen Pence in the Pound, fully rated; and the tax on the profits of trades and professions, with other taxes, do, I suppose, make full Half a Crown in the Pound. . . .

Q. Do not you think the people of America would submit to pay the stamp duty, if it was moderated?

A. No, never, unless compelled by force of arms. . . .

Q. How is the assembly composed? Of what kinds of people are the members, landholders or traders?

A. It is composed of landholders, merchants and artificers.

Q. Are not the majority landholders?

A. I believe they are.

Q. Do not they, as much as possible, shift the tax off from the land, to ease that, and lay the burthen heavier on trade?

A. I have never understood it so. I never heard such a thing suggested. And indeed an attempt of that kind could answer no purpose. The merchant or trader is always skilled in figures, and ready with his pen and ink. If unequal burthens are laid on his trade, he puts an additional price on his goods; and the consumers, who are chiefly landholders, finally pay the greatest part, if not the whole.

Q. What was the temper of America towards Great-Britain before the year 1763?

A. The best in the world. They submitted willingly to the government of the Crown, and paid, in all their courts, obedience to acts of parliament. Numerous as the people are in the several old provinces, they cost you nothing in forts, citadels, garrisons or armies, to keep them in subjection. They were governed by this country at the expence only of a little pen, ink and paper. They were led by a thread. They had not only a respect, but an affection, for Great-Britain, for its laws, its customs and manners, and even a fondness for its fashions, that greatly increased the commerce. Natives of Britain were always treated with particular regard; to be an Old England-man was, of itself, a character of some respect, and gave a kind of rank among us.

Q. And what is their temper now?

A. O, very much altered.

Q. Did you ever hear the authority of parliament to make laws for America questioned till lately?

A. The authority of parliament was allowed to be valid in all laws, except such as should lay internal taxes. It was never disputed in laying duties to regulate commerce. . . .

Q. In what light did the people of America use to consider the parliament of Great-Britain?

A. They considered the parliament as the great bulwark and security of their liberties and privileges, and always spoke of it with the utmost respect and veneration. Arbitrary ministers, they thought, might possibly, at times, attempt to oppress them; but they relied on it, that the parliament, on application, would always give redress. They remembered, with gratitude, a strong instance of this, when a bill was brought into parliament, with a clause to make royal instructions laws in the Colonies, which the house of commons would not pass, and it was thrown out.

Q. And have they not still the same respect for parliament?

A. No; it is greatly lessened.

Q. To what causes is that owing?

A. To a concurrence of causes; the restraints lately laid on their trade, by which the bringing of foreign gold and silver into the Colonies was prevented; the prohibition of making paper money among themselves; and then demanding a new and heavy tax by stamps; taking away, at the same time, trials by juries, and refusing to receive and hear their humble petitions.

Q. Don't you think they would submit to the stamp-act, if it was modified, the obnoxious parts taken out, and the duty reduced to some particulars, of small moment?

A. No; they will never submit to it. . . .

Q. What is your opinion of a future tax, imposed on the same principle with that of the stamp-act; how would the Americans receive it?

A. Just as they do this. They would not pay it.

Q. Have you not heard of the resolutions of this house, and of the house of lords, asserting the right of parliament relating to America, including a power to tax the people there?

A. Yes, I have heard of such resolutions.

Q. What will be the opinion of the Americans on those resolutions?

A. They will think them unconstitutional, and unjust.

Q. Was it an opinion in America before 1763, that the parliament had no right to lay taxes and duties there?

A. I never heard any objection to the right of laying duties to regulate commerce; but a right to lay internal taxes was never supposed to be in parliament, as we are not represented there.

Q. On what do you found your opinion, that the people in America made any such distinction?

A. I know that whenever the subject has occurred in conversation where I have been present, it has appeared to be the opinion of every one, that we could not be taxed in a parliament where we were not represented. But the payment of duties laid by act of parliament, as regulations of commerce, was never disputed.

Q. But can you name any act of assembly, or public act of any of your governments, that made such distinction?

A. I do not know that there was any; I think there was never an occasion to make any such act, till now that you have attempted to tax us; that has occasioned resolutions of assembly, declaring the distinction, in which I think every assembly on the continent, and every member in every assembly, have been unanimous. . . .

Q. You say the Colonies have always submitted to external taxes, and object to the right of parliament only in laying internal taxes; now can you shew that there is any kind of difference between the two taxes to the Colony on which they may be laid?

A. I think the difference is very great. An external tax is a duty laid on commodities imported; that duty is added to the first cost, and other charges on the commodity, and when it is offered to sale, makes a part of the price. If the people do not like it at that price, they refuse it; they are not obliged to pay it. But an internal tax is forced from the people without their consent, if not laid by their own representatives. The stamp-act says, we shall have no commerce, make no exchange of property with each other, neither purchase nor grant, nor recover debts; we shall neither marry, nor make our wills, unless we pay such and such sums, and thus it is intended to extort our money from us, or ruin us by the consequences of refusing to pay it.

Q. But supposing the external tax or duty to be laid on the necessaries of life imported into your Colony, will not that be the same thing in its effects as an internal tax?

A. I do not know a single article imported into the Northern Colonies, but what they can either do without, or make themselves.

Q. Don't you think cloth from England absolutely necessary to them?

A. No, by no means absolutely necessary; with industry and good management, they may very well supply themselves with all they want.

Q. Will it not take a long time to establish that manufacture among them? and must they not in the mean while suffer greatly?

A. I think not. They have made a surprising progress already. And I am of opinion, that before their old clothes are worn out, they will have new ones of their own making. . . .

Q. Did the Americans ever dispute the controling power of parliament to regulate the commerce?

A. No.

Q. Can any thing less than a military force carry the stamp-act into execution?

A. I do not see how a military force can be applied to that purpose.

Q. Why may it not?

A. Suppose a military force sent into America, they will find nobody in arms; what are they then to do? They cannot force a man to take stamps who chooses to do without them. They will not find a rebellion; they may indeed make one.

Q. If the act is not repealed, what do you think will be the consequences?

A. A total loss of the respect and affection the people of America bear to this country, and of all the commerce that depends on that respect and affection.

Q. How can the commerce be affected?

A. You will find, that if the act is not repealed, they will take very little of your manufactures in a short time.

Q. Is it in their power to do without them?

A. I think they may very well do without them.

Q. Is it their interest not to take them?

A. The goods they take from Britain are either necessaries, mere conveniences, or superfluities. The first, as cloth, &c. with a little industry they can make at home; the second they can do without, till they are able to provide them among themselves; and the last, which are much the greatest part, they will strike off immediately. They are mere articles of fashion, purchased and consumed, because the fashion in a respected country, but will now be detested and rejected. The people have already struck off, by general agreement, the use of all goods fashionable in mournings, and many thousand pounds worth are sent back as unsaleable. . . .

Q. Suppose an act of internal regulations, connected with a tax, how would they receive it?

A. I think it would be objected to.

Q. Then no regulation with a tax would be submitted to?

A. Their opinion is, that when aids to the Crown are wanted, they are to be asked of the several assemblies, according to the old established usage, who will, as they always have done, grant them freely. And that their money ought not to be given away without their consent, by persons at a distance, unacquainted with their circumstances and abilities. The granting aids to the Crown, is the only means they have of recommending themselves to their sovereign, and they think it extremely hard and unjust, that a body of men, in which they have no representatives, should make a merit to itself to giving and granting what is not its own, but theirs, and deprive them of a right they esteem of the utmost value and importance, as it is the security of all their other rights.

Q. But is not the post-office, which they have long received, a tax as well as a regulation?

A. No; the money paid for the postage of a letter is not of the nature of a tax; it is merely a quantum meruit for a service done; no person is compellable to pay the money, if he does not chuse to receive the service. A man may still, as before the act, send his letter by a servant, a special messenger, or a friend, if he thinks it cheaper and safer. . . .

Q. You say they do not object to the right of parliament in laying duties on goods to be paid on their importation; now, is there any kind of difference between a duty on the importation of goods, and an excise on their consumption?

A. Yes; a very material one; an excise, for the reasons I have just mentioned, they think you can have no right to lay within their country. But the sea is yours; you maintain, by your fleets, the safety of navigation in it; and keep it clear of pirates; you may have therefore a natural and equitable right to some toll or duty on merchandizes carried through that part of your dominions, towards defraying the expence you are at in ships to maintain the safety of that carriage. . . .

Q. What do you think a sufficient military force to protect the distribution of the stamps in every part of America?

A. A very great force; I can't say what, if the disposition of America is for a general resistance. . . .

Q. If the stamp act should be repealed, would not the Americans think they could oblige the parliament to repeal every external tax law now in force?

A. It is hard to answer questions of what people at such a distance will think.

Q. But what do you imagine they will think were the motives of repealing the act?

A. I suppose they will think that it was repealed from a conviction of its inexpediency; and they will rely upon it, that while the same inexpediency subsists, you will never attempt to make such another.

Q. What do you mean by its inexpediency?

A. I mean its inexpediency on several accounts; the poverty and inability of those who were to pay the tax; the general discontent it has occasioned; and the impracticability of enforcing it.

Q. If the act should be repealed, and the legislature should shew its resentment to the opposers of the stamp-act, would the Colonies acquiesce in the authority of the legislature? What is your opinion they would do?

A. I don't doubt at all, that if the legislature repeal the stamp-act, the Colonies will acquiesce in the authority.

Q. But if the legislature should think fit to ascertain its right to lay taxes, by any act laying a small tax, contrary to their opinion, would they submit to pay the tax?

A. The proceedings of the people in America have been considered too much together. The proceedings of the assemblies have been very different from those of the mobs, and should be distinguished, as having no connection with each other. The assemblies have only peaceably resolved what they take to be their rights; they have taken no measures for opposition by force; they have not built a fort, raised a man, or provided a grain of ammunition, in order to such opposition. The ringleaders of riots they think ought to be punished; they would punish them themselves, if they could. Every sober sensible man would wish to see rioters punished; as otherwise peaceable people have no security of person or estate. But as to any internal tax, how small soever, laid by the legislature here on the people there, while they have no representatives in this legislature, I think it will never be submitted to. They will oppose it to the last. They do not consider it as at all necessary for you to raise money on them by your taxes, because they are, and always have been, ready to raise money by taxes among themselves, and to grant large sums, equal to their abilities, upon requisition from the Crown. . . . America has been greatly misrepresented and abused here, in papers, and pamphlets, and speeches, as ungrateful, and unreasonable, and unjust, in having put this nation to immense expence for their defence, and refusing to bear any part of that expence. The Colonies raised, paid and clothed, near 25000 men during the last war, a number equal to those sent from Britain, and far beyond their proportion; they went deeply into debt in doing this, and all their taxes and estates are mortgaged, for many years to come, for discharging that debt. Government here was at that time very sensible of this. The Colonies were recommended to parliament. Every year the King sent down to the house a written message to this purpose, That his Majesty, being highly sensible of the zeal and vigour with which his faithful subjects in North-America had exerted themselves, in defence of his Majesty's just rights and possessions, recommended it to the house to take the same into consideration, and enable him to give them a proper compensation. You will find those messages on your own journals every year of the war to the very last, and you did accordingly give 200,000 Pounds annually to the Crown, to be distributed in such compensation to the Colonies. This is the strongest of all proofs that the Colonies, far from being unwilling to bear a share of the burthen, did exceed their proportion; for if they had done less, or had only equalled their proportion, there would have been no room or reason for compensation. Indeed the sums reimbursed them, were by no means adequate to the expence they incurred beyond their proportion; but they never murmured at that; they esteemed their Sovereign's approbation of their zeal and fidelity, and the approbation of this house, far beyond any other kind of compensation; therefore there was no occasion for this act, to force money from a willing people; they had not refused giving money for the purposes of the act; no requisition had been made; they were always willing and ready to do what could reasonably be expected from them, and in this light they wish to be considered. . . .

Q. If the act should pass, requiring the American assemblies to make compensation to the sufferers, and they should disobey it, and then the parliament should, by another act, lay an internal tax, would they then obey it?

A. The people will pay no internal tax; and I think an act to oblige the assemblies to make compensation is unnecessary, for I am of opinion, that as soon as the present heats are abated, they will take the matter into consideration, and, if it is right to be done, they will do it of themselves. . . .

Q. Does the distinction between internal and external taxes exist in the words of the [Pennsylvania] charter?

A. No, I believe not.

Q. Then may they not, by the same interpretation, object to the parliament's right of external taxation?

A. They never have hitherto. Many arguments have been lately used here to shew them that there is no difference, and that if you have no right to tax them internally, you have none to tax them externally, or make any other law to bind them. At present they do not reason so, but in time they may possibly be convinced by these arguments. . . .

Q. If the stamp-act should be repealed, would it induce the assemblies of America to acknowledge the rights of parliament to tax them, and would they erase their resolutions?

A. No, never.

Q. Is there no means of obliging them to erase those resolutions?

A. None that I know of; they will never do it unless compelled by force of arms.

Q. Is there a power on earth that can force them to erase them?

A. No power, how great soever, can force men to change their opinions. . . .

Q. What used to be the pride of the Americans?

A. To indulge in the fashions and manufactures of Great-Britain.

Q. What is now their pride?

A. To wear their old cloaths over again, till they can make new ones.

Lord Camden (Charles Pratt) Exhorts Parliament to Change Direction, 1766

I find that I have been very injuriously treated; have been considered as the broacher of new-fangled doctrines, contrary to the laws of this kingdom, and subversive of the rights of parliament. . . . As the affair is of the utmost importance, and in its consequences may involve the fate of kingdoms, I took the strictest review of my arguments; I re-examined all my authorities;

fully determined, if I found myself mistaken, publicly to own my mistake, and give up my opinion: but my searches have more and more convinced me, that the British parliament have no right to tax the Americans. I shall not therefore consider the Declaratory Bill now lying on your table . . . the very existence of which is illegal, absolutely illegal, contrary to the fundamental laws of nature, contrary to the fundamental laws of this constitution? A constitution grounded on the eternal and immutable laws of nature; a constitution whose foundation and centre is liberty, which sends liberty to every subject, that is or may happen to be within any part of its ample circumference. Nor, my lords, is the doctrine new, it is as old as the constitution; it grew up with it; indeed it is its support; taxation and representation are inseparably united; God hath joined them, no British parliament can separate them; to endeavour to do it, is to stab our very vitals. Nor is this the first time this doctrine has been mentioned; 70 years ago, my lords, a pamphlet was published, recommending the levying a parliamentary tax on one of the colonies; this pamphlet was answered by two others, then much read; these totally deny the power of taxing the colonies; and why? Because the colonies had no representatives in parliament to give consent; no answer, public or private, was given to these pamphlets, no censure passed upon them; men were not startled at the doctrine as either new or illegal, or derogatory to the rights of parliament. I do not mention these pamphlets by way of authority, but to vindicate myself from the imputation of having first broached this doctrine.

My position is this—I repeat it—I will maintain it to my last hour,—taxation and representation are inseparable;—this position is founded on the laws of nature; it is more, it is itself an eternal law of nature; for whatever is a man's own, is absolutely his own; no man hath a right to take it from him without his consent, either expressed by himself or representative; whoever attempts to do it, attempts an injury; whoever does it, commits a robbery; he throws down and destroys the distinction between liberty and slavery. Taxation and representation are coeval with and essential to this constitution. . . . As to Ireland, my lords, before that kingdom had a parliament as it now has, if your lordships will examine the old records, you will find, that when a tax was to be laid on that country, the Irish sent over here representatives; and the same records will inform your lordships, what wages those representatives received from their constituents. In short, my lords, from the whole of our history, from the earliest period, you will find that taxation and representation were always united; so true are the words of that consummate reasoner and politician Mr. Locke. I before alluded to his book; I have again consulted him; and finding what he writes so applicable to the subject in hand, and so much in favour of my sentiments, I beg your lordships' leave to read a little of this book.

"The supreme power cannot take from any man, any part of his property, without his own consent;" and B. 2. p. 136–139, particularly 140. Such are the words of this great man, and which are well worth your serious attention. His principles are drawn from the heart of our constitution, which he thoroughly understood, and will last as long as that shall last; . . . For these reasons, my lords, I can never give my assent to any bill for taxing the American colonies, while they remain unrepresented; for as to the distinction of a virtual representation, it is so absurd as not to deserve an answer; I therefore pass it over with contempt. The forefathers of the Americans did not leave their native country, and subject themselves to every danger and distress, to be reduced to a state of slavery: they did not give up their rights; they looked for protection, and not for chains, from their mother country; by her they expected to be defended in the possession of their property, and not to be deprived of it: for, should the present power continue, there is nothing which they can call their own; or, to use the words of Mr. Locke, "What property have they in that, which another may, by right, take, when he pleases, to himself?"

Parliament Repeals the Stamp Act but Declares Its Authority, 1766

Repeal Act, March 18, 1766

Whereas an Act was passed in the last session of Parliament entitled, An Act for granting and applying certain stamp duties, and other duties in the British colonies and plantations in America towards further defraying the expenses of defending, protecting, and securing the same; and for amending such parts of the several Acts of Parliament relating to the trade and revenues of the said colonies and plantations as direct the manner of determining and recovering the penalties and forfeitures therein mentioned; and whereas the continuance of the said Act would be attended with many inconveniencies, and may be productive of consequences greatly detrimental to the commercial interests of these kingdoms; . . . be it enacted by the king's most excellent Majesty, by and with the advice and consent of the Lords Spiritual and Temporal, and Commons, . . . that . . . the above-mentioned Act . . . is . . . hereby repealed.

The Declaratory Act of March 18, 1766

Whereas several of the houses of representatives in his Majesty's colonies and plantations in America, have of late, against law, claimed to themselves, or to the general assemblies of the same, the sole and exclusive right of imposing duties and taxes upon his Majesty's subjects in the said colonies and plantations; and have, in pursuance of such claim, passed certain votes, resolutions, and orders, derogatory to the legislative authority of Parliament, and inconsistent with the dependency of the said colonies and plantations upon the Crown of Great Britain: may it therefore . . . be declared, . . . in this present Parliament assembled, . . . that the said colonies and plantations in America have been, are, and of right ought to be, subordinate unto, and dependent upon the imperial Crown and Parliament of Great Britain; and that the . . . Parliament assembled, had, hath, and of right ought to have, full power and authority to make laws and statutes of sufficient force and validity to bind the colonies and people of America, subjects of the Crown of Great Britain, in all cases whatsoever.

II. And be it further declared and enacted by the authority aforesaid, that all resolutions, votes, orders, and proceedings, in any of the said colonies or plantations, whereby the power and authority of the Parliament of Great Britain, to make laws and statutes as aforesaid, is denied, or drawn into question, are, and are hereby declared to be, utterly null and void to all intents and purposes whatsoever.

John Dickinson Exhorts the Colonists to Opposition, 1767–1768

My Dear Countrymen,

[A] late act of parliament, which appears to me to be unconstitutional, and . . . destructive to the liberty of these colonies . . . is the act for granting the duties on paper, glass, etc.

The parliament unquestionably possesses a legal authority to *regulate* the trade of *Great Britain,* and all her colonies. Such an authority is essential to the relation between a mother country and her colonies; and necessary for the common good of all. He who considers these provinces as states distinct from the *British Empire,* has very slender notions of *justice,* or of their *interests.* We are but parts of a *whole;* and therefore there must exist a power somewhere, to preside, and preserve the connection in due order. This power is lodged in the parliament; and we are as much dependent on *Great Britain,* as a perfectly free people can be on another.

I have looked over *every statute* relating to these colonies, from their first settlement to this time; and I find every one of them founded on this principle, till the *Stamp Act* administration. *All before,* are calculated to regulate trade, and preserve or promote a mutually beneficial intercourse between the several constituent parts of the empire; and though many of them imposed duties on trade, yet those duties were always imposed *with design* to restrain the commerce of one part, that was injurious to another, and thus to promote the general welfare. The raising of a revenue thereby was never intended. . . . Never did the *British* parliament, till the period above mentioned, think of imposing duties in *America* FOR THE PURPOSE OF RAISING A REVENUE. Mr. *Greenville* first introduced this language. . . .

A few months after came the *Stamp Act.* . . .

The last act, granting duties upon paper, etc. carefully pursues these modern precedents. The preamble is, "Whereas it is expedient THAT A REVENUE SHOULD BE RAISED IN YOUR MAJESTY'S DOMINIONS IN AMERICA." . . .

This I call an innovation; and a most dangerous innovation. It may perhaps be objected, that *Great Britain* has a right to lay what duties she pleases upon her exports, and it makes no difference to us, whether they are paid here or there.

To this I answer. These colonies require many things for their use, which the laws of *Great Britain* prohibit them from getting any where but from her. Such are paper and glass. . . .

Our great advocate, Mr. *Pitt,* in his speeches on the debate concerning the repeal of the *Stamp Act,* acknowledged, that *Great Britain* could restrain our manufactures. His words are these—"This kingdom, as the supreme governing and legislative power, has ALWAYS bound the colonies by her regulations and RESTRICTIONS in trade, in navigation, in MANUFACTURES—in everything, *except that of taking their money out of their pockets* WITHOUT THEIR CONSENT." Again he says, "We may bind their trade, CONFINE THEIR MANUFACTURES, and exercise every power whatever, *except that of taking their money out of their pockets* WITHOUT THEIR CONSENT."

Here then, my dear countrymen, ROUSE yourselves, and behold the ruin hanging over your heads. If you ONCE admit, that *Great Britain* may lay duties upon her exportations to us, *for the purpose of levying money on us only,* she then will have nothing to do, but to lay those duties on the articles which she prohibits us to manufacture—and the tragedy of *American* liberty is finished. We have been prohibited from procuring manufactures, in all cases, any where but from *Great Britain* (excepting linens, which we are permitted to import directly from *Ireland*). We have been prohibited, in some cases, from manufacturing for ourselves; and may be prohibited in others. We are therefore exactly in the situation of a city besieged, which is surrounded by the works of the besiegers in every part *but one.* If *that* is closed up, no step can be taken, *but to surrender at discretion.* If *Great Britain* can order us to come to her for necessaries we want, and can order us to pay what taxes she pleases before we take them away, or when we land them here, we are as abject slaves as *France* and *Poland* can show in wooden shoes and with uncombed hair. . . .

A Farmer

My Dear Countrymen,
    . . . We feel too sensibly, that *any ministerial measures* relating to these colonies, are soon carried successfully through the parliament. Certain prejudices operate there so strongly against us, that it may be justly questioned, whether *all* the provinces united, will ever be able effectually to call to an account before the parliament, any minister who shall abuse the power by the late act given to the crown in *America.* He may divide the spoils torn from us in what manner he pleases, *and we shall have no way of making him responsible.* If he should order, that every *governor* shall have a yearly salary of 5,000£ sterling; every *chief justice* of 3,000£; every inferior officer in proportion; and should then reward the most profligate, ignorant, or needy dependents or himself or his friends, with places of the greatest trust, because they were of the greatest profit, this would be called an arrangement in consequence of the "adequate provision for defraying the charge of the administration of justice, and the support of the civil government": And if the taxes should prove at any time insufficient to answer all the expenses of the numberless offices, which ministers may please to create, surely the members of the house of commons will be so "*modest,*" as not to "contradict

a minister" who shall tell them, it is become necessary to lay a new tax upon the colonies, for the laudable purposes of defraying the charges of the "administration of justice, and support of civil government" among them. Thus, in fact, we shall be taxed by ministers. In short, it will be in their power to settle upon us any CIVIL, ECCLESIASTICAL, or MILITARY establishment, which they choose.

We may perceive, by the example of *Ireland,* how eager ministers are to seize upon any settled revenue, and apply it in supporting their own power. Happy are the men, and *happy the people who grow wise by the misfortunes of others.* Earnestly, my dear countrymen, do I beseech the author of all good gifts, that you may grow wise in this manner; and if I may be allowed to take such a liberty, I beg leave to recommend to you in general, as the best method of attaining this wisdom, diligently to study the histories of other countries. You will there find all the arts, that can possibly be practiced by cunning rulers, or false patriots among yourselves, so fully delineated, that, changing names, the account would serve for your own times.

It is pretty well known on this continent, that *Ireland* has, with a regular consistency of injustice, been cruelly treated by ministers in the article of *pensions.* . . .

Besides the burden of *pensions* in *Ireland,* which have enormously increased within these few years, almost all the *offices* in that poor kingdom, have been, since the commencement of the present century, and now are bestowed upon *strangers.* For tho' the merit of persons born there, justly raises them to places of high trust when they go abroad, as all *Europe* can witness, yet he is an uncommonly lucky *Irishman,* who can get a good post *in his* NATIVE *country.* . . .

In the same manner shall we unquestionably be treated, as soon as the late taxes laid upon us, shall make posts in the "government," and the "administration of justice" *here,* worth the attention of persons of influence in *Great Britain.* We know enough already to satisfy us of this truth. But this will not be the worst part of our case.

The *principals,* in all great offices, will reside in *England,* making some paltry allowance to deputies for doing the business *here.* Let any consider what an exhausting drain this must be upon us, when ministers are possessed of the power of creating what posts they please, and of affixing to such posts what salaries they please, and he must be convinced how destructive the late act will be. The injured kingdom lately mentioned, can tell us the mischiefs of ABSENTEES; and we may perceive already the same disposition taking place with us. The government of *New York* has been exercised by a deputy. That of *Virginia* is now held so; and we know of a number of secretaryships, collectorships, and other offices, held in the same manner. . . .

Surely therefore, those who wish the welfare of their country, ought seriously to reflect, what may be the consequence of such a new creation of offices, in the disposal of the crown. The *army,* the *administration of justice,* and the *civil government* here, with such salaries as the crown shall please to annex, will extend *ministerial influence* as much beyond its former bounds, as the late war did the *British* dominions.

But whatever the people of *Great Britain* may think on this occasion, I hope the people of these colonies will unanimously join in this sentiment, that the late act of parliament is injurious to their liberty, and that this sentiment will unite them in a firm opposition to it, in the same manner as the dread of the *Stamp Act* did.

Some persons may imagine the sums to be raised by it, are but small, and therefore may be inclined to acquiesce under it. A conduct more dangerous to freedom, as before has been observed, can never be adopted. Nothing is wanted at home but a PRECEDENT, the force of which shall be established, by the tacit submission of the colonies. With what zeal was the statute erecting the post office, and another relating to the recovery of debts in *America,* urged and tortured, as *precedents* in support of the *Stamp Act,* tho' wholly inapplicable. If the parliament succeeds in this attempt, other statutes will impose other duties. Instead of taxing ourselves, as we have been accustomed to do, from the first settlement of these provinces, all our usual taxes will be converted into parliamentary taxes on our importations; and thus the parliament will levy upon us such sums of money as they choose to take, *without any other* LIMITATION, *than their* PLEASURE. . . .

In short, if the late act of parliament takes effect, these colonies must dwindle down into "COMMON CORPORATIONS," as their enemies, in the debates concerning the repeal of the *Stamp Act, strenuously insisted they were;* and it seems not improbable that some future historian may thus record our fall. . . .

"Certain it is, that though they had before their eyes *so many illustrious examples* in their mother country, of the *constant* success attending *firmness* and *perseverance,* in opposition to dangerous encroachments on liberty, yet they quietly gave up a point of the LAST IMPORTANCE. From thence the decline of their freedom began, and its decay was extremely rapid; for *as money* was always raised upon them by the parliament, their *assemblies* grew immediately *useless,* and in a short time *contemptible:* And in less than one hundred years, the people sunk down into that *tameness* and *supineness* of spirit, by which they still continue to be distinguished." . . .
Remember your ancestors and your posterity.

A Farmer

My Dear Countrymen,

Some states have lost their liberty by *particular accidents:* But this calamity is generally owing to the *decay of virtue.* A *people* is travelling fast to destruction, when *individuals* consider *their* interests as distinct from *those of the public.* Such notions are fatal to their country, and to themselves. Yet how many are there, so *weak* and *sordid* as to *think* they perform *all the offices of life,* if they earnestly endeavor to increase their own *wealth, power,* and *credit,* without the least regard for the society, under the protection of which they live; who, if they can make an *immediate profit to themselves,* by lending their assistance to those, whose projects plainly tend to the injury of their country, rejoice in their *dexterity,* and believe themselves entitled to the character of *able politicians.* Miserable men! Of whom it is hard to say, whether they ought to be most the objects of *pity* or *contempt:* But whose opinions are certainly as *detestable,* as their practices are *destructive.*

Though I always reflect, with a high pleasure, on the integrity and understanding of my countrymen, . . . yet when I consider, that in every age and country there have been bad men, my heart, at this threatening period, is so full of apprehension, as not to permit me to believe, but that there may be some on this continent, *against whom you ought to be upon your guard*—Men, who either hold, or expect to hold certain advantages, by setting examples of servility to their countrymen.—Men, who trained to the employment, or self taught by a natural versatility of genius, serve as decoys for drawing the innocent and unwary into snares. It is not to be doubted but that such men will diligently bestir themselves on this and every like occasion, to spread the infection of their meanness as far as they can. On the plans *they* have adopted, this is *their* course. *This* is the method to recommend themselves to their *patrons.* . . .

Our *vigilance* and our *union* are *success* and *safety.* Our *negligence* and our *division* are *distress* and *death.* They are *worse*—They are *shame* and *slavery.* Let us equally shun the benumbing stillness of *overweening sloth,* and the feverish activity of that *ill informed zeal,* which busies itself in maintaining *little, mean* and *narrow* opinions. Let us, with a truly wise *generosity* and *charity,* banish and discourage all *illiberal distinctions,* which may arise from differences in *situation,* forms of *government,* or modes of *religion.* Let us consider ourselves as MEN—FREEMEN—CHRISTIAN FREEMEN—*separated from the rest of the world, and firmly bound together* by the *same rights, interests* and *dangers.* Let *these* keep our attention inflexibly fixed on the GREAT OBJECTS, which we must CONTINUALLY REGARD, in order to *preserve those rights, to promote those interests,* and to *avert those dangers.*

Let these *truths* be indelibly impressed on our minds—*that* we *cannot be* HAPPY, *without being* FREE—that we cannot be free, *without being secure in our property*—that *we* cannot be secure in our property, *if, without our consent, others may, as by right, take it away*—that *taxes imposed on us by parliament,* do thus take it away—that *duties laid for the sole purpose of raising money,* are taxes—that *attempts* to lay such duties *should be instantly and firmly opposed*—that this opposition can never be effectual, *unless it is the united effort of these provinces*—that therefore BENEVOLENCE *of temper towards each other,* and UNANIMITY *of counsels,* are essential to the welfare of the whole—and lastly, that for this reason, every man among us, who in any manner would encourage either *dissension, dissidence,* or *indifference,* between these colonies, is an enemy to *himself,* and *to his country.* . . .

Let us take care of our *rights,* and we *therein* take care of *our prosperity.* "SLAVERY IS EVER PRECEDED BY SLEEP." *Individuals* may be *dependent* on ministers, if they please. STATES SHOULD SCORN IT. . . .

You are assigned by divine providence, in the appointed order of things, the *protectors of unborn ages,* whose *fate* depends upon your *virtue.* Whether *they* shall arise the *generous* and *indisputable heirs* of the noblest patrimonies, or the *dastardly and hereditary drudges* of imperious task-masters, YOU MUST DETERMINE. . . .

For my part, I am resolved to contend for the liberty delivered down to me by my ancestors, but whether I shall do it effectually or not, depends on you, my countrymen. "How littlesoever one is able to write, yet when the liberties of one's country are threatened, it is still more difficult to be silent."

A Farmer

Charleston Merchants Outline a Plan of Nonimportation, 1769

We, his Majesty's dutiful and loving subjects, the inhabitants of South Carolina, being sensibly affected with the great prejudice done to Great Britain, and the abject and wretched condition to which the British colonies are reduced by several Acts of Parliament lately passed; by *some of which* the moneys that the colonists usually and cheerfully spent in the purchase of all sorts of goods imported from Great Britain, are now, to their great grievance, wrung from them, without their consent, or even their being represented, and applied by the ministry, in prejudice of, and without regard to, the real interest of Great Britain, or the manufactures thereof, almost totally, to the support of new-created commissioners of customs, placemen, parasitical and novel ministerial officers; and *by others of which acts* we are not only deprived of those invaluable rights, trial by our peers and the common law, but are also made subject to the arbitrary and oppressive proceedings of the civil law, justly abhorred and rejected by our ancestors, the freemen of England; and finding that the most dutiful and loyal petitions from the colonies alone, for redress of those grievances, have been rejected with contempt so that no relief can be expected from that method of proceedings; and being fully convinced of the absolute necessity of stimulating our fellow subjects and sufferers in Great Britain to aid us in this our distress, and of joining the rest of the colonies in some other loyal and vigorous methods that may most probably procure such relief, which we believe may be most effectually promoted by strict economy, and by encouraging the manufactures of America in general, and of this province in particular: we therefore, whose names are underwritten, do solemnly promise, and agree to and with each other, that, until the colonies be restored to their former freedom by the repeal of the said Acts, we will most strictly abide by the following[:]

Resolutions

I. That we will encourage and promote the use of North American manufactures in general, and those of this province in particular. And any of us who are vendors thereof, do engage to sell and dispose of them at the same rates as heretofore.

II. That we will upon no pretence whatsoever, either upon our own account or on commission, import into this province any of the manufactures of Great Britain, or any other European or East India goods, either from Great Britain, Holland, or any other place, other than such as may have been shipped in consequence of former orders; excepting only Negro cloth, commonly called white and coloured plains, not exceeding one shilling and six pence sterling per yard, canvas, bolting cloths, drugs and family medicines, plantation and workmen's tools, nails, firearms, bar steel, gunpowder, shot, lead, flints, wire cards and card-wire, mill and grindstones, fishhooks, printed books and pamphlets, salt, coals, and saltpeter. And exclusive of these articles, we do solemnly promise and declare that we will immediately countermand all orders to our correspondents in Great Britain for shipping any such goods, wares, and merchandise; and we will sell and dispose of the goods we have on hand, or that may arrive in consequence of former orders at the same rates as heretofore.

III. That we will use the utmost economy in our persons, houses, and furniture; particularly, that we will give no mourning, or gloves, or scarves at funerals.

IV. That from and after the 1st day of January, 1770, we will not import, buy, or sell any Negroes that shall be brought into this province from Africa; nor after the 1st day of October next, any Negroes that shall be imported from the West Indies, or any other place excepting from Africa as aforesaid; and that if any goods or Negroes shall be sent to us contrary to our agreement in this subscription, such goods shall be re-shipped or stored, and such Negroes re-shipped from this province, and not by any means offered for sale therein.

V. That we will not purchase from, or sell for, any masters of vessels, transient persons, or non-subscribers, any kind of European or East India goods whatever, excepting coals and salt, after the 1st day of November next.

VI. That as wines are subject to a heavy duty, we agree not to import any on our account or commission, or purchase from any master of vessel, transient person, or non-subscriber, after the 1st day of January next.

VII. Lastly, that we will not purchase any Negroes imported, or any goods or merchandise whatever, from any resident in this province, that refuses or neglects to sign this agreement within one month from the date hereof; excepting it shall appear he has been unavoidably prevented from doing the same. And every subscriber who shall not strictly and literally adhere to this agreement, according to the true intent and meaning hereof, ought to be treated with the utmost contempt.

✳ E S S A Y S

The Stamp Act and the Townshend Acts provided the political foundations for the central issues of the imperial crisis. As the following essays demonstrate, the basic conflict between parliamentary rule and colonial rights had emerged by 1765, although a full realization of the depth of the division became clear only after repeated political maneuvers and tests of will.

Edmund S. Morgan, a Pulitzer Prize–winning Yale professor emeritus, and his late wife Helen M. Morgan argue in the first essay that Prime Minister George Grenville deviously used the Stamp Act to establish the authority of Parliament in the colonies. Conciliatory Americans who wished to supply revenues to Britain by their own means were first encouraged but then brushed aside in a way that provoked stern resistance. In the second essay the Morgans explain how, following the repeal of the Stamp Act in 1766 and the simultaneous reassertion of Parliament's right to legislate for the colonies "in all cases whatsoever," the conflict was renewed over the Townshend Acts, a series of customs duties intended to achieve the same objectives as the Stamp Act but by a slightly more indirect route. Although the fundamental issue—Parliament's assertion of the right of taxation—remained unchanged, Pauline Maier, a professor of history at the Massachusetts Institute of Technology, argues in the third essay that this sequel to the Stamp Act changed the character of resistance, because the Townshend Acts dashed remaining colonial hopes for fairness. Although colonial leaders continued to intimidate their adversaries, Maier reports, they still normally regarded violence as an unnecessary and illegitimate tactic. At the same time, she shows that their non-importation associations became ever more ready to assert quasi–governmental authority. A pattern of mutual alienation, first evident in 1765–1766, came to characterize relations between imperial authorities and the leaders of colonial legislatures. As a result, though a kind of peace would be restored in 1770 by the repeal of most of the Townshend Acts, Britain and the colonies in fact were even further apart politically than when the Declaratory Act had been issued.

Grenville's Assertion of Parliamentary Control: The Stamp Act

EDMUND S. AND HELEN M. MORGAN

When George Grenville tightened up the administration of the colonial customs service and revised the rates to make them produce a revenue, he knew that he was only beginning, that the colonies could and should contribute more to the cost of their defence. During the summer of 1763 he had already begun to consider the possibility of a stamp tax, and had assigned two different individuals to prepare drafts of an American Stamp Act. When these were presented to him on September 30, 1763, and October 10, 1763, respectively, he found neither satisfactory. The men who drew them up simply did not know the details of American judicial procedures well enough

"Voices of the System" from *The Stamp Act Crisis: Prologue to Revolution* by Edmund S. and Helen M. Morgan. Published for the Institute of Early American History and Culture, Williamsburg, VA. © 1962 The University of North Carolina Press.

to name and describe the documents upon which a tax should be collected. In fact it is unlikely that anyone in the offices at Whitehall knew enough. Consequently, although Grenville was anxious to increase the revenue as rapidly as possible, a stamp tax would have to wait until the necessary information could be gathered.

Since he could not present Parliament with an American Stamp Act in the spring of 1764, why did Grenville offer his resolution that one might be proper in the future? Why not wait until he had it ready, before introducing the subject? . . . Grenville was worried, though probably not greatly, about the reaction to a stamp tax both in Parliament and in the colonies. . . . Legislative bodies are not fond of setting limits on their own competence, and Parliament had long since accustomed itself to the idea of its own omnipotence. Yet Grenville had heard hints dropped outside Parliament. Perhaps he knew that his great brother-in-law did not share the general view, and a view which William Pitt did not share was possibly not so general after all. One way to establish its acceptance, however, was by a Parliamentary resolution. Once Parliament agreed that it had the right to levy stamp duties in the colonies, it was not likely to reverse its opinion when asked to exercise the right. . . .

There was also the question of how a stamp act would be received in the colonies. Grenville saw a way to take care of this problem too with his advance resolution: when introducing it to Parliament he managed to maneuver the colonists into a position where a stamp act would appear to be the result of their own failure to come to the assistance of the mother country in an hour of need. . . . There is no official record of what he said in Parliament on March 9, 1764, and in the several accounts by private hands most of the space is devoted to his remarks on the deplorable condition of English finances and his explanation of the resolutions which were to form the basis of the Sugar Act. With regard to the fifteenth resolution (which affirmed that a stamp tax might be necessary), the accounts are meager, but a few facts stand out: Grenville announced that he wished no action on this subject until the next session, that his reason for delay was a desire to consult the ease, the interest (or the quiet), and the good will of the colonies, and that the colonies might take advantage of the delay to offer any objections they might have to the tax, or to suggest some more satisfactory tax, or— and here was the most misleading suggestion—to raise the money themselves in any way they saw fit. . . .

The report by Edward Montague, the agent of Virginia, stated . . . that Grenville had given the colonies this alternative: "Mr. G—— then suggested that this [his?] great object, being the relief of this kingdom from the burthen which in justice America should bear, it would be as satisfactory to him if the several provinces would among themselves, and in modes best suited to their circumstances, raise a sum adequate to the expense of their defence." . . .

Grenville definitely proposed in his speech of March 9, that the colonies might avert the stamp tax. If they would prefer to tax themselves rather than be taxed by Parliament they had a year in which to take action. Having made this magnanimous gesture, Grenville put in motion the machinery for drawing up a stamp bill to present to the next session of Parliament. For reasons that will become apparent Grenville was probably certain that the colonies would do nothing, and he wanted to have his bill ready by 1765. He gave to Thomas Whately in the treasury office the task of preparing it, and Whately wrote to persons he knew in America to get the necessary information. . . .

While Thomas Whately was busy preparing the Stamp Act, the colonial agents, to say nothing of the colonists, were puzzling over the meaning of the alternative proposal that Grenville had made in his speech of March 9. For a reason which is obvious enough if we assume that Grenville had already made up his mind to have a stamp tax, he had not communicated the proposal to the colonial assemblies through the channel normally used. Had he really intended to allow the colonies a chance to raise the money themselves, he would have made his offer in the regular manner by having the Secretary of State for the Southern Department write to the governors of the colonies. He had had Halifax write for the information about colonial judicial transactions needed in draughting the Stamp Act, but he made no communication on the subject of letting the colonial assemblies tax themselves. . . .

Yet in spite of the fact that Grenville did not make the offer in proper form, he did make it, and the agents did report it to their constituents. . . . It was only a short time after the speech, however, before the agents realized that the terms of the proposal they had communicated to the colonies were not entirely clear. Grenville had said that if the colonies would raise among themselves an adequate sum or sum equivalent to that expected from the stamp tax, he would accept it in lieu of a stamp tax. But how much was an "adequate" or "equivalent" sum? If the colonies were to lay an equivalent tax themselves, they would have to know either how much was needed in all, or else what were the intended taxable items and rates. Without this information it would be impossible for them to act upon Grenville's proposal. The agents, before they could have had time to hear from their constituents about it, decided to have a talk with the Minister. He met them on May 17, 1764, in a conference which was afterwards described in some detail by three of the participants.

Grenville opened by stating that he had not changed his mind, but he then proceeded to propose something he had not so much as mentioned in his speech. The agents were trying to find out "the sort of proposition, which would probably be accepted from them to Parliament," in other words how much he wanted the colonies to raise. But Grenville, rather than stating the sum he wanted from them, now proposed that they assent in advance to the Parliamentary tax and thereby set a precedent for being consulted about any future taxes! He also spoke strongly of the difficulties which "would have" attended any scheme of letting them tax themselves, as though that issue were closed. But he did not expressly repudiate his offer; and the agents, although they could not help seeing that he was discouraging action by the colonies, apparently did not recognize that he was precluding it. They did not, however, press for a statement of the exact sum with which the colonies might satisfy him. Grenville had steered the conference beyond that subject, and they probably feared to upset his evident good humor by insisting on a matter so obviously distasteful. They must prolong the conference and find out, if possible, the terms of the act he expected to bring in if the colonies did not raise the money themselves. They must know the terms, one of the agents explained, "in order that our respective constituents might have the whole, both substance and form under their deliberation, when they would be far better able to determine whether or how far, to approve or disapprove." But the details of the act were, of course, unknown to Grenville himself, for it had not yet been drawn up. Israel Mauduit [Massachusetts' agent] pointed out that to ask the colonies to assent in advance to a bill without giving the provisions of it was asking them "to assent to they did not know what." To this Grenville answered simply that it was not necessary to bother with details, "That everyone knew the stamp laws here; and that this Bill is intended to be formed upon the same plan." He did agree to consult with the agents on this matter just before the meeting of Parliament, provided that in the meantime the colonial assemblies should signify their assent to the general idea of a stamp tax. He warned that any protests based on the financial inability of the colonies to pay would carry little weight in Parliament. In his speech of March 9 he had already made it plain that he would listen to nothing which called in question the right of Parliament to levy the tax, so that he left the colonies very little room either for criticism or for constructive action.

It is evident from this conference that Grenville was determined upon a stamp tax. Though he was willing to make magnanimous gestures, he had no intention of allowing the colonies to prevent passage of his measure either by objections to it or by raising an "equivalent" sum. They would not thwart him by levying a substitute tax themselves: by withholding the necessary information he made sure of that. Nor would he be troubled by their objections: thanks to his foresighted resolution he could safely predict Parliament's unsympathetic reaction here. Grenville must have felt comfortably satisfied with all his maneuvers. He had made it useless for the colonies to attempt any action to avert the tax, and yet he had carried out his interview so smoothly, and expressed his affection for the colonies so convincingly, that the agents did not perceive, nor inform their clients, of the hopelessness of their efforts.

It was only when a colony set about to tax itself that the hollowness of Grenville's offer became apparent. Massachusetts made the attempt. Though Governor Bernard was convinced that the Ministry really intended to let the colonies raise all internal taxes themselves, yet when several members of the Assembly approached him in the summer of 1764, asking for a special session in order that the colony might tax itself to avoid being taxed by Parliament, Bernard refused, because he saw that nothing could be done without more information from Grenville. He related the entire incident to his friend Richard Jackson, in a letter dated at Boston, August 18, 1764. . . .

This letter shows plainly enough why the colonies did not take advantage of Grenville's offer to let them tax themselves. Not only was the offer never made them in a regular manner by letters from the Secretary of State, but it was never couched in terms that were definite enough to permit of action. Several colonies signified their willingness to contribute if requested in a regular manner for a specific sum, but such a request was never made.

What the colonies did do was to take up the challenge which Grenville had thrown to Parliament and which Parliament had endorsed and passed on to them. The Americans read the fifteenth resolution correctly, as a declaration of Parliament's right to tax them. And since the challenge was no more than a declaration, albeit by a body which regarded its own declarations as final, they replied in the mode, infuriating to omnipotence, of talking back. In the petitions to Parliament and letters to their agents . . . they denied that Parliament had any right to tax them. This denial was by no means limited to the dusky halls of legislative assemblies. The people at large were as much concerned over the measure as their representatives. Jared Ingersoll, in answer to Thomas Whately's inquiries, warned the man who was drafting the Stamp Act, that the minds of the people "are filled with the most dreadfull apprehensions from such a Step's taking place, from whence I leave you to guess how Easily a tax of that kind would be Collected; tis difficult to say how many ways could be invented to avoid the payment of a tax laid upon a Country without the Consent of the Legislature of that Country and in the opinion of most of the people Contrary to the foundation principles of their natural and Constitutional rights and Liberties. Dont think me impertinent, Since you desire Information, when I tell you that I have heard Gentlemen of the greatest property in Neighbouring Governments say, Seemingly very Cooly, that should such a Step take place they would immediately remove themselves with their families and fortunes into some foreign Kingdom." Ingersoll also told Whately, much as Bernard had told Jackson, that "If the King should fix the proportion of our Duty, we all say we will do our parts in the Common Cause, but if the Parliament once interpose and Lay a tax, tho' it may be a very moderate one . . . what Consequences may, or rather may not, follow?"

With his two secretaries, Jackson and Whately, receiving communications of this kind, and with other colonial agents spreading petitions and pamphlets to the same effect around London, Grenville could see for himself that the champions of colonial reorganization were right in crying that the authority of Parliament in America needed bolstering, but he did not therefore agree that reorganization would provide the best reinforcement. The way to get authority recognized was to exercise it, and Grenville was prepared to do just that with his stamp tax. Twenty-three years before, in 1742, Sir William Keith had proposed such a tax precisely because he thought it would establish among the Americans "a more just and favourable opinion of their dependency on a British Parliament, than what they generally have at present." And doubtless Thomas Whately voiced Grenville's own view when he called the Stamp Act "the great measure of the Sessions . . . on account of the important point it establishes, the Right of Parliament to lay an internal Tax upon the Colonies."

If Parliament was not as aware as Grenville that its authority in America needed support, the colonists themselves completed the awakening. As the protests from across the ocean poured into England, Parliamentary hackles rose, and the Minister could rejoice, for, as he had calculated, the members reacted to the denial of their authority with the wrath of injured dignity. The unfortunate colonial agents, fighting frantically to stave off the coming blow, saw that because of their clients' declarations the battle was being transformed into a test of Parliament's authority. The main issue was no longer raising a revenue, but putting the Americans in their place. . . .

By this time the situation was becoming desperate. Parliament was due to open, and though a good deal of propaganda had been published, most of it probably at the instigation of the agents, there was no organized opposition in the House of Commons to contest the bill when Grenville should bring it in. The agents decided to make one last attempt to stop the tax at its source and deputed four of their number to call on the Minister again and point out to him that most of the colonies had expressed their willingness to contribute to the British Treasury if called upon to do so in a regular, constitutional manner. The agents . . . met with Grenville on February 2, 1765. . . .

When the conference of February 2 was over the agents must have realized at last that Grenville's offer had never been made in good faith, that a year ago, even while making the offer, he had already made up his mind to levy a stamp tax. The willingness he had then expressed to let the colonies tax themselves or offer objections was nothing more than a rhetorical gesture, designed to demonstrate his own benevolence. In the conference of February 2, 1765, he even told the agents that "he had pledged his Word for Offering the Stamp Bill to the house." What he had given the colonies was not an opportunity to tax themselves but an opportunity to refuse to tax themselves.

In the time that was left the agents continued their preparation for the ensuing battle in Parliament, but the impudence of the Americans had so irritated the law-makers, that the issue was a foregone conclusion. . . . Even the most eloquent opponents of the tax spoke in terms of equity and expediency and did not venture to deny the absolute authority of Parliament.

The staunchest supporter of the colonies in this first debate was Colonel Isaac Barré, a veteran of the French and Indian War. According to one observer, "He most strongly recommended that if there must be a tax laid, tho' he could wish there was to be none, that the Provinces might be indulged with the liberty as heretofore of furnishing their quotas of any sums required and colecting it in their own modes." Barré, in other words, advocated the proposal that Grenville himself had first made but failed to carry through. Charles Townshend, author-to-be of the Townshend Duties, spoke with some warmth in the debate, asking on one occasion: "And now will these Americans, Children planted by our Care, nourished up by our Indulgence untill they are grown to a Degree of Strength and Opulence, and protected by our Arms, will they grudge to contribute their mite to relieve us from the heavy weight of that burden which we lie under?" To this Barré answered with words that would soon make him famous throughout the American Colonies:

> They planted by your Care? No! your Oppressions planted em in America. They fled from your Tyranny to a then uncultivated and unhospitable Country—where they exposed themselves to almost all the hardships to which human Nature is liable, and among others to the Cruelties of a Savage foe, the most subtle and I take upon me to say the most formidable of any People upon the face of Gods Earth. And yet, actuated by Principles of true english Lyberty, they met all these hardships with pleasure, compared with those they suffered in their own Country, from the hands of those who should have been their Friends.
>
> They nourished by *your* indulgence? they grew by your neglect of Em: as soon as you began to care about Em, that Care was Exercised in sending persons to rule over Em, in one Department and another, who were perhaps the Deputies of Deputies to some Member of this house—sent to Spy out their Lyberty, to misrepresent their Actions and to prey upon Em; men whose behaviour on many Occasions has caused the Blood of those Sons of Liberty to recoil within them; men promoted to the highest Seats of Justice, some, who to my knowledge were glad by going to a foreign Country to Escape being brought to the Bar of a Court of Justice in their own.
>
> They protected by *your* Arms? they have nobly taken up Arms in your defence, have Exerted a Valour amidst their constant and Laborious industry for the defence of a Country, whose frontier, while drench'd in blood, its interior Parts have yielded all its little Savings to your Emolument. And believe me, remember I this Day told you so, that same Spirit of freedom which actuated that people at first, will accompany them still.—But prudence forbids me to explain myself further. God knows I do not at this Time speak from motives of party Heat, what I deliver are the genuine Sentiments of my heart.

Even Barré's eloquence, which did not, after all, deny the authority of Parliament, could not alter the determination of the members to prove their unlimited authority by taxing the colonies. . . . The sentiment in favor of the tax was so strong that the opposition, instead of bringing the matter to a vote on the immediate question, tried to get through a vote to adjourn. . . . The motion was lost by a vote of 245 to 49, taken at about midnight, and on the following day the House of Commons passed, without a division, the fifty-five resolutions which formed the basis of the Stamp Act.

Grenville, having thus secured the approval of Parliament, brought in the bill itself on February 13. It received its first reading then and its second on February 15. This was the crucial reading, and the opposition prepared to present petitions against it. . . .

The refusal of Parliament to hear these petitions did not pass without debate. General Conway . . . was the principal defender of the colonies at this juncture. He made a telling point when he reminded the members that they had postponed the Stamp Act the preceding year in order to give the colonies time to send messages representing their objections to it. "This time has been given," said Conway. "The Representations are come from the Colonies; and shall we shut our Ears against that Information, which, with an Affectation of Candour, we allotted sufficient Time to reach us? . . . [F]rom whom, unless from themselves, are we to learn the Circumstances of the Colonies, and the fatal Consequences that may attend the imposing of this Tax?"

Conway's plea on February 15 was no more effective than Barré's had been on February 6; . . . and by March 22 the Stamp Act was a statute of the realm. It remained to be seen whether it would establish, or destroy, the authority of Parliament in America.

The Significance of the Stamp Act Resistance

EDMUND S. AND HELEN M. MORGAN

One of the principal arguments which the opposition had used against repeal of the Stamp Act was that the colonies would interpret it as a sign of weakness, that whatever reason Parliament assigned for repeal, the Americans would believe that their own resistance had been the real cause. The friends of the colonies took care to inform their correspondents in America that the violence against the stamp distributors had prolonged the struggle for repeal and had even threatened to prevent it entirely. Letters sent by the committee of merchants in London to the merchants of the principal towns and cities of North America urged the Americans not to exult in the victory as a point gained over Parliamentary authority. Any such attitude would surely strengthen the hand of Grenville and his followers, who might still return to power and undo the great work of reconciliation. The merchants had had a hard fight, in which they had "pawned their words" for the colonies, and "I hope," one of them wrote, "nothing will be done, that may make them ashamed of the assurances they have given, that all would return to quiet and good humour. A contrary behaviour will hurt the present ministry, who are your true friends; and if they fall, your enemies will succeed, from whom you have everything to fear." In order to prevent such a catastrophe, the committee urged the Americans to send over expressions of "filial duty and gratitude to your parent country."

These words were made more pointed by two protests issuing from the minority in the House of Lords against repeal of the Stamp Act. . . . Repeal of the Stamp Act, they said, was a surrender of Parliament's supreme jurisdiction. The reasons the Americans had assigned for disobedience to the Act would extend "to all other laws, of what nature soever, which that Parliament had enacted, or shall enact, to bind them in times to come, and must, if admitted, set them absolutely free from any obedience to the power of the British legislature." By the Declaratory Act, they said, Parliament only "more grievously injured its own dignity and authority by verbally asserting that right which it substantially yields up to its opposition." The total effect would be to push the colonies in the direction toward which they

From *The Stamp Act Crisis: Prologue to Revolution* by Edmund S. and Helen M. Morgan. © 1962 The University of North Carolina Press.

were already verging—independence. In the protests of the Lords the Americans could read the narrowness of their escape as well as their future peril, and they hastened to comply with the advice of the merchants, which had been seconded by Secretary Conway in sending official notice of the repeal. The assemblies of the various colonies drew up addresses of thanks to King and Parliament for their parental solicitude and gave assurance of their loyalty to the King and their submission to the authority of Parliament— though none of them specifically acknowledged that this authority included the right to tax them.

In spite of the loyal sentiments of their addresses, the colonists would have been a little more than human if they had not given themselves some of the credit for repeal. "Had we tamely submitted," they asked themselves, "would the Justice of our Cause have procured us Relief?" Probably few could find it in their hearts to say yes. . . . Thomas Hutchinson, looking back upon the period some years later thought that repeal was interpreted throughout the colonies, not as an act of favor, but as a concession to the colonial view that taxation was the power only of a representative body. The celebrations with which repeal was greeted were decent and orderly, as the committee of merchants had urged. . . . Up and down the Atlantic coast, houses were illuminated; paintings and verses composed for the occasion were exhibited; and toasts were drunk publicly to William Pitt and the other men who had championed the cause of the colonies in Parliament; but the most significant thing about the celebrations was that they were directed by the Sons of Liberty, the men responsible for the violent proceedings which according to the Committee of Merchants had hindered repeal. The Sons of Liberty showed no contrition for their sins. Not only did they direct celebrations of repeal in 1766, but they also staged celebrations upon the anniversary of repeal every year thereafter, until the Revolution began. In Boston they even celebrated the anniversary of August 14, the night of the first riot. Thus the Sons of Liberty kept alive the memory of the glorious days when Americans had risen up against the threat of tyranny and had successfully asserted their rights.

This misinterpretation of the repeal of the Stamp Act was rendered the more easy by the general terms in which Rockingham had couched the Declaratory Act. After the debate over Barré's motion to omit the words, "in all cases whatsoever," the meaning of the Act was plain to members of Parliament, so plain that one unofficial report of the resolves which formed the basis of the Act summarized it as saying "That the King, Lords, and Commons of this realm have always had, and ought to have the undoubted right to tax the colonies." But the session of Parliament in which the debate took place was a secret one with no visitors allowed. Hugh Hamersley, the secretary to Lord Baltimore, wrote to Governor Sharpe of Maryland that he could give him no report of what had happened in the House of Commons, because "they have throughout the business shut their doors against all strangers." Reports did reach the colonies from members of Parliament who happened to be colonial agents. Charles Garth sent a full report of the debate to the Maryland Assembly. But many colonists, unaware of what had passed in Parliament, were puzzled by the Declaratory Act. Though the early reports had said that it asserted Parliament's right to tax, when the actual texts of the resolution and of the Act were reported, it was apparent that Parliament had made no mention of taxation. Ezra Stiles noted that the Act "declared the most absolute parliamentary Authority in Legislation yet with a seeming Ambiguity, as to power of Taxation." John Adams, reading the resolve in the Boston newspapers, observed that it asserted Parliament's right "to make laws for the Colonies in all cases whatever," and wondered "whether they will lay a tax in consequence of that resolution, or what kind of a law they will make." James Otis, on the other hand, assured the Boston town meeting that the Act "had no relation to Taxes," or so at least Governor Bernard was told.

If Otis and others placed such an interpretation on the Act, it was not without reason. Rockingham had deliberately omitted any mention of taxation, and Conway in speaking to Dennys De Berdt, an agent of Massachusetts, told him that the Ministry had been opposed to any Declaratory Act but had been obliged to accept one in order to get a majority for repeal. Conway hoped that the Americans would understand the Act in that light. Richard Jackson, the other agent of Massachusetts, dismissed the Act as a formality. . . .

There is no evidence that the Americans, in rejoicing over repeal of the Stamp Act, accepted the right of Parliament to tax them. Many of their loyal addresses of thanks upon the repeal, were phrased so as to reject any such admission. . . . The vague terms of the Declaratory Act enabled them to accept it as a statement of their own position: that Parliament had supreme legislative authority, but that taxation was not a part of legislation.

William Pitt himself had spectacularly supported the American position in Parliament, and the American press like the British press gave to Pitt the credit for carrying the repeal. He had asserted plainly the power of Parliament in all branches of legislation whatsoever, but he had stoutly denied Parliament's right to tax. Upon reading his speech of January 14, John Adams wrote in his diary: "What has been said in America which Mr. Pitt has not confirmed? Otis, Adams, Hopkins, &c. have said no more." Since they believed that repeal was the work of Pitt many Americans must have found it hard to believe that the Declaratory Act should be interpreted as a denial of everything he had said. George Mason of Virginia observed that the Act asserted the "legislative authority" of Great Britain in all cases whatsoever, but he remembered that "a just and necessary Distinction between Legislation and Taxation hath been made by the greatest and wisest men in the Nation," for surely Pitt was one of the greatest and wisest. . . .

When the Americans did come to realize that the Declaratory Act was intended to affirm the right of taxation, they were by no means ready to accept it. . . .

Those who perceived the true meaning of the Declaratory Act also perceived that the Americans had small reason to display the gratitude which the merchants had insisted upon, for both Parliament and the merchants had been motivated by a concern for the welfare of England rather than

America. . . . George Mason ridiculed the merchants for speaking to the colonists like schoolboys, as if to say:

> We have with infinite difficulty and fatigue got you excused this one time; pray be a good boy for the future, do what your papa and mama bid you, and hasten to return them your most grateful acknowledgments for condescending to let you keep what is your own; and then all your acquaintance will love you, and praise you, and give you pretty things; . . . Is not this a little ridiculous, when applied to three millions of as loyal and useful subjects as any in the British dominions, who have been only contending for their birth-right, and have now only gained, or rather kept, what could not, with common justice, or even policy, be denied them?

Not all Americans were able to see . . . the implications of what Parliament had done, and even they missed the larger significance of the Declaratory Act. Perhaps even Rockingham failed to understand that his Act assigned a greater authority to Parliament than Grenville had originally claimed with his Stamp Act. Grenville had justified taxing the colonies on the ground that they were represented—virtually—in Parliament. Repeal of the Stamp Act, unaccompanied by the Declaratory Act, could have been utilized as a demonstration that virtual representation worked. Though the Americans did not elect a single member, Parliament had been sufficiently sensitive to their interests, as expressed through the British merchants, to repeal a measure they disliked. What better answer than this to the American claim that virtual representation could not cross the ocean? But the Declaratory Act precluded such an interpretation of repeal, for it rendered unnecessary the pretence of linking taxation and representation, and rested the authority of Parliament on a simple declaration of that body's sovereignty. . . . Officially there was no longer any doubt that Parliament had authority to tax the colonies, and there was no longer any need to justify that authority by the doctrine of virtual representation. The British government had abandoned the constitutional position which linked them with the Americans and had retreated to the heights of arbitrary declaration. . . .

As the years went by the government fell more and more into the grasp of men who believed with George Grenville that the Stamp Act should have been enforced instead of repealed. . . .

In the eyes of these men the Americans had been aiming at independence ever since the Peace of Paris. It was a common observation in the mid-eighteenth century that the colonies would not forever remain as dependencies of Great Britain. No one who considered the extent of the North American continent and the rate at which its population was increasing could doubt the truth of the observation, though the separation was scarcely expected to take place in the eighteenth century. Many Englishmen had warned before the Peace of Paris that if Canada were not returned to the French the Americans would no longer feel the need of the British army and navy to protect them and would turn their faces toward independence. When these warnings were ignored and the French menace was ended by the Peace of Paris, the prophets of doom saw their fears justified in the ensuing American resistance to the Stamp Act. Anti-Sejanus told the people of England that "The Americans imbibe notions of independence and liberty with their very milk, and will some time or other shake off all subjection. If we yield to them in this particular, by repealing the Stamp-Act, it is all over; they will from that moment assert their freedom." Rockingham and the merchants by arguing that the Americans objected only to internal taxation had been able to persuade a majority of Parliament that repeal of the Stamp Act would not encourage the movement of the colonies to independence. When the colonies next objected to the external taxes levied by the Townshend duties, many members of Parliament must have been convinced that Anti-Sejanus had been right. The Americans, it appeared, were working their way by gradual stages to the point where they would be completely independent, first freedom from internal taxes, then from external taxes. The Acts of Trade would be next. Little by little the supremacy of the mother country would be whittled away until the last bond was severed. The movement must be halted or at least retarded before it went any farther. Granted that America would one day become independent, there was no reason why that event should take place while the American population was little more than a quarter of Great Britain's.

As the English thought that they saw the Americans inching their way toward independence, the Americans thought that they saw a sinister party in England seeking by gradual degrees to enslave them. There had been rumors of a plan to reorganize the colonies ever since the fall of Quebec, and Governor Bernard had intimated that the Stamp Act was a part of that plan. Even so reasonable a man as William Samuel Johnson thought that the ministry must have had a "formal design" constantly in view for several years. "Fortunately," he wrote in January, 1766, "they have of late precipitated their Measures and by that means opened our Eyes. Had they proceeded by slow and sensible degrees as they have been wont to do perhaps in a course of years they might have effected their baneful purpose. But by pressing it too much and making more haste than good speed they have defeated the whole design and given such an Alarm as will forever keep America upon her guard."

With the repeal of the Stamp Act many Americans, misinterpreting the meaning of the Declaratory Act, believed that the plot had been foiled, and when Rockingham was replaced by Pitt, they rejoiced that their fastest friend was now in control. When the attempt to tax them was renewed under a ministry with Pitt at the head, they could see that the repeal was only a pause in the relentless advance of the plot to enslave them, and the vagueness of the Declaratory Act an effort to lull them into delusions of security, while stronger claims were fastened about them. . . .

Unfortunately the Stamp Act period had not merely created illusions about the aims of both Englishmen and Americans but had also impaired the disposition to compromise in both countries and had in some cases discredited the men who would have been willing to do so. The circumstances that enabled Lord North to retain power from 1770 to 1782 were complex, but undoubtedly one reason was the conviction of most members of Parliament after 1768 that the repeal of the Stamp Act had been a mistake. Certainly this conviction was expressed again and again on the floor of the House of Commons, and the Whigs felt obliged to apologize for the measure which had staved off revolution in 1766.

In America too the Stamp Act had discredited moderates and enabled extremists to gain greater influence than they had ever enjoyed before. . . . The withdrawal of these men from public life was accompanied by the rise of bolder and more aggressive politicians who had made their reputation in resistance to the Stamp Act. . . . It seems particularly significant that the parties which brought on the revolution in the two leading colonies, Massachusetts and Virginia, gained their ascendancy at the time of the Stamp Act. . . .

Besides disposing the colonies to accept radical leadership the Stamp Act period furnished those leaders with a method for bringing pressure to bear in England. Hitherto the colonies had never been able to unite for any purpose, not even for their own defense against the French and Indians. The Stamp Act, much to their own surprise, enabled them to act together. . . . The most spectacular achievement in unity was of course the Stamp Act Congress, but the non-importation agreements adopted by the merchants of Boston, New York, and Philadelphia were equally surprising and more effective. . . .

The colonies remembered the strength of union well enough, as they demonstrated later in their non-importation agreements against the Townshend Duties, in their continental congresses, and finally in their formation of a continental army. Yet in the last analysis the significance of the Stamp Act crisis lies in the emergence, not of leaders and methods and organizations, but of well-defined constitutional principles. The resolutions of the colonial and intercolonial assemblies in 1765 laid down the line on which Americans stood until they cut their connections with England. Consistently from 1765 to 1776 they denied the authority of Parliament to tax them externally or internally; consistently they affirmed their willingness to submit to whatever legislation Parliament should enact for the supervision of the empire as a whole. To be sure, by the time when the First Continental Congress was called in 1774 they had become convinced that Parliament had no more authority to legislate for them than to tax them (this had been the position of the most radical Americans in 1765). But even while thus extending their objections to Parliamentary authority, they agreed to waive their rights in this respect and submit to Parliament's supervisory legislation as they had before. In spite of the radical temper of the colonial leaders the position taken in 1765 would have served as a basis for reconciliation at any time until the Declaration of Independence. There was, however, no middle ground, no intermediate line to which the colonists were willing to retreat in the face of British efforts to tax them. They "stood bluff" in 1776 on the line they had drawn in 1765, and when the Ministry this time refused to recede from its demands, they fought.

The Townshend Acts and the Consolidation of Colonial Resistance, 1767–1770

PAULINE MAIER

Repeal of the Stamp Act did not, of course, finally resolve the Anglo-American conflict. Colonial opposition reawoke . . . over the Townshend Revenue Act of 1767. Never again, however, did the Americans relapse to the consternation of 1765 when they had lamented that "no similar Examples from former Times" existed to guide them. Colonists now simply revived and developed the tactics first evolved during the Stamp Act crisis and articulated by the Sons of Liberty. It was clear that legitimate resistance must involve the body of the people, must prefer peaceful over violent forms of action, and must confine whatever force was necessary within defined limits. Yet even as these limitations upon agitation were honored, colonial resistance moved beyond the model of 1765–6 toward a more serious threat to British authority as nonimportation associations increasingly assumed the functions of civil government. The portents of revolution in the final months of the Townshend agitation reflected, moreover, an important corrosion of that ultimate faith in British rule which had characterized the Stamp Act resistance, and which had survived even into the opening years of opposition to the Townshend Act.

I

In 1766, Jonathan Mayhew already grasped the potential significance of the Stamp Act resistance. Should a similar occasion recur, he said, the colonists' "late experience and success will teach them how to act in order to obtain the redress of grievances." He referred to the peaceful methods gradually settled upon in the course of the Stamp Act agitation: "joint, manly and spirited, yet respectful and loyal petitioning," backed up by commercial sanctions. The strategy of petition and nonimportation reappeared a year later in John Dickinson's "Letters from a Farmer in Pennsylvania." First published between December 1767 and February 1768, the Farmer's Letters rallied colonists against the new British legislation and more than any other source defined guidelines for the Americans' subsequent opposition to Britain. All "excesses and outrages" were condemned by Dickinson in 1767 just as they had been in 1766 by Mayhew. To talk of defending rights as if they could be upheld only by arms or by riots and tumults was "as much out of the way," Dickinson said, "as if a man having a choice of several roads to reach his journey's end, should prefer the worst for no other reason but because it *is* the worst." Free men should be spirited, ready to maintain their rights; but such efforts should for the time be channeled into "constitutional methods of seeking Redress," such as petitions or nonimportation, modes of opposition proposed as conscious alternatives to violence.

Accordingly, the colonists first petitioned Britain for relief from the Townshend Revenue Act. But during 1769, as it became clear that their petitions were unsuccessful, Americans gradually united behind nonimportation agreements similar to those already initiated in New England and New York. There were, however, significant local variations in the various nonimportation associations. In the Northern and middle colonies, merchants alone formed the covenant; while in the plantation colonies, which lacked so pre-eminent a commercial class, broader-based public bodies endorsed the agreements. . . . The lists of goods proscribed for importation also varied from colony to colony, and in the South agreements tended to emphasize nonconsumption more than nonimportation. . . .

Nonimportation was thus the successor of the Stamp Act resistance. . . . Continuity was evident in strategy, such as the nonimporters' concern for widening their base of support throughout the population. In the South, this goal was often explicit from the outset: Virginia's association of May 18, 1769, for example, invited "all Gentlemen, Merchants, Traders, and other Inhabitants of this Colony" to sign subscription lists. In the Northern colonies, however, the nonimportation associations only gradually involved the nonmercantile population. Massachusetts developments illustrated the slow widening of the movement. The original Boston agreement of March 1768 was drafted and signed only by merchants. In the fall of 1769, however, merchants circulated another subscription paper through the town, asking other inhabitants to pledge not to purchase goods imported contrary to the association and to support patriotic traders. . . . By April 1770, Thomas Hutchinson estimated that the representatives of seven-eighths of the provincial towns favored the agreement, and that "the majority of every order of men in government" had united with "the body of the people" on that issue. . . .

The effort to unite the people against Britain's "unconstitutional" legislation encouraged also the creation of popular institutions where none had previously existed. The virtues of the New England town meeting for "uniting the whole body of the people in the measures taken to oppose the Stamp Act induced other Provinces to imitate their example," Philadelphia's Charles Thomson later testified. Large public meetings provided important support for nonimportation in New York and Philadelphia. . . . In 1770, the South Carolinians sought to hold meetings as "*full* . . . as possible" so that their resolutions could be announced as "*the Sense of the Whole Body.*"

At the outset of the nonimportation effort, economic considerations encouraged widespread participation. A commercial depression afflicted the continent. Colonists suffered in part from a scarcity of hard currency, which, they said, had been drained from America by customs payments. New Englanders were particularly aware that trade law reform and economic retrenchment were necessary for recovery. In the South, nonimportation conferred an additional benefit, as George Washington understood, for it gave debt-ridden planters an honorable excuse for cutting back upon extravagant display. Meanwhile merchants could use the curtailment of imports to reduce their inventories of less desirable goods. Yet by late 1769 it had become clear that the association involved—as the town of Abington, Massachusetts, expressed it—"self-denial and public virtue" more than self-indulgence. Even artisans, who might have gained by the new emphasis upon domestic manufacturing, frequently suffered. Too often their trades depended upon imported materials, while occasional public efforts to support American manufacturing were for the most part limited to the production of essential articles such as paper or cloth.

The enduring arguments for nonimportation were, then, above all political. It offered the "wisest and only peaceable method" for Americans to recover their liberty, one, moreover, that was legal and seemed to promise success. As during the Stamp Act crisis, colonists argued that economic retrenchment would awaken the attention of [the] British. . . .

The claims for effectiveness were never disproven in the period through 1770. The movement's disintegration indicated only that any future nonimportation association would have to be more carefully designed—preferably with one identical plan for all the colonies—and less dependent upon the merchants than its predecessor. . . . Hence there was justification enough for the Continental Congress to revive the policy in 1774.

The notion that nonimportation afforded a peaceful and legal means to redress did, however, come into question. Proponents considered nonimportation peaceful in that it was nonviolent. But force was not condemned in general; even the docile John Dickinson considered the resort to forceful resistance in 1765, when there was no alternative but submission to the Stamp Act, "prudent and glorious." Admittedly, force was "always to be the very last means thought of, when every things else fails," and as of 1768 and 1769 it seemed possible to avoid it. . . .

Once again, as during the Stamp Act period, those who ignored or violated the patriotic agreements were coerced by social and economic boycotts which became harsher as the movement itself gained strength and intensity. . . . Whole colonies might be indicted: when Georgia failed to enforce its agreement, patriots in Charleston resolved that the colony ought "to be amputated from the rest of their brethren, as a rotten part that might spread a dangerous infection"; and attempts in Providence and Newport to withdraw from the agreement in May 1770 were cut short after New York, Philadelphia, and Boston imposed an absolute boycott on Rhode Island merchants. A mass of resolutions to boycott New York was also passed after that city finally defected from the movement in 1770.

The architects of nonimportation hoped that the movement could remain peaceful and still be effective. By publishing the names of those who violated the agreement or patronized violators as enemies of their country and greeting them with "every mark of infamy and reproach," Virginia's George Mason argued, associators could effectively play upon men's "sense of shame and fear of reproach." . . . More direct intimidation came only from the "indiscreet Zeal" of individuals and was by no means characteristic of the nonimporters as a whole.

Nonviolence was rarely if ever a passive achievement. In Boston, active efforts to contain popular exuberance were as necessary as they had been during the Stamp Act agitation. As early as 1767, Thomas Hutchinson understood that those who had been "very forward" in promoting the tumults of 1765 had decided to use other means against the Townshend duties. Mobbish incidents were successfully avoided that year. . . .

The efforts of Boston leaders to maintain peace continued into 1768. Effigies that appeared on Liberty Tree the morning of March 18—the anniversary of the Stamp Act's repeal—were taken down. . . . Rumors of an insurrection had circulated for days beforehand, Hutchinson wrote, but because the "Sons of Liberty . . . declared there should be no Riots, we had only such a mob as we have long been used to the 5 of November and other Holidays." . . . Again a year later, when a mob seemed intent upon revenging a brutal beating of Otis by a group of royalists, it was turned back by radicals who called out, "No violence, or you'll hurt the cause."

When violence did break out—in June 1768 during the *Liberty* riot— it was not a result of nonimportation. The incident culminated weeks of mounting tension over impressment between townsmen and the King's ship *Romney,* and was sparked off by the customsmen's method in seizing John Hancock's sloop *Liberty.* From the outset, leading Bostonians tried to stop the disorder. A mob pelting the comptroller's house with stones withdrew "by the advice of some prudent gentlemen that interposed"; and as the crowd burned a pleasure boat belonging to the customs collector, Joseph Harrison, "some gentlemen who had influence" with the mob—allegedly John Hancock, Samuel Adams, and Joseph Warren—persuaded the rioters to disperse. . . . Within the week William Molineux, the radical nonimportation supporter, wrote a letter of sympathy to Harrison, blaming the collector's losses upon a local minority of "such Sort of People" as inhabited "Every Great City perhaps in the World." . . .

Although violence was everywhere curtailed, coercion was not universally eschewed. Fear of mob reprisals forced Simon Cooley to confess his political sins and vow to honor the association at New York in July 1769, and a scaffold erected near Liberty Tree brought the submission of a jeweler, Thomas Richardson, in September. . . .

About [this] time . . . the Bostonians, it seems, began to use more forceful methods against importing merchants. One observer complained in October 1769 that the means taken to induce compliance were "really infamous." The nonsubscribers, he thought, were "in real danger of their Lives. Their property was actually unsafe, their Signs, Doors and Windows were daub'd over in the Night time with every kind of Filth, and one of them particularly had his person treated in the same manner." On October 28, the crowd turned against John Mein, publisher of the *Boston Chronicle* and leading opponent of the association, whom impending social stigma and economic ruin had failed to silence. Mein was first attacked by ten to twelve persons "of some considerable Rank." . . . Later, these assailants were joined by a mob of over a thousand persons which had gathered earlier to tar and feather a suspected customs informer. Mein received an ugly wound from an iron shovel . . . but managed to escape into the guardhouse, where he was shielded by royal troops.

In December, Lieutenant Governor Hutchinson reported that the province was "in a very calm state" although "discontents" continued in Boston. Then, in January, a group of merchants that included Hutchinson's sons Elisha and Thomas, Jr., decided to resume the sale of imported goods. The entire association was brought into peril and agitation revived. Association meetings voted to visit the offenders *en masse,* but these official visits were, as Hutchinson admitted, "without any degree of tumult." Committees were chosen before each visit, and the crowd normally marched to the offender's house with great order, then remained outside the gate while its leaders negotiated with its host. . . .

With the failure of peaceful mass pressure, more virulent forms of mob pressure were again revived. On three successive Thursdays—February 8, 15, and 22—signs and effigies mysteriously appeared pointing out "importers," particularly William Jackson and Theophilus Lillie. Crowds of boys and country people gathered, for it was marketing day, when schools were closed. Customers were intimidated from entering proscribed shops and sometimes pelted with dirt. During those weeks, importers' signs were defaced and their windows broken or "besmeared . . . with tar & feathers." On each occasion, efforts to remove the "importer" signs were repulsed: on the eighth, Jackson was turned back by "a Number of Idle people . . . standing by, with Clubs and sticks in their Hands"; soldiers who made a similar effort on the fifteenth were "beat of[f] and some of them much Hurt"; and finally, on the twenty-second, an attempt to remove an effigy over Lillie's door by Ebenezer Richardson, an ex–customs informer who was considered particularly obnoxious in Boston, resulted in bloodshed. Richardson was chased to his nearby home and besieged by a rock-throwing crowd until he fired shots into the street, hitting an eleven-year-old boy, Christopher Sneider. At that the crowd seized Richardson, dragged him through the streets, and some tried "to put a rope about his Neck and . . . execute him themselves."

Even within this surge of violence the hand of restraint was apparent. A line was usually drawn at lesser forms of harassment: window breaking, the "besmearing" of signs, suggestions of impending violence. . . . On other occasions, leaders intervened to curtail violence and to protect the persons of their enemies. In June 1770, for example, a mob was dissuaded from tarring and feathering Patrick McMasters when it became clear that he could not survive the ordeal. More important, Richardson was saved from his would-be murderers by William Molineux, who was probably responsible for turning the crowd against importers in the first place. Molineux in fact personified the ambiguity that persisted even in the extremes of Boston radicalism. He was the arch demagogue of nonimportation, believed to be "the first Leader of Dirty Matters," whose violence was a divisive factor even within the nonimportation movement in 1770; yet it was he who saved Richardson and also consoled Joseph Harrison after the *Liberty* riot. There were limits on the violence Molineux endorsed, and those limits were not wholly subjective. In January 1770, it was said, he claimed he would kill with his own hands every person who presumed to open imported goods— "were it not for the law."

Basic to Molineux's behavior there was, it seems, a distinction drawn between violence and coercion. While the destruction of persons and property was condemned as criminal, the resort to lesser forms of harassment for political purposes might be justifiable under criteria of collective necessity. Once force was used against importers, however, the immediate legality of nonimportation came increasingly into question. From the outset, proponents argued that the associations were lawful because their aims were lawful: no statute required colonists to purchase imported goods or to patronize importing merchants and their supporters. Local justices of the peace therefore denied Lieutenant Governor Hutchinson's claim that the association's meetings in Boston involved a "breach of law" unless—as the justices said in January 1770—"there should be something more disorderly than yet had been." If, however, the associations could be linked with illegal violence, all members would be in grave danger: since, as Hutchinson warned in January 1770, "their professed design [was] to reform the law by effecting the repeal of the revenue acts"—a public aim, beyond their personal grievances—"any violence from any of the inferior people who were among them would in my opinion involve them all in the guilt of high treason." . . .

The colonists' concern for acting within the law indicated a continued respect for British institutions. Like the Sons of Liberty during the Stamp Act crisis, the nonimporters insisted that their opposition to British authority was limited. The various associations usually provided for their own dissolution once the Townshend Revenue Act was repealed. An effort by Boston to extend the agreements to work for the repeal of earlier review acts as well, particularly that of 1764, failed completely. Even where royal control faced the greatest resistance, at Boston, the ligaments of British authority were loosened in only limited areas. "In other matters which have no relation to this dispute between the Kingdom and the Colonies," Hutchinson wrote as late as February 28, 1770, "Government retains its vigour and the administration of it is attended with no unusual difficulty."

Nonetheless, by 1770 the American agitation had clearly reached a stage of seriousness far beyond that of three years earlier. Escalation was marked by the increasing severity of reprisals: from mild economic boycotts, through public advertisements of importers as "enemies of their country" who deserved the contempt of their countrymen, to the violence of Boston, which was itself an act of desperation. The town's disorder, Hutchinson testified, came from a "general disposition . . . to favour the measures of the Merchants as the *only means* to preserve the Rights of the people and bring about the Repeal of the Revenue Acts and other Acts called unconstitutional." . . .

The inflamed rhetoric, the assertions that Parliament's unconstitutional acts justified colonial resistance, were reminiscent of the Stamp Act crisis. But even while precautions were taken to maintain the general framework of legal authority, resistance to the Townshend duties became a more serious threat to British authority than that to the Stamp Act. By nature, nonimportation committed partisans to a wider share of administrative responsibilities than had been exercised by the Sons of Liberty of 1765–6. In short, the associations increasingly exercised functions normally reserved to a sovereign state. Committees regularly demanded the right to inspect merchants' invoices and papers, to judge the guilt of suspected violators of the association, and to impose sanctions against the unyielding. . . .

As the number of adherents increased, and nonimporters could claim to speak for the body of the people, the various associations came to serve as social compacts, analogous to the formal constitutions that would be set up by the various colonies in the mid-1770's. The Virginia Association of June 1770, for example, outlined the structure and procedures of that colony's enforcement mechanisms. It took the form of a solemn agreement or compact among the subscribers—described simply as "his Majesty's most dutiful and loyal subjects of *Virginia*"—to adhere to its provisions, which were "binding on all and each" of them. Although their sphere of activity was limited, within that sphere the associations had, as Drayton charged in South Carolina, set up a new legislative power. . . .

As committees increasingly assumed the right to speak and act for the people, the associations' right to coerce nonconformers seemed ever more justified. The personal rights of opponents were not denied, but put in perspective. "The hardships of particulars are not to be considered," Christopher Gadsden wrote, "when the good of the whole is the object in view; as evidently it is, in the case before us." Eighteenth-century political thought had never emphasized individual rights so much as the corporate rights of the community; and patriotism itself was said to involve at core a willingness to sacrifice private interest for the public good. As such nonimportation, with its demand of self-sacrifice for the general welfare, seemed to institutionalize public virtue: "the little conveniences and comforts of life," George Mason wrote, "when set in competition with our liberty, ought to be rejected, not with reluctance, but with pleasure." Importers were, . . . as the Virginia Association of June 1770 put it, men who "preferred their own private emolument, by importing or selling articles prohibited by this association, to the destruction of the dearest rights of the people of this colony." To condemn nonimportation because it supposedly involved "infringing the right of others while . . . contending for liberty ourselves" was an "ill-founded" argument: "every member of society is in duty bound to contribute to the safety and good of the whole," Mason contended. . . .

Samuel Adams similarly compared the authority of the nonimportation supporters with that of regular institutions when he defended the Bostonians' actions against importer Patrick McMasters, who was banished from Boston by a mob in June 1770. In all states, Adams said, individuals were bound to act according to the common will of their fellow citizens or to leave. And in exceptional situations, like the present, the "will and pleasure of the society" was not "declared in its laws," but had to be imposed directly.

II

For most royal observers, the careful legal distinctions that colonial leaders tried to maintain were of no significance. The associators' claim that nonimportation was lawful seemed at best a pretense. In Boston, the fanatical

Tory Peter Oliver later claimed, inhabitants armed themselves with home-made "massy Clubs," since "Guns they imagined were Weapons of Death in the Eye of the Law, which the meanest of them was an Adept in; but Bludgeons were only Implements to beat out Brains with." Such constructions seemed only to circumvent the law.

The colonists' goals seemed as culpable as their methods, for in the eyes of British officials all resistance to Parliament's authority was unjustifiable. . . . The colonists' constitutional defenses, in short, seemed as facetious as their legal arguments. As a result, the Americans' painstaking distinction between just and unjust uprisings also became meaningless: all extra-legal uprisings were unjust.

The royal officials' insistence on the authority of Parliament and the Americans' criminality acquired particular shrillness and rigidity as they saw their own authority disintegrate. The failure of local magistrates and militias to support them during the Stamp Act period was not easily forgotten, particularly since the same situation was re-enacted during later incidents. Nor was the success of colonial political leaders in repressing or subduing violence of any consolation. Such authority was not their own; it was at the disposal of powers outside the legal British establishment, and as such seemed unreliable. . . .

As the dominant opinion in the colonies turned toward the radicals rather than toward London, royal officials had a ready explanation. They argued, as Thomas Jefferson later put it, "that the whole ferment has been raised and constantly kept up by a few principal men in every colony, and that it might be expected to subside in a short time either of itself, or by the assistance of a coercive power." The theory was readily adopted in England, where some Members of Parliament clamored for the arrest and punishment of the principal troublemakers. The argument appealed also to the King, who considered Parliament's right to bind the colonists "in all cases what-soever, as essential to the dignity of the crown, and a right appertaining to the state, which it was his duty to preserve entirely enviolate." He was therefore "greatly displeased" with colonial petitions and remonstrances that denied Parliament's absolute supremacy, and regretted that his subjects were so "misled"—again, by a handful of factious leaders. In retrospect this rhetoric of conspiracy, which the colonists themselves gradually adopted to explain England's actions, belied the gap between English and American political assumptions, for neither side could recognize the other as acting honestly upon legitimate principles different from its own. . . .

Sometimes haunted by fears for their own safety, conscious that the King's and Parliament's authority was at stake in their own persons, the governors and officials reverted to an old solution for their problems. Troops were necessary, not only to execute individual laws, but, as Georgia's Governor Wright wrote, to support His Majesty's authority from insults. . . . This call for soldiers became a standard theme, not only for governors, but for customs officials, particularly those on the American Board of Customs Commissioners, who arrived in November 1767 and within a year convinced

London to send a contingent of troops—uncalled for by local officials—to Boston. . . .

As early as the Stamp Act crisis, however, it seemed unlikely that troops could successfully remedy the officials' isolation. In part, the problem was a technical one of how many men Britain would engage in North America and where to locate them. The number of men General Gage could offer governors in 1765 was often so insufficient that the troops would have constituted a provocation more than a deterrent to insurrection; and Dr. Thomas Moffatt told a parliamentary committee that it would have taken ten weeks to send troops into Rhode Island. Any military solution was compromised as well by ingrained beliefs and expectations. For colonists, a standing army signaled that the government was pursuing ends other than the good of the governed. Thus, rather than augmenting the government's authority, the use of troops encouraged additional suspicion and hostility. Already in September 1765, the New York Council advised Colden that it would be "more safe for the Government to shew a Confidence in the People, than to discover its distrust of them by Calling any assistance to the Civil Power." . . . The wisdom in [this warning] was illustrated at New York in late 1765, where Colden's reinforcement of Fort George in effect aggravated the riot he was preparing to meet. The same lesson was repeated there in late 1769 and early 1770, when the presence of royal troops proved useless for protecting importers, while repeated frays between soldiers and citizens finally culminated in the so-called Battle of Golden Hill in January 1770. Again at Boston, the royal troops which arrived in October 1768 proved useless for protecting nonimportation opponents such as John Mein: "in Ireland perhaps where the people have been long used to the military upon an apprehension only of violence from the populace" regular soldiers might have been used for Mein's protection, Hutchinson commented; but "in the present state of the colonies I could not think it so. . . ." The troops were finally withdrawn when their continued presence threatened to occasion a battle worse even than that of March 5, 1770.

British suppositions also hindered any confident and effective use of troops against the colonists. Traditional ideas about the proper role of the army in a free country were as vivid for military commanders like Sir Jeffery Amherst or Thomas Gage as for John Adams, and even British ministers shared the Americans' misgivings. When Governor Wright of Georgia managed briefly to distribute stamps with the aid of regular troops, he earned not the thanks of his superiors but a word of admonition from Secretary of State Shelburne. . . . The secretary's sentiments here were not far different from those of New York's radical printer John Holt. In commenting upon a letter that anticipated the day when mobs would be suppressed and a proper respect for the laws impressed upon "the lower rank," Holt said simply that *"Not force, but justice will do it."*

Out of this impossibility of military rule arose in good part the peculiar conditions that gave the American Revolution its distinctive character. British authority could not be imposed upon an unwilling people. To be effective it had to be administered by men "reverenced and beloved by the people," as the *Boston Gazette* once said; its power had to flow directly from the governed who, when the laws seemed to promote their welfare, would both obey and enforce them. As these conditions ceased to be true, royal authority disintegrated; imperial officials became incapable of restraining hostility and disorderly outbreaks. But simultaneously, the function of maintaining order was assumed by their opponents. Both sides shared a respect for orderly, lawful procedures; they differed in their definitions of order and their conceptions of legitimacy. The colonists' progressive assumption of power paralleled their increasing conviction that Britain aspired to despotic power. Yet, ironically, it was not only British inability but also her remaining liberal traditions that prevented a simple forceful suppression of the American agitation.

III

The basic guidelines for American opposition to Britain were defined already during the Stamp Act crisis; but the nature of the Anglo-American conflict changed radically within the next decade. Signs of this transformation were already apparent in the nonimportation effort by 1770. The fixation of 1765–6 with buttressing British authority beyond the regions affected by the Stamp Act had to some extent been replaced by a conscious assumption of extra-legal political power. More important, the old Sons of Liberty's faith in Britain, her rulers and institutions had given way to a new desperation for American liberty, which was marked by a willingness to resort to ever more extreme methods to maintain the nonimportation association. By 1770, in short, the colonists had begun to advance along the road from resistance to revolution.

Disillusionment with Britain did not immediately follow the Declaratory Act of 1766, which asserted Parliament's sovereign right "to make Laws . . . to bind the Colonists and People of America . . . in all Cases whatsoever." Most colonists apparently interpreted the enactment as a face-saving device upon which Parliament did not intend to act. Colonists remained strongly confident of British justice in late 1767, when John Dickinson's "Letters from a Farmer in Pennsylvania" were readily accepted as expressing the views of his countrymen. In words strikingly like those of Jonathan Mayhew a year earlier, Dickinson stressed that the Americans had "an excellent prince" in whose "good dispositions they could confide"; they had a "generous, sensible and humane nation" to whom they could apply for redress from their newest grievances. Separation was the least desirable outcome of the conflict—"Torn from the body, to which we are united by religion, liberty, laws, affections, relation, language and commerce, we must bleed at every vein."

Attitudes toward Britain changed, in short, most dramatically only after 1767. . . .

In assigning responsibility for continued "oppressive" policies, the colonists tended to accuse . . . familiar figures. . . . Newspapers of 1765 and

1766 continually repeated rumors that the Stamp Act had been proposed and promoted by British agents on the American continent. . . . Gradually, misrepresentations from "this side the water" became the entire explanation of British policy, as King and Parliament were allegedly led into ill-considered decisions by false information from the colonies. . . .

At first, several scattered individuals were singled out for attack. In 1764, Rhode Island's Governor Stephen Hopkins complained that royal customs officials were misrepresenting that colony. By 1765, fears centered on the Newport Junto. In Charleston, South Carolina, Christopher Gadsden complained of misrepresentation at the hands of local Scottish merchants. But after 1766, charges focused increasingly on one man, Massachusetts's Governor Francis Bernard. Opposition to the governor from within the Bay Colony had predated the Stamp Act agitation, then intensified and spread when Bernard asserted the absolute authority of Parliament before the provincial assembly in September 1765 and recommended submission to the Stamp Act. His stance assumed significance for other colonies, too, when he was cited by a dissenting faction in the House of Lords to buttress its opposition to the Stamp Act's repeal: "We are of Opinion," the Lords said, "that the total Repeal of that Law, especially while . . . Resistance continues would (as Governor Bernard says in their Intention) *make the Authority of Great Britain contemtible hereafter.*" . . .

Events thereafter only reinforced suspicions of the governor. Bernard presented a recommendation from England that victims of the Stamp Act riots be compensated for their losses in such a fashion that the assembly refused to honor it, whereupon he reported the incident so unfavorably that the colony's agent in London, Dennis De Berdt, immediately suspected that the account was "a slander on the Province." . . .

But why should Bernard and his fellow royal officials misrepresent the colonists as factious, disposed to riot, disloyal? . . . Was it not perhaps to justify military rule? . . . Had not the customsmen exacerbated the *Liberty* riot of June 1768, which led to the stationing of regular troops in the town? . . . For colonists this military build-up was unnecessary. Boston was not in a state of anarchy; incidents before the *Liberty* riot had been trivial, and even that more serious incident had been brought under control by the steady efforts of native Bostonians. Eventually, the British government came to much the same conclusion.

In the immediate aftermath of the troops' arrival, colonists throughout the American continent with increasing unanimity indicted Crown officials in the Bay Colony. In October 1768, Pennsylvania Chief Justice William Allen wrote correspondents in England that "the gross Misrepresentations of Governor Bernard (who, was his true Character as well known with you as it is in America, would be little regarded) have very undeservedly inflamed the Nation." New Yorkers burned Bernard in effigy two months later, and as late as 1770 the Portsmouth Town Meeting blamed misrepresentation for America's grievances. "It is the Opinion of this Town," it resolved, "That our King, and many of the principal Men in the Nation, have been greatly deceived by the false and malicious Accounts sent from America by Governor

Bernard, the Commissioners [of Customs] and other wicked designing Persons who expected to enrich themselves on the Spoils of America."

A belief in misrepresentation was, however, insufficient to transform American opposition from resistance to revolution. Its implications were reformist, not revolutionary. . . . Moreover, misrepresentation absolved officials in London of any guilt for their actions. This was true for the dispatch of troops to Boston. . . . The protraction of grievances was "not to be imputed to an unkind disposition in Lord Hillsborough towards us," it said, "but altogether to the malicious and false representations of an infamous faction on this side the water."

For the radical movement to become revolutionary, more extreme conclusions were necessary. The Americans must become convinced, as John Dickinson put it, that "mistake or passion" could not explain Britain's wrongheaded actions. It had to appear "UNDOUBTED that an inveterate resolution is formed to annihilate the liberties of the governed," one that involved the King, Parliament, and ministry as centrally as their servants in the colonies. And to arrive at such a conclusion, colonists had to turn their eyes from their own continent to London, to examine the actions of King, Parliament, and ministry. In that fact lay the truth of a statement continually repeated by colonists during the frenetic days of the Stamp Act crisis—that only Great Britain could force America toward independence.

✷ *F U R T H E R   R E A D I N G*

John Brooke, *The Chatham Administration, 1766–1768* (1956)

Robert J. Chaffin, "The Townshend Acts of 1767," *William and Mary Quarterly*, 3d ser., 27 (1970), 90–121

Oliver M. Dickerson, *The Navigation Acts and the American Revolution* (1951)

Joseph A. Ernst, "The Currency Act Repeal Movement: A Study of Imperial Politics and Revolutionary Crisis, 1764–1767," *William and Mary Quarterly*, 3d ser., 25 (1968), 177–211

Lawrence H. Gipson, "The Great Debate in the Committee of the Whole House of Commons on the Stamp Act, 1766, as Reported by Nathaniel Ryder," *Pennsylvania Magazine of History* 86 (1962), 10–41

———, *The Triumphant Empire: The Rumbling of the Coming Storm, 1766–1770* (1965)

———, *The Triumphant Empire: Thunder-Clouds Gather in the West, 1763–1766* (1961)

Michael Kammen, *A Rope of Sand: The Colonial Agents, British Politics, and the American Revolution* (1968)

Bernhard Knollenberg, *Origin of the American Revolution, 1759–1766* (1960)

Jesse Lemisch, "Radical Plot in Boston (1770): A Study in the Use of Evidence," *Harvard Law Review* 84 (1970), 485–504

Pauline Maier, *From Resistance to Revolution: Colonial Radicals and the Development of American Opposition to Britain, 1765–1776* (1972)

Edmund S. Morgan, "Colonial Ideas of Parliamentary Power, 1764–1766," *William and Mary Quarterly*, 3d ser., 5 (1948), 311–341

———, ed., *Prologue to Revolution: Sources and Documents on the Stamp Act Crisis, 1764–1766* (1959)

———, and Helen M. Morgan, *The Stamp Act Crisis: Prologue to Revolution* (1953)

Arthur M. Schlesinger, *The Colonial Merchants and the American Revolution, 1763–1776* (1918)

Glenn C. Smith, "An Era of Non-Importation Associations, 1768–1773," *William and Mary Quarterly,* 2d ser., 20 (1940), 84–98

Neil R. Stout, *The Royal Navy in America: A Study of Enforcement of Colonial Policy in the Era of the American Revolution* (1973)

Peter D. G. Thomas, *British Politics and the Stamp Act Crisis: The First Phase of the American Revolution, 1763–1767* (1975)

————, *The Townshend Duties Crisis: The Second Phase of the American Revolution, 1767–1773* (1987)

Carl Ubbelohde, *The Vice-Admiralty Courts and the American Revolution* (1960)

John J. Waters and John A. Schutz, "Patterns of Colonial Politics: The Writs of Assistance and the Rivalry Between the Otis and Hutchinson Families," *William and Mary Quarterly,* 3d ser., 24 (1967), 543–567

Derek Watson, "The Rockingham Whigs and the Townshend Duties," *English Historical Review* 84 (1969), 561–565

Robert M. Weir, "North Carolina: Reaction to the Currency Act of 1764," *North Carolina Historical Review* 40 (1963), 183–199

Hiller B. Zobel, *The Boston Massacre* (1970)

When Worlds Collide: From the Tea Act to the Declaration of Independence, 1773–1776

⨯

When Parliament passed the Tea Act on May 10, 1773, it unwittingly supplied the catalyst that would revive united colonial resistance to British rule. The law aimed to relieve the East India Company's huge oversupply of tea by enabling the company to market the popular consumer product directly in America and Ireland at a reduced price. Members of Parliament never supposed that by providing tea—which had been taxed since 1767—more cheaply to America, they would cause a storm of protest. But when patriot leaders explained the meaning of the Tea Act, colonists from Charleston, South Carolina, to Boston, Massachusetts, became convinced that the new law was a deceptive scheme intended to enforce the collection of taxes in America. By giving the East India Company a monopoly on the importation of tea into the colonies, Parliament was pushing out untaxed tea from Dutch sources that enterprising colonists previously had smuggled in. And whereas taxes on East India Company tea formerly had been paid by shippers in England, now revenues would be collected in America by the East India Company's loyal, hand-picked agents. With the principle of collecting taxes in America thus established, patriots argued that Parliament might not only raise the tea duty at some later point but impose similar taxes on other commodities, and even on land. Because of these threats, patriots were able to mobilize effective resistance to the landing of the tea in all the major colonial ports. Everywhere, colonists returned the tea to Britain before it was unloaded on shore or taxed—everywhere, that is, except Boston. There Governor Thomas Hutchinson, whose son was an East India Company agent, refused to allow the tea ship to sail back to England with its savory cargo. So in a carefully executed protest, patriots disguised as Indians dumped the tea into the harbor.

As John Adams among others recognized immediately, the patriots' "tea party" was a critical action. Parliament retaliated with the Coercive Acts, by which it intended to establish control over Massachusetts while sending a stern message to the other colonies. Americans' subsequent decision to treat Massachu-

setts as suffering in the common cause led to the creation of the Continental Congress, which not only supported Massachusetts but, in October 1774, enacted a trade embargo (the Continental Association) against Britain. Later, after fighting broke out at Lexington and Concord, the Congress would back Massachusetts.

Reconciliation now receded further and further from the reach of leaders on both sides of the Atlantic. As imperial politics became polarized and positions hardened, in the colonists' eyes, an open break from England seemed more and more necessary. Parliament effectively declared war on the colonists as rebels by passing the Prohibitory Act in December 1775. In response, the colonists turned to independence as a reasonable policy. Although it was never possible for the colonists as a whole to achieve unanimity—too many different interests and too much diversity prevailed among them—in the Continental Congress the tide of opinion swept rapidly toward independence.

✕ D O C U M E N T S

In the first document, John Adams's private response to the Tea Party, the patriot leader reveals the depth of colonial resistance to the Tea Act, while the parliamentary debates reprinted in the second selection show how differently the same event was viewed in Britain. The colonists had a few friends in Parliament—Sir George Saville and General Conway, for example—but the weight of parliamentary opinion and numbers favored restrictions, if not outright punishment, for Boston and the rest of Massachusetts. Britain's considered response was the Coercive Acts, excerpted here as the third selection. This legislation so threatened all the colonies that they banded together in the Continental Congress to protest.

Virginia, along with Massachusetts, emerged as an advocate of vigorous resistance. The reasoning of the Virginia patriots is set forth in Jefferson's *Summary View* (the fourth document), a tract that anticipated Thomas Paine's *Common Sense* and the *Declaration of Independence.* By the time of the battles of Lexington and Concord in April 1775, few politicians on either side believed in conciliation, and after blood was shed, both sides hardened. See the fifth selection for two contrasting reports on the skirmishes—one, the official patriot account, and the other, the description of a loyalist woman. For Britain the decisive measure that doomed talk of reconciliation was the American Prohibitory Act, the sixth document, which inflicted commercial punishment on the colonies, treating them and their trade as enemies. In America objections to independence were being swept aside by powerful arguments such as those expressed in *Common Sense,* which is excerpted in document seven. This January 1776 pamphlet by an anonymous English immigrant rapidly circulated among tens of thousands of households and gave the once-frightening idea of independence legitimacy. A few leaders, among them Pennsylvania's John Dickinson, still argued that the time for declaring independence had not yet come, as the next selection, from Dickinson's writings, shows. Congress nevertheless adopted and proclaimed the Declaration of Independence, document nine, which Thomas Jefferson, in committee with John Adams, Benjamin Franklin, John Jay, and Roger Sherman, had drafted. Grounding the Declaration on both natural rights and the rights of Englishmen under the British Constitution, they asserted American independence on a narrow, legalistic basis quite different from Thomas Paine's sweeping rejection of monarchy and the whole corrupt British system. When Congress finally voted the Declaration, John Adams exulted, as is revealed in the final selection, Adams's explanation to his wife, Abigail, that though the struggle would be painful and arduous, its purpose was glorious.

John Adams Reflects on the Boston Tea Party, 1773

Last Night 3 Cargoes of Bohea Tea were emptied into the Sea. This Morning a Man of War sails.

This is the most magnificent Movement of all. There is a Dignity, a Majesty, a Sublimity, in this last Effort of the Patriots, that I greatly admire. The People should never rise, without doing something to be remembered—something notable And striking. This Destruction of the Tea is so bold, so daring, so firm, intrepid and inflexible, and it must have so important Consequences, and so lasting, that I cant but consider it as an Epocha in History.

This however is but an Attack upon Property. Another similar Exertion of popular Power, may produce the destruction of Lives. Many Persons wish, that as many dead Carcasses were floating in the Harbour, as there are Chests of Tea:—a much less Number of Lives however would remove the Causes of all our Calamities. . . .

What Measures will the Ministry take, in Consequence of this?—Will they resent it? will they dare to resent it? will they punish Us? How? By quartering Troops upon Us?—by annulling our Charter?—by laying on more duties? By restraining our Trade? By Sacrifice of Individuals, or how.

The Question is whether the Destruction of this Tea was necessary? I apprehend it was absolutely and indispensably so.—They could not send it back, the Governor, Admiral and Collector and Comptroller would not suffer it. It was in their Power to have saved it—but in no other. It could not get by the Castle, the Men of War &c. Then there was no other Alternative but to destroy it or let it be landed. To let it be landed, would be giving up the Principle of Taxation by Parliamentary Authority, against which the Continent have struggled for 10 years, it was loosing all our labour for 10 years and subjecting ourselves and our Posterity forever to Egyptian Taskmasters—to Burthens, Indignities, to Ignominy, Reproach and Contempt, to Desolation and Oppression, to Poverty and Servitude.

But it will be said it might have been left in the Care of a Committee of the Town, or in Castle William. To this many Objections may be made.

Deacon Palmer and Mr. Is. Smith dined with me, and Mr. Trumble came in. They say, the Tories blame the Consignees, as much as the Whiggs do—and say that the Governor will loose his Place, for not taking the Tea into his Protection before, by Means of the Ships of War, I suppose, and the Troops at the Castle.

Letters and texts of John Adams reprinted by permission of the publishers from *Diary and Autobiography of John Adams*, Volumes 2 and 4, L. H. Butterfield, Editor, Leonard C. Faber and Wendell D. Garrett, Assistant Editors, Cambridge, Mass.: The Belknap Press of Harvard University Press, © 1961 Massachusetts Historical Society.

Parliament Debates the Coercive Acts, 1774

Sir George Saville said . . . that the measure now before the house was a very doubtful and dangerous one; doubtful as to the propriety of regulation, and dangerous as to its consequence; that charters by government were sacred things, and are only to be taken away by a due course of law, either as a punishment for an offence, or for a breach of the contract, and that can only be by evidence of the facts; nor could he conceive that in either of those cases there could be any such thing as proceeding without a fair hearing of BOTH parties. This measure before us seems to be a most extraordinary exertion of legislative power. . . . You are now going to alter the charter because it is convenient. In what manner does the house mean to take away this charter, when in fact they refuse to hear the parties, or to go through a legal course of evidence of the facts. Chartered rights have, at all times, when attempted to be altered or taken away, occasioned much bloodshed and strife. . . .

Mr. Welbore Ellis. . . . I differ from the honorable gentleman who spoke last; . . . I think, sir, that chartered rights are by no means those sacred things which never can be altered; they are vested in the crown as a prerogative, for the good of the people at large; if the supreme legislature find that those charters so granted, are both unfit and inconvenient for the public utility, they have a right to make them fit and convenient. . . . Is a charter, not consistent with the public good, to be continued? . . .

General Conway. What I intend to say will not delay the house long. . . . The consequence of this bill will be very important and dangerous. Parliament cannot break into a right without hearing the parties. The question then is simply this:—Have they been heard? What! because the papers say a murder had been committed, does it follow they have proved it? . . . Gentlemen will consider, that this is not only the charter of Boston, or of any particular part, but the charter of ALL America. Are the Americans not to be heard? . . . I do think, and it is my sincere opinion, that we are the AGGRESSORS and INNOVATORS, and NOT the COLONIES. We have IRRITATED and FORCED laws upon them for these six or seven years last past. We have enacted such a variety of laws, with these new taxes, together with a refusal to repeal the *trifling* duty on tea; all these things have served no other purpose but to *distress* and *perplex.* I think the Americans have done *no more* than *every* subject *would* do in an *arbitrary* state, where laws are imposed against their will. In my conscience, I think, *taxation* and *legislation* are in this case *inconsistent.* Have you not a legislative right over Ireland? And yet no one will *dare* to say we have a right to tax. These acts respecting America, will *involve* this country and its ministers in *misfortunes,* and I wish I may not add, in *ruin.*

Lord North. I do not consider this matter of regulation to be taking away their charters in such manner as is represented; it is a regulation of government to assist the crown; it appears to me not to be a matter of political expediency, but of necessity. If it does not stand upon that ground, it stands on nothing. . . . Gentlemen say, let the colony come to your bar, and be heard in their defence; though it is not likely that they will come, when they deny your authority in every instance, can we remain in this situation long? We must effectually take some measures to correct and amend the defects of that government. . . . The Americans have tarred and feathered your subjects, plundered your merchants, burnt your ships, denied all obedience to your laws and authority; yet so clement and forbearing has our conduct been, that it is incumbent upon us now to take a different course. Whatever may be the consequence, we must risque something; if we do not, all is over. . . .

Sir George Young. It remains to me, sir, . . . that the parties should be heard, though even at a twelve-month hence. Nothing, sir, but *fatal* necessity can countenance this measure. No body of men ought to be proceeded against without being heard, much less ought the regulation of a whole government to take place, without the parties attending in their defence against such alterations. . . .

Mr. C. Jenkinson. I rise, sir, only to observe, that if the colony has not that power within itself to maintain its own peace and order, the legislature should, and ought to have. Let me ask, sir, whether the colony took any step, in any shape, to quell the riots and disturbances? No, they took none. . . . It is not only in the late proceedings, but in all former, that they have denied your authority over them; they have refused protection to his majesty's subjects, and in every instance disobeyed the laws of this country; either let this country forsake its trade with America, or let us give that due protection to it which safety requires.

Mr. Harris. I cannot see, sir, any reason for so wide a separation between America and England as other gentlemen are apt to think there ought to be; that country, sir, was hatched from this, and I hope we shall always keep it under the shadow of our wings. It has been said, no representation, no taxation. This was the system formerly adopted, but I do not find it authorised in any book of jurisprudence, nor do I deem it to be a doctrine either reasonable or constitutional. I insist upon it, they are bound to obey both the crown and parliament. The last twelve years of our proceedings have been a scene of lenity and inactivity. Let us proceed and mend our method. . . .

Governor Pownal. . . . Things are now come to action; and I must be free to tell the house, that the Americans will resist these measures: they are prepared to do it. I do not mean by arms, but by the conversation of public town meetings; they now send their letters by couriers, instead of the post, from one town to another; and I can say your post office will very soon be deprived of its revenue. With regard to the officers who command the militia of that country, they will have them of their own appointment, and not from government; but I will never more give an opinion concerning America in this house; those I have given have been disregarded.

Mr. Rigby. Upon my word, sir, what was just now said, is very worthy the consideration of this house; . . . it appears, *that America is preparing to arms; and that the deliberations of their town meetings tend chiefly to oppose the measures of this country by force.* He has told you, sir, that the Americans will appoint other officers than those sent by government to command their troops. He has told you that the post office is established on their account from town to town, in order to carry their traitorous correspondence from one to another. He has told you the post office revenue will soon be annihilated. If these things are true, sir, I find we have been the aggressors, by continually doing acts of lenity for these twelve years last past. . . . I think this country has a right to tax America; but I do not say that I would put any new tax on at this particular crisis; but when things are returned to a peaceable state, I would then begin to exercise it. And I am free to declare my opinion, that I think we have a right to tax Ireland, if there was a necessity so to do, in order to help the mother country. If Ireland was to rebel and resist our laws, I would tax it. The mother country has an undoubted right and controul over the whole of its colonies. Again, sir, a great deal has been said concerning requisition. Pray, in what manner is it to be obtained? Is the king to demand it, or are we, the legislative power of this country, to send a very *civil polite gentleman* over to treat with their assemblies? . . . Is he to tell the speaker that we have been extremely ill used by our neighbors the French; that they have attacked us in several quarters; that the finances of this country are in a bad state; and therefore we desire you will be *kind* enough to assist us, and give us some money? Is this to be the language of this country to that; and are we thus to go cap in hand? I am of opinion, that if the administration of this country had not been changed soon after passing the stamp-act, that tax would have been collected with as much ease as the land-tax is in Great Britain. . . .

  Mr. C. Fox. I am glad to hear from the honorable gentleman who spoke last, that *now* is not the time to tax America; that the only time for that is, when all these disturbances are quelled, and they are returned to their duty; so, I find taxes are to be the reward of obedience; and the Americans, who are considered to have been in open rebellion, are to be rewarded by acquiescing to their measures. When will be the time when America ought to have heavy taxes laid upon it? The honorable gentleman (Mr. Rigby) tells you, that that time will be when the Americans are returned to peace and quietness. The hon. gentleman tells us also, that we have a right to tax Ireland; however I may agree with him in regard to the principle, it would not be policy to exercise it; I believe we have no more right to tax the one than the other. I believe America is wrong in resisting against this country, with regard to legislative authority. . . . But, sir, there has been a constant conduct practised in this country, consisting of violence and weakness; I wish those measures may not continue; nor can I think that the stamp-act would have been submitted to without resistance, if the administration had not been changed; the present bill before you . . . irritates the minds of the people, but does not correct the deficiencies of that government.

  Sir Gilbert Elliot arose to answer Mr. C. Fox, which he did in a very masterly manner, by stating that there was not the least degree of absurdity in taxing your own subjects, over whom you have declared you had an absolute right; though that tax should, through necessity, be enacted at a time when peace and quietness were the reigning system of the times; you declare you have that right, where is the absurdity in the exercise of it?

Sir Richard Sutton read a copy of a letter, relative to the government of America, *from a governor in America,* to the board of trade, shewing that, at the most quiet times, the dispositions to oppose the laws of this country were strongly ingrafted in them, and that all their actions conveyed a spirit and wish for independence. If you ask an American who is his master? he will tell you he has none, nor any governor but Jesus Christ. I do believe it, and it is my firm opinion, that the opposition to the measures of the legislature of this country, is a determined prepossession of the idea of total independence.

The Coercive Acts, 1774

1. *The Boston Port Act*

Whereas dangerous commotions and insurrections have been fomented and raised in the town of Boston, in the province of Massachusetts Bay in New England, by divers ill-affected persons, to the subversion of his Majesty's government and to the utter destruction of the public peace and good order of the said town; in which commotions and insurrections certain valuable cargoes of teas, being the property of the East India Company and on board certain vessels lying within the bay or harbour of Boston, were seized and destroyed; and whereas, in the present condition of the said town and harbour the commerce of his Majesty's subjects cannot be safely carried on there, nor the customs payable to his Majesty duly collected; and it is therefore expedient that the officers of his Majesty's customs should be forthwith removed from the said town: . . . be it enacted . . . [that it is unlawful to load on any vessel goods for shipment to any other part of the province or to any other colony or country, and that it is unlawful to unload goods from any other part of the province or any other colony or country in the town of Boston and in the bay called the harbour of Boston. Penalty for violation is forfeiture of ship and goods] . . . until it shall be certified to his Majesty in Council by the governor or lieutenant-governor of the said province, that reasonable satisfaction hath been made to the officers of his Majesty's revenue, and others, who suffered by the riots and insurrections above mentioned, in the months of November and December, in the year one thousand seven hundred and seventy-three, and in the month of January, in the year one thousand seven hundred and seventy-four.

2. *The Massachusetts Government Act*

Whereas [the Massachusetts Bay Charter of 1692 provides that the twenty-eight members of the Governor's Council should be chosen by the Assembly each year, and that method] has been so far from contributing to the attainment of the good ends and purposes thereby intended, and to the promoting of the internal welfare, peace, and good government of the said province, or to the maintenance of the just subordination to, and conformity with, the laws of Great Britain that the manner of exercising the powers, authorities, and privileges aforesaid, by the persons so annually elected, hath for some time past been such as had the most manifest tendency to obstruct, and, in great measure, defeat, the execution of the laws; to weaken the attachment of his Majesty's well-disposed subjects . . . and to encourage the ill-disposed among them to proceed even to acts of direct resistance to, and defiance of, his Majesty's authority; and it hath accordingly happened that an open resistance to the execution of the laws hath actually taken place in the town of Boston and the neighbourhood thereof, within the said province; and whereas it is, under these circumstances, become absolutely necessary, in order to the preservation of the peace and good order of the said province, the protection of his Majesty's well-disposed subjects therein resident, the continuance of the mutual benefits arising from the commerce and corre- spondence between this kingdom and the said province, and the maintaining of the just dependence of the said province upon the Crown and Parliament of Great Britain that the said method of annually electing the councillors or assistants of the said province should no longer be suffered to continue but that the appointment of the said councillors or assistants should hence- forth be put upon the like footing as is established in such other of his Majesty's colonies or plantations in America. . . . Be it therefore enacted . . . that . . . the council or court of assistants of the said province for the time being, shall be composed of such of the inhabitants or proprietors of lands within the same as shall be thereunto nominated and appointed by his Majesty, . . . agreeable to the practice now used in respect to the appoint- ment of councillors in such of his Majesty's other colonies in America. . . .

II. And it is hereby further enacted, that the said assistants or councillors, so to be appointed as aforesaid, shall hold their offices respectively, for and during the pleasure of his Majesty. . . .

III. And be it further enacted, . . . that . . . it shall and may be lawful for his Majesty's governor . . . to nominate and appoint, under the seal of the province, from time to time, and also to remove, without the consent of the council, all judges of the inferior courts of common pleas, commis- sioners of oyer and terminer, the attorney general, provosts, marshals, jus- tices of the peace, and other officers to the council or courts of justice belonging. . . .

V. And be it further enacted . . . that . . . it shall and may be lawful for his Majesty's governor . . . to nominate and appoint the sheriffs without the consent of the council, and to remove such sheriffs with such consent, and not otherwise.

VI. And be it further enacted . . . that upon·every vacancy of the offices of chief justice and judges of the Superior Court . . . the governor . . . shall have full power and authority to nominate and appoint the persons to succeed to the said offices, who shall hold their commissions during the pleasure of his Majesty. . . .

VII. And whereas, . . . [town meetings have been called at the discretion of local officials] and whereas a great abuse has been made of the power of calling such meetings, and the inhabitants have, contrary to the design of their institution, been misled to treat upon matters of the most general concern, and to pass many dangerous and unwarrantable resolves; for remedy whereof, be it enacted, that from and after the said first day of August, one thousand seven hundred and seventy-four, no meeting shall be called by the selectmen, or at the request of any number of freeholders of any township, district, or precinct, without the leave of the governor . . . in writing, expressing the special business of the said meeting, first had and obtained, except the annual meeting in the months of March or May, for the choice of selectmen, constables, and other officers, . . . and that no other matter shall be treated of at such meetings, except the election of their aforesaid officers or representatives, nor at any other meeting, except the business expressed in the leave given by the governor. . . .

VIII. And whereas the method at present used in the province of Massachusetts Bay in America, of electing persons to serve on grand juries, and other juries, by the freeholders and inhabitants of the several towns, affords occasion for many evil practices, and tends to pervert the free and impartial administration of justice; for remedy whereof, be it further enacted . . . that . . . jurors . . . shall not be elected, nominated, or appointed, by the freeholders and inhabitants of the several towns within the said respective counties, nor summoned or returned by the constables of the said towns; but that, from thenceforth, the jurors . . . shall be summoned and returned by the sheriffs of the respective counties within the said province. . . .

3.   The Administration of Justice Act

Whereas in his Majesty's province of Massachusetts Bay, in New England, an attempt has lately been made to throw off the authority of the Parliament of Great Britain over the said province, and an actual and avowed resistance by open force, to the execution of certain Acts of Parliament, has been suffered to take place, uncontrolled and unpunished, in defiance of his Majesty's authority, and to the utter subversion of all lawful government; and whereas, in the present disordered state of the said province it is of the utmost importance to the general welfare thereof, and to the re-establishment of lawful authority throughout the same, that neither the magistrates acting in support of the laws, nor any of his Majesty's subjects aiding and assisting them therein, or in the suppression of riots and tumults raised in opposition to the execution of the laws and statutes of this realm, should be discouraged from the proper discharge of their duty by an apprehension that in case of their being questioned for any acts done therein, they may be liable to be brought to trial for the same before persons who do not acknowledge the validity of the laws, in the execution thereof, or the authority of the magistrate in the support of whom such acts had been done: in order therefore to remove every such discouragement from the minds of his Majesty's subjects, and to induce them, upon all proper occasions, to exert themselves in support of the public peace of the province, and of the authority of the king and Parliament of Great Britain over the same, be it enacted . . . that if any inquisition or indictment shall be found, or if any appeal shall be sued or preferred against any person for murder, or other capital offence, in the province of Massachusetts Bay, and it shall appear by information given upon oath to the governor, . . . that the fact was committed by the person . . . either in the execution of his duty as a magistrate for the suppression of riots, or in the support of the laws of revenue, or in acting in his duty as an officer of revenue, or in acting under the direction and order of any magistrate for the suppression of riots, or for the carrying into effect the laws of revenue, or in aiding and assisting in any of the cases aforesaid; and if it shall also appear to the satisfaction of the said governor . . . that an indifferent trial cannot be had within the said province; in that case it shall and may be lawful for the governor . . . to direct, with the advice and consent of the council, that the inquisition, indictment, or appeal shall be tried in some other of his Majesty's colonies, or in Great Britain. . . .

4.   The Quartering Act

Whereas doubts have been entertained, whether troops can be quartered otherwise than in barracks . . . within his Majesty's dominions in North America; and whereas it may frequently happen, from the situation of such barracks that, if troops should be quartered therein they would not be stationed where their presence may be necessary and required: be it therefore enacted . . . that, in such cases it shall and may be lawful . . . to cause any officers or soldiers in his Majesty's service to be quartered and billeted in such manner as is now directed by law, where no barracks are provided by the colonies.

II. And be it further enacted . . . that . . . it shall and may be lawful for the governor of the province to order and direct such and so many uninhabited houses, outhouses, barns, or other buildings, as he shall think necessary to be taken (making a reasonable allowance for the same) and make fit for the reception of such officers and soldiers, and to put and quarter such officers and soldiers therein for such time as he shall think proper. . . .

Thomas Jefferson Asserts American Rights, 1774

Resolved, that . . . when assembled in general congress with the deputies from the other states of British America, . . . an humble and dutiful address be presented to his majesty, begging leave to lay before him, as chief magistrate of the British empire, the united complaints of his majesty's subjects in America; complaints which are excited by many unwarrantable encroachments and usurpations, attempted to be made by the legislature of one part of the empire, upon those rights which God and the laws have given equally and independently to all. To represent to his majesty that these his states have often individually made humble application to his imperial throne to obtain, through its intervention, some redress of their injured rights, to none of which was ever even an answer condescended; humbly to hope that this their joint address, penned in the language of truth, and divested of those expressions of servility which would persuade his majesty that we are asking favours, and not rights, shall obtain from his majesty a more respectful acceptance. And this his majesty will think we have reason to expect when he reflects that he is no more than the chief officer of the people, appointed by the laws, and circumscribed with definite powers, to assist in working the great machine of government, erected for their use, and consequently subject to their superintendence. And in order that these our rights, as well as the invasions of them, may be laid more fully before his majesty, to take a view of them from the origin and first settlement of these countries.

To remind him that our ancestors, before their emigration to America, were the free inhabitants of the British dominions in Europe, and possessed a right which nature has given to all men, of departing from the country in which chance, not choice, has placed them, of going in quest of new habitations, and of there establishing new societies, under such laws and regulations as to them shall seem most likely to promote public happiness. That their Saxon ancestors had, under this universal law, in like manner left their native wilds and woods in the north of Europe, had possessed themselves of the island of Britain, then less charged with inhabitants, and had established there that system of laws which has so long been the glory and protection of that country. Nor was ever any claim of superiority or dependence asserted over them by that mother country from which they had migrated; and were such a claim made, it is believed that his majesty's subjects in Great Britain have too firm a feeling of the rights derived to them from their ancestors, to bow down the sovereignty of their state before such visionary pretensions. And it is thought that no circumstance has occurred to distinguish materially the British from the Saxon emigration. America was conquered, and her settlements made, and firmly established, at the expence of individuals, and not of the British public. Their own blood was spilt in acquiring lands for their settlement, their own fortunes expended in making that settlement effectual; for themselves they fought, for themselves they conquered, and for themselves alone they have right to hold. Not a shilling was ever issued from the public treasures of his majesty, or his ancestors, for their assistance, till of very late times, after the colonies had become established on a firm and permanent footing. That then, indeed, having become valuable to Great Britain for her commercial purposes, his parliament was pleased to lend them assistance against an enemy, who would fain have drawn to herself the benefits of their commerce, to the great aggrandizement of herself, and danger of Great Britain. Such assistance, and in such circumstances, they had often before given to Portugal, and other allied states, with whom they carry on a commercial intercourse; yet these states never supposed, that by calling in her aid, they thereby submitted themselves to her sovereignty. . . .

That the exercise of a free trade with all parts of the world, possessed by the American colonists, as of natural right, and which no law of their own had taken away or abridged, was next the object of unjust encroachment. . . . The trade of the colonies was laid under such restrictions, as shew what hopes they might form from the justice of a British parliament, were its uncontrouled power admitted over the states. History has informed us that bodies of men, as well as individuals, are susceptible of the spirit of tyranny. A view of these acts of parliament for regulation, as it has been affectedly called, of the American trade, if all other evidence were removed out of the case, would undeniably evince the truth of this observation. . . . That these acts prohibit us from carrying in quest of other purchasers the surplus of our tobaccoes remaining after the consumption of Great Britain is supplied; so that we must leave them with the British merchant for whatever he will please to allow us, to be by him reshipped to foreign markets, where he will reap the benefits of making sale of them for full value. That to heighten still the idea of parliamentary justice, and to shew with what moderation they are like to exercise power, where themselves are to feel no part of its weight, we take leave to mention to his majesty certain other acts of British parliament, by which they would prohibit us from manufacturing for our own use the articles we raise on our own lands with our own labour. By an act passed in the 5th Year of the reign of his late majesty king George the second, an American subject is forbidden to make a hat for himself of the fur which he has taken perhaps on his own soil; an instance of despotism to which no parallel can be produced in the most arbitrary ages of British history. By one other act, passed in the 23d year of the same reign, the iron which we make we are forbidden to manufacture, and heavy as that article is, and necessary in every branch of husbandry, besides commission and insurance, we are to pay freight for it to Great Britain, and freight for it back again, for the purpose of supporting not men, but machines, in the island of Great Britain. . . . We do not point out to his majesty the injustice of these acts, with intent to rest on that principle the cause of their nullity; but to shew that experience confirms the propriety of those political principles which exempt us from the jurisdiction of the British parliament. The true ground on which we declare these acts void is, that the British parliament has no right to exercise authority over us.

That these exercises of usurped power have not been confined to instances alone, in which themselves were interested, but they have also intermeddled with the regulation of the internal affairs of the colonies. The act of the 9th [year] of [the reign of Queen] Anne for establishing a post office in America seems to have had little connection with British convenience, except that of accommodating his majesty's ministers and favourites with the sale of a lucrative and easy office.

That thus have we hastened through the reigns which preceded his majesty's, during which the violations of our right were less alarming, because repeated at more distant intervals than that rapid and bold succession of injuries which is likely to distinguish the present from all other periods of American story. Scarcely have our minds been able to emerge from the astonishment into which one stroke of parliamentary thunder has involved us, before another more heavy, and more alarming, is fallen on us. Single acts of tyranny may be ascribed to the accidental opinion of a day; but a series of oppressions, begun at a distinguished period, and pursued unalterably through every change of ministers, too plainly prove a deliberate and systematical plan of reducing us to slavery.

That the act passed in the 4th year of his majesty's reign, intitled "An act for granting certain duties in the British colonies and plantations in America, &c."

One other act, passed in the 5th year of his reign, intitled "An act for granting and applying certain stamp duties and other duties in the British colonies and plantations in America, &c."

One other act, passed in the 6th year of his reign, intitled "An act for the better securing the dependency of his majesty's dominions in America upon the crown and parliament of Great Britain;" and one other act, passed in the 7th year of his reign, intitled "An act for granting duties on paper, tea, &c." form that connected chain of parliamentary usurpation, which has already been the subject of frequent applications to his majesty, and the houses of lords and commons of Great Britain; and no answers having yet been condescended to any of these, we shall not trouble his majesty with a repetition of the matters they contained.

But that one other act, passed in the same 7th year of the reign, having been a peculiar attempt, must ever require peculiar mention; it is intitled "An act for suspending the legislature of New York." One free and independent legislature hereby takes upon itself to suspend the powers of another, free and independent as itself; thus exhibiting a phœnomenon unknown in nature, the creator and creature of its own power. Not only the principles of common sense, but the common feelings of human nature, must be surrendered up before his majesty's subjects here can be persuaded to believe that they hold their political existence at the will of a British parliament. Shall these governments be dissolved, their property annihilated, and their people reduced to a state of nature, at the imperious breath of a body of men, whom they never saw, in whom they never confided, and over whom they have no powers of punishment or removal, let their crimes against the American public be ever so great? Can any one reason be assigned why 160,000 electors in the island of Great Britain should give law to four millions in the states of America, every individual of whom is equal to every individual of them, in virtue, in understanding, and in bodily strength? Were this to be admitted, instead of being a free people, as we have hitherto supposed, and mean to continue ourselves, we should suddenly be found the slaves, not of one, but of 160,000 tyrants, distinguished too from all others by this singular circumstance, that they are removed from the reach of fear, the only restraining motive which may hold the hand of a tyrant.

That by "an act to discontinue in such manner and for such time as are therein mentioned the landing and discharging, lading or shipping, of goods, wares, and merchandize, at the town and within the harbour of Boston, in the province of Massachusetts Bay, in North America," which was passed at the last session of British parliament; a large and populous town, whose trade was their sole subsistence, was deprived of that trade, and involved in utter ruin. Let us for a while suppose the question of right suspended, in order to examine this act on principles of justice: An act of parliament had been passed imposing duties on teas, to be paid in America, against which act the Americans had protested as inauthoritative. The East India company, who till that time had never sent a pound of tea to America on their own account, step forth on that occasion the assertors of parliamentary right, and send hither many ship loads of that obnoxious commodity. The masters of their several vessels, however, on their arrival in America, wisely attended to admonition, and returned with their cargoes. In the province of New England alone the remonstrances of the people were disregarded, and a compliance, after being many days waited for, was flatly refused. Whether in this the master of the vessel was governed by his obstinacy, or his instructions, let those who know, say. There are extraordinary situations which require extraordinary interposition. An exasperated people, who feel that they possess power, are not easily restrained within limits strictly regular. A number of them assembled in the town of Boston, threw the tea into the ocean, and dispersed without doing any other act of violence. If in this they did wrong, they were known and were amenable to the laws of the land, against which it could not be objected that they had ever, in any instance, been obstructed or diverted from their regular course in favour of popular offenders. They should therefore not have been distrusted on this occasion. But that ill fated colony had formerly been bold in their enmities against the house of Stuart, and were now devoted to ruin by that unseen hand which governs the momentous affairs of this great empire. On the partial representations of a few worthless ministerial dependents, whose constant office it has been to keep that government embroiled, and who, by their treacheries, hope to obtain the dignity of the British knighthood, without calling for a party accused, without asking a proof, without attempting a distinction between the guilty and the innocent, the whole of that antient and wealthy town is in a moment reduced from opulence to beggary. Men who had spent their lives in extending the British commerce, who had invested in that place the wealth their honest endeavours had merited, found themselves and their families thrown at once on the world for subsistence by its charities. Not the hundredth part of the inhabitants of that town had been concerned in the act complained of; many of them were in Great Britain and in other parts beyond sea; yet all were involved in one indiscriminate ruin, by a new executive power, unheard of till then, that of a British parliament. A property, of the value of many millions of money, was sacrificed to revenge, not repay, the loss of a few thousands. This is administering justice with a heavy hand indeed! and when is this tempest to be arrested in its course? . . .

By the act for the suppression of riots and tumults in the town of Boston, passed also in the last session of parliament, a murder committed there is, if the governor pleases, to be tried . . . in the island of Great Britain. . . . And the wretched criminal, if he happen to have offended on the American side, stripped of his privilege of trial by peers of his vicinage, removed from the place where alone full evidence could be obtained, without money, without counsel, without friends, without exculpatory proof, is tried before judges predetermined to condemn. The cowards who would suffer a countryman to be torn from the bowels of their society, in order to be thus offered a sacrifice to parliamentary tyranny, would merit that everlasting infamy now fixed on the authors of the act! . . .

That these are the acts of power, assumed by a body of men, foreign to our constitutions, and unacknowledged by our laws, against which we do, on behalf of the inhabitants of British America, enter this our solemn and determined protest; and we do earnestly entreat his majesty, as yet the only mediatory power between the several states of the British empire, to recommend to his parliament of Great Britain the total revocation of these acts, which, however nugatory they be, may yet prove the cause of further discontents and jealousies among us.

That we next proceed to consider the conduct of his majesty, as holding the executive powers of the laws of these states, and mark out his deviations from the line of duty: By the constitution of Great Britain, as well as of the several American states, his majesty possesses the power of refusing to pass into a law any bill which has already passed the other two branches of legislature. His majesty, however, and his ancestors, conscious of the impropriety of opposing their single opinion to the united wisdom of two houses of parliament, while their proceedings were unbiassed by interested principles, for several ages past have modestly declined the exercise of this power in that part of his empire called Great Britain. But by change of circumstances, other principles than those of justice simply have obtained an influence on their determinations; the addition of new states to the British empire has produced an addition of new, and sometimes opposite interests. It is now, therefore, the great office of his majesty, to resume the exercise of his negative power, and to prevent the passage of laws by any one legislature of the empire, which might bear injuriously on the rights and interests of another. Yet this will not excuse the wanton exercise of this power which we have seen his majesty practise on the laws of the American legislatures. For the most trifling reasons, and sometimes for no conceivable reason at all, his majesty has rejected laws of the most salutary tendency. The abolition of domestic slavery is the great object of desire in those colonies, where it was unhappily introduced in their infant state. But previous to the enfranchisement of the slaves we have, it is necessary to exclude all further importations from Africa; yet our repeated attempts to effect this by prohibitions, and by imposing duties which might amount to a prohibition, have been hitherto defeated by his majesty's negative: Thus preferring the immediate advantages of a few African corsairs to the lasting interests of the American states, and to the rights of human nature, deeply wounded by this infamous practice. Nay, the single interposition of an interested individual against a law was scarcely ever known to fail of success, though in the opposite scale were placed the interests of a whole country. That this is so shameful an abuse of a power trusted with his majesty for other purposes, as if not reformed, would call for some legal restrictions.

With equal inattention to the necessities of his people here has his majesty permitted our laws to lie neglected in England for years, neither confirming them by his assent, nor annulling them by his negative; so that such of them as have no suspending clause we hold on the most precarious of all tenures, his majesty's will. . . .

That in order to enforce the arbitrary measures before complained of, his majesty has from time to time sent among us large bodies of armed forces, not made up of the people here, nor raised by the authority of our laws: Did his majesty possess such a right as this, it might swallow up all our other rights whenever he should think proper. But his majesty has no right to land a single armed man on our shores, and those whom he sends here are liable to our laws made for the suppression and punishment of riots, routs, and unlawful assemblies; or are hostile bodies, invading us in defiance of law. . . .

To render these proceedings still more criminal against our laws, instead of subjecting the military to the civil powers, his majesty has expressly made the civil subordinate to the military. But can his majesty thus put down all law under his feet? Can he erect a power superior to that which erected himself? He has done it indeed by force; but let him remember that force cannot give right.

That these are our grievances which we have thus laid before his majesty, with that freedom of language and sentiment which becomes a free people claiming their rights, as derived from the laws of nature, and not as the gift of their chief magistrate: Let those flatter who fear; it is not an American art. . . . Kings are the servants, not the proprietors of the people. Open your breast, sire, to liberal and expanded thought. Let not the name of George the third be a blot in the page of history. You are surrounded by British counsellors, but remember that they are parties. You have no ministers for American affairs, because you have none taken from among us, nor amenable to the laws on which they are to give you advice. It behoves you, therefore, to think and to act for yourself and your people. The great principles of right and wrong are legible to every reader; to pursue them requires not the aid of many counsellors. The whole art of government consists in the art of being honest. Only aim to do your duty, and mankind will give you credit where you fail. No longer persevere in sacrificing the rights of one part of the empire to the inordinate desires of another; but deal out to all equal and impartial right. Let no act be passed by any one legislature which may infringe on the rights and liberties of another. This is the important post in which fortune has placed you, holding the balance of a great, if a well poised empire. . . .

Two Views of the Battles of Lexington and Concord, 1775

Official Patriot Account, April 26, 1775

To the Inhabitants of Great Britain.
Friends and Fellow-Subjects:
    Hostilities are at length commenced in this colony by the troops under

the command of General Gage, and it being of the greatest importance that an early, true, and authentic account of this inhuman proceeding should be known to you, the congress of this colony have transmitted the same and from want of a session of the honourable Continental Congress, think it proper to address you on this alarming occasion.

By the clearest depositions relative to this transaction, it will appear that on the night preceding the 19 of April instant, a body of the king's troops, under the command of Colonel Smith, were secretly landed at Cambridge with an apparent design to take or destroy the military and other stores provided for the defence of this colony, and deposited at Concord; that some inhabitants of the colony on the night aforesaid, whilst travelling peaceably on the road between Boston and Concord, were seized and greatly abused by armed men who appeared to be officers of General Gage's army; that the town of Lexington by these means was alarmed, and a company of the inhabitants mustered on the occasion; that the regular troops on their way to Concord marched into the said town of Lexington, and the said company, on their approach, began to disperse; that, notwithstanding this, the regulars rushed on with great violence and first began hostilities by firing on said Lexington Company, whereby they killed eight and wounded several others; that the regulars continued their fire until those of said company who were neither killed nor wounded had made their escape; that Colonel Smith with the detachment then marched to Concord, where a number of provincials were again fired on by the troops, and two of them killed, and several wounded, before the provincials fired on them; and that these hostile measures of the troops produced an engagement that lasted through the day in which many of the provincials, and more of the regular troops, were killed and wounded.

To give a particular account of the ravages of the troops as they retreated from Concord to Charlestown, would be very difficult, if not impracticable. Let it suffice to say that a great number of the houses on the road were plundered and rendered unfit for use; several were burnt; women in childbed were driven by the soldiery naked into the streets; old men, peaceably in their houses were shot dead; and such scenes exhibited as would disgrace the annals of the most uncivilized nation.

These, brethren, are marks of ministerial vengeance against this colony for refusing, with her sister colonies, submission to slavery, but they have not yet detached us from our royal sovereign. We profess to be his loyal and dutiful subjects, and so hardly dealt with as we have been, are still ready with our lives and fortunes to defend his person, family, crown, and dignity. Nevertheless, to the persecution and tyranny of his cruel ministry, we will not tamely submit. Appealing to Heaven for the justice of our cause, we determine to die or be free. . . .

We sincerely hope that the great Sovereign of the universe who hath so often appeared for the English nation, will support you in every rational and manly exertion with these colonies for saving it from ruin, and that in a constitutional connection with the mother country we shall be altogether a free and happy people.

A Loyalist Lady's Account, April 1775

On the 18th instant at 11 at night, about 800 grenadiers and light infantry were ferried across the bay to Cambridge, from whence they marched to Concord, about 20 miles. The congress had been lately assembled at that place, and it was imagined that the general had intelligence of a magazine being formed there and that they were going to destroy it.

The people in the country (who are all furnished with arms and have what they call minute companies in every town ready to march on any alarm) had a signal, it's supposed, by a light from one of the steeples in town, upon the troops embarking. The alarm spread through the country so that before daybreak the people in general were in arms and on their march to Concord. About daybreak a number of the people appeared before the troops near Lexington. They were called to, to disperse, when they fired on the troops and ran off. Upon which the light infantry pursued them and brought down about fifteen of them. The troops went on to Concord and executed the business they were sent on, and on their return found two or three of their people lying in the agonies of death, scalped and their noses and ears cut off and eyes bored out, which exasperated the soldiers exceedingly, a pro-digious number of people now occupying the hills, woods, and stone walls along the road. The light troops drove some parties from the hills but all the road being enclosed with stone walls served as a cover to the rebels, from whence they fired on the troops still running off whenever they had fired, but still supplied by fresh numbers who came from many parts of the country. In this manner were the troops harassed in their return for seven [or] eight miles. They were almost exhausted and had expended near the whole of their ammunition when to their great joy they were relieved by a brigade of troops under the command of Lord Percy with two pieces of artillery. The troops now combated with fresh ardour and marched in their return with undaunted countenances, receiving sheets of fire all the way for many miles, yet having no visible enemy to combat with, for they never would face 'em in an open field, but always skulked and fired from behind walls and trees, and out of windows of houses, but this cost them dear for the soldiers entered those dwellings and put all the men to death. Lord Percy has gained great honour by his conduct through this day of severe service; he was exposed to the hottest of the fire and animated the troops with great coolness and spirit. Several officers are wounded and about 100 soldiers. The killed amount to near 50; as to the enemy we can have no exact account but it is said there was about ten times the number of them engaged and that near 1,000 of 'em have fallen.

The troops returned to Charlestown about sunset after having some of 'em marched near fifty miles, and being engaged from daybreak in action, without respite or refreshment, and about ten in the evening they were brought back to Boston. The next day the country poured down its thou-sands, and at this time from the entrance of Boston Neck at Roxbury round by Cambridge to Charlestown is surrounded by at least 20,000 men, who are raising batteries on three or four different hills. We are now cut off from all communication with the country and many people must soon perish with famine in this place. Some families have laid in store of provisions against a siege. We are threatened, that whilst the outlines are attacked, with a rising of the inhabitants within, and fire and sword, a dreadful prospect before us, and you know how many and how dear are the objects of our care. The Lord preserve us all and grant us an happy issue out of these troubles.

Britain Declares Commercial War on the Colonies: The American Prohibitory Act, 1775

Whereas many persons in the colonies of New Hampshire, Massachusetts Bay, Rhode Island, Connecticut, New York, New Jersey, Pennsylvania, the three lower counties on Delaware, Maryland, Virginia, North Carolina, South Carolina, and Georgia, have set themselves in open rebellion and defiance to the just and legal authority of the king and Parliament of Great Britain, to which they ever have been, and of right ought to be, subject; and have assembled together an armed force, engaged his Majesty's troops, and attacked his forts; have usurped the powers of government, and prohibited all trade and commerce with this kingdom and the other parts of his Majesty's dominions; for the more speedily and effectually suppressing such wicked and daring designs, and for preventing any aid, supply, or assistance being sent thither during the continuance of the said rebellious and treasonable commotions, be it therefore declared and enacted . . . that all manner of trade and commerce is and shall be prohibited with the colonies of New Hampshire, Massachusetts Bay, Rhode Island, Connecticut, New York, New Jersey, Pennsylvania, the three lower counties on Delaware, Maryland, Virginia, North Carolina, South Carolina, and Georgia; and that all ships and vessels of or belonging to the inhabitants of the said colonies, together with their cargoes, apparel, and furniture, and all other ships and vessels whatsoever, together with their cargoes, apparel, and furniture, which shall be found trading in any port or place of the said colonies, or going to trade, or coming from trading, in any such port or place, shall become forfeited to his Majesty, as if the same were the ships and effects of open enemies. . . .

And, for the encouragement of the officers and seamen of his Majesty's ships of war, be it further enacted, that the flag officers, captains, commanders, and other commissioned officers in his Majesty's pay, and also the seamen, marines, and soldiers on board shall have the sole interest and property of and in all and every such ship, vessel, goods, and merchandise, which they shall seize and take. . . .

Thomas Paine Calls for Common Sense, 1776

Introduction

Perhaps the sentiments contained in the following pages, are not *yet* sufficiently fashionable to procure them general favor; a long habit of not thinking a thing *wrong,* gives it a superficial appearance of being *right,* and raises at first a formidable outcry in defence of custom. But the tumult soon subsides. Time makes more converts than reason. . . .

The cause of America is in a great measure the cause of all mankind. Many circumstances hath, and will arise, which are not local, but universal, and through which the principles of all Lovers of Mankind are affected, and in the Event of which, their Affections are interested. The laying a Country desolate with Fire and Sword, declaring War against the natural rights of all Mankind, and extirpating the Defenders thereof from the Face of the Earth, is the Concern of every Man to whom Nature hath given the Power of feeling; of which Class, regardless of Party Censure, is the

AUTHOR.

Of the Origin and Design of Government in General. With Concise Remarks on the English Constitution

Some writers have so confounded society with government, as to leave little or no distinction between them; whereas they are not only different, but have different origins. Society is produced by our wants, and government by our wickedness; the former promotes our happiness *positively* by uniting our affections, the latter *negatively* by restraining our vices. The one encourages intercourse, the other creates distinctions. The first is a patron, the last a punisher.

Society in every state is a blessing, but government even in its best state is but a necessary evil; in its worst state an intolerable one; for when we suffer, or are exposed to the same miseries *by a government,* which we might expect in a country *without government,* our calamity is heightened by reflecting that we furnish the means by which we suffer. Government, like dress, is the badge of lost innocence; the palaces of kings are built on the ruins of the bowers of paradise. For were the impulses of conscience clear, uniform, and irresistibly obeyed, man would need no other lawgiver; but that not being the case, he finds it necessary to surrender up a part of his property to furnish means for the protection of the rest; and this he is induced to do by the same prudence which in every other case advises him out of two evils to choose the least. *Wherefore,* security being the true design and end of government, it unanswerably follows, that whatever *form* thereof appears most likely to ensure it to us, with the least expence and greatest benefit, is preferable to all others.

In order to gain a clear and just idea of the design and end of government, let us suppose a small number of persons settled in some sequestered part of the earth, unconnected with the rest, they will then represent the first peopling of any country, or of the world. In this state of natural liberty, society will be their first thought. A thousand motives will excite them thereto, the strength of one man is so unequal to his wants, and his mind so unfitted for perpetual solitude, that he is soon obliged to seek assistance and relief of another, who in his turn requires the same. Four or five united would be able to raise a tolerable dwelling in the midst of a wilderness, but *one* man might labour out the common period of life without accomplishing any thing; when he had felled his timber he could not remove it, nor erect it after it was removed; hunger in the mean time would urge him from his work, and every different want call him a different way. Disease, nay even misfortune would be death, for though neither might be mortal, yet either would disable him from living, and reduce him to a state in which he might rather be said to perish than to die.

Thus necessity, like a gravitating power, would soon form our newly arrived emigrants into society, the reciprocal blessings of which, would supersede, and render the obligations of law and government unnecessary while they remained perfectly just to each other; but as nothing but heaven is impregnable to vice, it will unavoidably happen, that in proportion as they surmount the first difficulties of emigration, which bound them together in a common cause, they will begin to relax in their duty and attachment to each other; and this remissness will point out the necessity of establishing some form of government to supply the defect of moral virtue.

Some convenient tree will afford them a State-House, under the branches of which, the whole colony may assemble to deliberate on public matters. It is more than probable that their first laws will have the title only of REGULATIONS, and be enforced by no other penalty than public disesteem. In this first parliament every man, by natural right, will have a seat.

But as the colony increases, the public concerns will increase likewise, and the distance at which the members may be separated, will render it too inconvenient for all of them to meet on every occasion as at first, when their number was small, their habitations near, and the public concerns few and trifling. This will point out the convenience of their consenting to leave the legislative part to be managed by a select number chosen from the whole body, who are supposed to have the same concerns at stake which those have who appointed them, and who will act in the same manner as the whole body would act, were they present. If the colony continue increasing, it will become necessary to augment the number of the representatives, and that the interest of every part of the colony may be attended to, it will be found best to divide the whole into convenient parts, each part sending its proper number; and that the *elected* might never form to themselves an interest separate from the *electors,* prudence will point out the propriety of having elections often; because as the *elected* might by that means return and mix again with the general body of the *electors* in a few months, their fidelity to the public will be secured by the prudent reflexion of not making a rod for themselves. And as this frequent interchange will establish a common interest with every part of the community, they will mutually and naturally support each other, and on this (not on the unmeaning name of king) depends the *strength of government, and the happiness of the governed.*

Here then is the origin and rise of government; namely, a mode rendered necessary by the inability of moral virtue to govern the world; here too is the design and end of government, viz. freedom and security. And however our eyes may be dazzled with show, or our ears deceived by sound; however prejudice may warp our wills, or interest darken our understanding, the simple voice of nature and of reason will say, it is right.

I draw my idea of the form of government from a principle in nature, which no art can overturn, viz. that the more simple any thing is, the less liable it is to be disordered, and the easier repaired when disordered; and with this maxim in view, I offer a few remarks on the so much boasted constitution of England. That it was noble for the dark and slavish times in which it was erected, is granted. When the world was overrun with tyranny the least remove therefrom was a glorious rescue. But that it is imperfect, subject to convulsions, and incapable of producing what it seems to promise, is easily demonstrated.

Absolute governments (tho' the disgrace of human nature) have this advantage with them, that they are simple; if the people suffer, they know the head from which their suffering springs, know likewise the remedy, and are not bewildered by a variety of causes and cures. But the constitution of England is so exceedingly complex, that the nation may suffer for years together without being able to discover in which part the fault lies; some will say in one and some in another, and every political physician will advise a different medicine.

I know it is difficult to get over local or long standing prejudices, yet if we will suffer ourselves to examine the component parts of the English constitution, we shall find them to be the base remains of two ancient tyrannies, compounded with some new republican materials.

First.—The remains of monarchical tyranny in the person of the king.

Secondly.—The remains of aristocratical tyranny in the persons of the peers.

Thirdly.—The new republican materials in the persons of the commons, on whose virtue depends the freedom of England. . . .

That the crown is this overbearing part in the English constitution, needs not be mentioned, and that it derives its whole consequence merely from being the giver of places and pensions, is self-evident, wherefore, though we have been wise enough to shut and lock a door against absolute monarchy, we at the same time have been foolish enough to put the crown in possession of the key.

The prejudice of Englishmen in favour of their own government by king, lords and commons, arises as much or more from national pride than reason. Individuals are undoubtedly safer in England than in some other countries, but the *will* of the king is as much the *law* of the land in Britain as in France, with this difference, that instead of proceeding directly from his mouth, it is handed to the people under the more formidable shape of an act of parliament. For the fate of Charles the First hath only made kings more subtle—not more just.

Wherefore, laying aside all national pride and prejudice in favour of modes and forms, the plain truth is, that *it is wholly owing to the constitution of the people, and not to the constitution of the government,* that the crown is not as oppressive in England as in Turkey. . . .

Of Monarchy and Hereditary Succession

Mankind being originally equals in the order of creation, the equality could only be destroyed by some subsequent circumstance; the distinctions of rich, and poor, may in a great measure be accounted for, and that without having recourse to the harsh, ill-sounding names of oppression and avarice. Oppression is often the *consequence,* but seldom or never the *means* of riches; and though avarice will preserve a man from being necessitously poor, it generally makes him too timorous to be wealthy.

But there is another and greater distinction, for which no truly natural or religious reason can be assigned, and that is, the distinction of men into KINGS and SUBJECTS. Male and female are the distinctions of nature, good and bad the distinctions of heaven; but how a race of men came into the world so exalted above the rest, and distinguished like some new species, is worth inquiring into, and whether they are the means of happiness or of misery to mankind.

In the early ages of the world, according to the scripture chronology, there were no kings; the consequence of which was, there were no wars; it is the pride of kings which throw mankind into confusion. Holland without a king hath enjoyed more peace for this last century than any of the monarchical governments in Europe. Antiquity favours the same remark; for the quiet and rural lives of the first patriarchs hath a happy something in them, which vanishes away when we come to the history of Jewish royalty.

Government by kings was first introduced into the world by the Heathens, from whom the children of Israel copied the custom. It was the most prosperous invention the Devil ever set on foot for the promotion of idolatry. The Heathens paid divine honors to their deceased kings, and the Christian world hath improved on the plan, by doing the same to their living ones. How impious is the title of sacred majesty applied to a worm, who in the midst of his splendor is crumbling into dust!

As the exalting one man so greatly above the rest cannot be justified on the equal rights of nature, so neither can it be defended on the authority of scripture; for the will of the Almighty, as declared by Gideon and the prophet Samuel, expressly disapproves of government by kings. All antimonarchical parts of scripture have been very smoothly glossed over in monarchical governments, but they undoubtedly merit the attention of countries which have their governments yet to form. *"Render unto Caesar the things which are Caesar's"* is the scripture doctrine of courts, yet it is no support of monarchical government, for the Jews at that time were without a king, and in a state of vassalage to the Romans.

Near three thousand years passed away from the Mosaic account of the creation, till the Jews under a national delusion requested a king. Till then their form of government (except in extraordinary cases, where the Almighty interposed) was a kind of republic administered by a judge and the elders of the tribes. Kings they had none, and it was held sinful to acknowledge any being under that title but the Lord of Hosts. And when a man seriously reflects on the idolatrous homage which is paid to the persons of kings, he need not wonder that the Almighty, ever jealous of his honor, should disapprove of a form of government which so impiously invades the prerogative of heaven.

Monarchy is ranked in scripture as one of the sins of the Jews, for which a curse in reserve is denounced against them. The history of that transaction is worth attending to.

The children of Israel being oppressed by the Midianites, Gideon marched against them with a small army, and victory, thro' the divine interposition, decided in his favour. The Jews, elate with success, and attributing it to the generalship of Gideon, proposed making him a king, saying, *Rule thou over us, thou and thy son's son.* Here was temptation in its fullest extent; not a kingdom only, but an hereditary one, but Gideon in the piety of his soul replied, *I will not rule over you, neither shall my son rule over you,* THE LORD SHALL RULE OVER YOU. Words need not be more explicit; Gideon doth not decline the honor, but denieth their right to give it; neither doth he compliment them with invented declarations of his thanks, but in the positive stile of a prophet charges them with disaffection to their proper Sovereign, the King of heaven. . . .

That the almighty hath here entered his protest against monarchical government, is true, or the scripture is false. And a man hath good reason to believe that there is as much of king-craft, as priest-craft, in withholding the scripture from the public in Popish countries. For monarchy in every instance is the Popery of government.

To the evil of monarchy we have added that of hereditary succession; and as the first is a degradation and lessening of ourselves, so the second, claimed as a matter of right, is an insult and an imposition on posterity. For all men being originally equals, no *one* by *birth* could have a right to set up his own family in perpetual preference to all others for ever, and though himself might deserve *some* decent degree of honors of his contemporaries, yet his descendants might be far too unworthy to inherit them. One of the strongest *natural* proofs of the folly of hereditary right in kings, is, that nature disapproves it, otherwise she would not so frequently turn it into ridicule by giving mankind an *Ass for a Lion.*

Secondly, as no man at first could possess any other public honors than were bestowed upon him, so the givers of those honors could have no power to give away the right of posterity. And though they might say, "We choose you for *our* head," they could not, without manifest injustice to their children, say "that your children and your childrens children shall reign over *ours* for ever." Because such an unwise, unjust, unnatural compact might (perhaps) in the next succession put them under the government of a rogue or a fool. Most wise men, in their private sentiments, have ever treated hereditary right with contempt; yet it is one of those evils, which when once established is not easily removed; many submit from fear, others from superstition, and the more powerful part shares with the king the plunder of the rest.

This is supposing the present race of kings in the world to have had an honorable origin; whereas it is more than probable, that could we take off the dark covering of antiquity, and trace them to their first rise, that we should find the first of them nothing better than the principal ruffian of some restless gang, whose savage manners or pre-eminence in subtilty obtained him the title of chief among plunderers. . . .

England, since the conquest, hath known some few good monarchs, but groaned beneath a much larger number of bad ones; yet no man in his senses can say that their claim under William the Conqueror is a very honorable one. A French bastard landing with an armed banditti, and establishing himself king of England against the consent of the natives, is in plain terms a very paltry rascally original.—It certainly hath no divinity in it. However, it is needless to spend much time in exposing the folly of hereditary right; if there are any so weak as to believe it, let them promiscuously worship the ass and lion, and welcome. I shall neither copy their humility, nor disturb their devotion.

Yet I should be glad to ask how they suppose kings came at first? The question admits but of three answers, viz. either by lot, by election, or by usurpation. If the first king was taken by lot, it establishes a precedent for the next, which excludes hereditary succession. . . . If the first king of any country was by election, that likewise establishes a precedent for the next; for to say, that the *right* of all future generations is taken away, by the act of the first electors, in their choice not only of a king, but of a family of kings for ever, hath no parallel in or out of scripture but the doctrine of original sin, which supposes the free will of all men lost in Adam; and from such comparison, and it will admit of no other, hereditary succession can derive no glory. For as in Adam all sinned, and as in the first electors all men obeyed; as in the one all mankind were subjected to Satan, and in the other to Sovereignty; as our innocence was lost in the first, and our authority in the last; and as both disable us from reassuming some former state and privilege, it unanswerably follows that original sin and hereditary succession are parallels. Dishonorable rank! Inglorious connexion! Yet the most subtile sophist cannot produce a juster simile.

As to usurpation, no man will be so hardy as to defend it; and that William the Conqueror was an usurper is a fact not to be contradicted. The plain truth is, that the antiquity of English monarchy will not bear looking into.

But it is not so much the absurdity as the evil of hereditary succession which concerns mankind. Did it ensure a race of good and wise men it would have the seal of divine authority, but as it opens a door to the *foolish,* the *wicked,* and the *improper,* it hath in it the nature of oppression. Men who look upon themselves born to reign, and others to obey, soon grow insolent; selected from the rest of mankind their minds are early poisoned by importance; and the world they act in differs so materially from the world at large, that they have but little opportunity of knowing its true interests, and when they succeed to the government are frequently the most ignorant and unfit of any throughout the dominions.

Another evil which attends hereditary succession is, that the throne is subject to be possessed by a minor at any age; all which time the regency, acting under the cover of a king, have every opportunity and inducement to betray their trust. The same national misfortune happens, when a king, worn out with age and infirmity, enters the last stage of human weakness. In both these cases the public becomes a prey to every miscreant, who can tamper successfully with the follies either of age or infancy.

The most plausible plea, which hath ever been offered in favour of hereditary succession, is, that it preserves a nation from civil wars; and were this true, it would be weighty; whereas, it is the most barefaced falsity ever imposed upon mankind. The whole history of England disowns the fact. Thirty kings and two minors have reigned in that distracted kingdom since the conquest, in which time there have been (including the Revolution) no less than eight civil wars and nineteen rebellions. Wherefore instead of making for peace, it makes against it, and destroys the very foundation it seems to stand on. . . .

In short, monarchy and succession have laid (not this or that kingdom only) but the world in blood and ashes. 'Tis a form of government which the word of God bears testimony against, and blood will attend it.

If we inquire into the business of a king, we shall find that in some countries they have none; and after sauntering away their lives without pleasure to themselves or advantage to the nation, withdraw from the scene, and leave their successors to tread the same idle ground. In absolute monarchies the whole weight of business, civil and military, lies on the king; the children of Israel in their request for a king, urged this plea "that he may judge us, and go out before us and fight our battles." But in countries where he is neither a judge nor a general, as in England, a man would be puzzled to know what *is* his business. . . .

In England a king hath little more to do than to make war and give away places; which in plain terms, is to impoverish the nation and set it together by the ears. A pretty business indeed for a man to be allowed eight hundred thousand sterling a year for, and worshipped into the bargain! Of more worth is one honest man to society and in the sight of God, than all the crowned ruffians that ever lived.

Thoughts on the Present State of American Affairs

In the following pages I offer nothing more than simple facts, plain arguments, and common sense; and have no other preliminaries to settle with the reader, than that he will divest himself of prejudice and prepossession, and suffer his reason and his feelings to determine for themselves; that he will put *on,* or rather that he will not put *off* the true character of a man, and generously enlarge his views beyond the present day.

Volumes have been written on the subject of the struggle between England and America. Men of all ranks have embarked in the controversy, from different motives, and with various designs; but all have been ineffectual, and the period of debate is closed. Arms, as the last resource, decide the contest; the appeal was the choice of the king, and the continent hath accepted the challenge. . . .

The sun never shined on a cause of greater worth. 'Tis not the affair of a city, a county, a province, or a kingdom, but of a continent—of at least one eighth part of the habitable globe. 'Tis not the concern of a day, a year, or an age; posterity are virtually involved in the contest, and will be more or less affected, even to the end of time, by the proceedings now. Now is the seed-time of continental union, faith and honor. The least fracture now will be like a name engraved with the point of a pin on the tender rind of a young oak; the wound will enlarge with the tree, and posterity read it in full grown characters.

By referring the matter from argument to arms, a new æra for politics is struck; a new method of thinking hath arisen. All plans, proposals, &c. prior to the nineteenth of April, *i.e.*, to the commencement of hostilities, are like the almanacks of the last year; which, though proper then are superseded and useless now. Whatever was advanced by the advocates on either side of the question then, terminated in one and the same point, viz. a union with Great-Britain; the only difference between the parties was the method of effecting it; the one proposing force, the other friendship; but it hath so far happened that the first hath failed, and the second hath withdrawn her influence.

As much hath been said of the advantages of reconciliation, which, like an agreeable dream, hath passed away and left us as we were, it is but right, that we should examine the contrary side of the argument, and inquire into some of the many material injuries which these colonies sustain, and always will sustain, by being connected with, and dependent on Great-Britain: To examine that connexion and dependence, on the principles of nature and common sense, to see what we have to trust to, if separated, and what we are to expect, if dependent.

I have heard it asserted by some, that as America hath flourished under her former connexion with Great-Britain, that the same connexion is necessary towards her future happiness, and will always have the same effect. Nothing can be more fallacious than this kind of argument. We may as well assert that because a child has thrived upon milk, that it is never to have meat, or that the first twenty years of our lives is to become a precedent for the next twenty. But even this is admitting more than is true, for I answer roundly, that America would have flourished as much, and probably much more, had no European power had any thing to do with her. The commerce, by which she hath enriched herself, are the necessaries of life, and will always have a market while eating is the custom of Europe.

But she has protected us, say some. That she has engrossed us is true, and defended the continent at our expence as well as her own is admitted, and she would have defended Turkey from the same motive, viz. the sake of trade and dominion.

Alas, we have been long led away by ancient prejudices, and made large sacrifices to superstition. We have boasted the protection of Great-Britain, without considering, that her motive was *interest* not *attachment;* that she did not protect us from *our enemies* on *our account,* but from *her enemies* on *her own account,* from those who had no quarrel with us on any *other account,* and who will always be our enemies on the *same account.* Let Britain wave her pretensions to the continent, or the continent throw off the dependence, and we should be at peace with France and Spain were they at war with Britain. The miseries of Hanover last war ought to warn us against connexions. . . .

But Britain is the parent country, say some. Then the more shame upon her conduct. Even brutes do not devour their young, nor savages make war upon their families; wherefore the assertion, if true, turns to her reproach; but it happens not to be true, or only partly so, and the phrase *parent* or *mother country* hath been jesuitically adopted by the king and his parasites, with a low papistical design of gaining an unfair bias on the credulous weakness of our minds. Europe, and not England, is the parent country of America. This new world hath been the asylum for the persecuted lovers of civil and religious liberty from *every part* of Europe. Hither have they fled, not from the tender embraces of the mother, but from the cruelty of the monster; and it is so far true of England, that the same tyranny which drove the first emigrants from home, pursues their descendants still.

In this extensive quarter of the globe, we forget the narrow limits of three hundred and sixty miles (the extent of England) and carry our friendship on a larger scale; we claim brotherhood with every European Christian, and triumph in the generosity of the sentiment. . . .

Much hath been said of the united strength of Britain and the colonies, that in conjunction they might bid defiance to the world. But this is mere presumption; the fate of war is uncertain, neither do the expressions mean any thing; for this continent would never suffer itself to be drained of inhabitants, to support the British arms in either Asia, Africa, or Europe.

Besides what have we to do with setting the world at defiance? Our plan is commerce, and that, well attended to, will secure us the peace and friendship of all Europe; because, it is the interest of all Europe to have America a *free port.* Her trade will always be a protection, and her barrenness of gold and silver secure her from invaders.

I challenge the warmest advocate for reconciliation, to shew, a single advantage that this continent can reap, by being connected with Great-Britain. I repeat the challenge, not a single advantage is derived. Our corn will fetch its price in any market in Europe, and our imported goods must be paid for buy them where we will.

But the injuries and disadvantages we sustain by that connection, are without number; and our duty to mankind at large, as well as to ourselves, instruct us to renounce the alliance: Because, any submission to, or dependence on Great-Britain, tends directly to involve this continent in European wars and quarrels; and sets us at variance with nations, who would otherwise seek our friendship, and against whom, we have neither anger nor complaint. As Europe is our market for trade, we ought to form no partial connection with any part of it. It is the true interest of America to steer clear of European contentions, which she never can do, while by her dependence on Britain, she is made the make-weight in the scale of British politics.

Europe is too thickly planted with kingdoms to be long at peace, and whenever a war breaks out between England and any foreign power, the trade of America goes to ruin, *because of her connection with Britain.* . . . Every thing that is right or natural pleads for separation. The blood of the slain, the weeping voice of nature cries, 'TIS TIME TO PART. Even the distance at which the Almighty hath placed England and America, is a strong and natural proof, that the authority of the one, over the other, was never the design of Heaven. The time likewise at which the continent was discovered, adds weight to the argument, and the manner in which it was peopled encreases the force of it. The reformation was preceded by the discovery of America, as if the Almighty graciously meant to open a sanctuary to the persecuted in future years, when home should afford neither friendship nor safety. . . .

It is the good fortune of many to live distant from the scene of sorrow; the evil is not sufficient brought to *their* doors to make *them* feel the precariousness with which all American property is possessed. But let our imaginations transport us for a few moments to Boston, that seat of wretchedness will teach us wisdom, and instruct us for ever to renounce a power in whom we can have no trust. . . .

Men of passive tempers look somewhat lightly over the offences of Britain, and, still hoping for the best, are apt to call out, *"Come, come, we shall be friends again, for all this."* But examine the passions and feelings of mankind, bring the doctrine of reconciliation to the touchstone of nature, and then tell me, whether you can hereafter love, honor, and faithfully serve the power that hath carried fire and sword into your land? If you cannot do all these, then are you only deceiving yourselves, and by your delay bringing ruin upon posterity. Your future connexion with Britain, whom you can neither love nor honor, will be forced and unnatural, and being formed only on the plan of present convenience, will in a little time fall into a relapse more wretched than the first. But if you say, you can still pass the violations over, then I ask, Hath your house been burnt? Hath your property been destroyed before your face? Are your wife and children destitute of a bed to lie on, or bread to live on? Have you lost a parent or a child by their hands, and yourself the ruined and wretched survivor? If you have not, then are you not a judge of those who have? But if you have, and still can shake hands with the murderers, then are you unworthy the name of husband, father, friend, or lover, and whatever may be your rank or title in life, you have the heart of a coward, and the spirit of a sycophant.

This is not inflaming or exaggerating matters, but trying them by those feelings and affections which nature justifies, and without which, we should be incapable of discharging the social duties of life, or enjoying the felicities of it. I mean not to exhibit horror for the purpose of provoking revenge, but to awaken us from fatal and unmanly slumbers, that we may pursue determinately some fixed object. It is not in the power of Britain or of Europe to conquer America, if she do not conquer herself by *delay* and *timidity.* The present winter is worth an age if rightly employed, but if lost or neglected, the whole continent will partake of the misfortune; and there is no punishment which that man will not deserve, be he who, or what, or where he will, that may be the means of sacrificing a season so precious and useful.

It is repugnant to reason, to the universal order of things, to all examples from former ages, to suppose, that this continent can longer remain subject to any external power. The most sanguine in Britain does not think so. The utmost stretch of human wisdom cannot, at this time, compass a plan short of separation, which can promise the continent even a year's security. Reconciliation is *now* a fallacious dream. Nature hath deserted the connexion, and Art cannot supply her place. For, as Milton wisely expresses, "never can true reconcilement grow, where wounds of deadly hate have pierc'd so deep."

Every quiet method for peace hath been ineffectual. Our prayers have been rejected with disdain; and only tended to convince us, that nothing flatters vanity, or confirms obstinacy in Kings more than repeated petitioning—and nothing hath contributed more than that very measure to make the Kings of Europe absolute: Witness Denmark and Sweden. Wherefore, since nothing but blows will do, for God's sake, let us come to a final separation, and not leave the next generation to be cutting throats, under the violated unmeaning names of parent and child.

To say, they will never attempt it again is idle and visionary, we thought so at the repeal of the stamp-act, yet a year or two undeceived us; as well may we suppose that nations, which have been once defeated, will never renew the quarrel.

As to government matters, it is not in the power of Britain to do this continent justice: The business of it will soon be too weighty, and intricate, to be managed with any tolerable degree of convenience, by a power so distant from us, and so very ignorant of us; for if they cannot conquer us, they cannot govern us. To be always running three or four thousand miles with a tale or a petition, waiting four or five months for an answer, which when obtained requires five or six more to explain it in, will in a few years be looked upon as folly and childishness—There was a time when it was proper, and there is a proper time for it to cease.

Small islands not capable of protecting themselves, are the proper objects for kingdoms to take under their care; but there is something very absurd, in supposing a continent to be perpetually governed by an island. In no instance hath nature made the satellite larger than its primary planet, and as England and America, with respect to each other, reverses the common order of nature, it is evident they belong to different systems; England to Europe, America to itself.

I am not induced by motives of pride, party, or resentment to espouse the doctrine of separation and independence; I am clearly, positively, and conscientiously persuaded that it is the true interest of this continent to be so; that every thing short of *that* is mere patchwork, that it can afford no lasting felicity,—that it is leaving the sword to our children, and shrinking back at a time, when, a little more, a little farther, would have rendered this continent the glory of the earth. . . .

No man was a warmer wisher for reconciliation than myself, before the fatal nineteenth of April 1775,* but the moment the event of that day was made known, I rejected the hardened, sullen tempered Pharaoh of England for ever; and disdain the wretch, that with the pretended title of FATHER OF HIS PEOPLE can unfeelingly hear of their slaughter, and composedly sleep with their blood upon his soul.

But admitting that matters were now made up, what would be the event? I answer, the ruin of the continent. And that for several reasons.

First. The powers of governing still remaining in the hands of the king, he will have a negative over the whole legislation of this continent. And as he hath shewn himself such an inveterate enemy to liberty, and discovered such a thirst for arbitrary power; is he, or is he not, a proper man to say to these colonies, "*You shall make no laws but what I please.*" . . .

America is only a secondary object in the system of British politics, England consults the good of *this* country, no farther than it answers her *own* purpose. Wherefore, her own interest leads her to suppress the growth of *ours* in every case which doth not promote her advantage, or in the least interferes with it. A pretty state we should soon be in under such a second-hand government, considering what has happened! Men do not change from enemies to friends by the alteration of a name: And in order to shew that reconciliation *now* is a dangerous doctrine, I affirm, *that it would be policy in the king at this time, to repeal the acts for the sake of reinstating himself in the government of the provinces;* in order, that HE MAY ACCOMPLISH BY CRAFT AND SUBTILTY, IN THE LONG RUN, WHAT HE CANNOT DO BY FORCE AND VIOLENCE IN THE SHORT ONE. Reconciliation and ruin are nearly related.

Secondly. That as even the best terms, which we can expect to obtain, can amount to no more than a temporary expedient, or a kind of government by guardianship, which can last no longer than till the colonies come of age, so the general face and state of things, in the interim, will be unsettled and unpromising. . . .

But the most powerful of all arguments, is, that nothing but independence, i.e., a continental form of government, can keep the peace of the continent and preserve it inviolate from civil wars. I dread the event of a reconciliation with Britain now, as it is more than probable, that it will be followed by a revolt somewhere or other, the consequences of which may be far more fatal than all the malice of Britain. . . .

If there is any true cause of fear respecting independence, it is because no plan is yet laid down. Men do not see their way out—Wherefore, as an opening into that business, I offer the following hints; at the same time modestly affirming, that I have no other opinion of them myself, than that they may be the means of giving rise to something better. Could the straggling thoughts of individuals be collected, they would frequently form materials for wise and able men to improve into useful matter.

Let the assemblies be annual, with a President only. The representation

* Massacre at Lexington.

more equal. Their business wholly domestic, and subject to the authority of a Continental Congress.

Let each colony be divided into six, eight, or ten, convenient districts, each district to send a proper number of delegates to Congress, so that each colony send at least thirty. The whole number in Congress will be at least 390. . . . And in order that nothing may pass into a law but what is satisfactorily just, not less than three fifths of the Congress to be called a majority—He that will promote discord, under a government so equally formed as this, would have joined Lucifer in his revolt.

But as there is a peculiar delicacy, from whom, or in what manner, this business must first arise, and as it seems most agreeable and consistent, that it should come from some intermediate body between the governed and the governors, that is, between the Congress and the people, let a CONTINENTAL CONFERENCE be held. . . .

. . . [L]et their business be to frame a CONTINENTAL CHARTER, or Charter of the United Colonies; (answering to what is called the Magna Charta of England) fixing the number and manner of choosing members of Congress, members of Assembly, with their date of sitting, and drawing the line of business and jurisdiction between them: (Always remembering, that our strength is continental, not provincial:) Securing freedom and property to all men, and above all things, the free exercise of religion, according to the dictates of conscience; with such other matter as is necessary for a charter to contain. Immediately after which, the said Conference to dissolve, and the bodies which shall be chosen conformable to the said charter, to be the legislators and governors of this continent for the time being: Whose peace and happiness may God preserve, Amen. . . .

But where, says some, is the King of America? I'll tell you. Friend, he reigns above, and doth not make havoc of mankind like the Royal Brute of Britain. Yet that we may not appear to be defective even in earthly honors, let a day be solemnly set apart for proclaiming the charter; let it be brought forth placed on the divine law, the word of God; let a crown be placed thereon, by which the world may know, that so far we approve of monarchy, that in America THE LAW IS KING. For as in absolute governments the King is law, so in free countries the law *ought* to be King; and there ought to be no other. But lest any ill use should afterwards arise, let the crown at the conclusion of the ceremony, be demolished, and scattered among the people whose right it is.

A government of our own is our natural right: And when a man seriously reflects on the precariousness of human affairs, he will become convinced, that it is infinitely wiser and safer, to form a constitution of our own in a cool deliberate manner, while we have it in our power, than to trust such an interesting event to time and chance. . . . Ye that oppose independence now, ye know not what ye do; ye are opening a door to eternal tyranny, by keeping vacant the seat of government. There are thousands, and tens of thousands, who would think it glorious to expel from the continent that barbarous and hellish power, which hath stirred up the Indians and Negroes to destroy us; the cruelty hath a double guilt, it is dealing brutally by us, and treacherously by them. . . .

Ye that tell us of harmony and reconciliation, can ye restore to us the time that is past? Can ye give to prostitution its former innocence? Neither can ye reconcile Britain and America. The last cord now is broken, the people of England are presenting addresses against us. There are injuries which nature cannot forgive; she would cease to be nature if she did. As well can the lover forgive the ravisher of his mistress, as the continent forgive the murders of Britain. The Almighty hath implanted in us these unextinguishable feelings for good and wise purposes. They are the guardians of his image in our hearts. They distinguish us from the herd of common animals. The social compact would dissolve, and justice be extirpated the earth, or have only a casual existence were we callous to the touches of affection. The robber, and the murderer, would often escape unpunished, did not the injuries which our tempers sustain, provoke us into justice.

O ye that love mankind! Ye that dare oppose, not only the tyranny, but the tyrant, stand forth! Every spot of the old world is overrun with oppression. Freedom hath been hunted round the globe. Asia, and Africa, have long expelled her—Europe regards her like a stranger, and England hath given her warning to depart. O! receive the fugitive, and prepare in time an asylum for mankind.

Of the Present Ability of America, with Some Miscellaneous Reflexions

I have never met with a man, either in England or America, who hath not confessed his opinion, that a separation between the countries, would take place one time or other: And there is no instance, in which we have shewn less judgment, than in endeavouring to describe, what we call the ripeness or fitness of the Continent for independence.

As all men allow the measure, and vary only in their opinion of the time, let us, in order to remove mistakes, take a general survey of things, and endeavour, if possible, to find out the *very* time. But we need not go far, the inquiry ceases at once, for, the *time hath found us*. The general concurrence, the glorious union of all things prove the fact.

It is not in numbers, but in unity, that our great strength lies; yet our present numbers are sufficient to repel the force of all the world. The Continent hath, at this time, the largest body of armed and disciplined men of any power under Heaven; and is just arrived at that pitch of strength, in which no single colony is able to support itself, and the whole, when united, can accomplish the matter, and either more, or, less than this, might be fatal in its effects. Our land force is already sufficient, and as to naval affairs, we cannot be insensible, that Britain would never suffer an American man of war to be built, while the continent remained in her hands. Wherefore, we should be no forwarder an hundred years hence in that branch, than we are now; but the truth is, we should be less so, because the timber of the country is every day diminishing, and that, which will remain at last, will be far off and difficult to procure.

Were the continent crowded with inhabitants, her sufferings under the present circumstances would be intolerable. The more seaport towns we had, the more should we have both to defend and to lose. Our present numbers are so happily proportioned to our wants, that no man need be idle. The diminution of trade affords an army, and the necessities of an army create a new trade.

Debts we have none; and whatever we may contract on this account will serve as a glorious memento of our virtue. Can we but leave posterity with a settled form of government, an independent constitution of its own, the purchase at any price will be cheap. But to expend millions for the sake of getting a few vile acts repealed, and routing the present ministry only, is unworthy the charge, and is using posterity with the utmost cruelty; because it is leaving them the great work to do, and a debt upon their backs, from which they derive no advantage. Such a thought is unworthy a man of honor, and is the true characteristic of a narrow heart and a peddling politician.

The debt we may contract doth not deserve our regard, if the work be but accomplished. No nation ought to be without a debt. A national debt is a national bond; and when it bears no interest, is in no case a grievance. Britain is oppressed with a debt of upwards of one hundred and forty millions sterling, for which she pays upwards of four millions interest. And as a compensation for her debt, she has a large navy; America is without a debt, and without a navy; yet for the twentieth part of the English national debt, could have a navy as large again. . . .

No country on the globe is so happily situated, or so internally capable of raising a fleet as America. Tar, timber, iron, and cordage are her natural produce. We need go abroad for nothing. Whereas the Dutch, who make large profits by hiring out their ships of war to the Spaniards and Portuguese, are obliged to import most of their materials they use. We ought to view the building a fleet as an article of commerce, it being the natural manufactory of this country. It is the best money we can lay out. A navy when finished is worth more than it cost. And is that nice point in national policy, in which commerce and protection are united. Let us build; if we want them not, we can sell; and by that means replace our paper currency with ready gold and silver.

In point of manning a fleet, people in general run into great errors; it is not necessary that one fourth part should be sailors. . . . A few able and social sailors will soon instruct a sufficient number of active landmen in the common work of a ship. Wherefore, we never can be more capable to begin on maritime matters than now, while our timber is standing, our fisheries blocked up, and our sailors and shipwrights out of employ. Men of war of seventy and eighty guns were built forty years ago in New-England, and why not the same now? Ship-building is America's greatest pride, and in which she will in time excel the whole world. . . .

In point of safety, ought we to be without a fleet? We are not the little people now, which we were sixty years ago; at that time we might have trusted our property in the streets, or fields rather; and slept securely without locks or bolts to our doors or windows. The case now is altered, and our methods of defence ought to improve with our increase of property. A common pirate, twelve months ago, might have come up the Delaware, and laid the city of Philadelphia under instant contribution, for what sum he pleased; and the same might have happened to other places. Nay, any daring fellow, in a brig of fourteen or sixteen guns might have robbed the whole continent, and carried off half a million of money. These are circumstances which demand our attention, and point out the necessity of naval protection. . . .

The English list of ships of war, is long and formidable, but not a tenth part of them are at any one time fit for service, numbers of them not in being; yet their names are pompously continued in the list, if only a plank be left of the ship: and not a fifth part of such as are fit for service, can be spared on any one station at one time. The East and West Indies, Mediterranean, Africa, and other parts over which Britain extends her claim, make large demands upon her navy. From a mixture of prejudice and inattention, we have contracted a false notion respecting the navy of England, and have talked as if we should have the whole of it to encounter at once, and for that reason, supposed, that we must have one as large; which not being instantly practicable, have been made use of by a set of disguised Tories to discourage our beginning thereon. Nothing can be farther from truth than this; for if America had only a twentieth part of the naval force of Britain, she would be by far an overmatch for her; because, as we neither have, nor claim any foreign dominion, our whole force would be employed on our own coast, where we should, in the long run, have two to one the advantage of those who had three or four thousand miles to sail over, before they could attack us, and the same distance to return in order to refit and recruit. . . .

In almost every article of defence we abound. Hemp flourishes even to rankness, so that we need not want cordage. Our iron is superior to that of other countries. Our small arms equal to any in the world. Cannon we can cast at pleasure. Saltpetre and gunpowder we are every day producing. Our knowledge is hourly improving. Resolution is our inherent character, and courage hath never yet forsaken us. . . .

Another reason why the present time is preferable to all others, is, that the fewer our numbers are, the more land there is yet unoccupied, which instead of being lavished by the king on his worthless dependents, may be hereafter applied, not only to the discharge of the present debt, but to the constant support of government. No nation under heaven hath such an advantage as this.

The infant state of the Colonies, as it is called, so far from being against, is an argument in favor of independence. We are sufficiently numerous, and were we more so, we might be less united. . . .

Youth is the seed time of good habits, as well in nations as in individuals. It might be difficult, if not impossible, to form the Continent into one government half a century hence. The vast variety of interests, occasioned by an increase of trade and population, would create confusion. Colony would be against colony. Each being able might scorn each other's assistance:

and while the proud and foolish gloried in their little distinctions, the wise would lament, that the union had not been formed before. Wherefore, the *present time* is the *true time* for establishing it. The intimacy which is contracted in infancy, and the friendship which is formed in misfortune, are, of all others, the most lasting and unalterable. Our present union is marked with both these characters: we are young, and we have been distressed; but our concord hath withstood our troubles, and fixes a memorable æra for posterity to glory in.

The present time, likewise, is that peculiar time, which never happens to a nation but once, *viz.* the time of forming itself into a government. Most nations have let slip the opportunity, and by that means have been compelled to receive laws from their conquerors, instead of making laws for themselves. First, they had a king, and then a form of government; whereas, the articles or charter of government, should be formed first, and men delegated to execute them afterward: but from the errors of other nations, let us learn wisdom, and lay hold of the present opportunity—*To begin government at the right end.* . . .

To CONCLUDE, however strange it may appear to some, or however unwilling they may be to think so, matters not, but many strong and striking reasons may be given, to shew, that nothing can settle our affairs so expeditiously as an open and determined declaration for independence. Some of which are,

First.—It is the custom of nations, when any two are at war, for some other powers, not engaged in the quarrel, to step in as mediators, and bring about the preliminaries of a peace: but while America calls herself the Subject of Great-Britain, no power, however well disposed she may be, can offer her mediation. Wherefore, in our present state we may quarrel on for ever.

Secondly.—It is unreasonable to suppose, that France or Spain will give us any kind of assistance, if we mean only, to make use of that assistance for the purpose of repairing the breach, and strengthening the connection between Britain and America; because, those powers would be sufferers by the consequences.

Thirdly.—While we profess ourselves the subjects of Britain, we must, in the eye of foreign nations, be considered as rebels. The precedent is somewhat dangerous to *their peace*, for men to be in arms under the name of subjects; we, on the spot, can solve the paradox: but to unite resistance and subjection, requires an idea much too refined for common understanding.

Fourthly.—Were a manifesto to be published, and despatched to foreign courts, setting forth the miseries we have endured, and the peaceable methods we have ineffectually used for redress; declaring, at the same time, that not being able, any longer, to live happily or safely under the cruel disposition of the British court, we had been driven to the necessity of breaking off all connections with her; at the same time, assuring all such courts of our peaceable disposition towards them, and of our desire of entering into trade with them: Such a memorial would produce more good effects to this Continent, than if a ship were freighted with petitions to Britain.

Under our present denomination of British subjects, we can neither be received nor heard abroad: The custom of all courts is against us, and will be so, until, by an independence, we take rank with other nations.

These proceedings may at first appear strange and difficult; but, like all other steps which we have already passed over, will in a little time become familiar and agreeable; and, until an independence is declared, the Continent will feel itself like a man who continues putting off some unpleasant business from day to day, yet knows it must be done, hates to set about it, wishes it over, and is continually haunted with the thoughts of its necessity.

John Dickinson Opposes Independence, 1776

The consequences involved in the motion now lying before you are of such magnitude that I tremble under the oppressive honour of sharing in its determination. . . . My conduct this day I expect will give the finishing blow to my once too great, and my integrity considered now, too diminished popularity. It will be my lot to know that I had rather vote away the enjoyment of that dazzling display, that pleasing possession, than the blood and happiness of my countrymen—too fortunate amidst their calamities, if I prove (a truth known in Heaven) that I had rather they should hate me than that I should hurt them. I might indeed practise an artful, an advantageous reserve upon this occasion. But thinking as I do on the subject of debate, silence would be guilt. I despise its arts, I detest its advantages. . . .

It was a custom in a wise and virtuous state to preface propositions in council with a prayer, that they might redound to the public benefit. . . . And I do most humbly implore Almighty God, with whom dwells wisdom itself, so to enlighten the members of this house that their decision may be such as will best promote the liberty, safety, and prosperity of these colonies, and for myself, that his divine goodness may be graciously pleased to enable me to speak the precepts of sound policy on the important question that now engages our attention.

Sir, gentlemen of very distinguished abilities and knowledge differ widely in their sentiments upon the point now agitated. They all agree that the utmost prudence is required in forming our decision, but immediately disagree in their notion of that prudence. Some cautiously insist that we ought to obtain that previous information which we are likely quickly to obtain, and to make those previous establishments that are acknowledged to be necessary. Others strenuously assert that though regularly such information and establishment ought to precede the measure proposed, yet, confiding in our fortune more boldly than Caesar himself, we ought to brave the storm in a skiff made of paper.

In all such cases where every argument is adorned with an eloquence that may please and yet mislead, it seems to me the proper method of discovering the right path, to inquire which of the parties is probably the most warmed by passion. Other circumstances being equal or nearly equal, that consideration would have influence with me. I fear the virtue of Americans. Resentment of the injuries offered to their country may irritate them to counsels and to actions that may be detrimental to the cause they would die to advance.

What advantages could it be claimed would follow from the adoption of this resolution? (1) It might animate the people. (2) It would convince foreign powers of our strength and unanimity and we would receive their aid in consequence thereof. As to the first point, it is unnecessary. The preservation of life, liberty, and property is a sufficient motive to animate the people. The general spirit of America is animated. As to the second, foreign powers will not rely on words.

The event of the campaign will be the best evidence of our strength and unanimity. This properly the first campaign. Who has received intelligence that such a proof of our strength and daring spirit will be agreeable to France? . . . She and Spain must perceive the immediate danger of their colonies lying at our doors, their seat of empire is in another world. . . .

It would be more respectful to act in conformity to the views of France. Let us take advantage of their pride; let us give them reason to believe that we confide in them; that we desire to act in conjunction with their policies and interests. Let us know how they would regard this stranger in the states of the world. People are fond of what they have attained in producing; they regard it as a child. A cement of affection exists between them. Let us allow them the glory of appearing the vindicators of liberty. It will please them.

It is treating them with contempt to act otherwise, especially after the application made to France which by this time has reached them. . . . What will they think if now so quickly afterwards, without waiting for their determination, totally slighting their sentiments on such a prodigious issue, we haughtily pursue our own measures?

May they not say to us: Gentlemen, you falsely pretended to consult us and disrespectfully proceeded without waiting our resolution. You must abide the consequences. We are not ready for a rupture. You should have negotiated till we were. We will not be hurried by your impetuosity. We know it is our interest to support you but we shall be in no haste about it. Try your own strength and resources in which you have such confidence. We know now you dare not look back. Reconciliation is impossible without declaring independence, now that you have reached the stage you have. Yours is the most rash and at the same time, the most contemptible senate that ever existed on earth! Suppose on this event Great Britain should offer Canada to France and Florida to Spain with an extension of the old limits. Would not France and Spain accept them? Gentlemen say the trade of all America is more valuable to France than Canada. I grant it; but suppose she may get both? If she is politic, and none doubt that, I aver she has the easiest game to play for attaining both that ever presented itself to a nation.

When we have bound ourselves to a stern quarrel with Great Britain by a declaration of independence, France has nothing to do but to hold back and intimidate Great Britain till Canada is put into her hands; then to intimidate us into a most disadvantageous grant of our trade. It is my firm opinion these events will take place, and arise naturally from our declaring independence.

As to aid from foreign powers: our declaration can procure us none during this present campaign though made today. It is impossible.

Now let us consider if all the advantages expected from foreign powers cannot be attained in a more unexceptional manner. Is there no way of giving notice of a nation's resolution than by proclaiming it to all the world? Let us in the most solemn manner inform the House of Bourbon, at least France, that we wait only for her determination to declare our independence. We must not talk generally of foreign powers but only of those we expect to favour us. Let us assure Spain that we never will give any assistance to her colonies. Let France become guarantee for us in arrangements of this kind.

Besides, first we ought to establish our governments and take the regular form of a state. These preventive measures will show deliberation, wisdom, caution, and unanimity.

It is our interest to keep Great Britain in the opinion that we mean reconciliation as long as possible. The wealth of London, etc., is poured into the treasury. The whole nation is ardent against us. We oblige her by our attitude to persevere in her spirit. . . .

Suppose we shall ruin her. France must rise on her ruins. Her ambition. Her religion. Our dangers from thence. . . . We shall be overwhelmed with debt. . . .

The war will be carried on with more severity. The burning of towns, the setting loose of Indians on our frontiers has not yet been done. Boston might have been burned, though it was not.

What advantage is to be expected from a declaration? (1) The animating of our troops? I answer, it is unnecessary. (2) Union of the colonies? I answer, this is also unnecessary. It may weaken that union when the people find themselves engaged in a cause rendered more cruel by such a declaration without prospect of an end to their calamities, by a continuation of the war.

People are changeable. In bitterness of soul they may complain against our rashness and ask why we did not apply first to foreign powers; why we did not settle differences among ourselves; why we did not take care to secure unsettled lands for easing their burdens instead of leaving them to colonies; why we did not wait till we were better prepared, or till we had made an experiment of our strength.

(3) A third advantage to be expected from a declaration is said to be the proof it would furnish of our great strength of spirit. But this is possibly only the first campaign of the war. France and Spain may be alarmed and provoked with each other. . . .

A partition of these colonies will take place if Great Britain can't conquer us. To escape from the protection we have in British rule by declaring independence would be like destroying a house before we have got another in winter with a small family; then asking a neighbour to take us in and finding he is unprepared.

(4) It is claimed that the spirit of the colonies calls for such a declaration. I answer that the spirit of the colonies is not to be relied on. Not only treaties with foreign powers but among ourselves should precede this dec-

laration. We should know on what grounds we are to stand with regard to one another. . . . And too, the committee on confederation dispute almost every article. Some of us totally despair of any reasonable terms of confederation.

We cannot look back. Men generally sell their goods to most advantage when they have several chapmen. We have but two to rely on. We exclude one by this declaration without knowing what the other will give.

Great Britain after one or more unsuccessful campaigns may be induced to offer us such a share of commerce as would satisfy us, to appoint councillors during good behaviour, to withdraw her armies, to protect our commerce, establish our militias—in short to redress all the grievances complained of in our first petition. Let us know if we can get terms from France that will be more beneficial than these. If we can, let us declare independence. If we cannot, let us at least withhold that declaration till we obtain terms that are tolerable. . . .

When our enemies are pressing us so vigorously; when we are in so wretched a state of preparation; when the sentiments and designs of our expected friends are so unknown to us, I am alarmed at this declaration being so vehemently presented. A worthy gentleman told us that people in this house have had different views for more than a twelvemonth. This is amazing after what they have so repeatedly declared in this house and private conversations, that they meant only reconciliation. But since they can conceal their views so dextrously, I should be glad to read a little more in the Doomsday Book of America—not all—that, like the Book of Fate, might be too dreadful—title page—binding. I should be glad to know whether in 20 or 30 years this commonwealth of colonies may not be thought too unwieldy, and Hudson's River be a proper boundary for a separate commonwealth to the northward. I have a strong impression on my mind that this will take place.

The Declaration of Independence, 1776

When, in the course of human events, it becomes necessary for one people to dissolve the political bands which have connected them with another, and to assume, among the powers of the earth, the separate and equal station to which the laws of nature and of nature's God entitle them, a decent respect to the opinions of mankind requires that they should declare the causes which impel them to the separation.

We hold these truths to be self-evident, that all men are created equal; that they are endowed by their Creator with certain unalienable rights; that among these are life, liberty, and the pursuit of happiness. That, to secure these rights, governments are instituted among men, deriving their just powers from the consent of the governed; that, whenever any form of government becomes destructive of these ends, it is the right of the people to alter or to abolish it, and to institute a new government, laying its foundation on such principles, and organizing its powers in such form, as to them shall seem most likely to effect their safety and happiness. Prudence, indeed, will dictate that governments long established should not be changed for light and transient causes; and, accordingly, all experience hath shown, that mankind are more disposed to suffer, while evils are sufferable, than to right themselves by abolishing the forms to which they are accustomed. But, when a long train of abuses and usurpations, pursuing invariably the same object, evinces a design to reduce them under absolute despotism, it is their right, it is their duty, to throw off such government, and to provide new guards for their future security. Such has been the patient sufferance of these colonies, and such is now the necessity which constrains them to alter their former systems of government. The history of the present King of Great Britain is a history of repeated injuries and usurpations, all having, in direct object, the establishment of an absolute tyranny over these states. To prove this, let facts be submitted to a candid world:

He has refused his assent to laws the most wholesome and necessary for the public good.

He has forbidden his governors to pass laws of immediate and pressing importance, unless suspended in their operation till his assent should be obtained; and, when so suspended, he has utterly neglected to attend to them.

He has refused to pass other laws for the accommodation of large districts of people, unless those people would relinquish the right of representation in the legislature; a right inestimable to them, and formidable to tyrants only.

He has called together legislative bodies at places unusual, uncomfortable, and distant from the depository of their public records, for the sole purpose of fatiguing them into compliance with his measures.

He has dissolved representative houses repeatedly, for opposing, with manly firmness, his invasions on the rights of the people.

He has refused, for a long time after such dissolutions, to cause others to be elected; whereby the legislative powers, incapable of annihilation, have returned to the people at large for their exercise; the state remaining, in the meantime, exposed to all the danger of invasion from without, and convulsions within.

He has endeavored to prevent the population of these States; for that purpose, obstructing the laws for naturalization of foreigners, refusing to pass others to encourage their migration hither, and raising the conditions of new appropriations of lands.

He has obstructed the administration of justice, by refusing his assent to laws for establishing judiciary powers.

He has made judges dependent on his will alone, for the tenure of their offices, and the amount and payment of their salaries.

He has erected a multitude of new offices, and sent hither swarms of officers to harass our people, and eat out their substance.

He has kept among us, in time of peace, standing armies, without the consent of our legislatures.

He has affected to render the military independent of, and superior to, the civil power.

He has combined, with others, to subject us to a jurisdiction foreign to our Constitution, and unacknowledged by our laws; giving his assent to their acts of pretended legislation:

For quartering large bodies of armed troops among us:

For protecting them by a mock trial, from punishment, for any murders which they should commit on the inhabitants of these States:

For cutting off our trade with all parts of the world:

For imposing taxes on us without our consent:

For depriving us, in many cases, of the benefit of trial by jury:

For transporting us beyond seas to be tried for pretended offenses:

For abolishing the free system of English laws in a neighboring province, establishing therein an arbitrary government, and enlarging its boundaries, so as to render it at once an example and fit instrument for introducing the same absolute rule into these colonies:

For taking away our charters, abolishing our most valuable laws, and altering, fundamentally, the forms of our governments:

For suspending our own legislatures, and declaring themselves invested with power to legislate for us in all cases whatsoever.

He has abdicated government here, by declaring us out of his protection, and waging war against us.

He has plundered our seas, ravaged our coasts, burnt our towns, and destroyed the lives of our people.

He is, at this time, transporting large armies of foreign mercenaries to complete the works of death, desolation, and tyranny, already begun, with circumstances of cruelty and perfidy scarcely paralleled in the most barbarous ages, and totally unworthy the head of a civilized nation.

He has constrained our fellow-citizens, taken captive on the high seas, to bear arms against their country, to become the executioners of their friends and brethren, or to fall themselves by their hands.

He has excited domestic insurrections amongst us, and has endeavored to bring on the inhabitants of our frontiers, the merciless Indian savages, whose known rule of warfare is an undistinguished destruction of all ages, sexes, and conditions.

In every stage of these oppressions, we have petitioned for redress, in the most humble terms; our repeated petitions have been answered only by repeated injury. A prince, whose character is thus marked by every act which may define a tyrant, is unfit to be the ruler of a free people.

Nor have we been wanting in attention to our British brethren. We have warned them, from time to time, of attempts by their legislature to extend an unwarrantable jurisdiction over us. We have reminded them of the circumstances of our emigration and settlement here. We have appealed to their native justice and magnanimity, and we have conjured them, by the ties of our common kindred, to disavow these usurpations, which would inevitably interrupt our connections and correspondence. They, too, have been deaf to the voice of justice and consanguinity. We must, therefore, acquiesce in the necessity which denounces our separation, and hold them, as we hold the rest of mankind, enemies in war, in peace, friends.

We, therefore, the representatives of the United States of America, in general Congress assembled, appealing to the Supreme Judge of the world for the rectitude of our intentions, do, in the name, and by the authority of the good people of these colonies, solemnly publish and declare, that these united colonies are, and of right ought to be, free and independent states; that they are absolved from all allegiance to the British Crown, and that all political connection between them and the state of Great Britain is, and ought to be, totally dissolved; and that, as free and independent states, they have full power to levy war, conclude peace, contract alliances, establish commerce, and to do all other acts and things which independent states may of right do. And, for the support of this declaration, with a firm reliance on the protection of Divine Providence, we mutually pledge to each other our lives, our fortunes, and our sacred honour.

John Adams Celebrates Independence, 1776

[To Mrs. Abigail Adams]

Had a declaration of independence been made seven months ago, it would have been attended with many great and glorious effects. We might, before this hour, have formed alliances with foreign states. We should have mastered Quebec, and been in possession of Canada. . . .

But, on the other hand, the delay of this declaration to this time has many great advantages attending it. The hopes of reconciliation, which were fondly entertained by multitudes of honest and well meaning, though short-sighted and mistaken people, have been gradually, and at last totally, extinguished. Time has been given for the whole people maturely to consider the great question of independence, and to ripen their judgment, dissipate their fears, and allure their hopes, by discussing it in newspapers and pamphlets—by debating it in assemblies, conventions, committees of safety and inspection—in town and county meetings, as well as in private conversations; so that the whole people, in every colony, have now adopted it as their own act. This will cement the union, and avoid those heats, and perhaps convulsions, which might have been occasioned by such a declaration six months ago.

But the day is past. The second day of July, 1776, will be a memorable epocha in the history of America. I am apt to believe that it will be celebrated by succeeding generations, as the great Anniversary Festival. It ought to be commemorated, as the day of deliverance, by solemn acts of devotion to God Almighty. It ought to be solemnized with pomp, shews, games, sports, guns, bells, bon-fires and illuminations, from one end of the continent to the other, from this time forward forever.

You will think me transported with enthusiasm; but I am not. I am well aware of the toil, and blood, and treasure, that it will cost us to maintain this declaration, and support and defend these states. Yet, through all the gloom, I can see the rays of light and glory; I can see that the end is more than worth all the means, and that posterity will triumph, although you and I may rue, which I hope we shall not.

✄ E S S A Y S

No two colonies responded to the crisis in imperial affairs in exactly the same way. Although elite leadership prevailed in every colony, economic interests, political circumstances, and cultural traditions varied. In the first essay, Thomas M. Doerflinger, a securities analyst and the author of *A Vigorous Spirit of Enterprise: Merchants and Economic Development in Revolutionary Philadelphia* (1986), examines the variety of factors that influenced the men who led Pennsylvania into the Revolution at a more gradual pace than Massachusetts or Virginia. In the second selection, Thad W. Tate, director emeritus of the Institute of Early American History and Culture and professor at the College of William and Mary, considers the interplay of political and economic motives that shaped Virginia's leaders for more than a decade, from the conflict over payment of the clergy (Twopenny Act of 1758) to independence. Clearly, although their paths and their motives differed, by July 1776 leaders from the thirteen colonies arrived at the same conclusion—to fight for independence.

The Mixed Motives of Merchant Revolutionaries

THOMAS M. DOERFLINGER – Neo-Whig

Philadelphia merchants before the Revolution . . . genuinely feared British encroachments on American rights and were willing to make real financial sacrifices to oppose them. Yet their opposition was qualified and inconsistent, their attitudes complex and conflicted; the merchants never offered sustained, united support for the resistance and Revolutionary movements. They neither strenuously lobbied against the Sugar Act, nor led the opposition to the Stamp Act, nor initiated the boycott of 1769–1770, nor supported strongly the convening of the Continental Congress. If it had been left to the city's merchants, the Revolutionary movement would have been more circumspect and cautious, more judicious and temperate, less eager to make the final break with Britain. In short, it would not have been a revolutionary movement at all. One reason for this ambivalence was that Philadelphia's economy was not especially disordered or depressed between 1760 and 1775, as some neo-Progressive historians have suggested; indeed, the period offered notable entrepreneurial opportunities. The merchants thus had no compelling financial reason to break with England. Quite to the contrary, they were restrained by a variety of countervailing factors. They had close commercial and personal ties with England; they wished to avoid disruption of their trade by boycotts and protests; and the Quakers among them not only discountenanced tumultuous extralegal protests but also feared that the Revolutionary movement would sweep Pennsylvania's turbulent Presbyterian faction into power.

The merchants' ambivalence is significant, first, because it shows that they did not propel the Revolutionary movement forward, and, second, because it illuminates the complex relationship in the pre-war years between

From "Philadelphia Merchants and the Logic of Moderation, 1760–1775," by Thomas Doerflinger from *William and Mary Quarterly*, 80, 1983. Reprinted by permission of the author.

ideas and interest—between the merchants' conception of their constitutional rights and their specific economic, social, and religious concerns. Although some scholars have attempted to identify the socioeconomic roots of Revolutionary ideologies, it seems more useful in the present case to explore how financial self-interest, religious affiliation, and social conservatism inhibited the emergence of a radical commitment among most merchants. This pattern is of more than local interest, because it throws light on an important regional dynamic of the Revolutionary era—that the Middle Atlantic area was consistently a center of political conservatism.

Historians have recently identified Philadelphia's dry goods trade with England as the center of a pre-Revolutionary economic crisis. It has been suggested that "English capital and English decisions increasingly dominated the colonial economy," as aggressive English firms sold huge quantities of merchandise on credit and undercut American merchant firms by selling directly to American shopkeepers and auction houses. The weight of evidence suggests that the dry goods trade was indeed overstocked during the period 1760–1775, following a profitable boom during the Seven Years' War. . . .

Although the relevant data are not fully consistent, it appears that the years 1764–1768 were indeed ones of severe commercial stagnation. Dry goods imports drifted in these years; the West Indies trade was unprofitable; and the volume of shipping activity in the port was low. In addition, merchants were frustrated by a serious "shortage of cash" caused by the withdrawal of provincial paper money from circulation and the movement of specie to England to finance the heavy wartime imports. As a result of these problems, the amount of shipping tonnage registered by merchants plunged in the second half of the 1760s, and the number of bankruptcies in Philadelphia peaked in 1767.

This downturn ended decisively in 1769, however, when flour and bread exports to the West Indies and southern Europe surged 128 percent above their 1768 levels. Philadelphia's provision trade continued to prosper until 1776. . . .

What we have, then, is a mixed picture: a dry goods market that was glutted as usual, but a strong housing market and a generally buoyant provision trade. The commercial downturn in the mid-1760s was followed by impressive expansion after 1768. This hardly adds up to a structural economic crisis that would have turned conservative businessmen into revolutionaries. The merchants, in fact, fared relatively well in this period, as a number of documents show. The number of carriage owners in Philadelphia increased from twenty-nine in 1761 to eighty-four in 1772, and in the latter year forty-four of them were merchants. Shipping records tell a similar story. . . .

Thus, despite the downturn of the mid-1760s, the pre-Revolutionary period offered good opportunities for the shrewd trader. This assessment does not imply that Philadelphia society was free from inequality and social strain in the decade and a half before Independence. It is, in fact, consistent with the argument that the distribution of wealth became increasingly unequal during the later colonial period. How else than through an expansion of commercial profits could merchants have financed the "urban mansions built during the 1760s" or purchased the "four-wheeled coaches and carriages imported from London"?

As the favorable commercial outlook in Philadelphia tended to moderate the merchants' attitudes toward the Revolutionary crisis, so too did their political orientation. Although they viewed encroachments of British power with as much dismay as other Philadelphians, politics was not the major concern of most traders. Moreover, the merchants feared that radical initiatives might sever their close and valuable ties with England and the empire.

There is a plethora of evidence, both private and public, that Philadelphia's merchants sincerely believed that parliamentary taxation of Americans was unconstitutional. In 1768 a committee of Philadelphia traders wrote to a group of leading English merchants that "the Statutes imposing Duties on Paper, Glass, Tea, &c. being a Tax on the Americans, without their Consent, we look upon, [as] Unconstitutional and destructive of our Rights, as your Brethren and Subjects." When the English merchants admitted that the Townshend duties might be "inexpedient," the Philadelphians pointedly insisted that they were unconstitutional as well. This belief was repeated again and again in the private correspondence not only of leading whig traders but of merchants who were loyalist or neutral during the Revolution. . . .

Grounded in the merchants' conceptions of their rights as Englishmen, these constitutional fears were sharpened by their problems as businessmen. The tightening of the customs administration after 1763 greatly complicated life for Philadelphia's smugglers, and both the Sugar Act and the Stamp Act required payment of taxes in specie at just the moment when the Currency Act of 1764 forbade colonial legislatures to issue legal tender paper money. All three of these acts coincided with the commercial downturn of the mid-1760s, when exchange rates were high and large amounts of specie were shipped to England to extinguish sterling debts. The result was a severe shortage of money in Pennsylvania. . . .

Even in the absence of an economic crisis, one might have expected these constitutional grievances to have aligned the merchants unambiguously behind the radical cause. A major task facing the historian, then, is to discern the factors that tended to moderate their political stance. Certainly one factor was the speed with which some of the merchants' major complaints were defused. The Stamp Act was never enforced; the Sugar Act was greatly revised in 1766. The Currency Act did not wreck Pennsylvania's paper currency but allowed the legislature to keep outstanding paper in circulation until its regular expiration date, and the colony was able to issue £102,000 of new money that was not legal tender. This was enough to meet most, though not all, of the colony's monetary needs.

A second reason for the merchants' caution may have been that they were more apolitical than the concept of a "merchant aristocracy" implies. To be sure, such traders as Charles Thomson, Thomas Mifflin, George Clymer, Thomas Wharton, and George Bryan were political activists, and many others had clear political affiliations. But before the Revolution merchants did not dominate political life. The men who articulated the colonists'

constitutional position in pamphlets, broadsides, and newspaper articles usually were not active merchants, and Pennsylvania's party chieftains were
generally wealthy lawyers, clerics, and landed gentlemen, rather than
traders. . . .

It is clear that many merchants, whether or not politically oriented,
identified closely with the British Empire, which was, after all, a commercial
construct. Merchants were the engineers of commerce who took risks to
move goods across the Atlantic; without them, the empire was only an inert
bureaucratic entity. As the Philadelphia traders wrote to their English colleagues, "We consider the Merchants here and in England as the Links of
the Chain that binds both Countries together. They are deeply concerned
in preserving the Union and Connection." . . .

This identification with the empire was challenged by a key instrument
of the Revolutionary movement, the boycotts of 1765–1766, 1768–1770, and
1774–1776. Although the stated aim of nonimportation was to exert pressure
for the repeal of particular measures, its actual reach was far wider. It was
in fact a tentative declaration of American economic independence, and its
enforcement by local committees gave rise to some of the earliest extralegal
Revolutionary governments in the colonies. The boycotts played an important ideological role as well, for they translated into action the moral component of a republican ideology that rejected the debilitating vices and
luxuries of the Old World. Nonimportation thus provided a means of atoning
for the sins of avarice and materialism in an increasingly secular age.

Philadelphia dry goods merchants, particularly the Quakers, did not
necessarily reject these attitudes *in toto.* In 1769 John Reynell donned a
leather jacket and set his wife to turning out homespun. . . . But the merchants could hardly overlook the fact that they were the conduit by which
pernicious luxuries poured into the Delaware Valley and that not a few of
the choicest extravagances ended up in their own parlors and pantries. If
fully executed, nonimportation entailed nothing less than repudiation of their
profession and destruction of the elaborate trading networks they had la-
boriously constructed. In this respect the merchants viewed the imperial
connection quite differently from Virginia planters, who found that they
were increasingly financing their expensive tastes with debt rather than tobacco shipments.

The merchants' moderate outlook was also fostered by the interrelated
issues of religion and social control, for the Revolutionary movement in
Pennsylvania was shaped at every step by bitter antagonism among religious
groups, especially between Quakers and Presbyterians. Anglicans and Quakers each composed over a third of the merchant community, and they dominated its upper stratum even more. . . . Presbyterians, on the other hand,
accounted for less than a fifth of the merchants and included few traders of
the first rank. Thus the economic muscle of the merchant group, the power
to make or break a boycott, rested with the conservative congregations of
the Friends' Meeting House and of Christ and St. Peter's churches.

The principles of the Society of Friends were ill-suited to governing
during an era of war and revolution, for the Quaker peace testimony not

only forbade military activity but discouraged riots, rallies, boycotts, and smuggling. . . . Many years of control of Pennsylvania's government, together with their commercial prominence and civic leadership, gave the Friends a conservative, rather complacent outlook. In this respect they resembled many Anglican merchants, who favored the status quo because they had close political and family ties with the colony's proprietors, British descendants of William Penn. The Anglicans' connections with England were also strong because the ministers of the church were ordained in London, and because the church in America depended on financial support from England.

The colony's Presbyterians, on the other hand, were of Scottish descent and had long resisted English domination. They traced their political lineage back to the Civil Wars, which had overthrown both bishop and king, and they felt little love for either. Indeed, Presbyterian ministers, especially those of a New Light persuasion, preached a distinctly republican message, emphasizing "the idea of a fundamental constitution based on law, of inalienable rights which were God-given and therefore natural, of government as a binding compact made between rulers and peoples, of the right of people to hold their rulers to account and to defend their rights against all oppression." The concentration of Presbyterians in Pennsylvania's underrepresented frontier counties minimized their influence in the assembly, but they hoped that their political power would grow as their share of the colony's population increased. . . .

The march of the Paxton Boys [a group of Scotch-Irish frontiersmen who marched on Philadelphia in order to reverse Pennsylvania policy friendly to the Indians] triggered a vicious political battle in Pennsylvania. To many Quakers, William Penn's once peaceful province seemed to be lurching toward anarchy as unruly Presbyterians tried to overrun the colony. These fears were heightened in 1765 when a band of Scotch-Irishmen in Cumberland County seized and destroyed a large shipment of goods that a Quaker mercantile firm was sending to Pittsburgh. Fundamental structural change—elimination of proprietary control of the colony—seemed to offer the only solution to the crisis. Therefore in 1765 the assembly dispatched Benjamin Franklin to London to persuade the British ministry that order could be maintained in Pennsylvania in no other way than by making it a royal colony. . . .

Fear of Presbyterian hegemony was a major factor in the Quaker merchants' view of the Revolutionary movement. They perceived an inexorable logic to the Revolutionary process that had nothing to do with commercial problems, parliamentary taxation, or ministerial tyranny. Like their forebears of the seventeenth century, the Presbyterians were evidently using discontent over constitutional issues to seize power for themselves and deny their fellow Christians freedom of conscience.

The prosperity of most merchants, a habitual detachment from political affairs, close ties with England, and fear of a rising Presbyterian faction all combined to moderate the merchants' political stance between 1764 and 1776. Although they clearly disliked the Sugar Act, their response to it was very restrained, perhaps in part because they were absorbed by the local political tumults of 1764. The Stamp Act crisis of the following year was powerfully shaped by the contingencies of provincial politics. . . .

Since the attacks on stamp agents constituted the chief form of resistance to the tax, it cannot be said that merchants as a group led the opposition to parliamentary taxation in 1765, as has been suggested. In reality, the trading community was split: Quaker merchants generally did not oppose the Stamp Act, while Anglican and Presbyterian merchants of the proprietary faction did. The one instance in which merchants united to oppose the act was the boycott of British imports, organized in November 1765. Even here, there is evidence that some merchants joined the boycott under duress. . . .

Despite their divisions in 1765, the merchants could have played a major role in opposing the Townshend Acts of 1767. . . . Primary opposition to the duties took the form, not of riots, but of a major commercial boycott from March 1769 to September 1770, in which the traders actively participated. According to some analysts, the merchants' causal role was indeed central. Neo-Progressive historians have argued that . . . the merchants initiated the boycott primarily to gain an eighteen-month respite from the relentless cascade of British capital and goods, during which they could sell off inventories, pay debts to English suppliers at favorable exchange rates, and build up cash reserves. Such a formulation is elegantly logical, and there is enough evidence to demonstrate that this consideration definitely was in the minds of some traders. At issue, however, is the causation of a revolution: the question is whether these concerns determined the pace and pattern of events.

The answer to this question is an unequivocal "no," for the neo-Progressives have overlooked one devastating detail. Far from leading the non-importation movement in Philadelphia, dry goods merchants stubbornly opposed it throughout 1768, steadfastly ignoring the increasingly vituperative demands of radicals that they place the public welfare above private interests. Pressure steadily mounted on importers to join the boycott, which Boston and New York had already agreed to start. In pamphlets, speeches, and newspaper articles the Philadelphia radicals, led by John Dickinson, showered the merchants with abuse. They even tried to force the issue by enlisting individual merchants, but the intransigence of "eight or ten" wealthy importers scotched the effort. Although questioning the constitutionality of the Townshend Acts, conservative merchants evidently opposed precipitate action that would violate the Quaker peace testimony and offend valuable correspondents in England.

By the same token, however, it is clear that overt loyalism of the kind shown by the royalist faction in Boston was not behind the merchants' caution. Once the boycott began in March 1769, its legitimacy was generally accepted, and there were few enforcement problems. . . . [W]hen three vessels from "the little dirty Colony of Rhode Island" (the first defector from the boycott) sailed into Delaware Bay, they were barred by the merchants from unloading their wares.

This stance demonstrates true commitment to the patriot cause, for by the spring of 1770 the stoppage of trade was a real burden to the importers, whose stocks were depleted. . . .

Although merchants were willing to shoulder the financial burdens of nonimportation, the drift of events made the sacrifice seem ever more pointless. In May 1770 most of the duties were repealed, and shortly thereafter Rhode Island defected from the agreement, as did New York in July. The agreements of Maryland, Massachusetts, and New York were less restrictive than Pennsylvania's, and there were well-documented reports that Bostonians were freely importing large quantities of tea. Worse still, the boycott seemed to be having little impact on the English economy. For all these reasons, by May 1770 many merchants wanted to end the boycott. Nevertheless, it dragged on until September—too late to import many goods until the following spring. . . .

Nonimportation shows clearly how patriotism was shaded by self-interest and by the circumspection of the mercantile mind. Anxious not to offend their correspondents in England, the merchants took their time in entering the boycott. Once the initiative was under way, however, they supported it to the point of foregoing profits as their inventories dwindled during 1770. But sacrifice had its limits; when other colonies abandoned the boycott and some of the Townshend duties were repealed, they became eager to get on with their trade. Of course the radicals in Philadelphia accused the moderates of being motivated by crass self-interest. To this charge the moderates replied, with some justice, that wet goods merchants were pressing for extension of a boycott that did not affect their own business even as they paid into the royal treasury duties on wine and rum. And their major allies in Philadelphia, the mechanics, benefited tremendously from the suspension of trade with England. Republican ideology was thus tempered and twisted by the realities of the marketplace.

Merchants approached with similar ambivalence the British East India Company's plan to unload its huge supply of tea in America. Many undoubtedly viewed it as a trick to seduce Americans into importing a dutied commodity, but it is apparent that some merchants had financial reasons for attacking the tea scheme. In addition to injuring directly those few traders who smuggled Dutch tea into Philadelphia, the company's plan concentrated power in the hands of a small number of prominent traders who had good connections in England. . . .

When news of the Coercive Acts reached Philadelphia in May 1774, wealthy Anglican and Quaker merchants attempted, as one said, "to keep the transactions of our City within the limits of Moderation and not Indecent or offensive to our parent State." They insisted that Boston should pay for the ruined tea and strongly opposed resumption of nonimportation, knowing by now that a boycott was far easier to start than to stop. The convening of the Continental Congress in September 1774, however, deprived them of the power to shape events as they had in the past. In particular, they could not delay the third boycott of the Revolutionary movement, the Association formulated by Congress, which banned imports after December 1, 1774, and exports after September 10, 1775.

Some traders—Charles Thomson, Thomas Mifflin, and George Clymer, for instance—enthusiastically promoted the Revolutionary cause as it moved forward in 1774 and 1775. Yet many wealthy merchants looked on with dismay as Independence drew near and the familiar social and political landscape was transformed. . . . Religious antagonisms continued to be a potent concern, especially for Quakers. James and Drinker discerned a common Presbyterian spring to events in Philadelphia and Boston in 1773: had not the "hasty and violent resolves" of Charles Thomson and other local Presbyterians inspired the intransigence of the Bostonians that led to the destruction of the tea? If Presbyterians finally managed to seize control of Pennsylvania, the freedom of conscience that had long graced the colony's constitution would disappear. . . . In the past, Quakers had battled in the political arena to hold back the Presbyterian tide, but by 1775 the forces of change were too strong, the political environment too turbulent, to justify this approach, and Friends defiantly retired from politics. For these various reasons—economic, social, religious, and political—a substantial proportion of the Philadelphia merchant community refused to enlist in the patriot cause.

The case of Philadelphia's merchants reminds us that interest may temper rather than intensify ideological commitment. While socioeconomic concerns may have made some Americans particularly receptive to a republican ideology, such factors had the opposite effect in Philadelphia's trading community. In the first place, the merchants did not face an economic crisis in the 1760s and 1770s. Despite the nearly chronic glut of the dry goods market and the stagnation of the provision trade between 1764 and 1768, the merchants were reasonably prosperous in the fifteen years before the War for Independence. They resented and feared English efforts to tax Americans and were willing to make sacrifices to defend their liberties, but these sentiments did not turn them into Revolutionaries because other factors intervened. Contingencies of local politics, close personal and commercial ties with England, fear of Presbyterian hegemony, and economic self-interest all conspired to moderate their stance. While the merchants did not mirror public opinion throughout the colony, neither were they an isolated group of rich reactionaries. A great many other Pennsylvanians viewed the prospect of Independence with equal misgiving. As late as May 1776, for instance, an election in Philadelphia that amounted to a referendum on the question of Independence favored the conservative position by a small margin.

The behavior of the merchants illustrates the limits of an ideological or intellectual explanation of the origins of the Revolution. By itself, such an approach explains too much; it lacks the specificity intrinsic to the problem at hand. The ideas of John Trenchard and Thomas Gordon, John Locke, and James Harrington were widely publicized throughout the colonies, yet they had far greater resonance in some colonies than in others. To understand fully the origins of the Revolution, we must determine what specific local and regional factors made particular areas more or less receptive to these ideas. The relative prosperity of the Middle Colonies, for example, in conjunction with a substantial Quaker influence and the presence of a large non-English-speaking population, may have predisposed this section toward conservatism. . . .

Regional differences continued to operate after 1776. The same pragmatism, elitism, and materialism that had hitherto made Philadelphia merchants reluctant Revolutionaries predisposed some of them to lead the Revolution in its later, more conservative phase. . . .

The Causes of the Revolution in Virginia: Britain's Challenge to the Ruling Class

THAD W. TATE

Contemplating the approach of independence in May 1776, Landon Carter, Virginia planter and retired Burgess, recorded in his diary that the Revolution was an unfortunate contest which Great Britain "certainly began with America by attempting to tax her out of the constitutional road." Carter took a view of the predominant issue leading to the American Revolution that every Patriot leader in Virginia shared. All the major public resolutions, addresses, and petitions of the colony spoke against a threat to "ancient, legal, and constitutional Rights."

The final statement, a bill of indictment against George III in the preamble of the 1776 constitution, comprised twenty-two charges, which stand as an official summary of the issues as the colony saw them. Five of the twenty-two related to punitive actions taken after the beginning of hostilities by Dunmore or by British military authorities elsewhere and did not, therefore, concern basic issues from which the conflict had arisen. Two other accusations were too general to relate to specific grievances. Of the remaining fifteen allegations, which were the heart of the case, fourteen attacked British political or military policies. Nine of the fourteen criticized restrictions on colonial legislatures, two objected to abridgment of legal rights of the individual, and three dealt with threats to liberty from the use of armed force. Only a single article from the entire list concerned economic conditions— a complaint against the restriction of colonial trade with non-British ports. Apparently the Virginia protest explained the Revolution as a defense of constitutional rights against their subversion by the British government. Moreover, it made no distinction between measures that affected Virginia directly and those that seemed, by their threat to another colony, to raise the prospect of future tyranny over all. The Virginians seemed content to say they fought over a common issue.

Many historians have been dissatisfied with this answer. In part, they have been influenced by broad currents in historical writing, such as the imperialist view of the colonial period, the economic interpretation of history, and the belief that the American Revolution was primarily an internal con-

From "The Coming of the Revolution in Virginia: Britain's Challenge to Virginia's Ruling Class, 1763–1776," by Thad W. Tate, *William and Mary Quarterly*, Third Series, 19, 1962. Reprinted by permission of the author.

flict, all of which have questioned the traditional constitutional explanation. Doubt has come, too, from certain local characteristics of the Revolution in Virginia. It has not been easy to understand why a colony with Virginia's reputation for conservatism and loyalty reacted with such force and rapidity, when the actual burdens of the British acts fell more lightly upon Virginia than upon many other colonies. . . . Such considerations have caused speculation about the candor of Virginia Patriots and about the accuracy of interpreting the Revolution in that colony solely as a contest for political liberty.

Although no one has made a full-scale attack on the constitutional interpretation as it applied to Virginia, a number of scholars have emphasized other issues. Among the additional sources of conflict to which they have pointed are the existence of earlier disputes, antedating the taxation measures of George Grenville; the massive indebtedness of the planters to British merchants; the clash between imperial policy and speculative interests of Virginians in western lands; and the divisions between radical Patriots of the stripe of Patrick Henry and the entrenched leadership of the House of Burgesses. The over-all effect has been to reduce the importance of the issue of colonial rights, as it developed after 1763, by suggesting either that it was only one among a number of points in dispute or that it was largely an expression of deeper-seated and more material grievances.

Those who believe that there were important beginnings of the Revolution in Virginia before the peace of 1763 have placed their emphasis upon the only serious political controversy at this time—the disputes over the Twopenny Acts, otherwise known as the Parsons' Cause. In the disallowance of these laws they have seen the making of an imperial dispute that commenced as early as 1759 and led directly to Virginia's involvement in the Revolution.

The Twopenny Acts were passed by the Assembly in 1755 and again in 1758 to relieve taxpayers of the necessity of satisfying their public obligations in tobacco during two years of short crops and abnormally high prices. Both laws permitted the commutation of such payments at a rate of two pence per pound of tobacco—well below its market value. The 1755 law was to remain in effect only ten months, and the 1758 law, twelve. Among the obligations affected were the salaries of the clergy of the Established Church, which had been fixed at sixteen thousand pounds of tobacco yearly by a 1748 law that had been confirmed by the Crown. Although the royal instructions stipulated that laws thus confirmed could not be altered without the consent of the Crown and required the insertion of a suspending clause in any amending acts, the Virginia legislature included no such clause in either of the Twopenny Acts. To have done so, as defenders of the measure later pointed out, would have kept them from going into immediate effect and would have defeated the whole purpose of the legislation. Lieutenant Governor Francis Fauquier realized that he was violating his instructions in assenting to the 1758 measure, but he readily approved it because there had been no repercussions from the approval of the 1755 law by his predecessor Robert Dinwiddie.

Passage of the 1758 act immediately evoked strong opposition from the clergy. Had the law not been enacted, the high-priced tobacco would have meant a substantial addition to their income. To avoid its loss a number of ministers determined to resist the Twopenny legislation. Their opposition took several forms: a convention of some, though not all, of the clergy; a petition to the Privy Council requesting that the 1758 act be declared null and void from its inception; a series of lawsuits for the recovery of the full market value of their assigned quota of tobacco, and a pamphlet and newspaper controversy. In all of these measures the chief clerical spokesman was the Reverend John Camm, Professor of Divinity at the College of William and Mary and rector of Yorkhampton Parish in nearby York County. It was he who largely instigated the complaints to England, carried the test suit to the Privy Council on appeal, and defended the clerical position in writing against two outspoken burgesses, Landon Carter and Richard Bland.

The resultant controversy continued from 1759 until 1766, and in its course the clerics directly challenged the competence of the Virginia Assembly to pass the Twopenny Acts. Both the timing—its later stages coincided with the taxation dispute with the home government—and the underlying issue—the limits of the legislative power of a colonial assembly—have made it easy to see the Parsons' Cause as one of the first steps of approaching revolution. Patrick Henry's vehement argument in the best-known of the clerical suits that a king who would annul a beneficial law degenerated into a tyrant seems to support this view. The same is true of the more sober arguments advanced by Carter and Bland. They justified the Twopenny Acts on several grounds that touched upon the nature of the imperial constitution: the necessity of the legislation to protect the welfare of the colony, the right of the people to be governed by laws made by their elected representatives, and the claim that a governor's instructions from the Crown were not obligatory and did not have the force of law.

Yet it is possible to see the Parsons' Cause in a much different light by considering its full scope, including the progress of the dispute in England as well as in the colony. . . . [This shows] the Parsons' Cause as primarily a dispute between the colony and its clergy, not between colony and mother country. . . .

The Parsons' Cause is sometimes also seen as an economic issue, in which Virginians took a first step toward revolution by their reaction to alleged British interference with an effort at debtor relief. But . . . the British action did not have any practical economic effect. Still the question of whether planter debts influenced the coming of the Revolution, being far broader than a single incident, demands further consideration. Certainly the endless discussions of increasing debts, depressed tobacco prices, and shortages of currency that occupy so large a part of the surviving correspondence of Virginians suggests the possibility of a link between economic conditions in the colony and the Revolutionary movement. Indeed, by 1763 planter debts were already an issue of long standing, as the running controversy in the 1750s over the rate of exchange between Virginia currency and sterling money attested.

In the 1760s and 1770s there are two aspects of the debt question. One centers around the Currency Act of 1764, which extended to the other continental colonies the 1751 restrictions on New England forbidding further emissions of paper money as legal tender. . . .

The second part of the debt question concerns the debts themselves— the ever increasing sums due British merchants as a consequence of the fortunes of the tobacco trade. If a link does exist between them and the Revolutionary protest, it is not easy to establish, for the Virginians never included complaints about economic conditions in their petitions and resolutions. Between 1764 and 1766 Virginians occasionally grumbled about debts. Governor Fauquier found the people "uneasy, peevish, and ready to murmur at every Occurrence" because of their debts, and he attributed some of the continued unrest after repeal of the Stamp Act to economic hardship. Again, most of the hostility seemed directed against the merchants; the debts were not the occasion for any contests with the government. Probably debtors welcomed the closing of the courts that had occurred while the Stamp Act was in force, because it prevented suits by creditors and put pressure on merchants to work for repeal of the stamp duties. But the benefit to debtors was almost certainly a by-product and not a cause of the suspension of the courts, which had occurred very widely to avoid the use of stamped paper. A number of inferior courts, moreover, reopened in Virginia before the repeal of the Stamp Act. . . .

The attitude of Virginians concerning their debts grew harsher in the spring and summer of 1774. These months mark a distinct shift to a new phase of the debt question. The commercial system was still not an object of criticism, but there was frank discussion of withholding the payment of debts. . . . The next year British subjects, permitted to return home by the Virginia Convention, were forbidden to take with them papers or account books belonging to anyone in Great Britain.

The closing of the courts—the most substantial of these actions since it blocked suits for debts—may have served as a weapon in the political struggle, as it had in part in 1765. Some merchants in Virginia conceded that its principal purpose was simply to force the merchants in Great Britain to use their influence against the repressive measures of the ministry instead of supporting them. Any exact apportionment between its political and economic purposes is impossible, but obviously political pressure on the merchants played some part. On the other hand, the atmosphere in 1774 did differ from that of 1765. There was more open complaint about debts, and by 1773 the tobacco trade had entered a new period of depression, bringing a consequent restriction on credit. If there was, however, a genuine economic conflict, it appeared at a late stage in the advance toward revolution, when public sentiment had become sufficiently inflamed to aggravate latent grievances.

In sum, there seems little doubt that there was—and had been for a long time—feeling by the planters on the subject of their financial obligations. That it constituted a basic issue in bringing on the Revolution is questionable. Virginians directed hostility over the debts against the merchants rather than against the economic policies of the government, which in all its measures after 1763 actually exerted less pressure on the matter of debts than it had sometimes done earlier. For most of these years the colonists agitated the debt issue correspondingly less. And in the last five years of the 1760s the Assembly even enacted a few minor safeguards against efforts of debtors to escape their obligations. Only with the interruption of the courts in 1774 did hostility grow notably sharper and did Virginia move to obstruct outright the collection of debts. The debt issue, in short, does not loom particularly large in the years of political conflict with Great Britain. At best, the planter debts were an underlying source of difficulty brought to the surface only late in the Revolutionary crisis under the stimulus of a deepening political crisis.

Virginia had another economic interest—speculation in western lands—which the post-1763 measures of the imperial government affected more directly. The land claims of Virginia were sweeping, and many of the leaders of the colony had acquired a stake in their exploitation. The series of British directives, beginning with the Proclamation Line of 1763, that restricted the confirmation of new grants or the establishment of new settlements in the West ran counter to the plans of Virginians for further acquisitions and profitable sales. Even where lands were to be opened, Virginia investors faced a contest with British rivals. Yet, the West no more figured as an initial issue in the Revolutionary controversy in Virginia than did planter debts. On land questions the colony could usually count upon the royal governor to take its side. Furthermore, the British allowed settlement in some areas west of the mountains by 1769 and never effectively interfered with it elsewhere. And Virginians, willing to trust their bargaining power with the home government, never questioned the Crown's rights to issue land grants.

Only in the already explosive situation of 1774 did the problem of the West attract complaints. In February of that year Dunmore, along with the other governors, received instructions to sell lands only at public auction, at a quintupled minimum price, and at twice the old rate for quitrents. These requirements, unpopular to a degree that had not been true of earlier British actions in the West, were the first to which Patriot leaders in Virginia seriously protested. As a potential grievance that failed to reach important proportions until the last stages of the controversy, the issue of the West developed in a manner similar to that of the debt question.

Internal divisions appear to have been no more important in bringing on the Revolution. The image of a band of radicals ceaselessly contending against a powerful conservative bloc to move the Revolution at a faster pace and to achieve a stronger voice in the colonial government does not hold for Virginia. At no time during the 1760s and 1770s were there organized or rival groups that might be legitimately classified as factions or parties. In fact, once events moved beyond the apparent challenge by Patrick Henry to the old guard of the House of Burgesses over the Stamp Act Resolves of 1765, it is difficult to find evidence of serious internal disputes among Virginia Patriots. . . . On only one later occasion, the closing of the courts, in 1774, did Virginians appear close to splitting, and then the minority quickly bowed to the popular decision. Nearly all the various committees and delegations elected in Virginia—the Committee of Correspondence of 1773, the first Committee of Safety, the members of the First Continental Congress—included men labeled both radical and conservative by modern scholars. As the Revolutionary controversy progressed, potential conflicts among the Patriots lessened rather than increased.

What remains as the fundamental issue in the coming of the Revolution, then, is nothing more than the contest over constitutional rights. None of the other potential issues seems to have applied in Virginia at the opening of the struggle. Perhaps after all the Virginians had stated their grievances reasonably accurately. In 1763 there was a tradition of jealously guarded rights and privileges, but no lingering issues capable in themselves of instigating new conflicts. The Revolution did not open in force until the announcement of the Stamp Act. From then until the beginning of armed conflict with Dunmore in the fall of 1775 political or constitutional issues were the occasion for every outbreak of protest within the colony. The Virginians reacted, moreover, to actions affecting other colonies—the suspension of the New York legislature, the threat to Massachusetts after the Circular Letter, the Gaspee incident in Rhode Island—almost as readily as to measures that applied directly to their own colony. They were apparently moved as much by the over-all conflict as by local considerations. . . .

In its concentration upon the broader aspects of the constitutional conflict with the mother country, the Revolutionary movement in Virginia appeared lacking in local issues of prime relevance. Yet local conditions and circumstances in Virginia, as well as elsewhere, almost certainly gave distinctive characteristics to the development of this common issue. One such influence was the structure and distribution of political power within the colonies. The Revolution marked not only a clash of constitutional theories but also a contest between rival blocs of power, the British seeing a need to extend their control over the colonies and the Americans determined to preserve the degree of autonomy they had enjoyed. As early as May 1764, Richard Henry Lee referred to the "iron hand of power" raised against the colonies. Although Virginians may have exaggerated in charging that the ministerial policies represented a determined system to reduce them to slavery, they correctly assessed the intent of Great Britain as an over-all decrease in colonial political power. Indeed, American constitutional theories were to some extent a rationalization of the power struggle, not in the sense of attempting to hide narrow self-interest but in the sense of explaining why some degree of political power was essential for the protection of liberty.

The operation of the British challenge upon the structure of power in Virginia did as much as anything to shape the Revolutionary controversy there. The nature of political control within the colony is generally familiar. The catch phrase is planter aristocracy. Historians have described a small, able ruling group, largely members of the planter class and frequently related by family ties. These men governed both through the Council and to an even larger extent through the House of Burgesses, and their dominance of the county courts and the Anglican parish vestries provided additional bases of local power. A further concentration of influence in the hands of a few leading Burgesses meant that a dozen or so men might dominate the government of the colony. At the same time a relatively wide franchise for the election of Burgesses prevented the ruling elite from completely ignoring the will of the populace and suggested a wide assent to the government of the colony.

In this situation there was little chance for factionalism to arise among the Patriots—the unanimity with which Virginians acted was largely unavoidable. Since there were no separate sources of local power, the Revolutionary movement most likely was directed from the center outward to the counties. . . . Moreover, the situation in Virginia left no room for the development of native Loyalist leadership. Loyalist claimants for British compensation after the Revolution numbered only thirteen persons born in Virginia. Even the Council, drawn from the same planter class as the Burgesses, was far from being a center of royalist sympathies. Several councilors were outspoken Patriots, and the others were more properly neutralist than Loyalist. The real explanation for the weakness of Loyalism within the colony may lie deeper than in the common assumption that Dunmore's antics alienated strong potential support for the Crown. It may be attributable instead to the lack of an avenue to political power other than the one already monopolized by the planters.

This combination of unanimity and concentration of political power probably accounts for many characteristic features of the Revolution in Virginia—features that have, at least, given a distinctive coloration to the central issue of political and constitutional rights. For example, the emphasis upon interference with the colonial legislatures in the charges against George III is perhaps a clue to the Virginians' preoccupation with threats to a political power that was centered in the House of Burgesses. Similarly, it suggests less concern about the rights of the individual than we commonly associate with the American Revolution. This may seem a risky supposition to make in the face of George Mason's classic defense of individualism in the Virginia Declaration of Rights, but Virginians may very well have thought they possessed individual liberty in sufficient degree and that their rights were endangered only to the extent that colonial self-government itself was in danger. Certainly, the changes that occurred in Virginia, with the exception of the achievement of religious freedom, had little to do with the extension of individual liberty. The two great consequences of the Revolution within Virginia were the elimination of all British control and the further predominance of the legislative branch of government.

The Virginia leaders, then, did not go far wrong in their attribution of the fateful dispute with Great Britain to an invasion of constitutional rights. The one thing they might perhaps have added, though for them it could hardly have needed to be made explicit, was that the new turn in imperial policy directly challenged an established ruling class who would not lightly give up its power and privileges of self-government. If one is seeking the material and substantial interests that represent the reality behind constitutional principle, this political power is substance enough.

✄ F U R T H E R   R E A D I N G

David Ammerman, *In the Common Cause: American Response to the Coercive Acts of 1774* (1974)

Bernard Bailyn, *The Ideological Origins of the American Revolution* (1967)

Richard D. Brown, *Revolutionary Politics in Massachusetts: The Boston Committee of Correspondence and the Towns, 1772–1774* (1970)

Roger Champagne, "New York and the Intolerable Acts, 1774," *New-York Historical Society Quarterly* 45 (1961), 195–207

Bernhard Donoughue, *British Politics and the American Revolution: The Path to War, 1773–1775* (1964)

Eric Foner, *Tom Paine and Revolutionary America* (1976)

Lawrence H. Gipson, *The Triumphant Empire: Britain Sails into the Storm, 1770–1776* (1965)

Robert A. Gross, *The Minutemen and Their World* (1976)

Ira D. Gruber, "The American Revolution as a Conspiracy," *William and Mary Quarterly*, 3d ser., 26 (1969), 360–372.

Richard M. Ketchum, *Decisive Day: The Battle for Bunker Hill* (1974)

Benjamin W. Labaree, *The Boston Tea Party* (1964)

William R. Leslie, "The Gaspee Affair: A Study of Its Constitutional Significance," *Mississippi Valley Historical Review* 39 (1952–1953), 233–256

Pauline Maier, *From Resistance to Revolution: Colonial Radicals and the Development of American Opposition to Britain* (1972)

Jerrilyn Greene Marston, *King and Congress: The Transfer of Political Legitimacy, 1774–1776* (1987)

Charles H. Metzger, *The Quebec Act: A Primary Cause of the American Revolution* (1936)

John A. Neunschwander, *The Middle Colonies and the Coming of the Revolution* (1973)

John Phillip Reid, *In Defiance of the Law: The Standing-Army Controversy, the Two Constitutions, and the Coming of the American Revolution* (1981)

——, *In a Rebellious Spirit: The Argument of Facts, the Liberty Riot, and the Coming of the American Revolution* (1979)

Richard Alan Ryerson, *The Revolution Is Now Begun: The Radical Committees of Philadelphia, 1765–1776* (1978)

Peter Shaw, *American Patriots and the Rituals of Revolution* (1981)

Robert E. Toohey, *Liberty and Empire: British Radical Solutions to the American Problem, 1774–1776* (1978)

Arthur Bernon Tourtellot, *William Diamond's Drum* (1959)

Robert W. Tucker and David C. Hendrickson, *The Fall of the First British Empire: Origins of the War of American Independence* (1982)

John W. Tyler, *Smugglers and Patriots: Boston Merchants and the Advent of the American Revolution* (1986)

Robert M. Weir, *"A Most Important Epocha": The Coming of the Revolution in South Carolina* (1970)

Garry Wills, *Inventing America: Jefferson's Declaration of Independence* (1978)

CHAPTER
5

Forging a National Army and Framing an International Alliance, 1776–1778

❎

In July 1776 opposition to British control came to a climax with the Declaration of Independence, but the challenge of defending the Revolution and creating a viable nation was only beginning. Facing the thirteen former colonies—now states—was the most formidable military power in the world, the British nation, with a navy so huge that it could deploy tens of thousands of well-provisioned and well-equipped professional troops anywhere along the Atlantic seaboard. No American port was safe; indeed, most settlements were within striking distance from the coast and inland waterways.

Their own military legacy and the influence of Whig political theory had led the colonists to rely on locally raised militia companies, citizen-soldiers who could rise swiftly in defense of their communities, as they had done at Lexington and Concord. And it was militiamen alone who enabled the Revolution to muster large armies at Bunker Hill in 1775 and Saratoga in 1777. But during most military operations, these part-time amateurs had limited value. In training and discipline they were deficient, and, most important, they could not be trusted to stay for the weeks, months, and even years that campaigning against Britain required. They would rise briefly to defend their own localities, but they were unwilling to travel long distances to fight away from home, nor would they leave their families, farms, and workshops for prolonged, indefinite periods. As a result, the Continental Congress had to turn away from colonial tradition. Working through the state governments, which possessed exclusive power to tax, it had to raise, equip, provision, and train a regular army that could go anywhere to fight, year after year.

This was an immense practical challenge of great political and financial complexity. It would occupy Congress's best energies until 1782. And it would be closely connected to the formation of American foreign policy. From the beginning of the war, Congress recognized that outside help was crucial and that the traditional enemy, France, was the nation most likely to supply assistance because of its eagerness to harass and humiliate Britain. The Catholic monarchy *that Americans had excoriated during the French and Indian wars of the 1740s and 1750s could supply money, military equipment, and ultimately troops and a naval squadron. It could also threaten Britain directly and thus divert forces from America and raise Britain's military expenses. Moreover, a long-term commercial connection with France would be mutually advantageous. Thus, even before the colonists declared independence, they had begun secret talks with France—negotiations that were encouraged immediately by covert French material support.*

But as eager as the Americans were for open military and commercial treaties with France, for a time French policymakers were reluctant to commit France publicly to the United States. Not only did a reconciliation between the British and the American colonists still seem possible, but there was a great chance that the American fight for independence would collapse. Under these circumstances France, not Britain, would taste humiliation. So the French government continued its covert assistance, avoiding any public commitments.

The American victory at Saratoga, New York, in October 1777 tipped the diplomatic balance. Here a well-trained, well-equipped British army of about 8,000 men under General John Burgoyne was surrounded by an American army that combined properly drilled continental units with regional militiamen so as to achieve superior strength and numbers. The American commanders— Philip Schuyler, Horatio Gates, and Benedict Arnold—wrangled among themselves over tactics and leadership, but their troops forced Burgoyne's surrender. This, the first great victory for the Americans, would prove a turning point in the war. After Saratoga, France and the United States would proclaim their alliance, and though the poorly financed, continually improvised American military effort was still struggling, Britain's prospects fell as its burden of international warfare mounted sharply.

✕ *D O C U M E N T S*

The difficulty of forming a national army—a challenge in both practical and theoretical terms—is illustrated in the correspondence of John Adams, General George Washington, and the Congress that composes the first few documents in this chapter. Such efforts permitted the United States to respond effectively to the British invasion from Canada led by General Burgoyne. The British general expressed his propaganda effort in his proclamation of July 2, 1777, which is reprinted here as the seventh selection. Designed to demoralize Americans along Burgoyne's route and to elicit loyalist support, the proclamation, in its tone and mixed messages, was in the end counterproductive and so helped to rally Vermont and Massachusetts militiamen. The veteran's account of one of the Saratoga battles, in the eighth document, reminds us that warfare is not an abstract chess game but a grim, bloody, human experience in which individuals, as well as nations, pay the price of victory and defeat.

The American diplomatic reports that compose the ninth and tenth documents reveal the connection between the Saratoga victory and the achievement of the Franco-American alliance. The texts of the treaties, reprinted as the final documentary selection, make clear the kinds of objectives that brought two dissimilar nations together in the joint enterprise of waging war on Britain. These documents reinforce the old saying that war is an extension of diplomacy and that politics makes strange bedfellows.

John Adams Discusses Military Preparations, 1776

Philadelphia Aug. 3, 1776

Dear Sir . . .

We have now a Nation to protect and defend; and I can easily see the Propriety of the observation . . . from the Prussian Hero, that the Prosperity of a State depends upon the Discipline of its Army. This Discipline reared the Roman Empire and the British: and the American will Stand or fall, in my Opinion, according as it adheres to or deviates from the Same Discipline. . . .

The Army must be well officered, Armed, disciplined, fed, cloathed, covered, and paid. In these Respects We do, as well as We can. . . . I am in more Anxiety for Cloaths and Tents than any Thing. Because the Health as well as Discipline of the Army, depend much upon them.

We shall never do well, untill We get a regular Army, and this will never be, untill Men are inlisted for a longer Duration, and that will never be effected untill We are more generous in our Encouragement to Men. But I am convinced that Time alone, will perswade Us to this Measure: and in the mean Time We shall, very indiscreetly waste a much greater Expence than would be necessary for this great Purpose in temporary Calls upon Militia, besides risquing the Loss of many Lives, and much Reputation.

John Adams to Henry Knox

Philadelphia August 25, 1776

Dear Sir . . .

Able Officers, are the Soul of an Army. Gentlemen of Sense, and Knowledge, as well as valour, must be advanced. I wish you would give me in Confidence a List of the best Officers from the Massachusetts, with their Characters. . . . Pray give me, your Sentiments frankly, and candidly. We have been delicate too long. Our Country, is too much interested, in this Subject. Men of Genius and Spirit, must be promoted, wherever they are. . . .

I am a constant Advocate for a regular Army, and the most masterly Discipline, because, I know, that without these We cannot reasonably hope to be a powerfull, a prosperous, or a free People, and therefore, I have been constantly labouring to obtain an handsome Encouragement for inlisting a permanent Body of Troops. But have not as yet prevailed, and indeed, I despair of ever Succeeding, unless the General, and the Officers from the Southward, Should convince Gentlemen here; or unless two or three horrid Defeats, Should bring a more melancholly Conviction, which I expect and believe will one day, or other be the Case.

Letters and texts of John Adams reprinted by permission of the publishers from *Diary and Autobiography of John Adams,* Volumes 2 and 4, L. H. Butterfield, Editor, Leonard C. Faber and Wendell D. Garret, Assistant Editors, Cambridge, MA.: The Belknap Press of Harvard University Press, Copyright © 1961 Massachusetts Historical Society.

Samuel Holden Parsons Reports to John Adams on Massachusetts Officers, 1776

I know I may write in Confidence to you, and therefore will endeavor to give the Characters of your [Massachusetts] Officers as I am able from my Acquaintance, tho' I think the Task hard and not the most agreable.

Colonels

Whitcomb	has no Trace of an Officer, his Men under no Government
Reed	A good Officer not of the most extensive Knowledge but far from being low or despicable
Prescot	A Good Soldier to fight no Sense after Eight o'Clock A.M.
Little	A Midling Officer and of tolerable Genius, not great
Serjeant	has a pretty good Character but I have no Acquaintance
Glover	is said to be a good Officer but am not acquainted
Hutchinson	An easy good Man not of great Genius
Baley	is Nothing
Baldwin	a Personable Man but not of the first Character
Learned	Was a good Officer, is old, Superanuated and Resigned
Greaton	An excellent Disciplinarian his Courage has been questioned, but I dont know with what Justice
Bond	I dont know him
Patterson	A Good Officer of a liberal Education, ingenious and Sensible

Lt. Colonels

Shephard	an excellent Officer none before him, of good Understanding and good common Learning
Jacobs	is less than Nothing
Wesson	An Able Officer
Clap	Pretty good
Reed	Pretty good
Moulton	Am not acquainted
Henshaw	Am not acquainted
Johonnot	Very good a fine Soldier and an extensive Acquaintance

Majors

Sprout	a good, able, Officer
Brooks	an Officer, Soldier, Gentleman and Scholar of the first Character
Smith	a midling Officer
Haydon	a good Officer faithful and prudent not of the most Learning or great Knowledge of the World

Lt. Col. Nixon I had forgot he is a discreet good Officer not of the greatest Mind.

Col. Ward is a diligent faithful Man and a good Soldier.

These are all the Field Officers from your State which I at present recollect with whom I have any Acquaintance; amongst them all tis my Opinion Lt. Col. Shephard would make as good an Officer as any at the Head of a Regiment and that Major Brooks would Honor any Command he Should be appointed to, he is now a Major of Col. Wibb's Regiment and as fit to command a Regiment as any Man in the Lines. Thus you have my Opinion without disguise and I am sure you will make no improper Use of it.

John Adams to Joseph Hawley

Philadelphia Aug. 25, 1776

Dear Sir . . .

We have been apt to flatter ourselves, with gay Prospects of Happiness to the People Prosperity to the State, and Glory to our Arms, from those free Kinds of Governments, which are to be erected in America.

And it is very true that no People ever had a finer opportunity to settle Things upon the best Foundations. But yet I fear that human Nature will be found to be the Same in America as it has been in Europe, and that the true Principles of Liberty will not be Sufficiently attended to.

Knowledge is among the most essential Foundations of Liberty. But is there not a Jealousy or an Envy taking Place among the Multitude of Men of Learning, and, a Wish to exclude them from the public Councils and from military Command? I could mention many Phenomena, in various Parts of these States, which indicate such a growing Disposition. To what Cause Shall I attribute the Surprizing Conduct of the Massachusetts Bay? How has it happened that such an illiterate Group of General and Field Officers, have been thrust into public View, by that Commonwealth which as it has an indisputable Superiority of Power to every other, in America as well as of Experience and Skill in War, ought to have set an Example to her sisters, by sending into the Field her best Men. Men of the most Genius Learning, Reflection, and Address. Instead of this, every Man you send into the Army as a General or a Collonell exhibits a Character, which nobody ever heard of before, or an aukward, illiterate, ill bred Man. . . .

This Conduct is Sinking the Character of the Province, into the lowest Contempt, and is injuring the service beyond description. Able Officers are the Soul of an Army. Good Officers will make good Soldiers, if you give them human Nature as a Material to work upon. But ignorant, unambitious, unfeeling unprincipled Officers, will make bad soldiers of the best Men in the World. . . .

If this is the Effect of popular Elections it is but a poor Pangyrick, upon such Elections. I fear We shall find that popular Elections are not oftener determined, upon pure Principles of Merit, Virtue, and public Spirit, than the Nominations of a Court, if We dont take Care. I fear there is an infinity of Corruption in our Elections already crept in. All kinds of Favour, Intrigue and Partiality in Elections are as real, Corruption in my Mind, as Treats and Bribes. A popular Government is the worse Curse, to which human Nature can be devoted when it is thoroughly corrupted. Despotism is better. A Sober, conscientious Habit, of electing for the public good alone must be introduced, and every Appearance of Interest, Favour, and Partiality, reprobated, or you will very soon make wise and honest Men wish for Monarchy again, nay you will make them introduce it into America.

There is another Particular, in which it is manifest that the Principles of Liberty have not sufficient Weight in Mens Minds, or are not well understood.

Equality of Representation in the Legislature, is a first Principle of Liberty, and the Moment, the least departure from such Equality takes Place, that Moment an Inroad is made upon Liberty. Yet this essential Principle is disregarded, in many Places, in several of these Republicks. Every County is to have an equal Voice altho some Counties are six times more numerous, and twelve times more wealthy. The Same Iniquity will be established in Congress. R.I. will have an equal Weight with the Mass. The Delaware Government with Pensilvania and Georgia with Virginia. Thus We are sowing the Seeds of Ignorance Corruption, and Injustice, in the fairest Field of Liberty, that ever appeared upon Earth, even in the first Attempts to cultivate it.

General George Washington Asks Congress for an Effective Army, 1776

To John Hancock, the President of Congress

Colonel Morris's, on the Heights of Harlem,

September 24, 1776

Sir:

From the hours allotted to Sleep, I will borrow a few Moments to convey my thoughts on sundry important matters to Congress. . . .

We are now as it were, upon the eve of another dissolution of our Army; . . . unless some speedy, and effectual measures are adopted by Congress, our cause will be lost.

It is in vain to expect, that any (or more than a trifling) part of this Army will again engage in the Service on the encouragement offered by Congress. When Men find that their Townsmen and Companions are receiving 20, 30, and more Dollars, for a few Months Service, (which is truely the case) it cannot be expected; without using compulsion; and to force them into the Service would answer no valuable purpose. When Men are irritated, and the Passions inflamed, they fly hastely and chearfully to Arms; but after the first emotions are over, to expect, among such People, as compose the bulk of an Army, that they are influenced by any other principles than those of Interest, is to look for what never did, and I fear never will happen; the Congress will deceive themselves therefore if they expect it.

A Soldier reasoned with upon the goodness of the cause he is engaged in, and the inestimable rights he is contending for, hears you with patience, and acknowledges the truth of your observations, but adds, that it is of no more Importance to him than others. The Officer makes you the same reply, with this further remark, that his pay will not support him, and he cannot ruin himself and Family to serve his Country, when every Member of the community is equally Interested and benefitted by his Labours. The few therefore, who act upon Principles of disinterestedness, are, comparatively speaking, no more than a drop in the Ocean. It becomes evidently clear then, that as this Contest is not likely to be the Work of a day; as the War must be carried on systematically, and to do it, you must have good Officers, there are, in my Judgment, no other possible means to obtain them but by establishing your Army upon a permanent footing; and giving your Officers good pay; this will induce Gentlemen, and Men of Character to engage; and till the bulk of your Officers are composed of such persons as are actuated by Principles of honour, and a spirit of enterprize, you have little to expect from them.—They ought to have such allowances as will enable them to live like, and support the Characters of Gentlemen; and not be driven by a scanty pittance to the low, and dirty arts which many of them practice, to filch the Public of more than the difference of pay would amount to upon an ample allowe. Besides, something is due to the Man who puts his life in his hands, hazards his health, and forsakes the Sweets of domestic enjoyments. . . . There is nothing that gives a Man consequence, and renders him fit for Command, like a support that renders him Independant of every body but the State he Serves.

With respect to the Men, nothing but a good bounty can obtain them upon a permanent establishment; and for no shorter time than the continuance of the War, ought they to be engaged; as Facts incontestibly prove, that the difficulty, and cost of Inlistments, increase with time. When the Army was first raised at Cambridge, I am persuaded the Men might have been got without a bounty for the War: after this, they began to see that the Contest was not likely to end so speedily as was immagined, and to feel their consequence, by remarking, that to get the Militia In, in the course of last year, many Towns were induced to give them a bounty. . . . I shall therefore take the freedom of giving it as my opinion, that a good Bounty be immediately offered, aided by the proffer of at least 100, or 150 Acres of Land and a suit of Cloaths and Blankt, to each non-Comd. Officer and Soldier; as I have good authority for saying, that however high the Men's pay may appear, it is barely sufficient in the present scarcity and dearness of all kinds of goods, to keep them in Cloaths, much less afford support to their Families. If this encouragement then is given to the Men, and such Pay allowed the Officers as will induce Gentlemen of Character and liberal Sentiments to engage; and proper care and precaution are used in the nomination (having more regard to the Characters of Persons, than the Number of Men they can Inlist) we should in a little time have an Army able to cope with any that can be opposed to it, as there are excellent Materials to form one out of: but while the only merit an Officer possesses is his ability to raise Men; while those Men consider, and treat him as an equal; and (in the Character of an Officer) regard him no more than a broomstick, being mixed together as one common herd; no order, nor no discipline can prevail; nor will the Officer ever meet with that respect which is essentially necessary to due subordination.

To place any dependance upon Militia, is, assuredly, resting upon a broken staff. Men just dragged from the tender Scenes of domestick life; unaccustomed to the din of Arms; totally unacquainted with every kind of Military skill, which being followed by a want of confidence in themselves, when opposed to Troops regularly train'd, disciplined, and appointed, superior in knowledge, and superior in Arms, makes them timid, and ready to fly from their own shadows. Besides, the sudden change in their manner of living, (particularly in the lodging) brings on sickness in many; impatience in all, and such an unconquerable desire of returning to their respective homes that it not only produces shameful, and scandalous Desertions among themselves, but infuses the like spirit in others. Again, Men accustomed to unbounded freedom, and no controul, cannot brook the Restraint which is indispensably necessary to the good order and Government of an Army; without which, licentiousness, and every kind of disorder triumphantly reign. To bring Men to a proper degree of Subordination, is not the work of a day, a Month or even a year; and unhappily for us, and the cause we are Engaged in, the little discipline I have been labouring to establish in the Army under my immediate Command, is in a manner done away by having such a mixture of Troops as have been called together within these few Months.

Relaxed, and unfit, as our Rules and Regulations of War are, for the Government of an Army, the Militia (those properly so called, for of these we have two sorts, the Six Months Men and those sent in as a temporary aid) do not think themselves subject to 'em, and therefore take liberties, which the Soldier is punished for; this creates jealousy; jealousy begets dissatisfaction, and these by degrees ripen into Mutiny; keeping the whole Army in a confused, and disordered State; rendering the time of those who wish to see regularity and good Order prevail more unhappy than Words can describe. Besides this, such repeated changes take place, that all arrangement is set at nought, and the constant fluctuation of things, deranges every plan, as fast as adopted.

These Sir, Congress may be assured, are but a small part of the Inconveniences which might be enumerated and attributed to Militia; but there is one that merits particular attention, and that is the expence. Certain I am, that it would be cheaper to keep 50, or 100,000 Men in constant pay than to depend upon half the number, and supply the other half occasionally by Militia. The time the latter is in pay before and after they are in Camp, assembling and Marching; the waste of Ammunition; the consumption of Stores, which in spite of every Resolution, and requisition of Congress they must be furnished with, or sent home, added to other incidental expences consequent upon their coming, and conduct in Camp, surpasses all Idea, and destroys every kind of regularity and œconomy which you could establish among fixed and Settled Troops; and will, in my opinion prove (if the scheme is adhered to) the Ruin of our Cause.

The Jealousies of a standing Army, and the Evils to be apprehended from one, are remote; and in my judgment, situated and circumstanced as we are, not at all to be dreaded; but the consequence of wanting one, according to my Ideas, formed from the present view of things, is certain, and inevitable Ruin. . . .

Another matter highly worthy of attention, is, that other Rules and Regulations may be adopted for the Government of the Army than those now in existence, otherwise the Army, but for the name, might as well be disbanded. For the most attrocious offences, (one or two Instances only excepted) a Man receives no more than 39 Lashes; and these perhaps (thro' the collusion of the Officer who is to see it inflicted), are given in such a manner as to become rather a matter of sport than punishment. . . . Of late, a practice prevails . . . of Plundering, for under the Idea of Tory property, or property which may fall into the hands of the Enemy, no Man is secure in his effects, and scarcely in his Person; for in order to get at them, we have several Instances of People being frightned out of their Houses under pretence of those Houses being ordered to be burnt, and this is done with a view of seizing the Goods; nay, in order that the villany may be more effectually concealed, some Houses have actually been burnt to cover the theft.

I have with some others, used my utmost endeavours to stop this horrid practice, but under the present lust after plunder, and want of Laws to punish Offenders, I might almost as well attempt to remove Mount Atlas.— I have ordered instant corporal Punishment upon every Man who passes our Lines, or is seen with Plunder. . . .

An Army formed of good Officers moves like Clock-Work; but there is no Situation upon Earth, less enviable, nor more distressing, than that Person's who is at the head of Troops, who are regardless of Order and discipline; and who are unprovided with almost every necessary.

Congress Calls on the States to Support the Continental Army, 1776

PHILADA. Sept. 24th, 1776.

Gentlemen,

You will perceive by the inclosed Resolves, which I have the honor to forward, in obedience to the Commands of Congress, that they have come to a determination to augment our Army, and to engage the Troops to serve during the War. As an Inducement to enlist on these Terms, the Congress have agreed to give, besides a Bounty of twenty dollars, a Hundred Acres of Land to each soldier; and in Case he should fall in Battle, they have resolved that his children, or other Representatives, shall succeed to such Land. . . .

The heavy and enormous expences consequent upon calling for the Militia, the Delay attending their Motions, and the Difficulty of keeping them in the Camp, render it extremely improper to place our whole dependence upon them. Experience hath uniformly convinced us of this, some of the Militia having actually deserted the Camp, at the very moment their services were most wanted. In the mean time the strength of the British Army which is great is rendered much more formidable by the Superior Order and Regularity which prevail in it.

Under these circumstances, and in this Situation of our affairs, it is evident that the Only Means left us of preserving our Liberties, is the Measure which the Congress have now adopted, and which I am ordered most earnestly to recommend to you, to carry into immediate effect. Without a well disciplined Army, we can never expect success agst veteran Troops; and it is totally impossible we should have a well disciplined Army, unless our Troops are engaged to serve during the war. To attain therefore this most desirable End, I am to request you will at once, and without a moments delay, bend all your attention to raise your Quota of the American army. . . .

British General John Burgoyne Tells Americans That His Cause Is Just and That the Patriots Are Vicious, 1777

The forces entrusted to my command, are designed to act in concert, and upon a common principle, with the numerous armies and fleets which already display in every quarter of America, the power, the justice, and, when properly sought, the mercy of the king.

The cause in which the British arms is thus exerted, applies to the most affecting interests of the human heart; and the military servants of the crown, at first called forth for the sole purpose of restoring the rights of the constitution, now combine with love of their country, and duty to their sovereign, the other extensive incitements, which form a due sense of the general privileges of mankind. To the eyes and ears of the temperate part of the public, and the breasts of suffering thousands, in the provinces, be the melancholy appeal, whether the present unnatural rebellion has not been made a foundation for the completest system of tyranny that ever God, in his displeasure, suffered for a time to be exercised over a forward and stubborn generation.

Arbitrary imprisonment, confiscation of property, persecution, and torture, unprecedented in the inquisition of the Romish church, are among the palpable enormities that verify the affirmative. These are inflicted, by assemblies and committees, who dare to profess themselves friends to liberty, upon the most quiet subjects, without distinction of age or sex, for the sole crime, often for the sole suspicion, of having adhered in principle to the government under which they were born, and to which, by every tie, divine and human, they owe allegiance. To consummate these shocking proceedings, the profanation of religion is added to the most profligate prostitution of common reason, the consciences of men are set at nought; and multitudes are compelled not only to bear arms, but also to swear subjection to an usurpation they abhor. . . .

The intention of this address is to hold forth security, not depredation to the country. To those, whom spirit and principle may induce to partake the glorious task of redeeming their countrymen from dungeons, and re-establishing the blessings of legal government, I offer encouragement and employment; and, upon the first intelligence of their association, I will find means to assist their undertakings. The domestic, the industrious, the infirm, and even the timid inhabitants, I am desirous to protect, provided they remain quietly at their houses; that they do not suffer their cattle to be removed, nor their corn or forage to be secreted or destroyed; that they do not break up their bridges or roads; nor by any other act, directly or indirectly, endeavor to obstruct the operations of the king's troops, or supply or assist those of the enemy.

Every species of provision, brought to my camp, will be paid for at an equitable rate, and in solid coin.

In consciousness of christianity, my royal master's clemency, and the honor of soldiership, I have dwelt upon this invitation, and wished for more persuasive terms to give it impression. And let not people be led to disregard it, by considering their distance from the immediate situation of my camp. I have but to give stretch to the Indian forces under my direction—and they amount to thousands—to overtake the hardened enemies of Great Britain and America. I consider them the same, wherever they may lurk.

If, notwithstanding these endeavors, and sincere inclinations to effect them, the phrenzy of hostility should remain, I trust I shall stand acquitted in the eyes of God and men in denouncing and executing the vengeance of the state against the wilful outcasts. The messengers of justice and of wrath await them in the field: and devastation, famine, and every concomitant horror, that a reluctant, but indispensable prosecution of military duty must occasion, will bar the way to their return.

A Veteran Remembers the Battle of Saratoga, 1777

About the tenth day of August, 1777, he was enrolled as a volunteer soldier in a military company under the command of said Capt. Asa Bray at said Southington [in Connecticut] and marched with them through Albany to Saratoga. . . . He would further state that while in this service at Saratoga he was engaged in the battle fought by the hostile armies on the seventh of October, the following particulars of which, together with many others which might be related, he distinctly remembers: viz., that about eleven o'clock in the forenoon of that day, the British troops advanced under the command of General Fraser, who led up the grenadiers, drove in our pickets and advanced guards, and made several unsuccessful charges with fixed bayonets upon the line of the Continental troops at the American redoubts on Bemis Heights, near the headquarters of General Gates. But meeting a repulse at this point of attack, the grenadiers commenced a slow but orderly retreat, still keeping up a brisk fire. After falling back two or three hundred yards, this part of the hostile army met and joined with the main body of the royal troops commanded by Lord Balcarres and General Riedesel. Here, on a level piece of ground of considerable extent called Freeman's Farms, thinly covered with yellow pines, the royal army formed an extensive line with the principal part of their artillery in front. By this time the American line was formed, consisting of Continentals, state troops, and militia. The fire immediately became general through the line with renewed spirit, and nearly the whole force on both sides was brought into action. General Fraser, mounted on a gray horse a little to the right of their center and greatly distinguishing himself by his activity, received a rifle shot through his body (supposed to be from one of Colonel Morgan's sharpshooters), of which he died the next morning at eight o'clock at the Smith house, then the headquarters of General Burgoyne. Soon after this occurrence, the British grenadiers began reluctantly to give ground, and their whole line, within a few minutes, appeared broken. Still, they kept up a respectable fire, both of artillery and musketry.

At about this stage in the action, General Arnold, while galloping up and down our line upon a small brown horse which he had that day borrowed of his friend Leonard Chester of Wethersfield, received a musket ball which broke his leg and killed the horse under him. He was at that moment about forty yards distant from this applicant and in fair view. Isaac Newell of said Southington, since deceased, and one or two others assisted this applicant to extricate Arnold from his fallen horse, placed him on a litter, and sent him back to the headquarters of General Gates.

A regiment of the royal grenadiers, with the brave Major Ackland at their head, in conducting the retreat came to a small cultivated field enclosed by a fence. Here they halted, formed, and made a stand, apparently determined to retrieve what they had lost by their repulse at the redoubts in the commencement of the action. They placed in their center and at each flank a strong battery of brass fieldpieces. The carnage became frightful, but the conflict was of short duration. Their gallant major received a musket ball through both legs, which placed him hors de combat. Retreat immediately ensued, leaving their killed and some of their wounded with two brass fieldpieces on the ground. Ackland, leaning upon a stump of a tree in the corner of the fence, was made prisoner by Adjutant General Wilkinson and his servant, who were passing by. They dismounted from their horses and, placing the major on the servant's horse, sent him to General Gates's headquarters to have his wounds dressed.

The retreat, pursuit, and firing continued till eight o'clock. It was then dark. The royal army continued their retreat about a mile further and there bivouacked for the night. Ours returned to camp, where we arrived between nine and ten o'clock in the evening. About two hundred of our wounded men, during the afternoon, and by that time in the evening, were brought from the field of battle in wagons, and for want of tents, sheds, or any kind of buildings to receive and cover them, were placed in a circular row on the naked ground. It was a clear, but cold and frosty, night. The sufferings of the wounded were extreme, having neither beds under them nor any kind of bed clothing to cover them. Several surgeons were busily employed during the night extracting bullets and performing other surgical operations. This applicant, though greatly fatigued by the exercise of the day, felt no inclination to sleep, but with several others spent the whole night carrying water and administering what other comforts were in our power to the sufferers, about seventy of whom died of their wounds during the night.

The next day (October 8th), this applicant was detached from our company to assist others detached from other companies in burying the dead remaining on the field of battle. This was a sad and laborious day's work. On the cleared field already mentioned and within the compass of a quarter of an acre of ground we found and assisted to bury between twenty and thirty dead bodies of the royal grenadiers. The brigade in which this term of service was performed was commanded by Gen. Oliver Wolcott [one of Connecticut's signers of the Declaration of Independence] of Litchfield. . . .

American Diplomats Press for a French Alliance, 1777

Passy, Dec. 8. 1777

To his Excellency the Count de Vergennes.

The Commissioners from the Congress of the United States of America, beg leave to represent to your Excellency, that it is near a year since they had the Honour of putting into your Hands the Propositions of the Congress for a Treaty of Amity and Commerce with this Kingdom, to which, with sundry other Propositions contained in subsequent Memorials, requesting the Aid of Ships of War, and offering Engagements to unite the Forces of the said States with those of France and Spain in acting against the Dominions of Great Britain, and to make no Peace but in Conjunction with those Courts, if Britain should declare War with them; to all which they have yet received no determinate Answer; and apprehending that a Continuance of this State of Uncertainty with regard to those Propositions, together with the Reports that must soon be spread in America of rigorous Treatment met with by our Armed Ships in the Ports of these Kingdoms, may give Advantage to our Enemies in making ill Impressions on the Minds of our People, who, from the Secrecy enjoyn'd us, cannot be informed of the Friendly and essential Aids that have been so generously but privately afforded us; the Commissioners conceive that, the present Circumstances considered, the compleating such a Treaty at this Time would have the most happy Effect, in raising the Credit of the United States abroad, and strengthening their Resolutions at Home; as well as discouraging and diminishing their internal Enemies, and confirming their Friends that might otherwise waver: And the Commissioners are further of Opinion that the Aid of Ships desired might at this Juncture be employed to great Advantage in America, which when honour'd with a Conference they could more particularly explain. They therefore request your Excellency most earnestly to resume the Consideration of those Affairs, and appoint them some speedy Day of Audience thereupon.

They also pray that their grateful Acknowledgements may be presented to the King for the additional Aid of three Millions which he has been so graciously pleased to promise them; and that his Majesty may be assured whatever Engagements they may enter into in behalf of the United States, in pursuance of the full Powers they are vested with, will be executed with the most punctual Good Faith by the Congress, who believing their Interests to be the same, and that a secure Increase of the Commerce, Wealth and Strength of France and Spain will be one Consequence of their Success in this Contest, wish for nothing so much, after establishing their own Liberty, as a firm and everlasting Union with these Nations.

American Diplomats Report Success, 1777

Passy, Dec. 18. 1777.

Gentlemen,

Since our last of Nov. 30, a Copy of which is herewith sent you, we received your Dispatches of Oct. 6. from York Town. They came to us by a Packet from Boston, which brought the great News of Burgoynes Defeat and Surrender, News that apparently occasion'd as much general Joy in France, as if it had been a Victory of their own Troops over their own Enemies; such is the universal warm and sincere Goodwill and Attachment to us and our Cause in this Nation.

We took the Opportunity of pressing the Ministry by a short Memorial to the Conclusion of our propos'd Treaty which had so long lain under their Consideration, and been from time to time postponed: A Meeting was had accordingly on friday the 12th Inst. in which some Difficulties were mention'd and remov'd, some Explications ask'd and given, to Satisfaction. As the Concurrance of Spain is necessary, we were told, that a Courier should be dispatch'd the next Day to obtain it, which we are since assured was done; and in three Weeks from the Time the Answer is expected.

On signifying to the Ministry the Importance it might be of at this Juncture, when probably Britain would be making some Propositions of Accomodation, that the Congress should be inform'd explicitly, what might be expected from France and Spain, M. Gerard, one of the Secretaries, came Yesterday to inform us by order of the King, that after long and full Consideration of our Affairs and Propositions in Council, it was decided and his Majesty was determined to acknowledge our Independence and make a Treaty with us of Amity and Commerce; that in this Treaty no Advantage would be taken of our present Situation to obtain Terms from us which otherwise would not be convenient for us to agree to, his Majesty desiring that the Treaty once made should be durable, and our Amity subsist forever, which could not be expected if each Nation did not find its Interest in the Continuance as well as in the Commencement of it. It was therefore his

Intention that the Terms of the Treaty should be such as we might be willing to agree to, if our State had been long since established, and in the fullness of Strength and Power, and such as we shall approve of when that time shall come. That his Majesty was fix'd in his Determination, not only to acknowledge but to support our Independence, by every means in his Power. That in doing this he might probably be soon engag'd in War, with all the Expences, Risque and Damage usually attending it; yet he should not expect any Compensation from us on that Account, nor pretend that he acted wholly for our Sakes, since besides his real Goodwill to us and our Cause, it was manifestly the Interest of France that the Power of England should be diminish'd by our Separation from it. He should moreover not so much as insist, that if he engag'd in a War with England on our Account we should not make a separate Peace, he would have us be at full Liberty to make a peace for ourselves, whenever good and advantageous Terms were offered to us: The only Condition he should require and rely on would be this, that we in no Peace to be made with England should give up our Independency, and return to the Obedience of that Government. . . .

It is sometime since we obtain'd a Promise of an additional Aid of three Millions of Livres, which we shall receive in January. Spain we are told will give an equal Sum but finding it inconvenient to remit here, she purposes sending it from the Havana in specie to the Congress. What we receive here will help to get us out of Debt.

Our Vessels laden with Supplies have by various means been delay'd, particularly by fear of falling into the Hands of the English cruizing Ships, who swarm in the Bay and Channel. At length it is resolv'd they shall sail together, as they are all provid'd for Defence, and we have obtain'd a King's Ship to convoy them out of the Channel, and we hope quite to America. They will carry we think to the amount of £70,000 Sterling and sail in a few Days. Also, in Consideration of the late frequent Losses of our Dispatches and the Importance of the present, we have apply'd for and obtain'd a Fregate to carry them. These extraordinary Favours, of a Nature provoking to Great Britain, are marks of the Sincerity of this Court, and seem to demand the Thanks of the Congress. . . .

The Supplies now going out from hence, and what we have sent and are sending from Spain, tho' far short of your Orders (which we have executed as far as we are able) will we hope, with private Adventures encourag'd by us, and others, put you into pretty good Circumstances as to Clothing, Arms, &c. if they arrive: And we shall continue to send, as Ability and Opportunity may permit. . . .

B. FRANKLIN   SILAS DEANE   ARTHUR LEE

The Treaties of Alliance with France, 1778

LEWIS, by the grace of God king of France and Navarre, to all who shall see these presents, Greeting.

The Congress of the thirteen United States of North America having made known to us, by their plenipotentiaries residing at Paris, their desire to establish between us and our dominions a good understanding, and a perfect correspondence; and having for that purpose proposed to conclude with us a treaty of amity and commerce; and we having thought it our duty to give to the said states a sensible proof of our affection, by a determination to accept of their proposals: . . .

In testimony whereof, we have hereunto set our seal.

Done at Versailles, this thirtieth day of January, in the year of our Lord, one thousand seven hundred and seventy-eight, and the fourth year of our reign.

Signed,   Louis.
By the King.
Gravier de Vergennes.

Treaty of Amity and Commerce

The most Christian King and the thirteen United States of North America, viz. New Hampshire, Massachusetts Bay, Rhode Island, Connecticut, New York, New Jersey, Pennsylvania, Delaware, Maryland, Virginia, North Carolina, South Carolina and Georgia, willing to fix in an equitable and permanent manner the rules which ought to be followed relative to the correspondence and commerce which the two parties desire to establish between their respective countries, states, and subjects; his most christian majesty and the said United States have judged that the said end could not be better obtained, than by taking, for the basis of their agreement, the most perfect equality and reciprocity, and by carefully avoiding all those burdensome preferences which are usually sources of debate, embarrassment, and discontent, by leaving also each party at liberty to make, respecting navigation and commerce, those interiour regulations which it shall find most convenient to itself, and by founding the advantage of commerce solely upon reciprocal utility and the just rules of free intercourse, reserving withal to each party the liberty of admitting, at its pleasure, other nations to a participation of the same advantages. . . .

Article I. There shall be a firm, inviolable and universal peace, and a true and sincere friendship between the most christian king, his heirs, and successors, and the United States of America, and the subjects of the most christian king and of the said states, and between the countries, islands, cities and towns situated under the jurisdiction of the most christian king, and of the said United States. . . .

Art. II. The most christian king and the United States engage, mutually, not to grant any particular favour to other nations in respect to commerce and navigation, which shall not immediately become common to the other party. . . .

Art. III. The subjects of the most christian king shall pay in the ports, havens, roads, countries, islands, cities or towns of the United States, or any of them, no other greater duties or imposts, of what nature soever they may be, or by what name soever called, than those which the nations most favoured are, or shall be obliged to pay. . . .

Art. IV. The subjects, people and inhabitants of the said United States, and each of them, shall not pay in the ports, havens, roads, isles, cities and places under the domination of his most christian majesty, in Europe, any other or greater duties or imposts, of what nature soever they may be, or by what name soever called, than those which the most favoured nations are or shall be obliged to pay. . . .

Art. VI. The most christian king shall endeavour, by all the means in his power, to protect and defend all vessels and the effects belonging to the subjects, people, or inhabitants of the said United States, or any of them, being in his ports, havens or roads, or on the seas near to his countries, islands, cities or towns. . . .

Art. VII. In like manner the said United States, and their ships of war sailing under their authority, shall protect and defend, conformably to the tenor of the preceding article, all the vessels and effects belonging to the subjects of the most christian king. . . .

Art. XXXI. The two contracting parties grant, mutually, the liberty of having each in the ports of the other, consuls, vice-consuls, agents and commissaries. . . .

Art. XXXII. And the more to favour and facilitate the commerce which the subjects of the United States may have with France, the most christian king will grant them, in Europe, one or more free ports, where they may bring and dispose of all the produce and merchandise of the thirteen United States; and his majesty will also continue to the subjects of the said states the free ports which have been and are open in the French Islands of America; of all which free ports, the said subjects of the United States shall enjoy the use, agreeable to the regulations which relate to them.

Art. XXXIII. The present treaty shall be ratified on both sides, and the ratifications shall be exchanged, in the space of six months, or sooner if possible.

In faith whereof the respective plenipotentiaries have signed the above articles, both in the French and English languages; declaring, nevertheless, that the present treaty was originally composed and concluded in the French language. And they have thereto set their seals.

Done at Paris, the sixth day of February, 1778.

C. A. Gerard
B. Franklin
Silas Deane
Arthur Lee

Treaty of Alliance, Eventual and Defensive

The most Christian King, and the United States of North America . . . having this day concluded a treaty of amity and commerce, for the reciprocal advantage of their subjects and citizens, have thought it necessary to take into consideration the means of strengthening those engagements, and of rendering them useful to the safety and tranquillty of the two parties; particularly in case Great Britain, in resentment of that connexion and of the good correspondence which is the object of the said treaty, should break the peace with France, either by direct hostilities, or by hindering her commerce and navigation in a manner contrary to the rights of nations, and the peace subsisting between the two crowns. And his majesty and the said United States, having resolved, in that case, to join their counsels and efforts against the enterprises of their common enemy . . . determined on the following articles.

Article I. If war should break out between France and Great Britain, during the continuance of the present war between the United States and England, his majesty and the said United States shall make it a common cause, and aid each other mutually with their good offices, their counsels, and their forces, according to the exigence of conjunctures, as becomes good and faithful allies.

Art. II. The essential and direct end of the present defensive alliance is, to maintain effectually the liberty, sovereignty, and independence absolute and unlimited of the said United States, as well in matters of government as of commerce.

Art. III. The two contracting parties shall, each on its own part, and in the manner it may judge most proper, make all the efforts in its power against their common enemy, in order to attain the end proposed.

Art. IV. The contracting parties agree, that in case either of them should form any particular enterprise in which the concurrence of the other may be desired, the party whose concurrence is desired shall readily, and with good faith, join to act in concert for that purpose, as far as circumstances, and its own particular situation, will permit; and in that case, they shall regulate, by a particular convention, the quantity and kind of succour to be furnished, and the time and manner of its being brought into action, as well as the advantages which are to be its compensation.

Art. V. If the United States should think fit to attempt the reduction of the British power remaining in the northern parts of America, or the islands of Bermudas, those countries or islands, in case of success, shall be confederated with, or dependent upon, the said United States.

Art. VI. The most christian king renounces for ever the possession of the islands of Bermudas, as well as of any part of the continent of North America which, before the treaty of Paris in 1763, or in virtue of that treaty, were acknowledged to belong to the crown of Great Britain, or to the United States heretofore called British colonies, or which are at this time, or have lately been, under the power of the king and crown of Great Britain.

Art. VII. If his most christian majesty shall think proper to attack any of the islands situated in the gulf of Mexico, or near that gulf, which are at present under the power of Great Britain, all the said isles, in case of success, shall appertain to the crown of France.

Art. VIII. Neither of the two parties shall conclude either truce or peace with Great Britain, without the formal consent of the other first obtained; and they mutually engage not to lay down their arms until the independence of the United States shall have been formally, or tacitly, assured by the treaty or treaties, that shall terminate the war.

Art. IX. The contracting parties declare, that, being resolved to fulfil, each on its own part, the clauses and conditions of the present treaty of alliance, according to its own power and circumstances, there shall be no after claim of compensation on one side or the other, whatever may be the event of the war.

Art. X. The most christian king and the United States agree to invite or admit other powers, who may have received injuries from England, to make common cause with them, and to accede to the present alliance, under such conditions as shall be freely agreed to and settled between all the parties.

Art. XI. The two parties guarantee, mutually, from the present time and forever, against all other powers, to wit, the United States to his most christian majesty, the present possessions of the crown of France in America, as well as those which it may acquire by the future treaty of peace; and his most christian majesty guarantees, on his part, to the United States, their liberty, sovereignty, and independence, absolute and unlimited, as well in matters of government as of commerce, and also their possessions, and the additions or conquests that their confederation may obtain during the war, from any of the dominions now or heretofore possessed by Great Britain in North America. . . .

Art. XIII. The present treaty shall be ratified on both sides; and the ratification shall be exchanged in the space of six months or sooner if possible.

In faith whereof the respective plenipotentiaries, to wit, on the part of the most christian king, Conrad Alexander Gérard, royal syndic of the city of Strasburg, and secretary of his majesty's council of state; and on the part of the United States, Benjamin Franklin, deputy of the general Congress from the state of Pennsylvania and president of the convention of the said State, Silas Deane, heretofore deputy from the state of Connecticut, and Arthur Lee, counsellor at law, have signed the above articles, both in the French and English languages; declaring, nevertheless, that the present treaty was originally composed and concluded in the French language; and they have hereunto affixed their seals.

Done at Paris, this 6th day of February, one thousand seven hundred and seventy-eight.

C. A. GERARD
B. FRANKLIN
SILAS DEANE
ARTHUR LEE

✕ *E S S A Y S*

In the first essay, John W. Shy, the distinguished University of Michigan scholar of war and society in early America, explores the complex interplay of interests confronting Congress and American soldiers during the war. By comparing myths and realities in his essay on "Long Bill" Scott, Shy reveals that the question of motive—why men fought—may be answered at several levels. In the second essay, Alexander DeConde's analysis of how historians have explained the French alliance reveals the complexities of international politics in the Revolutionary era.

Professor DeConde, of the University of California, Santa Barbara, has been a scholar of American diplomacy for over thirty years and has specialized in Franco-American relations in the early national era.

Hearts and Minds: The Case of "Long Bill" Scott

JOHN W. SHY

Armed force, and nothing else, decided the outcome of the American Revolution. . . . Crude, obvious, and unappealing as this truism may be, it is still true; without war to sustain it, the Declaration of Independence would be a forgotten, abortive manifesto. Writing about an earlier revolutionary war, Thomas Hobbes rammed home the point when he said that "covenants without swords are but words."

But the cynicism of Hobbes can too easily mask a second, equally important truism, perhaps best expressed a century later by David Hume. "As force is always on the side of the governed," Hume wrote, "the governors have nothing to support them but opinion." For all their peculiar aggressiveness, even human beings do not kill and risk death for no reason. Beneath the raw irrationality of violence lies motive—some psychic web spun from logic, belief, perception, and emotion that draws people to commit terrible acts and to hazard everything they possess. . . . If Hobbes—like all his fellow cynics down through history—is right in believing that public opinion is a fairly fragile flower which can seldom survive the hot wind of violence, Hume reminds us that no one, not even a soldier, uses force without somehow being moved to do so.

John Adams put his finger on this matter of motivation when he said that the real American Revolution, the revolution that estranged American hearts from old British loyalties and readied American minds to use (and to withstand) massive violence, was over before the war began. But Adams also opined that a third of the American people supported the Revolutionary cause, another third remained more or less loyal to Britain, and that the rest were neutral or apathetic. Clearly, Adams conceded that not all hearts and minds had been permanently affected in the same way. Many British observers thought that the real American Revolutionaries were the religious Dissenters, Congregationalists and Presbyterians who had always been secretly disloyal to the Crown because they rejected the whole Anglican Establishment, whose head was the king; and that these Revolutionaries persuaded poor Irishmen, who poured into the American colonies in great numbers during the middle third of the eighteenth century, to do most of the dirty business of actual fighting. American Whigs, on the other hand, generally assumed that all decent, sane people supported the Revolution, and that those who did not could be categorized as timid, vicious, corrupt, or deluded. . . .

Like these stock opinions, we have two standard images of the popular response to the Revolutionary War. One is of whole towns springing to arms as Paul Revere carried his warning to them in the spring of 1775. The other is of a tiny, frozen, naked band of men at Valley Forge, all that are left when everyone else went home in the winter of 1778. Which is the true picture? Both, evidently. But that answer is of no use at all when we ask whether the Revolution succeeded only by the persistence of a very small group of people, the intervention of France, and great good luck; or whether the Revolution was—or became—unbeatable because the mass of the population simply would not give up the struggle, and the British simply could not muster the force and the resolution to kill them all or break their will or sit on all or even any large proportion of them. This problem posed by the motivation for violence breaks down into more specific questions: Who actually took up arms and why? How strong was the motivation to serve, and to keep serving in spite of defeat and other adversities? What was the intricate interplay and feedback between attitude and behavior, events and attitude? Did people get war weary and discouraged, or did they become adamant toward British efforts to coerce them? If we could answer these questions with confidence, not only would we know why the rebels won and the government lost, but we would also know important things about the American society that emerged from seven years of armed conflict. . . .

The essential difficulty in answering these questions lies less in the lack of evidence than in the nature of the subject. Violence, with all its ramifications, remains a great mystery for students of human life, while the deeper motivational sources of human behavior—particularly collective behavior under conditions of stress—are almost equally mysterious. . . .

A suitably humble approach to these difficult questions lies at hand in a book written by Peter Oliver, who watched the Revolution explode in Boston. Oliver descended from some of the oldest families of Massachusetts Bay, he was a distinguished merchant and public official, and he became a bitter Tory. His book, *The Origin and Progress of the American Rebellion,* . . . is a fascinatingly unsympathetic version of the Revolution, and in it Oliver makes an attempt to answer some of our questions. . . . Oliver asked a wounded American lieutenant, who had been captured at Bunker Hill, how he had come to be a rebel. The American officer allegedly replied as follows:

> The case was this Sir! I lived in a Country Town; I was a Shoemaker, & got my Living by my Labor. When this Rebellion came on, I saw some of my Neighbors get into Commission, who were no better than myself. I was very ambitious, & did not like to see those Men above me. I was asked to enlist, as a private Soldier. My Ambition was too great for so low a Rank; I offered to enlist upon having a Lieutenants Commission; which was granted. I imagined my self now in a way of Promotion: if I was killed in Battle, there would an end of me, but if my Captain was killed, I should rise in Rank, & should still have a Chance to rise higher. These Sir! were the only Motives of my entering into the Service; for as to the Dispute

between great Britain & the Colonies, I know nothing of it; neither am I capable of judging whether it is right or wrong.

Now the lieutenant was not a figment of Oliver's embittered imagination. His name is given by Oliver as Scott, and American records show that Lieutenant William Scott, of Colonel Paul Sargent's regiment, was indeed wounded and captured at Bunker Hill. Scott turns out, upon investigation, to have been an interesting character. Perhaps the first thing to be said about him is that nothing in the record of his life down to 1775 contradicts anything in Oliver's account of the interview. Scott came from Peterborough, New Hampshire, a town settled in the 1730s by Irish Presbyterians. Scott's father had served in the famous Rogers' Rangers during the French and Indian War. At the news of the outbreak of fighting in 1775, a cousin who kept the store in Peterborough recruited a company of local men to fight the British. Apparently the cousin tried to enlist our William Scott—known to his neighbors as "Long Bill," thus distinguishing him from the cousin, "Short Bill." But "Long Bill"—our Bill—seems to have declined serving as a private, and insisted on being a lieutenant if cousin "Short Bill" was going to be a captain. "Short Bill" agreed. So far the stories as told by Oliver and as revealed in the New Hampshire records check perfectly. Nor is there any reason to think that "Long Bill" had a deeper understanding of the causes of the Revolution than appear in Oliver's version of the interview.

What Peter Oliver never knew was the subsequent life history of this battered yokel, whose view of the American rebellion seemed so pitifully naive. When the British evacuated Boston, they took Scott and other American prisoners to Halifax, Nova Scotia. There, after more than a year in captivity, Scott somehow managed to escape, to find a boat, and to make his way back to the American army just in time for the fighting around New York City in 1776. Captured again in November, when Fort Washington and its garrison fell to a surprise British assault, Scott escaped almost immediately, this time by swimming the Hudson River at night—according to a newspaper account—with his sword tied around his neck and his watch pinned to his hat. He returned to New Hampshire during the winter of 1777 to recruit a company of his own; there, he enlisted his two eldest sons for three years or the duration of the war. Stationed in the Boston area, he marched against Burgoyne's invading army from Canada, and led a detachment that cut off the last retreat just before the surrender near Saratoga. Scott later took part in the fighting around Newport, Rhode Island. But when his light infantry company was ordered to Virginia under Lafayette in early 1781, to counter the raiding expedition led by Benedict Arnold, Scott's health broke down; long marches and hot weather would make the old Bunker Hill wounds ache, and he was permitted to resign from the army. After only a few months of recuperation, however, he seems to have grown restless, for we find him during the last year of the war serving as a volunteer on a navy frigate.

What would Scott have said if Oliver had been able to interview him again, after the war? We can only guess. Probably he would have told Oliver that his oldest son had died in the army, not gloriously, but of camp fever, after six years of service. Scott might have said that in 1777 he had sold his Peterborough farm in order to meet expenses, but that the note which he took in exchange turned into a scrap of paper when the dollar of 1777 became worth less than two cents by 1780. He might also have said that another farm, in Groton, Massachusetts, slipped away from him, along with a down payment that he had made on it, when his military pay depreciated rapidly to a fraction of its nominal value. He might not have been willing to admit that when his wife died he simply turned their younger children over to his surviving elder son, and then set off to beg a pension or a job from the government. Almost certainly he would not have told Oliver that when the son—himself sick, his corn crop killed by a late frost, and saddled with three little brothers and sisters—begged his father for help, our hero told him, should all else fail, to hand the children over to the selectmen of Peterborough—in short, to put them on welfare.

In 1792, "Long Bill" Scott once more made the newspapers: he rescued eight people from drowning when their small boat capsized in New York harbor. But heroism did not pay very well. At last, in 1794, Secretary of War Henry Knox made Scott deputy storekeeper at West Point; and a year later General Benjamin Lincoln took Scott with him to the Ohio country, where they were to negotiate with the Indians and survey the land opened up by Anthony Wayne's victory at Fallen Timbers. At last he had a respectable job, and even a small pension for his nine wounds; but Lincoln's group caught something called "lake fever" while surveying on the Black River, near Sandusky. Scott, ill himself, guided part of the group back to Fort Stanwix, New York, then returned for the others. It was his last heroic act. A few days after his second trip, he died, on September 16, 1796.

Anecdotes, even good ones like the touching saga of "Long Bill" Scott, do not make history; . . . yet the story of his life leads us directly—and at the level of ordinary people—toward crucial features of the process.

Peterborough, New Hampshire, in 1775 had a population of 549. Town, state, and federal records show that about 170 men were credited to Peterborough as performing some military service during the Revolution. In other words, almost every adult male, at one time or another, carried a gun in the war. But of these 170 participants, less than a third performed extensive service; that is, service ranging from over a year up to the whole eight years of the war. And only a fraction of these—less than two dozen—served as long as Bill Scott. In Scott we are not seeing a typical participant, but one of a small "hard core" of revolutionary fighters—the men who stayed in the army for more than a few months or a single campaign. As we look down the list of long-service soldiers from Peterborough, they seem indeed to be untypical people. A few, like Scott and his cousin "Short Bill" and James Taggart and Josiah Munroe, became officers or at least sergeants, and thereby acquired status and perhaps some personal satisfaction from their prolonged military service. But most of the hard core remained privates, and they were an unusually poor, obscure group of men, even by the rustic standards of Peterborough. Many—like John Alexander, Robert Cunningham, William Ducannon, Joseph Henderson, Richard Richardson, John Wallace, and Thomas Williamson—were recruited from outside the town, from among men who never really lived in Peterborough. Whether they lived *anywhere*—in the strict legal sense—is a question. Two men—Zaccheus Brooks and John Miller—are simply noted as "transients." At least two—James Hackley and Randall McAllister—were deserters from the British army. At least two others—Samuel Weir and Titus Wilson—were black men, Wilson dying as a prisoner of war. A few, like Michael Silk, simply appear, join the army, then vanish without a documentary trace. Many more reveal themselves as near the bottom of the socioeconomic ladder: Hackley, Benjamin Allds, Isaac Mitchell, Ebenezer Perkins, Amos Spofford, Jonathan Wheelock, and Charles White were legal paupers after the Revolution, Joseph Henderson was a landless day-laborer, Samuel Spear was jailed for debt, and John Miller was mentally deranged.

We can look at the whole Peterborough contingent in another way, in terms of those in it who were, or later became, prominent or at least solid citizens of the town. With a few exceptions, like "Short Bill" Scott and "Long Bill" 's son John, who survived frost-killed corn and a parcel of unwanted siblings to become a selectman and a leader of the town, these prominent men and solid citizens had served in the war for only short periods—a few months in 1775, a month or two in the Burgoyne emergency of 1777, maybe a month in Rhode Island or a month late in the war to bolster the key garrison of West Point. The pattern is clear, and it is a pattern that reappears wherever the surviving evidence has permitted a similar kind of inquiry. Lynn, Massachusetts; Berks County, Pennsylvania; Colonel Smallwood's recruits from Maryland in 1782; several regiments of the Massachusetts Line; a sampling of pension applicants from Virginia— all show that the hard core of Continental soldiers, the Bill Scotts who could not wrangle commissions, the soldiers at Valley Forge, the men who shouldered the heaviest military burden, were something *less* than average colonial Americans. As a group, they were poorer, more marginal, less well anchored in the society. Perhaps we should not be surprised; it is easy to imagine men like these actually being attracted by the relative affluence, comfort, security, prestige, and even the chance for satisfying human relationships offered by the Continental army. Revolutionary America may have been a middle-class society, happier and more prosperous than any other in its time, but it contained a large and growing number of fairly poor people, and many of them did much of the actual fighting and suffering between 1775 and 1783: A very old story.

The large proportion of men, from Peterborough and other communities, who served only briefly might thus seem far less important to our subject than the disadvantaged minority who did such a large part of the heavy work of revolution. This militarily less active majority were of course the militiamen. One could compile a large volume of pithy observations, beginning with a few dozen from Washington himself, in which the military value of the militia was called into question. The nub of the critique was that these part-time soldiers were untrained, undisciplined, undependable, and very expensive, consuming pay, rations, clothing, and weapons at a great rate in return for short periods of active service. . . .

To understand the Revolutionary militia and its role, we must go back to the year before the outbreak of fighting at Lexington and Concord. Each colony, except Pennsylvania, had traditionally required every free white adult male, with a few minor occupational exceptions, to be inscribed in a militia unit, and to take part in training several times a year. . . . Their real function might be described as a hybrid of draft board and modern reserve unit—a modicum of military training combined with a mechanism to find and enlist individuals when they were needed. But the colonial militia did not simply slide smoothly into the Revolution. Militia officers, even where they were elected, held royal commissions, and a significant number of them were not enthusiastic about rebellion. Purging and restructuring the militia was an important step toward revolution, one that deserves more attention than it has had.

When the news reached America that Parliament would take a very hard line in response to the Boston Tea Party, and in particular had passed a law that could destroy, economically and politically, the town of Boston, the reaction in the colonies was stronger and more nearly unanimous than at any time since the Stamp Act. No one could defend the Boston Port Act; it was an unprecedented, draconian law, the possible consequences of which seemed staggering. Radicals, like Samuel Adams, demanded an immediate and complete break in commercial relations with the rest of the Empire. Boycotts had worked effectively in the past, and they were an obvious response to the British hard line. More moderate leaders, however, dreaded a hasty confrontation that might quickly escalate beyond their control, and they used democratic theory to argue that nothing ought to be done without a full and proper consultation of the popular will. Like the boycott, the consultative congress had a respectable pedigree, and the moderates won the argument. When Congress met in September 1774 there were general expectations in both Britain and America that it would cool and seek to compromise the situation.

Exactly what happened to disappoint those expectations is even now not wholly clear; our own sense that Congress was heading straight toward revolution and independence distorts a complex moment in history, when uncertainty about both ends and means deeply troubled the minds of most decision-makers. Congress had hardly convened when it heard that the British had bombarded Boston. For a few days men from different colonies, normally suspicious of one another, were swept together by a wave of common fear and apprehension. Though the report was quickly proved false, these hours of mutual panic seem to have altered the emotional economy of the Congress. Soon afterward it passed without any serious dissent a resolution in favor of the long-advocated boycott, to be known as the Association. Local committees were to gather signatures for the Association, and were to take necessary steps to enforce its provisions. The Association was the vital link in transforming the colonial militia into a revolutionary organization. . . .

In some places, like Peterborough, the same men who were enrolled in the militia became the strong right arm of the local committee; reluctant militia officers were ignored because, after all, not the militia as such but a voluntary association of militia members was taking the action. . . . The new Revolutionary militia might look very much like the old colonial militia, but it was, in its origins, less a draft board and a reserve training unit than a police force and an instrument of political surveillance. Although the boycott could be defended to moderate men as a constitutional, non-violent technique, its implementation had radical consequences. Adoption by Congress gave it a legitimacy and a unity that it could have gained in no other way. . . .

It is difficult to overestimate the importance of what happened in 1775 to engage mass participation on the side of the Revolution. The new militia, which repeatedly denied that it was in rebellion and proclaimed its loyalty to the Crown, enforced a boycott intended to make Britain back down; Britain did not back down, but the attempt drew virtually everyone into the realm of politics. Enlistment, training, and occasional emergencies were the means whereby dissenters were identified, isolated, and dealt with. Where the new militia had trouble getting organized, there, Revolutionary activists could see that forceful intervention from outside might be needed. Connecticut units moved into the New York City area; Virginia troops moved into the Delmarva peninsula; in Pennsylvania, men from Reading and Lancaster marched into Bucks County. Once established, the militia became the infrastructure of revolutionary government. It controlled its community, whether through indoctrination or intimidation; it provided on short notice large numbers of armed men for brief periods of emergency service; and it found and persuaded, drafted or bribed, the smaller number of men needed each year to keep the Continental army alive. After the first months of the war, popular enthusiasm and spontaneity could not have sustained the struggle; only a pervasive armed organization, in which almost everyone took some part, kept people constantly, year after year, at the hard task of revolution. While Scott and his sons, the indigent, the blacks, and the otherwise socially expendable men fought the British, James and Samuel Cunningham, Henry Ferguson, John Gray, William McNee, Benjamin Mitchell, Robert Morison, Alexander and William Robbe, Robert Swan, Robert Wilson, and four or five men named Smith—all militiamen, but whose combined active service hardly equalled that of "Long Bill" Scott alone—ran Peterborough, expelling a few Tories, scraping up enough recruits for the Continental army to meet the town's quota every spring, taking time out to help John Stark destroy the Germans at the battle of Bennington.

The mention of Tories brings us, briefly, to the last aspect of our subject. . . . Peterborough had little trouble with Tories; the most sensational case occurred when the Presbyterian minister, the Rev. John Morrison, who had been having difficulties with his congregation, deserted his post as chaplain to the Peterborough troops and entered British lines at Boston in June 1775. But an informed estimate is that a half million Americans can be counted as loyal to Britain. Looking at the absence of serious Loyalism in Peterborough, we might conclude that Scotch-Irish Presbyterians almost never were Tories. That, however, would be an error of fact, and we are impelled to seek further for an explanation. What appears as we look at places like Peterborough, where Tories are hardly visible, and at other places where Toryism was rampant, is a pattern—not so much an ethnic, religious, or ideological pattern, but a pattern of raw power. Wherever the British and their allies were strong enough to penetrate in force—along the seacoast, in the Hudson, Mohawk, and lower Delaware valleys, in Georgia, the Carolinas, and the transappalachian West—there Toryism flourished. But geographically less exposed areas, if population density made self-defense feasible—most of New England, the Pennsylvania hinterland, and piedmont Virginia—where the enemy hardly appeared or not at all, there Tories either ran away, kept quiet, even serving in the rebel armies, or occasionally took a brave but hopeless stand against Revolutionary committees and their gunmen. After the war, of course, men remembered their parts in the successful Revolution in ways that make it difficult for the historian to reconstruct accurately the relationship between what they thought and what they did.

The view here presented of how armed force and public opinion were mobilized may seem a bit cynical—a reversion to Thomas Hobbes. True, it gives little weight to ideology, to perceptions and principles, to grievances and aspirations, to the more admirable side of the emergent American character. Perhaps that is a weakness; perhaps I have failed to grasp what really drove Bill Scott. But what strikes me most forcibly in studying this part of the Revolution is how much in essential agreement almost all Americans were in 1774, both in their views of British measures and in their feelings about them. What then is puzzling, and thus needs explaining, is why so many of these people behaved in anomalous and in different ways. Why did so many, who did not intend a civil war or political independence, get so inextricably involved in the organization and use of armed force? Why did relatively few do most of the actual fighting? Why was a dissenting fifth of the population so politically and militarily impotent, so little able to affect the outcome of the struggle? Answers to these questions cannot be found in the life of one obscure man, or in the history of one backwoods town. But microscopic study does emphasize certain features of the American Revolution: the political structuring of resistance to Britain, the play of social and economic factors in carrying on that resistance by armed force, and the brutally direct effects on behavior, if not on opinions, of military power.

The Meaning of the French Alliance

ALEXANDER DECONDE

In the past two hundred years historians have created a considerable literature pertaining to the Franco-American alliance of 1778, viewed by some scholars, such as Edmund S. Morgan, as "the greatest diplomatic victory the United States has ever achieved." This volume of scholarly activity is understandable because that alliance, even when stripped of high-flying rhetoric, holds a position of fundamental importance in the founding of the American nation. The story of the alliance is well known and the only areas of disagreement among scholars concern facts that are hazy, motivation that is uncertain, or speculation that derives from weak circumstantial data. . . .

What follows is the gist of the conventional account of the origins of the alliance.

After defeating France and Spain in the Seven Years' War ending in 1763, Great Britain emerged as the world's preeminent imperial power. Accustomed to the acceptance of their own country as the most powerful and civilized on earth, French leaders felt such deep humiliation that they could not adjust to the reality of British ascendancy. They brooded and sought an opportunity to avenge the losses of 1763. Most prominent in working out this policy of revenge were two men who carried major responsibility for France's foreign affairs after the defeat in 1763, Etienne François, duc de Choiseul, and Charles Gravier, comte de Vergennes. They assumed that much of Britain's wealth and power came from trade with her North American colonies and that, if Britain were deprived of this fountain of wealth, her power would diminish. Both ministers sent agents to North America to foment rebellion in the colonies against British rule. Astute colonials understood well the objectives of French policy. "I fancy," Benjamin Franklin observed of France in 1767, "that intriguing nation would like very well to meddle on occasion, and blow up the coals between Britain and her colonies; but I hope we shall give them no opportunity."

Americans finally did provide such an opportunity in 1775, when resistance to British measures burst into open conflict. Those rebel leaders who viewed their struggle in an international as well as a local context expected foreign assistance, especially from France. In November the Second Continental Congress established a Committee of Secret Correspondence, a kind of foreign office, to explore the possibilities of obtaining help from foreign nations. Early in March 1776 this committee decided to send an agent to Paris to solicit arms and to explore the possibility of an alliance. It chose Silas Deane, a businessman from Connecticut, to carry out this mission, explaining in his instructions that France was "the power whose friendship it would be fittest for us to obtain and cultivate."

Before Deane set foot on French soil, Vergennes put in motion a plan to help the American rebels. Persuaded by the arguments of Vergennes and others, Louis XVI authorized the expenditure of one million livres, or several million dollars, in secret aid to Americans. The king took this step despite the risk of war with Britain and a financial system so weak that France courted bankruptcy. Six weeks later Charles III, king of Spain, put up an equivalent sum to support the Revolution. In August a fictitious trading company, *Rodrigue Hortalez et Cie,* funded by the Bourbon monarchs and headed by the playwright, adventurer, and diplomatic agent Caron de Beaumarchais, began supplying American fighters with money, guns, and munitions.

Simultaneously, American leaders decided that they needed more than secret aid. They assumed they could elicit more because Vergennes and other French statesmen were so eager to see England humbled that they would not hesitate to commit France to the American cause even without a reciprocal obligation. These Americans also considered the potential flow of commerce to and from North America to be so valuable it would give them considerable leverage in bargaining with France. Consequently, they believed that the French would be content to help disrupt Britain's empire and destroy her trade in North America without exacting a heavy price beforehand. Later, France would be grateful for an opportunity to take over that commerce for herself. Thomas Paine's pamphlet of January 1776, *Common Sense,* gave considerable publicity to this design. He called not only for independence but also for foreign assistance without political strings attached to it.

Other Americans felt that they could not attract large-scale French help without an alliance and that they must declare independence as a means of obtaining it. "It is not choice then, but necessity," Richard Henry Lee of Virginia wrote, "that calls for Independence, as the only means by which foreign Alliance can be obtained." On June 7 he offered a resolution in Congress calling for independence, confederation, and "foreign alliances." Four days later Congress appointed a committee to draft a declaration of independence, and on the next day created another committee to prepare a plan of treaties to be proposed to foreign powers. This latter committee presented Congress with a plan and the model of a treaty, drafted by John Adams, to be submitted to France. That model called for a commercial agreement containing no political commitment from the United States.

At this point Adams and other revolutionaries did not necessarily construe the word *alliance* to mean a military obligation. They sometimes used the term *commercial alliance* as the equivalent of a trade agreement. "I am not for soliciting any political connection," Adams wrote privately, "or military assistance, or indeed naval, from France. I wish for nothing but commerce, a mere marine treaty with them." Congress adopted the committee's plan, after making amendments, on September 17, 1776.

Nine days later Congress appointed three commissioners to negotiate agreements with European nations according to the principles of the Model Treaty. "It is highly probable," their instructions read, "that France means not to let the United States sink in the present Contest." The most prominent of the commissioners, seventy-year-old Benjamin Franklin, landed in France early in December. Although received cordially, the American emissaries in Paris failed to secure either recognition of the United States or more aid. Since at the same time the war was going badly for Americans, Congress put aside fears of a political connection and sent new instructions to its agents in France authorizing them to secure military alliances with that country and with Spain.

Even though Vergennes and other officials desired such an alliance, they hesitated since a treaty would mean war with a Britain which still commanded the seas and which still retained the loyalty of many in North America. If France did not move cautiously, she might repeat the disaster of the Seven Years' War. She "feared lest the colonists might all at once desist, and resume all their ancient relations with England." Vergennes decided to wait until Americans demonstrated not only a will to fight but also the skill to do so successfully and an ability to remain independent of Britain over the long pull.

The need for waiting ended early in December 1777, when Vergennes learned the results of Saratoga. There, on October 17, a British army under the command of Gen. John Burgoyne capitulated to American forces under Gen. Horatio Gates. This news, along with information that the British were now willing to offer concessions that Americans might accept, persuaded the French to proceed with the alliance which Americans desired. Otherwise Americans might end their Revolution and return to the British Empire.

The British, understandably, tried to defeat the alliance. Through special agents in Paris, Lord North, head of the British government, attempted several times in December 1777 and January 1778 to obtain terms for a reconciliation from Franklin. One agent said that the British government was now willing to grant Americans everything they might ask "except the word *independence.*" North's agents also reminded Americans that they had nothing in common with the French. As in the past, loyalists insisted, France remained America's natural enemy rather than friend. These tactics failed.

On February 6, 1778, representatives of France and the United States signed three agreements in Paris. In the first, a treaty of amity and commerce, France formally recognized the United States as an independent country. In return, Americans promised special trading privileges that were potentially valuable. The second document, a treaty of alliance, provided that when Britain responded to France's recognition with war, the new allies would fight together in "common cause." Each pledged to conclude neither truce nor peace with Britain "without the formal consent of the other first obtained." France promised, as her prime purpose, to wage war until American independence was assured. She also renounced claim to territory in North America that she had lost in 1763. In exchange, the United States said it would defend French possessions in the Caribbean. The term of the alliance was "forever." The third instrument, held secret, reserved a place for Spain in the alliance.

Dissenters challenge several aspects of the conventional account up to this point, usually focusing on the motivation of the French in making the alliance. Regardless of how skilled, historians cannot pinpoint what actuates a nation. Often, however, they can ascertain what drives those who have the power to make decisions. From this knowledge scholars can speculate broadly on why a nation or government behaved in a particular manner. Even with such evidence, knowledge cannot be precise, mainly because historians generally use selective personal data—letters, diaries, and statements—from those few people in positions of power whose documents survive, or are accessible, for wide-ranging conjectures.

Such data support the conventional theory that French leaders could not ignore the splendid opportunity presented by the American Revolution to avenge the losses of 1763. They desired the alliance as the instrument of their revenge. Critics of this thesis argue from various perspectives, but they have in common the general idea that nations do not shape policy to gratify the emotion of anger or inflict injury on other countries merely to be vindictive, as revenge implies. In addition to revenge, or in place of it, theories of motivation emphasize such factors as desire for power in Europe, national survival, territory in North America, response to alleged popular support for liberal ideas, and hope for commercial advantage.

Most persuasive is the hypothesis advanced by Edward S. Corwin and others, maintaining that France entered the alliance for reasons of prestige and power. Her leaders, notably Choiseul and Vergennes, wished to weaken England, create a new balance of power in Europe, and restore France to her former greatness. They expected war, and planned for it, to attain this goal. Not all French leaders accepted such reasoning. Louis XVI's minister of finance, Anne Robert Jacques Turgot, for instance, argued that an alliance risked too much for too little. France's finances could not sustain a war with Britain. In time, moreover, Britain would lose her colonies and her empire would collapse. Turgot concluded, therefore, that Americans did not need French help to achieve independence, and France did not require war to enhance her power. . . .

As the varying interpretations indicate, historians still differ as to the nature of French motivation, but few who investigate the subject in depth seem satisfied with the conventional revenge thesis.

Yet this concern with motivation, especially with revenge, leads readily to the theory that Frenchmen, not Americans, took the initiative in drawing up the alliance. Some writers suggest that France desired war with England and hence from the beginning of her secret aid she looked forward to an alliance. . . .

The conventional view insists, however, that Americans, rather than Frenchmen, made the initial overtures, that they declared independence mainly to attract an alliance. . . . When insurgent leaders realized that commercial incentives, as in the terms of the Model Treaty, would not bring immediate French recognition, they pressed for a military agreement. Americans needed foreign aid in any form but desired a firm and sustained commitment to their cause, as in a treaty of alliance, and that is what their representatives in France and Spain sought.

In support of this conventional analysis, . . . scholars point out that Benjamin Franklin used the possibility of a reconciliation with England to goad the French into an alliance. . . .

This argument in favor of American initiative seems particularly convincing when linked to the impact of Saratoga. . . . John Adams, as well as other contemporaries, was convinced that "it determined the wavering counsels of France to an alliance." In this view the Battle of Saratoga marked a major turning point in the American Revolution. It signaled the beginning of warfare by Europeans against England in various parts of the globe. . . .

This intervention, as told in the conventional narrative, developed just about as the French had planned. On March 13, 1778, the French ambassador in London informed the British government of what it already knew, that his country had recognized the United States. Four days later England reacted to this provoking announcement with a declaration of war on France.

The French government drew up plans for an invasion of England. Across the Atlantic on May 4 the Continental Congress, meeting in York, Pennsylvania, spurned British overtures for reconciliation and voted unanimous approval of the French treaties. Hostilities between the great powers began on June 17 when two British warships attacked a French frigate in the English Channel.

At last, as Americans had hoped and assumed it would, the French alliance transformed their Revolution from a local uprising into a key element in an international war. Later, Spain and the Netherlands also fought against England. France sent armies and fleets to North America, subsidized the United States government with loans and gifts, and braced a sagging economy. American soldiers carried muskets made in France, fired French cannon, and received pay from French sources. France also provided the naval and military superiority at the siege of Yorktown that forced surrender of Gen. Charles Cornwallis's army on October 19, 1781, and that brought victory to the allies in North America.

In this victory as in the general achievement of American independence, the alliance proved the essential element or "deciding factor." Diplomatic historians appear to consider this judgment virtually as dogma; few depart from it. Without the alliance, they say, the Revolution would have failed, since "without France the Americans were completely helpless."

✳ *F U R T H E R   R E A D I N G*

Samuel Flagg Bemis, *The Diplomacy of the American Revolution* (1935)
George Athan Billias, ed., *George Washington's Opponents: British Generals and Admirals in the American Revolution* (1969)
R. Arthur Bowler, *Logistics and the Failure of the British Army in America, 1775–1783* (1975)
Richard Buel, Jr., *Dear Liberty: Connecticut's Mobilization for War* (1980)
E. Wayne Carp, *To Starve the Army at Pleasure: Continental Army Administration and American Political Culture, 1775–1783* (1984)
Jonathan R. Dull, *A Diplomatic History of the American Revolution* (1985)
———, *The French Navy and American Independence: A Study of Arms and Diplomacy* (1975)
William M. Fowler, Jr., *Rebels Under Sail: The American Navy During the Revolution* (1976)
Robert A. Gross, *The Minutemen and Their World* (1976)
Ira D. Gruber, *The Howe Brothers and the American Revolution* (1972)
Don Higginbotham, *War and Society in Revolutionary America: The Wider Dimensions of the Conflict* (1988)
———, *The War of American Independence: Military Attitudes, Policies, and Practice, 1763–1789* (1971)
Ronald Hoffman and Peter J. Albert, eds., *Arms and Independence: The Military Character of the American Revolution* (1984)
———, *Diplomacy and Revolution: The Franco-American Alliance of 1778* (1981)
Ronald Hoffman, Thad W. Tate, and Peter J. Albert, eds., *An Uncivil War: The Southern Backcountry During the American Revolution* (1985)
James H. Hutson, *John Adams and the Diplomacy of the American Revolution* (1980)
Piers Mackesy, *The War for America, 1775–1783* (1964)

James Kirby Martin and Mark E. Lender, *A Respectable Army: The Military Origins of the Republic* (1982)

Jan Willem Schulte Nordholt, *The Dutch Republic and American Independence* (1982)

Stephen E. Patterson, *Political Parties in Revolutionary Massachusetts* (1973)

Howard H. Peckham, ed., *The Toll of Independence: Engagements and Battle Casualties of the American Revolution* (1974)

Hugh F. Rankin, *The North Carolina Continentals* (1971)

Eric Robson, *The American Revolution in Its Political and Military Aspects* (1955)

Steven Rosswurm, *Arms, Country, and Class: The Philadelphia Militia and the "Lower Sort" During the American Revolution* (1987)

Charles Royster, *A Revolutionary People at War: The Continental Army and American Character* (1979)

John E. Selby, *The Revolution in Virginia, 1775–1783* (1988)

John Shy, *A People Numerous and Armed: Reflections on the Military Struggle for American Independence* (1976)

Marshall Smelser, *The Winning of Independence* (1972)

Jack M. Sosin, *The Revolutionary Frontier, 1763–1783* (1967)

Gerald Stourzh, *Benjamin Franklin and American Foreign Policy*, 2d ed. (1969)

Willard M. Wallace, *Appeal to Arms: A Military History of the Revolution* (1951)

CHAPTER

6

Struggling Toward Victory,
1779–1783

✕

The victory at Saratoga and France's entry into the war as a U.S. ally were great triumphs, but they did not win the war. The British government remained unyielding, while in America war weariness set in. Perhaps, Americans hoped, France would now carry the major burden. As a consequence of such wishful thinking, the army continued near starvation, and recurrent unrest stirred among the troops. After Saratoga, the British shifted the main theater of warfare to the south, where, if anything, Americans faced an even more difficult military challenge than before. Here, not only were settlers more thinly scattered through the countryside, but the revolutionary governments were threatened by Native American attacks, loyalist troops, and slave unrest in addition to British invasions.

As in the north earlier, the course of the fighting was generally inconclusive. Although the Americans scored a few notable victories and defeated the Native American and loyalist threats, the British army succeeded in moving through the southern states, capturing any town it wished. True, the British often paid a high price in casualties and supplies, but in most battles the redcoats won the field. As a result, during 1779, 1780, and 1781, the battle for independence became a war of attrition—a test of British, American, and French willpower as well as material resources.

In the summer and fall of 1781, Washington finally fashioned the crucial victory at Yorktown, thanks to French military assistance on land and sea. Now, for the first time in the war, Washington attacked a British army with superior numbers, while a French fleet under DeGrasse cut off its escape route. At Yorktown there were more French troops under Rochambeau and Lafayette than there were Americans under Washington—and for the moment the sea belonged to France—yet this campaign proved to be the decisive American triumph. After London learned of the loss of a second army—Burgoyne's had been the first—the North ministry fell, and Britain sought to negotiate a peace with the United States.

The peace negotiations were complicated. The United States Congress was not entirely united in its priorities as to boundaries, trade, and fishing rights.

*France, now bound to honor the objectives of its other ally, Spain, also had
multiple, and not always compatible, goals. And Britain maneuvered so that it
could retain as much as possible or at least prevent the shift of any advantages
to France or Spain. Under these circumstances the negotiations took time. Ultimately the American diplomats Benjamin Franklin, John Adams, and John Jay
used their discretion to negotiate terms with Britain, leaving France and its
Spanish ally to accept American realpolitik. In light of the United States' pledge
to France not to sign a separate treaty, this was not the most elegant or idealistic note on which to end the war for American independence; but the United
States, like other nations, faced hard realities at home and abroad that made an
early peace imperative. To most Americans, the 1783 Treaty of Paris was cause
for celebration.*

✳ D O C U M E N T S

Patriotic mythology emphasizes only the dedicated heroism of Revolutionary soldiers, as if they were incapable of base or selfish thoughts. In reality, however,
the Revolution displayed the ignoble side of human nature as well. In the later
years of the war, mutinies among the troops—officers as well as enlisted men—
seriously threatened the American cause. Inadequate supplies, payless paydays,
and broken promises of government support led to a restless cynicism that sometimes erupted into open revolt. A Connecticut soldier's vantage point is expressed
in the reminiscences in the first document of Joseph Plumb Martin, who was a
participant in some of the restiveness that troubled the leadership. General Washington's inventory of the difficulties facing the army is revealed in the second selection, a plea for help. Congressman James Duane promises that help is on the
way in the third selection.

When sufficient help did not come, in 1781 full-scale mutinies erupted among
New Jersey and Pennsylvania troops. The fourth document is an official account
of the New Jersey mutiny by General Robert Howe to General Washington. In
the next selection, Washington responds by praising the loyalty and dedication of
the men who suppressed the incipient revolt. Later that year, Congress had more
promising news to report respecting military, political, and diplomatic affairs, as
the sixth document reveals. A climax came with the victory at Yorktown, here
described by Benjamin Gilbert, a lieutenant from Massachusetts, and Sarah Os-
borne, a soldier's wife who was employed by the army as a cook and washer-
woman (see the two-part seventh selection).

This victory soon led to peace negotiations and to the widespread expectation
in 1782 that the war was all but over. The provisions of the Treaty of Paris, reprinted here as the final document, reveal the scope of the American victory in
concrete terms.

A Soldier Views Mutiny Among American Troops, 1780

We left Westfield [New Jersey] about the twenty-fifth of May and went to
Basking Ridge to our old winter cantonments. . . . The men were now
exasperated beyond endurance; they could not stand it any longer. . . . What
was to be done? Here was the army starved and naked, and there their
country sitting still and expecting the army to do notable things while fainting

from sheer starvation. All things considered, the army was not to be blamed. . . .

We had borne as long as human nature could endure, and to bear longer we considered folly. Accordingly, one pleasant day, the men spent the most of their time upon the parade, growling like soreheaded dogs. At evening roll call they began to show their dissatisfaction by snapping at the officers and acting contrary to their orders. After their dismissal from the parade, the officers went, as usual, to their quarters, except the adjutant, who happened to remain, giving details for next day's duty to the orderly sergeants, or some other business, when the men, none of whom had left the parade began to make him sensible that they had something in train. He said something that did not altogether accord with the soldiers' ideas of propriety, one of the men retorted; the adjutant called him a mutinous rascal, or some such epithet, and then left the parade. This man, then stamping the butt of his musket upon the ground, as much as to say, I am in a passion, called out, "Who will parade with me?" The whole regiment immediately fell in and formed.

We had made no plans for our future operations, but while we were consulting how to proceed, the Fourth Regiment, which lay on our left, formed, and came and paraded with us. We now concluded to go in a body to the other two regiments [the Third and Sixth] that belonged to our brigade and induce them to join with us. These regiments lay forty or fifty rods in front of us, with a brook and bushes between. We did not wish to have anyone in particular to command, lest he might be singled out for a court-martial to exercise its clemency upon. We therefore gave directions to the drummers to give certain signals on the drums; at the first signal we shouldered our arms, at the second we faced, at the third we began our march to join with the other two regiments, and went off with music playing.

By this time our officers had obtained knowledge of our military maneuvering and some of them had run across the brook, by a nearer way than we had taken, it being now quite dark, and informed the officers of those regiments of our approach and supposed intentions. The officers ordered their men to parade as quick as possible *without* arms. When that was done, they stationed a camp guard, that happened to be near at hand, between the men and their huts, which prevented them from entering and taking their arms, which they were very anxious to do. Colonel [Return Jonathan] Meigs, of the Sixth Regiment, exerted himself to prevent his men from obtaining their arms until he received a severe wound in his side by a bayonet in the scuffle, which cooled his courage at the time. He said he had always considered himself the soldier's friend and thought the soldiers regarded him as such, but had reason now to conclude he might be mistaken. Colonel Meigs was truly an excellent man and a brave officer. The man, whoever he was, that wounded him, doubtless had no particular grudge against him; it was dark and the wound was given, it is probable, altogether unintentionally. . . .

When we found the officers had been too crafty for us we returned with grumbling instead of music, the officers following in the rear growling in concert. One of the men in the rear calling out, "Halt in front," the officers seized upon him like wolves on a sheep and dragged him out of the ranks, intending to make an example of him for being a "mutinous rascal," but the bayonets of the men pointing at their breasts as thick as hatchel teeth, compelled them quickly to relinquish their hold of him. We marched back to our own parade and then formed again. The officers now began to coax us to disperse to our quarters, but that had no more effect upon us than their threats. One of them slipped away into the bushes, and after a short time returned, counterfeiting to have come directly from headquarters. Said he, "There is good news for you, boys, there has just arrived a large drove of cattle for the army." But this piece of finesse would not avail. All the answer he received for his labor was, "Go and butcher them," or some such slight expression. The lieutenant colonel of the Fourth Regiment now came on to the parade. He could persuade *his* men, he said, to go peaceably to their quarters. After a good deal of palaver, he ordered them to shoulder their arms, but the men taking no notice of him or his order, he fell into a violent passion, threatening them with the bitterest punishment if they did not immediately obey his orders. After spending a whole quiver of the arrows of his rhetoric, he again ordered them to shoulder their arms, but he met with the same success that he did at the first trial. He therefore gave up the contest as hopeless and left us and walked off to his quarters, chewing the cud of resentment all the way, and how much longer I neither knew nor cared. The rest of the officers, after they found that they were likely to meet with no better success than the colonel, walked off likewise to their huts. . . .

After our officers had left us to our own option, we dispersed to our huts and laid by our arms of our own accord, but the worm of hunger gnawing so keen kept us from being entirely quiet. We therefore still kept upon the parade in groups, venting our spleen at our country and government, then at our officers, and then at ourselves for our imbecility in staying there and starving in detail for an ungrateful people who did not care what became of us, so they could enjoy themselves while we were keeping a cruel enemy from them. . . .

Our stir did us some good in the end, for we had provisions directly after, so we had no great cause for complaint for some time.

General George Washington Explains Army Problems and Calls for Help, 1780

Gen. George Washington's Circular to the States

> Head Quarters, near the Liberty Pole, in
> Bergen County, August 27, 1780.

Sir:

The Honble: the Committee of Co-operation having returned to Congress, I am under the disagreeable necessity of informing you that the Army is again reduced to an extremity of distress for want of provision. The greater part of it had been without Meat from the 21st. to the 26th. To endeavour to obtain some relief, I moved down to this place, with a view of stripping the lower parts of the County of the remainder of its Cattle, which after a most rigorous exaction is found to afford between two and three days supply only, and those, consisting of Milch Cows and Calves of one or two years old. When this scanty pittance is consumed, I know not what will be our next resource, as the Commissary can give me no certain information of more than 120 head of Cattle expected from pennsylvania and about 150 from Massachusetts. I mean in time to supply our immediate wants. Military coercion is no longer of any avail, as nothing further can possibly be collected from the Country in which we are obliged to take a position, without depriving the inhabitants of the last morsel. This mode of subsisting, supposing the desired end could be answered by it, besides being in the highest degree distressing to individuals, is attended with ruin to the Morals and discipline of the Army; during the few days which we have been obliged to send out small parties to procure provision for themselves, the most enormous excesses have been committed.

It has been no inconsiderable support of our cause, to have had it in our power to contrast the conduct of our Army with that of the enemy, and to convince the inhabitants that while their rights were wantonly violated by the British Troops, by ours they were respected. This distinction must unhappily now cease, and we must assume the odious character of the plunderers instead of the protectors of the people, the direct consequence of which must be to alienate their minds from the Army and insensibly from the cause. We have not yet been absolutely without Flour, but we have *this* day but *one* days supply in Camp, and I am not certain that there is a single Barrel between this place and Trenton. I shall be obliged therefore to draw down one or two hundred Barrels from a small Magazine which I have endeavoured to establish at West point, for the security of the Garrison in case of a sudden investiture.

From the above state of facts it may be foreseen that this army cannot possibly remain much longer together, unless very vigorous and immediate measures are taken by the States to comply with the requisitions made upon them. The Commissary General has neither the means nor the power of procuring supplies; he is only to receive them from the several Agents. Without a speedy change of circumstances, this dilemma will be involved; either the Army must disband, or what is, if possible, worse, subsist upon the plunder of the people. . . . Altho' the troops have upon every occasion hitherto borne their wants with unparralled patience, it will be dangerous to trust too often to a repetition of the causes of discontent.

A Congressman Offers Encouragement, 1780

James Duane to George Washington

PHILADELPHIA 9th December 1780.

My Dear General, . . .

Amidst pressing distresses it will give your Excellency pleasure to be assured that Congress have deliberated with unanimity, and decided with firmness; and that every thing within their power is nearly accomplished for vigorous Efforts in the Course of the next year. If the States will draw forth their Resources: if our Ally will seriously cooperate by assuming a naval superiority in the American Seas: if we are seasonably furnished with the Clothing Arms and Ammunition which we have reason to expect; and obtain the aid of money which we have once more attempted to borrow: if these Circumstances in any tolerable degree Combine, your Excellency will at last see a prospect, under the divine blessing of finishing the war with Glory.

But it is obvious that we have many difficulties to encounter. Government instead of possessing the Confidence and the Dignity necessary to enforce its Counsels, is surrounded by clamorous Creditors and insidious speculators, and what is worse the Intemperance of our Friends conspires with the malice of our Enemies to render it odious. . . .

Another great difficulty which embarrasses us is the absolute Dependence which we are compelled to place on the Exertions of the States *individually*. A failure in *one* may draw upon us insupportable distress. If the supplies of provisions should be punctually furnished the transportation alone is an Expence of such magnitude that I never think of it but with anxiety. . . . There is a remedy but whether we have a sufficient degree of public spirit to apply it can only be known by Experiment. Why shou'd not the opulent contribute, the whole or a large proportion of their plate? Why shou'd not the Farmer break in upon his Capital if his annual produce is incompetent? Nothing is clearer than that this wou'd be the truest Oeconomy, as a foundation wou'd be laid to terminate the war by a great and decisive Effort. These are Resources in the power of every Legislature, and I shall think them inexcuseable if, seeing the necessity to be so urgent, they shrink from the Burthen. A Duty on Imports Exports and prizes will be strongly recommended by Congress; and if approved by the States, it must produce a considerable Revenue.

General Robert Howe Reports on the New Jersey Mutiny, 1781

Ringwood, 27 January, 1781.

Sir,

In obedience to your Excellency's commands I arrived at this place yesterday evening, and found that the mutineers were returning to their

From Burnett, C., ed.: *Letters of Members of Continental Congress,* 8 vols., Peter Smith Publisher, Inc.: 1963 Gloucester, MA. Reprinted by permission.

huts. Colonel Dayton had offered them pardon for their offences, provided
they immediately would put themselves under the command of their officers,
and would behave in future consistently with that subordination so essential
to military discipline. To this they seemingly acceded, but soon demonstrated
by their conduct, that they were actuated by motives exceedingly distinct
from those they had professed; for, though in some respects they would
suffer a few particular officers to have influence over them, yet it was by
no means the case in general, and what they did do, appeared rather like
following advice than obeying command.

Arrived at their huts, they condescended once to parade when ordered,
but were no sooner dismissed than several officers were insulted. One had
a bayonet put to his breast, and upon the man's being knocked down for
his insolence, a musket was fired, which being their alarm-signal, most of
them paraded in arms. In short, their whole behaviour was such as cried
aloud for chastisement, and made it evident, that they had only returned
to their huts, as a place more convenient for themselves, where they meant
to negotiate with the committee appointed, previous to their meeting, to
inquire into their grievances, and to whom they thought to have dictated
their own terms.

Having long been convinced, that in cases of insurrection no medium
lies, either for civil or military bodies, between dignity and servility, but
coercion, and that no other method could be possibly fallen upon without
the deepest wound to the service, I instantly determined to adopt it. We
marched from Ringwood about midnight, and having, by the assistance of
Colonels Shreve and Barber, made myself acquainted with the situation of
their encampment, I thought it proper to occupy four different positions
about it. Lieutenant-Colonel-Commandant Sprout, with one party and a
piece of artillery, was ordered to take post on their left; Lieutenant-Colonel
Miller, with another party and two pieces, on their right; Major Oliver, with
his men, in front of their encampment; Major Throop, with his, in the rear
of it. Major Morril, who, with the New Hampshire detachment, had been
ordered to Pompton by the way of King's Ferry and was arrived, was directed
to post himself upon the Charlottenberg road, about half a mile above the
first bridge.

Thus was every avenue secured, and in this position the mutineers found
us when day-light appeared. Colonel Barber, of the Jersey line, was sent to
them with orders immediately to parade without arms, and to march to the
ground pointed out for them. Some seemed willing to comply, but others
exclaimed, "What! No conditions? Then if we are to die, it is as well to die
where we are as anywhere else." Some hesitation happening among them,
Colonel Sprout was directed to advance, and only five minutes were given
the mutineers to comply with the orders, which had been sent to them. This
had its effect, and they, to a man, marched without arms to the ground
appointed for them. The Jersey officers gave a list of those, whom they
thought the most atrocious offenders, upon which I desired them to select
three (one of each regiment), which was accordingly done. A field court-
martial was presently held, and they received sentence of death by the

unanimous decree of the court. Two of them were executed on the spot; the third I have reprieved, because the officers inform me, that they were guided in their naming him more by his having been the commanding officer of the party, than from any circumstances of aggravation in his own conduct; and because it appeared in evidence, that, though he had been compelled to take the command, he had endeavoured to prevail upon the men to return to their duty. These reasons, Sir, induced me to spare him, which I am persuaded your Excellency will approve. I thought it would have a good effect to appoint the executioners from among those most active in the mutiny.

After the execution, the officers were ordered to parade the men regimentally, and to divide them into platoons, each officer to take his platoon. In this situation they were directed to make, and they made, proper concessions to their officers, in the face of the troops, and promised by future good conduct to atone for past offences. I then spoke to them by platoons, representing to them, in the strongest terms I was capable of, the heinousness of their guilt, as well as the folly of it, in the outrage they had offered to that civil authority, to which they owed obedience, and which it was their incumbent duty to support and maintain. They showed the fullest sense of their guilt, and such strong marks of contrition, that I think I may venture to pledge myself for their future good conduct.

I take pleasure in expressing, Sir, the warmest approbation of the conduct of the detachments of every line detailed for this command. The rapid march made by each on the several routes they took in very inclement weather, through a depth of snow, and upon an occasion, which, from the nature of it, nothing but a sense of duty and love of their country could render pleasing, is a very meritorious instance of their patriotism, as well as of their zeal for the service.

General Washington Responds to Howe, 1781

Head Quarters, New Windsor,
Tuesday, January 30, 1781.

The General returns his thanks to Major General Howe for the judicious measures he pursued and to the officers and men under his command for the good conduct and alacrity with which they executed his orders for suppressing the late Mutiny in a part of the New Jersey line. It gave him inexpressible pain to have been obliged to employ their arms upon such an occasion and convinced that they themselves felt all the Reluctance which former Affection to fellow Soldiers could inspire. He considers the patience with which they endured the fatigues of the march through rough and mountainous roads rendered almost impassable by the depth of the Snow and the cheerfulness with which they performed every other part of their duty as the strongest proof of their Fidelity, attachment to the service, sense of subordination and abhorrence of the principles which actuated the Mutineers in so daring and atrocious a departure from what they owed to their Country, to their Officers to their Oaths and to themselves.

The General is deeply sensible of the sufferings of the army. He leaves no expedient unessayed to relieve them, and he is persuaded Congress and the several States are doing every thing in their power for the same purpose. But while we look to the public for the fullfilment of its engagements we should do it with proper allowance for the embarrassments of public affairs. We began a Contest for Liberty and Independence ill provided with the means for war, relying on our own Patriotism to supply the deficiency. We expected to encounter many wants and distresses and We should neither shrink from them when they happen nor fly in the face of Law and Government to procure redress. There is no doubt the public will in the event do ample justice to men fighting and suffering in its defence. But it is our duty to bear present Evils with Fortitude looking forward to the period when our Country will have it more in its power to reward our services.

History is full of Examples of armies suffering with patience extremities of distress which exceed those we have suffered, and this in the cause of ambition and conquest not in that of the rights of humanity of their country, of their families of themselves; shall we who aspire to the distinction of a patriot army, who are contending for every thing precious in society against every thing hateful and degrading in slavery, shall We who call ourselves citizens discover less Constancy and Military virtue than the mercenary instruments of ambition? Those who in the present instance have stained the honor of the American soldiery and sullied the reputation of patient Virtue for which they have been so long eminent can only atone for their pusillanimous defection by a life devoted to a Zealous and examplary discharge of their duty. Persuaded that the greater part were influenced by the pernicious advice of a few who probably have been paid by the enemy to betray their Associates; The General is happy in the lenity shewn in the execution of only two of the most guilty after compelling the whole to an unconditional surrender, and he flatters himself no similar instance will hereafter disgrace our military History. It can only bring ruin on those who are mad enough to make the attempt; for lenity on any future occasion would be criminal and inadmissible.

Congress Reports Progress at Home and Abroad, 1781

John Sullivan to George Washington

PHILADELPHIA Jany 29, 1781.

Dear General,

. . . I know it is a Trying time with the Americans in General but above all I Lament The Tryals you are compelled to go Through. But I am Convinced we Shall Soon be in better Circumstances. our Political Disorder has in my opinion Come to a Crisis and the next Campaign we Shall See the Republick rising into Action with new vigor we are now making Some

Arrangements which Evidence the Recovery of our Reason. A Minister of Foreign Affairs, one of Finance, a Minister of War and of Marine are to be appointed. Maryland has Acceeded to the Association. Virginia has granted Congress all the Lands west of the Ohio our Plan of Finance is Nearly Through we mean to try for a Loan of Coined Specie and Plate from Individuals in which I Doubt not we Shall Succeed as we Mean to Convince them that they will be repaid in Specie by this Means we Intend Establishing a Bank to Support Paper for though paper Bills may well Enough Represent Silver and Gold That really does Exist yet when they are used as a Circulating Medium to represent Silver and Gold which does not Exist and probably never may this medium is but the Shadow of a Shade. If the Loan, can be obtained and Colo. Laurens Should be Successful in France I am Convinced we Shall be in a very respectable Situation next year and Even if he is unsuccessful, in a much better than we have been for years Past. I promise myself much from our Present and past Distresses. I find that Congress and assemblies begin to Rouse from their Slumber and Individuals are now alarmed for the Publick Safety who have for years past been Employed in amassing wealth. America has undoubtedly abundant Resources but we Seem to have had neither Efficient Powers or skill to call them forth. I wish Your Excellency would be so oblidging (when you have Liesure to favor me with another Letter) as to give me Yr. opinion with respect to Colo. Hamilton as a Financier.

Your Excellencys Letter with a Flying Seal was Delivered to the President and immediately read in Congress and I think you may rest assured that Every Exertion will be made to prevent Similar Disturbances. I am happy to find that amidst all the Disorders in the Pensylvania Line they gave Such undeniable Evidence of their attachment to the Cause of their Country even if it answered no other purpose but those of preventing unfavorable Impressions in Europe. I have the Honor to be very respectfully

Dear General Your Excellencys most obedient Servant
JNO. SULLIVAN

John Sullivan to George Washington

PHILADELPHIA May 28th 1781.

My Dear General, . . .

. . . The Reinforcement from France though far short of what was intended, will (I trust) enable us to undertake offensive operations by Land and Sea. the Generous Donation of his most Christian Majesty with the measures adopted by Congress and by our Financier will enable us to pay and supply our Army. The Cloathing Arrived and now on its passage will enable us to Cloathe our Army. the Measures adopted by the French Court will furnish us with the necessary Munitions of war. The Exertions of Mr. R : Morris will in a few Days give you a permanent Supply of provisions Independant of the Supplies expected from the States. The Late important discoveries made by Congress have at Length convinced them that Honesty is the best policy; These will restore our Lost credit. The prospects of a peace being Dictated to us by an armed neutrality will rouse Congress and the States to Exertions which may put us on a footing to negotiate on Terms of Equality. The scrupulous adherence of his Christian Majesty to the Terms of the Alliance; The favorable Disposition of the Spanish Court; and the interest which the powers of Europe have discovered in our becoming an Independant Nation promise us every thing in a Negociation which our Exertions and their political Interest may Dictate. but amidst all those flattering prospects we are now called upon to make our Last desperate Struggle to pave the way to that peace and Independance for which we have so long contended. Congress do and I am convinced the States will feel the necessity to exert every nerve at this critical moment and I do not entertain a Doubt of the Success.

Two Views of the Battle of Yorktown, 1781

Letters from an American Soldier (Benjamin Gilbert)

To His Father and Stepmother

Maubin Hills [Malvern Hill, Va.]   18 July 1781

Honoured Parents

Since writing my last, the Army under Marquis de la fayatte moved towards James Town, where Cornwallis encamped his Troops and on the 6th Instant, a small part of our army, Detached as a front Guard, fell in with the Enemies Piquet, and drove them into their lines, on which their whole army formed for Action, began the attackt on our detachments. Our Army being at that time from Eight to fifteen miles from the field of action, no immediate support could be lent them, but they maintaining their ground with unexampled Braverey, kept the Enemy at such a distance, as gave time for six Hundred of Pensilvania line to come to their assistance. The Enemies front line at that time conssisted of 2100, our 700 often changing 4 or 5 shots of a side. The Enemy made a violent charge with Bayonetts, and being 3 to 1 they flanked our troops to that degree, that they gave way, and retreated with the loss of all their Dead and two field peices. Our killed, wounded, and missing is 111, some of which Deserted to the enemy in time of Action. The Enemies loss we are not able to assertain, but are informed it is very considerable.* Next Day they crossed the river, leaving all our wounded that fell into their hands on the place of Action. After they had Crossed the River the foot marched toward Portsmouth, and the Horse thro the Center of the Country towards Carolina, where we are in Daily expectations of marching. But I dread the march, our men having not more than

---

* This action is known as the Battle of Green Spring. Howard H. Peckham (ed.), *The Toll of Independence* (Chicago, 1974), p. 87, gives the American losses as 28 killed, 99 wounded, and 12 missing, British losses as 75 killed and wounded.

one pair of shoes or Hose to Eight men, and the sands are so hot in the middle of the Day that it continually raises Blisters on the mens feet.

To Lieutenant Park Holland

[August 1781]

Dear Park

I shall not attempt to give you any perticular account of the strength or sittuation of the Enemy. They ly at York[town] and in its Vicinity. Our army are lying in different parts of Kings County upwards of thirty miles from them, and are daily marching. Our Provision is very Indifferent but the duty is not hard. We are Ragged and destitute of Cash which prevents our makeing so great an aquaintence as we should do, were we other ways provided for. The Inhabitints are Exceeding polite and Hospitable which ennables us to make more acquaintence than could be expected with persons in our situation. The Ladies are exceeding Amouris but not So Beautifull as at the Northward, tho there is some rare Beauties amongst them. Amouris Intrigues and Gallantry are every where approved of in this State, and amongst the Vulgar any man that is given to concupcience may have his fill. The Ladies are Exceeding fond of the Northern Gentleman, Esspecially those of the Army. Daily Invitations are given by the Inhabitints for our Gentleman to dine and dring grogg with them where they are generally entertained with musick and the conversation of the Ladies. Yet notwithstanding these diversions, my want of Clothes and Cash and the unwholesomeness of the Climent makes me anxious to return to Head Quarters where I shall Injoye the Company and agreable conversation of my old friends.

To His Father

Camp near Williamsburg   September 19th 1781

Honoured Sir,

Military affairs in this Quarter bears a more favourable Aspect than it has for some time passt. Count De Grass has arived from the West Indias with Twenty eight sail of the line and five Thousand two Hundred french Troops. His Excellency [General Washington] has Arived from Whites plains with Count Rochambeau and has Eight Thousand Troops French and Americans on their way for this place, some of which are arived, the others hourly Expected. Nine Ships of the line with six Hundred french Troops and a large Quantity of Artillerey have arived in the James River. What Troops Pensilvania Maryland and Virginia have Raised this sumer are with us so that a morderate computation makes our strength sixteen Thousand Regulars beside Artilerey Cavalry and Militia. The French fleet has shut Lord Cornwallis into York River and he is fortifying himself in york Town wheir we shall soon lay seige to him. If the French fleet continues long enough and the smile of Providence we shall give as good an account of him as we did of Burgoyine. Nothing but the warmest Expectations of capturing Cornwallis keeps my spirits hight, my Cloths being almost worne out, and no money to get new ones, having Received but 25 Dollars since March Eighty which passed six for one and no expectations of getting any sone.

Recollections of an Army Cook and Washerwoman
(Sarah Osborne)

They [the American troops], however, marched immediately for a place called Williamsburg, as she thinks, deponent [Sarah Osborn] alternately on horseback and on foot. There arrived, they remained two days till the army all came in by land and then marched for Yorktown, or Little York as it was then called. The York troops were posted at the right, the Connecticut troops next, and the French to the left. In about one day or less than a day, they reached the place of encampment about one mile from Yorktown. . . . Deponent's attention was arrested by the appearance of a large plain between them and Yorktown and an entrenchment thrown up. She also saw a number of dead Negroes lying round their encampment, whom she understood the British had driven out of the town and left to starve, or were first starved and then thrown out. Deponent took her stand just back of the American tents, say about a mile from the town, and busied herself washing, mending, and cooking for the soldiers, in which she was assisted by the other females; some men washed their own clothing. She heard the roar of the artillery for a number of days, and the last night the Americans threw up entrenchments, it was a misty, foggy night, rather wet but not rainy. Every soldier threw up for himself, as she understood, and she afterwards saw and went into the entrenchments. Deponent's said husband was there throwing up entrenchments, and deponent cooked and carried in beef, and bread, and coffee (in a gallon pot) to the soldiers in the entrenchment.

On one occasion when deponent was thus employed carrying in provisions, she met General Washington, who asked her if she "was not afraid of the cannonballs?"

She replied, "No, the bullets would not cheat the gallows," that "It would not do for the men to fight and starve too."

They dug entrenchments nearer and nearer to Yorktown every night or two till the last. While digging that, the enemy fired very heavy till about nine o'clock next morning, then stopped, and the drums from the enemy beat excessively. Deponent was a little way off in Colonel Van Schaick's or the officers' marquee and a number of officers were present, among whom was Captain Gregg, who, on account of infirmities, did not go out much to do duty.

The drums continued beating, and all at once the officers hurrahed and swung their hats, and deponent asked them, "What is the matter now?"

One of them replied, "Are not you soldier enough to know what it means?"

Deponent replied, "No."

They then replied, "The British have surrendered."

Deponent, having provisions ready, carried the same down to the entrenchments that morning, and four of the soldiers whom she was in the habit of cooking for ate their breakfasts.

Deponent stood on one side of the road and the American officers upon the other side when the British officers came out of the town and rode up to the American officers and delivered up [their swords, which the deponent] thinks were returned again, and the British officers rode right on before the army, who marched out beating and playing a melancholy tune, their drums covered with black handkerchiefs and their fifes with black ribbands tied around them, into an old field and there grounded their arms and then returned into town again to await their destiny. Deponent recollects seeing a great many American officers, some on horseback and some on foot, but cannot call them all by name. Washington, Lafayette, and Clinton were among the number. The British general at the head of the army was a large, portly man, full face, and the tears rolled down his cheeks as he passed along. She does not recollect his name, but it was not Cornwallis. She saw the latter afterwards and noticed his being a man of diminutive appearance and having cross eyes.

Provisions of the Peace Treaty of Paris, 1783

Article I

His Britannic Majesty acknowledges the said United States, viz. New Hampshire, Massachusetts Bay, Rhode Island, and Providence Plantations, Connecticut, New York, New Jersey, Pennsylvania, Delaware, Maryland, Virginia, North Carolina, South Carolina, and Georgia, to be free, sovereign and independent States; that he treats with them as such, and for himself, his heirs and successors, relinquishes all claims to the Government, propriety and territorial rights of the same, and every part thereof.

Article II

And that all disputes which might arise in future, on the subject of the boundaries of the said United States may be prevented, it is hereby agreed and declared, that the following are, and shall be their boundaries, viz: From the northwest angle of Nova Scotia, viz. that angle which is formed by a line drawn due north from the source of Saint Croix River to the Highlands; along the said Highlands which divide those rivers that empty themselves into the river St. Lawrence, from those which fall into the Atlantic Ocean, to the northwesternmost head of Connecticut River; thence down along the middle of that river, to the forty-fifth degree of north latitude; from thence, by a line due west on said latitude, until it strikes the river Iroquois or Cataraquy; thence along the middle of said river into Lake Ontario, through the middle of said lake until it strikes the communication by water between that lake and Lake Erie; thence along the middle of said communication into Lake Erie, through the middle of said lake until it arrives at the water communication between that lake and Lake Huron; thence along the middle of said water communication into the Lake Huron; thence through the middle of said lake to the water communication between that lake and Lake Superior; thence through Lake Superior northward of the Isles Royal and Phelipeaux, to the Long Lake; thence through the middle of said Long Lake, and the water communication between it and the Lake of the Woods, to the said Lake of the Woods; thence through the said lake to the most northwestern point thereof, and from thence on a due west course to the river Mississippi; thence by a line to be drawn along the middle of the said river Mississippi until it shall intersect the northernmost part of the thirty-first degree of north latitude. South, by a line to be drawn due east from the determination of the line last mentioned, in the latitude of thirty-one degrees north of the Equator, to the middle of the river Apalachicola or Catahouche; thence along the middle thereof to its junction with the Flint River; thence straight to the head of St. Mary's River; and thence down along the middle of St. Mary's River to the Atlantic Ocean. East, by a line to be drawn along the middle of the river St. Croix, from its mouth in the Bay of Fundy to its source, and from its source directly north to the aforesaid Highlands, which divide the rivers that fall into the Atlantic Ocean from whose which fall into the river St. Lawrence; comprehending all islands within twenty leagues of any part of the shores of the United States, and lying between lines to be drawn due east from the points where the aforesaid boundaries between Nova Scotia on the one part, and East Florida on the other, shall respectively touch the Bay of Fundy and the Atlantic Ocean; excepting such islands as now are, or heretofore have been, within the limits of the said province of Nova Scotia.

Article III

It is agreed that the people of the United States shall continue to enjoy unmolested the right to take fish of every kind on the Grand Bank, and on all the other banks of Newfoundland; also in the Gulph of Saint Lawrence, and at all other places in the sea where the inhabitants of both countries used at any time heretofore to fish. And also that the inhabitants of the United States shall have liberty to take fish of every kind on such part of the coast of Newfoundland as British fishermen shall use (but not to dry or cure the same on that island) and also on the coasts, bays, and creeks of all other of His Britannic Majesty's dominions in America; and that the American fishermen shall have liberty to dry and cure fish in any of the unsettled bays, harbours, and creeks of Nova Scotia, Magdalen Islands, and Labrador, so long as the same shall remain unsettled; but so soon as the same or either of them shall be settled, it shall not be lawful for the said fishermen to dry or cure fish at such settlement, without a previous agreement for that purpose with the inhabitants, proprietors, or possessors of the ground.

Article IV

It is agreed that creditors on either side shall meet with no lawful impediment to the recovery of the full value in sterling money, of all bona fide debts heretofore contracted.

Article V

It is agreed that the Congress shall earnestly recommend it to the legislatures of the respective States, to provide for the restitution of all estates, rights, and properties which have been confiscated, belonging to real British subjects, and also of the estates, rights, and properties of persons resident in districts in the possession of His Majesty's arms, and who have not borne arms against the said United States. And that persons of any other description shall have free liberty to go to any part or parts of any of the thirteen United States, and therein to remain twelve months, unmolested in their endeavours to obtain the restitution of such of their estates, rights, and properties as may have been confiscated; and that Congress shall also earnestly recommend to the several States a reconsideration and revision of all acts or laws regarding the premises, so as to render the said laws or acts perfectly consistent, not only with justice and equity, but with that spirit of conciliation which, on the return of the blessings of peace, should universally prevail. And that Congress shall also earnestly recommend to the several States, that the estates, rights, and properties of such last mentioned persons, shall be restored to them, they refunding to any persons who may be now in possession, the bona fide price (where any has been given) which such persons may have paid on purchasing any of the said lands, rights, or properties, since the confiscation. And it is agreed, that all persons who have any interest in confiscated lands, either by debts, marriage settlements, or otherwise, shall meet with no lawful impediment in the prosecution of their just rights.

Article VI

That there shall be no future confiscations made, nor any prosecutions commenc'd against any person or persons for, or by reason of the part which he or they may have taken in the present war; and that no person shall, on that account, suffer any future loss or damage, either in his person, liberty, or property; and that those who may be in confinement on such charges, at the time of the ratification of the treaty in America, shall be immediately set at liberty, and the prosecutions so commenced be discontinued.

Article VII

There shall be a firm and perpetual peace between His Britannic Majesty and the said States, and between the subjects of the one and the citizens of the other, wherefore all hostilities, both by sea and land, shall from henceforth cease: All prisoners on both sides shall be set at liberty, and His

Britannic Majesty shall, with all convenient speed, and without causing any destruction, or carrying away any negroes or other property of the American inhabitants, withdraw all his armies, garrisons, and fleets from the said United States, and from every port, place, and harbour within the same; leaving in all fortifications the American artillery that may be therein: And shall also order and cause all archives, records, deeds, and papers, belonging to any of the said States, or their citizens, which, in the course of the war, may have fallen into the hands of his officers, to be forthwith restored and deliver'd to the proper States and persons to whom they belong.

Article VIII

The navigation of the river Mississippi, from its source to the ocean, shall forever remain free and open to the subjects of Great Britain, and the citizens of the United States.

Article IX

In case it should so happen that any place or territory belonging to Great Britain or to the United States, should have been conquer'd by the arms of either from the other, before the arrival of the said provisional articles in America, it is agreed, that the same shall be restored without difficulty, and without requiring any compensation.

Article X

The solemn ratifications of the present treaty, expedited in good and due form, shall be exchanged between the contracting parties, in the space of six months, or sooner if possible, to be computed from the day of the signature of the present treaty. In witness thereof, we the undersigned, their Ministers Plenipotentiary, have in their name and in virtue of our full powers, signed with our hands the present definitive treaty, and caused the seals of our arms to be affix'd thereto.

Done at Paris, this third day of September, in the year of our Lord one thousand seven hundred and eighty-three.

D. HARTLEY
JOHN ADAMS
B. FRANKLIN
JOHN JAY

✂ E S S A Y S

In the first essay, the much celebrated and much maligned role of the militia is analyzed in its historical context by Professor Don Higginbotham, a Revolutionary War scholar at the University of North Carolina, Chapel Hill. Gregg L. Lint, a scholar of the diplomatic history of the American Revolution and an associate editor of the Adams Papers, with particular responsibility for the papers of John Adams, writes in the second essay on the treaty that ended the war.

The Strengths and Weaknesses of the Militia

DON HIGGINBOTHAM

"There, my lads, are the Hessians! Tonight our flag floats over yonder hill, or Molly Stark is a widow." Those were the famous words of General John Stark to his militiamen on the eve of the Battle of Bennington, and thanks to them Molly Stark did not lose her vain and volatile husband. For on August 16, 1777, Stark's New Hampshire and Vermont followers smashed a column of Germans from General John Burgoyne's British army, a little gem of a triumph with far-reaching consequences.

Before we sing Stark's praises, other more sobering facts are in order. The Continental Congress had recently rebuked Stark for failing to unite his band with the American northern army and place himself under the jurisdiction of its commander. If we are inclined to agree with the historian who commented that this was one occasion when insubordination achieved splendid results, we might look ahead to October 7 of that same year: within minutes of General Horatio Gates's climactic battle of the Saratoga campaign against Burgoyne, Stark departed from Gates's camp with his entire militia because their enlistments had expired. These episodes illustrate the complexity of analyzing the performance of militia in the War of Independence.

My purpose in examining the militia is several-fold: to put in historical perspective the approach of previous generations to this subject and, more importantly, to weave together recent strands of scholarship and to add something of my own—to achieve, all told, a kind of overview. . . .

There is a decidedly negative image of the militia in most of our historical literature. Taking as a prime case in point Stark's irresponsibility at Saratoga, C. H. Van Tyne, in his Pulitzer Prize–winning account of the war, declared that "few events . . . so proved the utter failure of the militia system."

When did this view originate? One must commence with Washington and his generals of the Continental Army who labored strenuously and for the most part futilely to secure a long-term professional army modeled in important respects after contemporary European systems. Only such a formidable, well-structured military arm could exchange blow for blow with the legions of Gage, Howe, and Clinton. The militia were seen as poorly trained, ill-disciplined, and unreliable. They were, complained General Nathanael Greene, "people coming from home with all the tender feelings of domestic life" and "not sufficiently fortified with natural courage to stand the shocking scenes of war. To march over dead men, to hear without concern the groans of the wounded, I say few men can stand such scenes unless steeled by habit or fortified by military pride."

The temporary soldiers were wasteful of supplies and weapons. General John Lacey of Pennsylvania, himself a state-level officer, conceded in 1777 that departing militia "had left their camp equipage strewed everywhere—Muskets, Cartouch-boxes, Camp kettels, and blankets—some in and some out of the huts the men had left, with here and there a Tent—some standing and some fallen down." Local units made off with so many Continental weapons that Washington implored "that every possible means may be used to recover them [for] the public and no more delivered to Militia."

Small wonder, given these attitudes, that serious friction erupted between Continentals and militia. To Joseph Reed, president of the Executive Council of Pennsylvania, "the jealousy which has taken place in this State, between the Continental troops and them, very much" resembled "the behaviour of the [British] Regulars and our Provincials" in the French and Indian War. Reed cautioned Nathanael Greene that, if the Rhode Island general had in fact been guilty of criticizing militia (as was reported in Philadelphia), he might be more guarded in his future comments. More openly contemptuous was a Colonel Jackson of the Continental line, who, in sending a detachment of regulars to Dorchester, Massachusetts, in 1777, instructed the captain in charge to take no orders from Colonel Thomas Crafts of the militia. . . .

. . . Jackson was scarcely the only Continental colonel who looked askance at taking orders from a militia general. "I have the fullest confidence that you will not put me in a Situation to be commanded by General Herkimer" of the militia, pleaded Colonel Goose Van Schaick, a regular, to Governor George Clinton of New York in 1777. These sentiments were echoed in 1780 by Colonel Daniel Morgan of the Continentals, who warned General Gates that he would find it humiliating to take orders from Virginia militia brigadiers.

Such condescension seemed so well founded that in the postwar years the militia were all but totally excluded from a rightful place in the Revolutionary firmament. Histories of the period focused upon the Continental Army, commanded by Washington, who quite understandably drew the spotlight to events associated with him. Furthermore, the narrator's task was simplified by staying center stage, avoiding the briars and brambles of the wings or peripheral areas where the militia usually operated. Finally, much of our military history was penned by professional soldiers, like Emory Upton, with an ax to grind for a professional military establishment. In our day, however, this traditionally harsh portrait of Revolutionary militia is being challenged. The impact of guerrilla or irregular warfare in the post-1945 world has spawned a desire to understand the place of nonregulars in the winning of independence.

Let us now turn to three somewhat interrelated questions. Who were the militia? What were their functions in the war? And which of those functions did they handle best? The first query sounds easier than it really is. To be sure, the English colonies had included most free white males within the militia structure, and this near universal requirement did not change in 1775 or 1776. Several current researchers have stated or implied that the actual composition of the state militias and the Continental Army was considerably different; that the productive citizens preferred service in the local military outfit, which would normally remain fairly close to home; that the Continentals came substantially from the lower echelons of American society—indentured servants, paid substitutes, farm laborers, unemployed persons, and transients, to say nothing of Blacks and British deserters.

These configurations have led to the conclusion that the long-suffering Continentals at Valley Forge and elsewhere were, rather than freedom fighters, mercenaries not much unlike those in European armies. Perhaps so; there is no need to sugarcoat our history. Still, if enlistees counted the monetary features of shouldering muskets as the overwhelming attraction, why were American armies always so short of manpower? . . .

Undoubtedly motivation for service—both militia and Continentals—must be examined in several contexts, including time and place. The patriotic response early in the war tended to be enthusiastic, especially that of the New England militia; but at the same time the Continental rifle companies to be raised in the frontier counties from Virginia to Pennsylvania were quickly filled, with many would-be volunteers left behind. Recruiting for Continental and state establishments as well probably suffered in areas—Philadelphia and parts of Maryland, for example—where the dominant political elites were unpopular and where class divisions worsened as a result of economic friction over war profiteering and the hoarding of goods.

Militia officers too are worth some analysis. Colonial Americans had actively sought commissions in the militia, as much for reasons of prestige as anything else. Even Jefferson, of all people, was a county lieutenant in Virginia. Whereas in New England there was a tradition of electing militia officers, the conflict with Britain saw the extension of that practice, especially below field grade, to New York, New Jersey, Pennsylvania, Maryland, and southward. The demand for officers was infinitely greater than ever—than for any of the colonial wars or, quite obviously, for the periods of peace, since militia organizations had deteriorated or become virtually extinct between imperial conflicts. Then, too, some former officers declined to serve in the revamped patriot forces because they were loyalists; while others, accused of being on the king's side, were squeezed out. Consequently, the officer ranks were opened dramatically, as in Maryland. . . .

Expanding the social range of militia officers had significant democratic implications in Maryland and elsewhere. Because local tensions engendered uneven support for the war, Maryland officers at times found their men extremely difficult to control, and officers themselves, willingly or through duress, took positions held by the rank and file. On the other hand, in New England, with its strong whig fervor, militia companies not only picked their officers, but sometimes members of a company adopted a document—a kind of covenant—stating their concerns and principles, their rules of behavior, and their limits or restrictions upon their officers' authority. "What you have," writes Alfred F. Young, "is not quite Cromwell's soldiers debating around the campfires (although maybe some of that) but a democratic soldiery with all the implications of that word."

The election of officers scarcely ever resulted in elevating the ablest men to leadership positions. Thus the New York provincial congress urged in December 1775 that militia officers be picked subsequently "according to their true merit and ability to serve the public." Few newly chosen officers were as self-effacing as a Mr. Beeker of Tryon County, New York, who, it was reported, "modestly declined" appointment to command a company, "alleging his want of education and experience for a station involving so much responsibility." Instead, Beeker proposed a Mr. Luke, who evidently had some military background and who was then "elected by a large majority." Once the training began, so our informant continues, French and Indian War veterans "were particularly engaged in giving instruction and advice," as was also true in Philadelphia and elsewhere. . . .

Officers with the most extensive experience in earlier wars often accepted Continental commissions. Later the leadership of the militia was bolstered by officers who resigned from the regular army, returned home, and took rank in the militia. . . .

But, for the most part, such individuals came home to continue their military careers in the state constabularies. And that, not infrequently, brought political gain from their militia exploits. . . .

When Virginians replaced Jefferson as the state's chief executive in 1781, they tapped General Thomas Nelson, head of the militia since 1777; and Nelson was elevated principally because of his military reputation. Another governorship appears to bear militia-versus-Continental overtones: the 1777 election in New York of Brigadier General George Clinton of the militia over Major General Philip Schuyler of the Continental line, with Clinton projecting the image—synonymous with the militia—of being a man of the people, militantly anti-tory.

Now for our second question: the function of the militia in the War of Independence. It is abundantly clear what that institution could not do: namely, carry the brunt of the conflict. Militia units, John Shy reminds us, had done relatively little fighting as regular formations in the colonial wars. Their previous responsibilities were more "a hybrid of draft board and modern reserve unit—a modicum of military training combined with a mechanism to find and enlist individuals when they were needed." Therefore, the Continental Congress opted to wage war by means of a Continental army, whose general favored minimal reliance upon militia. From the army's camp at Cambridge in 1775, Nathanael Greene asserted, "With regard to the Militia we have no occasion for them. We have here as many of the Province Militia as we know what to do with." Greene's feelings had not changed, only deepened, when he vowed some months later that "all the force in America should be under one Commander raised and appointed by the same Authority, subjected to the same Regulations and ready to be detacht where ever Occasion may require."

Even if Congress and the states responded by raising a formidable army, Washington was a realist; his own forces would hardly be able to contest British regulars and to defend the colonies against their internal enemies as well. "The Militia," he counseled, in explaining his unwillingness to respond to various local crises, should be "more than competent to all purposes" of internal security. Actually, he probably intended to alert colony leaders that they would have to fend for themselves against loyalists, potentially hostile blacks in their midst, and Indians on their frontiers. To scatter his regiments, to be at all places at all times, would have reduced the Virginian to small-unit operations. Unable to openly contend with General William Howe and his successors, Washington would have had no alternative to guerrilla warfare, or what was known then as partisan war, or *la petite guerre.*

Washington instead advocated a response to the enemy that, in modern terminology, is known as the principle of concentration, or mass. "It is of the greatest importance to the safety of a Country involved in a defensive war," he explained, "to endeavor to draw their Troops together at some post at the opening of a Campaign, so central to the theater of War that they may be sent to the support of any part of the Country [that] the Enemy may direct their motions against."

His thinking made sense. To divide his own army would invite his adversaries to defeat it in detail. Besides, a guerrilla conflict had other disadvantages. One might harass and annoy the enemy effectively without its being beaten decisively or driven from the country. That kind of aggressiveness was a tall order, but Congress wanted it. The lawmakers wished the army to stand and fight; and Washington was combative by instinct, although after 1776 he became more cautious, endeavoring to choose the moment and the place that would provide him the greatest advantage and the smallest risk. Then, too, a guerrilla struggle would pose internal dangers to the cause: such physical destruction, such savagery and bloodletting, that the internal institutions of the country, along with the political and legal processes, might fall sacrifice to the war. And in the main, the Revolution's leaders were conservative in both political and military outlook; their principal aims were to preserve and build rather than to tear down and destroy. Finally, the presence of the Continental Army intact offered Americans a symbol of unity and an object of national feeling, just as it was to the outside world—where the patriots hoped to get tangible support—a sign of conventional military strength.

So, in Washington's view, the Continentals and militia had separate, although mutually supportive, roles to play. To improve the militia's effectiveness and to create a degree of uniformity everywhere, Congress made recommendations to the colonies as to the size and organization of regiments. If these proposals were disregarded, they were still definitely in order; for although the patriot militias were to resemble closely their colonial predecessors, the Americans encountered problems in reviving that military instrument. Initial laws were enacted in such haste that they had to be amended or superseded with more comprehensive statutes.

Maryland is a case in point. In December 1774, the Maryland convention passed a resolution for establishing "a well regulated" militia. While the convention instructed the inhabitants between the ages of sixteen and fifty to form themselves into sixty-eight-man companies and to elect their officers, it made no provision for the machinery of mobilization, for officers of field grades, or for specific civil oversight. Was the militia to receive orders only from the convention, the colony-wide council, or the local committees of observation—or might all exercise a controlling and perhaps overlapping and conflicting hand? Following Lexington and Concord, the convention provided the answers and called for artillery units and minute companies. Minute companies there and elsewhere did not work out in actual practice to be satisfactory, and after a time many simply faded out of the picture or, as in New Jersey and New York, were expressly abolished. . . .

As an institution . . . the militia proved deficient. The law-making bodies of the colony-states were never able to bring these military organizations up to meeting their responsibilities. The reason in part is that, as time passed, those responsibilities were vastly enlarged—to the point of embracing just about everything of a military nature. If we are mindful of this all-encompassing role they were asked to play, then we can better understand their limitations and their failures. If, as Washington said, the militia were best suited to control the home front, the problem was that the pressures of the war never allowed them to so restrict themselves.

Only initially, in the first year or so, were the militias able to confine the scope of their duties—to enforce the 1774 Continental Association of Congress on non-importation, to compel people to take sides, to put down loyalist uprisings, to seize military stores from royal governors, and to keep the slave population under control. Increasingly thereafter the state forces were involved in repelling Indian incursions, taking the offensive against the tribesmen, and engaging British coastal raiding parties. Besides, wartime demands, especially the manpower deficiencies of the Continental Army, prompted drafts—usually of short-term duration—to flesh out the ranks of the regulars; they also resulted in drafts, on a large scale, from existing militia units, which then were reorganized into new regiments; and, unlike the trend of the colonial wars, already established militia regiments were sometimes thrust into service. All of these various contingents were not infrequently asked to fight next to Washington's soldiers in formalized engagements. When required to stay for extended lengths in the field far from home, when mixed closely with sizable bodies of Continentals, and when performing against redcoats in open combat—the militia were at their worst. Nothing in their modest training, not to mention their normally deficient equipment and supplies, prepared them for these duties.

If Washington against his better judgment had to throw militia on the front lines with Continentals, there were also situations when part-time defenders had to oppose the enemy alone, particularly when British raiding parties descended upon the coast of a state and, now and then, penetrated inland. So it was in Virginia, which between 1779 and 1781 reeled from a succession of blows. British Generals Edward Mathew, Alexander Leslie, Benedict Arnold, William Phillips, and Lord Cornwallis roamed and pillaged over sections of the tidewater and even into the piedmont. Time and time the counties were urged to turn out their militia, of whom—wailed Jefferson—"there is not a single man who has ever seen the face of an Enemy."

Simultaneously, the state's resources were being drained southward, for it was serving as a troop-and-supply center for American operations in the Carolinas.

The greenness of the defenders and the repeated demands upon their services, combined with shortages of weapons, equipment, and transportation in an overwhelmingly rural, agricultural society, made it impossible to keep the militia in the field for protracted periods. . . . Even so, in Pennsylvania, New Jersey, New York, and other states the civilian leadership made repeated efforts to make the militia more resilient. No one labored harder at this task than Virginia's Governor Thomas Nelson in 1781. Nelson advocated for some of the militia "constant training, notwithstanding the expense." Here was the notion of a kind of "standing" militia, well trained and ready to go anywhere on sudden notice. Nelson's scheme never gained acceptance, but as chief executive he received from the legislature an enlargement of the governor's powers over the militia. With the consent of his council, the governor could assemble as many of the militia as he thought necessary and could hasten them to any part of the state; he could also employ them to impress supplies and to act in various other ways. Deserters could now receive the death penalty, while others who failed to come forward could be given six months' additional service.

In a more limited way, both Washington and Congress sought to invigorate the militia without appreciably weakening the regular forces. The most common form of succor was to detach Continental officers for duty with the militia in their home states in times of alarm, as, for example, when Generals George Weedon and Peter Muhlenberg returned to Virginia in 1780. North Carolina's only active brigadier general during the last three years of the conflict, Jethro Sumner, directed the state's militia in harassing the enemy. To keep the militia in arms at crucial moments Congress might even offer to pay the militia and maintain their upkeep, as it did for New York detachments garrisoning Fort Schuyler.

All these endeavors did not dramatically change the performance of the militia. When we seek to find what was revolutionary about the American Revolution, as scholars have done since the days of J. F. Jameson, there is no reason to look to the militia, which institutionally remained very similar to what it had been in the colonial period. Yet, as we have seen, its duties in a sense were revolutionary: it was expected to perform virtually every military function imaginable. Indeed, for this very reason—that so much was demanded of the local contingents—I believe the overall impression of the militia should be one of admiration, not derision.

Where specifically did the militia earn their highest marks? We find that answer in their own backyards, in operations within their own immediate districts, and sometimes in colony- or state-wide endeavors. These activities were always exceedingly important, but in the months before and after the outbreak of hostilities at Lexington and Concord they were absolutely essential to the launching and the continuation of the Revolution as a war. The militia's use of muscle guaranteed that the patriots would maintain

control of the political and law-enforcing machinery in every colony. Therefore, from a military point of view, these months were quite likely the most
crucial period of the Revolution. If one result of this militia-backed take-
over was that the loyalists were to remain permanently on the defensive,
surely another consequence was that virtually everywhere British armies
landed they encountered a hostile environment. That circumstance helps
explain why enormous quantities of supplies and provisions for royal regiments had to come from the mother country, 3,000 miles away, rather than
from the mainland colonies. . . .

Both propositions invite closer scrutiny, although the first one has been
expressed on several occasions of late. It was probably Walter Millis in 1956
who initially stressed the local role of the militia in the opening rounds of
the struggle: "the much despised and frequently unwarlike" militia's choking
off any chance of a loyalist "counter-revolution," as he phrased it. Whatever
their methods—and they ranged from intimidation to violence—these home
guards did the job. Most of those who publicly spoke or acted against the
edicts of the community committees, provincial congresses, or Continental
Congress were punished or else they recanted, as did Robert Davis of Anne
Arundel County in Maryland. When whig militiamen sought to interrogate
him, he shouted from behind closed doors, "You damned rebel sons of
bitches—I will shoot you if you come any nearer." When his tormentors
prepared to storm his house, Davis's threats turned to hollow rhetoric. He
meekly consented to come before the committee of safety, where he apol-
ogized for his verbal indiscretion.

The second proposition, concerning the British army's inhospitable sur-
roundings, needs more extended commentary. British columns, except for
Burgoyne's, usually advanced relatively unimpeded from one fixed point to
another. But the redcoats and their loyalist allies had minimal accomplishments outside or beyond those fixed points, which were the cities and occasional towns and fortified geographical locations. One accomplishment that
historians, however grudgingly, have conceded to the militia as irregulars is
their hit-and-run activity against British patrols and outposts *behind the lines,*
with the South Carolina trio of Marion, Sumter, and Pickens receiving most
of the limelight. But, as the observation about fixed points suggests, the
areas of effective British control were scarcely expansive enough for the
expression *behind the lines* to have much meaning. In any event, we might
well examine more closely sectors that are clearly *between the lines:* broadly
speaking, between the contending armies or not completely in the hands of
either side. It was there that the loyalists were most aggressive; there, too,
that the British sought to obtain supplies, with forage generally the most
sought-after commodity. In seeking to checkmate the enemy in these broad
zones, the American militia made a most substantial contribution, second
only in magnitude to their sustaining local and provincial whig governmental
machinery at the onset of the Revolution. (And we may add, because of
their early strong-armed tactics, which were repeated later in the war whenever necessary, there was generally a somewhat secure, stable behind-the-
lines region for Continental armies.)

There were whig-tory clashes large and small between the lines, so many, in fact—they number in the hundreds—that the London-published *Annual Register* predicted that "by such skirmishes . . . the fate of America must be necessarily decided." Sizable, well-publicized encounters included Moore's Creek Bridge in 1776, where 1,400 North Carolinians killed or captured virtually an entire force of roughly the same strength, and King's Mountain in 1780, where again the opposing bands numbered over a thousand and again scarcely a soul among the king's friends escaped. Lesser known struggles also involved numerous participants, such as Kettle Creek near the Georgia-Carolina border in 1779, where 700 tories scattered before a much smaller whig party, or Ramsour's Mill in North Carolina in 1780, where another 700 loyalists were dispersed, although there were heavy casualties on both sides.

For illustrative purposes these encounters merit further comment. In all four instances the crown's followers, previously cowed by threats from local patriots, had mustered their courage because they foresaw the protection of British regulars. Moore's Creek Bridge was such a devastating setback for England in North Carolina (the loyalists had come forth in the belief they were to be aided by a royal expedition on the coast) that the tories kept their peace for over four years, that is, until they again saw the prospect of a British invasion of the state in 1780, when Lord Cornwallis's troops appeared in upper South Carolina. But after their premature rising and reversal at Ramsour's Mill, only thirty of them united with His Lordship at Camden. Also important were the results at Kettle Creek; most of the tories of the upper Savannah River region were fearful of showing their true colors for over a year, until the British capture of Charleston in 1780. And as for King's Mountain, the royalist defeat was a blow from which the cause of Britain in the western Carolinas never recovered.

If these battles were all in the South, there were obviously others above the Mason-Dixon line, most of which were less spectacular and involved fewer numbers, a remark that holds true for between-the-lines skirmishing during the British occupation of New York and Philadelphia. Describing "a five-year war of neighbors" across from Manhattan Island in the Hackensack Valley (of Bergen County, New Jersey, and lower Orange County, New York), a local historian declared that while the "militia daily risked brushes with . . . raiders from New York," all too many Continentals remained in their cold-weather encampments and "did not hear a gun fired in battle from one year to the next."

The statement, if exaggerated, is not without some validity, although militia units themselves were often dazed and demoralized by initial British invasions. Yet they did revive, particularly after the crimson-clad regiments settled into winter quarters or congregated at fixed points. . . .

British and German diarists say not only that the rebel militia harassed and bloodied the tories, but that the American amateurs made it necessary for their foraging parties combing the countryside to be escorted by anywhere between several hundred and several thousand regulars. It was such a scavenging expedition—detached from Burgoyne's army in search of food and horse—that was crushed by Stark at Bennington. The preponderance of these encounters were only skirmishes; but to the British they were nasty affairs, expensive in time and matériel and successful in limiting the effectiveness of the foragers. British Lieutenant Colonel Charles Stuart complained that the conflict over forage "kept the army the whole winter [of 1776–1777] in perpetual harassment, and upon a modest computation has lost us more men than the last campaign."

To John Ewald, a German officer serving in the middle states, this "partisan war," as he termed it, "was carried on constantly in full force." The finest troops were deployed against the whig marauders, whom he variously described as "the country people" and "uncivilized mountaineers." But the best—"the Jäger Corps, the light infantry, and the Queen's Rangers"—were themselves bedeviled by the intruders, were compelled to get their rest at midday "because rest can seldom be enjoyed at night and in the morning."

What of a remedy for these raids, ambushes, and nocturnal intrusions? Ewald felt that when the British entered an area, large segments of the army, not just the light units, should be sent out: search and destroy missions, in the language of recent warfare, against roving rebel bands. That was a doubtful cure. In any case, a solution was never found, not by Howe or Clinton in the North, not by Cornwallis in the South. "I will not say much in praise of the militia of the Southern Colonies," confided Cornwallis, "but the list of British officers and soldiers killed and wounded by them . . . proves but too fatally that they are not wholly contemptible." . . .

Outside of New York and Pennsylvania the part-time soldiers held their own against the Indians. In 1776, state-supported columns from Virginia and the Carolinas devastated the settlements of the Cherokee, who were never again a serious threat. And the expeditions of George Rogers Clark, if they did not win the West as his biographers have claimed, did save Kentucky. Even in standardized confrontations with British veterans, the militia occasionally provided much needed help: at Princeton, Savannah, Cowpens, Eutaw Springs, and Springfield. Why did militia stand tall in some battles and not in others? It depended on how they were employed and how they were led. There is an old axiom that civilian-soldiers would go just as far on the battlefield as their officers would take them. Officers like Daniel Morgan and Andrew Pickens would take them quite a distance.

Today, quite properly, the pendulum has swung back toward a more favorable image of the militia and their contributions to American independence. But we may wish to halt its movement before it swings too far, before it denies Washington's Continentals their just desserts. John Shy has accurately spoken of the "triangularity of the struggle," of two armed forces contending "less with each other than for the support and control of the civilian population." Generally . . . I think the Continentals did a reasonably good job—better than the British army—of behaving with propriety, even sensitivity, toward the noncombatant elements. Generals like Washington,

Greene, Gates, Schuyler, and Lincoln recognized this delicate dimension to the conflict.

Not so the militia. Nothing so reminds us that the Revolution was also a civil war as certain activities of the home-front defenders. Their very éclat as a constabulary and enforcer of conformity posed a threat. As the war dragged on and as animosities increased, the ruthlessness of the whig militia—and their careless lack of discrimination between friend and foe—to say nothing of their dabbling in local politics—alarmed both state and congressional authorities. The Reverend James Caldwell of Springfield, New Jersey, a staunch patriot whose wife was killed in a British raid, was himself shot down by a trigger-happy militiaman; the minister had gone into enemy-controlled country to bring out a young woman and was returning under a flag of truce when his senseless death occurred. Pennsylvania's General Lacey acknowledged the destructiveness of his own men and agreed with a friend who complained that "Numbers of the Inhabitants begin to be more afraid of our own [militia] than the Army of General Howe." General Greene in the South was equally concerned about the extreme retribution that whig civilian-soldiers inflicted upon tories and alleged royalist sympathizers, fearing it would alienate myriad potential friends. . . .

Greene's concern elicits another observation. Continental officers not only sought to hold down militia atrocities in day-to-day military campaigning; they additionally may have had a strong hand in persuading the patriot inhabitants to accept the loyalists back into the American fold as the war slowly drew to an end. The process of reassimilation, having never received more than passing investigation, warrants careful scrutiny. For despite the deep bitterness in both camps, the patriots, however grudgingly, allowed most of the tories to return to their own communities. . . .

The experiences of the Revolution indicated that a strong dose of central control was required to upgrade the militias of the states. Although reforms such as those proposed by Washington, Steuben, and others failed to impress the Confederation government of the 1780s, the military provisions of the Constitution appeared to represent a triumph of those ideas. The new political instrument contained authority for a radically different kind of militia system. The Congress, in the language of the Constitution, "shall have Power" to call "forth the Militia [of the states] to execute the Laws of the Union, suppress Insurrections and repel Invasions." These passages recognized the wide range of militia endeavors in the recent war; but now they might be carried out under federal rather than state control. Whereas the training of the Revolutionary militia had been sorely deficient, Congress was to have the power "to provide for organizing, arming, and disciplining the Militia," although "reserving to the States, respectively, the appointment of the Officers, and the Authority of training the Militia according to the discipline prescribed by Congress." . . .

Whatever the later vicissitudes of the militia, that institution, for all its frailties, made its finest contributions to the nation in the Revolution. Seldom has an armed force done so much with so little—providing a vast reservoir of manpower for a multiplicity of military needs, fighting (often unaided by Continentals) in the great majority of the 1,331 land engagements of the war. Surely in retrospect we can be as charitable toward the militia as Joseph Reed, who had watched the semi-soldiers throughout the war and who declared, "In short, at this time of day, we must say of them as [of the] Price of a wife: Be to their faults a little blind, And to their virtues very kind."

Franco-American Diplomacy and the Treaty of Paris

GREGG L. LINT

The War of the American Revolution was a conflict between the Old World and the New. It was, of course, primarily a struggle by the American colonies to achieve confirmation of their independence from Great Britain. But it was also a struggle by the Americans to obtain a peace treaty achieving objectives that were, in some cases, at odds with those of France and Spain. In an examination of this tripartite conflict among the United States, France, and Spain, the goals of each party must first be defined and then the differing perceptions of the path to peace explored.

The accurate determination of national objectives, here, peace objectives, is a difficult process for the historian. One must identify the individuals or groups he believes to have been the most instrumental in determining foreign policy, and upon that basis define what he perceives to have been the interest of a given nation at a specific time. This is a subjective process, however, and the question arises whether the definition is truly representative of the national interest or is only the view of a relatively small elite.

For France and Spain this task is made easier because both countries were relatively unified and homogeneous. . . . Moreover, the two foreign ministers, the comte de Vergennes and the conde de Floridablanca, were essentially the sole enunciators of foreign policy, and even if they occasionally resorted to questionable justifications for their policies, it was still clear what they believed their ultimate objectives to be.

With the United States the undertaking is more difficult. Representing thirteen independent states, the members of the Continental Congress were themselves divided on foreign policy. A vital objective to one section or interest group was unimportant to another, and thus the peace ultimatums adopted by Congress were the product of compromise. This situation was complicated by the fact that it would not be Congress that negotiated the peace but rather its peace commissioners, 3,000 miles away and far more aware of the realities of and opportunities presented by the European po-

"Preparing for Peace: The Objectives of the United States, France, and Spain in the War of the American Revolution," by Gregg L. Lint, in *Peace and Peacemakers: The Treaty of 1783,* Ronald Hoffman and Peter J. Albert, eds. Copyright © 1986, reprinted by permission of the University Press of Virginia.

litical situation. Thus a second set of objectives, those of the commissioners, came to equal and then surpass in importance those of the Congress, a result of both the disorderly (when compared with the French or Spanish) American political system and the decision to negotiate in Europe. . . .

The Declaration of Independence asserted that the United States was an independent, sovereign state. . . . The basic issue of the Anglo-American war for the United States became, therefore, not the achievement, but rather the confirmation of independence and thus the legitimacy of the new American government. This was to be achieved, first, by the agreement of Britain to treat with American negotiators as representatives of a sovereign state and, second, by a precise statement acknowledging that condition in a treaty of peace. . . .

Except for this political decision concerning the basis upon which negotiations could begin, the Continental Congress made no formal attempt to define its objectives before February 1779. . . . With the conclusion of the alliance, however, it became clear that the treaty would be negotiated in Europe by peace commissioners named by Congress and that, accordingly, the American peace ultimatums would have to be defined in advance.

Despite the new situation, Congress might not have undertaken the task even then without French intervention. In October 1778 Vergennes instructed Conrad Alexandre Gérard to press for congressional action and outlined his position on the various American objectives then being informally discussed. Gérard placed the demand before Congress in his letter of February 9, 1779. Ostensibly, Gérard's request reflected France's desire that the United States be prepared for negotiations in the event that the then ongoing Spanish mediation effort succeeded. There was, however, another motive: France wished to limit American objectives in order to bring them into line with her own and to remove obstacles to Spain's entry into the war. . . .

On February 23, 1779, a congressional committee presented a draft report on American peace objectives that, in light of later changes, represents the most determined effort by that body to serve the fundamental interests of the United States. The report declared that the United States was not to join the mediation without a prior acknowledgment of independence by Britain. Negotiations could then proceed with the American commissioners insisting on boundaries extending north to Canada and including the portion of present-day Ontario between Lakes Ontario and Huron, west to the Mississippi, and south to the Floridas; evacuation of all places held by British forces; acknowledgment of American fishing rights on the Grand Banks; free commerce to some port on the Mississippi south of the boundary; and, if its allies would support it by continuing hostilities, the cession or independence of Nova Scotia. Nova Scotia could be given up if the fisheries could not be otherwise obtained; if neither could be achieved, then Bermuda was to be claimed. The report also provided that if adequate compensation was made, the United States would not engage in trade with the East Indies or in slaves, would not allow settlement beyond the treaty boundaries, would cede Florida to Spain if ceded to the United States by Britain, and would enter into a reciprocal guarantee of possessions. It would not agree to a truce except during the negotiations.

Except for the portion dealing with British recognition of American independence, these objectives were in conflict with those of France and Spain. The basic problems concerned Canada, the Newfoundland fishery, and western boundaries, none of which were explicitly dealt with in the treaties of 1778. The French position was made clear on May 22, 1779, when Gérard informed Congress that France was committed only to the achievement of British recognition of American independence and would not prolong the war to achieve ends not specifically mentioned in the Franco-American treaties. He added that the boundaries could not be settled until the final peace treaty, and thus the French guarantee of American territory could not come into force until such time as peace was concluded.

There had been an awareness of the probable conflict between French and American objectives long before Congress formally defined the latter in 1779. In a memorandum written in April 1776, Vergennes stated that it was "very probable that as a result of events we could recover a part of the possessions which England took away from us in America, such as the shore fishery, that of the Gulf of St. Lawrence, Cape Breton Island, etc. etc. We are not speaking of Canada." Vergennes could renounce Canada because France lacked the resources to regain it, the general belief that the economic return was not worth the effort of reconquest, and the knowledge that such an undertaking would alienate the Americans. A formal renunciation was proposed by the United States in the Model Treaty, or treaty plan, of 1776 and was accepted by France in the alliance of 1778.

For the United States this was an important concession. Canada had long been a major American goal, as was indicated by the unsuccessful Arnold expedition of 1775. . . . For John Adams, Canada was necessary because "we shall have perpetual wars with Britain while she has a foot of ground in America."

France's renunciation of Canada did not mean that it favored substituting American for British rule, however. Vergennes informed Gérard on March 29, 1778, less than two months after signature of the Franco-American treaties, that France wished Canada to remain in British hands to assure American dependence on French support. And on October 26, 1778, Vergennes wrote to Gérard that "it would be . . . very useful if Congress's ultimatum included . . . a renunciation of Canada and Nova Scotia or at least Canada." Peace should not depend on so secondary a cause as Canada. . . .

With regard to the western boundary, Vergennes, in his instruction of October 26, was unsure of the precise Spanish position. He doubted whether Spain would accept American claims to the Mississippi and thought that Congress should consider the interests of Spain in drawing up its ultimatums. Gérard was directed to accept guidance on the matter from the unofficial Spanish representative at Philadelphia, Don Juan de Miralles. Congress already had indicated the extent of its probable willingness to satisfy Spain.

Revised instructions regarding the treaty plan, which were adopted in December 1776, provided that if Spain would join the war, the United States would "assist in reducing to the possession of Spain the town and harbour of Pensacola, *provided the citizens and inhabitants of the United States shall have the free and uninterrupted navigation of the Mississippi and use of the harbour of Pensacola.*" The United States had even been willing to go to war with Portugal if such were desired by Spain. Any hopes that such concessions, or indeed any others that Congress was likely to make, would satisfy Spain vanished when Gérard met with that body on February 15, 1779, and, according to William Henry Drayton, stated that "Spain wishes to see the territorial claims of the United States terminated. She wishes to have the navigation of the Mississippi shut, and possession of the Floridas."

Considering France's position on Canada and the fisheries and its desire that the United States recognize Spanish interests in its peace ultimatums, it is . . . remarkable . . . that French pressure and the acrimonious debate, inside Congress and outside of it, which stretched over six months, did not produce greater changes. The requirement that American independence be recognized before negotiations could begin as well as the provision defining boundaries remained. Free navigation of the Mississippi became an objective to be sought by John Jay in a treaty with Spain, and the acquisition of Canada and Nova Scotia became desirable objects in a peace treaty rather than ultimatums. Although not an ultimatum, the confirmation of American fishing rights was to be a major objective in an Anglo-American commercial treaty. The proposal for such a treaty was in line with the long-term American objective of seeking to widen its trading opportunities, but it was more immediately the result of the need to compromise over the question of the fisheries in order to obtain any ultimatums at all. Such a solution was satisfactory to France since the negotiation of a commercial treaty seemed a doubtful undertaking and thus was unlikely to affect France's own interests or objectives.

It is significant, however, that no specific American objective was formally renounced. That, together with the appointment of John Adams as the sole American peace commissioner, indicated that there were limits to France's ability to influence the American position regarding peace negotiations.

On April 12, even as debates in Congress continued over American peace objectives, France and Spain signed the Convention of Aranjuez that brought Spain into the war. A Spanish belligerency had always been an objective of the United States and France, . . . but more so for the French than the Americans. This was evident from the limited concessions that the United States was willing to make to accommodate Spanish interests as opposed to the concerted French efforts to limit American territorial acquisitions and ultimately was borne out by the terms of the Convention. There, because it needed the Spanish fleet, France undertook commitments in support of Spain that went far beyond what it expected from Spain, even to the extent of agreeing to terms that, if not directly in conflict with the Franco-American alliance, violated its spirit. . . .

For each of the three nations the peace objectives were but part of a larger policy. For France and Spain a favorable treaty would mark the end of an undertaking, for the United States a beginning. France hoped to reverse its position vis-à-vis Britain resulting from its defeat in the Seven Years' War and formalized in the Treaty of Paris of 1763. Spain sought to recover its lost territory, particularly Gibraltar, and to slow, if not reverse, its slide to the rank of a second-rate power. The United States sought to establish its independence and provide for its future prosperity by seeking trade with all nations while rejecting involvement in European political rivalries. . . .

The American Revolution seemed an opportunity for France to engage Britain on favorable terms and, initially, at little risk. According to prevailing mercantilist thought, the separation of the colonies from the mother country would deprive Great Britain of a trade—fully one-third of the total according to some sources—that could not be made up elsewhere. Britain would thus be so weakened that it would be reduced, perhaps, to the level of a second-rate power. The prospect of such an outcome, particularly if it promised to enhance French commerce by permitting entry into the American market, induced France to assume the objective of American independence as its own, despite the obvious incongruity of an absolute monarchy supporting the revolt of subjects against their king.

The initial French commitment was small, but soon expanded. Turgot, the finance minister, warned, prophetically as it turned out, that although clandestine aid could be provided at relatively little risk, it could not long continue, even in the absence of an open and declared Anglo-French war, without severely straining French finances. Vergennes, either not understanding or ignoring France's financial plight, saw the small initial cost of the aid as of no importance. Even if the Americans were overcome, the extent to which the war could be prolonged would increase British expenditures and the defeated colonies would be considerably less lucrative and governable than previously. For Vergennes, financial considerations were always opposed to "reasons of state" and it was the latter that "assured triumphs."

The moment of truth came with the arrival of news concerning the battles at Saratoga and Germantown. The outcome of those engagements permitted the American commissioners to argue that Britain might now be willing to negotiate and that the absence of a more substantial French commitment forced the United States to look with favor on such an opportunity. At that point, according to a memorandum of January 13, 1778, unsigned but presumably reflecting his thoughts, Vergennes saw only two possible options: total abandonment or full support. Abandonment was unacceptable because "England will take advantage of it by making a reconciliation, and in that case she will either preserve her supremacy wholly or partially, or she will gain an ally. Now it is known that she is disposed to sacrifice that supremacy and propose simply a sort of family compact, that is to say, a league against the House of Bourbon. The result of this will be that the Americans will become our perpetual enemies, and we must expect to see them turn all their efforts against our possessions, and against those of Spain." . . .

If Vergennes's assessment was unrealistic in the short run, it contained an element of truth in the event of a protracted war. When the treaty plan of 1776 was drafted, Congress expected that opening the American market would be enough to induce France to provide aid without a political or military alliance, but France needed a stronger attachment and thus the alliance was concluded. The initial lack of enthusiasm by the United States for such an agreement raised questions about its long-term commitment, and France might well be uneasy because the achievement of its objectives depended to a considerable degree on American adherence to the alliance. Of even more significance was the fact that the United States was fighting the war less to defeat Great Britain than to maintain its independence until Britain would agree to end the conflict and confirm what already existed. Such a recognition was Britain's to give regardless of French participation in the war, and, considering the enthusiasm on all sides in Britain for a war with France, it was never outside the realm of possibility that it would be granted. This was not a problem in late 1777 or 1778, but it always loomed as a possibility, one which Vergennes continually had to consider.

Statements by Benjamin Franklin and John Adams, both of whom were involved in the drafting of the treaty plan and would become peace commissioners, lend credence to French fears. . . . The implication was that if Britain were willing to make an acceptable offer, the United States, despite any obligations to France, would be willing to consider it. In 1780, after Vergennes had rejected his plan to disclose formally his commissions to Britain, John Adams observed that the alliance with France would last no longer than the war and that, in effect, it was in Britain's interest to make peace as soon as possible so as to remove the threat posed by it.

If France had doubts about the United States as an instrument to achieve its objectives, the Convention of Aranjuez posed questions about the American reliance on France. The obligation not to make peace until Gibraltar was taken put France in a curious situation. The United States could not be expected to delay peace for that objective since it did not constitute one of the provisions of the treaty of alliance. Nor could Spain be expected to continue the war until American independence was recognized since the Convention of Aranjuez put it under no obligation to do so even tacitly, and such an outcome ran against its own interests. At the point at which either the United States obtained recognition of its independence or Spain took Gibraltar, France would be faced with the question of what to do in regard to its other ally. This was what in fact happened in 1782 with the signature by the American peace commissioners of the preliminary articles. . . .

For the United States the continuation of the war influenced its conception of what was possible in a peace. In February 1781, following Virginia's acquiescence, Jay was instructed to agree to a treaty with Spain that did not contain a provision guaranteeing the right to free navigation on the Mississippi. By June 1781 Adams had been joined by additional peace commissioners and new instructions were issued. No longer was recognition of the United States a prerequisite to negotiations, nor were the boundaries delineated in previous instructions to be regarded as an ultimatum. Even a truce was permissible if peace could be obtained in no other way. Most importantly, the new instructions declared that "you are to make the most candid and confidential communication upon all subjects to the ministers of our generous ally, the King of France; to undertake nothing in the negotiations for peace or truce without their knowledge and concurrence; and ultimately to govern yourselves by their advice and opinion."

When these instructions were adopted they were understandable. There were genuine doubts in the minds of many members of Congress about the ability of the United States to continue the war, and, in any case, it could not do so without continued aid from France. Despite this, France in demanding such instructions overplayed its hand and created the conditions most conducive to producing the situation it feared. It would not be a Congress under the domination of a French minister, naively accepting his interpretation of events, that would negotiate the peace but rather peace commissioners 3,000 miles away. Franklin might be seen by some as too eager to appease France, but he was an experienced diplomat and an expansionist, well aware of where American interests lay. Certainly it was questionable whether Adams, if he received support from others and if conditions warranted it, would feel himself bound by the instructions. But it was Jay who provided the strongest evidence that Vergennes's policy was in jeopardy. Writing to the president of Congress on September 20, 1781, he declared that "as an American I feel an interest in the dignity of my country, which renders it difficult for me to reconcile myself to the idea of the sovereign independent States of America submitting, in the persons of their ministers, to be absolutely governed by the advice and opinions of the servants of another sovereign, especially in a case of such national importance." Moreover, the instructions put "out of the power of your ministers to improve those chances and opportunities which in the normal course of human affairs happens more or less frequently to all men."

The question posed by the new instructions, addressed by Jay and ultimately settled by the separate negotiations leading to the peace treaty of 1783, was that of legitimacy. The United States could accept aid from France and even guidance as to its objectives, but to allow France to determine the terms under which it was to exist, which was what the peace treaty was about, meant that the United States became a creature of France. Whatever standing it would have on the world stage would then be dependent upon continued French support. Such dependence was in line with French policy, but could not be accepted by the United States, particularly in view of its desire to remain outside the political system of Europe, enjoy the benefits of neutrality in its wars, and, for all intents and purposes, terminate the alliance with France at the end of the war.

It was also an important domestic issue. After the victory at Yorktown some members of Congress sought to modify the instructions of 1781 to bring them into line with American interests. This was not done because of the implications for the French alliance while the war continued and French aid remained necessary. It showed, however, an awareness that the terms of a peace treaty would be important domestically, particularly if it appeared that concessions had been made unnecessarily and sectional interests had been needlessly sacrificed. If such were perceived to be the case, then it would have a profound effect on the acceptance of the treaty and possibly even the continued cohesion of the United States under the Articles of Confederation.

The decision of Adams, Franklin, and Jay to negotiate separately and secretly had a profound effect on the achievement of peace objectives. The United States did not obtain Canada and Nova Scotia, but, by reverting to the objectives of 1779, it achieved almost everything else. The French believed that Britain bought, rather than negotiated, a peace, but there was a logic to the British concessions. Once the decision had been made to grant independence and begin serious negotiations, there was little reason to limit American boundaries to the Proclamation Line or to restrict access to the fisheries. Indeed, one can discern a certain desire for revenge, for by setting the boundary on the Mississippi and sharing the right to the free navigation of the river derived from the treaty of 1763, Britain left Spain with exactly the problem that it and France had hoped to avoid through the limitation of American objectives. By granting the Americans extensive fishing rights on the Grand Banks of Newfoundland, Britain worked a division of the fishery between itself and the United States, leaving France no better off than it had been before.

France and Spain found themselves in essentially the same position that they had occupied vis-à-vis Great Britain before the war began. France did achieve the separation of the American colonies from Britain and the removal of the British commissioner from Dunkirk, but it was unable to achieve an exclusive access to the fisheries and made no major gains in the West Indies. Also it had been unable to achieve the decisive victory that it needed to reverse the results of the treaty of 1763, and ended the war in far worse financial condition than at the start. Spain gained Minorca, but even with French help, it could not conquer Gibraltar, an object that Spain might still have obtained had it been willing to give up something suitable in return, such as Puerto Rico.

The preliminary peace treaty signed in 1782 was a triumph for American self-interest, made necessary by the conflict between the objectives of the United States and those of France and Spain. For the United States the Franco-American alliance and its tenuous connection with Spain were viable only so long as they provided a means to achieve the short-term objectives set down in the ultimatums of 1779 and did not permanently prevent the new nation from pursuing the long-term objective of remaining apart from European political affairs, with neutrality the foundation of its foreign policy. The instructions of 1781, in the minds of the American negotiators, threatened the achievement of both sets of objectives. Therefore, a separate peace was concluded in violation of the alliance, dashing French hopes of exerting significant influence over the future policies of the United States and, for all intents and purposes, ending the French alliance.

✷ *F U R T H E R   R E A D I N G*

Samuel Flagg Bemis, *The Diplomacy of the American Revolution* (1935)
George Athan Billias, ed., *George Washington's Opponents: British Generals and Admirals in the American Revolution* (1969)
R. Arthur Bowler, *Logistics and the Failure of the British Army in America, 1775–1783* (1975)
Richard Buel, Jr., *Dear Liberty: Connecticut's Mobilization for War* (1980)
E. Wayne Carp, *To Starve the Army at Pleasure: Continental Army Administration and American Political Culture, 1775–1783* (1984)
Burke Davis, *The Campaign That Won America: The Story of Yorktown* (1970)
Jonathan R. Dull, *A Diplomatic History of the American Revolution* (1985)
——, *The French Navy and American Independence: A Study of Arms and Diplomacy* (1975)
William M. Fowler, Jr., *Rebels Under Sail: The American Navy During the Revolution* (1976)
Robert A. Gross, *The Minutemen and Their World* (1976)
Ira D. Gruber, *The Howe Brothers and the American Revolution* (1972)
Don Higginbotham, *War and Society in Revolutionary America: The Wider Dimensions of the Conflict* (1988)
——, *The War of American Independence: Military Attitudes, Policies, and Practice, 1763–1789* (1971)
Ronald Hoffman and Peter J. Albert, eds., *Arms and Independence: The Military Character of the American Revolution* (1984)
——, eds., *Peace and the Peacemakers: The Treaty of 1783* (1986)
Ronald Hoffman, Thad W. Tate, and Peter J. Albert, eds., *An Uncivil War: The Southern Backcountry During the American Revolution* (1985)
James H. Hutson, *John Adams and the Diplomacy of the American Revolution* (1980)
Richard H. Kohn, *Eagle and Sword: The Beginnings of the Military Establishment in America* (1975)
Piers Mackesy, *The War for America, 1775–1783* (1964)
James Kirby Martin and Mark E. Lender, *A Respectable Army: The Military Origins of the Republic* (1982)
Richard B. Morris, *The Peacemakers: The Great Powers and American Independence* (1965)
Jan Willem Schulte Nordholt, *The Dutch Republic and American Independence* (1982)
Stephen E. Patterson, *Political Parties in Revolutionary Massachusetts* (1973)
Howard H. Peckham, ed., *The Toll of Independence: Engagements and Battle Casualties of the American Revolution* (1974)
Hugh F. Rankin, *The North Carolina Continentals* (1971)
Eric Robson, *The American Revolution in Its Political and Military Aspects* (1955)
Steven Rosswurm, *Arms, Country, and Class: The Philadelphia Militia and the "Lower Sort" During the American Revolution* (1987)
Charles Royster, *A Revolutionary People at War: The Continental Army and American Character* (1979)
John E. Selby, *The Revolution in Virginia, 1775–1783* (1988)
John Shy, *A People Numerous and Armed: Reflections on the Military Struggle for American Independence* (1976)
Marshall Smelser, *The Winning of Independence* (1972)
Jack M. Sosin, *The Revolutionary Frontier, 1763–1783* (1967)
William C. Stinchcombe, *The American Revolution and the French Alliance* (1969)
Gerald Stourzh, *Benjamin Franklin and American Foreign Policy*, 2d ed. (1969)
Willard M. Wallace, *Appeal to Arms: A Military History of the Revolution* (1951)

Casualties of Revolution: The Native Americans and the Loyalists

⋇

Most Americans today view the Revolution as a heroic, triumphant episode. The independent nation it created, with its representative system of government and its unusually broad access to economic and social opportunity, has commanded the allegiance and admiration of generations of Americans since the era of George Washington. The Revolution was painful, and, yes, it demanded great sacrifices, but most of us believe that it turned out well in the end. This is the history of the Revolution from the perspective of the winners.

Some Americans, however, regarded the Revolution as a catastrophe—an unrelieved disaster. The liberty of native Americans, for example, was threatened, not bolstered, by the patriots' victory. Seeking only to be left alone on lands guaranteed to them by treaty, native Americans cared little about the colonists' conflict with Britain except insofar as it led the United States and Britain to interfere with the status quo. Although both sides urged neutrality on the woodland peoples and formally encouraged them to stay aloof from the imperial quarrel, in actuality both sides sought a ''benevolent'' neutrality that would allow them to move troops freely through native American lands. Moreover, when particular disputes over trade and territorial issues led to physical conflicts, native Americans were drawn into the fighting, usually on the British side. Consequently, when Britain lost, the native Americans also lost. Moreover, after the war, because of the growing white population's irrepressible appetite for land, the national and state governments offered scant protection to native Americans, even those who had fought on behalf of the United States. Although the Revolutionaries did not aim to ravage the peoples of the eastern woodlands, at the least, American independence accelerated their ruin.

The other conspicuous losers in the Revolution were the active loyalists. In contrast to the native Americans, the loyalists rightly understood the Revolution as their own quarrel, and as partisans they stood to gain or lose according to the success of British arms. Thousands of them fought for the King and Parlia-

*ment, and thousands more evacuated their homes to seek shelter in British-
occupied strongholds like New York City or in Britain, Canada, or the West Indies. Castigated in the 1770s by their patriot enemies, subsequently they have
often been ignored. As a result, we have mistakenly tended to think of the Revolution as a consensus movement against British rule that displaced only a tiny
imperial elite. In fact, however, loyalty to Britain commanded substantial support in the colonies, and loyalists expressed political ideas that clearly set them
apart from the patriots. Understanding who they were and what they believed
enables us to grasp more accurately the character of the Revolution, as both a
political movement and a social experience.*

*Examining the loyalists also invites us to consider the path not taken in the
eighteenth century and to wonder whether the competitive, individualistic, and
antiauthoritarian aspects of post-Revolutionary American society would have
flourished without the ouster (between 1775 and 1783) of leaders who promoted
paternalistic, conservative principles. What seems evident from the experiences of
native Americans and loyalists in the Revolution is not only that some people
gained while others lost but also that the direction of American society and culture was significantly affected by these victories and defeats.*

✗ D O C U M E N T S

The first two documents treat the Continental Congress's policy toward native
Americans at the outset of the war. John Adams's letter makes clear that
Congress was never friendly to the native Americans and that calculations of self-
interest lay at the core of American policy. In light of Adams's remarks, the formal congressional address to the Six Iroquois Nations a month later is revealing.

The remaining documents, which concern the loyalists, are of three kinds:
patriot attacks, which show the sources and intensity of the hostility they faced;
loyalist addresses, one of them (by Governor William Franklin of New Jersey)
delivered to Americans and inviting them to reconsider their actions and the other
a plea to Britain to recognize loyalist achievements, sacrifices, and loyalty; and
finally, an analysis of who the loyalists were and how they differed from the patriots, written by the Philadelphia physician and patriot Benjamin Rush.

John Adams Reports on Congress's Strategy Toward the Native Americans, 1775

Phyladelphia June 7. 1775

Dear Sir

We have been puzzled to discover, what we ought to do, with the
Canadians and Indians. . . .

Whether We Should march into Canada with an Army Sufficient to
break the Power of Governor [of Quebec Guy] Carlton, to overawe the
Indians, and to protect the French has been a great Question. It Seems to
be the general Conclusion that it is best to go, if We can be assured that
the Canadians will be pleased with it, and join.

The Nations of Indians inhabiting the Frontiers of the Colonies, are numerous and warlike. They seem disposed to Neutrality. None have as yet taken up the Hatchet against us; and We have not obtained any certain Evidence that Either Carlton or [Guy] Johnson [superintendent of Indians in the northern department] have directly attempted to persuade them to take up the Hatchet. Some Suspicious Circumstances there are.

The Indians are known to conduct their Wars, So entirely without Faith and Humanity, that it would bring eternal Infamy on the Ministry throughout all Europe, if they should excite these Savages to War. The French disgraced themselves last War, by employing them. To let loose these blood Hounds to scalp Men, and to butcher Women and Children is horrid. Still it [is] Such Kind of Humanity and Policy as we have experienced, from the Ministry.

Congress Explains Patriot Reasoning and Calls for Native American Neutrality, 1775

A Speech to the Six Confederate Nations, MOHAWKS, ONEIDAS, TUSCARORAS, ONONDAGAS, CAYUGAS, SENECAS, *from the Twelve United Colonies, convened in Council at* PHILADELPHIA.

Brothers, Sachems, and Warriors! We, the Delegates from the twelve United Provinces . . . now sitting in General Congress at *Philadelphia,* send this talk to you our Brothers. We are sixty-five in number, chosen and appointed by the people throughout all these Provinces and Colonies, to meet and sit together in one great Council, to consult together for the common good of the land, and speak and act for them.

Brothers! In our consultation we have judged it proper and necessary to send you this talk, as we are upon the same island, that you may be informed of the reasons of this great Council, the situation of our civil Constitution, and our disposition towards you our *Indian* brothers of the *Six Nations* and their allies.

Brothers and Friends, now attend! When our fathers crossed the great water and came over to this land, the King of *England* gave them a talk, assuring them that they and their children should be his children, and that if they would leave their native country and make settlements, and live here, and buy and sell, and trade with their brethren beyond the water, they should still keep hold of the same covenant chain and enjoy peace; and it was covenanted, that the fields, houses, goods and possessions which our fathers should acquire, should remain to them as their own, and be their children's forever, and at their sole disposal.

Trusting that this covenant should never be broken, our fathers came a great distance beyond the great water, laid out their money here, built houses, cleared fields, raised crops, and through their own labour and industry grew tall and strong. . . .

Brothers and Friends, open a kind ear! We will now tell you of the quarrel betwixt the Counsellors of King *George* and the inhabitants and Colonies of *America.*

Many of his Counsellors are proud and wicked men. They persuade the King to break the covenant chain, and not to send us any more good Talks. A considerable number have prevailed upon him to enter into a new covenant against us, and have torn asunder and cast behind their backs the good old covenant which their ancestors and ours entered into, and took strong hold of.

They now tell us they will slip their hand into our pocket without asking, as though it were their own; and at their pleasure they will take from us our Charters, or written Civil Constitution, which we love as our lives; also our plantations, our houses and goods, whenever they please, without asking our leave; that our vessels may go to this island in the sea, but to this or that particular island we shall not trade any more; and in case of our non-compliance with these new orders, they shut up our harbours.

Brothers, this is our present situation; thus have many of the King's Counsellors and servants dealt with us. If we submit, or comply with their demands, you can easily perceive to what state we will be reduced. If our people labour on the field, they will not know who shall enjoy the crop. If they hunt in the woods, it will be uncertain who shall taste of the meat, or have the skins. If they build houses, they will not know whether they may sit round the fire, with their wives and children. They cannot be sure whether they shall be permitted to eat, drink, and wear the fruits of their own labour and industry.

Brothers and Friends of the SIX NATIONS, *attend!* We upon this island have often spoke and entreated the King and his servants the Counsellors, that peace and harmony might still continue between us; that we cannot part with or lose our hold of the old covenant chain which united our fathers and theirs; that we want to brighten this chain, and keep the way open as our fathers did; that we want to live with them as brothers, labour, trade, travel abroad, eat and drink in peace. We have often asked them to love us, and live in such friendship with us as their fathers did with ours.

We told them again that we judged we were exceedingly injured, that they might as well kill us, as take away our property and the necessaries of life. We have asked why they treat us thus? What has become of our repeated addresses and supplications to them? Who hath shut the ears of the King to the cries of his children in *America?* No soft answer, no pleasant voice from beyond the water has yet sounded in our ears.

Brothers, thus stands the matter betwixt old *England* and *America.* You *Indians* know how things are proportioned in a family—between the father and the son—the child carries a little pack. *England* we regard as the father; this island may be compared to the son.

The father has a numerous family—both at home and upon this island. He appoints a great number of servants to assist him in the government of his family. In process of time, some of his servants grow proud and ill-natured; they were displeased to see the boy so alert and walk so nimbly with his pack. They tell the father, and advise him to enlarge the child's pack; they prevail; the pack is increased; the child takes it up again—as he thought it might be the father's pleasure—speaks but few words—those very small—for he was loth to offend the father. Those proud and wicked servants, finding they had prevailed, laughed to see the boy sweat and stagger under his increased load. By and by, they apply to the father to double the boy's pack, because they heard him complain; and without any reason, said they, he is a cross child; correct him if he complains any more. The boy entreats the father; addresses the great servants in a decent manner, that the pack might be lightened; he could not go any farther; humbly asks, if the old fathers, in any of their records, had described such a pack for the child; after all the tears and entreaties of the child, the pack is redoubled; the child stands a little while staggering under the weight, ready to fall every moment. However, he entreats the father once more, though so faint he could only lisp out his last humble supplication; waits a while; no voice returns. The child concludes the father could not hear; those proud servants had intercepted his supplications, or stopped the ears of the father. He therefore gives one struggle and throws off the pack, and says he cannot take it up again; such a weight would crush him down and kill him, and he can but die if he refuses.

Upon this, those servants are very wroth; and tell the father many false stories respecting the child; they bring a great cudgel to the father, asking him to take it in his hand and strike the child.

This may serve to illustrate the present condition of the King's *American* subjects or children.

Amidst these oppressions we now and then hear a mollifying and reviving voice from some of the King's wise Counsellors, who are our friends, and feel for our distresses; when they heard our complaints and our cries, they applied to the King; also told those wicked servants, that this child in *America* was not a cross boy; it had sufficient reason for crying, and if the cause of its complaint was neglected, it would soon assume the voice of a man, plead for justice like a man, and defend its rights and support the old covenant chain of the fathers.

Brothers, listen! Notwithstanding all our entreaties, we have but little hope the King will send us any more good Talks, by reason of his evil Counsellors; they have persuaded him to send an army of soldiers and many ships-of-war, to rob and destroy us. They have shut up many of our harbours, seized and taken into possession many of our vessels; the soldiers have struck the blow; killed some of our people; the blood now runs of the *American* children. They have also burned our houses and Towns, and taken much of our goods.

Brothers! We are now necessitated to rise, and forced to fight, or give up our Civil Constitution, run away, and leave our farms and houses behind us. This must not be. Since the King's wicked Counsellors will not open their ears, and consider our just complaints, and the cause of our weeping, and hath given the blow, we are determined to drive away the King's Soldiers, and to kill and destroy all those wicked men we find in arms against the peace of the twelve United Colonies upon this island. We think our cause is just; therefore hope *God* will be on our side. We do not take up the hatchet and struggle for honour and conquest; but to maintain our Civil

Constitution and religious privileges, the very same for which our forefathers left their native land and came to this Country.

Brothers and Friends! We desire you will hear and receive what we have now told you, and that you will open a good ear and listen to what we are now going to say. This is a family quarrel between us and *Old England.* You *Indians* are not concerned in it. We don't wish you to take up the hatchet against the King's Troops. We desire you to remain at home, and not join on either side, but keep the hatchet buried deep. In the name and behalf of all our people, we ask and desire you to love peace and maintain it, and to love and sympathize with us in our troubles; that the path may be kept open with all our people and yours, to pass and repass, without molestation.

Brothers! We live upon the same ground with you. The same island is our common birthplace. We desire to sit down under the same tree of peace with you; let us water its roots and cherish its growth, till the large leaves and flourishing branches shall extend to the setting sun, and reach the skies.

Brothers, observe well! What is it we have asked of you? Nothing but peace, notwithstanding our present disturbed situation; and if application should be made to you by any of the King's unwise and wicked Ministers to join on their side, we only advise you to deliberate with great caution, and in your wisdom look forward to the consequences of a compliance. For, if the King's Troops take away our property, and destroy us, who are of the same blood with themselves, what can you, who are *Indians,* expect from them afterwards?

Therefore, we say, Brothers, take care; hold fast to your covenant chain. You now know our disposition towards you, the *Six Nations* of *Indians,* and your allies. Let this our good Talk remain at *Onondaga,* your central Council-House. We depend upon you to send and acquaint your allies to the northward, the seven Tribes on the River *St. Lawrence,* that you have this Talk of ours at the Great Council Fire of the *Six Nations.* And when they return, we invite your great men to come and converse farther with us at *Albany,* where we intend to rekindle the Council Fire, which your and our ancestors sat round in great friendship.

Brothers and Friends! We greet you all farewell.

Brothers! We have said we wish you *Indians* may continue in peace with one another, and with us the white people. Let us both be cautious in our behaviour towards each other at this critical state of affairs. This island now trembles; the wind whistles from almost every quarter; let us fortify our minds and shut our ears against false rumours; let us be cautious what we receive for truth, unless spoken by wise and good men. If any thing disagreeable should ever fall out between us, the twelve *United Colonies,* and you, the *Six Nations,* to wound our peace, let us immediately seek measures for healing the breach. From the present situation of our affairs, we judge it wise and expedient to kindle up a small Council Fire at *Albany,* where we may hear each other's voice, and disclose our minds more fully to each other.

Ordered, That a similar Talk be prepared for the other *Indian* Nations, preserving the tenour of the above, and altering it so as to suit the *Indians* in the several Departments.

Patriots Intimidate a New Jersey Loyalist, 1775

The 6th of December, at Quibble Town, Middlesex County, Pisquata Township, New Jersey, Thomas Randolph, Cooper, who had publicly proved himself an enemy to his country, by reviling and using his utmost endeavors to oppose the proceedings of the Continental and Provincial Conventions and Committees, in defence of their rights and liberties; and he being adjudged a person of no consequence enough for a severer punishment, was ordered to be stripped naked, well coated with tar and feathers, and carried in a wagon publicly round the town—which punishment was accordingly inflicted; and as he soon became duly sensible of his offence, for which he earnestly begged pardon, and promised to atone as far as he was able, by a contrary behavior for the future, he was released and suffered to return to his house in less than half an hour. The whole was conducted with that regularity and decorum, that ought to be observed in all public punishments.

A Patriot Urges Congress to Execute Loyalists, 1776

Northampton, July 17, 1776.

Dear Sir:

I have often said that I supposed a Declaration of Independence would be accompanied with a declaration of high treason. Most certainly it must immediately, and without the least delay, follow it. Can we subsist—did any State ever subsist, without exterminating traitors? . . . Our whole cause is every moment in amazing danger for want of it. The common understanding of the people, like unerring instinct, has long declared this; and from the clear discerning which they have had of it, they have been long in agonies about it. They expect that effectual care will now be taken for the general safety, and that all those who shall be convicted of endeavouring, by overt act, to destroy the State, shall be cut off from the earth.

Thomas Paine Calls for Patriotism and Attacks the Loyalists, 1776

December 23, 1776

These are the times that try men's souls: The summer soldier and the sunshine patriot will, in this crisis, shrink from the service of his country; but he that stands it NOW, deserves the love and thanks of man and woman. Tyranny, like hell, is not easily conquered; yet we have this consolation with us, that the harder the conflict, the more glorious the triumph. What we obtain too cheap, we esteem too lightly: 'Tis dearness only that gives every thing its value. Heaven knows how to put a proper price upon its goods; and it would be strange indeed, if so celestial an article as FREEDOM should not be highly rated. Britain, with an army to enforce her tyranny, has declared that she has a right (*not only to* TAX) but "*to* BIND *us in* ALL CASES WHATSOEVER," and if being *bound in that manner,* is not slavery, then is there not such a thing as slavery upon earth. Even the expression is impious, for so unlimited a power can belong only to GOD. . . .

Why is it that the enemy have left the New-England provinces, and made these middle ones the seat of war? The answer is easy: New-England is not infested with tories, and we are. I have been tender in raising the cry against these men, and used numberless arguments to shew them their danger, but it will not do to sacrifice a world to either their folly or their baseness. The period is now arrived, in which either they or we must change our sentiments, or one or both must fall. And what is a tory? Good GOD! what is he? I should not be afraid to go with an hundred whigs against a thousand tories, were they to attempt to get into arms. Every tory is a coward, for a servile, slavish, self-interested fear is the foundation of toryism; and a man under such influence, though he may be cruel, never can be brave.

But, before the line of irrecoverable separation be drawn between us, let us reason the matter together: Your conduct is an invitation to the enemy, yet not one in a thousand of you has heart enough to join him. Howe is as much deceived by you as the American cause is injured by you. He expects you will all take up arms, and flock to his standard with muskets on your shoulders. Your opinions are of no use to him, unless you support him personally, for 'tis soldiers, and not tories, that he wants.

I once felt all that kind of anger, which a man ought to feel, against the mean principles that are held by the tories: A noted one, who kept a tavern at Amboy, was standing at his door, with as pretty a child in his hand, about eight or nine years old, as most I ever saw, and after speaking his mind as freely as he thought was prudent, finished with this unfatherly expression, *"Well! give me peace in my day."* Not a man lives on the continent but fully believes that a separation must some time or other finally take place, and a generous parent should have said, *"If there must be trouble, let it be in my day that my child may have peace;"* and this single reflection, well applied, is sufficient to awaken every man to duty. Not a place upon earth might be so happy as America. Her situation is remote from all the wrangling world, and she has nothing to do but to trade with them. A man may easily distinguish in himself between temper and principle, and I am as confident, as I am that GOD governs the world, that America will never be happy till she gets clear of foreign dominion. Wars, without ceasing, will break out till that period arrives, and the continent must in the end be conqueror; for though the flame of liberty may sometimes cease to shine, the coal never can expire.

A Newspaper Attack on Loyalists, 1779

Among the many errors America has been guilty of during her contest with Great Britain, few have been greater, or attended with more fatal consequences to these States, than her lenity to the Tories. At first it might have been right, or perhaps political; but is it not surprising that, after repeated proofs of the same evils resulting therefrom, it should still be continued? We are all crying out against the depreciation of our money, and entering into measures to restore it to its value; while the Tories, who are one principal cause of the depreciation, are taken no notice of, but suffered to live quietly among us. We can no longer be silent on this subject, and see the independence of the country, after standing every shock from without, endangered by internal enemies. Rouse, America! your danger is great—great from a quarter where you least expect it. The Tories, the Tories will yet be the ruin of you! 'Tis high time they were separated from among you. They are now busy engaged in undermining your liberties. They have a thousand ways of doing it, and they make use of them all. Who were the occasion of this war? The Tories! Who persuaded the tyrant of Britain to prosecute it in a manner before unknown to civilized nations, and shocking even to barbarians? The Tories! Who prevailed on the savages of the wilderness to join the standard of the enemy? The Tories! Who have assisted the Indians in taking the scalp from the aged matron, the blooming fair one, the helpless infant, and the dying hero? The Tories! Who advised and who assisted in burning your towns, ravaging your country, and violating the chastity of your women? The Tories! Who are the occasion that thousands of you now mourn the loss of your dearest connections? The Tories! Who have always counteracted the endeavors of Congress to secure the liberties of this country? The Tories! Who refused their money when as good as specie, though stamped with the image of his most sacred Majesty? The Tories! Who continue to refuse it? The Tories! Who do all in their power to depreciate it? The Tories! Who propagate lies among us to discourage the Whigs? The Tories! Who corrupt the minds of the good people of these States by every specie of insidious counsel? The Tories! Who hold a traitorous correspondence with the enemy? The Tories! Who daily sends them intelligence? The Tories! Who take the oaths of allegiance to the States one day, and break them the next? The Tories! Who prevent your battalions from being filled? The Tories! Who dissuade men from entering the army? The Tories! Who persuade those who have enlisted to desert? The Tories! Who harbor those who do desert? The Tories! In short, who wish to see us conquered, to see us slaves, to see us hewers of wood and drawers of water? The Tories!

And is it possible that we should suffer men, who have been guilty of all these and a thousand other calamities which this country has experienced, to live among us! To live among us, did I say? Nay, do they not move in on our assemblies? Do they not insult us with their impudence? Do they not hold traitorous assemblies of their own? Do they not walk the streets at noon day, and taste the air of liberty? In short, do they not enjoy every privilege of the brave soldier who has spilt his blood, or the honest patriot who has sacrificed his all in our righteous cause? Yes—to our eternal shame be it spoken—they do. . . . 'Tis time to rid ourselves of these bosom vipers. An immediate separation is necessary. I dread to think of the evils every moment is big with, while a single Tory remains among us. . . . Awake, Americans, to a sense of your danger. No time to be lost. Instantly banish every Tory from among you. Let America be sacred alone to freemen.

Drive far from you every baneful wretch who wishes to see you fettered with the chains of tyranny. Send them where they may enjoy their beloved slavery to perfection—send them to the island of Britain; there let them drink the cup of slavery and eat the bread of bitterness all the days of their existence—there let them drag out a painful life, despised and accursed by those very men whose cause they have had the wickedness to espouse. Never let them return to this happy land—never let them taste the sweets of that independence which they strove to prevent. Banishment, perpetual banishment, should be their lot.

Governor William Franklin Admonishes the New Jersey Legislature, 1776

I shall take my leave of you, and the good people you represent—perhaps for the last time. Permit me, before we part, to recommend it to you to defend your constitution in all its branches. Let me exhort you to avoid, above all things, the traps of Independency and Republicanism now set for you, however temptingly they may be baited. Depend upon it you can never place yourselves in a happier situation than in your ancient constitutional dependency on Great-Britain. No Independent State ever was or ever can be so happy as we have been, and might still be, under that government. I have early and often warned you of the pernicious designs of many pretended patriots; who, under the mask of zeal for Reconciliation, have been from the first insidiously promoting a system of measures, purposely calculated for widening the breach between the two countries, so far as to let in an Independent Republican Tyranny—the worst and most debasing of all possible tyrannies. They well know that this has not even a chance of being accomplished, but at the expence of the lives and properties of many thousands of the honest people of this country—yet *these,* it seems, are as nothing in the eyes of such desperate gamesters! But remember, Gentlemen, that I now tell you, that should they (contrary to all probability) accomplish their baneful purpose, yet their government will not be lasting. It will never suit a people who have once tasted the sweets of British Liberty under a British Constitution. When the present high fever shall abate of its warmth, and the people are once more able cooly to survey and compare their past with their then situation, they will, as naturally as the sparks fly upwards, wreak their vengeance on the heads of those who, taking advantage of their delirium, had plunged them into such difficulties and distress.

This, Gentlemen, I well know, is not language to the times. But it is better, it is honest truth flowing from a heart that is ready to shed its best blood for this country. A real patriot can seldom or ever speak popular language. A false one will never suffer himself to speak anything else. The last will often be popular because he will always conform himself to the present humour and passions of the people, that he may the better gratify his private ambition, and promote his own sinister designs. The first will most generally be unpopular, because his conscience will not permit him to be guilty of such base compliances, and because he will even serve the people, if in his power, against their own inclinations, though he be sure that he thereby risks his ruin or destruction. . . . As to my own part, I have no scruple to repeat at this time what I formerly declared to the Assembly— *That no Office or Honour in the Power of the Crown to bestow, will ever influence me to forget or neglect the Duty I owe my Country, nor the most furious Rage of the most intemperate Zealots induce me to swerve from the Duty I owe His Majesty.*

Loyalists Plead Their Cause to the King, Parliament, and the British People, 1782

We, his majesty's most dutiful and faithful subjects, the loyal inhabitants of America, . . . animated with the purest principles of duty and allegiance to his majesty and the British parliament, beg leave, with the deepest humility and reverence, on the present calamitous occasion of public and national misfortune, in the surrender of lord Cornwallis, and the army under his lordship's command, at York-Town, humbly to entreat that your majesty, and the parliament, would be graciously pleased to permit us to offer this renewed testimony of loyalty and attachment to our most gracious sovereign, and the British nation and government; and thus publicly to repeat our most heart-felt acknowledgments for the infinite obligations we feel ourselves under for the heavy expenses that have been incurred, and the great national exertions that have been made, to save and rescue us, and your American colonies, from impending ruin, and the accumulated distresses and calamities of civil war. . . . We revere, with a kind of holy enthusiasm, the ancient constitution of the American colonies; and that we cannot but lament every event, and be anxiously solicitous to remove every cause or suspicion, that might have the most distant tendency to separate the two countries, or in any remote degree to lessen the claim we have to the present aid and continued exertions of Great Britain; especially if it should arise from any misrepresentation or distrust, either of our fidelity or numbers, to entitle us to the future countenance and protection of that sovereign and nation, whose government and laws, we call God to witness, that, in the integrity of our souls, we prefer to all others. . . .

Unhappy, indeed, for ourselves, and we cannot but think unfortunately too for Great Britain, the number of well affected inhabitants in America to the parent country, cannot, for obvious reasons, be exactly ascertained. . . . The penalty under which any American subject enlists into his majesty's service, is no less than the immediate forfeiture of all his goods and chattels, lands and tenements; and if apprehended, and convicted by the rebels, of having enlisted, or prevailed on any other person to enlist into his majesty's service, it is considered as treason, and punished with death: Whereas, no forfeiture is incurred, or penalty annexed, to his entering into the service of congress; but, on the contrary, his property is secured, and himself rewarded.

In the former case, he withdraws himself from his family and relations, without any possibility of receiving any assistance from, or affording any relief to either. In the latter, he is subject to no such peculiar self-denials, and real distresses. . . .

The desultory manner also in which the war has been carried on, by first taking possession of Boston, Rhode Island, Philadelphia, Portsmouth, Norfolk, in Virginia, Wilmington, in North Carolina, &c. &c. and then evacuating them, whereby many thousand inhabitants have been involved in the greatest wretchedness, is another substantial reason why more loyalists have not enlisted into his majesty's service, or openly espoused and attached themselves to the royal cause; yet, notwithstanding all these discouraging circumstances, there are *many more men in his majesty's provincial regiments, than there are in the continental service.* Hence it cannot be doubted but that there are more loyalists in America than there are rebels; and also, that their zeal must be greater, or so many would not have enlisted into the provincial service, under such very unequal circumstances. Other reasons might be enumerated, why many more have not enlisted into his majesty's provincial service, if we were not prevented from it by motives of delicacy and tenderness to the character of the person to whose management the business of that department was principally committed. . . .

If it should be said, if such is the number and disposition of the loyalists in America, how comes it to pass that they have not been of more importance to his majesty's service? We answer, might it not with equal propriety be enquired, why his majesty's forces have not more fully answered the just expectations of the nation?—And might not the question with greater propriety be put to his majesty's commanders in America? A due deference to whom, we trust, will be thought the most decent apology for our waving the mention of many more of the true and undeniable causes which we have it in our power to assign. And permit us to add, that it is only from modesty, and a wish to avoid both the appearance and imputation of selfish ostentation, that we decline entering into a particular enumeration of such proofs of allegiance and fidelity, from the conduct and sufferings of American loyalists, as have never been equalled by any people, in any age, or in any country. We cannot, however, refrain from hinting at some incontestible advantages the loyalists have been of, in affording supplies to the royal army,—by acting as guides and pilots, and (independent of those employed in the provincial line) as militia and partizan troops. As corps of Refugees, they have been too often distinguished by the zeal and gallantry of their behavior, to need the mention of any particular instance; if they did, we might refer to the affair of the Block-house, opposite Fort Knyphausen, where captain Ward, with about 70 Refugees, withstood and repulsed the attack of general Wayne, at the head of three chosen brigades of continentals. As a militia, acting by themselves (for we take no notice of the many thousands that, at different times, particularly in Georgia and South Carolina, have attached themselves to the royal army) a small party, some time ago, under the command of one Bunnion, went from Long Island to Connecticut, and there surprised and took prisoner a rebel major general, named Silliman, and several other officers.

A party of militia also not long ago went from Wilmington, in North Carolina, 60 or 70 miles into the country, and took major general Ashe, with two or three field officers, and some other persons, and brought them prisoners to his majesty's garrison at Wilmington. Another party of militia lately went near 200 miles up into the country from Wilmington, to a place called Hillsborough, and with a body of 6 or 700 militia, attacked a party of rebel troops, who were there as a guard to the rebel legislature, then sitting at that place, and took the rebel governor, Mr. Burke, several of his council, 11 continental officers, and about 120 of the troops prisoners, whom the militia delivered to major Craig, who commanded the king's troops at Wilmington. Other more voluntary alerts, performed by the loyalists in South Carolina and elsewhere, might be mentioned without number. Surely such are not *timid friends!* . . .

Relying with the fullest confidence upon national justice and compassion to our fidelity and distresses, we can entertain no doubts but that Great Britain will prevent the ruin of her American friends, at every risk short of certain destruction to herself. But if compelled, by adversity or misfortune, from the wicked and perfidious combinations and designs of numerous and powerful enemies abroad, and more criminal and dangerous enemies at home, an idea should be formed by Great Britain of relinquishing her American colonies to the usurpation of congress, we thus solemnly call God to witness, that we think the colonies can never be so happy or so free as in a constitutional connexion with, and dependence on Great Britain; convinced, as we are, that to be a British subject, with all its consequences, is to be the happiest and freest member of any civil society in the known world—we, therefore, in justice to our members, in duty to ourselves, and in fidelity to our posterity, must not, cannot refrain from making this public declaration and appeal to the faithful subjects of every government, and the compassionate sovereign of every people, in every nation and kingdom of the world, that our principles are the principles of the virtuous and free; that our sufferings are the sufferings of unprotected loyalty, and persecuted fidelity; that our cause is the cause of legal and constitutional government, throughout the world; that, opposed by principles of republicanism, and convinced, from recent observation, that brutal violence, merciless severity, relentless cruelty, and discretionary outrages are the distinguished traits and ruling principles of the present system of congressional republicanism, our aversion is unconquerable, irreconcileable.—That we are attached to monarchical government, from past and happy experience—by duty, and by choice. That, to oppose insurrections, and to listen to the requests of people so circumstanced as we are, is the common interest of all mankind in civil society. That to support our rights, is to support the rights of every subject of legal government; and that to afford us relief, is at once the duty and security of every prince and sovereign on earth. Our appeal, therefore, is just; and our claim to aid and assistance is extensive and universal. But if, reflecting on the uncertain events of war, and sinking under the gloomy prospect of public affairs, from the divisions and contests unhappily existing in the great councils of the nation, any apprehensions should have been excited in our breasts with respect to the issue of the American war, we humbly hope it cannot, even by the most illiberal, be imputed to us as an abatement of our unshaken loyalty to our most gracious sovereign, or of our unalterable predilection in favor of the British nation and government, whom may God long protect and preserve, if, in consequence thereof, we thus humbly implore that your majesty, and the parliament, would be graciously pleased, in the tenderness of our fears, and in pity to our distresses, to solicit, by your ambassadors at the courts of foreign sovereigns, the aid of such powerful and good allies, as to your majesty and parliament, in your great wisdom and discretion, may seem meet. Or if such a measure should in any manner be thought incompatible with the dignity and interest of our sovereign and the nation, we most humbly and ardently supplicate and entreat, that, by deputies or ambassadors, nominated and appointed by your majesty's suffering American loyalists, they may be permitted to solicit and obtain from other nations that interference, aid and alliance, which, by the blessing of Almighty God, may, in the last fatal and ultimate extreme, save and deliver us, his majesty's American loyalists, who, we maintain, in every one of the colonies, compose a great majority of the inhabitants, and those too the first in point of opulence and consequence, from the ruinous system of congressional independence and republican tyranny, detesting rebellion as we do, and preferring a subjection to any power in Europe, to the mortifying debasement of a state of slavery, and a life of insult, under the tyranny of congressional usurpation.

Benjamin Rush Contrasts Loyalists and Patriots, 1777*

. . . Tories and Whigs were actuated by very different motives in their conduct, or by the same motives acting in different degrees of force. . . . There were Tories (1) from an attachment to power and office. (2) From an attachment to the British commerce which the war had interrupted or annihilated. (3) From an attachment to kingly government. (4) From an attachment to the hierarchy of the Church of England, which it was supposed would be abolished in America by her seperation from Great Britain. This motive acted chiefly upon the Episcopal clergy, more especially in the Eastern states. (5) From a dread of the power of the country being transferred into the hands of the Presbyterians. This motive acted upon many of the Quakers in Pennsylvania and New Jersey, and upon the Episcopalians in several of those states where they had been in possession of power, or of a religious establishment.

It cannot be denied, but that private and personal consideration actuated some of those men who took a part in favor of the American Revolution. There were Whigs (1) from a desire of possessing, or at least sharing, in

---

* Drawing on notes composed in 1777, Rush made this analysis in his later *Autobiography*.

the power of our country. It was said there were Whigs (2) from an expectation that a war with Great Britain would cancel all British debts. There certainly were Whigs (3) from the facility with which the tender laws enabled debtors to pay their creditors in depreciated paper money. (4) A few men were Whigs from ancient or hereditary hostility to persons, or families who were Tories. But a great majority of the people who took part with their country were Whigs (5) from a sincere and disinterested love of liberty and justice.

Both parties differed as much in their conduct as they did in the motives which actuated them. There were (1) furious Tories who had recourse to violence, and even to arms, to oppose the measures of the Whigs. (2) Writing and talking Tories. (3) Silent but busy Tories in disseminating Tory pamphlets and news papers and in circulating intelligence. (4) Peaceable and conscientious Tories who patiently submitted to the measures of the governing powers, and who shewed nearly equal kindness to the distressed of both parties during the war.

The Whigs were divided by their conduct into (1) Furious Whigs, who considered the tarring and feathering of a Tory as a greater duty and exploit than the extermination of a British army. These men were generally cowards, and shrunk from danger when called into the field by pretending sickness or some family disaster. (2) Speculating Whigs. These men infested our public councils, as well as the army, and did the country great mischief. A colonel of a regiment informed a friend of mine that he had made a great deal of money by buying poor horses for his waggon, and selling them again for a large profit after he had fattened them at the public expense. (3) Timid Whigs. The hopes of these people rose and fell with every victory and defeat of our armies. (4) Staunch Whigs. These were moderate in their tempers, but firm, inflexible, and persevering in their conduct. There was, besides these two classes of people, a great number of persons who were neither Whigs nor Tories. They had no fixed principles and accommodated their conduct to their interest, to events, and to their company. They were not without their uses. They protected both parties in many instances from the rage of each other, and each party always found hospitable treatment from them.

Perhaps the inhabitants of the United States might have been divided nearly into three classes, viz. Tories, Whigs, and persons who were neither Whigs nor Tories. The Whigs constituted the largest class. The 3rd class were a powerful reinforcement to them after the affairs of America assumed a uniformly prosperous appearance. . . .

[M]any of the children of Tory parents were Whigs; so were the Jews in all the States. . . .

✳ E S S A Y S

Anthony F. C. Wallace's account in the first essay of the hazards that the Iroquois encountered in their diplomacy with Congress reveals the tenuousness of their situation, placed as they were between the two combatants. Wallace, a University of Pennsylvania historical anthropologist, was one of the first scholars to analyze the conflict by drawing on native American primary sources. Historian Gary Nash of the University of California, Los Angeles, has long been interested in the historical experience of common people and those located near the bottom of the social spectrum. In the second essay, his discussion of native Americans and African Americans reveals that the patriots and the Revolutionary cause looked questionable to people who were not citizens of the new republic. Ironically, their fight for liberty could place them at odds with a Revolution fought in the name of liberty.

One of the most perceptive analysts of the loyalists has been historian William H. Nelson of the University of Toronto. The third essay, Nelson's description of the varied origins of loyalists, comes from his 1960 book, *The American Tory*. Janice Potter, another Canadian historian, uses the published arguments of loyalists in New York and Massachusetts to trace the political outlook they espoused. Her discussion in the final selection suggests that whatever political, material, and social differences may have separated patriots and loyalists, questions of ideology also mattered.

The Iroquois and the Revolution: The Neutrality Policy

ANTHONY F. C. WALLACE

The Continental Congress early considered what role the Iroquois, probably the most formidable single body of fighting men in the colony of New York, should play in the developing war. In July 1775, the Congress passed an act dividing the Indian country into three departments, with three commissioners for the northern department and one each for the others. The Continental policy, like that of the British in the years before the French were defeated, was to secure, if not the assistance, at least the neutrality of the Six Nations and their dependents. . . .

In August 1775, the Continental commissioners met with the Iroquois at Albany, where they explained at length, and most pathetically, the moral justifications for the colonists' recourse to arms, and said again that this was a family quarrel between them and Old England, in which the Indians were not concerned. They did not want the Iroquois to take up the hatchet against the King's troops but rather urged them to remain at home, not joining either side and to keep the hatchet buried deep. The Six Nations replied, through Little Abraham, the notable Mohawk speaker, in clear language: "the determination of the Six Nations [is] not to take any part; but as it is a family affair, to sit still and see you fight it out."

But the Six Nations, by no means naive in this sort of diplomacy, set certain conditions upon the agreement to remain neutral. Specifically, the military activities of the Continentals should be confined to the coast. The free passage of Iroquois hunters from fort to fort, from trading post to trading post, within their wide country, was not to be interrupted (rumor

"The Iroquois and the Revolution: The Neutrality Policy" from *The Death and Rebirth of The Seneca* by Anthony F. C. Wallace. Reprinted by permission of Alfred A. Knopf, Inc.

had it that the road to Fort Stanwix was to be closed by Continental troops). Further, Sir John Johnson [son of the British Indian administrator Sir William Johnson], an outspoken loyalist, was not to be disturbed, nor was the Reverend Mr. Stewart, the loyalist missionary among the Mohawk, although both of them were being threatened with reprisals by the patriots. The Six Nations also made the satisfaction of their generations-old land claims against New York a part of their understanding of the agreement—an interpretation that was not so far-fetched as might appear, since the commissioners had made much of the renewal of the old covenant between the people of Albany and the Six Nations, which was celebrated on the occasion.

The suspicions so quietly expressed by Little Abraham were not ill-founded. Doubt of Albany people had been traditional among Iroquoians for a century, and for good reason; and now the reply of the commissioners was equivocal and therefore ominous. Congress would give no assurance that their territory would not be invaded. The missionary to the Mohawk was assured of his security (actually, he was forced to flee into Canada). An open trade was promised at Albany and Schenectady. And in answer to the request for settlement of ancient Mohawk land claims, the commissioners asserted that "the accusation is groundless," and anyway was a matter for the Albany people to discuss. To this Little Abraham replied evenly, "In case I was to answer that part of your speech, it might perhaps draw us into an argument." He went on briefly to advise the commissioners that Sir Guy's advice at the western and northern councils had been "not to take any part in this dispute, as it was a quarrel between brothers."

And "We are very glad," said Little Abraham, "that your language and Colonel Johnson's so well agree."

Thus it appears that the settled policy of the Six Nations, in response to the official requests for their neutrality made both by Johnson and the Continental commissioners, was to wait and watch. Hotheads there were, like Joseph Brant, who argued for an early involvement on the British side; a few high-spirited warriors committed themselves to minor campaigns, some (primarily Oneida and Stockbridge) on the American side, some (primarily the Caughnawaga Mohawk in Canada) on the British. But in the main, at first, the Six Nations avoided military alliance. The neutrality was, however, conditional upon the contending parties' refraining from encroaching upon their trade, their travel, or their land. The tribes had, in effect, implemented the classic play-off policy again; they would fight *against* whoever first invaded their territory, interfered with their trade and travel, injured their people, or demanded their alliance, and *for* whoever had not upset the *status quo*. . . .

The official policy of the Iroquois was still neutrality when, in the fall of 1775, a council was held at Pittsburgh between the Congressional commissioners and the Seneca, Wyandot, Shawnee, and Delaware. The commissioners wished to obtain from these western nations a firm commitment to neutrality. Guyasuta, the old Seneca half-king, speaking for the dependent nations, promised neutrality; and although the leader of a Delaware faction, White Eyes, defiantly announced the independence of the Delaware, the council as a whole agreed in an intention to remain neutral. Guyasuta promised to use his influence on the confederate council of the Six Nations to endorse the neutral policy. . . . In July 1776, at Fort Pitt, another council was held, and Guyasuta again announced the policy that the Six Nations had formulated at Oswego and expressed at Albany: they would be neutral, but neither British nor Americans were to be permitted to pass through the territory of the Six Nations. "I am appointed," he said, "to take care of this country, that is of the nations on the other side of the Ohio, and I desire you will not think of an expedition against Detroit, for I will repeat, we will not suffer any army to pass through our country."

It was inevitable that the Americans would sooner or later break with the Six Nations, however, for they were revolutionaries attacking the established system and could not tolerate a neutrality that maintained the *status quo.* Patriotic fervor, indeed, sometimes verged on the paranoid, interpreting almost any sort of detachment or verbal disagreement as evidence of conspiracy. A loyalist Mohawk sachem, Peter Nickus, was wounded and then hacked to pieces by patriotic white swordsmen about 1775—the first war casualty in the valley. In 1775 the Americans had seized Oswego, in defiance of the Six Nations' warnings at Albany, and captured some Mohawk warriors. In 1776, on the basis of perjurous accusations, General Schuyler besieged and imprisoned Sir John Johnson (son of the old friend of the Mohawk, Sir William Johnson), after brushing aside Mohawk objections that the Albany treaty provided for his freedom and that this same treaty prohibited the "closing of the road" with armed men. The accusation on which Johnson's arrest was based was that he was secreting a small arsenal for a loyalist campaign against the patriots. Although this accusation was proven false, the arms not being found where the informer swore they were hidden, Johnson was not exonerated but was placed on "parole." A few months later General Schuyler, who suspected, no doubt sincerely but almost certainly mistakenly, that Johnson was attempting to persuade the Indians to massacre the patriots, sent men to seize and imprison him. Johnson, presumably considering this to be a violation by Schuyler of the parole agreement, thereupon gathered together his friends, and various official records and papers and in May 1776, fled through the forests to Canada. He was declared by the Continentals to have broken his parole, his estates were confiscated, and his wife, Lady Johnson, was seized and held as a hostage in Albany. Johnson thereafter became a militant antirevolutionary, a colonel commanding Indian and ranger detachments. . . .

The Six Nations, who had in fact kept steadfastly neutral, took Johnson's seizure and other events of that order as a sure sign that "the road was closed," in violation of the Albany agreement. More and more of the Mohawk slipped away from the Mohawk Valley; a few remained for a time, nervously guarding their homes and wondering how soon the patriots, now throwing off all restraints, would serve them ill. On May 20, 1776, some of the Mohawk, led by the firebrand Joseph Brant (who was acting without general Six Nations' sanction), fought against the Americans at the Battle of the Cedars, in which the American forces retreating from their invasion of Canada were disastrously beaten. Lurid, if false, atrocity stories were circulated concerning this affair, and Congress denounced the British for their outrageous use of Indian troops. At the same moment, however, and before news of the Cedars could have reached Philadelphia, Congress itself was preparing to use Indian troops. On May 25 Congress resolved that "it was highly expedient to engage the Indians in the service of the United Colonies," and authorized the Commander-in-Chief to recruit two thousand paid Indian auxiliaries. This resolution flatly contradicted the neutrality injunctions issued at Albany the year before, and news of it no doubt reinforced a growing Iroquois sense of the undependability of the Continental Congress. Indeed, this resolution was passed one day after an Iroquois deputation, then in Philadelphia, was exhorted to remain neutral. Few Indian warriors ever joined the American army, however, and most of those few were Oneida, Tuscarora, and Stockbridge, from the Reverend Mr. Kirkland's congregation.

The Forgotten Experience: Indians, Blacks, and the American Revolution

GARY B. NASH

The American Revolution was more than a struggle between highly principled American colonists and a tyrannical, corrupt mother country. It was more, even, than a war of national liberation overlaid by an internal struggle among patriots concerning the kind of society that should emerge if the war was won. Seen most broadly, the Revolution was an era of social upheaval and military conflict in which a bewildering variety of people was swept into a whirlpool of ideas and events, forced to decide what it was they believed in, and obliged—as happens to few of us in the modern age—to risk everything in defense of those beliefs. Some of these people were white; some were black, and some were red. . . .

What has been largely lost in our recording of American history is the fact that for many of the people of North America the struggle for life, liberty, and the pursuit of happiness in the 1770s and 1780s was carried on by fighting with the British and against those American patriots upon whom our patriotic celebrations have always exclusively focused. . . .

An example of the "other" patriots was Thomas Peters. In 1759, . . . he was an Egba of the Yoruba tribe, living in what is now Nigeria. . . . But a year later he was in the New World, having been kidnapped by slave traders, carried across the Atlantic, and sold at auction in French Louisiana. Peters lost not only his Egba name and his family and friends but also his liberty, his dreams of happiness, and very nearly his life. Shortly thereafter, he started his own revolution in America because, without benefit of a written language or constitutional treatises, he had been deprived of what he considered his natural rights. Three times he tried to escape from the grasp of another human being who called him chattel property. He thus proclaimed, within the context of his own experience, that all men are created equal. Three times he paid the price of unsuccessful black revolutionaries—first whippings, then branding, and finally ankle shackles.

By the early 1770s, Peters had been sold to a plantation owner in Wilmington, North Carolina, perhaps because his former master had wearied of trying to snuff out the yearning for freedom that seemed to beat irrepressibly in his breast. On the eve of the Revolution, then in his thirties and well acculturated to the ways of the New World slave colonies, Peters struck his next blow for freedom. Pamphleteers all over the colonies were crying out against British oppression, British tyranny, and British plans to enslave the Americans. But in November 1775, in Norfolk, Virginia, about two hundred miles from Peters's master's plantation, the royal governor, Lord Dunmore, proclaimed lifelong freedom to any American slave or indentured servant "able and willing to bear arms" who escaped his master and made it to the British lines. Peters broke the law of North Carolina, redefined himself as man instead of chattel property, and made good his escape. For the remainder of the war he fought in the British Regiment of Black Guides and Pioneers, was twice wounded, and was promoted to sergeant. He made a wartime marriage to another black freedom fighter, a slave woman who had escaped her master in Charleston, South Carolina, about the time the colonial delegates to the Second Continental Congress were gathering in Philadelphia to sign the great document by which they collectively emancipated themselves from their masters.

At the end of the war, Peters, his wife, and hundreds of other members of the Black Guides and Pioneers were evacuated from New York City to Nova Scotia by the British. There could be no staying in the land of the victorious American revolutionaries because only Vermont, among the territories of the new republic, had ended slavery. Those who had fought with the British were particularly hated and subject to retaliation; to remain in America meant running the risk of reenslavement. Moreover, the British promised land, tools, and rations for three years to those who had fought alongside them against the rebellious colonists. But in Nova Scotia the dream of life, liberty, and happiness became a nightmare. Some 3,000 ex-slaves found that they were segregated in impoverished villages, given small scraps of often untillable land, deprived of rights normally extended to British subjects, and reduced to peonage by a white population. . . . White Nova Scotians were no more willing than the Americans to accept blacks as better than slaves, and this was made abundantly clear less than a year after Peters and his people arrived from New York. Hundreds of disbanded British soldiers, who were taking up settlement in Nova Scotia, attacked black villages, burned and looted, and pulled down the houses of free blacks who underbid their labor in the area.

After several years of frustration, Peters determined to journey to England to put the case of the black Nova Scotians before the British government. He sailed in July 1790 and in London met with leaders of the English abolitionist movement—Granville Sharp, Thomas Clarkson, and William Wilburforce. These men were already working to establish a free black colony on the west coast of Africa, especially for ex-slaves, many of them refugees from America, living in poverty in London. By 1792 the plan was perfected. The colony was to be called Sierra Leone, and its capital city would be Freetown. Peters, accompanied by John Clarkson, the younger brother of Thomas, returned to Nova Scotia and spread the word of a return to the homeland; he also played a galvanizing role in organizing the pilgrimage back to the part of the world from whence many of his compatriots had started half a lifetime before. In January 1792, fifteen ships with some 1,200 black Canadians weighed anchor, set their sails to the east, and followed this black Moses away from the New World. . . .

Peters . . . waged an epic half-century struggle for the most basic political rights, for social equity, and for human dignity. For Peters, as for a large number of Afro-Americans in the 1770s, this struggle involved a reckoning of which side of the family quarrel to take in order to pursue their personal freedom as opposed to the nation's freedom. As Benjamin Quarles has said, the "major loyalty [of black revolutionaries] was not to a place nor a people but to a principle." If the principle could best be achieved by joining the British, then why should it matter whether the king and Parliament were taxing the Americans without representation or quartering troops in Boston? Such infringements of white rights paled by comparison to the violation of black rights by these same Americans, as even some white revolutionaries admitted. If, on the other hand, the British army was nowhere near, then service on the American side might earn a slave his freedom. So black Americans made their choices according to the circumstances in which they found themselves, and in many of the colonies they were quick to petition the legislatures for their freedom even before the fighting began. They were helped along by scores of white revolutionaries who, like the clergyman Samuel Hopkins of Connecticut, called for "universal liberty to white and black" and pointed out "the shocking, the intolerable, the . . . gross bare-faced practiced inconsistence" between the patriots inveighing against the slavery imposed by king and Parliament on the colonies, while at the same time they consigned to "unutterable wretchedness" many thousands of poor blacks "who have as good a claim to liberty as themselves." But black Americans quickly learned in the early years of the war that the chances for a general emancipation were almost nil. Many white patriots, throughout the colonies, believed that slavery was a grotesque contradiction of the revolutionary credo. But they regarded the social and economic costs of emancipation as too high a price to pay. Thus blacks learned not to look to white society for their liberty, but to seize the moment, whenever and wherever it presented itself, to liberate themselves.

It is not surprising, then, that in almost every part of the colonies, black Americans took advantage of wartime disruption to obtain their freedom in any way they could. Sometimes they joined the American army, often serving in place of their masters who gladly gave black men freedom in order not to risk life and limb for the cause. Sometimes they served with their masters on the battlefield as orderlies and hoped for the rewards of freedom at war's end. Such was the case of William Lee, Washington's slave, who appears at the General's side in many paintings of the period but had to wait until Washington's death in 1799 to collect his reward. Sometimes black Americans served with such heroism that white society gladly gave them freedom for services rendered. Such was the case of James Armistead, who enlisted under General Lafayette in 1781, infiltrated Cornwallis's camp at Yorktown, providing valuable information for the revolutionary army, and lived, a free man after the war, to greet the French general when he returned to America in 1824 to visit his friend, Thomas Jefferson. Sometimes Afro-Americans tried to burst the shackles of slavery by fleeing all the white combatants and seeking refuge among the trans-Allegheny Indian tribes. But most frequently, freedom was sought by joining the British whenever their regiments were close enough to reach. . . . Black Americans took up arms, so far as we can tell, in as great a proportion to their numbers as did white Americans. . . .

Perhaps only 20 percent or less of the American slaves gained their freedom and survived the war—and many of them faced years of travail and even reenslavement thereafter in Nova Scotia, England, the West Indies, and British Florida. But their story is an extraordinarily important part of a tradition of black protest and struggle that did not die with the Peace of Paris in 1783. The American Revolution was the first large-scale rebellion of American slaves, and we must link their quest with the struggles of nineteenth-century black abolitionists and resistant slaves who drew inspiration from their work. It was a rebellion, to be sure, that was carried on individually rather than collectively for the most part, because circumstances favored individualized struggles for freedom. But out of thousands of separate acts grew a legend of black strength, black vision for the future, black resistance to slavery and institutionalized white racism.

Personified in the lifelong struggle of Thomas Peters, this new determination reemerged after the war, surfacing in the first successful efforts to build black institutions in America: the African Baptist and Methodist Episcopal churches founded by sons of the revolution such as David George, Andrew Bryan, Peter Williams, and Absalom Jones; and black schools and fraternal societies in the North. "We are determined to seek out for ourselves," wrote Richard Allen of Philadelphia, "the Lord being our helper." In the closing decades of the eighteenth century, among both free and slave Afro-Americans, this spirit could not be stifled. The task of a generation of black leaders, who for the most part had seized the opportunities inherent in wartime disruption to gain their own freedom and carve out their own destinies, was to lay the foundations of modern Afro-American culture. Their task was even more formidable because white society, after the war, abandoned the antislavery impulse of the early revolutionary years and entered an era of intensified prejudice against black Americans. . . .

For some 200,000 Native Americans living between the Atlantic Ocean and the Mississippi River, the American Revolution was also a time to "try men's souls." Thayendanegea, known in the English communities as Joseph Brant, stands as an illuminating example. Thayendanegea was a Mohawk, born about the same time as Thomas Peters but in an Iroquois village on the other side of the world. His sister married the prominent William Johnson, . . . a baronial landowner in New York, the king's superintendent of Indian Affairs for the northern colonies, and an honorary member of the Mohawk tribe. Thayendanegea spoke English fluently, for he had been educated in Eleazar Wheelock's Indian school in Connecticut, later to become Dartmouth College. He had translated part of the Bible into Mohawk, at age 13 served the Anglo-American cause by fighting with William Johnson against the French at Crown Point in 1755, and four years later aided the colonists again by battling Pontiac's Indian insurgents, who were determined in the wake of the defeat of the French during the Seven Years' War to expel the British soldiers and their encroaching American cousins from the Ohio country. Thayendanegea was a man who lived in two worlds—red and white. Bilingual and bicultural, he gravitated between the two.

As he matured in the 1760s, Thayendanegea grew to understand that despite the trading alliance the Iroquois had maintained with the northern colonies for generations and despite the close ties that the Mohawks (the easternmost of the six Iroquois nations) maintained with William Johnson, his people were now seriously threatened by the rapidly growing white population. Barely 20,000 white colonists inhabited New York in 1700, but by 1740 their number had increased to 65,000 and by 1770 to 160,000. Many times in the twilight of the colonial period, the Mohawks had been swindled out of land by rapacious New York land speculators and frontiersmen. So as the war clouds gathered in 1775, Thayendanegea, 33 years old, took ship to London to see what the English king would offer the Iroquois for their support in a war that, while still not formally declared, had been in the shooting stage since early in the year. Like his grandfather, Chief Hendrick, who had been among the Iroquois chiefs who travelled to London to consult with Queen Anne 65 years before, Thayendanegea was greeted as royalty in England. He was feted by the king, written about in the *London Universal Magazine,* and had his portrait painted by Romney. But his mission was to determine how life, liberty, and the protection of property might best be preserved by his people. His decision, made before leaving London, augured the reckoning of a vast majority of Indian tribes in the next few years—that only by fighting against the independence-seeking Americans could Indian tribes themselves remain independent. He returned to New York a few weeks after the Declaration of Independence had been signed at Philadelphia, served with the British General, George Howe, at Long Island in the first major defeat of Washington's army, and then in November 1776 began a long trek through the lands of the Iroquois and their confederates in the Ohio country to spread the message, as he wrote, that "their own Country and Liberty" were "in danger from the Rebels." Thayendanegea's diplomatic mission was crucial in bringing most of the Iroquois into the war on the British side in the summer of 1777.

During the war Thayendanegea was everywhere—at Oriskany in August 1777 when the British and their Indian allies, in perhaps the bloodiest battle of the Revolution, defeated the Americans who were trying to reach the besieged Fort Stanwix, which controlled access to the western Mohawk Valley and the Great Lakes; at Cherry Valley in the summer of 1778 when the Iroquois drove thousands of American farmers from their fields in southern New York and northern Pennsylvania; and at a dozen battles in the campaign of 1779 when the American general, John Sullivan, invaded the Iroquois country, burning towns and scorching the earth. For the entire war, Thayendanegea played a leading role in virtually eliminating the New York and Pennsylvania back-country (a major grain and cattle-growing area upon which the Continental army had depended for supplies) from contributing much to the war effort. "A thousand Iroquois warriors and five hundred Tory rangers," writes one historian, "were able to lay in waste nearly 50,000 square miles of colonial territory."

Though never militarily defeated during the war, the Iroquois were abandoned by their British allies at the peace talks in Paris and left, in 1783, to cope with an aggressive, combat-experienced, and land-hungry American people. Confronting insurmountable odds, the Iroquois signed dictated treaties that dispossessed them of most of their land and consigned them to reservations that within a generation became "slums in the wilderness." Thayendanegea spent the last twenty years of his life trying to lead the Iroquois in adjusting to the harsh new realities by which a proud and independent people found that the pursuit of happiness by white Americans required red Americans to surrender life, liberty, and property.

The story of Thayendanegea and the Iroquois encapsulates important facets of the Indians' American Revolution. At the heart of this red struggle were the twin goals of political independence and territorial defense. Black Americans, who had neither liberty nor land, fought for the former in order someday to gain the latter. Red Americans, who had both, struggled to preserve both. Like most black Americans, almost all Indian tribes concluded that their revolutionary goals could best be achieved through fighting *against* the side that proclaimed the equality of all men and with the side that the Americans accused of trampling on their natural, irreducible rights. The logic of nearly two hundred years of abrasive contact with colonizing Europeans compelled the choice, for it was the settler-subjects of the English king who most threatened Indian autonomy, just as it was the royal power that, before the Revolution, had attempted to protect Indian land from white encroachment by means of the Proclamation Line of 1763 and the regulation of trade. . . .

In the end, the Indians were disastrously the losers in the war of the American Revolution. Partly this was because they were less successful than the thirteen white tribes in overcoming intertribal factionalism; partly because the supplies of European trade goods upon which they depended—especially guns, powder, and shot—were seriously disrupted during the war; and partly because they were abandoned to the Americans by their British allies at war's end. Facing a white society in 1783 that was heavily armed and obsessed with the vision of western lands, tribes such as the Iroquois and Cherokee were forced to cede most of their land. The prewar white population buildup, which had caused worsening economic conditions in many older communities along the coastal plain, was relieved as thousands of settlers spilled across the mountains after 1783, frequently in violation of treaties contracted by their own elected governments. Aiding these frontiersmen, many of them war veterans, were state and national governments that understood that the western lands, once the native inhabitants had been driven away, were the new nation's most valuable resource. The sale of western lands would provide the revenue both to liquidate the huge war debt and to underwrite the expenses of a nation of tax-shy people. . . .

Most Americans were no more willing to apply the principles emblazoned on the revolutionary banners to relations with the Indian inhabitants of the trans-Allegheny region than they were to fulfill the revolutionary ideal of abolishing slavery. Indian land, like black slave labor, was one of the new republic's preeminently important resources. To forego its exploitation was beyond the collective will of a people whose colonial background had inculcated the ideal of individualistic, material aggrandizement alongside the ideals of political freedom and religious liberty.

The pro-British stance of the Native Americans cannot be counted as a failure of judgment on their part. Had they sided with the Americans they would have fared no better, as the dismal postwar experience of several pro-American tribes, such as the Tuscaroras and Oneidas, demonstrates. . . .

The republic's greatest wartime hero, now its first president, captured the national mood when he wrote, "The gradual extension of our settlements will as certainly cause the Savage as the Wolf to retire; both being beasts of prey tho' they differ in shape."

In studying the Revolution, we need to broaden our perspective so as to recognize that the conflict—fought by white Americans for life, liberty, and the pursuit of happiness—compelled many nonwhite Americans to take the British side in quest of the same goals. The red and black people of this land were animated by the doctrine of natural rights as surely as were the minutemen at Concord Bridge or the signers of the Declaration of Independence; and they were as moved by self-interest as were white revolutionaries. Most of them took the other side to gain or preserve these rights and to pursue their own interests, which had been defined by generations of interaction among red, white, and black people in America. In their struggle against the white revolutionaries, most of them lost, at least in the proximate sense. What they won, however, was a piece of history, for they kept lit the lamp of liberty and passed on their own revolutionary heritage to their children and their children's children. . . . In this sense, the American Revolution is far from over.

The Tory Rank and File

WILLIAM H. NELSON

Of all the approaches that might be used in an attempt to separate intelligibly the Loyalists from their Patriot kinsmen, that of occupation or social class

Excerpted from the *The American Tory* by William H. Nelson. Copyright © 1961 by Oxford University Press. Reprinted by permission.

seems the least fruitful. There was indeed a Tory oligarchy, but there was also a Whig oligarchy, and if in New England the Tory proportion of ruling families was greater than the Tory proportion of the total population, in the Southern Colonies the reverse was true. Even in New England the Loyalists were hardly the gentry pictured in legend. When an Act of Banishment was passed against some three hundred Loyalists in Massachusetts in 1778, they were listed by trade or profession. About a third were merchants, professional men, and gentlemen; another third were farmers, and the rest were artisans or labourers with a sprinkling of small shopkeepers.

Most random lists of Loyalists show even less evidence of gentility than this. Always the gentlemen, esquires, merchants, and the like are far outnumbered by the yeomen, cordwainers, tailors, labourers, masons, blacksmiths, and their fellows. . . . Clearly, none of the simpler economic determinants was at work separating Whigs from Tories. Economic influences, however, may account in part for the pattern of geographical distribution that appears when the Loyalist strongholds are considered. The main centres of Tory strength fall into two distinct regions: The first was along the thinly settled western frontier, from Georgia and District Ninety-Six in South Carolina, through the Regulator country of North Carolina and the mountain settlements of Virginia, Pennsylvania, and New York, to the newly-occupied Vermont lands. The other was the maritime region of the Middle Colonies, including western Long Island and the counties of the lower Hudson Valley, southern New Jersey, the three old counties of Pennsylvania around Philadelphia, and the peninsula between Delaware and Chesapeake Bays. There were also locally important concentrations of Tories elsewhere along the Atlantic seaboard: at Charleston, around Wilmington and Norfolk, and around Newport and Portsmouth in New England.

In the West and in the tidal region of the Middle Colonies Loyalists and neutrals may have formed a majority of the population. In the areas of dense agricultural settlement, however, including the plantation country of the Southern Colonies, the thickly settled parts of the Piedmont, and most of New England, Loyalists were comparatively scarce. All that the Tory regions, the mountain and maritime frontiers, had in common was that both suffered or were threatened with economic and political subjugation by richer adjoining areas. The geographical concentration of the Tories was in peripheral areas, regions already in decline, or not yet risen to importance.

It is not difficult to explain the Loyalism of the West. The Appalachian frontiersmen—hunters, trappers, and fur traders—feared the advance of close settlement which would destroy their economy. Like the Indians of the region, many of the frontiersmen were loyal to Britain because the British government was the only force they could rely on to check the rapid advance of agricultural settlement. The tidal region of the Middle Colonies, on the other hand, still had political power, but was in danger of losing it to the more populous districts inland. Moreover, this region formed part of an Atlantic community. It looked eastward; its ties with Britain were closer than its ties with the new West. Even in New England the truly maritime regions seem to have been less than enthusiastic in their support of the

Revolution. Newport lacked zeal; Nantucket and Martha's Vineyard were opportunist or neutral, and the Maine coast grew steadily less faithful to the Revolution, until Nova Scotia's Loyalism of necessity was reached.

Whether the St. Lawrence Valley should be considered a separate province, or whether it merely combined the characteristics of a thinly settled and a maritime region, it too was indifferent or hostile to the Revolution. Undoubtedly some of Vermont's capriciousness during the period may be ascribed to the pull of the St. Lawrence. In any case, wherever regions newly or thinly settled touched the sea, there the Revolution was weakest: in Quebec, in Nova Scotia, in Georgia, and in New York where the Hudson carried the Atlantic world into the mountains. Wherever sailors and fishermen, trappers and traders outnumbered farmers and planters, there Tories outnumbered Whigs.

Of course a major insufficiency of such a geographical analysis is that it takes no account of important cultural influences, differences in nationality and religion mainly, that played a great role in the Revolution. The Canadians of the St. Lawrence Valley were suspicious of the Revolution, not only because they lived far outside its physical homeland, but also because they were French and Catholic, and the Revolution seemed to them English and Protestant. No geographic or economic considerations can explain the Tory villages on Long Island, intermingled with Whig villages. The Tory villages were Dutch, while the others had been settled by New Englanders. Here again, legend has done a disservice to students of the Revolution. The Loyalists were seldom more English than the patriots. There were, of course, many British-born Tories whose allegiance to England was habitual and natural. But, apart from these, the Tories more commonly drew their recruits from the non-English than from the English parts of the community. The two most purely English provinces, Virginia and Massachusetts, were the strongholds of the Revolution. It was in the patchwork societies of Pennsylvania and New York that the Tories were strongest.

Among almost all cultural minorities, the proportion of Tories seems to have been clearly higher than among the population at large. The Dutch and Germans seem to have inclined towards supporting the Revolution where they were already anglicized, but not where they had kept their language and separate outlook. In New York, for example, the English-speaking Dutch Reformed congregation was Whiggish, but the Dutch-speaking congregation was Tory, and on such cordial terms with the Anglicans that they were allowed to use St. George's chapel during the British occupation. The Tories praised the loyalty of the French Calvinists at New Rochelle, the only place in the colonies where they had preserved their language, while elsewhere the descendants of the Huguenots were conspicuously active revolutionists.

There seems to have been reason for John Witherspoon's lament that his fellow Scots made bad revolutionists, whether Highlanders in the back country of New York and North Carolina, or Lowlanders along the Virginia and Carolina coast. Even the Ulstermen were tainted with Toryism in the Regulator districts of North Carolina and in the frontier districts of South

Carolina. The Loyalism of the Indians is well known, and contemporary opinion held that the Negroes were dangerously Toryfied. Of course people like the Brooklyn Dutch or the South Carolina Germans and Scots may have remained loyal to Britain partly out of political quietism. It is difficult not to believe, however, that they were Loyalists also because they thought Britain would protect them from the cultural aggression of an Anglo-American majority.

In religion, the lines that divided Tories from Whigs were quite clearly drawn. Adherents of religious groups that were in a local minority were everywhere inclined towards Loyalism, while adherents of the dominant local denomination were most often Patriots. In New England not many Congregationalists, in the Middle Colonies not many Presbyterians, in the South not many Episcopalians, were Tories. Conversely, most of the Anglicans in the North were Tories; so were many Presbyterians in the Episcopalian South. Of the smaller religious groups, most of the Quakers and German Pietists were passive Loyalists, and in New England even the Baptists were accused of "not being hearty" in the American cause. The reputation the Methodists had for being poor rebels was perhaps not entirely due to the influence of Wesley and other English ministers.

The Catholics and Jews apparently form an exception to the rule that religious minorities leaned towards Toryism. Both seem generally to have supported the Revolution, although among the Jews there were notable exceptions like the Hart family in Newport and the Franks family in Philadelphia. Jonathan Boucher observed that although the Maryland Catholics supported the Revolution in its later stages, they had taken little part at first. It is possible that the Jews and Catholics were in such suspect and habitual minority, that they felt obliged to follow what seemed majority opinion for their own safety.

Taking all the groups and factions, sects, classes, and inhabitants of regions that seem to have been Tory, they have but one thing in common: they represented conscious minorities, people who felt weak and threatened. The sense of weakness, which is so marked a characteristic of the Tory leaders, is equally evident among the rank and file. Almost all the Loyalists were, in one way or another, more afraid of America than they were of Britain. Almost all of them had interests that they felt needed protection from an American majority. Being fairly certain that they would be in a permanent minority (as Quakers or oligarchs or frontiersmen or Dutchmen) they could not find much comfort in a theory of government that assured them of sovereign equality with other Americans *as individuals*. Not many Loyalists were as explicit in their distrust of individualism as, say, Jonathan Boucher, but most of them shared his suspicion of a political order based on the "common good" if the common good was to be defined by a numerical majority.

A theory that the Loyalists were compounded of an assortment of minority groups does not, of course, preclude their having in total constituted a majority of Americans. Without the social and religious homogeneity, without the common purpose, and without the organic and efficient leadership of the revolutionists, the Loyalists might still have outnumbered them.

In this case the Revolution would have been, as it has sometimes been claimed to have been, the achievement of an organized and wilful minority. The problem of discovering how many Tories there were is complicated, moreover, by there having been, between avowed supporters and avowed opponents of the Revolution, a great middle group of passive citizens who had no clear point of view, who hoped perhaps that one side or the other would win, but who wanted above all not to be disturbed. There must have been many like the New Jersey shopkeeper who stood in his door and prayed that whatever happened, he might have peace in his time. There were probably also a good number of sceptics who thought as John Ross of Philadelphia did: "Let who would be king, he well knew that he should be subject."

An old and symmetrical guess that a third of Americans were revolutionists, another third Loyalists, and a third neutral, has long been accepted by historians as reasonable. It goes back, presumably, to John Adams's assignment of these relative proportions. But Adams may have been trying, unconsciously, to gain distinction for the revolutionists by maintaining they were a wise minority. In Connecticut, the only colony for which anything like an exact estimate of Tory strength has been made, the hard core of Tories seems to have numbered only about six per cent of the population. But then, Connecticut was one of two or three colonies where the Tories were weakest. During the Revolutionary War perhaps half as many Americans were in arms for the King, at one time or another, as fought on the side of the Congress. Only in New York is it reasonably certain that the Loyalists numbered half the population. Throughout the Middle Colonies, including New York, the Loyalists may have been almost as numerous as their opponents. In the South, however, they could hardly have amounted to more than a fourth or a third of the population, and in New England to scarcely a tenth. A more reasonable guess than Adams's would be that the Loyalists were a third, and the revolutionists two-thirds of the politically active population of the colonies. No reliable estimate is possible until more precise studies of individual colonies have been made.

The outbreak of open war between the British and the Massachusetts militia threw the Tories, temporarily at least, entirely on the defensive. The shock of the news of Lexington and Concord was shortly transformed into anger at those who did not immediately drop all argument and join the fight against the British. Except along the western frontier, and in parts of the Middle Colonies, there was no doubt that Britain and America, not merely Britain and Massachusetts, were at war, and the Tories, who were now calling themselves Loyalists, were beginning to be regarded as traitors. When the news of the Battle of Lexington reached New York, the mob, after almost ten years' confinement, slipped its chains, looted the arsenal, and raged through the streets. While a few weeks earlier it had been said of the New York Whigs that "no one dares among gentlemen, to support them," it was now possible for John Adams to write, "The tories put to flight here . . . such a spirit was never seen in New York."

As the Whigs luxuriated in their sudden release from the bonds of sober argument, they began to look on the Tories with real impatience. To people with a new faith, especially one being forged in the heat of war, the adherents of the old beliefs are either wicked and will not see, or are superstitious and cannot see. George Washington thought the Loyalists were wicked, and denounced them as "parricides." Other revolutionists were more charitable, like one who wrote, "We may say of Toryism as of Popery, that it is always the same. There are worthy individuals among the professors of both; and a few rare instances of real converts from each, through an increase of knowledge, but the prevailing spirit of the parties is uniform and abiding."

Just after the adjournment of the First Continental Congress, the local committees of inspection had begun to enforce compliance with the Association. In some localities the whole adult population signed the oath. Everywhere it was used to force Tories either to acquiesce in the measures of the Congress, or to declare themselves open "enemies of American liberty" and face ostracism. As a Maryland revolutionist put it, the Association acted "as a powerful emetick to our Tories." The efficiency of the committees' work rested on years of experience in informal government, going back in many cases to the committees that had enforced the Non-Importation Agreement in 1768. . . .

Everywhere then, in 1775, the Tories were intimidated, disarmed, and defeated, even in districts where they had overwhelming local superiority. Lack of organization, of course, contributed to their failure. This is clear, for example, in the absence of any co-ordination of the several abortive western risings. Had a concerted attack by Tories and Indians been made all along the frontier from New York to Georgia, it might have proved embarrassing to the Congress. Here, however, not only their lack of organization, but also the inherent disparateness of the Tories handicapped them. The alliance between the Cherokees and the South Carolina frontiersmen was uneasy if not unsound. In North Carolina the Regulators and Scots Highlanders mistrusted each other, and none of the frontier Tories had much in common with the stolid farmers of Long Island, or the Chesapeake fishermen.

The Tories were willing enough to fight for their principles and prejudices, as they showed later in the war. But separate grievances can make common cause only when they have a common standard to rally around. The failure, in years gone by, of Tory leaders to provide such a standard was decisive now. In 1775 only the British could have given leadership to the various Tory groups, supplied and reinforced them, and led them into common purpose; this the British were as yet unwilling to attempt. . . .

The Loyalists' Conservatism

JANICE POTTER

Although Loyalist writers were addressing problems of immediate concern and were trying to persuade readers, not philosophize, their arguments were based on a number of key assumptions—often only implied—which distin-

Reprinted by permission of the publishers from *The Liberty We Seek: Loyalist Ideology in Colonial New York and Massachusetts* by Janice Potter, Cambridge, Mass.: Harvard.

guished them from Patriots. . . . It is not surprising that the general outlines of a common ideology existed in the colonies. Views about basic concepts like the nature of man mold an individual's response to events, but they also flow from the world in which the ideology functions. In other words, the Loyalists' sharing of certain basic beliefs in part reflected the fact that they were all living in the same society, experiencing the same changes, and reacting in similar ways to the social and political realities they confronted. Thus Loyalist ideas and anxieties can only be fully appreciated if they are related to contemporary changes in the colonies.

Reason and Passion

Patriots were more likely to view man in universal terms and to stress the equality, potential, and features common to all. The universalism of Thomas Paine's approach was revealed in his remark that Americans were championing "the natural rights of all mankind" and that the "cause of America" was "the cause of all mankind." . . . A tendency to see man in abstract terms led Alexander Hamilton to write, "All men have one common original . . . one common nature . . . one common right." And Hamilton, along with other Patriots like John Adams, were more inclined than were Loyalists to emphasize man's potential rather than the discrepancies between human capabilities and his actual behavior.

The Loyalists' view of man was more historical. They tended to look to the past for truths about fundamental concepts like man's nature. History, for Peter Van Schaack, was the "grand fountain of instruction." To Jonathan Sewall and other Loyalists, knowledge about human nature was to be found in the "experience of former ages and Nations."

One lesson gleaned from history was that men were unequal creatures. Although there was no general consensus about the nature or cause of these inequalities, Loyalists placed less emphasis than did Patriots on the features common to all men and more on their differences and inequalities. Societies were usually depicted as incorporating diverging classes or interests. Some writers described a hierarchical, corporate, and organic society, reminiscent of seventeenth-century Puritan ideals, where each person existed as part of a larger social body and had a duty to contribute to the well-being of the whole in accord with his own abilities and station in the hierarchy. Others merely described pluralistic societies comprising disparate social, economic, or religious interest groups. Most recognized the necessity or inevitability of disparities amongst men in socioeconomic condition, talents, or potential for good or evil. Some stressed that society was divided into leaders—those whose merit and accomplishments fitted them to guide the community—and followers, whose role it was to defer to the superior wisdom of their leaders. Virtually all Loyalist spokesmen included in society the weak and the strong, the wise and the less prudent, and the relatively good and evil.

The other vital lesson taught by history was that man was imperfect. This belief was part and parcel of Loyalist attitudes toward passion and reason. Though to most eighteenth-century Americans passion usually had pejorative connotations, some Patriots exalted it. "Powerful and sublime passion," wrote a New York Patriot, "by depriving man in some measure of his natural feelings prompts him to love his country independently of himself." Thomas Paine also praised feelings as the "guardians of his [God's] image in our hearts." "The social compact," he proclaimed, "would dissolve, and justice be extirpated from the earth . . . were we callous to the touches of affection." Other Patriots, however, would have been as critical of passion as were Loyalists, the crucial difference being one of emphasis. Loyalists were more acutely conscious of the tension between man's potential for good—to use his reason and act morally and wisely—and for evil—to succumb to the pull of passion—and the fear of passion was more central to Loyalist ideology. . . .

Because reason was man's highest potential, it was considered to be the source of his freedom and morality. This belief flowed from the assumption that freedom or independence consisted in utilizing the rational faculties that God endowed man with to perceive the truth of a situation and then to act on the basis of this reasoned judgment. Making decisions in this way was considered to be acting in accord with one's conscience. As Daniel Leonard explained, important decisions could not be taken "without first settling with . . . [one's] conscience, in the retired moments of reflection, the important question respecting the justice of . . . [one's] cause." To do this, one had to "hear and weigh every thing that is fairly adduced, on either side of the question, with equal care and attention" and avoid the "disposition to drink in with avidity, what favours our hypothesis, and to reject with disgust whatever contravenes it." . . .

Perhaps the Loyalist who wrestled most earnestly with the claims of individual conscience was Peter Van Schaack. In 1777 at the age of thirty, Van Schaack could look back on a career which began auspiciously enough when he graduated first in his class from King's College and went on to become a lawyer. Although an active supporter of the Patriot side until 1776, he refused to support independence because he sincerely believed that the Lockean compact theory of government did not justify it. In defending his views to the Provincial Convention he argued that because of the seriousness of deciding whether or not government had abrogated its trust and could legitimately be overthrown, each person had to make the decision for himself since "every individual must one day answer for the part he now acts"; he then went on to state that "if he must *answer* for the part he acts, which certainly presupposes the right of private judgment, he can never be justifiable in the sight of God or man, if he acts against the light of his own conviction. In such a case no majority, however respectable, can decide for him." The concept of conscience, as defined by Van Schaack and others, helps to explain more fully why Loyalist spokesmen were so outraged at Patriot repression of dissent. The Patriots were guilty of nothing less than depriving them of their right to use their noblest faculty, reason, to decide the merits of the British-American dispute, and to act according to their own consciences. . . .

Loyalists who believed that reason was the source of man's freedom, morality, and peace of mind were equally certain that passion—a weakness that all men were susceptible to—undermined freedom and morality. An unmanly weakness, passion was equated with many undesirable emotions or baser instincts, like malice, envy, the desire for revenge, or prejudice. When men were gripped by the malevolent appeal of passion, it was contended, their reason was disturbed and their judgment distorted. . . . Passion was so dangerous because it divested man of both his freedom and morality. It made man a slave because it disordered his mind and prevented him from using his reason to perceive independently the truth of a situation. It led to immoral conduct because men, blinded by their passions, were incapable of exercising their God-given ability to arrive at a rational and independent judgment by which to guide their behavior.

Passion, it was stressed, also led to unruly, impetuous, and uncontrollable behavior, which was aesthetically abhorrent to many Loyalists. . . . As a result of the impassioned conduct of irrational creatures, the colonies had sacrificed the contentment and order, the "mutual support and affection," which many Loyalists prized highly, for what was variously described as a state of "enthusiastic frenzy," libertinism, and "Tumult, Disorder and confusion." Thus, behavior guided by passion upset the order of the universe and introduced in its place ugly, ungainly and uncontrollable anarchy and confusion.

Basic to Loyalist ideology, then, was a keen awareness that man was equally capable of noble and rational conduct, dictated by reason, which allowed man to act freely and morally; and of ignoble behavior, determined by passion, which undermined both freedom and morality. And while behavior based on reason was wise, moderate, and restrained, impassioned conduct was unruly, uncontrollable, and senseless.

This acute sensitivity to passion and reason helps to clarify the Loyalists' perception of the people. One ambiguity in the Loyalist argument was their assumption on the one hand that the people were rational, and on the other hand, that the Revolution occurred because the people were deluded. . . . The Revolution came about because the masses, easily swayed and vulnerable to appeals to their passions or baser instincts, were duped by a crafty and unscrupulous cabal. This apparent contradiction can be explained by the Loyalist assumption that the people were volatile and malleable. . . .

Self-Interest and Faction

Along with man's vulnerability to passion, Loyalist spokesmen were also bothered by man's tendency to pursue his own self-interest. An underlying theme in Loyalist literature was that American society was approaching a crisis because of the growth of personal ambition and the all-consuming desire of individuals to advance their own interests rather than promote the public good. Some Loyalists explicitly acknowledged ambition and selfishness as undesirable but irrepressible human traits. . . . Avarice and ambition, it was asserted, were the two main contemporary evils which sprang from the quest for wealth and power. Other Loyalists merely noted with uneasiness the prevalence of the pursuit of private goals and ambitions at the expense of the public welfare. An important theme in the Loyalist history of the Revolution was that the Patriots had no concern for the public good and were motivated instead by their own ambitions and desire to advance their interests.

For some Loyalists self-interested behavior was a source of anxiety because it conflicted with their social ideals, which were more holistic than those of the Patriots. A society in which it was acceptable for individuals to pursue their own interests would be an individualistic community in which the public interest would be synonymous with the sum of individual interests. Some Loyalists decried such a community and advanced the opposing ideal that when men united to form a society, certain claims of the social whole were established which transcended the aspirations of its individual members. Man in society, according to Sewall, "no longer considers himself as an *individual,* absolutely unaccountable and uncontroulable, but as one of a community, every member of which is bound to consult and promote the general good." . . . Some also rejected what has been called "possessive individualism," the idea that the individual possessed certain abilities or talents which he could use exclusively for his own betterment. Instead, they stressed the belief that man has a duty to use his talents in a public-spirited way to promote the general, as well as his own individual, welfare.

Many Loyalists were also concerned because self-interest was spreading into public life in the form of factionalism. Several expressed alarm about party faction and the excesses of party spirit, zeal or "designs." Factions were worrisome because their sole *raison d'être* was self-interest without any strong commitment to shared political ideals or beliefs. . . .

What exactly was it that bothered Loyalists most about the growth of faction—or the pursuit of self-interest—in politics? . . . Their concern . . . was with the *effects* of factional politics. One alarming byproduct of faction for many Loyalists was a lessening of private and public morality. By their very nature, factions were amoral in that they were formed solely to acquire power and to advance special interests, and this was reflected, it was argued, in their members' behavior. Political leaders who sought gain at the expense of their country and blatantly "set up their particular interests in opposition to the true interests of their country" were not only acting immorally themselves, they were also setting a bad example for others. Moreover, factions were believed to encourage unprincipled behavior. "There is not anything more astonishing than the unblushing face of party," one Loyalist wrote sadly; "without the smallest confusion she paints the most notorious falsehoods and without the least remorse, attempts to darken the brightest of characters." Party leaders, in other words, only took public positions because of the perceived political advantage of doing so; truth or "national virtue" were irrelevant considerations. Partisanship, or party spirit, and party presses "wholly employed in prosecuting party designs" were intrinsic parts of factional politics, leading to an abandonment of reason in favor of appeals to popular passions and prejudices.

Equally, if not more devastating, were the squabbling and rancor produced by factions. A "partial, vindictive, virulence of spirit," one Loyalist lamented, replaced the "generous warmth and sober firmness of an honest love for our country," as communities were divided along party lines. Animosities and mutual distrusts resulted, another regretted, from the prejudice and partisanship promoted by factions. Several Loyalists feared that if not restrained, factions could reduce communities to virtual anarchy. One, for example, proclaimed that "societies have often been thrown into confusion and disorder, by the turbulence of factious demagogues, who have abused the licence of the press, and credulity of the people, to serve their own interested or ambitious purposes". . . .

Thus many Loyalist spokesmen were alarmed about the ways in which self-interested behavior affected their society, political practices, and attitudes. They were seriously concerned with the prospect of social fragmentation. Many writers feared that as individuals increasingly pursued their own self-interest with no regard for the common good or for previously accepted standards of morality, there would be no social cohesion, no bonds to unite the community, no moral guidelines to regulate the behavior of its members. Society would fragment and consist of nothing more than a number of isolated, amoral, self-seeking, and purposeless individuals. Self-interested behavior was also perceived as a major threat to colonial politics. Underlying Loyalist critiques of faction, which to them virtually institutionalized self-interest, was the fear that politics or public life was degenerating into nothing more than an immoral scramble by a myriad of interest groups for place and power. . . . Loyalists feared that a society based on self-interest would lack a central focus, a common bond. It would be an unstable and potentially anarchic community.

How legitimate were these Loyalist anxieties? How relevant were their ideas to contemporary colonial society? . . . In the first place, their perception that ambition and self-interested behavior were becoming more common and accepted was accurate. The North American environment, it could be argued, had always fostered ambition, because the widespread availability of land meant greater opportunities for advancement in the colonies than in Europe. But ambition and the pursuit of self-interest were especially nurtured by the economic conditions of the time. Between 1720 and 1760 the colonies experienced rapid population growth, economic expansion, and diversification. Colonial society became more individualistic and competitive, and there was greater economic and geographic mobility. Enhanced opportunities to prosper heightened people's ambitions, whetted appetites for a growing array of consumer goods, and encouraged them to act in unabashedly self-interested ways. Americans might still talk about the desirability of subordinating private interests to the general good, but their actions showed that their primary concern was with "the protection and facilitation of group interests and individual enterprise."

Economic behavior also began to affect attitudes about self-interest. Previously considered a weakness or vice which was at odds with public spirit, self-interest came, as early as the seventeenth century in England, to take on more positive connotations. The generally accepted right of the individual to be secure in his property gradually came to encompass as well the right to prosper and advance himself. Moreover, the pursuit of self-interest was increasingly seen as being not only legitimate but also beneficial. Allowing individuals from all walks of life the economic freedom to advance themselves was upheld in some circles as an incentive to individual industry and creativity, which produced economic growth and expansion. Releasing the individual from past restraints could, it seemed, benefit all: ambitions to rise in the economic ladder could be satisfied at the same time as the economy expanded and society prospered. Such views of self-interest laid the foundations for Adam Smith's justification of the market economy. Assuming that profit-seeking was a basic and irreversible part of human nature, Smith argued that there was a natural order which regulated economic activity so that the "actions of self-seeking individuals balanced one another to produce a natural harmony and a momentum toward the maximization of productivity."

There were grounds for the Loyalist view that self-interested conduct was growing and there was also some justification for their concern about social fragmentation and political instability. One of the most significant changes occurring in Britain and America at the time of the Revolution was the emergence of what has been called the market economy. . . . One effect of the emergence of the market economy, it has been argued, was the atomization of society. The focus in economic theory and in practice was increasingly on the individual, on his right to use his abilities for his own betterment, and on the benefits to society of allowing him to make economic decisions. Of secondary importance at best was the ideal that the individual had a duty or responsibility to society. If one did not share Adam Smith's belief in a natural balancing mechanism which ensured that economic decisions made by individuals served the public interest, then it was legitimate to ask what would bind together members of the community and prevent it from fragmenting into hundreds of competing interest groups. . . .

Certain characteristics of contemporary American politics also fostered uncertainty and volatility. Colonial political institutions, though modeled on those of the mother country, lacked the solid grounding of their English counterparts. Political practices of the eighteenth century merely accentuated the instability. Political factions developed in almost all of the colonies in the course of the century, and very much as Loyalists described them, they were based not on differing political philosophies, but represented various economic and sectional interests. As competing factions curried favor with the electorate, there was greater popular involvement in politics, which in turn added a volatile dimension to public life. Moreover, the press, used increasingly for partisan political purposes, became a powerful propaganda tool that could be used to sway public opinion. And the mob—an accepted part of the political process—presumed to mete out justice often in defiance of the law, and increasingly the lower classes used it to vent their grievances and achieve their goals.

Thus, when Loyalists worried openly about self-interested behavior, instability, and the lack of cohesion in the community, they were reflecting some very real changes occurring in their midst, and this fact sheds new light on their ideology. In the first place, it sets their response to the Revolution in a broader context. In light of the challenges to social unity and political order posed by the development of the market economy and the lessening of influence of the church and family, it is not surprising that Loyalists were deeply concerned when government, the final bastion of order in colonial society, also came under attack. Seen from this vantage point, the Revolution, which swept away the last vestiges of government power, represented the final blow to social unity and political order in America.

Secondly, the fact that there was some substance to Loyalist anxieties about instability affects any assessment of the relevance of their ideology to contemporary Americans, which has been largely overlooked. The Patriots, it has been pointed out, in warning of the dangers of British tyranny, were striking a responsive chord with their readers who had deeply rooted fears about the threat power posed to liberty. But the whole thrust of the Loyalist argument was that anarchy and popular tyranny were more imminent threats to America than was the arbitrary power of British or colonial governments. The Loyalist appeal was to anxieties about instability—the absence of a sense of unity, cohesion, order, and continuity in colonial life. The immediate circumstances of the mid-1770s, when lawlessness, violence, and mob activity were common, fed such fears, as did the more general changes taking place at the time. The growth of individualism and the prominence, even acceptance, of self-interested behavior challenged long-established norms about desirable behavior and fostered concerns about the effects of such conduct on community order. Factions fostered acrimony in public life, and their very existence was at odds with the traditional belief that leaders should act in public-spirited ways to promote social harmony. In the Revolutionary period, then, when there were some signs of instability, uncertainty, and confusion about basic values, Americans were just as likely to be apprehensive about social fragmentation and political instability and their attendant evils as they were to fear tyranny.

Patriots, it should be pointed out, did not share these Loyalist concerns because their ideology was more consistent with self-interested behavior. Loyalists did not believe there were, or could ever be, natural bonds uniting a society of individuals pursuing their own self-interest. Patriots, on the other hand, embraced the ideal of an individualistic society whose members joined together voluntarily and were united by a consensus about basic values. Loyalists could not share this ideal because it was so inconsistent with their beliefs about man and the people. Assuming men were unequal, diverse creatures ruled as easily by passion as by reason, a society that allowed individuals the greatest possible freedom, and left it up to them to find a common basis for their union would be a nightmare, as was the hypothetical state of nature to many Loyalists. Conflict would rage uncontrolled; the stronger members of society would victimize the weaker. And rather than consensus, only disagreement and disorder would result. Underlying Loyalist ideology, then, was the implicit premise that man was too imperfect and the people too unpredictable to be left entirely to their own devices. Loyalists lacked the Patriots' faith in the individual and the people; they had, instead, confidence in the unifying and stabilizing influence of institutions generally and of governments specifically.

Liberty and Government

Loyalist attitudes toward government and other institutions must be studied in relation to Patriot ideology. The American Revolution was premised on a liberal vision of society, and part of this vision was what might be called a positive view of liberty. Associated with freedom from restraint or control over one's destiny, liberty was highly prized by Patriots, who assumed that there was perpetual tension between it and power. To ensure that liberty was not overwhelmed by power required vigilance. Government, from this perspective, was best described by Thomas Paine as a "necessary evil" or a "badge of lost innocence". . . .

The Loyalists' view of liberty, on the other hand, could be called negative in that the stress was not on maximizing individual freedom but on controlling or setting bounds to freedom. This emphasis on restraining rather than liberating the individual was expressed aptly by an unknown writer. "As much liberty as is consistent with good order and government, is the right of subjects in common," he began. "But more liberty," he asserted, "is destructive: and [breeds] a spirit of licentiousness and insolence, in the lower classes of the people, to say nothing of the higher, [it] is in every view criminal and most commonly proves fatal." While Patriots worried that power would be transformed into tyranny, Loyalists feared that liberty would degenerate into licentiousness. . . .

Other writers advocated more specific limits on individual freedom. Several granted that criticisms of government were legitimate or even beneficial, but effectively limited the freedom to criticize authority by insisting that critics could not "advance anything in dimunition of the peace and good order of society." . . . The belief that individual freedom had to be controlled was consistent with the idea that man was an imperfect being vulnerable to the pull of passion as well as the higher call of reason; to allow unrestrained freedom to such creatures would be to invite disorder, instability, and irrationality.

The other side of a limited view of liberty was a more positive view, based on two main ideas, of institutions generally and of government specifically. One idea was that institutions were essential to the happiness and freedom of individuals; the other was that institutions and their authority were seen not as potentially threatening but as benign or salutary.

Relative to the Patriots, the Loyalist approach to institutions was historical. Patriots were more likely to posit the law of nature as a universal principle that should be applied to all institutions, regardless of considerations like the nature of the population or its stage of development. Loyalists like Charles Inglis, however, saw institutions less as the creations of a single generation and more as traditions and practices which unfolded over time to meet the peculiar "genius, manners, disposition and other circumstances of the people." Leonard justified the Quebec Act on the grounds that it was "adapted to the genius and manners of the Canadians." Institutions which evolved gradually over the course of many generations preserved the "wisdom of ages," as Inglis put it, and at the same time had the flexibility to change in response to new circumstances. . . . From this perspective, institutions were almost like a mirror of a society; ideally, they retained the wisdom of the past and adjusted to meet the needs of the future. They had for this reason continuity and an enduring quality. For many Loyalists, institutions were unifying and stabilizing forces which embodied the shared experiences of a people, had been tested by time, and were to be esteemed at least as highly as the reasoning of one generation of imperfect individuals.

A common assumption in Loyalist tributes to church and family was that these institutions should use their moral authority to bring out man's potential to act rationally and unselfishly and to discourage or even repress man's baser instincts. . . . Mothers should stress the importance of authority, obedience, and awe and reverence for authority. The church also had the responsibility for encouraging virtue and discouraging vice and more specifically, for inculcating the importance of deference and respect for authority. . . .

More common than tributes to the family or church was praise for government, whose positive role was supported for a wide variety of reasons. For many Loyalists the necessity for government was rooted firmly in man's nature. As Charles Inglis explained, the state of nature was a fiction, and "a state of society is the *natural state of man.*" . . . As Inglis put it, man "is born in *society,* whose ends cannot be obtained, but by *subordination, order,* and *the regulation of laws,* and where these are, there is government."

Loyalist writers also saw government as essential to man's well-being because it was a unifying and even paternalistic force which regulated conflict and maintained order. . . . The task of harmonizing disparate interests was part and parcel of government's broader function of preserving order. Loyalists frequently associated government and laws with peace, order, and security. Government was to secure to individuals their rights and freedoms, foster a peaceful, stable society, and promote order.

Such views of government and law were remarkably secular and modern. Laws were not seen as tools to punish sin and nurture good Christians but as instruments to maintain social and political order and make good citizens. Some Loyalists went so far as to argue that laws need not be consistent with "natural justice." In other words, the law was to be obeyed not because it was consistent with universal moral principles, but because it was the means by which government regulated society and preserved order. . . . According to Samuel Seabury, "Government was intended for the security of those who live under it;—to protect the weak against the strong;—the good against the bad;—to preserve order and decency among men, preventing every one from injuring his neighbour." For these reasons, "Every person, then, owes obedience to the laws of the government under which he lives and is obliged in honour and duty to support them."

The Significance of the Loyalists' Conservatism

Thus a fundamental ideological division between Loyalists and Patriots lay in their differing views of liberty and government. Whereas a Patriot like Josiah Quincy Junior might assert that "it is much easier to restrain liberty from running into licentiousness than power from swelling into tyranny and oppression," Loyalist writers assumed exactly the opposite. . . . Neither side condoned anarchy or tyranny, but their disagreement about which evil was more serious was fundamental. Patriot thought was premised on an almost obsessive fear of tyranny and a pervasive distrust of power. Patriots placed a high priority on individual freedom and assumed an inherent tension between liberty and power. Government authority, therefore, had to be restricted and controlled so that it could not endanger individual liberty.

Loyalist ideas about liberty and government were more conservative. The duty of the state was to protect the lives, liberties, and property of the individual. But because man was happiest, most secure, and freest in a society under government and law, it was also the duty of individuals to uphold the authority of government. In other words, while Patriots believed that individual liberty had to be protected from government power, Loyalists felt that it was government that ensured the security and freedom of the individual. . . .

Loyalist ideas about government were neither backward-looking nor totally ill-suited to contemporary American society. The liberal ideology of the Patriots, it is true, was more compatible with the individualistic behavior that was an intrinsic part of the emerging market economy. The Loyalists' more conservative ideology, however, was in tune with other contemporary changes. Their attitudes toward political conflict and the law were remarkably modern and well suited to a pluralistic society, characterized increasingly by conflict among differing individuals or interest groups. Their political ideas were more elitist and antidemocratic than those of the Patriots, but they reflected the social structure and distribution of wealth that was becoming more common in the colonies. By the 1770s colonial society resembled its British counterpart in that it was a stratified structure topped by affluent and politically powerful elites. In New York, especially, the foundations for a hierarchical and deferential society were in the making as the growing demand for land enhanced the profitability of the huge manorial estates. Even in the political sphere, the trend was not entirely in the direction of greater democratization—a larger role for the people or their representatives in the political process. In Massachusetts, for example, evidence suggests that power was in fact gravitating away from popularly elected officials and in the direction of royal appointees like justices of the peace.

The point quite simply is that although the Patriot ideal of a liberal society—stressing individualism and a limited government—triumphed, this was not inevitable. Loyalists offered Americans a more conservative ideology based on a positive view of the state and a distrust of the masses that was also consistent with some aspects of colonial society. The importance of this ideology as an alternative to Patriot ideas is accentuated when it is considered that neither their world view nor their critique of American society were new to their readers; both were rooted in British political theory and in the previous decade of colonial experience.

✳ *F U R T H E R   R E A D I N G*

Native Americans

Colin G. Calloway, *Crown and Calumet: British-Indian Relations, 1783–1815* (1987)
David H. Corkran, *The Creek Frontier, 1540–1783* (1967)
Barbara Graymont, *The Iroquois in the American Revolution* (1972)
Reginald Horsman, *Expansion and American Indian Policy* (1967)
Francis Jennings, *Empire of Fortune: Crowns, Colonies, and Tribes in the Seven Years' War* (1988)
Isabel Thompson Kelsay, *Joseph Brant, 1743–1807: Man of Two Worlds* (1984)
William G. McLoughlin, *Cherokee Renascence in the New Republic* (1986)
James H. O'Donnell III, *Southern Indians in the American Revolution* (1973)
Francis Paul Prucha, *American Indian Policy in the Formative Years: The Indian Trade and Intercourse Acts, 1780–1834* (1962)
Daniel K. Richter and James H. Merrell, eds., *Beyond the Covenant Chain: The Iroquois and Their Neighbors in Indian North America* (1987)
Anthony F. C. Wallace, *The Death and Rebirth of the Seneca* (1970)

Loyalists

Robert S. Allen, ed., *The Loyal Americans: The Military Role of Loyalist Provincial Corps and Their Settlement in British North America, 1775–1784* (1983)
Bernard Bailyn, *The Ordeal of Thomas Hutchinson* (1974)
Carol Berkin, *Jonathan Sewall: Odyssey of an American Loyalist* (1974)
Wallace Brown, *The Good Americans: The Loyalists in the American Revolution* (1969)
———, *The King's Friends: The Composition and Motives of the American Loyalist Claimants* (1965)
Robert McCluer Calhoon, *The Loyalists in Revolutionary America, 1760–1781* (1973)
Elizabeth P. McCaughey, *From Loyalist to Founding Father: The Political Odyssey of William Samuel Johnson* (1980)
William H. Nelson, *The American Tory* (1961)
Mary Beth Norton, *The British-Americans: The Loyalist Exiles in England, 1774–1789* (1972)
William Pencak, *America's Burke: The Mind of Thomas Hutchinson* (1982)
Janice Potter, *The Liberty We Seek: Loyalist Ideology in Colonial New York and Massachusetts* (1983)
Philip Ranlet, *The New York Loyalists* (1986)
Paul H. Smith, *Loyalists and Redcoats: A Study in British Revolutionary Policy* (1964)
James W. St. G. Walker, *The Black Loyalists: The Search for a Promised Land in Nova Scotia and Sierra Leone, 1783–1870* (1976)
Ellen Gibson Wilson, *The Loyal Blacks* (1976)
Esther Clark Wright, *The Loyalists of New Brunswick* (1955)
Anne Y. Zimmer, *Jonathan Boucher: Loyalist in Exile* (1978)

CHAPTER 8

Defining the Boundaries
of Liberty for Women
and African-Americans

✕

"We hold these truths to be self-evident, that all men are created equal," Congress proclaimed, "that they are endowed by their Creator with certain unalienable rights, that among these are life, liberty, and the pursuit of happiness." Where did that leave the women of the Revolutionary era? Were they to be denied a full share of natural rights because they were not literally men? And what about African-Americans, most of them held in slavery? Did "all men" mean whites only? These questions have haunted the history of liberty in the United States since 1776. The fact that male dominance remained the rule in American law and public life and that slavery not only survived independence but also was permanently protected by the Constitution has led many to wonder whether the grand ideals of the Revolution were a cruel rhetorical hoax. No patriotic pieties or platitudes can conceal the historical reality that Thomas Jefferson, John Adams, Benjamin Franklin, and their revered colleagues had no intention of including women or African-Americans in their declaration of rights.

In an open society, such a dynamic and soul-stirring idea as natural liberty is hard to contain. Indeed, even before independence was formally voted, a few women, a few blacks, and a few white men were articulating challenges to the prevailing rules of subordination. Already the Revolution had released a "contagion of liberty" that would carry the United States, and with it men like Jefferson and Adams, into new ways of thinking and acting. The noble words of their Declaration would unexpectedly subvert long-established customs and institutions.

By 1775 many Revolutionary leaders recognized that their protests against British tyranny were hard to reconcile with African slavery. "How is it," one Englishman asked, "that we hear the loudest yelps for liberty among the drivers of Negroes?" Here natural rights ran head-on into a stone wall of economic and social privilege. The men who enjoyed the benefits of the slave system were not about to give it up, and they were vital to the success of the Revolutionary coalition. The slavery question that Jefferson himself had raised in Congress in June 1776 was pushed aside, ever after to remain an unwelcome problem in national councils; the critics of slavery lost the struggle. Yet they kept the issue alive, even though the national government would not protect African-American rights. Indeed, for generations, the promise of the Declaration supplied the leverage necessary to keep African-American liberty on the public agenda.

Revolutionary Americans generally failed even to see that there was a contradiction between the ideals of the Declaration and the continuance of women's subordination. Some women recognized it and spoke out in protest, as did a very few men. But eighteenth-century Americans so widely accepted the assignment of a domestic role to women that such responsibility often seemed like a . natural law. Under these circumstances, it was hard to bring women's rights into the political arena, although in some states the issue was raised, and old-fashioned patriarchy was consequently challenged on part of its turf, in the home and the community. In these areas relations between men and women, domestic responsibilities, and the whole subject of gender—that is, of socially constructed roles based on sex—were freshly scrutinized in public discussion that was transatlantic in scope. So although there was a kind of political quarantine by a ''gentlemen's agreement'' against the spread of the contagion of liberty to include women's rights, the foundations of that quarantine were gradually undermined by egalitarian thinking and female activism in the generations leading to the assertion of women's political rights in the 1840s.

✂ D O C U M E N T S

The first set of documents, letters written by Abigail and John Adams in 1776 before Independence, reveal the fundamental challenge that the Revolution posed for conventional modes of thought and behavior. The movement called customary political roles into question, as is evident in the second document, "The Sentiments of an American Woman," published in 1780. The full realization of Revolutionary ideology is brilliantly expounded in the third selection, the 1848 Declaration of Sentiments issued by the women's rights convention that met in Seneca Falls, New York.

As the fourth document reveals, the Revolutionary challenge to slavery began even earlier, in 1773, as slaves employed ideas about natural rights to press the Massachusetts legislature to end their bondage. By 1775 one Massachusetts county, Worcester, took up the cause, which is spelled out in the fifth document. The following year, a twenty-three-year-old mulatto minuteman, Lemuel Haynes from western Massachusetts, drafted an essay using Revolutionary ideas to attack slavery. Although Haynes's essay, reprinted here as the sixth document, was never completed and was first printed as recently as 1983, it is testimony to the power of the contagion of liberty. Ironically, the British commander of troops in Virginia, Lord Dunmore, who had no use for Revolutionary principles, promised freedom to slaves who would join his army. His proclamation did indeed free several hundred slaves, but because it threatened to incite a slave uprising it also cemented planter attachment to the patriot cause.

Abigail and John Adams Debate Women's Rights, 1776

Abigail Adams to John Adams

Braintree March 31 1776

. . . I long to hear that you have declared an independancy—and by the way in the new Code of Laws which I suppose it will be necessary for you to make I desire you would Remember the Ladies, and be more generous and favourable to them than your ancestors. Do not put such unlimited power into the hands of the Husbands. Remember all Men would be tyrants if they could. If perticuliar care and attention is not paid to the Laidies we are determined to foment a Rebelion, and will not hold ourselves bound by any Laws in which we have no voice, or Representation.

That your Sex are Naturally Tyrannical is a Truth so thoroughly established as to admit of no dispute, but such of you as wish to be happy willingly give up the harsh title of Master for the more tender and endearing one of Friend. Why then, not put it out of the power of the vicious and the Lawless to use us with cruelty and indignity with impunity. Men of Sense in all Ages abhor those customs which treat us only as the vassals of your Sex. Regard us then as Beings placed by providence under your protection and in immitation of the Supreem Being make use of that power only for our happiness.

John Adams to Abigail Adams

Ap. 14. 1776

. . . As to your extraordinary Code of Laws, I cannot but laugh. We have been told that our Struggle has loosened the bands of Government every where. That Children and Apprentices were disobedient—that schools and Colledges were grown turbulent—that Indians slighted their Guardians and Negroes grew insolent to their Masters. But your Letter was the first Intimation that another Tribe more numerous and powerfull than all the rest were grown discontented.—This is rather too coarse a Compliment but you are so saucy, I wont blot it out.

Depend upon it, We know better than to repeal our Masculine systems. Altho they are in full Force, you know they are little more than Theory. We dare not exert our Power in its full Latitude. We are obliged to go fair, and softly, and in Practice you know We are the subjects. We have only the Name of Masters, and rather than give up this, which would compleatly subject Us to the Despotism of the Peticoat, I hope General Washington, and all our brave Heroes would fight. . . . I begin to think the Ministry as deep as they are wicked. After stirring up Tories, Landjobbers, Trimmers, Bigots, Canadians, Indians, Negroes, Hanoverians, Hessians, Russians, Irish Roman Catholicks, Scotch Renegadoes, at last they have stimulated the [text missing] to demand new Priviledges and threaten to rebell.

Abigail Adams to John Adams

B[raintre]e May 7 1776

. . . I can not say that I think you very generous to the Ladies, for whilst you are proclaiming peace and good will to Men, Emancipating all Nations, you insist upon retaining an absolute power over Wives. But you must remember that Arbitrary power is like most other things which are very hard, very liable to be broken—and notwithstanding all your wise Laws and Maxims we have it in our power not only to free ourselves but to subdue our Masters, and without voilence throw both your natural and legal authority at our feet—

> Charm by accepting, by submitting sway
> Yet have our Humour most when we obey.

I thank you for several Letters which I have received since I wrote Last. They alleviate a tedious absence, and I long earnestly for a Saturday Evening, and experience a similar pleasure to that which I used to find in the return of my Friend upon that day after a weeks absence. The Idea of a year dissolves all my Phylosophy. . . .

Johnny and Charls have the Mumps, a bad disorder, but they are not very bad. Pray be kind enough to remember me at all times and write as often as you possibly can.

John Adams to James Sullivan

Philadelphia May. 26. 1776

Dear Sir

. . . Our worthy Friend, Mr. Gerry has put into my Hand, a Letter from you, of the Sixth of May, in which you consider the Principles of Representation and Legislation, and give us Hints of Some Alterations, which you Seem to think necessary, in the Qualification of Voters. . . .

It is certain in Theory, that the only moral Foundation of Government is the Consent of the People. But to what an Extent Shall We carry this Principle? Shall We Say, that every Individual of the Community, old and young, male and female, as well as rich and poor, must consent, expressly to every Act of Legislation? No, you will Say. This is impossible. How then does the Right arise in the Majority to govern the Minority, against their Will? Whence arises the Right of the Men to govern Women, without their Consent? Whence the Right of the old to bind the Young, without theirs.

But let us first Suppose, that the whole Community of every Age, Rank, Sex, and Condition, has a Right to vote. This Community, is assembled— a Motion is made and carried by a Majority of one Voice. The Minority will not agree to this. Whence arises the Right of the Majority to govern, and the Obligation of the Minority to obey? from Necessity, you will Say, because there can be no other Rule. But why exclude Women? You will Say, because their Delicacy renders them unfit for Practice and Experience, in the great Business of Life, and the hardy Enterprizes of War, as well as the arduous Cares of State. Besides, their attention is So much engaged with the necessary Nurture of their Children, that Nature has made them fittest for domestic Cares. And Children have not Judgment or Will of their own. True. But will not these Reasons apply to others? Is it not equally true, that Men in general in every Society, who are wholly destitute of Property, are also too little acquainted with public Affairs to form a Right Judgment, and too dependent upon other Men to have a Will of their own? If this is a Fact, if you give to every Man, who has no Property, a Vote, will you not make a fine encouraging Provision for Corruption by your fundamental Law? Such is the Frailty of the human Heart, that very few Men, who have no Property, have any Judgment of their own. They talk and vote as they are directed by Some Man of Property, who has attached their Minds to his Interest. . . .

Harrington has Shewn that Power always follows Property. This I believe to be as infallible a Maxim, in Politicks, as, that Action and Re-action are equal, is in Mechanicks. Nay I believe We may advance one Step farther and affirm that the Ballance of Power in a Society, accompanies the Ballance of Property in Land. The only possible Way then of preserving the Ballance of Power on the side of equal Liberty and public Virtue, is to make the Acquisition of Land easy to every Member of Society: to make a Division of the Land into Small Quantities, So that the Multitude may be possessed of landed Estates. If the Multitude is possessed of the Ballance of real Estate, the Multitude will have the Ballance of Power, and in that Case the Multitude will take Care of the Liberty, Virtue, and Interest of the Multitude in all Acts of Government. . . .

The Same Reasoning, which will induce you to admit all Men, who have no Property, to vote, with those who have, for those Laws, which affect the Person will prove that you ought to admit Women and Children: for generally Speaking, Women and Children, have as good Judgment, and as independent Minds as those Men who are wholly destitute of Property: these last being to all Intents and Purposes as much dependent upon others, who will please to feed, cloath, and employ them, as Women are upon their Husbands, or Children on their Parents.

As to your Idea, of proportioning the Votes of Men in Money Matters, to the Property they hold, it is utterly impracticable. There is no possible Way of Ascertaining, at any one Time, how much every Man in a Community, is worth; and if there is, So fluctuating is Trade and Property, that this State of it, would change in half an Hour. The Property of the whole Community, is Shifting every Hour, and no Record can be kept of the Changes.

Society can be governed only by general Rules. Government cannot accommodate itself to every particular Case, as it happens, nor to the Circumstances of particular Persons. It must establish general, comprehensive Regulations for Cases and Persons. The only Question is, which general Rule, will accommodate most Cases and most Persons.

Depend upon it, sir, it is dangerous to open So fruitfull a Source of Controversy and Altercation, as would be opened by attempting to alter the

Qualifications of Voters. There will be no End of it. New Claims will arise. Women will demand a Vote. Lads from 12 to 21 will think their Rights not enough attended to, and every Man, who has not a Farthing, will demand an equal Voice with any other in all Acts of State. It tends to confound and destroy all Distinctions, and prostrate all Ranks, to one common Levell.

The Sentiments of an American Woman, 1780

On the commencement of actual war, the Women of America manifested a firm resolution to contribute as much as could depend on them, to the deliverance of their country. Animated by the purest patriotism, they are sensible of sorrow at this day, in not offering more than barren wishes for the success of so glorious a Revolution. They aspire to render themselves more really useful; and this sentiment is universal from the north to the south of the Thirteen United States. Our ambition is kindled by the fame of those heroines of antiquity, who have rendered their sex illustrious, and have proved to the universe, that, if the weakness of our Constitution, if opinion and manners did not forbid us to march to glory by the same paths as the Men, we should at least equal, and sometimes surpass them in our love for the public good. I glory in all that which my sex has done great and commendable. I call to mind with enthusiasm and with admiration, all those acts of courage, of constancy and patriotism, which history has transmitted to us: The people favoured by Heaven, preserved from destruction by the virtues, the zeal and the resolution of Deborah, of Judith, of Esther! The fortitude of the mother of the Macchabees, in giving up her sons to die before her eyes: Rome saved from the fury of a victorious enemy by the efforts of Volumnia, and other Roman Ladies: So many famous sieges where the Women have been seen forgetting the weakness of their sex, building new walls, digging trenches with their feeble hands, furnishing arms to their defenders, they themselves darting the missile weapons on the enemy, resigning the ornaments of their apparel, and their fortune, to fill the public treasury, and to hasten the deliverance of their country; burying themselves under its ruins; throwing themselves into the flames rather than submit to the disgrace of humiliation before a proud enemy.

Born for liberty, disdaining to bear the irons of a tyrannic Government, we associate ourselves to the grandeur of those Sovereigns, cherished and revered, who have held with so much splendour the scepter of the greatest States, The Batildas, the Elizabeths, the Maries, the Catharines, who have extended the empire of liberty, and contented to reign by sweetness and justice, have broken the chains of slavery, forged by tyrants in times of ignorance and barbarity. . . .

. . . We are at least certain, that he cannot be a good citizen who will not applaud our efforts for the relief of the armies which defend our lives, our possessions, our liberty? . . . And shall we hesitate to evidence to you our gratitude? Shall we hesitate to wear a cloathing more simple; hair dressed less elegant, while at the price of this small privation, we shall deserve your benedictions. Who, amongst us, will not renounce with the highest pleasure, those vain ornaments, when she shall consider that the valiant defenders of America will be able to draw some advantage from the money which she may have laid out in these. . . . The time is arrived to display the same sentiments which animated us at the beginning of the Revolution, when we renounced the use of teas, however agreeable to our taste, rather than receive them from our persecutors; when we made it appear to them that we placed former necessaries in the rank of superfluities, when our liberty was interested; when our republican and laborious hands spun the flax, prepared the linen intended for the use of our soldiers; when [as] exiles and fugitives we supported with courage all the evils which are the concomitants of war. Let us not lose a moment; let us be engaged to offer the homage of our gratitude at the altar of military valour, and you, our brave deliverers, while mercenary slaves combat to cause you to share with them, the irons with which they are loaded, receive with a free hand our offering, the purest which can be presented to your virtue, By AN AMERICAN WOMAN.

The Declaration of Sentiments of the Seneca Falls Convention, 1848

When, in the course of human events, it becomes necessary for one portion of the family of man to assume among the people of the earth a position different from that which they have hitherto occupied, but one to which the laws of nature and of nature's God entitle them, a decent respect to the opinions of mankind requires that they should declare the causes that impel them to such a course.

We hold these truths to be self-evident: that all men and women are created equal; that they are endowed by their Creator with certain inalienable rights; that among these are life, liberty, and the pursuit of happiness; that to secure these rights governments are instituted, deriving their just powers from the consent of the governed. Whenever any form of government becomes destructive of these ends, it is the right of those who suffer from it to refuse allegiance to it, and to insist upon the institution of a new government, laying its foundation on such principles, and organizing its powers in such form, as to them shall seem most likely to effect their safety and happiness. Prudence, indeed, will dictate that governments long established should not be changed for light and transient causes; and accordingly all experience hath shown that mankind are more disposed to suffer, while evils are sufferable, than to right themselves by abolishing the forms to which they were accustomed. But when a long train of abuses and usurpations, pursuing invariably the same object evinces a design to reduce them under absolute despotism, it is their duty to throw off such government, and to provide new guards for their future security. Such has been the patient sufferance of the women under this government, and such is now the necessity which constrains them to demand the equal situation to which they are entitled.

The history of mankind is a history of repeated injuries and usurpations on the part of man toward woman, having in direct object the establishment of an absolute tyranny over her. To prove this, let facts be submitted to a candid world.

He has never permitted her to exercise her inalienable right to the elective franchise.

He has compelled her to submit to laws, in the formation of which she had no voice.

He has withheld from her rights which are given to the most ignorant and degraded men—both natives and foreigners.

Having deprived her of this first right of a citizen, the elective franchise, thereby leaving her without representation in the halls of legislation, he has oppressed her on all sides.

He has made her, if married, in the eye of the law, civilly dead.

He has taken from her all right in property, even to the wages she earns.

He has made her, morally, an irresponsible being, as she can commit many crimes with impunity, provided they be done in the presence of her husband. In the covenant of marriage, she is compelled to promise obedience to her husband, he becoming, to all intents and purposes, her master—the law giving him power to deprive her of her liberty, and to administer chastisement.

He has so framed the laws of divorce, as to what shall be the proper causes, and in case of separation, to whom the guardianship of the children shall be given, as to be wholly regardless of the happiness of women—the law, in all cases, going upon a false supposition of the supremacy of man, and giving all power into his hands.

After depriving her of all rights as a married woman, if single, and the owner of property, he has taxed her to support a government which recognizes her only when her property can be made profitable to it.

He has monopolized nearly all the profitable employments, and from those she is permitted to follow, she receives but a scanty remuneration. He closes against her all the avenues to wealth and distinction which he considers most honorable to himself. As a teacher of theology, medicine, or law, she is not known.

He has denied her the facilities for obtaining a thorough education, all colleges being closed against her.

He allows her in Church, as well as State, but a subordinate position, claiming Apostolic authority for her exclusion from the ministry, and, with some exceptions, from any public participation in the affairs of the Church.

He has created a false public sentiment by giving to the world a different code of morals for men and women, by which moral delinquencies which exclude women from society, are not only tolerated, but deemed of little account in man.

He has usurped the prerogative of Jehovah himself, claiming it as his right to assign for her a sphere of action, when that belongs to her conscience and to her God.

He has endeavored, in every way that he could, to destroy her confidence in her own powers, to lessen her self-respect, and to make her willing to lead a dependent and abject life.

Now, in view of this entire disfranchisement of one-half the people of this country, their social and religious degradation—in view of the unjust laws above mentioned, and because women do feel themselves aggrieved, oppressed, and fraudulently deprived of their most sacred rights, we insist that they have immediate admission to all the rights and privileges which belong to them as citizens of the United States.

In entering upon the great work before us, we anticipate no small amount of misconception, misrepresentation, and ridicule; but we shall use every instrumentality within our power to effect our object. We shall employ agents, circulate tracts, petition the State and National legislatures, and endeavor to enlist the pulpit and the press in our behalf. We hope this Convention will be followed by a series of Conventions embracing every part of the country.

Massachusetts Slaves Argue for Freedom, 1773

Boston, April 20th, 1773

Sir, The efforts made by the legislative of this province in their last sessions to free themselves from slavery, gave us, who are in that deplorable state, a high degree of satisfaction. We expect great things from men who have made such a noble stand against the designs of their *fellow-men* to enslave them. We cannot but wish and hope Sir, that you will have the same grand object, we mean civil and religious liberty, in view in your next session. The divine spirit of *freedom,* seems to fire every humane breast on this continent, except such as are bribed to assist in executing the execrable plan.

We are very sensible that it would be highly detrimental to our present masters, if we were allowed to demand all that of *right* belongs to us for past services; this we disclaim. Even the *Spaniards,* who have not those sublime ideas of freedom that English men have, are conscious that they have no right to all the services of their fellow-men, we mean the *Africans,* whom they have purchased with their money; therefore they allow them one day in a week to work for themselves, to enable them to earn money to purchase the residue of their time, which they have a right to demand in such portions as they are able to pay for (a due appraizement of their services being first made, which always stands at the purchase money.) We do not pretend to dictate to you Sir, or to the Honorable Assembly, of which you are a member. We acknowledge our obligations to you for what you have already done, but as the people of this province seem to be actuated by the principles of equity and justice, we cannot but expect your house will again take our deplorable case into serious consideration, and give us that ample relief which, *as men,* we have a natural right to.

But since the wise and righteous governor of the universe, has permitted our fellow men to make us slaves, we bow in submission to him, and determine to behave in such a manner as that we may have reason to expect the divine approbation of, and assistance in, our peaceable and lawful attempts to gain our freedom.

We are willing to submit to such regulations and laws, as may be made relative to us, until we leave the province, which we determine to do as soon as we can, from our joynt labours procure money to transport ourselves to some part of the Coast of *Africa,* where we propose a settlement. We are very desirous that you should have instructions relative to us, from your town, therefore we pray you to communicate this letter to them, and ask this favor for us.

In behalf of our fellow slaves in this province, and by order of their Committee.

Peter Bestes
Sambo Freeman
Felix Holbrook
Chester Joie

Worcester County, Massachusetts, Calls for the Abolition of Slavery, 1775

Whereas the Negroes in the counties of Bristol and Worcester, the 24th of March last, petitioned the Committees of Correspondence for the county of Worcester (then convened in Worcester) to assist them in obtaining their freedom. Therefore, In County Convention, June 14th, 1775. Resolved, that we abhor the enslaving of any of the human race, and particularly of the NEGROES in this country. And that whenever there shall be a door opened, or opportunity present, for anything to be done toward emancipating the NEGROES: we will use our influence and endeavor that such a thing may be effected.

A New England Mulatto Attacks Slavery, 1776

Liberty Further Extended: Or Free thoughts on the illegality of Slave-keeping; Wherein those arguments that Are used in its vindication Are plainly confuted. Together with an humble Address to such as are Concearned in the practise.

> We hold these truths to be self-Evident, that all men are created Equal, that they are Endowed By their Creator with Ceartain unalienable rights, that among these are Life, Liberty, and the pursuit of happyness.
>
> *Congress.*

. . . Liberty is a Jewel which was handed Down to man from the cabinet of heaven, and is Coaeval with his Existance. And as it proceed from the Supreme Legislature of the univers, so it is he which hath a sole right to take away; therefore, he that would take away a mans Liberty assumes a prerogative that Belongs to another, and acts out of his own domain.

One man may bost a superorety above another in point of Natural previledg; yet if he can produse no convincive arguments in vindication of this preheminence his hypothesis is to Be Suspected. To affirm, that an

Englishman has a right to his Liberty, is a truth which has Been so clearly Evinced, Especially of Late, that to spend time in illustrating this, would be But Superfluous tautology. But I query, whether Liberty is so contracted a principle as to be Confin'd to any nation under Heaven; nay, I think it not hyperbolical to affirm, that Even an affrican, has Equally as good a right to his Liberty in common with Englishmen. . . .

It hath pleased god to *make of one Blood all nations of men, for to dwell upon the face of the Earth.* Acts 17, 26. And as all are of one Species, so there are the same Laws, and aspiring principles placed in all nations; and the Effect that these Laws will produce, are Similar to Each other. Consequently we may suppose, that what is precious to one man, is precious to another, and what is irksom, or intolarable to one man, is so to another, consider'd in a Law of Nature. Therefore we may reasonably Conclude, that Liberty is Equally as pre[c]ious to a *Black man,* as it is to a *white one,* and Bondage Equally as intollarable to the one as it is to the other: Seeing it Effects the Laws of nature Equally as much in the one as it Does in the other. But, as I observed Before, those privileges that are granted to us By the Divine Being, no one has the Least right to take them from us without our consen[t]; and there is Not the Least precept, or practise, in the Sacred Scriptures, that constitutes a Black man a Slave, any more than a white one.

Shall a mans Couler Be the Decisive Criterion whereby to Judg of his natural right? or Becaus a man is not of the same couler with his Neighbour, shall he Be Deprived of those things that Distuingsheth [Distinguisheth] him from the Beasts of the field? . . . O *Sirs!* Let that pity, and compassion, which is peculiar to mankind, Especially to English-men, no Longer Lie Dormant in your Breast: Let it run free thro' Disinterested Benevolence. then how would these iron yoaks Spontaneously fall from the gauled Necks of the oppress'd! And that Disparity, in point of Natural previlege, which is the Bane of Society, would Be Cast upon the utmost coasts of Oblivion. . . . "O when shall America be consistantly Engaged in the Cause of Liberty!" If you have any Love to yourselves, or any Love to this Land, if you have any Love to your fellow-men, Break these intollerable yoaks, and Let their names Be remembered no more, Least they Be retorted on your own necks, and you Sink under them: for god will not hold you guiltless.

Lord Dunmore Promises Freedom to Slaves Who Fight for Britain, 1775

I do, in virtue of the power and authority to *me* given, by his *majesty,* determine to execute martial law, and cause the same to be executed throughout this colony; and to the end that peace and good order may the sooner be restored, I do require every person capable of bearing arms to resort to his *majesty's* standard, or be looked upon as traitors to his *majesty's* crown and government, and thereby become liable to the penalty the law inflicts upon such offences; such as forfeiture of life, confiscation of lands, &c. &c. And I do hereby further declare all indented servants, negroes, or others (appertaining to rebels) free, that are able and willing to bear arms, they joining his majesty's troops as soon as may be, for the more speedily reducing this colony to a proper sense of their duty to *his majesty's* crown and dignity. . . .

"Given under my hand, on board the ship William, off Norfolk, the 7th day of November, in the 16th year of his majesty's reign.

"DUNMORE.

"GOD save the KING."

✷ *E S S A Y S*

Mary Beth Norton, the Mary Donlon Alger Professor of American history at Cornell University, has written the leading general work on women and the American Revolution. The first selection here reveals her sense that, although the Revolution did not liberate women, it opened the door to significant changes for them, both immediately and in the long term. This perspective is fundamentally different from the argument of Professor Joan Hoff Wilson of Indiana University, who contends in the second essay that the Revolution diminished women's power and place while enhancing men's.

In the third essay, historian Ira Berlin of the University of Maryland takes up African-American experiences during the Revolutionary generation to show that blacks did achieve some significant advances. Finally, the fundamentally problematic relationship between property rights and human rights—both of which the Founders believed were natural rights—supplies the backdrop for William W. Freehling's analysis of the politics of slavery. In a now-classic article, reprinted here as the last essay, the Johns Hopkins University professor of history argues that the Revolutionary generation's choices were profoundly important for America's future.

Revolutionary Advances for Women

MARY BETH NORTON

The decade of turbulence that preceded the Revolution touched the lives of colonial women as well as men. . . . When American leaders decided to use economic boycotts in their struggle against Great Britain, women's domestic roles took on political significance. The chosen tactics could succeed only if white housewives and their daughters refused to purchase imported goods and simultaneously increased their production of homespun. Even the work assignments of female slaves would have to be changed if the colonial policy was to be fully effective. Thus the attention of male political leaders had to focus on the realm of the household, and the public recognition accorded the female role irreversibly altered its inferior status. Although traditional denigrating attitudes would continue to be voiced as late as the

Text by Mary Beth Norton "We Commenced Perfect Statesmen" and "Conclusion" in *Liberty's Daughters,* 1980, pp. 155–185, 187–193, 296–298. Reprinted with permission Little, Brown and Company.

1790s, the reevaluation of domesticity that began during the revolutionary years would eventually culminate in nineteenth-century culture's glorification of woman's household role.

In addition, during the revolutionary decades the boundaries of the feminine sphere itself began to change. White women, who in the mid-1760s offered profuse apologies whenever they dared to discuss politics, were by the 1780s reading widely in political literature, publishing their own sentiments, engaging in heated debates over public policy, and avidly supporting the war effort in a variety of ways. Indeed, some females were so unstinting in their activism that disagreements over politics during the war led to broken marriages and friendships. Moreover, their commitment to the Revolution caused a number of Philadelphia women to attempt to establish the first nationwide female organization. Even though they had only limited success, the very fact that women embarked upon such an ambitious, unprecedented venture revealed the extent to which their lives had been reshaped during the preceding years.

I

The activism of female patriots found particular expression in their support of the colonial boycott of tea and other items taxed by the Townshend Act of 1767. Male leaders recognized that they needed women's cooperation to ensure that Americans would comply with the request to forgo the use of tea and luxury goods until the act was repealed. Accordingly, newspaper essays urged women to participate in the boycott, and American editors frequently praised those females who refused to drink foreign Bohea tea, substituting instead coffee or local herbal teas. A gathering of New Hampshire women, for example, won applause for having "made their Breakfast upon Rye Coffee," and it was reported that in Newport a group of ladies "most judiciously rejected the poisonous Bohea, and unanimously, to their great honour, preferred the balsamic Hyperion." . . .

To the female readers of this and other similar patriotic calls to action, the stress upon the vital significance of their participation must have been novel and refreshing. For women to be told, even in an obvious hyperbole, that their activities could be more important to America's future than the efforts of male committees and congresses, represented an extraordinary departure from the past American devaluation of the feminine role. Consequently, one can understand the possible psychological as well as political motivations for women's abstention from the use of tea.

In their verses, female poets demonstrated a clear comprehension of the political implications of the nonconsumption movement. "Farewell the Tea Board, with its gaudy Equipage," wrote one whose words were published in the *Virginia Gazette* in early 1774, "because I'm taught (and I believe it true) / Its use will fasten slavish Chains upon my country." . . . Still another woman . . . urged her female compatriots: "Stand firmly resolved and bid Grenville to see / That rather than Freedom, we'll part with our Tea." And she had another purpose as well: "Thus acting—we point out their Duty to men." To her, then, American women were leading the struggle against parliamentary policy; although men might be "strip'd of their Freedom, and rob'd of their Right," women would never surrender to British tyranny. . . .

In a marked departure from the tradition of feminine noninvolvement in public affairs, women occasionally formalized their agreements not to purchase or consume imported tea. Most notably, the *Boston Evening Post* reported in February 1770 that more than three hundred "Mistresses of Families" had promised to "totally abstain" from the use of tea, "Sickness excepted." Their statement showed that they understood the meaning of their acts: the women spoke of their desire to "save this abused Country from Ruin and Slavery" at a time when their "invaluable Rights and Privileges are attacked in an unconstitutional and most alarming Manner." In the South, groups of women went even further by associating themselves generally with nonimportation policies, not confining their attention to the tea issue alone. The meeting satirized in the famous British cartoon of the so-called Edenton Ladies' Tea Party fell into this category. The agreement signed in October 1774 by fifty-one female North Carolinians—among them two sisters and a cousin of Hannah Johnston Iredell—did not mention tea. Instead, the women declared their "sincere adherence" to the resolves of the provincial congress and proclaimed it their "duty" to do "every thing as far as lies in our power" to support the "publick good."

This apparently simple statement had unprecedented implications. The Edenton women were not only asserting their right to acquiesce in political measures, but they were also taking upon themselves a "duty" to work for the common good. Never before had female Americans formally shouldered the responsibility of a public role, never before had they claimed a voice—even a compliant one—in public policy. Accordingly, the Edenton statement marked an important turning point in American women's political perceptions, signaling the start of a process through which they would eventually come to regard themselves as participants in the polity rather than as females with purely private concerns.

Yet the North Carolina meeting and the change it embodied aroused amusement among men. . . . Nowhere was this made clearer than in a well-known exchange between Abigail and John Adams. . . . Abigail asked her husband in March 1776 to ensure that the new nation's legal code included protection for wives against the "Naturally Tyrannical" tendencies of their spouses. In reply John declared, "I cannot but laugh" at "your extraordinary Code of Laws." . . . He commented, "[O]ur Masculine systems . . . are little more than Theory. . . . In Practice you know We are the subjects. We have only the Name of Masters." Adams . . . failed to come to terms with the implications of the issues raised by the growing interest in politics among colonial women. He could deal with his wife's display of independent thought only by refusing to take it seriously.

American men's inability to perceive the alterations that were occurring in their womenfolk's self-conceptions was undoubtedly heightened by the superficially conventional character of feminine contributions to the protest movement. Women participating in the boycott simply made different decisions about what items to purchase and consume; they did not move beyond the boundaries of the feminine sphere. Likewise, when colonial leaders began to emphasize the importance of producing homespun as a substitute for English cloth, they did not ask women to take on an "unfeminine" task: quite the contrary, for spinning was the very role symbolic of femininity itself. But once the context had changed, so too did women's understanding of the meaning of their traditional tasks.

Because the pattern of home manufactures in the colonies showed considerable regional variation, differences also appeared in Americans' responses to calls for expanded domestic cloth production. In the plantation South, which had long been heavily dependent on imported cloth, home manufactures did not readily take hold. Planters were reluctant to reassign female slaves from field work to spinning and weaving, believing both that the change would be expensive and that, as a North Carolinian declared during a 1775 congressional debate on nonimportation, the women were "best employed about Tobacco." Consequently, it was not until late 1774 and early 1775 that planters acquiesced in the inevitable and began to establish large-scale cloth manufactories on their lands. . . .

The shift to home manufacturing in the South was undeniably successful. In 1778, a Virginia merchant reported that his neighbors were "manufactoring so much of the necessary wear that the demand will be but triffling till a change of times & Measures," and a year later a visitor noted that in Virginia spinning was now "the chief employment of the female negroes." Planters in the Carolinas and Georgia likewise made an extensive commitment to the domestic production of cloth. After the war, white southerners continued to use skilled black female spinners and weavers until machine-made American textiles became available following the War of 1812. . . .

Farther north, home manufactures had to be increased by persuasion, not by giving orders to slaves. Political leaders had to convince individual adult white women, and especially their daughters, of the importance of producing more homespun. In the process the men were forced to reevaluate the importance of a crucial component of the feminine domestic role. One of the most common, and indeed most tedious, household tasks took on a high social and political value for the first time. Again, men did not anticipate the consequences.

Initially, the authors of newspaper articles recommending an expansion of home manufactures did not single out women for special attention. . . . But this neglect did not continue beyond the end of 1768, for, as a writer in the *Providence Gazette* had noted late the previous year, "[W]e must after all our efforts depend greatly upon the female sex for the introduction of oeconomy among us." The first months of 1769 brought an explosion in the newspaper coverage of women's activities, especially in New England. Stories about spinning bees, which had been both rare and relegated to back pages, suddenly became numerous and prominently featured. . . .

The formal spinning groups had a value more symbolic than real. They . . . were ideological showcases: they were intended to convince American women that they could render essential contributions to the struggle against

Britain, and to encourage them to engage in increased cloth production in the privacy of their own homes. Sometimes the newspaper accounts made this instructional function quite explicit. The fact that many of the participants came from "as *good families* as any in town," one editor remarked, showed that "it was no longer a disgrace for one of our fair sex to be catched at a spinning wheel." Women's private papers provide confirmations of the success of the campaign.

Betsy Foote, the Connecticut farm girl whose ordinary chores included spinning and weaving, found her tasks invested with new significance. In October 1775 she proudly recorded in her diary that she had carded all day, then spun ten knots of wool in the evening, "& felt Nationly into the bargain."

Charity Clarke, a New York City teenager who eagerly knitted "stock-ens" from homespun yarn supplied by a friend, showed in letters to an English cousin that she too "felt Nationly." . . . But despite her political fervor, Charity Clarke worried about how her cousin would react to her words. Perhaps they would change "the Idea you should have of female softness in me," she told him worriedly in late 1769. Politics as a subject was "out of my province," she admitted, and so she felt uneasy about expressing her opinions, though, she asserted, "I cannot help them, nor can I by any means think them seditious." In her hesitancy Clarke resembled her female compatriots. Like her, they discovered by the late 1760s that the new role they had assumed brought them into conflict with one of the primary limitations on the feminine sphere: their exclusion from the world of politics. In the chaos of the revolutionary period they accordingly began the process of developing an innovative conception of their relationship to the public realm.

II

Before the mid-1760s, most men and women accepted without question the standard dictum that political discussion, like direct political participation, fell outside the feminine sphere. As Esther Burr observed in 1755, "[T]he Men say . . . that Women have no business to concern themselves about em [politics] but trust to those that know better." Accordingly, when such issues became (in the words of Sally Logan Fisher) "the prevaling topic of Conversation," women found themselves in a quandary. They all agreed that political discussion was "not our province," yet at the same time, Sarah Franklin told her father in the fall of 1765, "[N]othing else is talked of, the Dutch talk of the stompt ack the Negroes of the tamp, in short every body has something to say." Were women to deny themselves the ability to comment on what a New Englander called "the most animating Subject," one that "Concerns us all"? . . .

As the years passed and women more frequently engaged in political discourse, the apologies tended to disappear. Simultaneously, men began to change their minds about women's political capacities. The transition can be seen clearly in the correspondence of Samuel Adams and his wife, Betsy.

Early in 1776 Samuel "for once" included a "political anecdote" in a letter to her. Later that same year, prefacing his remarks with the accurate observation, "it has not been usual for me to write to you of War or Politicks," Samuel nevertheless transmitted the most recent political and military news because he knew, he said, "how deeply you have always interested your self in the Welfare of our Country." Although in 1780 he was still wondering whether he should "trouble" her with his reflections on public affairs, the following year he formally challenged the conventional outlines of the feminine sphere by declaring, "I see no Reason why a Man may not communicate his political opinions to his wife, if he pleases."

By 1783, wartime circumstances had created a generation of women who, like the North Carolinian Elizabeth Steele, described themselves as "great politician[s]." Several years after the event, Eliza Wilkinson, a resident of the South Carolina sea islands, recalled that during the British invasion of her state in 1780 "none were greater politicians than the several knots of ladies, who met together. All trifling discourse of fashions, and such low chat was thrown by, and we commenced perfect statesmen." Women read newspapers and pamphlets as eagerly as their male counterparts, repeatedly asked their husbands to keep them supplied with accurate information on military affairs, and followed the progress of war and diplomacy throughout the world, not just on the American continent. . . .

Interest in public affairs and partisan commitments were not confined to women of the middling and better sorts. In 1774, a Boston seamstress firmly aligned herself with the "libe[r]ty boys" against what she called the "tyranny [that] rides in our harbour and insults us in our fields and streets." Travelers regularly encountered politically committed landladies, and British prisoners of war found themselves verbally and sometimes physically assaulted by female Americans. . . . Loyalist women from all social ranks were no less firmly committed to their political position. . . .

That political allegiance had come to be of major importance to American women was demonstrated by the large number of friendships broken by divergent beliefs. . . . In New York City, Helena Kortwright Brasher recalled in later years, the "most intimate friends became the most inveterate enemies." . . . Marriages, too, broke under the strain of political differences. . . .

The same partisanship that led to broken marriages and friendships also caused women to take active roles in the conflict. Camp followers like the woman called Molly Pitcher are today the most famous of the female activists, yet it is impossible to know whether those wives who followed their spouses to the armies of both sides were merely deprived of alternative means of support by their husbands' enlistments, or whether their participation in the war may be attributed to their own political beliefs. When women acted independently, on the other hand, one can be fairly certain they did so out of political conviction. Innumerable anecdotes recount the exploits of such female patriots as Deborah Sampson, who disguised herself as a man to fight in the revolutionary army; Nancy Hart, the Georgian who single-handedly captured a group of Tories; Patience Wright, Lydia Darragh, and other spies; and teenaged messengers like Emily Gieger and Deborah Champion. Such well-known tales dramatically reveal a few women's intense commitment, but they provide no basis for estimating the extent of female partisan activity. By studying the 468 claims submitted by loyalist refugee women, though, one can gain a better idea of the proportion of activists and of the ways in which they contributed to their chosen side.

Paul Smith has argued persuasively that about 15 percent of adult white male loyalists took up arms for the British cause. The percentage of activist women was significantly smaller: only twenty-six, or 5.5 percent, of the female refugees said that they had directly assisted the British. Of these, some of whom contributed in more than one way, six aided loyalists, nine helped British soldiers (including those being held as prisoners of war), six carried letters through the lines, and eight served as spies. In addition, two women from upstate New York worked to prevent the Iroquois from allying themselves with the rebels. . . .

To argue that . . . politicization and partisanship . . . was common among women is not to contend that it was universal. After all, the vast majority of female loyalist claimants gave no indication that they had taken positive steps on behalf of the British cause. To be sure, many of them fled their homes at an early stage of the conflict and so could not have contributed actively to the war effort, but some evidence suggests that for many women home and family remained the sole concern throughout the period of the war.

Such a conclusion emerges [as well] from an examination of the pension petitions submitted in the 1830s and 1840s by the elderly widows of Revolutionary War soldiers. . . .

But those who adhered wholly to the traditional domestic realm were anomalous. The change in women's political perceptions wrought by revolutionary circumstances was truly momentous. For the first time, women became active—if not equal—participants in discourse on public affairs and in endeavors that carried political significance. As they discussed politics with men and among themselves during the twenty years from the mid-1760s to the mid-1780s, they gained both sophistication in political analysis and a new sense of their own role—one they expressed most fully in the summer of 1780 when they attempted to form a nationwide organization.

III

Charleston, South Carolina, fell to besieging British forces on May 12, 1780, striking a heavy blow to American hopes for an end to the war in the foreseeable future. Galvanized into action by the disaster, Philadelphia merchants and government officials took steps to support the inflated Pennsylvania currency and began soliciting funds for enlistment bounties to pay new army recruits. In this time of crisis their wives and daughters too adopted "public spirited measures," to use the words of the *Pennsylvania Gazette*: they signaled their intention to found the first large-scale women's association in American history. . . .

The campaign began on June 10, 1780, with the publication of a broadside, *The Sentiments of an American Woman*. The broadside was composed by the thirty-three-year-old Esther DeBerdt Reed, who was to become president of the Ladies Association. The daughter of a prominent English supporter of America, Esther had lived in Pennsylvania only since her 1770 marriage to Joseph Reed, but she was nonetheless a staunch patriot. . . . Recognizing that in proposing an active political role for women she was challenging the boundaries of the feminine sphere, Mrs. Reed built her case carefully.

She began by reviewing the history of women's patriotic activity, referring to female monarchs, Roman matrons, and Old Testament women. Linking herself explicitly to such foremothers, she declared, "I glory in all which my sex has done great and commendable. I call to mind with enthusiasm and with admiration, all those acts of courage, of constancy and patriotism, which history has transmitted to us." Mrs. Reed especially held up Joan of Arc as an appropriate model, for she had driven from France "the ancestors of these same British, whose odious yoke we have just shaken off, and whom it is necessary that we drive from this Continent."

Esther Reed then addressed the question of propriety. Some men might perhaps "disapprove" women's activity, she admitted. But in the current dismal state of public affairs anyone who raised this objection would not be "a good citizen." Any man who truly understood the soldiers' needs, she wrote, could only "applaud our efforts for the relief of the armies which defend our lives, our possessions, our liberty." By thus hinting that critics of her scheme would be unpatriotic, Mrs. Reed cleverly defused possible traditionalist objections even before they could be advanced.

Finally, she outlined her plan. Recalling the contributions women had made to the nonimportation and home manufacture movements, Esther Reed recommended that female Americans renounce "vain ornaments," donating the money they would no longer spend on extravagant clothing and elaborate hairstyles to the patriot troops as *"the offering of the Ladies."*

Her appeal drew an immediate response. Three days after the publication of the broadside, thirty-six Philadelphia women met to decide how to implement its suggestions. The results of their deliberations were printed as an appendix to *Sentiments* when it appeared in the June 21 issue of the *Pennsylvania Gazette*. Entitled "Ideas, relative to the manner of forwarding to the American Soldiers, the Presents of the American Women," the plan proposed the mobilization of the entire female population. Contributions would be accepted from any woman, in any amount. A "Treasuress" appointed in each county would oversee the collection of money, keeping careful records of all sums received. Heading each state's county treasuresses would be the wife of its governor, who would serve as "Treasuress-General." Ultimately, all contributions would be sent to Martha Washington to be used for the benefit of the troops. Only one restriction was placed on the employment of the contributions: "It is an extraordinary bounty intended to render the condition of the soldier more pleasant, and not to hold place of the things which they ought to receive from the Congress, or from the States."

The Philadelphians set to work collecting funds even before the publication of their "Ideas." Dividing the city into ten equal districts, they assigned between two and five of their number to each area. Traveling in pairs, the canvassers visited every house, requesting contributions from "each woman and girl without any distinction." . . .

By the time the Philadelphia canvass was completed in early July, more than $300,000 continental dollars had been collected from over 1600 persons. Because of inflation, this amount when converted to specie equaled only about $7500, but even that represented a considerable sum. In financial terms, the city canvass was a smashing success. It was a success in other ways as well, for the Philadelphia women sought and achieved symbolic goals that went far beyond the collection of money. . . .

In July, newspapers throughout the country reprinted *Sentiments,* usually accompanied by the detailed collection plan, and editors occasionally added exhortations of their own to the women's call for action. Thus the *Continental Journal* of Boston declared on July 13, "[I]f ever an Army deserved every Encouragement from the Country it protects, it is that of America: And nothing could make a deeper Impression on the Minds of those brave men, . . . than such a Mark of Gratitude, and Regard, as is proposed from the FAIRER HALF of the United States." . . .

Successful as this publicity was in spreading the news of the Philadelphians' plan, Esther Reed and her fellow organizers did not rely solely upon print. . . . After they completed the city collections the women decided to write circular letters to their acquaintances in other counties and towns: "[W]e have it in charge to keep up this correspondence until the whole subscription shall be completed." . . .

The women of Trenton, New Jersey, were the first to copy the Philadelphians' lead. . . . Ambitiously, they proposed to establish coordinating committees in each county, and when they announced their scheme in the newspapers they published "Sentiments of a Lady in New Jersey" in deliberate imitation of the Philadelphians. "Let us animate one another to contribute from our purses in proportion to our circumstances towards the support and comfort of the brave men who are fighting and suffering for us on the field," the author exhorted her female compatriots. . . . In mid-July . . . [they] forwarded nearly $15,500 to George Washington as an initial contribution to the fund.

Maryland women also responded quickly to the Philadelphians' request. Mrs. Thomas Sim Lee, the wife of the governor, wrote to friends in each county to ask them to serve as treasuresses, and by July 14 the organization was actively soliciting money in Annapolis. In that city alone, even though many residents had left town for the summer, more than $16,000 in currency was collected, with additional sums in specie. . . . Some months later, writing with particular reference to the Marylanders, the editor of the *Pennsylvania Packet* rhapsodized that "the women of every part of the globe are under

obligations to those of America, for having shown that females are capable
of the highest political virtue."

Only for one other state, Virginia, is there evidence of successful activity
connected with the Ladies Association. . . . A public announcement of the
campaign appeared in the *Virginia Gazette*. Given the diffuse pattern of
settlement in the state, a house-to-house solicitation would have been impossible, so the plan specified that collections would be made in the churches.
. . . Fragmentary records . . . indicate that county treasuresses gathered total
currency contributions ranging from £1,560 (Albemarle) to $7,506 (Prince
William). . . .

Although the women's association found active participants only in Pennsylvania, New Jersey, Maryland, and Virginia, still it collected substantial
sums of money. Its organizers next had to decide how to disburse the funds
in accordance with their original aim, which was to present the American
soldiers with "some extraordinary and unexpected relief, . . . *the offering
of the Ladies.*" Since Martha Washington had returned to Virginia by the
time the collection was completed, the association's leaders agreed to leave
the disposition of the funds to her husband. There was only one problem:
George Washington had plans for the money that differed sharply from
theirs. "Altho' the terms of the association seem in some measure to preclude
the purchase of any article, which the public is bound to find," General
Washington told Joseph Reed in late June, "I would, nevertheless, recommend a provision of shirts in preference to any thing else." . . .

In February 1781 Washington offered profuse thanks to the members
of the committee that had succeeded Esther Reed as leaders of the Ladies
Association. The organization's contributions, he declared, entitled its participants "to an equal place with any who have preceded them in the walk
of female patriotism. It embellishes the American character with a new trait;
by proving that the love of country is blended with those softer domestic
virtues, which have always been allowed to be more peculiarly *your own.*"

Washington's gratitude was genuine, and the army certainly needed the
shirts, but the fact remains that the members of the association, who had
embarked on a very unfeminine enterprise, were ultimately deflected into
a traditional domestic role. The general's encomium on their contributions
made this explicit by its references to "female patriotism" and "those softer
domestic virtues," which presumably included the ability to sew. Ironically
and symbolically, the Philadelphia women of 1780, who had tried to chart
an independent course for themselves and to establish an unprecedented
nationwide female organization, ended up as what one amused historian has
termed "General Washington's Sewing Circle."

The amusement has not been confined to subsequent generations, for
male revolutionary leaders, too, regarded the women's efforts with droll
condescension. Benjamin Rush and John Adams exchanged wry comments
on the association, with Adams proclaiming, "The Ladies having undertaken
to support American Independence, settles the point." Women, on the other
hand, saw nothing to smile at in the affair. Kitty Livingston, whose mother
was a participant in the New Jersey group, sent a copy of *The Sentiments*

of an American Woman to her sister Sarah Jay, then in Spain. "I am prouder than ever of my charming countrywomen," Sarah told her husband in forwarding the broadside to him, and she later repeated that message to Kitty when she thanked her for the information. Abigail Adams had a similar reaction, one that stands in sharp contrast to her husband's. . . . To her, the women's activities proved that "America will not wear chains while her daughters are virtuous." Not for Abigail were any references to "female patriotism" or "softer virtues." She saw female Americans as equal participants in the war effort. . . .

The proud sense of involvement in public affairs evident in these comments and in women's observations on their private contributions to the war effort carried over into the postwar years, for the return of peace did not bring with it a retreat from politics on the part of American women. Quite the contrary; their interest in the affairs of state continued unabated.

IV

In 1782, Eliza Wilkinson took up the cudgel on behalf of her sex. "The men say we have no business with them [politics], it is not in our sphere!" she told a friend angrily. "I won't have it thought that because we are the weaker sex as to *bodily* strength, my dear, we are capable of nothing more than minding the dairy, visiting the poultry-house, and all such domestic concerns. . . . They won't even allow us the liberty of thought, and that is all I want. . . . Surely we may have sense enough to give our opinions to commend or discommend such actions as we may approve or disapprove; without being reminded of our spinning and household affairs as the only matters we are capable of thinking or speaking of with justness and propriety."

The serious interest in politics that lay behind Mrs. Wilkinson's tirade was not hers alone. In the late 1780s and 1790s women whose appetite for public affairs had been whetted by the events of the Revolution kept themselves abreast of political happenings through newspapers, conversations, and correspondence. . . . From the French traveler who in 1791 encountered two young Virginia women eagerly taking part in political debates, to the New England girl who at a 1788 dance proudly pronounced herself a "politician" to a youth wishing to discuss the new Constitution, to Debby Logan, who in 1799 found it notable that during a visit to Philadelphia she had "scarsly spoke a Political Sentence," the indications are unanimous: after the Revolution women no longer regarded politics as falling outside their sphere. As Abigail Adams put it in 1799, "If a woman does not hold the reigns [*sic*] of Government, I see no reason for her not judging how they are conducted." . . .

But Mrs. Adams believed that a woman should express her political opinions only in private, rather than by taking part in public debates. Others of her female contemporaries were less traditionally minded. Letitia Cunningham, a Philadelphia widow who had bought government bonds during the war, published in 1783 a closely reasoned, well-researched pamphlet, *The Case of the Whigs Who Loaned their Money on the Public Faith Fairly*

Stated, arguing on behalf of herself and other investors—but especially widows—that they were entitled to full interest payments on the loans. Likewise, Anne Willing Bingham, a niece of Elizabeth Willing Powel, openly challenged Thomas Jefferson's belief that American women should be "too wise to wrinkle their foreheads with politics." To Jefferson, the ideal feminine role was "to soothe and calm the minds of their husbands returning ruffled from political debate," and he criticized French women for meddling publicly in political affairs. Mrs. Bingham saw the matter quite differently. "The Women of France interfere in the politics of the Country, and often give a decided Turn to the Fate of Empires," she told Jefferson in 1787. As a result, "they have obtained that Rank of Consideration in society, which the Sex are intitled to, and which they in vain contend for in other countries." . . .

Although many American men were willing to allow women private political influence of the sort advocated and exercised by Abigail Adams, only in one state did the postrevolutionary era bring a real, if temporary, recognition of women's potential public role. In 1790, New Jersey adopted an election law that explicitly referred to voters as "he or she," thereby instituting a formal experiment with woman suffrage more than a century prior to the adoption of the Nineteenth Amendment to the Constitution.

The origins of the New Jersey law are obscure. The state constitution of 1776 neither specifically disfranchised women nor enfranchised them, defining voters vaguely as "all free inhabitants" meeting property and residence requirements. Although this broad wording could conceivably have been intended to encompass eligible widows and spinsters as well as free black males, the constitution's phraseology probably represented a simple oversight on the part of its framers, as the opponents of woman and black suffrage later claimed. The electoral clause aroused no special comment at the constitutional convention; if deliberate, such a novel extension of the suffrage would surely have elicited considerable debate. Even so, the state constitution's lack of specificity allowed the newly politicized property-holding women of New Jersey to seize the initiative, and they successfully claimed the right to vote in local elections during the 1780s. The 1790 statute, and similarly worded election laws passed later that same decade, thus simply acknowledged and legitimized extant practice. By 1800, woman suffrage was so well established in the state that the legislature rejected an amendment providing for female voting in congressional races on the grounds that it was unnecessary. As one legislator said, "Our Constitution gives this right to maids or widows *black or white.*"

One well-documented election in which women played a prominent role was the heated contest in 1797 over the seat for the town of Elizabeth in the legislature. Reportedly, seventy-five female Federalists appeared at the polls to vote against the Democratic-Republican candidate, John Condict. Although Condict won, Federalist newspapers celebrated the women's activism, declaring their party's intention to "not only preach the 'Rights of Woman' but boldly push it into practice." . . .

Yet not all male New Jerseyites greeted woman suffrage with such exuberant glee. In his 1798 commentary on the state constitution William Griffith remarked that he found it a "mockery," even "perfectly disgusting," to watch female voters casting their ballots. . . . In 1807, relying on the persistence of such traditional attitudes among his colleagues in the legislature, John Condict had his revenge for his near-defeat at the hands of female voters ten years earlier: he introduced the bill that successfully disfranchised both women and blacks. . . .

New Jersey men had never displayed a strong commitment to the principle of woman suffrage; they had merely left a loophole in their constitution that allowed the boldest among their female fellow citizens to express directly a new sense of public responsibility. That the experiment was formalized at all was a tribute to the wartime politicization of the state's female population, and, indeed, illustrated the possible long-term consequences of that politicization. But even though the women of the revolutionary generation enthusiastically exercised their newfound public role, there are indications that many of their daughters and granddaughters reverted to a more traditional understanding of woman's place. . . .

In 1798, Judith Sargent Murray confidently predicted the dawn of "a new era of female history." "The partial distribution of advantages which has too long obtained, is, in this enlightened age, rapidly giving place to a more uniform system of information," she asserted. Women were at last "emerging from the clouds which have hitherto enveloped them, and *the revolution of events is advancing in that half of the human species, which hath hitherto been involved in the night of darkness, toward the irradiating sun of science.*"

Most of Murray's contemporaries were less optimistic. The "American Lady" who wrote the "Second Vindication of the Rights of Women" in 1801 pointed out that, although men "do professedly condescend to acknowledge an equality which is evidently founded in nature; yet, they are by no means willing to ab[b]reviate their pretences to superiority." As a result, she observed accurately, woman's improvement could at present "answer no particular purpose in life." Seen in this perspective, an educated woman in 1800 had only a modicum more control over her destiny than her uneducated grandmother had had in 1750: she could, if she wished, teach school for a few years before marriage, decide not to marry at all, choose a husband without consulting her parents, or raise her children in accordance with republican principles. But she could not, realistically, aspire to leave the feminine sphere altogether. . . .

Yet if the white women who lived in early nineteenth-century America could not escape the constraints of femininity, the precise nature of those constraints differed subtly, but significantly, from the limits that had governed their colonial grandmothers. As the nature of American government and society had changed during the half-century that witnessed the Revolution, so too had American notions of womanhood. Not the least of those changes was the very attempt to place the feminine role in the context of society as a whole. Prior to the Revolution, when the private realm of the household was seen as having little connection with the public world of politics and economics, woman's secular role was viewed solely in its domestic setting. That individual women could have a positive—or negative—effect on their husbands, suitors, or perhaps children, was widely recognized, but no one, male or female, wrote or thought about the possibility that women might affect the wider secular society through their individual or collective behavior. In theory, their sexual identity was a barrier that separated them from the public world. Femininity, it was believed, placed them one step removed from the imperatives and obligations that ruled the white male population.

The war necessarily broke down the barrier which seemed to insulate women from the realm of politics, for they, no less than men, were caught up in the turmoil that enveloped the entire populace. . . . But to recognize that women had a role to fulfill in the wider society was not to declare that male and female roles were, or should be, the same. Not even Judith Sargent Murray conceived of an androgynous world; men's and women's functions were to be equal and complementary, not identical. And so the citizens of the republic set out to discover and define woman's public role. They found it not in the notion that women should directly participate in politics, New Jersey's brief experiment with woman suffrage to the contrary. Rather, they located woman's public role in her domestic responsibilities, in her obligation to create a supportive home life for her husband, and particularly in her duty to raise republican sons who would love their country and preserve its virtuous character.

The ironies of this formulation were manifest. On the one hand, society had at last formally recognized women's work as valuable. No longer was domesticity denigrated; no longer was the feminine sphere subordinated to the masculine, nor were women regarded as inferior. The white women of nineteenth-century America could take pride in their sex in a way their female ancestors could not. The importance of motherhood was admitted by all, and women could glory in the special role laid out for them in the copious literature that rhapsodized about beneficent feminine influences both inside and outside the home.

But, on the other hand, the republican definition of womanhood, which began as a marked step forward, grew ever more restrictive as the decades passed. Woman's domestic and maternal role came to be seen as so important that it was believed women sacrificed their femininity if they attempted to be more (or other) than wives and mothers. Accordingly, the women who were most successful in winning society's acceptance of their extradomestic activities were those who—like teachers, missionaries, or charitable workers—managed to conceal their flouting of convention by subsuming their actions within the confines of an orthodox, if somewhat broadened, conception of womanhood and its proper functions.

In the prerevolutionary world, no one had bothered to define domesticity: the private realm seemed unimportant, and besides, women could not escape their inevitable destiny. In the postrevolutionary world, the social significance of household and family was recognized, and simultaneously women began to be able to choose different ways of conducting their lives. As a direct result, a definition of domesticity was at last required. The process of defining woman's proper role may well have stiffened the constraints that had always encircled female lives, but that definition also—by its very existence—signaled American society's growing comprehension of woman's importance within a sphere far wider than a private household or a marital relationship.

The legacy of the American Revolution for women was thus ambiguous. Republican womanhood eventually became Victorian womanhood, but at the same time the egalitarian rhetoric of the Revolution provided the women's rights movement with its earliest vocabulary, and the republican academies produced its first leaders. Few historical events can ever be assessed in absolute terms. With respect to its impact on women, the American Revolution is no exception.

The Illusion of Change: Women and the American Revolution

JOAN HOFF WILSON

To discuss individual women and the American Revolution is to talk about unrequited patriotism. To discuss individual women in relation to any specific historical event like a revolution, a depression, or any other major development in foreign and domestic policy is equally gratuitous. By themselves women seldom fit into the power and prestige categories that characterize standard textbook accounts of this nation's development. Their contributions to history and the important societal conditions affecting them and other subordinate, powerless groups in American history are largely evolutionary in nature. Consequently, they do not dovetail with such common periodizations as the Revolution, the Jacksonian period, Reconstruction, or the Progressive Era.

Therefore, no attempt simply to document the specific individual or group actions of American women between 1763 and 1783 will contribute significantly to assessing their historical importance. One must begin to hypothesize about their collective stage of socioeconomic development *before,* *during,* and *after* the events leading up to and immediately following the War for Independence. Hence, the time period under discussion will generally be the last half of the eighteenth century and first decade of the nineteenth century, with particular attention given to the years from the end of the French and Indian War in 1763 to 1800. It was a period of war, socioeconomic change, and political upheaval. . . .

I realize that no single conceptual framework or methodology is completely satisfactory to unravel the complexities of women's history. The application of a functional, comparative analysis will allow historians to more easily question the validity of behavior prescribed for women on the basis

Exerpts from Joan Hoff Wilson's "The Illusion of Change: Women and the American Revolution," in *The American Revolution: Explorations in the History of American Radicalism,* Alfred F. Young, ed. © 1976 by Northern Illinois University Press. Reprinted with permission of the publisher and author.

of standard patriarchal and often sexist value judgments about their contributions to history. By keeping in mind the differences among various
classes and races of women, as well as individual differences among women,
we may also move away from traditional generalizations about women as a
whole. . . . I will argue that certain types of female functions, leading either
to the well-known exploitation of working women or to the ornamental
middle-class housewife of the nineteenth century, were abetted by the American Revolution, although not caused by it.

This occurred because the functional opportunities open to women between 1700 and 1800 were too limited to allow them to make the transition
in attitudes necessary to insure high status performance in the newly emerging
nation. In other words, before 1776 women did not participate enough in
conflicts over land, religion, taxes, local politics, or commercial transactions.
They simply had not come into contact with enough worldly diversity to be
prepared for a changing, pluralistic, modern society. Women of the postrevolutionary generation had little choice but to fill those low status functions
prescribed by the small minority of American males who *were* prepared for
modernization by enough diverse activities and experiences.

As a result, the American Revolution produced no significant benefits
for American women. This same generalization can be made for other powerless groups in the colonies—native Americans, blacks, probably most
propertyless white males, and indentured servants. Although these people
together with women made up the vast majority of colonial population, they
could not take advantage of the overthrow of British rule to better their
own positions, as did the white, propertied males who controlled economics,
politics, and culture. By no means did all members of these subordinate
groups support the patriot cause, and those who did, even among whites,
were not automatically accorded personal liberation when national liberation
was won. . . .

Why didn't the experiences of the Revolution result in changing the
political consciousness of women? Part of the answer lies in the socialized
attitudes among female members of the revolutionary generation that set
them apart from their male contemporaries. Their attitudes had been molded
by the modernization trends encountered by most women in the course of
the eighteenth century. Out of the necessity wrought by the struggle with
England, women performed certain tasks that appeared revolutionary in
nature, just as they had performed nonfamilial tasks out of necessity throughout the colonial period. But this seemingly revolutionary behavior is not
necessarily proof of the acceptance of abstract revolutionary principles.

Despite their participation in greater economic specialization, despite
their experiences with a slightly smaller conjugal household where power
relations were changing, despite a limited expansion of the legal rights and
somewhat improved educational opportunities for free, white women, the
revolutionary generation of females were less prepared than most men for
the modern implications of independence. Their distinctly different experiential level, combined with the intellectually and psychologically limiting
impact of the Great Awakening and the Enlightenment on women, literally

made it impossible for even the best educated females to understand the political intent or principles behind the inflated rhetoric of the revolutionary era. Words like virtue, veracity, morality, tyranny, and corruption were ultimately given public political meanings by male revolutionary leaders that were incomprehensible or, more likely, misunderstood by most women. . . .

How does one prove such a generalization about attitudes behind the behavior of women during the Revolution? . . . Among the more articulate and educated women there is written testimony to at least an initial sense of pride and importance involved in their participation in the war effort. Thus a young Connecticut woman named Abigail Foote wrote in her diary in 1775 that carding two pounds of whole wool had made her feel "Nationly," while others recorded their contributions in similarly patriotic terms.

But the question remains: did their supportive actions prepare them to accept a vision of society anywhere near the version ultimately conveyed by James Madison's Federalist Number Ten in the fight over the Constitution of 1787? To date there is little evidence that this type of sophisticated political thought was present, either in the writings of women about the Revolution and its results or in the appeals made to them during or immediately following the war. . . .

The same lack of political astuteness appears to underlie even the least traditional and most overtly political activities of women, such as the fifty-one who signed the anti-tea declaration in Edenton, North Carolina, on 25 October 1774 (later immortalized in a London cartoon). The same could be said of the more than 500 Boston women who agreed on 31 January 1770 to support the radical male boycott of tea; of the Daughters of Liberty in general; and of the 1,600 Philadelphia women who raised 7,500 dollars in gold for the Continental Army. Even Mercy Otis Warren never perceived the modern political system that evolved from the Revolution. Instead she viewed the war and its aftermath as the "instrument of Providence that sparked a world movement, changing thought and habit of men to complete the divine plan for human happiness" largely through the practice of virtue.

Perhaps the most important aspect of the supportive activities among women for the patriot cause was the increase in class and social distinctions they symbolized. For example, it appears unlikely that poor white or black women joined Daughters of Liberty groups, actively boycotted English goods, or participated in any significant numbers in those associations of "Ladies of the highest rank and influence," who raised money and supplies for the Continental Army. On the contrary, it may well have been primarily "young female spinsters" from prominent families and well-to-do widows and wives who could afford the time or the luxury of such highly publicized activities. The vast majority, however, of middle-class female patriots (and, for that matter, Loyalists), whether single or married, performed such necessary volunteer roles as seamstresses, nurses, hostesses, and sometime spies, whenever the fighting shifted to their locales, without any undue fanfare or praise. The same is true of poorer women, with one important difference: they had no choice. . . .

Probably the classic example of housewifely efficiency and economic shrewdness is found in Abigail's management of the Adams's family and farm during John's long absences. But in this respect Abigail Adams stands in direct contrast to the women in the lives of other leading revolutionaries like Jefferson, Madison, and Monroe—all of whom were bankrupt by public service in part because their wives were not as capable at land management as she was. This even proved true of the most outspoken of all revolutionary wives, Mercy Otis Warren. Numerous lesser well-known women, however, proved equal to the increased domestic responsibilities placed upon them. Only the utterly impoverished could not resort to the traditional colonial task of household manager.

As the months of fighting lengthened into years, more and more poverty-stricken women left home to join their husbands, lovers, fathers, or other male relatives in the army encampments. Once there, distinctions between traditional male and female roles broke down. . . . These camp followers, as well as the women who stayed at home, complained about their plight privately and publicly, and on occasion they rioted and looted for foodstuffs. Women rioting for bread or other staples never became a significant or even a particularly common revolutionary act in the New World as it did in Europe, largely because of the absence of any long-term, abject poverty on the part of even the poorest colonials. . . .

There is still no clear indication of an appreciable change in the political consciousness of such women. . . . In addition, except for camp followers and female vagabonds, the principal concern of most members of this generation of primarily rural women remained the home and their functions there. During the home-spinning drives and during the war when their men were away, their domestic and agricultural duties became all the more demanding, but not consciousness-raising. . . .

Once independence was won, however, these same women, particularly those forced to become camp followers, naturally welcomed the chance to withdraw to what had been their more normal prewar private lives within the physical and psychic safety of their homes. Collective validation and vicarious fulfillment through their families, rather than individual assertion, continued to satisfy most of them. In fact, their desire to end the increased familial hardships and dislocation created by the Revolution is clearly indicated in the one common characteristic all women exhibited regardless of class: an affective response not only to the Revolution specifically, but also to all legal-political matters in general—and most important, to one another. . . .

Lastly, in explaining the failure of the equalitarian ideals of the Revolution to bear even limited fruit for women, one must analyze the narrow ideological parameters of even those few who advocated women's rights, persons such as Abigail Adams, Judith Sargent Murray, Elizabeth Southgate Bowne, Elizabeth Drinker, and Mercy Otis Warren.

These women . . . were not feminists. Like most of the better organized, but no less unsuccessful Républicaines of France, they seldom, if ever, aspired to complete equality with men except in terms of education. Moreover, none challenged the institution of marriage or defined themselves "as other than mothers and potential mothers." They simply could not conceive of a society whose standards were not set by male, patriarchal institutions, nor should they be expected to have done so. Instead of demanding equal rights, the most articulate and politically conscious American women of this generation asked at most for privileges and at least for favors—not for an absolute expansion of their legal or political functions, which they considered beyond their proper womanly sphere. Man was indeed the measure of equality to these women, and given their societal conditioning, such status was beyond their conception of themselves as individuals.

Ironically it is this same sense of their "proper sphere" that explains why the most educated female patriots did not feel obliged to organize to demand more from the Founding Fathers. It is usually overlooked that in the famous letter of 31 March 1776 where Abigail asks John Adams to "Remember the Ladies," she justified this mild request for "more generous and favourable" treatment on the grounds that married women were then subjected to the "unlimited power" of their husbands. She was not asking him for the right to vote, only for some legal protection of wives from abuses under common law practices. "Regard us then," she pleaded with her husband, "as Beings placed by providence under your protection and in imitation of the Supreme Being make use of that power only for our happiness." Despite an earlier statement in this letter about the "Ladies" being "determined to foment a Rebelion" and refusing to be "bound by any Laws in which we have no voice, or Representation," Abigail Adams was not in any sense demanding legal, let alone political or individual, equality with men at the beginning of the American Revolution. If anything, her concept of the separateness of the two different spheres in which men and women operated was accentuated by the war and the subsequent trials of the new republic between 1776 and 1800. . . .

It is true that Abigail Adams was an extremely independent-minded person who firmly criticized books by foreign authors who subordinated the female sphere to that of the male. Writing to her sister Elizabeth Shaw Peabody in 1799, she said that "I will never consent to have our sex considered in an inferior point of light. Let each planet shine in their own orbit, God and nature designed it so—if man is Lord, woman is *Lordess*—that is what I contend for." . . . Such a strong belief in equal, but separate, spheres is indeed admirable for the times, but it should not be confused with feminism. . . .

To have asked for individual or political equality with men would not only have violated their belief in two separate, but equal, spheres of duty, but it also would have automatically meant asking for a role in the public realm that was literally considered a physical impossibility by most eighteenth-century women. Their dawn-to-dusk domestic duties as household managers, and their health problems from frequent childbirth and inadequate diets relegated all classes of colonial women to lives of domesticity in the broadest sense of that term. This was philosophically reinforced by the political theories and physical laws of the universe associated with the Enlightenment that deemed it "natural" for public affairs to be conducted exclusively by men. . . .

A final factor that helps to explain the absence of feminism in the behavior of women during the Revolution and in their attitudes afterward is related to the demographic changes that were taking place within the family unit between 1760 and 1800. Middle- and upper-class women were increasingly subjected to foreign and domestic literature stressing standards of femininity that had not inhibited the conduct of their colonial ancestors. While the rhetoric of this new literature was that of the Enlightenment, its message was that of romantic love, glamorized dependence, idealized motherhood, and sentimentalized children within the ever-narrowing realm of family life. At poorer levels of society a new family pattern was emerging as parental control broke down, and ultimately these two trends would merge, leaving all women in lower status domestic roles than they had once occupied.

In general it appears that the American Revolution retarded those societal conditions that had given colonial women their unique function and status in society, while it promoted those that were leading toward the gradual "embourgeoisement" of late eighteenth-century women. By 1800 their economic and legal privileges were curtailed; their recent revolutionary activity minimized or simply ignored; their future interest in politics discouraged; and their domestic roles extolled, but increasingly limited. . . .

For women, the American Revolution was over before it ever began. Their "disinterested" patriotism (or disloyalty, as the case may be) was accorded identical treatment by male revolutionaries following the war: conscious neglect of female rights combined with subtle educational and economic exploitation. The end result was increased loss of function and authentic status for all women whether they were on or under the proverbial pedestal.

The Revolution in Black Life

IRA BERLIN

The years between 1770 and 1810 were a formative period for Afro-American culture. The confluence of three events—freedom for large numbers of blacks with the abolition of slavery in the North and large-scale manumission in parts of the South; the maturation of a native-born Afro-American population after more than a century of American captivity; and a new, if short-lived, flexibility in white racial attitudes—made these years the pivot point in the development of black life in the United States. The social patterns and institutions established during the revolutionary era simultaneously confirmed the cultural transformation of the preceding century and shaped black

Exerpts from Ira Berlin's "The Revolution in Black Life," in *The American Revolution: Explorations in the History of American Radicalism,* Alfred F. Young, ed. © 1976 Northern Illinois University Press. Reprinted with permission of the publisher and the author.

life well into the twentieth century. In many ways, the revolutionary era, far more than the much studied Reconstruction period, laid the foundation for modern Afro-American life.

The events and ideas of the revolutionary years radically altered the structure of black society and the substance of Afro-American culture. The number of blacks enjoying freedom swelled under the pressure of revolutionary change, from a few thousand in the 1760s to almost two-hundred thousand by the end of the first decade of the nineteenth century. Freedom, even within the limited bounds of white domination, enhanced black opportunities by creating new needs and allowing blacks a chance to draw on the rapidly maturing Afro-American culture to fulfill them. But the revolution in black life was not confined to those legally free. The forces unleashed by the American Revolution soon reached beyond the bounds of free black society and deeply influenced the course of slave life in the critical years before the great migration to the Lower South. Most importantly, the revolution in black life created new and enlarged older regional distinctions between the black populations, free and slave, of the North, the Upper South, and the Lower South. In each of these regions, differences in the size, character, and dynamics of development of the free and slave black populations bred distinctive patterns of relations with whites and among blacks, shaping the development of black life and American race relations during the nineteenth century and beyond.

The growth of the free Negro population was one of the most far reaching events of the revolutionary era. Before the Revolution only a tiny fraction of the black population enjoyed liberty in English mainland North America. A 1755 Maryland census, one of the few enumerations of colonial freemen, counted slightly more than 1,800 free Negroes, who composed about 4 percent of the colony's black population and less than 2 percent of its free population. Moreover, over 80 percent of these freemen were of mixed racial origin, and more than one-fifth were cripples or old folk deemed "past labour." Few full-blooded Africans found their way to freedom. . . . Although colonial freemen demand further study, it appears that Maryland's free Negroes typified those found throughout the mainland English colonies. . . .

Although few in number and much like whites in appearance, free Negroes raised white fears of subversion. During the colonial years, lawmakers steadily gnawed at the freemen's liberty, taxing them with numerous proscriptions on their civil, political, and social rights. On the eve of the Revolution, few whites, even those who opposed slavery, showed any inclination to increase the number of Negro freemen. But the events of the revolutionary years moved in unpredictable and uncontrollable ways. As the war dragged on, military necessity forced the British and then, more reluctantly, Americans to muster black slaves into their armies by offering them freedom in exchange for their services.

The British, who had no direct interest in slavery, first offered the exchange. In November 1775, Lord Dunmore, the royal governor of Virginia, declared martial law and freed all slaves that were able and willing to bear arms in His Majesty's service. Even though this declaration shook colonial Virginians, it came as no surprise. Dunmore and other British officials had been threatening such action for several months. Slaves, ever alive to the possibilities of liberty, quickly picked up these first rumblings of freedom. Some months earlier, a group of blacks had visited Dunmore and offered to join him and take up arms. At that time, Dunmore brusquely dismissed them. But the blacks would not be put off, and when Dunmore officially tendered the promise of liberty, they flocked to British headquarters in Norfolk harbor.

Defeat deflated Dunmore's promise of liberty. In December, about a month after his proclamation, patriot troops routed Loyalist forces, including a large number of blacks wearing sashes emblazoned with the words "Liberty to Slaves." The loss broke the back of Dunmore's attempt to discipline rebellious Virginians. . . .

The manpower shortage that forced Dunmore to use black troops worsened as the war dragged on. British commanders, despite popular opposition in England, increasingly followed Dunmore's lead and recruited slaves. When the war turned south in 1778, thousands of blacks flocked to the British standard. General Henry Clinton, the British commander-in-chief, officially promised liberty to all slaves who deserted their masters for British service. In the years that followed, British reliance on black manpower increased, and the proponents of utilizing black military might on a massive scale grew ever more vocal. . . .

Colonial commanders and policymakers were considerably more chary about accepting slave recruits. Many were large slaveholders who had much to lose from any disruption of slavery. Most feared that a servile revolt or a mass defection of slaveholders would follow the arming of blacks. Although blacks had occasionally served in colonial militias and distinguished themselves in the first battles of the Revolution, the Continental Congress, at South Carolina's instigation, barred them from the Continental army. But patriots proved no more immune to the exigencies of war than the British. As the struggle for independence lengthened and manpower grew critically short, the patriot policy shifted. The northern states, led by New England, began to solicit black recruits, and Rhode Island created a black regiment. When the war moved south, Upper South states grudgingly adopted a similar course of action, in spite of their larger black populations and greater dependence on slave labor. Maryland authorized slave enlistments and eventually subjected free Negroes to the draft. Virginia allowed black freemen to serve in its army and navy, and Delaware and North Carolina, following Virginia, occasionally permitted slaves to stand as substitutes for their masters. In the Lower South, however, white resistance to arming blacks stiffened. The numerical superiority of blacks in the lowland rice swamps, the large numbers of newly arrived African slaves, and the commonplace absenteeism bred an overpowering fear of slave rebellion. Despite the pleas of the Continental Congress and the urgings of commanders in the field,

South Carolina and Georgia rejected the hesitant measures adopted in the Upper South. . . .

Almost everywhere, the war widened opportunities for blacks to gain their liberty. When the British left America at the end of the war, they carried thousands of blacks to freedom in Great Britain, the West Indies, Canada, and, eventually, Africa. Hundreds, perhaps thousands, of others that were freed by British wartime policy eluded their masters and remained in the United States. There is "reason to believe," petitioned angry white Virginians in 1781, "that a great number of slaves which were taken by the British Army are now passing in this Country as free men." Many blacks who fought with the patriots also secured their liberty. Some grateful masters freed their slaves, and occasionally state legislatures liberated individual bondsmen by special enactment. . . .

Whatever the effects of official British and American policy, the chaos created by rampaging armies did even more to expand a slave's chances for liberty. The actions of soldiers of both belligerents, and the often violent disputes between patriot and Tory militiamen, created near anarchic conditions, revealed the limits of slaveholder authority, and encouraged slaves to take their freedom. Runaways, previously few in number, increased rapidly in the confusion of the war. This was especially true in the Upper South, where the nature of agriculture had allowed second and third generation Afro-Americans to gain broad familiarity with the countryside. At war's end, these fugitives also passed into the growing free black population.

The war did not last long enough to destroy slavery, but the libertarian ideology that patriots used to justify their rebellion continued to challenge it when the war ended. If all men were created equal, why were some men still slaves? . . .

Slavery fell first in New England, where blacks were few in number and never an important part of the labor force or a threat to white dominance. In the Middle Atlantic states, where blacks were more numerous and bondage more deeply entrenched than in New England, slavery proved more resistant to revolutionary change. But an influx of white immigrant workers assured employers of an adequate supply of labor, and undermined the most persuasive argument against abolition. By 1804, every northern state had provided for eventual emancipation.

Still, slavery died hard. In 1810, almost 30,000 blacks—almost a quarter of the region's black population—remained in chattel bondage. Although that number fell dramatically in succeeding decades, slavery continued. There were over 1,000 bondsmen in the "free" states in 1840. Moreover, in many of the new northern states, slaveholders and their allies tried to overthrow the antislavery provisions of the Northwest Ordinance and reinstate the peculiar institution. Failing that, they enacted various forms of long-term indentureships, which allowed chattel bondage to flourish covertly until the Civil War. Nevertheless, slavery was doomed, and the mass of Northern black people had been freed.

South of Pennsylvania, emancipation faced still greater obstacles, and, in the long run, these difficulties proved insuperable. But the Christian equalitarianism unleashed by the evangelical revivals of the mid-eighteenth century complemented and strengthened the idealism of the Revolution in many parts of the South. Like revolutionary ideology, the religious awakenings transcended sectional boundaries. Methodists and Baptist evangelicals crisscrossed the southern states and, in hundreds of camp meetings, made thousands of converts. Propelled by the revolutionary idea that all men were equal in the sight of God, they frequently accepted black and white converts with equal enthusiasm. The equality of the communion table proved contagious, and some evangelicals broke the confines of other-worldly concerns to make the connection between spiritual and secular equality. Methodists, Baptists, and other evangelical sectarians joined with Quakers to become the mainstays of the southern antislavery movement. Like their northern counterparts, they organized antislavery societies, petitioned legislatures, and aided freedom suits.

Economic changes in the Upper South, especially in Maryland, Delaware, and northern Virginia, offered emancipationists an opening wedge. Beginning in the 1760s, the increased worldwide demand for foodstuff encouraged planters to expand cereal production. Dislocations in mercantile ties, resulting from the war and the depression that accompanied independence, further speeded the shift from tobacco to cereal agriculture in many parts of the Chesapeake region. This change reduced the demand for slaves, since wheat culture on small units under the existing technology thrived on free labor. Many farmers found themselves burdened with a surplus of slaves. Moreover, the agricultural transformation and the resultant establishment of new methods of processing and development of new patterns of marketing quickened the pace of commerce, stimulated the growth of light industry, and swelled urban centers. Baltimore, Richmond, Fredericksburg, and Petersburg grew as never before. In all, changes in the agricultural landscape increased commercial activity, and nascent urbanization and industrialization profoundly altered the region. Many Americans believed that the Upper South would follow the pattern of development exemplified by Pennsylvania, and not the states farther south. As the price of slaves sagged under the weight of these changes, the future of slavery became an open question. . . .

The economic transformation of the Upper South supported freedom in other less direct ways. The growing number of tenant farmers and independent tradesmen in the region, often in need of an extra hand and rarely in a position to purchase slaves, frequently employed blacks, with few questions asked. The ability to find a safe haven, even for a few days, could make the difference between a successful flight and a return to bondage. The success of many fugitives, like relatively indiscriminate manumission, not only enlarged the free black population, but darkened it as well. The larger, darker-skinned free Negro population camouflaged fugitives, increased their chances of success, and encouraged still other blacks to make their way from slavery to freedom. The increase in runaways begun during the tumult of the Revolution continued into the postwar years.

Slavery easily survived the increase of manumissions and runaways, recovered its balance, and in most places continued to grow. But the social changes of the revolutionary era profoundly altered the size and character of the free Negro population in the Upper South, and sent reverberations of liberty into the region's slave quarters.

The growth of the free Negro population can be most clearly viewed in Maryland. Between 1755 and 1790, the number of free Negroes in that state increased almost 350 percent, to about 8,000, and in the following decade it again more than doubled. By 1810, almost a quarter of Maryland's blacks were free, numbering nearly 34,000. Although not immediately apparent, slavery in Maryland had been dealt a mortal blow.

Free Negroes registered similar gains throughout the Upper South. In 1782, the year Virginia legalized private manumissions, St. George Tucker estimated the number of freemen in his state at about 2,000. By 1790, Virginia's free Negroes had increased to 12,000. Ten years later, Negro freemen numbered 20,000, and by 1810, the total stood at over 30,000. During the twenty years between 1790 and 1810, the free Negro population of Virginia more than doubled. In all, the number of Negro freemen in the Upper South grew almost 90 percent between 1790 and 1800, and another 65 percent in the following decade, so that freemen now composed more than 10 percent of the region's black population. . . .

The social forces that transformed black society in the North and in the Upper South met stern resistance in the Lower South. There, economic and demographic considerations countered the ideology of the Revolution and the great revivals. . . . Following the war, Lower South whites imported thousands of slaves from the states to the north and, in 1803, South Carolina reopened the slave trade with Africa. Not until the 1790s, when the successful black revolution in Saint Domingue sent hundreds of light-skinned *gens de couleur* fleeing for American shores, did the number of free Negroes increase significantly in the Lower South. Thus, unlike northern and Upper South freemen, Lower South free people of color remained a tiny mulatto fragment of the larger black population.

In transforming the structure of black society, the events of the revolutionary years created new, and enlarged older, regional distinctions between the black populations of the North, the Upper South, and the Lower South.

Free Negro Population, 1790–1810

	1790	1800	1810
United States	59,466	108,395	186,466
North	27,109	47,154	78,181
South	32,357	61,241	108,265
Upper South	30,158	56,855	94,085
Lower South	2,199	4,386	14,180*

---

* Increase in the Lower South between 1800 and 1810 is largely due to the accession of Louisiana.
Source: *Population of the United States in 1860* (Washington, D.C., 1864), pp. 600–601.

By the end of the century, northern whites had committed themselves to emancipation, and the great majority of blacks enjoyed freedom. Upper South slavery, on the other hand, withstood the challenges of the revolutionary years, but its free black population expanded rapidly during the period, so that better than one black in ten was free by 1800. Slavery in the Lower South, although greatly disrupted by the war, never faced the direct emancipationist pressures present in the North or even the Upper South. It stood almost unchallenged throughout the postwar period, quickly recouped its wartime losses, and entered into a period of its greatest expansion. Lower South free people of color remained as they had been in the colonial era, a small appendage to a rapidly increasing slave population. . . . These regional distinctions in the structure of both slave and free black societies reflected and influenced white racial attitudes and shaped the development of black life in the years to come. . . .

Structural and cultural changes in black society profoundly influenced white attitudes and behavior. In the long run, they stiffened white racism. With so many blacks in possession of freedom, whites could no longer rely on their status alone to distinguish themselves from a people they despised. They began to grope for new ways to subordinate Negro freemen and set themselves apart from all blacks. Thus as the free Negro population grew, whites curbed their mobility, limited their economic opportunities, all but obliterated many of their political rights, and schemed to deport freemen from the country. Yet, the Revolution, with its emphasis on equality, forced whites to reconsider their racial values. This reconsideration produced a new flexibility in the racial attitudes of some whites and a brief recession in the color line. The liberalization of manumission codes, the passage of antikidnapping laws, the increased number of free Negroes, and the challenge to slavery all reflected small, but real, changes in white racial attitudes. These changes allowed blacks some room to maneuver in a society that was often hostile to their very being. Nevertheless, racism remained a potent force in revolutionary America. The society and culture that emerged from this first attempt to remake black life in America represented an easing of white racial hostility within a system of continued racial oppression.

The cumulative impact of freedom, cultural maturation, and the new flexibility in white attitudes unleashed the creative energies of black people. Newly freed blacks moved at once to give meaning to their freshly won liberty and form to the cultural transformation of black life in America. They took new names, established new residential and occupational patterns, reconstructed their family life, chose the first recognizable leadership class, and developed new institutions and modes of social action. . . .

Although accompanied by proscription and exclusion, freedom also created new opportunities, often for slaves as well as freemen. It allowed some blacks to attain positions from which all blacks previously had been barred. Suddenly blacks took the role of a painter, poet, author, astronomer, minister, and merchant. The almanacs of Benjamin Banneker, the poems of Phillis Wheatly and Jupiter Hammon, and the portraits of Joshua Johnston stand not only as tributes to the achievements of talented men and women, but also as symbols of the cultural transformation of the revolutionary era.

The new opportunities of freedom also allowed some freemen to accumulate property and achieve a modicum of economic security. William Flora, a revolutionary veteran, purchased several lots in Portsmouth, Virginia, soon after his discharge from the army. Later he opened a livery stable, served Portsmouth for thirty years, and willed his property to his son. In 1783, James McHenry, a Maryland shoemaker, purchased his freedom, and four years later rented a farm for £35 a year and had "a house and other stock more than sufficient for his farm." Henry Carter, a Virginia freeman, was similarly successful. He was emancipated in 1811, and within six years not only had "funds sufficient to purchase his wife Priscilla but some other property, personal & real." Throughout the nation the growth of a black property-holding class followed the growth of the free Negro population. In some places, freemen controlled sizable businesses. The striking success of sea captain Paul Cuffee of New Bedford, Massachusetts, sail manufacturer James Forten of Philadelphia, and merchant Robert Sheridan of Wilmington, North Carolina, suggests how quickly blacks took advantage of the expanding, if still limited, opportunities created by freedom. Although most blacks remained, as in slavery, poor and propertyless, some freemen rose to modest wealth and respectability.

Slowly, a new black elite emerged: Prince Hall in Boston, Richard Allen in Philadelphia, Daniel Coker in Baltimore, Christopher McPherson in Richmond, Andrew Bryan in Savannah, and a host of others in black communities throughout the new republic. Born in the decade before the Revolution, these men came of age with the emergence of the free Negro population and the maturation of Afro-American culture. Many of them owed their liberty to the changes unleashed by the American Revolution, and they shared the optimism and enthusiasm that accompanied freedom. Wealthier and better educated than most blacks, they moved easily into positions of leadership within the black community and pressed whites to expand black liberty. Pointing to the ideas of the Declaration of Independence, the new black elite provided the leadership in petitioning Congress and state legislatures to abolish slavery and relieve free blacks of the disabilities that prevented them from enjoying their full rights as citizens. Norfolk freemen, in a typical action, requested that they be allowed to testify in court against whites so they could prove their accounts. Boston blacks demanded an equal share of the city's school fund so they might educate their children. South Carolina's free Negroes petitioned for relief from a special head tax that pushed them into a condition "but small removed from Slavery." And from Nashville, Tennessee, came a plea that free Negroes "ought to have the same opportunities of doing well that any Person being a citizen & free . . . would have, and that the door ought not be kept shut against them more than any other of the Human race." In the North, blacks, themselves but recently liberated, urged an end to the slave trade and the establishment of a universal emancipation. Occasionally, a few bold southern freemen like Baltimore's Daniel Coker added their voices to this public condemnation of slavery. These freemen protested in vain. Even the most restrained pleas led to harsher repression, further anchoring them to the bottom of free society. . . .

Frustrated by unyielding white hostility, freemen took two divergent courses. Some turned away from slaves in an effort to ingratiate themselves with whites, by trying to demonstrate they were more free than black. This strategy was especially evident in—although not limited to—the Lower South, where ties between freemen and slaves had never been strong and where many of the newly arrived *gens de couleur* had suffered heavy losses at the hands of the Haitian slave rebels. During the 1790s, the free people of color in Charleston established the Brown Fellowship Society, an organization limited to free brown people, and one which remained a symbol of mulatto exclusiveness throughout the antebellum period.

Most freemen, especially in the North and Upper South, took a different course. Increasingly, they turned inward and worked to strengthen the black community—free and slave. Freemen, frequently joined by slaves, established institutions where blacks might pray, educate their children, entertain, and protect themselves. African churches, schools, and fraternal societies not only served the new needs of the much expanded free Negro population and gave meaning to black liberty, but they also symbolized the emergence of Afro-American culture and represented the strongest effort to unite the black community.

Yet, even while they shouldered the new responsibilities of freedom, blacks did not immediately form separate institutions. The development of the African church, for example, was not merely a product of the emergence of the free Negro population. At first, most blacks looked to the white-dominated evangelical churches, which made acceptance of the gospel the only criterion for salvation and welcomed blacks into the fold. Free Negroes, along with slaves and poor whites, found this open membership policy, the emotional sermons, and the generous grants of self-expression an appealing contrast to the icy restrictiveness of the older, more staid denominations. Although racially mixed congregations were often forced to meet at odd hours to avoid hostile sheriffs and slave patrols, black membership in these churches grew rapidly. By the end of the eighteenth century, thousands of blacks, free and slave, had joined Methodist and Baptist churches.

The newness of the evangelical denominations together with their Christian equalitarianism fostered new racial patterns. In many such churches, blacks and whites seated themselves indiscriminately. It was not unusual for black churchmen to attend synods and association meetings with whites. In 1794, when one Virginia church called this practice into question, the Portsmouth Baptist Association firmly announced that "it saw nothing in the Word of God nor anything contrary to the rules of decency to prohibit a church from sending as a delegate, any male member they shall choose." Sometimes blacks served as preachers to a mixed congregation. John Chavis, a black Presbyterian circuit rider, enjoyed his greatest success among whites;

Fayetteville whites regarded Henry Evans, a black Methodist, as the "best preacher of his time in that quarter"; and when Richard Allen looked down from his Philadelphia pulpit he saw "Nearly . . . as many Whites as Blacks."

Yet the old racial patterns had remarkable resilience. Christian equalitarianism momentarily bent the color line, but could not break it. In most churches, membership did not assure blacks of equal participation. Indeed, whites usually placed blacks in a distant corner or gallery and barred them from most of the rights of church members. One Virginia congregation painted some of its benches black to avoid any possibility of confusion.

As blacks found themselves proscribed from white churches or discriminated against in mixed churches, they attempted the difficult task of forming their own religious institutions. In doing so, blacks not only lacked the capital and organizational experience, but they frequently faced fierce white opposition. This was especially true in the South, where whites identified freemen with slaves and seemed to see every meeting of free blacks, no matter how innocuous, as an insurrectionary plot. The abolition of slavery in the North, in large measure, had freed whites from this fear, allowing blacks greater organizational opportunities. Northern whites frequently took a benign view of black institutions and believed, along with Benjamin Rush, that it would "be much cheaper to build churches for them than jails."

Regional differences in white attitudes allowed blacks to act more openly in the North. While northern freemen quickly established their own churches and schools, southern free blacks, frequently joined by slaves, continued to meet intense opposition. . . . Despite the rising pitch of white opposition, the number of black churches increased steadily throughout the 1780s and 1790s. . . . The rank discrimination of white-dominated churches fostered black separatism, but some blacks welcomed the split. It allowed them, for the first time, full control over their own religious life. By the end of the century, black communities from Boston to Savannah boasted their own African churches. . . .

During the early years of the nineteenth century, blacks continued to establish new African churches in the northern and border slave states. In 1816, leading black churchmen from various parts of these regions joined together to form the first independent black denomination, the African Methodist Episcopal (AME) Church. But if the African church flourished in the North, it fell upon hard times in the South. While the abolition of slavery had freed northern whites from the fear of insurrection, those anxieties grew among white southerners. In 1800, when Gabriel Prosser's aborted insurrection in Virginia nearly transformed the worst fears of southern whites into a dreadful reality, the African church came under still greater pressure. Hysterical whites shut many black churches and forced black ministers to flee the South. Even white churchmen found themselves under attack for proselytizing blacks. When a white circuit rider tried to preach to a mixed congregation in Richmond in 1802, he was threatened with the lash and driven out of the city. Charleston Methodists similarly found themselves "watched, ridiculed, and openly assailed" for allowing blacks to attend their meetings. The growth of the African church in the South was abruptly halted during the first years of the nineteenth century. Later it would revive under very different conditions.

The early development of African schools followed the same tortuous path as that of the independent black churches. In the years immediately following the Revolutionary War, the momentary respite in racial hostility encouraged some freemen and sympathetic whites to establish integrated academies throughout the North and even in some border states. But the emotions and ideals that united poor whites and blacks in evangelical churches were absent from the founding of schools. Schools were middle- and upper-class institutions, and class distinctions alone doubtless excluded most free blacks. Handicapped by a lack of funds and surrounded by increasingly hostile whites, integrated schools languished. By the turn of the century, the ebbing of revolutionary equalitarianism forced those few remaining integrated schools to close their doors or segregate their classrooms. The support of black schools fell largely on black communities. African schools, usually attached to black churches, continued to meet in the North, and in some places increased in size and number. But in the South, they faced intense opposition from whites, who viewed them as nurseries of subversion. . . .

The dismantling of African churches and schools suggests the intensity of white opposition to the development of independent black institutions wherever slavery continued to exist. Yet, even as whites closed black churches and schools and slapped new proscriptions on black liberty in order to freeze blacks into a place of permanent social inferiority, they could not erase all the gains made in the first flush of freedom. In the North, African churches and schools continued to grow and occasionally flourish, and even in the South some of these institutions limped on, although often forced to accept white supervision or meet clandestinely.

On the surface, African churches and schools and allied benevolent and fraternal societies were but a weak imitation of those of the larger society. Often they reflected white values and mimicked the structure of their white counterparts. But, on closer inspection, they embodied an Afro-American culture that was over a century in the making. Whites who visited black church meetings or attended black funerals almost uniformly observed the striking difference between them and their own somber rituals. It was no accident that blacks called their churches African churches, their schools African schools, and their benevolent societies African benevolent societies.

These organizations provided an institutional core for black life throughout the nineteenth century and well into the twentieth. In African churches and schools, black people baptized their children, educated their youth, and provided for the sick, aged, and disabled. African churches strengthened black family life by insisting that marriages be solemnized, by punishing adulterers, and occasionally by reuniting separated couples. Leaders of these institutions, especially ministers, moved into dominant positions in the black community, and African churches, in turn, provided a means of advancement for ambitious black youth. More than this, these institutions gave the black community a sense of solidarity and common purpose. At no time was this more evident than in the postrevolutionary era, when slaves and freemen joined together to re-form black society and give shape to the cultural transformation of the preceding century. Later, free Negroes and slaves would drift apart, and many of the institutions formed during this earlier era would become identified with the free blacks and urban slave artisans who placed them at the center of black life in the North and urban South. But the new social and institutional forms established during the years after the Revolution were not lost for the mass of enslaved black people. The changes set in motion by the Revolution permeated slave life in ways that are only barely recognized now. The new occupational, religious, and familial patterns and the new social roles and modes of social action established by the convergence of changes in Afro-American and Anglo-American life during the revolutionary era continued to inform slave society, as the great cotton boom pulled slaves out of the seaboard states and into the Lower South. The revolution in black life spread across the continent. On the rich, loamy soils of the cotton South, slaves reshaped the cultural legacy of the revolutionary era to meet the new needs of plantation life. And with the Civil War, the Emancipation Proclamation, and the Thirteenth Amendment, the transformed institutional and cultural legacy of the revolutionary era emerged once again and stood at the center of black life.

The Founding Fathers and Slavery

WILLIAM W. FREEHLING

Years ago . . . no man needed to defend the Founding Fathers on slavery. However serious were their sins and however greedy seemed their pursuits, the men who made the American Revolution were deemed to have placed black slavery at bay. Patriots such as George Washington, historians used to point out, freed their slaves. If Jefferson emancipated few of his, the condemnation of Jeffersonian ideology and the curse of a declining economy were fast driving Virginia's slavery to smash. Only the fabulous profits made possible by Whitney's invention of the cotton gin and the reactionary abstractions perpetuated by Calhoun's repudiation of Jefferson breathed life into the system and waylaid the Fathers' thrust toward peaceful abolition.

This happy tale, once so important and so widely believed, now lies withered. . . . The Declaration of Independence, it is now argued, was a white man's document that its author rarely applied to his or to any slaves. The Constitution created aristocratic privilege while consolidating black bondage. Virginia shrank from abolition, for slave prices were too high and race fears too great. Jefferson himself suspected blacks were innately inferior. He bought and sold slaves; he advertised for fugitives; he ordered lashes well laid on. He lived in the grand manner, burying prayers for freedom under an avalanche of debt. In all these evasions and missed opportunities

"The Founding Fathers and Slavery" by William W. Freehling from *American Historical Review,* 77, 1972. Permission granted by William W. Freehling and the Gerard McCauley Agency, Inc.

Jefferson spoke for his age. For whatever the virtues of the Founding Fathers, concludes the new view, they hardly put slavery on the road to ultimate extinction. It seems fitting, then, that when Southerners turned their backs on the Declaration and swung toward reaction in the wake of the Missouri crisis, the sage of Monticello himself helped point the way.

Many admirers of Jefferson, aware of a brighter side, scorn this judgment and yearn for a reassessment. The following essay, while in sympathy with their position, is not written for their reasons. More is at stake than Thomas Jefferson; indeed Jefferson's agonized positions on slavery are chiefly important as the supreme embodiment of a generation's travail. Moreover, the historian's task is not to judge but to explain; and the trouble with the new condemnatory view is not so much that it is a one-sided judgment of the Founding Fathers as that it distorts the process by which American slavery was abolished. The new charge that the Founding Fathers did next to nothing about bondage is as misleading as the older notion that they almost did everything. The abolitionist process proceeded slowly but inexorably from 1776 to 1860: slowly in part because of what Jefferson and his contemporaries did not do, inexorably in part because of what they did. The impact of the Founding Fathers on slavery, like the extent to which the American Revolution was revolutionary, must be seen in the long run not in terms of what changed in the late eighteenth century but in terms of how the Revolutionary experience changed the whole of American antebellum history. Any such view must place Thomas Jefferson and his contemporaries, for all their ironies and missed opportunities, back into the creeping American antislavery process.

If men were evaluated in terms of dreams rather than deeds everyone would concede the antislavery credentials of the Founding Fathers. No American Revolutionary could square the principles of the Declaration with the perpetuation of human bondage. Only a few men of 1776 considered the evil of slavery permanently necessary. None dared proclaim the evil a good. Most looked forward to the day when the curse could be forever erased from the land. "The love of justice and the love of country," Jefferson wrote Edward Coles in 1814, "plead equally the cause of these people, and it is a moral reproach to us that they should have pleaded it so long in vain."

If the Founding Fathers unquestionably dreamed of universal American freedom, their ideological posture was weighed down equally unquestionably with conceptions of priorities, profits, and prejudices that would long make the dream utopian. The master passion of the age was not with extending liberty to blacks but with erecting republics for whites. Creative energies poured into designing a political City on the Hill; and the blueprints for utopia came to be the federal Constitution and American union. When the slavery issue threatened the Philadelphia Constitutional Convention the Deep South's ultimatums were quickly met. When the Missouri crisis threatened the Union Jefferson and fellow spirits beat a retreat. This pattern of valuing the Union more than abolition—of marrying the meaning of America to the continuation of a particular government—would persist, producing endless compromises and finally inspiring Lincoln's war.

The realization of the Founding Fathers' antislavery dream was blocked also by the concern for property rights articulated in their Declaration. Jefferson's document at once denounced slave chains as immoral and sanctioned slave property as legitimate. It made the slave's right to freedom no more "natural" than the master's right to property. Liberty for blacks became irrevocably tied to compensation for whites; and if some proposed paying masters for slaves, no one conceived of compensating South Carolina planters for the fabulous swamp estates emancipation would wreck.

The financial cost of abolition, heavy enough by itself, was made too staggering to bear by the Founding Fathers' racism, an ideological hindrance to antislavery no less important than their sense of priorities and their commitment to property. Here again Jefferson typified the age. As Winthrop Jordan has shown, Jefferson suspected that blacks had greater sexual appetites and lower intellectual faculties than did whites. This racism was never as hidebound as its twentieth-century varieties. Jefferson kept an open mind on the subject and always described innate differences as but his suspicion. Still it is significant, as Merrill Peterson points out, that Jefferson suspected blacks were inferior rather than suspecting blacks were equal. These suspicions, together with Jefferson's painfully accurate prophecy that free blacks and free whites could not live harmoniously in America for centuries, made him and others tie American emancipation to African colonization. The alternative appeared to be race riot and sexual chaos. The consequence, heaping the cost of colonization on the cost of abolition, made the hurdles to emancipation seem unsurmountable.

Jefferson and the men of the Revolution, however, continually dreamed of leaping ahead when the time was ripe. In 1814, while lamenting his own failure, Jefferson urged others to take up the crusade. "I had always hoped," he wrote Edward Coles, "that the younger generation receiving their early impressions after the flame of liberty had been kindled in every breast . . . would have sympathized with oppression wherever found, and proved their love of liberty beyond their own share of it." As late as 1824, five years after his retreat in the Missouri crisis, Jefferson suggested a federally financed postnati abolition scheme that would have ended slavery faster than the plan proposed by his grandson, Thomas Jefferson Randolph, in the famed Virginia slavery debate of 1832.

The ideological stance of Jefferson and other Founding Fathers on slavery, then, was profoundly ambivalent. On the one hand they were restrained by their overriding interest in creating the Union, by their concern for property rights, and by their visions of race war and miscegenation; on the other hand they embraced a revolutionary ideology that made emancipation inescapable. The question is, How was this theoretical ambivalence resolved in practical action?

The answer, not surprisingly, is also ambivalent. Whenever dangers to Union, property, or racial order seemed to them acute the Founding Fathers did little. In the short run, especially in those Deep Southern states where the going was stickiest, they did almost nothing. But whenever abolition dangers seemed to them manageable Jefferson and his contemporaries moved effectively, circumscribing and crippling the institution and thereby gutting its long-range capacity to endure.

The revisionist view of the Founding Fathers is at its best in emphasizing slavery's short-run strength in Jefferson's South. In Virginia both secure slave prices and frenzied race fears made emancipation a distant goal. Jefferson as legislator did no more than draft abolitionist resolutions, and his revisions of the Virginia slave code did little to ease the lot of slaves and something to intensify the plight of free blacks. Jefferson's proposed clause, requiring a white woman who had a black child to leave the state within a year or be placed "out of the protection of the laws," speaks volumes on why abolition came hard in Virginia. South of Virginia, where percentages of slaves and profits from staple crops ran higher, abolition was more remote. Planters who worked huge gangs of slaves in pestilential Georgia and South Carolina's lowlands never proposed peacefully accepting the end of their world.

The federal Constitution of 1787 also reflected slavery's short-run strength. Garrison's instinct to consign that document to the flames was exactly right, for the Constitution perpetually protected an institution the Fathers liked to call temporary. Safeguards included the three-fifths clause, destined to help make the minority South political masters of the nation for years, and the fugitive slave clause, destined to help return to thralldom men who had risked everything for freedom. Moreover, to lure Georgia and South Carolina into the Union, the Fathers agreed to allow any state to reopen the African slave trade for twenty years. When South Carolina seized the option from 1803 to 1807 the forty thousand imported blacks and their hundreds of thousands of slave descendants paid an awesome price for the creation of the white man's republic.

After the Constitution was ratified slavery again showed its strength by expanding over the West. "The years of slavery's supposed decline," Robert McColley points out, "were in fact the years of its greatest expansion." In the age of Jefferson black bondage spread across Kentucky and engulfed Alabama and Mississippi. Furthermore, Jefferson as president acquired slave Louisiana, and Jefferson as elder statesman gave his blessings to the resulting diffusion of the system. . . .

The old view, then, that slavery was dying in Jefferson's South cannot withstand the revisionist onslaught. The system was strong and, in places, growing stronger; and the combination of economic interest, concern for the Union, life style, and race prejudice made emancipationists rare in Virginia and almost nonexistent in South Carolina. . . . The point is crucial: long before Garrison, when Jefferson ruled, peaceful abolition was not possible.

What could be done—what Jefferson and his contemporaries did—was to attack slavery where it was weakest, thereby driving the institution south and vitiating its capacity to survive. In a variety of ways the Founding Fathers took positive steps that demonstrated their antislavery instincts and that, taken together, drastically reduced the slavocracy's potential area, population, and capacity to endure.

The first key reform took place in the North. When the American Revolution began slavery was a national institution, thriving both north and south of the Mason-Dixon line. Slaves comprised 14 per cent of the New York population, with other figures ranging from 8 per cent in New Jersey to 6 per cent in Rhode Island and 3 per cent in Connecticut and Pennsylvania. In these states, unlike Virginia, percentages of slaves were low enough to permit an unconvulsive variety of reform.

Still, prior to 1776, abolitionists such as John Woolman found the North barren soil for antislavery ideas. As John Jay recalled, "the great majority" of Northerners accepted slavery as a matter of course, and "very few among them even doubted the propriety and rectitude of it." The movement of 1776 changed all this. The humanitarian zeal of the Revolutionary era, together with nonslaveholder hatred of slave competition and universal acknowledgment that the economy did not need slavery, doomed Northern slavery to extinction. In some states the doom was long delayed as Northern slaveholders fought to keep their bondsmen. Slavery was not altogether ended in New York until 1827 and in New Jersey until well into the 1840s. By 1830, however, less than one per cent of the 125,000 Northern blacks were slaves. Bondage had been made a *peculiar* institution, retained alone in the Southern states.

No less important than abolition in old Northern states was the long and bitter fight to keep bondage from expanding. In 1784 Jefferson drafted a congressional ordinance declaring slavery illegal in all Western territories after 1800. The proposed law, keeping bondage out of Alabama and Mississippi no less than Illinois and Indiana, lost by a single vote, that of a New Jerseyite ill in his dwelling. Seldom has a lone legislator lost so good a chance to turn around the history of a nation. "The fate of millions unborn," Jefferson later cried, was "hanging on the tongue of one man, and heaven was silent in that awful moment."

Three years later, in the famed Northwest Ordinance of 1787, Congress decreed slavery illegal immediately in the upper Western territories. The new law left bondage free to invade the Southwest. But without the Northwest Ordinance slavery might have crept into Illinois and Indiana as well, for even with it bondage found much support in the Midwest.

In the years before 1809 Indiana settlers, led by William Henry Harrison and the so-called Virginia aristocrats, petitioned Congress again and again to allow Midwestern slavery. Indiana's pro-Harrison and anti-Harrison parties were both proslavery; they disagreed only on the tactical question of how to force Congress to budge. When Congress refused to repeal the ordinance, the Indiana legislature in 1805 passed a black indentured servitude act, in effect legalizing slavery. Indiana census takers, more honest than the legislature, counted 237 slaves in the territory in 1810 and 190 in 1820.

In 1809, when the part of Indiana that was most in favor of slavery split off as the new territory of Illinois, the battleground but not the issue shifted. The climax to the territorial phase of the Midwestern quest for slavery came in the Illinois Constitutional Convention of 1818, when proslavery forces, after winning a bitterly contested election to the convention, settled for a renewal of the territorial indentured servitude law because they feared that an explicit slavery law might jeopardize statehood.

With statehood secured the battle over slavery in Illinois continued in the 1820s. The hero of the antislavery forces was Edward Coles, an enlightened Virginian deeply influenced by Madison and Jefferson. Coles, who came to Illinois to free his slaves and stayed to protect the Northwest Ordinance, narrowly defeated his proslavery rival for governor in 1822. In 1824 he helped secure, by the close vote of 6,640–4,973, final victory in a referendum on a proslavery constitutional convention. With Coles's triumph slavery had again been restricted to the South.

The crusade for slavery in Illinois and Indiana, lasting over a quarter of a century and so often coming so close to victory, forms a dramatic example of the institution's expansive potential in the age of the Founding Fathers. The proslavery drive was turned back in part because of race phobias and economic desires that obsessed nonslaveholding Midwestern farmers. But in an area where victory came so hard no one can deny the importance of the Northwest Ordinance and Edward Coles's crusade in keeping slavery away.

A third antislavery victory of the Founding Fathers, more important than Northern abolition and the Northwest Ordinance, was the abolition of the African slave trade. This accomplishment, too often dismissed as a nonaccomplishment, shows more clearly than anything else the impact on antislavery of the Revolutionary generation. Furthermore, nowhere else does one see so clearly that Thomas Jefferson helped cripple the Southern slave establishment.

The drive to abolish the African slave trade began with the drafting of the Declaration of Independence. Jefferson, with the concurrence of Virginia and the upper South, sought to condemn King George for foisting Africans on his colonies. South Carolina and Georgia, less sure they had enough slaves, demanded the clause be killed. Jefferson acquiesced. Thus was prefigured, at the first moment of national history, the split between upper and lower South that less than a century later would contribute mightily to the disruption of the republic.

At the Constitutional Convention, as we have seen, lower South delegates again postponed a national decision on slave importations. This time a compromise was secured, allowing but not requiring Congress to abolish the trade after twenty years. A year before the deadline Jefferson, now presiding at the White House, urged Congress to seize its opportunity. "I congratulate you, fellow citizens," he wrote in his annual message of December 2, 1806, "on the approach of the period when you may interpose your authority constitutionally" to stop Americans "from all further participation in those violations of human rights which have been so long continued on the unoffending inhabitants of Africa, and which the morality, the reputation, and the best interests of our country have long been eager to proscribe." Although the law could not take effect until January 1, 1808, noted Jefferson, the reform, if passed in 1807, could make certain that no extra African was dragged legally across the seas. In 1807 Congress enacted Jefferson's proposal.

The new law, although one of the most important acts an American Congress ever passed, did not altogether end African importations. Americans illegally imported approximately one thousand blacks annually until 1860. This is, however, a tiny fraction of the number that could have been imported if the trade had been legal and considered legitimate. Brazil imported over a million and a half slaves from 1807 to 1860, and the Deep South's potential to absorb bondsmen was greater. South Carolina alone imported ten thousand blacks a year in the early nineteenth century, before the law of 1808 went into effect. Louisiana creole planters sought unsuccessfully to make Jefferson's administration grant them the same privilege. The desire of Virginia slaveholders to keep slave prices high no doubt helped feed the abolition of the trade, just as the desire of Illinois nonslaveholders to keep out blacks helped give Edward Coles his triumph. In both cases, however, the Revolutionary generation's conception of slavery as a moral disaster was of undeniable significance.

The law that closed the trade and saved millions of Africans from servitude on new Southwestern plantations also aided slaves already on those plantations. The great Southwestern boom came after the close of the African trade. Slaves could not be "used up," no matter how fantastic yearly profits were, for the restricted supply kept slave prices high. By mid-nineteenth century, moreover, almost all blacks were assimilated to the Southern way, making possible a paternal relationship between master and slave that could ease exploitation. One does not have to romanticize slave life or exaggerate planter paternalism to recognize that bondage would have been crueler if millions of Africans had been available in Mississippi and Louisiana to escalate profits. The contrast with nineteenth-century South America, where the trade remained open, makes the point with precision. Wherever Latin Americans imported so-called raw Africans by the boatload to open up virgin territories, work conditions reached a level of exploitation unparalleled in the New World. Easy access to fresh recruits led to using up laborers; and the fact that slaves were unassimilated foreigners precluded the development of the kind of ameliorating relationship that was possible between master and bondsman in North America.

The law profoundly affected North American whites as well as blacks. Most notably, it shut off the South's importation of labor during the period when immigrants were pouring into the North and the two societies were locked in mortal combat. If the trade had remained open, the operation of the three-fifths clause would have given the South greater congressional representation, and a massive supply of Africans might well have helped Southerners to compete more successfully in the race to Kansas and the campaign to industrialize. As it was, with the trade closed, fresh immigration fed the Northern colossus by the hour while Southerners fell ever more desperately behind.

Perhaps the most important long-run impact of closing the trade was to help push bondage deeper into the South, thereby continuing the work the Fathers had begun with Northern abolition and the Northwest Ordinance. Now that African markets were closed the new Southwest had to procure its slaves from Northern slave states. By 1860 the resulting slave drain had significantly reduced percentages of slaves and commitments to slavery throughout the border area stretching from Delaware through Maryland and Kentucky into Missouri. Whereas in 1790 almost 20 per cent of American slaves lived in this most northern tier of border slave states, the figure was down to 10 per cent and falling by 1860. On the other hand, in 1790 the area that became the seven Deep South states had 20 per cent of American slaves and by 1860 the figure was up to 54 per cent and rising. During the cotton boom the shift was especially dramatic. From 1830 to 1860 the percentage of slaves in Delaware declined from 4 to 1 per cent; in Maryland from 23 to 13 per cent; in Kentucky from 24 to 19 per cent; in Missouri from 18 to 10 per cent; and in the counties to become West Virginia from 10 to 5 per cent.

By both reducing the economic reliance on slavery and the psychic fear of blacks this great migration had political consequences. Antislavery politicians, echoing Hinton R. Helper's appeals to white racism, garnered thousands of votes and several elections, especially in Missouri, during the 1850s. It was only a beginning, but it was similar to the early stages of the demise of slavery in New York. . . .

Meanwhile, in two border states, manumission sabotaged the institution more insistently. Delaware, which had 9,000 slaves and 4,000 free blacks in 1790, had 1,800 slaves and 20,000 free blacks in 1860. Maryland, with 103,000 slaves and 8,000 free blacks in 1790, had 87,000 slaves and 84,000 free blacks in 1860. These two so-called slave states came close to being free Negro states on the eve of Lincoln's election. Indeed, the Maryland manumission rate compares favorably with those of Brazil and Cuba, countries that supposedly had a monopoly on Western Hemispheric voluntary emancipation.

The manumission tradition was slowly but relentlessly changing the character of states such as Maryland in large part because of a final Jeffersonian legacy: the belief that slavery was an evil that must some day be ended. Particularly in the upper South, this argument remained alive. It informed the works of so-called proslavery propagandists such as Albert T. Bledsoe; it inspired Missouri antislavery activists such as Congressman Frank Blair and the mayor of St. Louis, John M. Wimer; and it gnawed at the consciences of thousands of slaveholders as they made up their wills. Jefferson's condemnation of slavery had thrown the South forever on the defensive, and all the efforts of the George Fitzhughs could never produce a unanimously proslavery society.

In summary, then, the Revolutionary generation found slavery a national institution, with the slave trade open and Northern abolitionists almost unheard. When Jefferson and his contemporaries left the national stage they willed to posterity a crippled, restricted, peculiar institution. Attacking slavery successfully where it was weakest they swept it out of the North and kept it away from the Northwest. They left the antebellum South unable to secure more slaves when immigrants rushed to the North. Most important of all, their law closing the slave trade and their tradition concerning individual manumissions constituted a doubly sharp weapon superbly calculated to continue pushing slavery south. By 1860 Delaware, Maryland, Missouri, and the area to become West Virginia all had fewer slaves than New York possessed at the time of the Revolution, and Kentucky did not have many more. The goal of abolition had become almost as practicable in these border states as it had been in the North in 1776. As the Civil War began, slavery remained secure in only eleven of the fifteen slave states while black migration toward the tropics showed every capacity to continue eroding the institution in Virginia and driving slavery down to the Gulf.

If the Founding Fathers had done none of this—if slavery had continued in the North and expanded into the Northwest; if millions of Africans had been imported to strengthen slavery in the Deep South, to consolidate it in New York and Illinois, to spread it to Kansas, and to keep it in the border South; if no free black population had developed in Delaware and Maryland; if no apology for slavery had left Southerners on shaky moral grounds; if, in short, Jefferson and his contemporaries had lifted nary a finger—everything would have been different. Because all of this was done slavery was more and more confined in the Deep South as the nineteenth century progressed.

No one spied these trends better than the men who made the Southern revolution of 1860–61. Secessionist newspaper editorials in the 1850s can almost be summed up as one long diatribe against Jeffersonian ideology and the policy to which it led. Committed lower South slaveholders knew the world was closing in on them at the very time the more Northern slave states could not be relied on. Seeing the need not only to fight off Republicans from without but also to halt erosion from within, radical Southerners applauded the movement to re-enslave free blacks in Maryland; many of them proposed reopening the slave trade so that the Gulf states' hunger for slavery could be fed by imported Africans instead of black Virginians; and they strove to gain Kansas in large part to keep Missouri.

When this and much else failed and Lincoln triumphed, lower South disunionists believed they had reached the moment of truth. They could remain in the Union and allow the noose to tighten inexorably around their necks. They would then watch slavery slowly ooze out of the border South and permit their own domain to shrink to a handful of Gulf and lower Atlantic states. Or they could strike for independence while the upper South retained some loyalty to bondage, thereby creating a confrontation and forcing wavering slave states to make their choice. This view of the options helped to inspire the lower South's secession, in part a final convulsive effort to halt the insidious process the Founding Fathers helped begin.

When war came the lower South's confrontation strategy was half successful. Four of the eight upper South states seceded in the wake of Sumter. But four others remained loyal to the North. In the most Northern slave states, Delaware, Maryland, Kentucky, Missouri, and the area to become West Virginia, the slave drain and manumission processes had progressed too far. When the crunch came, loyalty to the Union outweighed loyalty to slavery. Abraham Lincoln is said to have remarked that while he hoped to have God on his side he had to have Kentucky. The remark, however apocryphal, clothes an important truth. In such a long and bitter war border slave states were crucial. If they, too, had seceded, the Confederacy might have survived. The long-run impact of the Founding Fathers' reforms, then, not only helped lead lower South slavocrats to risk everything in war but also helped doom their desperate gamble to failure.

Any judgment of the Founding Fathers' record on slavery must rest on whether the long or the short run is emphasized. In their own day the Fathers left intact a strong Southern slave tradition. The American Revolution, however, did not end in 1790. Over several generations, antislavery reforms inspired by the Revolution helped lead to Southern division, desperation, and defeat in war. That was not the most desirable way to abolish slavery, but that was the way abolition came. And given the Deep South's aversion to committing suicide, both in Jefferson's day and in Lincoln's, perhaps abolition could not have come any other way.

✕ *F U R T H E R   R E A D I N G*

Women

Mary Sumner Benson, *Women in Eighteenth-Century America: A Study of Opinion and Social Usage* (1935)

Ruth H. Bloch, "The Gendered Meanings of Virtue in Revolutionary America," *Signs, 13* (Autumn 1987), 37–58.

Joy Day Buel and Richard Buel, Jr., *The Way of Duty: A Woman and Her Family in Revolutionary America* (1984)

Nancy F. Cott, "Divorce and the Changing Status of Women in Eighteenth-Century Massachusetts," *William and Mary Quarterly,* 3d Ser., 33 (1976), 586–614.

———, *The Bonds of Womanhood: "Women's Sphere" in New England, 1780–1835* (1977)

Joan R. Gundersen, "Independence, Citizenship, and the American Revolution," *Signs, 13* (Autumn 1987), 59–77.

Ronald Hoffman and Peter J. Albert, eds., *Women in the Age of the American Revolution* (1989)

Janet Wilson James, *Changing Ideas About Women in the United States, 1776–1825* (1981)

Joan M. Jensen, *Loosening the Bonds: Mid-Atlantic Farm Women, 1750–1850* (1986)

Linda K. Kerber, *Women of the Republic: Intellect and Ideology in Revolutionary America* (1980)

Mary Beth Norton, *Liberty's Daughters: The Revolutionary Experience of American Women, 1750–1800* (1980)

Marylynn Salmon, *Women and the Law of Property in Early America* (1986)

Julia Cherry Spruill, *Women's Life and Work in the Southern Colonies* (1938)

African-Americans

Ira Berlin, *Slaves Without Masters: The Free Negro in the Antebellum South* (1974)
Ira Berlin and Ronald Hoffman, eds., *Slavery and Freedom in the Age of the American Revolution* (1983)
Philip D. Curtin, *The Atlantic Slave Trade: A Census* (1969)
David Brion Davis, *The Problem of Slavery in the Age of Revolution, 1770–1823* (1975)
James Essig, *Bonds of Wickedness: American Evangelicals Against Slavery, 1770–1808* (1982)
Lorenzo J. Greene, *The Negro in Colonial New England, 1620–1776* (1942)
A. Leon Higginbotham, Jr., *In the Matter of Color: Race and the American Legal Process, the Colonial Period* (1978)
James Hugo Johnston, *Race Relations in Virginia and Miscegenation in the South, 1776–1860* (1970)
Winthrop D. Jordan, *White over Black: American Attitudes Toward the Negro, 1550–1812* (1968)
Sidney Kaplan and Emma Nogrady Kaplan, *The Black Presence in the Era of the American Revolution*, rev. ed. (1989)
Allan Kulikoff, *Tobacco and Slaves: The Development of Southern Cultures in the Chesapeake, 1680–1800* (1986)
Robert McColley, *Slavery and Jeffersonian Virginia* (1964)
Duncan J. MacLeod, *Slavery, Race, and the American Revolution* (1974)
Edmund S. Morgan, *American Slavery, American Freedom: The Ordeal of Colonial Virginia* (1975)
Donald G. Nieman, "With Liberty for Some: The Old Constitution and the Rights of Blacks, 1776–1846," In Nieman, *Promises to Keep: African-Americans and the Constitutional Order, 1776 to the Present* (1991), 3–29.
Benjamin Quarles, *The Negro in the American Revolution* (1961)
James A. Rawley, *The Transatlantic Slave Trade: A History* (1981)
Donald L. Robinson, *Slavery in the Structure of American Politics, 1765–1820* (1971)
Mechal Sobel, *The World They Made Together: Black and White Values in Eighteenth-Century Virginia* (1987)
Jean R. Soderlund, *Quakers and Slavery: A Divided Spirit* (1985)
James W. St. G. Walker, *The Black Loyalists: The Search for a Promised Land in Nova Scotia and Sierra Leone, 1783–1870* (1976)
William M. Wiecek, *The Sources of Antislavery Constitutionalism in America, 1760–1848* (1977)
Ellen Gibson Wilson, *The Loyal Blacks* (1976)
Arthur Zilversmit, *The First Emancipation: The Abolition of Slavery in the North* (1967)

CHAPTER
9

The Challenge
of Religious Freedom
in a Christian Republic

✳

During the past generation, as historians have paid increased attention to the Revolution's social dimensions, the place of religion in public life—like the place of women and blacks, the subject of the previous chapter—has attracted renewed scrutiny. Moreover, because church-state relations are controversial in present-day politics, the historical record on religion is especially relevant. Congress and the Supreme Court make policy based on interpretation of the Constitution's First Amendment, which deals with church-state relations explicitly. In short, this branch of Revolutionary history has exceptional influence because of its direct, practical consequences.

In the Revolutionary era, as today, virtually everyone believed in religious liberty. But then, as now, there were significant differences of opinion as to what religious liberty exactly meant. While most voters believed that the vitality of religion was good for the country, they could not agree as to whether government power should be used to assist religion directly. In certain states, among them Massachusetts, a majority favored some form of public assistance to churches. In other states, including Virginia, the belief prevailed that neither religion nor liberty was safe when government—a secular, majority-controlled agency—took a hand in religion. The government should enable churches to operate on their own—but should do nothing more.

Until the advent of the Constitution in 1787–1788, these debates over religious issues occurred primarily at the state level, because no one supposed that the United States government, as weak and limited as it was, had any voice in the matter. The relationship of church and state became a national question only when Antifederalists voiced fears that the new national government, which they associated with an elite political establishment, might also create a religious establishment. The history of religious establishments in Britain and many of the colonies convinced the Antifederalists that such a development was a real possibility. As a result of Antifederalist arguments, Congress adopted the First

Amendment, using language that served immediate political needs but that also allowed for different later interpretations.

Americans worked out the relations between church and state in their new, experimental republic in a revolutionary way. Their solutions gave the United States a radical degree of religious freedom while providing a foundation for religion to flourish. American policies, as we shall see, were not entirely consistent, but they did convey the continuing power of the "contagion of liberty."

✴ D O C U M E N T S

The first three documents—the Massachusetts Declaration of Rights (1780) and the comments of Boston and Ashby (an inland country town)—reveal how complex the issue of religious freedom was and how divided Protestants were concerning the role of the government. In Massachusetts the ideal of religious freedom was compatible with compulsory support for churches. The enlightened clergyman and Yale college president Ezra Stiles, who delivered the annual sermon to the Connecticut legislature in 1783, which is reprinted as the fourth document, articulated the prevailing New England view that the American republic must also become a reformed Christian republic. He saw the well-being of the United States and of Presbyterianism as one.

The difficulty posed by applying such an outlook on a national scale is illustrated by the next four documents, drawn from Pennsylvania and Virginia. When Philadelphia's Jews objected to their exclusion from officeholding under Pennsylvania's 1776 Constitution, they raised the question of whether it was legitimate for government to prefer Christians over others who believed in God. James Madison's remonstrance against religious taxes and Thomas Jefferson's Virginia Statute of Religious Liberty express the radical implications of Revolutionary ideas for separating church and state. George Washington's pragmatic, nonideological position indicates a strain of thought and behavior that was crucial for finding political solutions in Virginia and elsewhere. The final document, the First Amendment to the Constitution, short enough to memorize easily, requires far more learning to interpret.

The Massachusetts Declaration of Rights, 1780

Art. I. All men are born free and equal, and have certain natural, essential, and unalienable rights; among which may be reckoned the right of enjoying and defending their lives and liberties; that of acquiring, possessing, and protecting property; in fine, that of seeking and obtaining their safety and happiness.

II. It is the right as well as the duty of all men in society, publicly, and at stated seasons, to worship the SUPREME BEING, the great creator and preserver of the universe. And no subject shall be hurt, molested, or restrained, in his person, liberty, or estate, for worshipping GOD in the manner and season most agreeable to the dictates of his own conscience; or for his religious profession or sentiments; provided he doth not disturb the public peace, or obstruct others in their religious worship.

III. As the happiness of a people, and the good order and preservation of civil government, essentially depend upon piety, religion and morality; and as these cannot be generally diffused through a community, but by the institution of the public worship of GOD, and of public instructions in piety, religion and morality: Therefore, to promote their happiness, and to secure the good order and preservation of their government, the people of this Commonwealth have a right to invest their legislature with power to authorize and require, and the legislature shall, from time to time, authorize and require, the several towns, parishes, precincts, and other bodies politic, or religious societies, to make suitable provision, at their own expense, for the institution of the public worship of GOD, and for the support and maintenance of public protestant teachers of piety, religion and morality, in all cases where such provision shall not be made voluntarily.

And the people of this Commonwealth have also a right to, and do, invest their legislature with authority to enjoin upon all the subjects an attendance upon the instructions of the public teachers aforesaid, at stated times and seasons, if there be any on whose instructions they can conscienciously and conveniently attend.

Provided notwithstanding, that the several towns, parishes, precincts, and other bodies politic, or religious societies, shall, at all times, have the exclusive right of electing their public teachers, and of contracting with them for their support and maintenance.

And all monies paid by the subject to the support of public worship, and of the public teachers aforesaid, shall, if he require it, be uniformly applied to the support of the public teacher or teachers of his own religious sect or denomination, provided there be any on whose instructions he attends; otherwise it may be paid towards the support of the teacher or teachers of the parish or precinct in which the said monies are raised.

And every denomination of christians, demeaning themselves peaceably, and as good subjects of the Commonwealth, shall be equally under the protection of the law; And no subordination of any one sect or denomination to another shall ever be established by law.

Boston's View of Religious Freedom, 1780

The only Article now to be attended to is the third in the Decleration of Rights, which Asserts that Piety, Religion and morality are essential to the happiness, Peace and Good order of a People and that these Principles are diffused by the Publick Worship of God, and by Publick Instructions &c— and in Consequence makes provision for their support. The alterations proposed here which you will Lay before the Convention were designed to Secure the Reights of Consience and to give the fullest Scope to religious Liberty In support of the proposition it urged that if Publick Worship and Publick teaching, did certainly (as was allowed) defuse a general Sence of Duty & moral Obligations, and, so secured the safety of our Persons and Properties, we ought chearfully to pay those from whose agency we derived such Advantages. But we are Attempting to support (it is said) the Kingdom of Christ; It may as well be said we are supporting the Kingdom of God, by institution of a Civil Goverment, which Declared to be an Ordinance to the Deity, and so refuse to pay the civil magistrate. What will be the consequence of such refusal—The greatest disorders, if not a Dissolution of Society. Suspend all provision for the inculation of Morality, religion and Piety, and confusion & every evil work may be justly dreaded; for it is found that with all the Restraints of religion induced by the Preaching of Ministers, and with all the Restraints of Goverment inforced by civil Law, the World is far from being as quiet an abode as might be wished. Remove the former by ceasing to support Morality, religion and Piety and it will be soon felt that human Laws were feble barriers opposed to the uninformed lusts of Passions of Mankind. But though we are not supporting the kingdom of Christ may we not be permitted to Assist civil society by an addoption, and by the teaching of the best set of Morals that were ever offered to the World. To Object to these Morrals, or even to the Piety and Religion we aim to inculcate, because they are drawn from the Gospel, must appear very singular to an Assembly generally professing themselves Christians. Were this really our intention, no Objection ought to be made to it provided, as in fact the case that equal Liberty is granted to every religious Sect and Denomination Whatever, and it is only required that every Man should pay to the support of Publick Worship In his own way. But should any be so Conscientious that they cannot pay to the support of any of the various denominations among us they may then alott their Money to the support of the Poor.

Ashby, Massachusetts, Opposes Religious Establishment, 1780

. . . The third Article lays a restraint: for those who cannot Concientiously or Convenantly attend upon any publick teachers are under restraint as to their Estates & so injurd as to their Liberty and property—

Reason 3 Religeous Societys as such have no voice in Chusing the Legeslature, the Legeslature therefore have no right to make Law binding on them as such; every religeous Society, as such, is intirely independant on any body politick, the Legeslature therefore have no more right to make Laws Binding on them, as such, then the Court of Great Britton have to make Laws binding on the Independant states of America— . . .

Reason 6. The Rivers of blood which has ran from the Veins of Marters! and all the torment which they have indured in the flames! was ocationed by the authority of Legeslature over religeous Society in consequence of the authority of the Legeslature or the authority arising from the authority of the Legeslature, the Feet of Paul & Silas where made fast in the stocks, the three Children Cast into the Furnace of fire, Daniel into the Lions Den, and many other such instances might be inumerated—

Reason 7. the third Article says the people of this common wealth have a right to invest their Legeslature with power to make Laws that are binding on religeous Society as (as we understand them) which is as much as to say we will not have Christ to reign over us that the Laws of this Kingdom are not sufficient to govern us, that the prosperity of his Kingdom is not eaqualy important with the Kingdoms of this world and that the Ark of God stands in need of Uzza's band to keep it from falling to the ground, butt lett us attend sereously to this important Truth that I will build my Church upon this Rock, and the Gates of Hell shall not prevail against it, now where resides this power in Christ only? or in the Legeslature?—it may be Objected against the Reasons here given that it leaves people two Louse and does not ingadge them to there duty & therby all religion will fall to the ground and this Objection indeed is very plausable because it may flow from an outward zeal for a form of Godliness without the power butt is it not founded upon this Supposition that men are not sufficiently ingadged to the practice of their Duty unless they doe somthing that God never required of them—

He that made us reasonable Creatures and Conferd upon us the Blessing of the Gospell has by this frame and situation laid us under the strongest Obligation to the practice of Piety, Religeon, and Morality that can posibly be conceived, & if this wont impress our minds to doe our Duty nothing will[.]

Rev. Ezra Stiles on the Place of Religion in the United States, 1783

He will then "make them high above all nations which he hath made, in praise, and in name, and in honor, and they shall become a holy people unto the Lord their God." . . .

I have assumed the text only as introductory to a discourse upon the political welfare of God's American Israel, and as allusively prophetic of the future prosperity and splendor of the United States. We may, then, consider—

I. What reason we have to expect that, by the blessing of God, these States may prosper and flourish into a great American Republic, and ascend into high and distinguished honor among the nations of the earth. "To make thee high above all nations which he hath made, in praise, and in name, and in honor."

II. That our system of dominion and civil polity would be imperfect without the true religion; or that from the diffusion of virtue among the people of any community would arise their greatest secular happiness: which will terminate in this conclusion, that holiness ought to be the end of all civil government. "That thou mayest be a holy people unto the Lord thy God."

The United States will embosom all the religious sects or denominations in Christendom. Here they may all enjoy their whole respective systems of worship and church government complete. Of these, next to the Presbyterians, the Church of England will hold a distinguished and principal figure. They will soon furnish themselves with a bishop in Virginia and Maryland, and perhaps another to the northward, to ordain their clergy, give confirmation, superintend and govern their churches,—the main body of which will be in Virginia and Maryland. . . . The *Unitas Fratrum* for above thirty years past have had Moravian bishops in America. . . . The Baptists, the Friends, the Lutherans, the Romanists, are all considerable bodies in all their dispersions through the states. The Dutch and Gallic and German Reformed or Calvinistic churches among us I consider as Presbyterian, differing from us in nothing of moment save in language. There is a considerable body of these in the states of New York, Jersey, Pennsylvania, and at Ebenezer, in Georgia. There is a Greek Church, brought from Smyrna; but I think it falls below these states. There are Westleians, Mennonists, and others, all which make a very inconsiderable amount in comparison with those who will give the religious complexion to America, which for the southern parts will be Episcopal, the northern, Presbyterian. All religious denominations will be independent of one another; . . . and having, on account of religion, no superiority as to secular powers and civil immunities, they will cohabit together in harmony, and, I hope, with a most generous catholicism and benevolence. The example of a friendly cohabitation of all sects in America, proving that men may be good members of civil society and yet differ in religion. . . .

Removed from the embarrassments of corrupt systems, and the dignities and blinding opulence connected with them, the unfettered mind can think with a noble enlargement, and, with an unbounded freedom, go wherever the light of truth directs. Here will be no bloody tribunals, no cardinal's inquisitors-general, to bend the human mind, forcibly to control the understanding, and put out the light of reason, the candle of the Lord, in man,—to force an innocent Galileo to renounce truths demonstrable as the light of day. Religion may here receive its last, most liberal, and impartial examination. Religious liberty is peculiarly friendly to fair and generous disquisition. Here Deism will have its full chance; nor need libertines more to complain of being overcome by any weapons but the gentle, the powerful ones of argument and truth. Revelation will be found to stand the test to the ten thousandth examination.

There are three coetaneous events to take place, whose futurition is certain from prophecy,—the annihilation of the pontificate, the reassembling of the Jews, and the fulness of the Gentiles. That liberal and candid disquisition of Christianity which will most assuredly take place in America, will prepare Europe for the first event, with which the other will be connected, when, especially on the return of the Twelve Tribes to the Holy Land, there will burst forth a degree of evidence hitherto unperceived, and of efficacy to convert a world. . . .

When we look forward and see this country increased to forty or fifty millions, while we see all the religious sects increased into respectable bodies, we shall doubtless find the united body of the Congregational, consociated, and Presbyterian churches making an equal figure with any two of them. . . . There is the greatest prospect that we shall become thirty out of forty millions. . . . In this country, out of sight of mitres and the purple, and removed from systems of corruption confirmed for ages and supported by the spiritual janizaries of an ecclesiastical hierarchy, aided and armed by the secular power, religion may be examined with the noble Berean freedom, the freedom of American-born minds. And revelation, both as to the true evangelical doctrines and church polity, may be settled here before they shall have undergone a thorough discussion, and been weighed with a calm and unprejudiced candor elsewhere. Great things are to be effected in the world before the millennium, which I do not expect to commence under seven or eight hundred years hence; and perhaps the liberal and candid disquisitions in America are to be rendered extensively subservient to some of the most glorious designs of Providence, and particularly in the propagation and diffusion of religion through the earth, in filling the whole earth with the knowledge of the glory of the Lord. A time will come when six hundred millions of the human race shall be ready to drop their idolatry and all false religion, when Christianity shall triumph over superstition, as well as Deism, and Gentilism, and Mohammedanism. They will then search all Christendom for the best model, the purest exemplification of the Christian church, with the fewest human mixtures. . . . And thus the American Republic, by illuminating the world with truth and liberty, would be exalted and made high among the nations, in praise, and in name, and in honor. I doubt not this is the honor reserved for us.

Philadelphia Jews Seek Equality Before the Law, 1783

To the honourable the Council of Censors, assembled agreeable to the Constitution of the State of Pennsylvania. The Memorial of . . . the Synagogue of the Jews at Philadelphia, . . . in behalf of themselves and their brethren Jews, residing in Pennsylvania,

Most respectfully showeth,

That by the tenth section of the Frame of Government of this Commonwealth, it is ordered that each member of the general assembly of representatives of the freemen of Pennsylvania, before he takes his seat, shall make and subscribe a declaration, which ends in these words, "I do acknowledge the Scriptures of the old and new Testament to be given by divine inspiration," to which is added an assurance, that "no further or other religious test shall ever hereafter be required of any civil officer or magistrate in this state."

Your memorialists beg leave to observe, that this clause seems to limit the civil rights of your citizens to one very special article of the creed; whereas by the second paragraph of the declaration of the rights of the inhabitants, it is asserted without any other limitation than the professing the existence of God, in plain words, "that no man who acknowledges the being of a God can be justly deprived or abridged of any civil rights as a citizen on account of his religious sentiments." But certainly this religious test deprives the Jews of the most eminent rights of freemen, solemnly ascertained to all men who are not professed Atheists.

May it please your Honors,

Although the Jews in Pennsylvania are but few in number, yet liberty of the people in one country, and the declaration of the government thereof, that these liberties are the rights of the people, may prove a powerful attractive to men, who live under restraints in another country. Holland and England have made valuable acquisitions of men, who for their religious sentiments, were distressed in their own countries.—And if Jews in Europe or elsewhere, should incline to transport themselves to America, and would, for reason of some certain advantage of the soil, climate, or the trade of Pennsylvania, rather become inhabitants thereof, than of any other State; yet the disability of Jews to take seat among the representatives of the people, as worded by the said religious test, might determine their free choice to go to New York, or to any other of the United States of America, where there is no such like restraint laid upon the nation and religion of the Jews, as in Pennsylvania. — Your memorialists cannot say that the Jews are particularly fond of being representatives of the people in assembly or civil officers and magistrates in the State; but with great submission they apprehend that a clause in the constitution, which disables them to be elected by their fellow citizens to represent them in assembly, is a stigma upon their nation and religion, and it is inconsonant with the second paragraph of the said bill of rights; otherwise Jews are as fond of liberty as their religious societies can be, and it must create in them a displeasure, when they perceive that for their professed dissent to doctrine, which is inconsistent with their religious sentiments, they should be excluded from the most important and honourable part of the rights of a free citizen.

Your memorialists beg further leave to represent, that in the religious books of the Jews, which are or may be in every man's hands, there are no such doctrines or principles established as are inconsistent with the safety and happiness of the people of Pennsylvania, and that the conduct and behaviour of the Jews in this and the neighbouring States, has always tallied with the great design of the Revolution; that the Jews of Charlestown, New York, New-Port and other posts, occupied by the British troops, have distinguishedly suffered for their attachment to the Revolution principles; and their brethren at St. Eustatius, for the same cause, experienced the most severe resentments of the British commanders. The Jews of Pennsylvania in proportion to the number of their members, can count with any religious society whatsoever, the Whigs among either of them; they have served some of them in the Continental army; some went out in the militia to fight the common enemy; all of them have cheerfully contributed to the support of the militia, and of the government of this State; they have no inconsiderable property in lands and tenements, but particularly in the way of trade, some more, some less, for which they pay taxes; they have, upon every plan formed for public utility, been forward to contribute as much as their circumstances would admit of; and as a nation or a religious society, they stand unimpeached of any matter whatsoever, against the safety and happiness of the people.

And your memorialists humbly pray, that if your honours, from any consideration than the subject of this address, should think proper to call a convention for revising the constitution, you would be pleased to recommend this to the notice of that convention.*

---

* When Pennsylvania revised its constitution in 1789–1790, the religious test was modified to accommodate Jews on an equal basis. Now the relevant passage stated: "That no person, who acknowledges the being of a God and a future state of rewards and punishments, shall, on account of his religious sentiments, be disqualified to hold any office or place of trust or profit under this commonwealth."

James Madison Protests Religious Taxes, 1785

*To the Honorable the General Assembly of the Commonwealth of
Virginia. A Memorial and Remonstrance.*

We, the subscribers, citizens of the said Commonwealth, having taken into
serious consideration, a Bill printed by order of the last Session of General
Assembly, entitled "A Bill establishing a provision for Teachers of the
Christian Religion," and conceiving that the same, if finally armed with the
sanctions of a law, will be a dangerous abuse of power, are bound as faithful
members of a free State, to remonstrate against it, and to declare the reasons
by which we are determined. We remonstrate against the said Bill,

1. Because we hold it for a fundamental and undeniable truth, "that
Religion or the duty which we owe to our Creator and the Manner of
discharging it, can be directed only by reason and conviction, not by force
or violence." The Religion then of every man must be left to the conviction
and conscience of every man; and it is the right of every man to exercise it
as these may dictate. This right is in its nature an unalienable right. It is
unalienable; because the opinions of men, depending only on the evidence
contemplated by their own minds, cannot follow the dictates of other men:
It is unalienable also; because what is here a right towards men, is a duty
towards the Creator. It is the duty of every man to render to the Creator
such homage, and such only, as he believes to be acceptable to him. This
duty is precedent both in order of time and degree of obligation, to the
claims of Civil Society. . . . True it is, that no other rule exists, by which
any question which may divide a Society, can be ultimately determined, but
the will of the majority; but it is also true, that the majority may trespass
on the rights of the minority.

2. Because if religion be exempt from the authority of the Society at
large, still less can it be subject to that of the Legislative Body. . . . The
preservation of a free government requires not merely, that the . . . bounds
which separate each department of power may be invariably maintained;
but more especially, that neither of them be suffered to overleap the great
Barrier which defends the rights of the people. The Rulers who are guilty
of such an encroachment, exceed the commission from which they derive
their authority, and are Tyrants. The People who submit to it are governed
by laws made neither by themselves, nor by an authority derived from them,
and are slaves.

3. Because, it is proper to take alarm at the first experiment on our
liberties. We hold this prudent jealousy to be the first duty of citizens, and
one of [the] noblest characteristics of the late Revolution. The freemen of
America did not wait till usurped power had strengthened itself by exercise,
and entangled the question in precedents. They saw all the consequences in
the principle, and they avoided the consequences by denying the principle.
We revere this lesson too much, soon to forget it. Who does not see that
the same authority which can establish Christianity, in exclusion of all other
Religions, may establish with the same ease any particular sect of Christians,

in exclusion of all other Sects? That the same authority which can force a citizen to contribute three pence only of his property for the support of any one establishment, may force him to conform to any other establishment in all cases whatsoever?

4. Because, the bill violates that equality which ought to be the basis of every law, and which is more indispensible, in proportion as the validity or expediency of any law is more liable to be impeached. If "all men are by nature equally free and independent," all men are to be considered as entering into Society on equal conditions; as relinquishing no more, and therefore retaining no less, one than another, of their natural rights. Above all are they to be considered as retaining an "*equal* title to the free exercise of Religion according to the dictates of conscience." Whilst we assert for ourselves a freedom to embrace, to profess and to observe the Religion which we believe to be of divine origin, we cannot deny an equal freedom to those whose minds have not yet yielded to the evidence which has convinced us. If this freedom be abused, it is an offence against God, not against man: To God, therefore, not to men, must an account of it be rendered. As the Bill violates equality by subjecting some to peculiar burdens; so it violates the same principle, by granting to others peculiar exemptions. Are the Quakers and Menonists the only sects who think a compulsive support of their religions unnecessary and unwarantable? Can their piety alone be intrusted with the care of public worship? Ought their Religions to be endowed above all others, with extraordinary privileges, by which proselytes may be enticed from all others? We think too favorably of the justice and good sense of these denominations, to believe that they either covet pre-eminencies over their fellow citizens, or that they will be seduced by them, from the common opposition to the measure.

5. Because the bill implies either that the Civil Magistrate is a competent Judge of Religious truth; or that he may employ Religion as an engine of Civil policy. The first is an arrogant pretension falsified by the contradictory opinions of Rulers in all ages, and throughout the world: The second an unhallowed perversion of the means of salvation.

6. Because the establishment proposed by the Bill is not requisite for the support of the Christian Religion. To say that it is, is a contradiction to the Christian Religion itself; for every page of it disavows a dependence on the powers of this world: it is a contradiction to fact; for it is known that this Religion both existed and flourished, not only without the support of human laws, but in spite of every opposition from them; and not only during the period of miraculous aid, but long after it had been left to its own evidence, and the ordinary care of Providence: Nay, it is a contradiction in terms; for a Religion not invented by human policy, must have pre-existed and been supported, before it was established by human policy. It is moreover to weaken in those who profess this Religion a pious confidence in its innate excellence, and the patronage of its Author; and to foster in those who still reject it, a suspicion that its friends are too conscious of its fallacies, to trust it to its own merits.

7. Because experience witnesseth that ecclesiastical establishments, in-

stead of maintaining the purity and efficacy of Religion, have had a contrary operation. During almost fifteen centuries, has the legal establishment of Christianity been on trial. What has been its fruits? More or less in all places, pride and indolence in the Clergy; ignorance and servility in the laity; in both, superstition, bigotry and persecution. . . .

8. Because the establishment in question is not necessary for the support of Civil Government. If it be urged as necessary for the support of Civil Government only as it is a means of supporting Religion, and it be not necessary for the latter purpose, it cannot be necessary for the former. If Religion be not within [the] cognizance of Civil Government, how can its legal establishment be said to be necessary to civil Government? What influence in fact have ecclesiastical establishments had on Civil Society? In some instances they have been seen to erect a spiritual tyranny on the ruins of Civil authority; in many instances they have been seen upholding the thrones of political tyranny; in no instance have they been seen the guardians of the liberties of the people. Rulers who wished to subvert the public liberty, may have found an established clergy convenient auxiliaries. A just government, instituted to secure & perpetuate it, needs them not. Such a government will be best supported by protecting every citizen in the enjoyment of his Religion with the same equal hand which protects his person and his property; by neither invading the equal rights of any Sect, nor suffering any Sect to invade those of another.

9. Because the proposed establishment is a departure from that generous policy, which, offering an asylum to the persecuted and oppressed of every Nation and Religion, promised a lustre to our country, and an accession to the number of its citizens. What a melancholy mark is the Bill of sudden degeneracy? Instead of holding forth an asylum to the persecuted, it is itself a signal of persecution. It degrades from the equal rank of Citizens all those whose opinions in Religion do not bend to those of the Legislative authority. Distant as it may be, in its present form, from the Inquisition it differs from it only in degree. The one is the first step, the other the last in the career of intolerance. . . .

10. Because, it will have a like tendency to banish our Citizens. The allurements presented by other situations are every day thinning their number. To superadd a fresh motive to emigration, by revoking the liberty which they now enjoy, would be the same species of folly which has dishonoured and depopulated flourishing kingdoms.

11. Because, it will destroy that moderation and harmony which the forbearance of our laws to intermeddle with Religion, has produced amongst its several sects. Torrents of blood have been spilt in the old world, by vain attempts of the secular arm to extinguish Religious discord, by proscribing all difference in Religious opinions. Time has at length revealed the true remedy. Every relaxation of narrow and rigorous policy, wherever it has been tried, has been found to assuage the disease. The American Theatre has exhibited proofs, that equal and compleat liberty, if it does not wholly eradicate it, sufficiently destroys its malignant influence on the health and prosperity of the State. If with the salutary effects of this system under our

own eyes, we begin to contract the bonds of Religious freedom, we know no name that will too severely reproach our folly. At least let warning be taken at the first fruits of the threatened innovation. The very appearance of the Bill has transformed that "Christian forbearance, love and charity," which of late mutually prevailed, into animosities and jealousies, which may not soon be appeased. What mischiefs may not be dreaded should this enemy to the public quiet be armed with the force of a law?

12. Because, the policy of the bill is adverse to the diffusion of the light of Christianity. The first wish of those who enjoy this precious gift, ought to be that it may be imparted to the whole race of mankind. Compare the number of those who have as yet received it with the number still remaining under the dominion of false Religions; and how small is the former! Does the policy of the Bill tend to lessen the disproportion? No; it at once discourages those who are strangers to the light of [revelation] from coming into the Region of it; and countenances, by example the nations who continue in darkness, in shutting out those who might convey it to them. Instead of levelling as far as possible, every obstacle to the victorious progress of truth, the Bill with an ignoble and unchristian timidity would circumscribe it, with a wall of defence, against the encroachments of error.

13. Because attempts to enforce by legal sanctions, acts obnoxious to so great a proportion of Citizens, tend to enervate the laws in general, and to slacken the bands of Society. If it be difficult to execute any law which is not generally deemed necessary or salutary, what must be the case where it is deemed invalid and dangerous? and what may be the effect of so striking an example of impotency in the Government, on its general authority.

14. Because a measure of such singular magnitude and delicacy ought not to be imposed, without the clearest evidence that it is called for by a majority of citizens: and no satisfactory method is yet proposed by which the voice of the majority in this case may be determined, or its influence secured. "The people of the respective counties are indeed requested to signify their opinion respecting the adoption of the Bill to the next Session of Assembly." But the representation must be made equal, before the voice either of the Representatives or of the Counties, will be that of the people. Our hope is that neither of the former will, after due consideration, espouse the dangerous principle of the Bill. Should the event disappoint us, it will still leave us in full confidence, that a fair appeal to the latter will reverse the sentence against our liberties.

15. Because, finally, "the equal right of every citizen to the free exercise of his Religion according to the dictates of conscience" is held by the same tenure with all our other rights. If we recur to its origin, it is equally the gift of nature; if we weigh its importance, it cannot be less dear to us; if we consult the Declaration of those rights which pertain to the good people of Virginia, as the "basis and foundation of Government," it is enumerated with equal solemnity, or rather studied emphasis. Either then, we must say, that the will of the Legislature is the only measure of their authority; and that in the plenitude of this authority, they may sweep away all our fundamental rights; or, that they are bound to leave this particular right un-

touched and sacred: Either we must say, that they may controul the freedom of the press, may abolish the trial by jury, may swallow up the Executive and Judiciary Powers of the State; nay that they may despoil us of our very right of suffrage, and erect themselves into an independant and hereditary assembly: or we must say, that they have no authority to enact into law the Bill under consideration. We the subscribers say, that the General Assembly of this Commonwealth have no such authority: And that no effort may be omitted on our part against so dangerous an usurpation, we oppose to it, this remonstrance; earnestly praying, as we are in duty bound, that the Supreme Lawgiver of the Universe, by illuminating those to whom it is addressed, may on the one hand, turn their councils from every act which would affront his holy prerogative, or violate the trust committed to them: and on the other, guide them into every measure which may be worthy of his [blessing, may re]dound to their own praise, and may establish more firmly the liberties, the prosperity, and the Happiness of the Commonwealth.

George Washington Accepts Religious Taxes, 1785

Letter to George Mason

Mount Vernon, 3 October, 1785.

Dear Sir, . . .

Although no man's sentiments are more opposed to any kind of restraint upon religious principles than mine are, yet I must confess, that I am not amongst the number of those, who are so much alarmed at the thoughts of making people pay towards the support of that which they profess, if of the denomination of Christians, or declare themselves Jews, Mahometans, or otherwise, and thereby obtain proper relief. As the matter now stands, I wish an assessment [tax] had never been agitated, and as it has gone so far that the bill could die an easy death; because I think it will be productive of more quiet to the State, than by enacting it into a law, which in my opinion would be impolitic, admitting there is a decided majority for it, to the disquiet of a respectable minority. In the former case, the matter will soon subside; in the latter, it will rankle and perhaps convulse the State.

Thomas Jefferson's Virginia Statute of Religious Liberty, 1786

I. Whereas Almighty God hath created the mind free; that all attempts to influence it by temporal punishments or burthens, or by civil incapacitations, tend only to beget habits of hypocrisy and meanness, and are a departure from the plan of the Holy author of our religion, who being Lord both of body and mind, yet chose not to propagate it by coercions on either, as was in his Almighty power to do; that the impious presumption of legislators and rulers, civil as well as ecclesiastical, who being themselves but fallible and uninspired men, have assumed dominion over the faith of others, setting up their own opinions and modes of thinking as the only true and infallible, and as such endeavouring to impose them on others, hath established and maintained false religions over the greatest part of the world, and through all time; that to compel a man to furnish contributions of money for the propagation of opinions which he disbelieves, is sinful and tyrannical; that even the forcing him to support this or that teacher of his own religious persuasion, is depriving him of the comfortable liberty of giving his contributions to the particular pastor whose morals he would make his pattern, and whose powers he feels most persuasive to righteousness, and is withdrawing from the ministry those temporary rewards, which proceeding from an approbation of their personal conduct, are an additional incitement to earnest and unremitting labours for the instruction of mankind; that our civil rights have no dependence on our religious opinions, any more than our opinions in physics or geometry; that therefore the proscribing any citizen as unworthy the public confidence by laying upon him an incapacity of being called to offices of trust and emolument, unless he profess or renounce this or that religious opinion, is depriving him injuriously of those privileges and advantages to which in common with his fellow-citizens he has a natural right, that it tends only to corrupt the principles of that religion it is meant to encourage, by bribing with a monopoly of worldly honours and emoluments, those who will externally profess and conform to it; that though indeed these are criminal who do not withstand such temptation, yet neither are those innocent who lay the bait in their way; that to suffer the civil magistrate to intrude his powers into the field of opinion, and to restrain the profession or propagation of principles on supposition of their ill tendency, is a dangerous fallacy, which at once destroys all religious liberty, because he being of course judge of that tendency will make his opinions the rule of judgment, and approve or condemn the sentiments of others only as they shall square with or differ from his own; that it is time enough for the rightful purposes of civil government, for its officers to interfere when principles break out into overt acts against peace and good order; and finally, that truth is great and will prevail if left to herself, that she is the proper and sufficient antagonist to error, and has nothing to fear from the conflict, unless by human interposition disarmed of her natural weapons, free argument and debate, errors ceasing to be dangerous when it is permitted freely to contradict them.

II. *Be it enacted by the General Assembly,* that no man shall be compelled to frequent or support any religious worship, place or ministry whatsoever, nor shall be enforced, restrained, molested, or burthened in his body or goods, nor shall otherwise suffer on account of his religious opinions or belief; but that all men shall be free to profess, and by argument to maintain, their opinion in matters of religion, and that the same shall in no wise diminish, enlarge or affect their civil capacities.

III. And though we well know that this assembly, elected by the people for the ordinary purposes of legislation only, have no power to restrain the acts of succeeding assemblies, constituted with powers equal to our own, and that therefore to declare this act to be irrevocable would be of no effect in law; yet as we are free to declare, and do declare, that the rights hereby asserted are of the natural rights of mankind, and that if any act shall hereafter be passed to repeal the present, or to narrow its operation, such act will be an infringement of natural right.

First Amendment to the United States Constitution, 1791

Congress shall make no law respecting an establishment of religion, or prohibiting the free exercise thereof; or abridging the freedom of speech, or of the press; or the right of the people peaceably to assemble, and to petition the government for a redress of grievances.

✳ *E S S A Y S*

Taking cognizance of a generation or more of previous scholarship, Professor Jon Butler of Yale University argues that, although the Revolution was informed by religious beliefs and had major consequences for religious organizations, it was primarily a secular episode. In the first essay, drawn from *Awash in a Sea of Faith* (1990), his history of religion in America, Butler takes issue with scholars who have claimed a causal link between the Great Awakening and the Revolution. William G. McLoughlin, a professor at Brown University, is the leading scholar of the Baptists and of religious dissent in early America. His analysis in the second essay places religion in a more central role in the Revolution, which, he argues, harnessed Protestantism to the national mission. Monsignor Thomas J. Curry of the Archdiocese of Los Angeles shows in the final essay that the First Amendment, which may seem clear and simple on its face, can be understood only in its historical context.

Was There a Revolutionary Millennium?

JON BUTLER

British colonists wrought momentous changes in America between 1760 and 1800. They confronted, then overthrew, the government they had known since colonization began. They established new governments and, some hoped, a new society as well. They were not wrong to trumpet their handiwork as "the new order of the ages." Nor were they wrong to worry about what they had accomplished. Benjamin Franklin warned his countrymen in 1776 that their republic would survive "if you can keep it." Part of the challenge, perhaps the most important part, lay in determining what kind of republic Americans intended. . . .

At its heart, the Revolution was a profoundly secular event. The causes that brought it into being and the ideologies that shaped it placed religious concerns more at its margins than at its center. Yet organized religion not

Reprinted by permission of the publishers from *Awash in a Sea of Faith: Christianizing the American People* by Jon Butler, Cambridge, Mass.: Harvard University Press, Copyright © 1990 by the President and Fellows of Harvard College.

only survived the revolutionary era but probably prospered from it, both because of the nature of the crisis and because of the deft way the denominations handled it. Despite their early hesitation and continuing anxiety about the process, the churches lent their weight to the American cause in a way that paid immense dividends in coming decades. Later, as new tensions arose in the new configuration of politics, society, and religion, the denominations moved to sacralize independence. . . .

Religion has not always interested historians of the American Revolution. Both David Ramsay and George Bancroft saw the Revolution as a thoroughly secular event, and their views represented the dominant opinion of their time. Antebellum revivalism and the approaching Civil War prompted some change in this perspective, though largely among historians of religion. . . .

More dramatic claims for religion's importance in the Revolution emerged a century later. Carl Bridenbaugh's *Mitre and Sceptre* (1962) drew attention to the "bishop question," in which Dissenters denounced alleged Anglican plots to install a colonial bishop while colonial assemblies were fighting off taxes and the escalation of imperial authority. Alan Heimert's seminal *Religion and the American Mind from the Great Awakening to the Revolution* (1966) substituted Calvinist evangelicalism for theological liberalism as the Revolution's principal theoretical foundation. Since then many historians—Gary Nash on the colonial cities, Rhys Isaac on eighteenth-century Virginia, Harry S. Stout on the New England sermon, Patricia Bonomi on denominational antiauthoritarianism—have stressed the importance of evangelical "style" in shaping the Revolution. In these accounts, evangelicalism underwrote economic discontent, fostered new modes of public address, and provoked confrontations with the standing order that eroded public confidence in the established government and played a substantial role in turning protest into rebellion. In the main, however, these accounts' view of the principal religious force that might have shaped the Revolution is unnecessarily narrow in their focus on evangelicalism. They bypass other religious issues and traditions that influenced revolutionary political discourse, exaggerate religion's general importance to the Revolution, and slight the difficulties that the Revolution posed for the American churches and that they ultimately overcame.

The Declaration of Independence provides clear-cut evidence of the secondary role that religion and Christianity played in creating the revolutionary struggle. The religious world invoked in the Declaration was a deist's world, at best; at worst, the Declaration was simply indifferent to religious concerns and issues. The god who appears in the Declaration is the god of nature rather than the God of Christian scriptural revelation, as when Jefferson wrote of "the laws of nature and nature's God." In other allusive appearances this god emerged as "the Supreme Judge of the world," to whom Americans would appeal "for the rectitude of our intentions," and as "Divine Providence," on whom they would rely for protection. Elsewhere, all was secular: taxes, troops, tyranny. Despite its length, not a single religious issue, including the dispute over the Anglican bishop, found a place in the "history of repeated injuries and usurpations" that closed the Declaration and that established the Revolution's most authoritative list of offensive British actions in America.

Yet the Declaration's remarkable silence on religious issues should not obscure the importance of religion in secondary issues. The bishop question, for example, carried significant long-term implications for revolutionary discontent because it undermined trust in British politicians and their motives. The dispute actually acknowledged the institutional progress that Anglicans had made in the eighteenth century. Dissenters feared a bishop, traditionally required for a full presence of the Church of England anywhere, precisely because they knew how well Anglicans had fared without one. When Dissenters counted, they found Anglican congregations in astonishing numbers: there were some four hundred by 1776. They knew all too well that these congregations were important not only in the colonial cities, where their presence had been visually commanding for many years, but especially in the countryside, where most colonists lived. . . .

The Anglican-Dissenter contest over a bishop for America escalated transatlantic political tensions for years. The controversy first appeared in the 1710s, abated until it flared in the 1750s, then flared again in 1761 when Anglicans purchased an extraordinarily large home in Cambridge, Massachusetts, which Dissenters gleefully named the "bishop's palace." After 1763 the Dissenters' argument was joined to the colonial protests against taxes and other English efforts at imperial centralization, and it climaxed in protests against the Quebec Act of 1774, through which the English government recognized the Catholic church in the conquered French territories of Canada.

The Quebec Act called forth another image: secret Catholicism, associated with every attempt at tyranny in England since the 1640s—the reigns of Charles I and James II and the rise of the Pretender in Scotland in 1745. The charges resonated clearly in a society where anti-Catholicism had been a staple crop for two centuries, even among Anglicans. Paul Revere expressed those fears in a superbly crafted engraving in 1774. In it the Devil, Anglican bishops, and England's most notorious politicians, Lord North and Lord Bute, form a cabal to effect their ultimate and long secret objective— Catholicizing the American colonies.

Protestant Christianity also reinforced the Whig political convictions that lay behind early revolutionary rhetoric. Whig sentiment extended throughout the colonies, where it was descended from eighteenth-century English political culture generally rather than from more narrow sources in revivalism or New England Calvinism. Religious support for the Whigs was thus not limited to New England or to evangelical Dissenters. The basic Whig texts— Locke's *Second Treatise of Government,* Benjamin Hoadley's *Origin and Institution of Civil Government Discussed,* and John Trenchard and Thomas Gordon's *Cato's Letters*—were disseminated throughout the colonies, and reached more than evangelicals. . . .

Political Whiggism appeared in colonial sermons in two especially important ways. First, the sermons reinforced the emphasis on virtue and morality that pervaded secular political discussion in eighteenth-century colonial and English society. Indeed, it was the very breadth and perfunctoriness of clerical allusions to politics that made the sermons useful in the political debates of the era. Listeners and clergy together, in a vast number of denominations and congregations, *assumed* that liberty proceeded from a virtuous citizenry. It was the ministers' duty to make sure that this virtue was a Christian virtue, of course. . . .

The clerics' constant emphasis on virtue, responsibility, and, especially, morality helped make sense of revolutionary rhetoric about corruption and evil among English politicians and society. The French and Indian War of 1758–1763 offered some Americans all too intimate a view of that immorality. The behavior of British "regulars" sent from England to fight in America repelled John Cleaveland, who witnessed their antics when he served as chaplain to Massachusetts's Third Regiment. "Profain swearing seems to be the naturalized language of the regulars," he wrote. Their "gaming, Robbery, Thievery, Whoring, bad-company-keeping, etc.," epitomized the evils he and other ministers lamented Sunday after Sunday. . . .

Second, as protest escalated, some ministers discussed Revolution politics specifically. . . . Both ironically (in view of the Revolution's frequent appeals to liberty) and surprisingly (in view of historians' recent emphasis on evangelical Dissent), the most common denominator among pro-Revolution ministers was a state church pulpit. . . . Though virtually all Anglican ministers in the northern and middle colonies, where Anglicans often had to act the role of "dissenters," became loyalists, a third of the Anglican clergy in Virginia and Maryland, where Anglicans held tax-supported pulpits, backed the Revolution. Elsewhere, prorevolutionary sentiment among ministers also coincided with a legally established, tax-supported ministry. In most colonies the Revolution pitted a colonial political establishment against an expanding imperial administration, and the colonial clergy often owed more to the former than to the latter, even if the clergy involved were Anglican. The kind of politically active colonists who led protest against British policy after 1763 usually supported the locally established congregation in colonies with state church systems; the established, tax-supported minister supported the Revolution. Moreover, like the colonial political elites who used local government as a base from which to launch revolutionary-era protest and rebellion, ministers in the state churches used their fast and thanksgiving day sermons in the war against British policies. In this way establishmentarian coercion, rather than Dissenting antiauthoritarian voluntarism, underwrote much of the American ministerial promotion of liberty and attack on Toryism. Most colonial ministers, however, remained silent about politics during the upheavals of the 1760s and 1770s. . . .

Most Presbyterian ministers simply did not participate in revolutionary politics. . . . The demand for obedience was as strong among colonial Presbyterians as it was among Anglicans, and the Presbyterian commitment had been tested only shortly before the Revolution. During the so-called Regulator Movement in North and South Carolina in the late 1760s, backcountry Presbyterian ministers, supported by German Lutheran and Anglican pastors, had not hesitated to use their pulpits to denounce rebellion against colonial governments dominated by tidewater planter elites and to cite the traditional Pauline texts in doing so. . . .

In their 1775 [pastoral] letter the members of the Philadelphia synod ultimately both instructed the Presbyterian laity on loyalty to George III and voiced support for Whig political principles. They expressed their "attachment and respect to our sovereign King George"; they also expressed their regard for "the revolution principles by which his august family was seated on the British throne." Still, as violence swirled around them, obedience preceded rebellion. The ministers explicitly upheld their allegiance to "the person of the prince," not merely to monarchy in the abstract. They believed that he may have been misled, but they also rejected "such insults as have been offered to the sovereign" by American protesters.

The Presbyterian statement suggested why loyalism so frequently had a dual religious foundation and extended beyond the ranks of Church of England ministers, two-thirds of whom departed for England after the Revolution began. One reason concerned the traditional emphasis on authority and obedience in colonial preaching. Loyalist clergymen could be found in every colonial denomination. . . .

A second reason centered on religious discrimination. The political elites who guided the Revolution in so many places also had frequently mistreated religious minorities in earlier times. Scottish and Scotch-Irish Presbyterians in North and South Carolina, English Baptists in Virginia, German Lutheran and German Reformed groups in Pennsylvania, and Anglicans in New England, together with small groups such as Wesley's Methodists or a sect like the Sandemanians of Rhode Island, had all experienced religious and political discrimination before the Revolution that ranged from minor annoyances to legal persecution. Most found the patriots' anti-Parliament protests ironic and even hypocritical. Some groups, like the Virginia Baptists, supported the Revolution anyway. But backcountry Presbyterians, German Lutheran and German Reformed settlers, and middle and northern colony Anglicans often found themselves drawn to loyalism not only out of political and religious principle but because of antagonisms with settlers who had earlier used the government and the law against them. . . .

The Revolution also shaped American religion, of course, and it did so in complex ways. This complexity emerges even in the story of Christian denominational decline and growth. The most serious erosion occurred in the Anglican congregations, which were often most numerous where other denominations were weakest and whose members had initiated the resurgence of public Christian worship at the beginning of the century. In parish after parish, Anglican ministers left because they openly supported the Crown, because they could not endure abuse by local patriots, or because they were no longer being paid by either the SPG [English Society for the Propagation of the Gospel] or their vestries. Fifty Anglican priests were working in Pennsylvania, New York, and New England before the Revolution; only nine remained afterward. About 100 of the 150 priests in the southern colonies also fled to England. As a result 75 percent of the Church of England parishes, built up so carefully in the previous half century, lost their clergymen and, with them, their principal leadership in sustaining public Christian worship. . . .

Yet in other settings Protestant denominations advanced during the Revolution. South Carolina's Charleston Baptist Association experienced significant growth. . . . Presbyterian statistics described similar growth after, though not before or during, the Revolution. . . .

Denominational statistics conveyed only part of the story, however. Methodism had the fewest difficulties, in part because it had the least to lose. Methodist missionaries had worked in America less than a decade, and all of them except Francis Asbury returned to England at John Wesley's command. Anglicans suffered most because they had the most to lose, in terms of both ministers and buildings. The physical destruction loosed on Anglican churches was reminiscent of sixteenth-century English anti-Catholic depredation. In parish after parish supporters of the Revolution stripped Anglican churches of their royal coats of arms, although usually they left the buildings and other fittings intact. . . .

Patriots attacked more than buildings. Isaac Backus noted the apparent murder in November 1776 of Ephraim Avery, a supporter of the Crown and the Anglican minister at Rye, New York. Those responsible contrived to make his death look like a suicide, an adroit move in a colony where loyalist sentiment ran high. Pennsylvania Quakers also experienced significant harassment for their pacifism and neutrality. . . . In May 1776 a stone-throwing mob forced Philadelphia Friends to observe a fast day that the Continental Congress had proclaimed. . . . Patriots celebrating the surrender of Cornwallis in October 1782 ransacked Quaker homes that had not displayed victory candles. . . .

Other dangers came from within patriot society. Clergymen who had struggled for a half century to advance Christian adherence could see much of their work lost in the turmoil of war. The Philadelphia synod continuously appointed fasts to relieve the "low and declining state of religion among us." Its letters spoke of "gross immoralities," "increasing decay of vital piety," "degeneracy of manners," even "want of public spirit." This feeling was not confined to English-speaking Americans or to the old middle colonies. German Reformed ministers, largely from western Pennsylvania, complained that the Revolution increased citizens' "vanity" and decreased their humility; they "indulge[d], without shame and decency, in the most abominable vices." Baptists in Virginia and South Carolina decried advancing sin and immorality amid the Revolution, and Isaac Backus worried deeply about morality in New England, something he too attributed to decline rather than to more persistent indifference to things moral and religious.

The religious tensions generated by the Revolution appeared with special force in the revolutionary army, where chaplains and soldiers were forced to reconstruct their lives and their religion outside of their normal settings. Chaplains were a traditional part of British military and political culture in both England and America. Colonial militias and British troops appointed chaplains during the French and Indian War, and some of these men served again during the Revolution. From a military perspective, chaplains were present primarily to promote discipline and only secondarily to preserve faith. During the French and Indian War, George Washington described a good chaplain as a "gentlemen of sober, serious and religious deportment, who would improve morale and discourage gambling, swearing, and drunkenness." Washington and other revolutionary commanders expected chaplains to serve the same ends, and the Continental Congress quickly approved chaplains for the army when it designated Washington commander-in-chief. . . .

Between the signing of the Declaration of Independence in 1776 and George Washington's death in 1799, American church and denominational leaders renewed efforts to stamp Christian values and goals on a now independent society. Three of these attempts proved especially important: powerful Christian explanations of the Revolution and of the proper political order that ought to govern American society; attacks on irreligion, especially on skepticism and deism; and the creation of new religious groups, which evinced principles that for the first time might be called distinctively American.

The association of society and government with Christianity was traditional in colonial political culture. But the Revolution strengthened the demand to associate society with Christianity in several ways—by revealing the previously shallow foundations of the association, by stressing a particular form of "republicanism" in government and society, and by stimulating a strong sense of cultural optimism that fitted certain religious themes, particularly American millennialism.

Dark concerns about America's religious future extended far beyond the chaplains working in the army camps. The destruction of church buildings, the interruption of denominational organization, the occasional decline in congregations and membership, the shattering of the Anglican church, and the rise of secular pride in revolutionary accomplishments all weighed on American religious leaders. Even as the Revolution advanced, denominational leaders often bemoaned rather than celebrated America's moral fiber. . . .

Republican political ideology heightened concern for moral and religious foundations. Republican principles had enormous importance for American religion because, though they were often vague and elusive, they placed great authority in the very laypeople with whom the clergy had long struggled. . . .

Contemporaries agreed that a successful republican society and government, by definition, depended on "a virtuous people." This sentiment did not take root in a reborn Puritanism but in more modern eighteenth-century principles. . . . The whole of society, not merely some of its parts, constituted the bedrock of the future. The contrast was particularly noticeable in Massachusetts. John Winthrop's Puritan society had been ordered by means of hierarchical responsibilities assigned among the people, "some highe and eminent in power and dignitie; others meane and in subjection." The 1780

Massachusetts constitution, however, rested order on a broader foundation: "The happiness of a people, and the good order and preservation of civil government, essentially depend upon piety, religion, and morality." It did not mention the "highe and eminent" or "others meane and in subjection."

Optimism fueled the new republic. . . . Progressive conceptions of time rooted in a secular, rather than a supernatural, view of life underwrote much of the new American optimism. . . . [Sermons], like those given with almost universal occurrence on July 4, simultaneously celebrated victory and independence. Fast and thanksgiving day sermons continued and even increased. Everywhere a torrent of ministers' words proclaimed American independence and Christianity together.

If claims measured God's approval, the clergy put the new nation in good stead. Providential rhetoric fixed God's sovereignty over the Revolution. . . . Joel Barlow asserted in his epic poem of American destiny, *The Vision of Columbus,* that Heaven approved independence as much as it had guided America's discoverers—"America" meaning the old mainland British colonies, of course, not the whole of the Western Hemisphere. Timothy Dwight proclaimed that only Israel had "experienced more extraordinary interpositions of Providence."

Millennialist rhetoric predicting Christ's return to earth also expanded. . . . Yet the very ubiquity of such predictions produced a bewildering variety of styles. No single millennialist vision emerged in the early national period. As Ruth Bloch has noted, proponents variously predicted the coming of true liberty and freedom, a rise in piety, American territorial expansion, and even freedom from hunger. Many propagandists hedged their predictions, just as their predecessors had done in the 1740s and 1750s. The few who provided definite dates for specific events usually developed different and sometimes exotic chronologies. As Americans experienced political, social, and economic setbacks after independence had been won, others turned to darker visions of the world and the new nation's place in it. New Hampshire's Samuel MacClintock warned against "luxury, and those other vices." New Jersey's Jacob Green foresaw "contentions, oppressions, and various calamities." New York's "Prophet Nathan" wrote that crop failure resulted from Americans' greed and disunity.

Despite, or perhaps because of, its inconsistencies, millennialist rhetoric performed important functions in revolutionary society. Above all, Christian millennialism played a significant role in rationalizing popular secular optimism, which it transformed more often than it confronted. Rather than make extensive critiques of secular optimism, millennialist propagandists offered a vision of optimistic progress that was made more understandable by Christian teleology. This progress took root not in man, whose imperfections were all too visible even amid the Revolution, but in God, whose perfection was highlighted by invisibility.

At the same time, apocalyptic thinking generally declined in the revolutionary period. . . . The Revolution was an event whose character and outcome seemed to have signaled the beginning of Christ's thousand-year reign, thus making the apocalypse either history or irrelevant.

Millennialism also had important political implications. Millennialist rhetoric secured an unwilling and often perplexed society to the Christian plow with the harness of Christian time. It demanded lay adherence in a society where the people were now sovereign. When New Englanders sought a unicameral legislature and an elected executive on the ground that "the voice of the people is the voice of God" (the view of the *New England Chronicle*), the rhetoric largely benefited the advancement of Christianity: a legislature that spoke for God should also listen to those who articulated Christian theology, morals, and ethics.

The millennialist incorporation of secular optimism in the revolutionary period was paralleled by equally adamant campaigns against irreligion in its intellectual disguises of skepticism, atheism, and deism. . . . But skepticism survived nonetheless, as American clergymen knew all too well. Its most prominent representatives—Franklin, Jefferson, Madison, and Washington, among others—seemed the apotheosis of the Enlightenment. Their support for Enlightenment discourse revealed a tolerance of skepticism, perhaps even irreligion, altogether dangerous in a new republic.

Deism became a chief object of attack in the war against irreligion. The choice proved particularly clever, not least because it clothed a familiar specter in new dress. Attacks on popular immorality were not novel, and atheism, meaning a sustained denial of the supernatural, was too rare to foster a believable campaign against it. Deism had the attraction of being relatively new yet suspiciously commonplace among the new nation's political and social leaders. The word itself dated only from the seventeenth century and had achieved a place in common vocabulary only in the early eighteenth century. Most important, deism offered extraordinary opportunities to its critics to demonstrate the need for real religion, meaning orthodox Christianity, in the new republic. This was possible because, to its critics, deism was the epitome of hypocrisy. It masqueraded as religion but was thoroughly irreligious. Deists admitted the justice of religious claims, but they made religion irrelevant to contemporary life. The deists' god was dead. At best, signs of his existence were found only in the distant past, not in the present.

As Americans turned from war making to nation making, clergymen turned to deism to explain their postrevolutionary failures and crises. Deism served as a new and dangerous label under which a broad list of evils, old and new, could be assembled. Thomas Paine's *Age of Reason,* published in 1794, was denounced far more than it was read. In 1798 Jedidiah Morse described why the deism Paine promoted should be so feared: "The existence of a God is boldly denied. Atheism and materialism are systematically professed. Reason and Nature are deified and adored. The Christian religion, and its divine and blessed author, are not only disbelieved, rejected and contemned, but even abhorred."

The eagerness to uncover deism produced two major campaigns of religious paranoia. One scare involved the so-called Bavarian Illuminati, rationalist compatriots of the Freemasons. The campaign encapsulated all the important themes common to later nineteenth- and twentieth-century American nativist crusades. The Illuminati were foreign, anti-Protestant, atheistic, secret, conspiratorial, and perverse. They were seen as having turned Masonic Christianity inside out, and as having hidden behind the respectability of the Freemasons, a group already worrisome to some evangelicals but not subject to massive attack until the 1830s and 1840s. Acting in concert with the French (who surely were atheists, Jesuits or both), the Illuminati would sacrifice any principle for power and, therefore, would subvert both independence and Christianity.

Thomas Jefferson's try for the presidency in 1800 brought out a second antideist campaign. It was particularly important because it focused on the potentially intimate relationship between a president's personal religious views and the fate of the American republic. Jefferson's actual religious views were complex. He was, indeed, a deist, and he also expressed a quiet regard for Christ and Christian ethics. But he rejected Christ's divinity and criticized religious coercion with a vigor that made some suspicious of his real religious views, despite the fact that evangelicals had long supported him for his efforts on behalf of religious freedom. Federalists linked Jefferson to anticlericalism and atheism in the by then notorious French Revolution; in their vocabulary, "Jacobin" meant atheist as well as democrat. Many ministers denounced Jefferson from their pulpits and decried the fate of the nation in the hands of a red-haired deist, an obvious agent of the Devil.

The campaign to advance Christianity after American independence was not wholly negative. Amid the anger directed against deism, skepticism, and rationalism, other Americans again sought religious renewal, reform, and revival. The most immediately impressive form of that quest emerged from rationalist liberal circles. Developed largely from what Henry May calls the "moderate Enlightenment" and centered in what would come to be called the Universalist and Unitarian movements, rationalist liberalism found itself an early beneficiary of the kind of revolution that had already reshaped American political life. Its principal doctrines—a largely positive view of man, universal salvation, rejection of the Trinity, fascination with science, and a trend toward systematization—closely fitted the political optimism of the times. Among a people simultaneously sweeping away the encrustations of the past and forging new constitutions to bring new states and a nation into being, an emphasis on simple, universal religious principles held considerable appeal. Religious reformers sought to locate Christianity's essentials in a few themes and doctrines, to dispense with the excess baggage of historical theology, and to embrace the new science, all in order to advance mankind and Christianity in a new society and a new age.

Unitarianism played a critical role in retaining Christian adherence among a critical segment of the new nation's political and cultural leadership. It was criticized by its contemporaries and subsequently by some historians for simplifications that seemed to strip away religious fervor. But this criticism, which generally reflects an evangelical conception of Christianity, also exposes the source of Unitarianism's importance in postrevolutionary America. As late as the 1790s it attracted more intellectual than popular attention. Between 1800 and 1830 as many as half of New England's tax-supported Congregationalist churches adopted Unitarian principles, sometimes after bitter local schisms that forced losers out of the old town or parish church. Unitarianism's admittedly elite following of literate, well-bred, and relatively affluent adherents, imbibing an abstract, distant theology, connected a significant Christianized element of the older colonial past to the more rambunctious, if not necessarily democratic, future. With little apparent sympathy for sectarian, disciplinarian, and revivalistic religious traditions, this element might easily have drifted into a far more aggressive secularism, perhaps not unlike that both publicly and privately expressed by so many of the Founding Fathers. However much evangelicals opposed Unitarian aloofness, Unitarianism kept a crucial elite moored to a Christian dock, no mean accomplishment in decades when enormous numbers of Europeans— including Europeans soon to be revolutionaries—abandoned Christianity altogether.

Emotion-laden revivals also emerged in postrevolutionary America. . . . The late eighteenth-century revivals exhibited three important characteristics linked to the Revolution. One was a marked tendency toward a reductionism and antitheologicalism, if not anti-intellectualism, which paralleled Unitarian rationalism but not Unitarian spiritual aloofness. . . . Second, revolutionary and postrevolutionary American revivalism had a tendency to involve dreams, visions, apparitions, and physical manifestations of divine intervention seen in some earlier eighteenth-century revivalism. The best-known example was that of the Shakers. Jesus had first appeared to Ann Lee, their apparent founder (and second manifestation of Christ on earth), and her associates in England, and in 1772 visions prompted them to emigrate to New England as the site of Christ's second kingdom. They arrived in New York in 1774. The Revolution only enhanced their millennialist visions, and the rightness of their celibacy came "to be transparent in their ideas in the bright and heavenly visions of God." For Shakers as well as for American revolutionaries, heaven began on earth.

The Shaker emphasis on dreams and visions was commonplace, not unique. [The Freewill Baptist] Benjamin Randel confirmed religious truth through out-of-body experiences and dreams: "I never could tell whether I was in the body or not . . . I saw a white robe brought down and put over me, which covered me, and I appeared as white as snow." Freeborn Garrettson and James Horton, Methodist itinerants, unashamedly shared accounts of their own divine dreams with their listeners, who in turn described equally compelling occurrences. . . .

In addition, postrevolutionary revivalism extended the fusion of indigenous and transatlantic dynamics that had been common to prerevolutionary Christian reform and revival. The "New Light Stir," Randel's Freewill Baptists, and even the emergence of the Unitarian movement reflected strong local dynamics whose importance only increased in the new republic. Transatlantic influences, too, pervaded postrevolutionary revivalism. Though the Shakers actually worked out their identity in the New York and New England wilderness, they did so by enhancing the millennialist, apocalyptic, and visionary themes they had earlier imbibed in England. Baptist revivalism throughout the southern states emerged as part of a vigorous Baptist revival that also occurred in late eighteenth-century England. The *Baptist Annual Register,* a London publication, advanced transatlantic revivals that involved blacks as well as whites in both the new states and the remaining British colonies in the Caribbean. Methodist itinerants similarly moved back and forth from England to America immediately after the Revolution, and their great success quickly produced a separate denominational structure that further invigorated the Methodists' national dynamism even as it deepened their transatlantic connections.

In all, Christianity recovered from the American Revolution with remarkable alacrity. The churches, though buffeted by a revolution whose battlefield and army camp experiences exposed the tenuousness of popular Christian adherence and reinforced the vigorous secularity of its political principles, emerged with renewed vigor in the 1780s. They sought to sacralize the Revolution and American society through a Christian rhetoric that pulled secular optimism within a Christian orbit. They experienced surprising growth in the 1780s and even greater growth in the 1790s. They found increasingly indigenous resonances in new religious movements, ranging from Unitarian rationalism to Baptist, Methodist, and Shaker ecstasy. In less than two decades, they demonstrated that religious groups that had not initiated the Revolution could nevertheless survive it. In the next half century, they would begin to master the new American environment by initiating a religious creativity that renewed spiritual reflection and perfected institutional power, all to serve Christian ends.

The Role of Religion in the Revolution

WILLIAM G. MCLOUGHLIN

The role of religion *in* the American Revolution cannot be understood apart from its role *before* and *after* the Revolution. If we define religion as the philosophical outlook, the set of fundamental assumptions, ideals, beliefs, and values about man's relationship to his neighbors, his environment, and his future, that provides the cultural cohesion for a community, then the Revolution was both a culmination and a beginning of the process that produced American cultural cohesion. In this sense the Revolution was a religious as well as a political movement.

The salient religious development of the Revolution has variously been referred to as disestablishment, the rise of religious liberty, the adoption of voluntaryism, or the separation of church and state (not all the same thing, but all closely related). From a moderately long-range view, this was an irreversible development in America from the time of the Great Awakening and reached one of its logical conclusions a century later with the final abolition of the system of compulsory religious taxes in Massachusetts. An even longer-range view would push the development back to Roger Williams, the Scrooby Separatists, or the Anabaptists of the Reformation and forward to today's problems over federal aid to parochial schools. In the more common and short-range view disestablishment began with George Mason's article on religious liberty in the Virginia Declaration of Rights in 1776 and was "substantially" complete, as J. Franklin Jameson said, by 1800, with the passage of the First Amendment and the abolition of religious tests for officeholding in most state constitutions.

I have chosen in this essay to take the moderately long-range view, concentrating upon the efforts to work out the principles and practical definitions of voluntaryism in the original states from 1776 to the middle of the nineteenth century. But this obliges me to begin with at least a cursory glance at the development of religious and political liberty in the period from 1740 to 1776.

As I see it, the Great Awakening, sometimes seen as a religious reaction to Arminianism and sometimes as the upthrust of the Enlightenment in the colonies, was really the beginning of America's identity as a nation—the starting point of the Revolution. The forces set in motion during the Awakening broke the undisputed power of religious establishments from Georgia to the District of Maine, but more than that, the Awakening constituted a watershed in the self-image and conceptualization of what it meant to be an American. The old assumptions about social order and authority that underlay colonial political economy and produced cultural cohesion dissolved. The corporate and hierarchical ideal of society began to yield to an individualistic and egalitarian one. While the medieval concept of a Christian commonwealth lingered, its social foundations crumbled.

A description of the complex forces that led to the breakdown of the old order and hastened the modernization of American institutions (of which the Revolution was the modus operandi) cannot be attempted here. Nor have I space to trace the subtle theological shifts that sustained this social reformation. But, in essence, between 1735 and 1790 the American colonists redefined their social principles into a cohesive structure sufficiently radical to necessitate a political break with the Old World and sufficiently conservative to sustain a new nation.

The historian of religion would stress three interrelated intellectual strands that gave the pattern to the new national consciousness: the new emphasis in evangelical Calvinism (the prevalent religious commitment of the people), stressing the individual's direct, personal, experiential relationship to God; the general acceptance of the deistic theory of inalienable natural rights and contractual self-government; and the resurgence of the radical whig ideology with its fear of hierarchical tyranny (the united despotism of church and state) epitomized in John Adams's *Dissertation on the Canon and Feudal Law.*

Before the Awakening most individuals gladly yielded their judgment and conscience to the superior claims and knowledge of their "betters," the ruling elite in church and state, who derived their authority from God and as his vicegerents administered the ordinances of government for the good of the people. After the Awakening this order of things became reversed: the state and church were considered by increasing numbers of Americans to be the creatures of the people and subject to their authority. Prior to the Awakening the king, his bishops, judges, and governors interpreted the will of God, and deference was their due. Afterwards the people considered themselves better able than any elite to interpret God's will and expected their elected officials to act as *their* vicegerents under God. The channel of authority no longer flowed from God to the rulers to the people but from God to the people to their elected representatives. State and church were henceforth to serve the needs of the people as defined by the people—or rather, by the people's interpretation of God's will. Intermediaries were dispensed with; every individual was assumed to be in direct relationship to God and responsible only to him, and therefore their collective will was God's will. Or so, in its extreme and logical form, this theory evolved by the time of Thomas Paine's *Common Sense* and came into practice by the age of Jackson. . . .

The religious and political establishments did not fall under these first radical onslaughts of pietistic individualism. But their authority eroded steadily before the rising tide of alienation. The Congregational establishments in New England, always under a measure of popular control, responded to the challenge by altering their posture—yielding power to the New Lights within the structure and granting greater religious liberty to those without. But the Anglican establishments turned more strongly than ever to authoritarian control, and that meant reliance upon the power of kings and bishops across the sea and insistence upon the need for bishops in America. Once the Revolution started, Anglican authority and power immediately ceased.

The Revolution—an essentially irrational impulse despite the eloquent rationalizations provided for it—combined this popular spirit of pietistic self-righteousness with a new commitment to inalienable natural rights (fostered by the Enlightenment). Both fed upon the heady fruits of a long-brewing commonwealth radicalism to produce an ecstatic enthusiasm for national self-assertion. Ostensible rationalists fervently upheld the innate, God-given rights of Englishmen and mankind against a despotic George III; evangelical pietists zealously insisted that Christ died, not for the divine right of kings or hierarchies, but for the Christian liberty of his saints. Both relied ultimately upon their own heartfelt judgments, for which God, but no one else, could hold them responsible. And when, in the final "appeal to heaven" after 1775, God judged for the patriots and pietists, it seemed proof positive that whatever divine right once existed within the British Empire had been corrupted beyond redemption. The power of crown and mitre had passed to the people, and the future site of the millennium had once again moved westward toward its final, and probably imminent, fulfillment. The Peace of Paris brought from the pietists cries of "Come quickly, Lord Jesus" and from the rationalists the belief that the United States of America were "God's last best hope" for mankind. . . .

Once the Rubicon was crossed and the break with Britain made, a new set of circumstances brought political and religious forces into conjunction. Rhetoric had to be put into practice in the construction of bills of rights and state constitutions. Undertaken in the midst of the struggle for independence, these formulations of the social contract required mutual give-and-take if harmony were to be maintained and the needs of all religious persuasions fairly met. The opportunity—the need—to do away with the old established churches necessitated cooperation in the creation of new religious structures in each state.

Having put the ideals of religious liberty into bills of rights, constitutions, and statutes, Americans had then to work them out in practice. Here the pragmatic temper of a frontier people, combined with the multiplicity of sects and a decentralized system of government, enabled a host of different ways of working out the frictions of religious pluralism. . . .

Ultimately the Revolution brought the dissenting sects out of their apolitical pietistic shells and within the pale of political power. Ceasing to be outgroups, they entered the mainstream of the nation as participating partners. The favored status of one Protestant denomination gave way to the equal status of all Protestants. In addition, as colonial boundaries broke down and the nation united, denominations formed interstate or national bodies and sometimes joined formally with other denominations in evangelistic or benevolent activities. Parochialism gave way to wider national horizons. Becoming respected and respectable, dissenters found men of rank and position willing now to join their churches. In the southern states Baptists, Methodists, and Presbyterians rapidly became the dominant denominations not only in numbers but in power and wealth.

These are only the most obvious and general ways in which the Revolution, by breaking the cake of custom and opening new opportunities, interacted with the ideals, the hopes, and the allegiances of all religious groups, uniting individual, sectarian, and local interests to those of the nation at large. . . . Under the urgent need to create one out of many, even Roman Catholics and Jews, the most extreme outsiders, found themselves included in the new nation. Many even talked as though Buddhists and Mohammedans would have been equally welcome.

Yet the harmony was deceptive. Beneath the abstract rhetoric and universal ideals of the Revolution—sufficiently powerful to break the vital bonds to the mother country—there yet remained assumptions, beliefs, and values that were far from universal or absolute. Americans did not cease at once to think like Englishmen, and their cultural heritage and homogeneity produced a very relativistic and ethnocentric definition of religious liberty. The Protestant establishment of the nineteenth century, so obvious to Tocqueville and Lord Bryce, may seem a betrayal of the Revolution if one thinks of Thomas Jefferson as its spokesman or if one reads the religious clauses of the bills of rights and the First Amendment with the deistic gloss that the Supreme Court has applied to them in the twentieth century. But, as I hope to indicate below, Americans were clearly committed to the establishment of a Protestant Christian nation. Religious liberty was to be granted to all, but the spiritual cement that was to hold the nation together had to be Protestant. . . .

The ambiguity of the Revolutionary generation toward religious duties (which were to be enforced) and religious liberty (which was to be untrammeled) has so often been noted that it hardly bears summary: laws requiring respect for the Sabbath and even church attendance were passed but seldom enforced; clergymen were admitted to state office despite prohibitions against it; Jefferson, Madison, and John Leland opposed the payment of federal and state chaplains although many Baptists and other evangelicals proudly accepted such posts; the Northwest Ordinance and Southwest Ordinance utilized federal funds for religious purposes despite the First Amendment; "In God We Trust" was placed on the coins but not in the Constitution; tax exemption was granted to all church property and often to ministers; national days of fasting, thanksgiving, and prayer were regularly proclaimed by some presidents and governors but objected to strenuously by others; and laws against gambling, dueling, theatergoing, and intemperance were debated with varying degrees of religious intensity in various parts of the country for the next century. . . . Heated arguments took place in the age of Jackson over the right of the state to deliver the mail on Sunday. Courts prosecuted citizens for blaspheming against the Christian religion until 1836, and most jurists throughout the nineteenth century believed that Christianity was part of the common law, Jefferson notwithstanding. . . .

The heart of these indecisions, inconsistencies, and contradictions lay in precisely what kinds of "friendly aids" the political fathers might give to the cause of Christianity. And, logically enough, the first great debate about the proper relationship of church and state in the new nation concerned a general assessment for the support of religion. The essence of this debate was encapsulated in the contrast between Jefferson's assertion in the preamble to his act for religious liberty "that even the forcing [a citizen] to support this or that teacher of his own religious persuasion is depriving him of the comfortable liberty of giving his contribution to the particular pastor whose morals he would make his pattern," and George Washington's negative reply to Madison's "Remonstrance": "I must confess that I am not amongst the number of those who are so much alarmed at the thoughts of making people pay toward the support of that which they profess. . . ."

According to the general-assessment concept every citizen would be required to pay a tax in proportion to his wealth for the support of religion (specifically for some form of Protestantism), but each taxpayer could specify to which particular church or minister he wished his religious assessment allocated (presumably to the church or minister he attended upon). Nothingarians, atheists, Roman Catholics, Jews, and other non-Protestants were equally responsible for paying such taxes, but sometimes in order to preserve their rights of conscience various alternatives were suggested for the allocation of their monies. In Virginia one general-assessment plan stated that the non-Protestant might allocate his money to the support of the poor, while another said his taxes would be allocated to public education; the Maryland plan exempted any Jew or Mohammedan who made a declaration of his belief before two justices; in Massachusetts those who did not attend any church had their taxes allocated to the oldest church in their parish (invariably the Congregational church—a fact that led many to assert that the Massachusetts general-assessment plan favored the old establishment). . . .

In view of the defeat of all efforts at general-assessment plans in the southern states, it has frequently been inferred that New England was backward and out of touch with the prevailing current for religious liberty and equality. But seen in the broader context the old Puritan states were going through precisely the same debate and on precisely the same terms. The reasons why the balance tipped in favor of the general-assessment system in New England can be attributed more to historical tradition and practice than to any significant difference of public opinion regarding the importance of compulsory tax support for religion. . . .

Other factors may also account for New England's willingness to try the general-assessment plan. First of all, there were far fewer dissenters in New England, probably less than a fifth in 1780; hence they did not have the votes or the influence to defeat it. Second, the New England Congregational system was a solid and thriving one that, despite the separations during the Great Awakening, remained in firm control of almost every parish. Third, the Congregational clergy, having been staunch supporters of the Revolution, attained increased respect and allegiance during that crisis. And finally, the rulers of Connecticut and Massachusetts may have been somewhat more fearful of social disruption than those of Virginia, where the upper class felt sufficiently secure to accept the dissolution of an ecclesiastical system that had never been very effective anyway. . . .

The avowed commitment of Americans to religious equality gradually produced a kind of tolerated status for Roman Catholics and Jews within the prevailing establishment (similar to that of Presbyterians in colonial Virginia or Anglicans in colonial Massachusetts), [but] Americans were unable to stretch their concept of religious liberty to include such extremes as Mormonism, the American Indian religions, Mohammedanism, or the various Oriental religions. The last two were prevented even from entering the country by one means or another (sometimes called "gentlemen's agreements") on the grounds that they were so outlandish as to be "unassimilable." The Mormons and Indians were forced to conform, the former by a combination of mob, martial, and judicial law, the latter by being treated as incompetent wards of the state whose education was turned over to the various denominations.

If religion in America, institutionalized as incorporated voluntaryism and the Protestant ethic, became so culture-bound as to constitute by the mid-nineteenth century a new form of official establishment, this does not mean that religion became one of the less important aspects of American life. If the American Revolution was a revival, the new nation became a church. Far from being an opiate, religion was an incredible stimulus to the American people.

The First Amendment and Religious Freedom

THOMAS J. CURRY

In 1789 the First Congress of the United States, responding to demands made by several states during the process of ratification of the federal Constitution, set about drawing up a Bill of Rights. By the end of 1791, the required three-fourths of the states had ratified this Bill of Rights in the form of a series of ten amendments to the Constitution. The first of these began with the statement, "Congress shall make no law respecting an establishment of religion, or prohibiting the free exercise thereof." This double declaration embodied the aspirations of many Americans during the colonial era, as well as the general thrust of American attitudes toward Church-State relations manifested during the revolutionary period. The meaning of so emphatic a statement should presumably have been clear; yet the question of the authors' intent has generated voluminous controversy, and the debates leading up to the passage by Congress of the First Amendment continue to raise problems ranging from paradoxical to impenetrable.

In endeavoring to determine the exact significance Congress and the states attached to the opening segment of the First Amendment, one must bear in mind the overall context of its enactment and ratification. . . . Americans in 1789 largely believed that issues of Church and State had been satisfactorily settled by the individual states. They agreed that the federal government had no power in such matters, but some individuals and groups wanted that fact stated explicitly. Granted, not all the states would have concurred on a single definition of religious liberty; but since they were denying power to Congress rather than giving it, differences among them on that score did not bring them into contention. . . .

In his [proposed] series of amendments [to the Constitution], Madison included two dealing with religion. The first proposed:

> The civil rights of none shall be abridged on account of religious belief or worship, nor shall any national religion be established, nor shall the full and equal rights of conscience be in any manner, or on any pretext, infringed.

The second stated that "no State shall violate the equal rights of conscience." . . .

In order to understand Americans' usage of "establishment of religion" in 1789, one has to dispense with two assumptions common to modern commentators, be they supporters or critics of the Supreme Court's definition of the Establishment clause. The first of these is that Americans during the colonial and revolutionary eras made a conscious distinction between two kinds of establishment of religion, between an exclusive state preference for one Church and a nonexclusive assistance to all churches—what historians have subsequently described as a "multiple establishment." The second is that Americans during the same periods actually experienced both kinds of establishment.

The dominant image of establishment Americans carried with them from the colonial period on was that of an exclusive government preference for one religion. Of course, New England Congregationalists, particularly in Massachusetts, contrasted their mild and equitable system with the English tyrannical one, what John Adams described as "creeds, tests, ceremonies, and tythes." Baptists, before and after the Revolution, disagreed with this. They regarded the New England ecclesiastical arrangements as an establishment of Congregationalism and the equivalent of the religious tyranny that Congregationalists decried in England.

After the advent of the Revolution, the supporters of a general assessment introduced a new idea into Church-State relations, a scheme that was genuinely designed to convey state support to the different Christian churches as distinct from the system in colonial New England, which was merely a cover for Congregational dominance. Opponents of a general assessment referred to it as an establishment, and at times its proponents did, too. Neither side, however, attempted to show that a general assessment constituted an essentially different kind of establishment or to differentiate it from an exclusive state preference for one religion. The parties to the general assessment dispute concerned themselves with showing whether it violated or did not violate freedom of religion. For its opponents in Virginia and Maryland, the common suspicion that a general assessment amounted to no more than a ruse to aid the Anglican Church only strengthened their assumption that it represented an extension of the traditional establishment. . . .

Moreover, during the revolutionary period, when Americans, irrespective of their stance on Church and State, spoke of banning the establishment of a particular sect or church in preference to others, they were not advocating a particular party viewpoint on establishment but employing an inherited terminology. Eighteenth-century American history offers abundant examples of writers using the concept of preference, when, in fact, they were referring to a ban on all government assistance to religion. . . .

This common image explains the discussion of establishment surrounding the Bill of Rights. James Madison and Patrick Henry, although they differed diametrically over the issue of government aid to religion, used the same words to describe establishment. When Madison spoke of prohibiting a "national" religion, he was not opening the door to the federal government's aid to religion in general. When Henry called for a ban on the establishment of one sect "in preference to others," he was not proposing that the federal government have the power to tax for a national general assessment. A purely literalist approach to the language used by Americans in colonial and revolutionary times in connection with the establishment of religion leads only to confusion. For instance, when Anti-Federalists in Pennsylvania petitioned the Pennsylvania Convention that "none should be compelled contrary to their principles . . . to hear or support the clergy of any one religion," they were certainly not implying that people could be compelled to hear and support the clergy of several or all religions. Similarly, when those connected with the passage of the Bill of Rights spoke or wrote of an establishment of religion as government imposition of one sect or articles of faith, they were not implying that government could favor all sects or sponsor religion short of imposing a creed on the populace. . . .

Thus the debate in Congress represented not a clash between parties arguing for a "broad" or "narrow" interpretation or between those who wished to give the federal government more or less power in religious matters. It represented rather a discussion about how to state the common agreement that the new government had no authority whatsoever in religious matters. . . .

The passage of the First Amendment constituted a symbolic act, a declaration for the future, an assurance to those nervous about the federal government that it was not going to reverse any of the guarantees for religious liberty won by the revolutionary states. Because it was making explicit the non-existence of a power, not regulating or curbing one that existed, Congress approached the subject in a somewhat hasty and absentminded manner. To examine the two clauses of the amendment as a carefully worded analysis of Church-State relations would be to overburden them. Similarly, to see the two clauses as separate, balanced, competing, or carefully worked out prohibitions designed to meet different eventualities would be to read into the minds of the actors far more than was there. Scholars sometimes argue, for instance, that the "Free Exercise" clause was intended to address different instances than the "Establishment" clause, and the Supreme Court has repeatedly struck down government interference with religion as a violation of the "Free Exercise" clause and government aid to religion as a violation of the "Establishment" clause.

The two clauses represented a double declaration of what Americans wanted to assert about Church and State. Congress settled on the wording of the Amendment because it probably found the phrases the most felicitous-sounding of those proposed; but any of the other formats offered would have served its substantive purpose equally well. . . .

The vast majority of Americans assumed that theirs was a Christian, i.e., Protestant, country, and they automatically expected that government would uphold the commonly agreed on Protestant ethos and morality. In many instances, they had not come to grips with the implications their belief in the powerlessness of government in religious matters held for a society in which the values, customs, and forms of Protestant Christianity thoroughly permeated civil and political life. The contradiction between their theory and their practice became evident to Americans only later, with the advent of a more religiously pluralistic society, when it became the subject of a disputation that continues into the present.

In a few specific areas, however, Americans did during the revolutionary period work out specific practical applications of their theories on Church and State. The inhabitants of all the states decided that government had no power to prohibit the free exercise of peaceable religion. All states agreed with Jefferson that civil government could interfere when "principles break out into overt acts against peace & good order"; but otherwise, citizens had a right to practice the religions of their choice, even the hated Catholicism, which had been proscribed in colonial America.

On one other question, the financial support of religion, Americans also clarified the application of their Church-State principles. The vast majority of them believed with the Continental Congress that "true religion and good morals are the only solid foundation of public liberty and happiness." Throughout the states, individuals and government bodies issued similar statements. From this premise, however, they drew differing conclusions. Some legislators, such as those in Massachusetts, decided that since good government depended on morality and piety, government should inculcate those virtues by seeing that churches and ministers were financially provided for. Others, such as those in Virginia, while agreeing with the necessity of virtue and religion for civil society, reasoned that if religion were to remain healthy, it had to remain free from the interfering hand of government. This, together with the secular viewpoint that "our civil rights have no dependence on our religious opinions," undergirded the argument for voluntarism.

Between these two positions the states divided sharply, and in 1785 a hint of this division surfaced over a plan of the Continental Congress for settling the western lands. A committee of that Congress, dominated by New Englanders, proposed that lot number twenty-nine of each township be set aside for the "support of religion" or for charitable purposes, the determination to be made by the majority of the male inhabitants of each township. The full Congress voted down this provision for the support of religion, and Madison, in a letter to James Monroe, wrote of it:

> How a regulation so unjust in itself, so foreign to the authority of Congress,
> so hurtful to the sale of public land, and smelling so strongly of antiquated
> bigotry, could have received the countenance of a committee is truly a
> matter of astonishment.

Even so, in July 1787, while Madison was attending the Constitutional Convention, Congress approved the sale of large tracts of land to a New England land speculator, the Reverend Manasseh Cutler, with the provision that lot number twenty-nine of each township be given for the support of religion.

Of the eleven states that ratified the First Amendment, nine (counting Maryland) adhered to the viewpoint that support of religion and churches should be voluntary, that any government financial assistance to religion constituted an establishment of religion and violated its free exercise. Some had done so from their earliest foundations; some arrived at that stance after the American Revolution. The Maryland constitution permitted a general assessment to support religion, but Marylanders firmly rejected a proposal to enact one. Of the ratifying states, only Vermont and New Hampshire adhered to the view that states could or should provide for tax-supported religion. On a whole range of other applications, however, Americans inherited traditions of government interference in religious matters. . . .

The meaning of free exercise of religion and establishment of religion in 1789 must be examined within the historical matrix that produced these concepts. . . . It meant at least this: that each citizen had a right to the free exercise of his or her religion as long as it did not "break out into overt acts against peace and order." Further, the people of almost every state that ratified the First Amendment believed that religion should be maintained and supported voluntarily. They saw government attempts to organize and regulate such support as a usurpation of power, as a violation of liberty of conscience and free exercise of religion, and as falling within the scope of what they termed an establishment of religion.

✕ F U R T H E R   R E A D I N G

Sidney E. Ahlstrom, *A Religious History of the American People* (1972)

John F. Berens, *Providence and Patriotism in Early America, 1640–1815* (1978)

Ruth H. Bloch, *Visionary Republic: Millennial Themes in American Thought, 1756–1800* (1985)

Patricia U. Bonomi, *Under the Cope of Heaven: Religion, Society, and Politics in Colonial America* (1986)

Carl Bridenbaugh, *Mitre and Sceptre: Transatlantic Faiths, Ideas, Personalities, and Politics, 1689–1775* (1962)

Thomas E. Buckley, *Church and State in Revolutionary Virginia, 1776–1787* (1977)

Jon Butler, *Awash in a Sea of Faith: Christianizing the American People* (1990)

Thomas J. Curry, *The First Freedoms: Church and State in America to the Passage of the First Amendment* (1986)

Nathan O. Hatch, *The Sacred Cause of Liberty: Republican Thought and the Millennium in Revolutionary New England* (1988)

———, *The Democratization of American Christianity* (1989)

Alan Heimert, *Religion and the American Mind from the Great Awakening to the Revolution* (1966)

Rhys Isaac, *The Transformation of Virginia, 1740–1790* (1982)

David S. Lovejoy, *Religious Enthusiasm in the New World: Heresy to Revolution* (1985)

William G. McLoughlin, *New England Dissent, 1630–1833: The Baptists and the Separation of Church and State* (1971)

Stephen A. Marini, *Radical Sects of Revolutionary New England* (1982)

Sidney E. Mead, *The Old Religion in the Brave New World: Reflections on the Relation Between Christendom and the Republic* (1977)

William Lee Miller, *The First Liberty: Religion and the American Republic* (1986)

Richard W. Pointer, *Protestant Pluralism and the New York Experience: A Study of Eighteenth-Century Religious Diversity* (1988)

Robert A. Rutland, *The Birth of the Bill of Rights, 1776–1791* (1955)

Charles B. Sanford, *The Religious Life of Thomas Jefferson* (1984)

Bernard Schwartz, *The Great Rights of Mankind: A History of the American Bill of Rights* (1977)

Sally Schwartz, *A Mixed Multitude: The Struggle for Toleration in Colonial Pennsylvania* (1987)

Harry S. Stout, *The New England Soul: Preaching and Religious Culture in Colonial New England* (1986)

Donald Weber, *Rhetoric and History in Revolutionary New England* (1988)

The Articles of
Confederation and the
Achievements of National Union,
1781–1787

✕

While Americans were confronting some of the unexpected social implications of their revolution, such as the place of women, African-Americans, and religion in the new republic, the mundane affairs of peacetime government went on. Commercial and foreign policy, public finance, and western land all demanded attention. In Congress, now sitting under the mandate of the Articles of Confederation (whose ratification was completed in 1781), all of these issues were addressed by delegates representing different interests and viewpoints. Although substantial obstacles, both political and structural, impeded their work, they made some headway in the formulation of national policy, especially in relation to western lands.

The history of this Confederation era, once called the critical period, has been dominated by the Federalist belief that the Articles of Confederation were a failure and that the Constitution of 1787 rescued the nation. Indeed, celebrating the Constitution is part of the national culture of the United States, whereas the Articles are widely forgotten, resurrected for praise mostly by champions of states' rights or critics of national policies. But the fact that the Articles of Confederation laid the foundation for the later Constitution and that the national government began during its tenure should lead to the recognition that this earlier blueprint for a national government shared much in common with the Constitution and was by no means its opposite. During the Constitution-ratification controversy and subsequently, it has been convenient rhetorically to picture the two frames of government as polar opposites: the Articles as weak, divided, and consensual; the Constitution as strong, united, and majoritarian. But in this case, the rhetoric clouds precise understanding.

In reality, strong continuities ran through the two governments. Considera-tion of the text of the Articles of Confederation, and of the politics surrounding government land policy, reveals the political principles and the practical realities of national government in the new republic of the 1780s. Complaints of frustra-tion were certainly part of an open, representative government, but so was the noteworthy achievement of the Northwest Ordinance.

✂ D O C U M E N T S

The first document, the Articles of Confederation, is a landmark in American constitutional history. Drafted by the Pennsylvanian John Dickinson (author of the *Farmer's Letters*) at the direction of Congress in 1777, the frame of govern-ment was finally ratified in 1781, after Maryland successfully insisted that states with western land claims cede them to the national government. Although the whole Confederation plan differs in some essential ways from the Constitution, several of its articles were brought into the later document almost intact. More-over, the principle of majority rule, not unanimous consensus, was clearly estab-lished in the plan.

The next two selections treat the controversy over the disposition of the west-ern lands—how they were to be surveyed, sold, and settled. The plan that Con-gress established in 1785, reprinted as the fourth selection, has had a powerful impact on the history and human ecology of the entire United States. The fifth and sixth documents, in which frustration with Congress's operations is evident, concern the Northwest Ordinance of 1787, the last major achievement of the Confederation. The Ordinance itself, the final selection, is notable for its provi-sions for the addition of future states, for its exclusion of slavery, and for its pro-tection of slavery elsewhere in its provision for the return of fugitive slaves.

The Articles of Confederation and Perpetual Union, 1781

Articles of Confederation and Perpetual Union Between the States of New Hampshire, Massachusetts Bay, Rhode Island and Providence Plantations, Connecticut, New York, New Jersey, Pennsylvania, Delaware, Maryland, Virginia, North Carolina, South Carolina, and Georgia

Article One

The style of this Confederacy shall be "The United States of America."

Article Two

Each State retains its sovereignty, freedom, and independence, and every power, jurisdiction, and right, which is not by this Confederation expressly delegated to the United States in Congress assembled.

Article Three

The said States hereby severally enter into a firm league of friendship with each other, for their common defence, the security of their liberties, and their mutual and general welfare, binding themselves to assist each other against all force offered to, or attacks made upon them, or any of them, on account of religion, sovereignty, trade, or any other pretence whatever.

Article Four

The better to secure and perpetuate mutual friendship and intercourse among the people of the different States in this Union, the free inhabitants of each of these States, paupers, vagabonds, and fugitives from justice excepted, shall be entitled to all the privileges and immunities of free citizens in the several States, and the people of each State shall have free ingress and regress to and from any other State, and shall enjoy therein all the privileges of trade and commerce, subject to the same duties, impositions, and restrictions as the inhabitants thereof respectively, provided that such restrictions shall not extend so far as to prevent the removal of property imported into any State, to any other State of which the owner is an inhabitant; provided also, that no imposition, duties, or restriction shall be laid by any State, on the property of the United States, or either of them.

If any person guilty of or charged with treason, felony, or other high misdemeanor in any State, shall flee from justice, and be found in any of the United States, he shall, upon demand of the governor or executive power of the State from which he fled, be delivered up and removed to the State having jurisdiction of his offence.

Full faith and credit shall be given in each of these States to the records, acts, and judicial proceedings of the courts and magistrates of every other State.

Article Five

For the more convenient management of the general interests of the United States, delegates shall be annually appointed in such manner as the legislature of each State shall direct, to meet in Congress on the first Monday in November, in every year, with a power reserved to each State to recall its delegates, or any of them, at any time within the year, and to send others in their stead, for the remainder of the year.

No State shall be represented in Congress by less than two, nor by more than seven members; and no person shall be capable of being a delegate for more than three years in any term of six years, nor shall any person, being a delegate, be capable of holding any office under the United States for which he or another for his benefit receives any salary, fees, or emolument of any kind.

Each State shall maintain its own delegates in a meeting of the States, and while they act as members of the committee of the States.

In determining questions in the United States, in Congress assembled, each State shall have one vote.

Freedom of speech and debate in Congress shall not be impeached or questioned in any court or place out of Congress, and the members of Congress shall be protected in their persons from arrests and imprisonments, during the time of their going to or from, and attendance on, Congress, except for treason, felony, or breach of the peace.

Article Six

No State, without the consent of the United States in Congress assembled, shall send any embassy to, or receive any embassy from, or enter into any conference, agreement, alliance, or treaty with, any king, prince, or state; nor shall any person holding any office of profit or trust under the United States, or any of them, accept of any present, emolument, office, or title of any kind whatever from any king, prince, or foreign state; nor shall the United States in Congress assembled, or any of them, grant any title of nobility.

No two or more States shall enter into any treaty, confederation, or alliance whatever between them, without the consent of the United States in Congress assembled, specifying accurately the purposes for which the same is to be entered into, and how long it shall continue.

No State shall lay any imposts or duties, which may interfere with any stipulations in treaties entered into by the United States in Congress assembled, with any king, prince, or state, in pursuance of any treaties already proposed by Congress, to the courts of France and Spain.

No vessels of war shall be kept in time of peace by any State, except such number only as shall be deemed necessary by the United States in Congress assembled, for the defence of such State or its trade; nor shall any body of forces be kept up by any State, in time of peace, except such number only as in the judgment of the United States in Congress assembled shall be deemed requisite to garrison the forts necessary for the defence of such State; but every State shall always keep up a well regulated and disciplined militia, sufficiently armed and accoutred, and shall provide and constantly have ready for use, in public stores, a due number of field-pieces and tents, and a proper quantity of arms, ammunition, and camp equipage.

No State shall engage in any war without the consent of the United States in Congress assembled, unless such State be actually invaded by enemies, or shall have received certain advice of a resolution being formed by some nation of Indians to invade such State, and the danger is so imminent as not to admit of a delay till the United States in Congress assembled can be consulted; nor shall any State grant commissions to any ships or vessels of war, nor letters of marque or reprisal, except it be after a declaration of war by the United States in Congress assembled, and then only against the kingdom or state, and the subjects thereof, against which war has been so declared, and under such regulations as shall be established by the United States in Congress assembled, unless such State be infested by pirates, in which case vessels of war may be fitted out for that occasion, and kept so long as the danger shall continue, or until the United States in Congress assembled shall determine otherwise.

Article Seven

When land forces are raised by any State for the common defense, all officers of or under the rank of colonel shall be appointed by the legislature of each State respectively, by whom such forces shall be raised, or in such manner as such State shall direct; and all vacancies shall be filled up by the State which first made the appointment.

Article Eight

All charges of war and all other expenses that shall be incurred for the common defence or general welfare, and allowed by the United States in Congress assembled, shall be defrayed out of a common treasury, which shall be supplied by the several States, in proportion to the value of all land within each State, granted to or surveyed for any person, and such land and the buildings and improvements thereon shall be estimated according to such mode as the United States in Congress assembled shall from time to time direct and appoint.

The taxes for paying that proportion shall be laid and levied by the authority and direction of the legislatures of the several States within the time agreed upon by the United States in Congress assembled.

Article Nine

The United States in Congress assembled shall have the sole and exclusive right and power of determining on peace and war, except in the cases mentioned in the sixth article—of sending and receiving ambassadors— entering into treaties and alliances, provided that no treaty of commerce shall be made whereby the legislative power of the respective States shall be restrained from imposing such imposts and duties on foreigners as their own people are subjected to, or from prohibiting the exportation or im- portation of any species of goods or commodities whatsoever—of estab- lishing rules for deciding, in all cases, what captures on land or water shall be legal, and in what manner prizes taken by land or naval forces in the service of the United States shall be divided or appropriated—of granting letters of marque and reprisal in times of peace—appointing courts for the trial of piracies and felonies committed on the high seas, and establishing courts for receiving and determining finally appeals in all cases of captures, provided that no member of Congress shall be appointed a judge of any of the said courts.

The United States in Congress assembled shall also be the last resort on appeal in all disputes and differences now subsisting or that hereafter may arise between two or more States concerning boundary, jurisdiction, or any other cause whatever; which authority shall always be exercised in the manner following:—Whenever the legislative or executive authority or lawful agent of any State in controversy with another shall present a petition to Congress stating the matter in question and praying for a hearing, notice thereof shall be given by order of Congress to the legislative or executive authority of the other State in controversy, and a day assigned for the appearance of the parties by their lawful agents, who shall then be directed to appoint, by joint consent, commissioners or judges to constitute a court for hearing and determining the matter in question; but if they cannot agree, Congress shall name three persons out of each of the United States, and from the list of such persons each party shall alternately strike out one, the petitioners beginning, until the number shall be reduced to thirteen; and from that number not less than seven nor more than nine names, as Congress shall direct, shall, in the presence of Congress, be drawn out by lot, and the persons whose names shall be so drawn, or any five of them, shall be commissioners or judges, to hear and finally determine the controversy, so always as a major part of the judges who shall hear the cause shall agree in the determination; and if either party shall neglect to attend at the day appointed, without showing reasons, which Congress shall judge sufficient, or, being present, shall refuse to strike, the Congress shall proceed to nominate three persons out of each State, and the Secretary of Congress shall strike in behalf of such party absent or refusing; and the judgment and sentence of the court to be appointed, in the manner before prescribed, shall be final and conclusive; and if any of the parties shall refuse to submit to the authority of such court, or to appear or defend their claim or cause, the court shall nevertheless proceed to pronounce sentence or judgment, which shall in like manner be final and decisive, the judgment or sentence and other proceedings being in either case transmitted to Congress, and lodged among the acts of Congress for the security of the parties concerned: provided that every commissioner, before he sits in judgment, shall take an oath, to be administered by one of the judges of the Supreme or Superior Court of the State where the cause shall be tried, *"well and truly to hear and determine the matter in question according to the best of his judgment, without favor, affection, or hope of reward,"* provided also that no State shall be deprived territory for the benefit of the United States.

All controversies concerning the private right of soil, claimed under different grants of two or more States, whose jurisdictions as they may respect such lands and the States which passed such grants are adjusted, the said grants or either of them being at the same time claimed to have originated antecedent to such settlement of jurisdiction, shall, on the petition of either party to the Congress of the United States, be finally determined as near as may be in the same manner as is before prescribed for deciding disputes respecting territorial jurisdiction between different States.

The United States in Congress assembled shall also have the sole and exclusive right and power of regulating the alloy and value of coin struck by their own authority, or by that of the respective States—fixing the standard of weights and measures throughout the United States—regulating the trade and managing all affairs with the Indians, not members of any of the States, provided that the legislative right of any State within its own limits be not infringed or violated—establishing and regulating post-offices from one State to another, throughout all the United States, and exacting such postage on the papers passing through the same as may be requisite to defray the expenses of the said office—appointing all officers of the land forces in the service of the United States, excepting regimental officers—appointing all the officers of the naval forces, and commissioning all officers whatever in the service of the United States—making rules for the government and regulation of the said land and naval forces, and directing their operations.

The United States in Congress assembled shall have authority to appoint a committee, to sit in the recess of Congress, to be denominated "A Committee of the States," and to consist of one delegate from each State; to appoint such other committees and civil officers as may be necessary for managing the general affairs of the United States under their direction; and to appoint one of their number to preside, provided that no person be allowed to serve in the office of president more than one year in any term of three years—to ascertain the necessary sums of money to be raised for the service of the United States, and to appropriate and apply the same for defraying the public expenses—to borrow money, or emit bills on the credit of the United States, transmitting every half-year to the respective States an account of the sums of money so borrowed or emitted—to build and equip a navy— to agree upon the number of land forces, and to make requisitions from each State for its quota, in proportion to the number of white inhabitants in such State; which requisition shall be binding, and thereupon the legislature of each State shall appoint the regimental officers, raise the men, and clothe, arm, and equip them in a soldier-like manner, at the expense of the United States, and the officers and men so clothed, armed, and equipped shall march to the place appointed, and within the time agreed on by the United States in Congress assembled; but if the United States in Congress assembled shall, on consideration of circumstances, judge proper that any State should not raise men, or should raise a smaller number than its quota, and that any other State should raise a greater number of men than the quota thereof, such extra number shall be raised, officered, clothed, armed, and equipped in the same manner as the quota of such State, unless the legislature of such State shall judge that such extra number cannot be safely spared out of the same, in which case they shall raise, officer, clothe, arm, and equip as many of such extra number as they judge can be safely spared: and the officers and men, so clothed, armed, and equipped shall march to the place appointed, and within the time agreed on, by the United States in Congress assembled.

The United States in Congress assembled shall never engage in a war, nor grant letters of marque and reprisal in time of peace, nor enter into any treaties or alliances, nor coin money, nor regulate the value thereof, nor ascertain the sums and expenses necessary for the defence and welfare of the United States, or any of them, nor emit bills, nor borrow money on the credit of the United States, nor appropriate money, nor agree upon the number of vessels of war to be built or purchased, or the number of land or sea forces to be raised, nor appoint a commander-in-chief of the army or navy, unless nine States assent to the same; nor shall a question on any other point, except for adjourning from day to day, be determined, unless by the votes of a majority of the United States in Congress assembled.

The Congress of the United States shall have power to adjourn to any time within the year, and to any place within the United States, so that no period of adjournment be for a longer duration than the space of six months, and shall publish the journal of their proceedings monthly, except such parts thereof relating to treaties, alliances, or military operations, as in their judgment require secrecy, and the yeas and nays of the delegates of each State on any question shall be entered on the journal, when it is desired by any delegate; and the delegates of a State, or any of them, at his or their request, shall be furnished with a transcript of the said journal, except such parts as are above excepted to lay before the legislatures of the several States.

Article Ten

The Committee of the States, or any nine of them, shall be authorized to execute, in the recess of Congress, such of the powers of Congress as the United States in Congress assembled, by the consent of nine States, shall from time to time think expedient to vest them with: provided that no power be delegated to the said Committee, for the exercise of which, by the Articles of Confederation, the voice of nine States in the Congress of the United States assembled is requisite.

Article Eleven

Canada, acceding to this Confederation, and joining in the measures of the United States, shall be admitted into and entitled to all the advantages of this Union; but no other colony shall be admitted into the same, unless such admission be agreed to by nine States.

Article Twelve

All bills of credit emitted, moneys borrowed, and debts contracted by or under the authority of Congress, before the assembling of the United States in pursuance of the present Confederation, shall be deemed and considered as a charge against the United States, for payment and satisfaction whereof the said United States and the public faith are hereby solemnly pledged.

Article Thirteen

Every State shall abide by the determinations of the United States in Congress assembled, on all questions which by this Confederation are submitted to them. And the Articles of this Confederation shall be inviolably observed by every State, and the Union shall be perpetual; nor shall any alteration at any time hereafter be made in any of them, unless such alteration be agreed to in a Congress of the United States, and be afterwards confirmed by the legislatures of every State.

AND WHEREAS it hath pleased the Great Governor of the world to incline the hearts of the legislatures we respectfully represent in Congress to approve of and to authorize us to ratify the said Articles of Confederation and perpetual Union, Know Ye, That we, the undersigned delegates, by virtue of the power and authority to us given for that purpose, do by these presents, in the name and in behalf of our respective constituents, fully and entirely ratify and confirm each and every of the said Articles of Confederation and perpetual Union, and all and singular the matters and things therein contained: and we do further solemnly plight and engage the faith of our respective constituents that they shall abide by the determinations of the United States in Congress assembled, on all questions which by the said Confederation are submitted to them. And that the Articles thereof shall be inviolably observed by the States we respectively represent, and the Union shall be perpetual.

A Virginia Congressman Reports on the Western Land Ordinance, 1785

William Grayson to George Washington

NEW YORK Ap'l 15th 1785

Dear Sir, . . .

The Ordnance was reported to Congress three days ago, and ordered to be printed, and I now take the earliest opportunity of sending you a copy; the idea of a sale by public Vendue, in such large quantities, appears at first view eccentric, and objectionable; I shall therefore mention to you the reasons which those who are advocates for the measure offer in it's support; They say this cannot be avoided with't affording an undue advantage to those whose contiguity to the territory has given them an opportunity of investigating the qualities of the land; That there certainly must be a difference in the value of the lands in different parts of the country, and that this difference cannot be ascertained with't an actual survey in the first instance and a sale by competition in the next.

That with respect to the quantity of land offered for sale in a township, it will not have the effects of injuring the poorer class of people, or of establishing monopolies in speculators and ingrossers: That experience is directly agt. the inference, for that the Eastern States, where lands are more equally divided than in any other part of the Continent were generally settled in that manner; That the idea of a township with the temptation of a support for religion and education, holds forth an inducement for neighborhoods of the same religious sentiments to confederate for the purpose of purchasing and settling together; That the Southern mode would defeat this end by introducing the idea of indiscriminate locations and settlements, which would have a tendency to destroy all those inducements to emigration which are derived from friendships, religion and relative connections; That the same consequence would result from sales in small quantities under the present plan;

That the advantages of an equal representation, the effect of laying off the country in this manner; the exemption from controversy on account of bounds to the latest ages; the fertility of the lands; the facilities of communication with the Atlantic through a variety of channels, as also with the British and Spaniards; the fur and peltry trade; and the right of forming free governments for themselves, must solicit emigrants from all parts of the world, and ensure a settlement of the country in the most rapid manner; That speculators and ingrossers, if they purchase the lands in the first instance cannot long retain them, on account of the high price they will be obliged to give and the consequent loss of interest while remaining in their hands uncultivated;

That if they however should make money by ingrossing, the great design of the land office is answered, which is revenue; and that this cannot affect any but European emigrants or those who were not at hand to purchase in the first instance; that if it is an evil, it will cure itself, which has been the case in Lincoln County Virginia, where the lands were first in the hands of Monopolists: but who were forced to part with them from a regard to the general defense. . . .

That the offering a small number of townships for sale at a time is an answer to the objection on account of delay and at the same time it prevents the price from being diminished on acct. of the Markets being overstocked. . . .

That the drawing for the townships and sending them on to the different States is conformable to the principles of the government, one State having an equal right to the best lands at its market with the other, as also of disposing of it's public securities in that way.

That if the Country is to be settled out of the bowels of the Atlantic States it is but fair the idea of each State's contributing it's proportion of emigrants should be countenanced by measures operating for that purpose.

That if the plan should be found by experience to be wrong, it can easily be altered by reducing the quantities and multiplying the surveys.

These were the principal reasonings on the Comm'ee in favor of the measure. . . . Some gentlemen looked upon it as a matter of revenue only and that it was true policy to get the money with't parting with inhabitants to populate the Country, and thereby prevent the lands in the original states from depreciating. Others (I think) were afraid of an interference with the lands now at market in the individual States. part of the Eastern Gentlemen wish to have the lands sold in such a manner as to suit their own people who may chuse to emigrate, of which I believe there will be great numbers particularly from Connecticut: But others are apprehensive of the consequences which may result from the new States taking their position in the

Confederacy. They perhaps wish that this event may be delayed as long as possible. Seven hundred men are agreed on, in Congress; to be raised for the purpose of protecting the settlers on the Western frontiers and preventing unwarrantable intrusions on the public lands; and for guarding the public stores.

William Grayson to James Madison

NEW YORK May 28th, 1785

Dear Sir, . . .

I inclose you a copy of the Ordinance: and if it is not the best in the world, it is I am confident the best that could be procured for the present: There was such a variety of interests most of them imaginary, that I am only surprised it is not more defective.

The Eastern people who before the revolution never had an idea of any quantity of Earth above a hundred acres, were for selling in large tracts of 30,000 acres while the Southern people who formerly could scarce bring their imaginations down so low as to comprehend the meaning of a hundred acres of ground were for selling the whole territory in lots of a mile square.

In this situation we remained for eight days, with great obstinacy on both sides, untill a kind of compromise took effect.

New Hampshire's Congressional Delegates Report on the Western Land Ordinance, 1785

New Hampshire Delegates to the President of New Hampshire (Meshech Weare)

NEW YORK May 29th, 1785

Sir,

We have the honor of transmitting to your Excellency . . . the ordinance opening a land office in the several states which passed . . . by the unanimous voice of all the States present—and we flatter ourselves is so adjusted as to give satisfaction to the State we have the honor to represent and at the same time we have the most confident expectation that in its operation it will considerably diminish the domestic debt by absorbing a great number of the public securities. The general opinion of the goodness of the soil in this western country and of the happy temperature of the climate, has been increasing with every new investigation of it, and we think it beyond a doubt that many of the creditors of the United States in the middle and southern parts of the Union have fixed their attention to this as a fund from which they shall soon be able to pay themselves. We submit it to the citizens of New Hampshire whether associations may not be formed for the purchase of townships in this territory for future settlements or dispositions with advantag[e] the distance notwithstanding. It was the inclination of the eastern states in conformity to the usual mode of locating lands in that part of the country by townships, to have adhered to that method throughout the whole country to be disposed of by the ordinance but as a different method had always been adopted to the southward, it became necessary to agree to alternate by lots and townships on the principle of compromise.

Congress Passes an Ordinance on Western Lands, 1785

An Ordinance for Ascertaining the Mode of Disposing of Lands in the Western Territory, May 20, 1785

Be it ordained by the United States in Congress assembled, that the territory ceded by individual States to the United States, which has been purchased of the Indian inhabitants, shall be disposed of in the following manner: . . .

The Surveyors, as they are respectively qualified, shall proceed to divide the said territory into townships of six miles square, by lines running due north and south, and others crossing these at right angles, as near as may be, unless where the boundaries of the late Indian purchases may render the same impracticable, and then they shall depart from this rule no farther than such particular circumstances may require; and each surveyor shall be allowed and paid at the rate of two dollars for every mile, in length, he shall run, including the wages of chain carriers, markers, and every other expense attending the same.

The first line, running north and south as aforesaid, shall begin on the river Ohio. . . .

The plats of the townships respectively, shall be marked by subdivisions into lots of one mile square, or 640 acres, in the same direction as the external lines, and numbered from 1 to 36; . . .

As soon as seven ranges of townships, and fractional parts of townships, in the direction from south to north, shall have been surveyed, the geographer shall transmit plats thereof to the board of treasury, who shall record the same, with the report, in well bound books to be kept for that purpose. . . . The Secretary at War shall have recourse thereto, and shall take by lot therefrom, a number of townships, . . . as will be equal to one seventh part of the whole of such seven ranges . . . for the use of the late continental army. . . . The board of treasury shall, from time to time, cause the remaining numbers, as well those to be sold entire, as those to be sold in lots, to be drawn for, in the name of the thirteen states respectively, according to the quotas in the last preceding requisition on all the states . . . provided, that none of the lands . . . be sold under the price of one dollar the acre, to be paid in specie, or loan office certificates, reduced to specie value . . . including interest, besides the expense of the survey and other charges thereon, which are hereby rated at thirty six dollars the township, in specie, or certificates as aforesaid, and so in the same proportion for a fractional part of a township, or of a lot, to be paid at the time of sales; on failure of which payment, the said lands shall again be offered for sale.

There shall be reserved for the United States out of every township, the four lots, being numbered 8, 11, 26, 29 . . . for future sale. There shall be reserved the lot N 16, of every township, for the maintenance of public schools, within the said township; also one third part of all gold, silver, lead and copper mines, to be sold, or otherwise disposed of as Congress shall hereafter direct.

A Virginia Representative Complains of General Congressional Inertia, 1787

Richard Henry Lee to Francis Lightfoot Lee

New York July 14th, 1787

My Dear Brother,

I arrived at this place [New York City] a week ago almost destroyed with heat and fatigue. Here I found [William] Grayson [a Virginia delegate] in the Chair of Congress . . . for the President who is absent. After some difficulty we passed an Ordinance for establishing a temporary Government beyond the Ohio as preparatory to the sale of that Country. And now we are considering an offer made to purchase 5 or 6 Millions of Acres with pub. Securities. I hope we shall agree with the Offer, but realy the difficulty is so great to get anything done, that it is not easy for the plainest propositions to succeed. We owe much money, the pressure of Taxes is very great and much complained of. we have now something to sell that will pay the debt and discharge the greatest part of the Taxes, and altho this something is in a fair way of being soon wrested from us by the Sons of Violence, yet we have a thousand *little* difficulties that prevent us from selling!

A Massachusetts Representative Reports Progress in Drafting the Northwest Ordinance, 1787

Nathan Dane to Rufus King

New York, July 16, 1787

Dear Sir, . . .

With pleasure I communicate to you what we are doing in Congress, not so much from a consciousness that what we do is well done, as from a desire that you may be acquainted with our proceedings. We have been much engaged in business for ten or twelve days, for a part of which we have had eight States. There appears to be a disposition to do business and the arrival of R. H. Lee is of considerable importance. I think his character serves, at least in some degree, to check the effects of the feeble habits and lax mode of thinking of some of his countrymen. We have been employed about several objects, the principal of which have been the government inclosed and the Ohio purchase; the former you will see is completed, and the latter will probably be completed tomorrow. . . . The Ohio company appeared to purchase a large tract of federal lands—about six or seven millions of acres—and we wanted to abolish the old system and get a better one for the government of the country, and we finally found it necessary to adopt the best system we could get. All agreed finally to the inclosed plan except A. Yates. He appeared in this case, as in most others, not to understand the subject at all. I think the number of free inhabitants, 60,000, which are requisite for the admission of a new State into the Confederacy, is too small; but, having divided the whole Territory into three States, this number appears to me to be less important. Each State in the common course of things must become important soon after it shall have that number of inhabitants. The Eastern State of the three will probably be the first, and more important than the rest, and will no doubt be settled chiefly by Eastern people; and there is, I think, full an equal chance of its adopting Eastern politics. When I drew the ordinance (which passed, a few words excepted, as I originally formed it) I had no idea the States would agree to the sixth article, prohibiting slavery, as only Massachusetts of the Eastern States, was present, and therefore omitted it in the draft; but finding the House favorably disposed on this subject, after we had completed the other parts, I moved the article, which was agreed to without opposition. We are in a fair way to fix the terms of our Ohio sale, etc. We have been upon it three days steadily. The magnitude of the purchase makes us very cautious about the terms of it and the security necessary to insure the performance of it.

The Northwest Ordinance, 1787

An Ordinance for the Government of the Territory of the United States Northwest of the River Ohio

Section 1. Be it ordained by the United States in Congress assembled, That the said territory, for the purposes of temporary government, be one district, subject, however, to be divided into two districts, as future circumstances may, in the opinion of Congress, make it expedient. . . .

Sec. 3. Be it ordained by the authority aforesaid, That there shall be appointed, from time to time, by Congress, a governor, whose commission shall continue in force for the term of three years, unless sooner revoked by Congress; he shall reside in the district, and have a freehold estate therein in one thousand acres of land, while in the exercise of his office.

Sec. 4. There shall be appointed from time to time, by Congress, a secretary, whose commission shall continue in force for four years, unless sooner revoked; he shall reside in the district, and have a freehold estate therein, in five hundred acres of land, while in the exercise of his office. . . . There shall also be appointed a court, to consist of three judges, any two of whom to form a court, who shall have a common-law jurisdiction, and reside in the district, and have each therein a freehold estate, in five hundred acres of land, while in the exercise of their offices; and their commissions shall continue in force during good behavior.

Sec. 5. The governor and judges, or a majority of them, shall adopt and publish in the district such laws of the original States, criminal and civil, as may be necessary, and best suited to the circumstances of the district, and report them to Congress from time to time, which laws shall be in force in the district until the organization of the general assembly therein, unless disapproved of by Congress; but afterwards the legislature shall have authority to alter them as they shall think fit.

Sec. 6. The governor, for the time being, shall be commander-in-chief of the militia, appoint and commission all officers in the same below the rank of general officers; all general officers shall be appointed and commissioned by Congress.

Sec. 7. Previous to the organization of the general assembly the governor shall appoint such magistrates, and other civil officers, in each county or township, as he shall find necessary for the preservation of the peace and good order in the same. After the general assembly shall be organized the powers and duties of the magistrates and other civil officers shall be regulated and defined by the said assembly; but all magistrates and other civil officers, not herein otherwise directed, shall, during the continuance of this temporary government, be appointed by the governor. . . .

Sec. 9. So soon as there shall be five thousand free male inhabitants, of full age, in the district, upon giving proof thereof to the governor, they shall receive authority, with time and place, to elect representatives from their counties or townships, to represent them in the general assembly: Provided, That for every five hundred free male inhabitants there shall be one representative, and so on, progressively, with the number of free male inhabitants, shall the right of representation increase, until the number of representatives shall amount to twenty-five; after which the number and proportion of representatives shall be regulated by the legislature: Provided, That no person be eligible or qualified to act as a representative, unless he shall have been a citizen of one of the United States three years, and be a resident in the district, or unless he shall have resided in the district three years; and, in either case, shall likewise hold in his own right, in fee-simple, two hundred acres of land within the same: Provided, also, That a freehold in fifty acres of land in the district, having been a citizen of one of the States, and being resident in the district, or the like freehold and two years' residence in the district, shall be necessary to qualify a man as an elector of a representative.

Sec. 10. The representatives thus elected shall serve for the term of two years; and in case of the death of a representative, or removal from office, the governor shall issue a writ to the county or township, for which he was a member, to elect another in his stead, to serve for the residue of the term.

Sec. 11. The general assembly, or legislature, shall consist of the governor, legislative council, and a house of representatives. The legislative council shall consist of five members, to continue in office five years, unless sooner removed by Congress. . . . And the governor, legislative council, and house of representatives shall have authority to make laws in all cases for the good government of the district, not repugnant to the principles and articles in this ordinance established and declared. And all bills, having passed by a majority in the house, and by a majority in the council, shall be referred to the governor for his assent; but no bill, or legislative act whatever, shall be of any force without his assent. The governor shall have power to convene, prorogue, and dissolve the general assembly when, in his opinion, it shall be expedient.

Sec. 12. The governor, judges, legislative council, secretary, and such other officers as Congress shall appoint in the district, shall take an oath or affirmation of fidelity, and of office; the governor before the President of Congress, and all other officers before the governor. As soon as a legislature shall be formed in the district, the council and house assembled, in one room, shall have authority, by joint ballot, to elect a delegate to Congress who shall have a seat in Congress, with a right of debating, but not of voting, during this temporary government.

Sec. 13. And for extending the fundamental principles of civil and religious liberty, which form the basis whereon these republics, their laws and constitutions, are erected; to fix and establish those principles as the basis of all laws, constitutions, and governments, which forever hereafter shall be formed in the said territory; to provide, also, for the establishment of States, and permanent government therein, and for their admission to a share in the Federal councils on an equal footing with the original States, at as early periods as may be consistent with the general interest:

Sec. 14. It is hereby ordained and declared, by the authority aforesaid, that the following articles shall be considered as articles of compact, between the original States and the people and States in the said territory, and forever remain unalterable, unless by common consent, to wit:

Article I

No person, demeaning himself in a peaceable and orderly manner, shall ever be molested on account of his mode of worship, or religious sentiments, in the said territories.

Article II

The inhabitants of the said territory shall always be entitled to the benefits of the writ of habeas corpus, and of the trial by jury; of a proportionate representation of the people in the legislature, and of judicial proceedings according to the course of common law. All persons shall be bailable, unless for capital offences, where the proof shall be evident, or the presumption great. All fines shall be moderate; and no cruel or unusual punishments shall be inflicted. No man shall be deprived of his liberty or property, but by the judgment of his peers, or the law of the land, and should the public exigencies make it necessary, for the common preservation, to take any person's property, or to demand his particular services, full compensation shall be made for the same. And, in the just preservation of rights and property, it is understood and declared, that no law ought ever to be made or have force in the said territory, that shall, in any manner whatever, interfere with or affect private contracts, or engagements, bona fide, and without fraud previously formed.

Article III

Religion, morality, and knowledge being necessary to good government and the happiness of mankind, schools and the means of education shall forever be encouraged. The utmost good faith shall always be observed towards the Indians; their lands and property shall never be taken from them without their consent; and in their property, rights, and liberty they never shall be invaded or disturbed, unless in just and lawful wars authorized by Congress; but laws founded in justice and humanity shall, from time to time, be made, for preventing wrongs being done to them, and for preserving peace and friendship with them.

Article IV

The said territory, and the States which may be formed therein, shall forever remain a part of this confederacy of the United States of America, subject to the Articles of Confederation, and to such alterations therein as shall be constitutionally made; and to all the acts and ordinances of the United States in Congress assembled, conformable thereto. . . .

Article V

There shall be formed in the said territory not less than three nor more than five States. . . . And whenever any of the said States shall have sixty thousand free inhabitants therein, such State shall be admitted, by its delegates, into the Congress of the United States, on an equal footing with the original States, in all respects whatever; and shall be at liberty to form a permanent constitution and State government: Provided, The constitution and government, so to be formed, shall be republican, and in conformity to the principles contained in these articles, and, so far as it can be consistent with the general interest of the confederacy, such admission shall be allowed at an earlier period, and when there may be a less number of free inhabitants in the State than sixty thousand.

Article VI

There shall be neither slavery nor involuntary servitude in the said territory, otherwise than in the punishment of crimes, whereof the party shall have been duly convicted: Provided always, That any person escaping into the same, from whom labor or service is lawfully claimed in any one of the original States, such fugitive may be lawfully reclaimed, and conveyed to the person claiming his or her labor or service as aforesaid. . . .

✳ E S S A Y S

Merrill M. Jensen (1905–1980), an influential professor of history at the University of Wisconsin for more than a generation, produced a trilogy of works on the Revolution, all of them displaying elements of the neo-Progressive view that class interests shaped the course of American politics. This selection from *The New Nation: A History of the United States During the Confederation, 1781–1789* (1950) expresses some of Jensen's reasons for believing that the United States was starting to thrive under the Articles, before the monied nationalists supplanted it. Professor of history Jack N. Rakove of Stanford University explores congressional politics during the war and through the 1780s in his *Beginnings of National Politics* (1979), from which the second essay is drawn. Although Rakove finds some successes in the measures of Congress under the Articles, he also points out the impediments to action, the growing recognition among congressmen of structural problems, and the declining stature of Congress.

The Achievements of the Confederation

MERRILL JENSEN

It is commonly believed that during the Confederation the government of the United States was a weak and incompetent affair, devoid of power and ideas, without a record of achievement, and sinking fast into oblivion. Certain basic ideas are set forth about it: it was difficult to get a quorum of Congress to do business; it had no income; it had no power to handle the country's ills, and so on. The government was "weak," of that there is no question. It had been created that way deliberately because its founders had feared, and during the 1780s they continued to fear, a strong central government as they had feared and fought against the British government before 1776.

Yet one cannot understand the history of the Confederation government if one talks of it only in terms of efforts to remedy its obvious weaknesses. To do so is to miss much of the point of the political history of the American Revolution. One misses also the fact that the central government struggled mightily with problems left by the war and with still others arising from the birth of a new nation. Furthermore, one loses sight of the fact that the government of the Confederation achieved a measure of success, at least according to the likes of those who believed in the kind of central government provided by the Articles of Confederation.

The Congress of the Confederation laid foundations for the administration of a central government which were to be expanded but not essentially altered in function for generations to come. The United States acquired a vast source of future wealth as the states ceded their claims to western lands. The national domain became a fact in 1784. Between then and 1787, in three great ordinances, Congress laid down the basic policies that were to be used as the United States spread westward to the Pacific. At the same time a permanent staff of government employees was built up. These men carried on the affairs of the central government whether Congress was in session or not. When the Washington administration took over in 1789, the members of the new administration in effect moved into front offices staffed with men who for years had handled the details of foreign affairs, finance, Indian relations, the post office, and the like. Many of these employees continued to do the basic work of the central government after 1789 as they had done before. The government under the Constitution of 1787 would have been as helpless without them as the Confederation would have been, yet this "bureaucracy" has been unknown to most of the people who have written of the Confederation.

The government of the Confederation struggled to straighten out the tangled mess that resulted from the financing of the war, and here too made progress. Finally, it faced the basic issue of the relationship of the balance of power between the central government and the states. That issue was before the people of the new nation from the outset of the war. After 1783 the believers in the federal system provided by the Articles of Confederation sought hard to solve its problems. They recognized that the central government needed more power and they sought to acquire that power, meanwhile carefully guarding against any basic change in the nature of the Articles of Confederation.

As one views the achievements of the Confederation, it is evident that the story is not a negative one, but a story of steady striving toward a goal. The "weakness" of the central government under the Confederation was the weakness of any government that must achieve its ends by persuasion rather than by coercion. There was a large group of the citizens of the new nation who believed in persuasion; a smaller but equally powerful group believed in a central government with coercive authority. The triumph of the latter group in the face of the achievements of the Confederation government was a victory for a dynamic minority with a positive program. It parallels in many ways the achievement of an equally dynamic, but quite different minority, in bringing about the war for independence and in writing the Articles of Confederation.

The Creation of the National Domain

The fact of expansion into new land loomed even larger in American thought and economy in the 1780s than it had in the colonial period. The dispute over the control of the West contributed to the tensions leading to the war for independence, but independence did not end the dispute, for Americans fought with one another as to whether the central government or the individual states should control the lands claimed by them on the basis of their ancient charters. . . .

The man chiefly responsible for the foundation of the first "colonial policy" of the United States was Thomas Jefferson. He had long been interested in the region west of the Alleghenies, not as a speculator, but as a statesman, a scientist, and a believer in agrarian democracy. Where others wanted to hand the West over to speculators, he wanted it to belong to actual settlers. Where others distrusted westerners as banditti and wanted them ruled by military force, he wanted them to govern themselves. Thus when he brought the Virginia cession to Congress, he had definite ideas about what should be done. He was made chairman of a committee to draft an ordinance for the government of the new public domain. He believed that the land should be given to the settlers, for they would have to pay their share of the national debt anyway. Why should they pay double? If settlers had to pay for the lands, they would dislike the union. Furthermore, they would settle the lands no matter what Congress did. One settler in the West would be worth twenty times what he paid for the land, and he would be worth that every year he lived on his farm.

Jefferson proposed that the domain be divided into ten districts which ultimately would become states. . . . There was to be self-government by the people, not arbitrary government by congressional appointees. Whenever Congress offered a piece of territory for sale, the settlers within it were to establish a temporary government and to adopt the constitution and laws of whatever state they chose. Whenever the territory had 20,000 people, they were to hold a convention, adopt a constitution, and send a delegate to Congress. When the population of the territory equalled that of the free inhabitants of the smallest of the thirteen states, the new state was to be admitted to the union as an equal partner. The new state must agree to remain a part of the United States; be subject to the central government exactly as the other states were; be liable for its share of the federal debt; maintain a republican form of government; and exclude slavery after 1800. Thus Jefferson planned a government for the national domain. When the Ordinance of 1784 was finally adopted by Congress, only a few changes were made. The reference to slavery was dropped and one new restriction was added: the future states might not tax federal lands nor interfere with their disposal.

It is too often said, and believed, that the Northwest Ordinance of 1787, which repealed the Ordinance of 1784, provided for democracy in the territories of the United States. The reverse is actually true. Jefferson's Ordinance provided for democratic self-government of western territories, and for that reason it was abolished in 1787 by the land speculators and their supporters who wanted congressional control of the West so that their interests could be protected from the actions of the inhabitants.

Meanwhile, with the Ordinance of 1784 adopted, the next step was to provide for the survey and sale of the lands. Jefferson was on the committee appointed to draft such a plan and here too he had ideas, although his belief that the West should be given to the actual settlers was soon lost sight of in the need of Congress for revenue and in the rise of new speculative groups.

Jefferson left for France to replace Franklin as minister before the Ordinance was completed. In its final form the Ordinance of 1785 provided that the West should be divided into townships, each containing thirty-six square miles. Four sections in each township were to be reserved for the

United States, and also one third of the gold, silver, and copper. In each township lot sixteen was set aside for public schools. Once surveyed, the lands were to be sold at public auction by the loan office commissioners in each of the states. The land could not be sold for less than a dollar an acre and payment was to be in specie, loan office certificates reduced to specie value, or certificates of the liquidated debt of the United States. Lands were reserved to provide the bounties promised the army during the war. This Ordinance was adopted by Congress 20 May 1785. . . .

But the Land Ordinance of 1785 was soon forgotten. New speculative interests swept down upon Congress and grabbed for enormous chunks of the public domain. The drive was spearheaded by New Englanders and by others who had few if any ties with the pre-revolutionary land companies. No group was more interested in the West than ex-army officers who saw in western lands an outlet for the desires and energies that had been so frustrated at the end of the war. . . .

What these men hoped for was a military colony in the Old Northwest such as they had proposed to Congress from Newburgh in the spring of 1783. But Congress soon made it plain that it was going to sell land, so the officers changed their plans. Early in 1786 Rufus Putnam and Benjamin Tupper issued a call to the Massachusetts officers and soldiers who had served in the Revolution. They proposed county meetings to choose delegates to a meeting at Boston to organize an association to be called the Ohio Company. The company was organized and shares of stock were sold. . . .

The Ohio Company asked for a virtual suspension of the Land Ordinance of 1785. Four ranges had been surveyed but had not been put up for sale when the Ohio Company appeared before Congress offering a million dollars for lands beyond the survey. . . .

The shift in tactics smoothed the way for the Ohio Company. . . . The price was to be not less than a dollar an acre payable in loan office certificates reduced to specie value and in other certificates of the liquidated debt of the United States. Up to one seventh of the total purchase price could be paid in the land bounty certificates issued to the officers and soldiers of the Continental Army. The price, however, was reduced by a third, for that much allowance was made for bad land and for incidental expenses. The purchase was an enormous bargain, for national debt certificates were selling for as little as ten cents on the dollar in the open market. In the final sale Congress held back some of the land. Section sixteen in each township was reserved for education. Section twenty-nine was set aside for "the purposes of religion." Sections eight, eleven, and twenty-six in each township were reserved by Congress for future sale. Not more than two townships were to be set aside for "the purposes of a university."

While the Ohio Company was making plans to exploit the West, the West itself was boiling with activity. Before surveys could be made, Congress must get the Indians to give up their claims. The result was a series of treaties. One treaty was signed at Fort McIntosh in 1785, but the Shawnee, the most important tribe, refused to come. A second treaty was negotiated at Fort Finney in 1786. The Shawnee attended and gave up some of their claims. There was no alternative to treaty-making except to kill the Indians, an alternative which the westerners tried their best to carry out.

Meanwhile, without regard for Congress or the Indians, settlers were moving beyond the Ohio and squatting on likely looking pieces of land. In 1785 Congress ordered the settlers to stay south of the Ohio. Troops were raised and sent to the frontier. They burned squatters' cabins but they could not kill the dogged hunger of men for land. When the troops moved on, the settlers came back and rebuilt their homes. John Armstrong, an officer given the task of removing the settlers, declared that they were "banditti whose actions are a disgrace to human nature." The settlers were defiant. . . . Such men fought both the soldiers and the Indians. South of Ohio the Kentuckians demanded help from both Congress and Virginia and carried on a bloody struggle all the while. Between 1783 and 1790 perhaps 1,500 Kentuckians were killed and 2,000 horses were stolen. No one knows how many Indians or squatters north of the river lost their lives.

Frontier warfare and the settlement of the land by more and more squatters convinced many a member of Congress that the westerners should be denied the right of self-government. "The emigrants to the frontier lands," wrote Timothy Pickering, "are the least worthy subjects in the United States. They are little less savage than the Indians; and when possessed of the most fertile spots, for want of industry, live miserably." Pickering's attitude was shared by many important leaders who had long feared the growth of the West and who distrusted all westerners. Very few easterners took much stock in Jefferson's ideal of self-government for the West as expressed in the Ordinance of 1784. By 1786 Congress was once more discussing the problem of government for the West. James Monroe, who had made a tour of the West with troops in 1785, declared that the question with regard to government was: "Shall it be upon colonial principles, under a governor, council and judges of the United States, removable at a certain period of time and they admitted to a vote in Congress with the common rights of the other states, or shall they be left to themselves until that event?"

The reconsideration of the Ordinance of 1784, which arose from the fear of westerners and the danger of Indian war, was given new urgency by the Ohio Company. These men wanted a guarantee of property rights and rigid political control. The result was the Northwest Ordinance of 1787. Richard Henry Lee put the whole case neatly when he said that the new Ordinance seemed necessary "for the security of property among uninformed, and perhaps licentious people, as the greater part of those who go there are, that a strong toned government should exist, and the rights of property be clearly defined." In another letter he said that "the form of this government . . . is much more tonic than our democratic forms on the Atlantic are."

Under the Ordinance of 1787, government was to be carried on by a governor, a secretary, and three judges appointed by Congress. These men were to adopt whatever laws they chose from those of the thirteen states. Whenever a district had 5,000 male inhabitants, the landowners could choose an assembly. The first task of this assembly was to nominate ten men from whom Congress would pick five to act as a legislative council. The assembly could pass laws, but the governor was to have an absolute veto on all legislation. The Northwest was to be divided into not more than five nor less than three districts. Whenever any one of those divisions had 60,000 free inhabitants it was to be admitted to Congress and then be free to write a constitution and establish a state government. The government of the West by Arthur St. Clair in the years after 1787 was an ample demonstration of both the westerners' dislike of eastern control, and of the clear purpose of eastern speculators to get and keep a position of pre-eminence.

So far as the government of the United States was concerned, the sale of land began to pave the way for the payment of the national debt. It was a matter of newspaper comment that such sales "must give an immediate rise to the current value of the securities of the United States, which are received in payment for the lands as specie." Congress was at last in a position to carry out the conviction of many Americans that the sale of the lands was all that was needed to solve the financial burden left by the Revolution. The conflict in policy had been decided in favor of sales rather than of settlers, although even so, the land was cheap by comparison with what lands farther east were selling for. Before 1789 the sales made by the United States amounted to 1,487,986 acres for which Congress got $839,203 in securities. In addition, bounty warrants for another 238,150 acres of land were taken in.

In the years to come the Land Ordinance of 1785 and the Ordinance of 1787 remained the basis for the sale and government of the national domain. By the 1830s the United States had sold more than forty-four million dollars worth of land and thus justified those men in the 1780s who had believed that the national domain alone would pay the foreign and domestic debt of the United States.

The Creation of a Bureaucracy

A second major achievement of the Confederation was the creation of a bureaucracy which carried on the day-to-day work of the central government. To talk of the Confederation government in terms only of Congress—of its difficulties in doing business, of the failure of some of the states to be fully represented—is to tell a distorted story, for the government continued to function whether Congress met or not. Congress was primarily a policy-making, not an administrative body, although administrative officers were elected by and responsible to it. This practice was reversed after 1789 when administrative officers were made responsible to the executive rather than to the legislature. The creation of a responsible staff of civil servants by the Confederation government is an almost unknown story. These men carried on the work of the departments of war, foreign affairs, finance, and the post office in season and out. Many of them continued to be employed after 1789. The best example of this was Joseph Nourse of Virginia who became register of the treasury in 1779, a post which he held until 1829 when he retired because of old age. He kept books and prepared innumerable reports for Robert Morris, the board of treasury, Alexander Hamilton, and the secretaries of the treasury who followed him. If it had not been for Nourse and men like him, with years of practical experience in the day-to-day affairs of government behind them, the Washington administration would have been badly hampered. . . .

The one figure who, more than any other, represented continuity throughout the Revolution was Charles Thomson, the Irish-born "Sam Adams of Philadelphia." He was elected secretary of the First Continental Congress by the radical element which had immediately sensed in him a fellow spirit. Thomson kept the Journals and all the other papers of Congress and saw to their printing. He performed every sort of job that Congress wanted done, even to serving for a time as president. His office carried on correspondence between Congress and the state governments; his signature and seal were placed on the official versions of ordinances, commissions, and treaties. At its peak, his office had a deputy secretary, two clerks, and a messenger, and all of them were overworked. Thomson plainly ranked, in the eyes of many congressmen, with the president, and with the heads of executive departments after 1781. . . . When the new government was established in 1789, Thomson was chosen to carry to Mt. Vernon the official notification of Washington's election to the presidency. . . .

The post office department was established by Congress in 1775. Benjamin Franklin, who had been deputy postmaster general for the American Colonies, was put in charge until he went to France. Beneath him were a secretary, a comptroller, and a growing number of deputy postmasters throughout the United States. The biggest problem was lack of funds because the Confederation Congress, like those of later days, kept rates low for political reasons. The officer who represented continuity was Ebenezer Hazard who held various offices from 1775 until 1782 when he became postmaster general, a post he held to the end of the Confederation. In 1782 the department had twenty-six riders carrying mail, and a variety of officials at headquarters in Philadelphia. Bad roads, poor ferry service, dishonest riders, and highwaymen all led to poor service.

There were constant congressional investigations, charges, and counter-charges as to the source of inefficient service. Furthermore, until the Confederation was ratified, the states paid little attention to Congress's desire for a monopoly of the postal business. Even after 1781, however, some states insisted that they had the power to establish postal service within their borders. . . . The post office department found it difficult to pay expenses out of income, but so does it now. Meanwhile the postal service expanded. By 1788 there were sixty-six deputy postmasters scattered from Maine to Georgia, and in the same year, Congress directed the postmaster to provide service to the Ohio Valley.

The war department was set up under a single executive in 1781, and General Benjamin Lincoln was appointed its head. . . . Early in March 1785, General Henry Knox was elected secretary from among several ambitious candidates. The most ardent of them was Timothy Pickering of Massachusetts, an earnest seeker of government jobs after 1783. However, Knox's friends had promoted him ever since Lincoln's resignation, and Knox had the enormous advantage of Washington's support. . . . As secretary, Knox had many duties. He was in charge of public stores, the disposition of troops, frontier defense, including the superintendents of Indian affairs who were ordered to obey his instructions, and the administration of the military bounty lands. In 1788 the department consisted of Knox, three clerks, and a messenger. Six hundred and seventy-nine men and officers were in the army. These men were stationed at various posts on the frontier. Arms and ammunition were located at various arsenals scattered from Massachusetts to South Carolina. Knox, both as a private individual and as secretary of war, heartily supported the ideals of the nationalists. He spoke of the "vile state governments" as "sources of pollution" and he worked actively in the suppression of Shays's Rebellion. Thus it was natural for the Washington administration to take him and his department over into the new government without a break in continuity of policy or personnel.

The first "Secretary for Foreign Affairs" was Robert R. Livingston of New York. . . . Then in May 1784 John Jay was elected before his return from Europe. . . . Congress moved to New York late in 1784 and Jay accepted the post. At once he made it clear that he intended to play an important role and that if Congress did not like it, he would resign. Congress soon agreed that all correspondence relating to foreign affairs should go through Jay's office, which was staffed with an undersecretary, a doorkeeper, a messenger, clerks, and three interpreters. Jay busied himself with problems of foreign trade, infractions of the Treaty of Peace, and negotiations with foreign powers. He attended Congress, served on committees, and debated on the floor. His prestige and power were great, although his popularity was uncertain. He represented, as no other man except Charles Thomson, continuity of policy because of the turnover of membership in Congress and the failure of many states to be represented during sessions. . . . Politically he was as much of a nationalist as Henry Knox, and his letters constantly refer to his hope of adding power to the central government. . . .

Robert Morris's name is well known, but the significance of his public life is but dimly realized. As a figure of the Revolution he is perhaps a more important symbol than Sam Adams, for the latter's work was finished in 1776, whereas Morris's greatness and influence began then and rose to its peak in 1781–1783, when he shaped the policies of government and dominated much of the economic life of the new nation. Beyond this, he was for a time the figure around which centered all those men who sought to give the new nation a powerful central government and who, in 1783, contemplated without many qualms the possibility of doing so by force. . . .

The final story of Morris's administration remains to be told. There is no question but that he was an extremely skillful manipulator of funds and credit and that he brought a measure of system into the chaos of Revolutionary finance. But in the course of doing so it seems evident that he did not distribute available funds with an even hand, that he did use his financial power to reward friends and partners while ignoring the claims of equally worthy citizens. . . .

When a man's enemies, his friends, and foreign observers all agree that he is using his office for private gain, even if the charge is completely unfounded, his tenure is apt to be uncertain or, at least, his usefulness slight. After repeated threats to do so, and long after he had lost control of Congress, Morris finally retired 1 November 1784.

As the campaign against Morris mounted, his enemies made plans to take over the treasury. The Massachusetts delegates, acting on their instructions, moved that the treasury be "revised." The result was a report which in effect slapped Morris, for it declared that if any of the proposed three commissioners engaged in trade directly or indirectly, they could never thereafter hold any office under the United States. Congress at first rejected the report, declaring that there had been "very great advantages" from the administration of Robert Morris. But the very next day the ordinance was passed. It provided that a board of treasury should exercise the powers of the superintendent of finance and suffer only loss of office if they engaged in trade. . . .

The duties of the new board were many. It supervised the treasury officials who were settling the accounts of the military departments, the continental loan officers in the states, the commissioners who were settling accounts between the United States and the states and between the United States and individuals. The multitudes of memorials sent to Congress were turned over to the board for investigation. The board called for documents, heard evidence, and reported back to Congress. . . .

In addition, . . . the board prepared endless reports to Congress on income and outgo. They paid the troops and the civil employees. They kept up a constant correspondence with state officials urging prompt payments of monies provided by state legislatures. The board worked out careful procedures for the conduct of the business of handling accounts. When Congress referred a question to the board, it examined the merits of the case and reported back to Congress. . . .

As the board struggled in the swamps of unsettled accounts and wrangled with the states, its members often sounded like the man whose administration they had so bitterly denounced. As they sat on the inside looking out, they too became concerned with acquisition of more power for the central government. Samuel Osgood declared that the management of money matters was a serious business. . . . He now believed that Congress either must have coercive power to collect money or to levy an impost. He admitted that the power to do justice would also involve the power to do injustice: "power must be lodged somewhere yet it should be done with a proper degree of caution and such checks" as to prevent misuse. He had once been opposed to such power, but experience had obliged him to change. Patriotism and public virtue "are no match in this country for dishonesty and intrigue. Americans have no more virtue than other people." Osgood had moved far since 1783. Arthur Lee too had moved as he faced the problems of finance.

. . . Money was desperately needed to pay interest on the foreign debt and the salaries of the employees of the Confederation government. Such men as Lee and Osgood, unlike their fellow officers Jay and Knox, did not want a "national" government, but they did want enough power lodged in Congress to maintain the Confederation. . . .

The Confederation: A Union Without Power

JACK N. RAKOVE

It has always been difficult to avoid viewing the political developments of the mid-1780s from any perspective other than the Constitutional Convention of 1787. However one assesses the true character of the four years separating the coming of peace from the assembling of the Convention, the framing and ratification of the Constitution indisputably marked the culminating event in the history of Revolutionary politics and political thinking. In one sense, then, it is of only secondary importance to determine whether the new republic actually lay at the brink of chaos—the admittedly exaggerated image we have inherited from John Fiske—or was a basically prosperous society recovering as rapidly as could be expected from the dislocations of the war, as Merrill Jensen persuasively argued some years ago. As Bernard Bailyn has recently written,

> Despite depressions, doubts, and fears for the future, and despite the universal easing of ideological fervor, the general mood remained high through all of these years. There was a freshness and boldness in the tone of the eighties, a continuing belief that the world was still open, that young, energetic, daring, hopeful, imaginative men had taken charge and were drawing their power directly from the soil of the society they ruled and not from a distant, capricious, unmanageable sovereign.

At last "free from the corruption and inflexibility of the tangled old-regime whose toils had so encumbered Americans in the late colonial period," the citizens of the newly independent United States discovered a "sense of enterprise and experimentation" whose impulses were expressed "in every sphere of life."

Such a portrait reminds us, of course, not merely that healthy societies experience political malaise, but also that politics may well have mattered little to an overwhelming majority of the population intent, as anyone would sensibly be, on returning to the private joys and ambitions of ordinary life. If Alexander Hamilton could retire from Congress to practice law and, it seems, ignore politics almost completely until 1786, one can only conclude that masses of his fellow citizens shared his relative unconcern.

Even so, some American leaders were consistently troubled by the visible debilities in the governments of the new republic. . . . This [selection] will briefly survey the major problems of policy and politics that troubled Congress during the mid-1780s. . . .

Capital

During the final years of the war, Congress had groped for ways to enhance its authority; in the first months of peace, it found itself struggling simply to maintain its dignity. The first insult came in late June 1783, when a small contingent of Pennsylvania soldiers mutinied, marched on Philadelphia, and surrounded the building where both Congress and the state council regularly met. After the council refused its request to call out the militia, Congress resolved to quit Philadelphia. The delegates adjourned to nearby Princeton, a college town that they soon discovered was no better prepared to accommodate Congress in a sudden flight than Baltimore and York had been in 1776 and 1777. . . .

Although some Philadelphians—including Charles Thomson, still secretary of Congress—hoped that conciliatory gestures could induce the delegates to return, public opinion in the nation's leading city turned against its former guests when resolutions to that effect narrowly failed to pass Congress. By late October, Benjamin Rush observed, Congress was being "abused, laughed at, pitied & cursed in every Company." Thomas Willing, a former delegate and merchant partner of Robert Morris, took the whole episode lightheartedly. "I have never said any thing to you about the removal of the Congress from this City," he wrote William Bingham; "it was not worth while. [W]e shall laugh at it hereafter over a glass of Wine." In the end, Willing believed, Congress "must finally sitt down *here,* & *here* only. The Bank itself, together with the enterprizing spirit of the people of Pennsylvania, will ever support their measures, better than they can be supported elsewhere." . . .

The ultimate location of the national capital was destined to remain unresolved until the famous Compromise of 1790 led to the planning and construction of Washington. Although hardly the most critical issue confronting the Continental Congress in the mid-1780s, this problem did symbolize several major aspects of the transition to peacetime politics. Its residence in five separate cities and towns during a period of little more than a year and a half did nothing to enhance the wounded dignity of Congress. The adamant opposition against returning to Philadelphia demonstrated the persistence of the partisan rancor nurtured during the final years of the war, when a small cluster of delegates centered on New England but abetted by Arthur Lee had been aroused against Robert Morris and the two principal interests he seemed to represent—the commercial ambitions of Philadelphia and the diplomatic designs of France. . . . Finally, the capital issue foreshadowed the role sectionalism would play in the politics of the mid-1780s. It was hardly surprising that sectional feelings influenced the outcome of this question. But other substantive issues soon arose that exposed the potential conflict among major regional interests in equally obvious but also more dangerous ways, ultimately raising the question of whether or not there was one common national interest the states could mutually support. The establishment of a national capital at least presupposed the survival of the confederation; other issues pertaining to commercial policy toward foreign powers and the settlement of the west seemed to point toward its dissolution.

Revenue

Finance, the great dilemma of the early 1780s, remained the central test of the authority Congress would be able to exercise after the peace. The revenue plan of April 1783 had embodied three major proposals: a revised impost, a request for supplemental funds to be appropriated by the states for the use of Congress, and a recommendation that population replace land values as the basis for apportioning the common expenses. Having framed a compromise that most members felt answered the reasonable objection of the states, Congress had agreed that none of these resolutions would take effect until all had been unanimously approved. This stringent condition apparently reflected an opinion that further modifications of this program would effectively reduce Congress to precisely the situation it sought to escape: a precarious dependence on the goodwill and efficiency of the states. Congress was anxious to deter individual states from attaching the sorts of restrictive conditions that had been incorporated in several of the acts ratifying the impost of 1781. As a result, the new revenue program remained a dead letter.

The impost nevertheless came close to adoption. It survived critical tests in Virginia, where Washington intervened in its behalf, and Massachusetts, where Robert Morris overcame forceful opposition by transmitting extracts from diplomatic dispatches in which John Adams had emphasized the importance of securing national credit. But Rhode Island remained obstinate and refused to ratify until 1785. In Connecticut feelings against the commutation of military pensions ran particularly high, and the impost was rejected twice before being approved in the spring of 1784. Georgia had never ratified the first impost—an omission largely overlooked during the furor over Rhode Island—and delayed ratifying the amended version until 1786.

By then New York was the only state that had yet to grant the impost in some form. . . . In 1785 the New York Senate rejected the impost, and when in 1786 the assembly did pass an act of ratification, it contained provisions that Congress deemed unacceptable. During the five years that an impost had been under consideration, all the states had accepted it at one time or another; but although Congress made a last futile effort to set it in operation, the New York rejection constituted the final verdict.

Other provisions of the program of 1783 also came to nothing. Congress did not receive unanimous approval for its amendment proposing the apportionment of expenses according to population. . . . To meet its current operating expenses, Congress continued to rely on requisitions on the states. The results were hardly satisfying. Remittances proved inadequate to the servicing of the foreign debt, which had remained the indisputable obligation of the confederation, and Congress was forced to postpone payments to major foreign creditors. The one sign of hope in this otherwise gloomy picture was the completion in 1784 of the major western land cessions, which finally enabled Congress to begin to plan for the disposition of the new national domain. Disagreements over the plans for settling and governing these territories prevented the immediate exploitation of this resource, however.

The desultory progress of these measures effectively defeated Robert Morris's plan to use the creation of a consolidated national debt to justify endowing Congress with independent revenues. Rather than provide the funds Congress wanted or wait until they were unanimously ratified, the states began to make separate provisions for satisfying the public creditors whom Morris had hoped to make dependent on Congress. State notes were issued in exchange for federal securities, making the states, in effect, the creditors of Congress. As the states responded to the demands of their own citizens by absorbing a substantial proportion of the domestic debt, the rationale for granting Congress independent revenues was progressively weakened. . . .

When Morris finally left office in the fall of 1784, his opponents were still cautiously optimistic about the financial prospects of Congress. [Arthur] Lee and [Samuel] Osgood soon comprised a majority of the new Board of Treasury, and while it was true, as Holten complained, that "there is not much pleasure in being a member of Congress, unless a man can bear duning very well," it now seemed possible that the states would grow less suspicious of Congress and more willing to support it. Osgood had his doubts on this score, but Lee was more optimistic. The prospective opening of the west, Lee believed, could yet do wonders. "With this fund well managed," he informed John Adams, "the public debt may soon be annihilated." Howell agreed. "The western world opens an amazing prospect as a national fund," he wrote in February 1784; ". . . it is equal to our debt."

By early 1786, however, the experience of administering the treasury was providing Lee and Osgood with evidence not of the inherent dangers of power but rather of the frustration of exercising it under the circumstances prevailing in the mid-1780s. As E. James Ferguson has observed, they eventually found themselves writing "diatribes against the states almost in the style of the Financier whom they had displaced." The conclusion seemed unavoidable that a financial system based on requisitions and the levying of state taxes would never work, as Osgood admitted in January 1786. . . . "I am clear in one point," Osgood observed,

> that the united states must be entrusted with Monies other than the scanty Pittance that they obtain from the annual Requisitions—Ten Months will more explicitly show all that we cannot exist as a Nation without more prompt & effectual Supplies—Congress must either be vested with coercive Powers as to the Collection of Money or with the Impost which last for many Years to come will not be equal to the Necessities of the Nation; they must therefore if vested with the last be vested with the former also— or cease to be a Congress of any Consequence to the Union.

For Osgood, once so fearful of the dangers of federal power, Congress was now a "Sovereign Body [which] ought always to have a Power to do Justice" to its creditors. . . . Now he was convinced that "Americans have no more Virtue than other People," and that "We must be governed by Laws, or we shall be no Nation at all." Although Osgood, like Lee, subsequently opposed the Constitution, his disillusionment in 1786 was profound; Gouverneur Morris could hardly have spoken more cynically. . . .

Dilemmas of Foreign Policy

The foreign policy problems of the mid-1780s . . . raised two major questions about the future of the confederation. First, would Congress enjoy sufficient authority and support to enable it to protect American interests in the world of nations? Second, and perhaps more disturbing, was there a general, coherent national interest that Congress could defend, or had the very success of the struggle for independence undermined the strongest foundation of American unity? Because the conduct of foreign policy was clearly the principal responsibility that Congress would exercise in time of peace, these posed the most alarming questions the delegates encountered between the Treaty of Paris and the calling of the Philadelphia Convention. Even the states' failure to supply the continental treasury could be subsumed under their larger inability to recognize the existence of a legitimate sphere of national interest. An impoverished Congress could neither satisfy foreign creditors nor keep up military forces capable of defending American claims and interests along its extensive frontiers, nor even maintain a diplomatic corps that European nations could take seriously. When the Committee of the States abruptly adjourned in August 1784, Charles Thomson was forced to reflect on how much Americans had yet to learn about the character of their mutual interests. "Whatever little politicians may think," . . .

> time will evince that it is of no small consequence to save appearances with foreign nations, and not to suffer the federal government to become invisible. A government without a visible head must appear a strange phenomenon to European politicians and will I fear lead them to form no very favourable opinion of our stability, wisdom or Union.

When critics of the Articles talked of amendments and reforms, what they had in mind were primarily these responsibilities of foreign relations, the great affairs of state as they were traditionally conceived.

These were concerns, however, that for the most part only experienced politicians could find deeply troubling, and that the majority of Americans deemed largely irrelevant to their own immediate interests. . . . The conversion from the wartime politics of patriotism to the candid pursuit of local and private interests foredoomed any attempt to secure the unanimous approval that amendments to the Articles required. The comparatively modest amendments Congress had proposed in April 1784 were never adopted, and there was little reason to believe that the broader commercial powers under consideration in 1785 and 1786 would soon enjoy a different reception.

Land

When, in 1785, James Monroe argued that a strategy of delaying agitation for major amendments was the wisest course Congress could take, he may well have been drawing lessons from the history of another issue that interested him intensely: the organization and development of the new national domain. The disposition of western lands had been among the most difficult questions Congress had confronted during the war, precisely because, like the issues of the mid-1780s, it had forced the states to balance considerations of self-interest against the pressing demands of national welfare. . . . If this issue, seemingly so intractable in 1776 and so intimately connected with the particular interests of the states, had finally been resolved in favor of the confederation, might it not provide a model for compromise and common sense on other matters as well?

So Monroe might have reasoned. The framing of a policy for the opening of the west *was* the one undisputed postwar achievement of Congress and, as several historians have recently argued, an achievement that represented not merely the visionary imprint of Thomas Jefferson (who played a leading role in the deliberations of 1784) but also the shared concerns of most delegates. Indeed, one of the most recent students of the evolution of the 1787 Ordinance has concluded that "its history is apparently nothing more or less than that of a rather ordinary piece of noncontroversial legislation," and that throughout the mid-1780s the "continuity and consensus of thought" about key provisions of territorial government "are obvious." Had other problems not intervened, the creation of the national domain might conceivably have fulfilled some of the expectations it had evoked within Congress all along, enhancing its influence, replenishing its treasury, and demonstrating that substantial power could be safely entrusted to the federal government, thereby weakening objections against the further revision of the Articles.

Yet the success of any western policy was itself contingent on the extent to which Congress could exercise authority in other matters, and by 1786 its debilities were threatening to undermine the anticipated results of the long struggle to acquire a national domain. The mere enactment of provisions for territorial government and settlement could not guarantee that Congress would be able to discharge its mandate effectively or retain the loyalty of western settlers. Would migrants to the west maintain their allegiance to the confederation if it proved incapable of defending the frontiers or forcing Spain to open the Mississippi? If the process of settlement proceeded as slowly as many members now believed it would, and if it were as carefully regulated as Congress intended, difficulties could presumably be avoided. Still, it was hard enough to imagine how the geographical barriers inhibiting the integration of the seaboard and the interior would be overcome even if political disputes between these disparate regions did not arise.

By the summer of 1786, the collapse of the revenue plan of 1783 and the bitter rift within Congress over the Mississippi converged to point toward more ominous conclusions. Even Rufus King, who was hardly an enthusiast for rapid western development, was alarmed when the Board of Treasury was forced to "explicitly declare their utter inability to make [a] pitiful advance" of $1,000 to transport ammunition to American posts along the Ohio River. Monroe and other southern delegates believed that the northern willingness to acquiesce in the closure of the Mississippi was designed "to break up . . . the settlements on the western waters, prevent any in future, and thereby keep the States southward as they now are"—that is, a numerical minority of the existing union. . . .

As the furor over the Mississippi subsided somewhat in early 1787, such fears receded as well, and Congress went ahead to complete the Northwest Ordinance. Nevertheless, far from being the notable exception to the otherwise pathetic history of Congress in the 1780s, the still problematic fate of its western policy indicated just how dangerous the unresolved difficulties of the confederation could become. If the confederation could not surmount its postwar lassitude and internal divisions, it was entirely conceivable that Britain and Spain would emerge as the dominant political forces in the interior of the continent, leaving the thirteen original states clinging to the ocean, deprived of the resources of the west, and still bickering over explosive issues of foreign affairs.

Reputation

Until the final months before the Philadelphia Convention, serious concern about the future of the confederation was in all probability confined to a small and elite circle of American politicians and their connections. Discussions of the peacetime plight of Congress appeared only infrequently in American newspapers and never developed into a full-fledged, much less incisive debate over the state of the union. . . . Americans probably knew as much if not more about Parliament, whose debates were often reprinted in their newspapers, as they did about Congress, which still sat behind closed doors even after the coming of peace effectively undercut the claim that its deliberations were best conducted in secret. . . .

One reason why Congress received so little attention was that it was often incapable of reaching decisions. Caught between various sources of sectional rivalry and the conflicting interests that periodically set Congress at loggerheads with the states, the delegates were hard pressed to frame policies they could realistically expect to be endorsed or executed by the states. But its constitutional handicaps hampered congressional efficiency in another way. Its lack of power could not make service at Congress attractive to veteran politicians whose own prestige might serve to enhance its precarious influence. When Jefferson expressed a belief that "the best effects [would be] produced by sending our young statesmen" to Congress, he hoped their exposure to national issues would eventually lead them to "befriend federal measures" whenever they returned to their states. But his statement also implied a certain doubt as to whether Congress would be able to do anything of real importance in the near future. In its weakened state, Congress could command neither the regular attendance nor the personal loyalties of many of its members, and both its reputation and the progress of business suffered accordingly.

From the time of its retreat to Princeton until the very demise of the confederation, Congress struggled almost constantly to maintain the quorum of seven states required by the Articles. The transaction of even minor business required the approval of all seven, and major decisions could be taken only with the affirmative vote of nine states. A state that was represented by two members—the minimum fixed by the Articles—always risked losing its vote if both disagreed, or whenever one member was ill, or decided he had more pressing business of his own to attend to, or left unexpectedly for home when his overdue relief failed to appear. Congress suffered as well, since the indisposition of a single delegate could prevent a quorum, while a divided delegation lessened any possibility of creating a majority. To have anything passed in Congress in the mid-1780s required a fair amount of luck and a substantial level of consensus. Neither came readily to hand. . . .

In its internal proceedings and its relations with the states, Congress was a victim of the clash of interests that shaped the course of politics in the mid-1780s. The major issues of these years—revenue, commerce, expansion—forced each state to calculate the benefits and costs that would flow from particular decisions. Freed from the patriotic constraints that had always operated, although unevenly, during the war, the states were no longer obliged to defer to the wisdom of Congress and the overriding demands of the common cause. The delegates, too, enjoyed greater liberty and, in a sense, a greater obligation to serve as the actual representatives of their constituents. They felt less impelled to subordinate the particular desires of their states to the larger good of the union. Most members agreed that Congress deserved greater support from the states than it was receiving—particularly after the influence of Robert Morris was, for better or worse, curtailed—but they themselves were often uncertain how far their personal loyalties to its interest extended. Few shared the sort of disinterested commitment that can be attributed to Madison. Until they grew more convinced that the problems of the union demanded a clear priority over the demands of the states, the task of strengthening Congress could only proceed on a piecemeal, gradual basis.

✖ *F U R T H E R   R E A D I N G*

Willi Paul Adams, *The First American Constitutions: Republican Ideology and the Making of the State Constitutions in the Revolutionary Era* (1980)

Edward Countryman, *A People in Revolution: The American Revolution and Political Society in New York, 1760–1790* (1981)

Philip A. Crowl, *Maryland During and After the Revolution: A Political and Economic Study* (1943)

Elisha P. Douglass, *Rebels and Democrats: The Struggle for Equal Political Rights and Majority Rule During the American Revolution* (1955)

E. James Ferguson, *The Power of the Purse: A History of American Public Finance, 1776–1790* (1961)

Robert A. Gross, *The Minutemen and Their World* (1976)

Van Beck Hall, *Politics Without Parties: Massachusetts, 1780–1791* (1972)

H. James Henderson, *Party Politics in the Continental Congress* (1974)

Ronald Hoffman and Peter J. Albert, eds., *Sovereign States in an Age of Uncertainty* (1982)

Reginald Horsman, *The Frontier in the Formative Years, 1783–1815* (1970)

Merrill Jensen, *The New Nation: A History of the United States During the Confederation, 1781–1789* (1950)

Donald S. Lutz, *Popular Consent and Popular Control: Whig Political Theory in the Early State Constitutions* (1980)

Richard P. McCormick, *Experiment in Independence: New Jersey in the Critical Period, 1781–1789* (1950)

Forrest McDonald, *E Pluribus Unum: The Formation of the American Republic, 1776–1790* (1965)

Jackson Turner Main, *Political Parties Before the Confederation* (1973)

———, *The Social Structure of Revolutionary America* (1965)

———, *The Sovereign States, 1775–1783* (1973)

———, *The Upper House in Revolutionary America* (1967)

James R. Morrill, *The Practice and Politics of Fiat Finance: North Carolina in the Confederation, 1783–1789* (1969)

Richard B. Morris, *The Forging of the Union, 1781–1789* (1987)

Allan Nevins, *The American States During and After the Revolution, 1775–1789* (1924)

Peter S. Onuf, *Statehood and Union: A History of the Northwest Ordinance* (1987)

Jack N. Rakove, *The Beginnings of National Politics: An Interpretive History of the Continental Congress* (1979)

John Philip Reid, *Constitutional History of the American Revolution: The Authority of Rights* (1986)

Malcolm J. Rohrbough, *The Trans-Appalachian Frontier: People, Societies, and Institutions, 1775–1850* (1978)

Alfred F. Young, *The Democratic-Republicans of New York: The Origins, 1763–1797* (1967)

CHAPTER 11

Political Unrest and the Movement for Constitutional Reform, 1786–1787

✕

From a long-term perspective, the future success of the United States may have been secured by the 1780s, but many of those who actually lived through 1786 and 1787 believed that there was a genuine crisis. Popular republicanism was working but not to the general satisfaction of all. In some places majorities appeared to be trampling the interests of minorities, and in others, entrenched, privileged minorities seemed determined to frustrate majority wishes. American independence, which had raised hopes of an ideal society, was producing a far more troubled politics than patriots had expected.

In Massachusetts there erupted Shays's Rebellion, a civil war involving pitched battles, bloodshed, and thousands of armed soldiers. Because Massachusetts possessed the most fully developed state constitution, drafted by John Adams and ratified by popular vote in 1780, this was a crucial test for republicanism. The Massachusetts constitution gave the governor veto power and carefully articulated the separation of powers between the executive, legislature, and judiciary. The state not only had literate voters but featured a broad, relatively equal distribution of property when compared to states like New York and Virginia. Truly, Massachusetts faced a crisis, one that seemed emblematic for the United States as a whole. If revolutionary republicanism failed in Massachusetts, where would it succeed?

The issues in Massachusetts, which pitted debtors against creditors and revolved around taxation, currency, and public finances, were problems throughout the new nation. Although they led to warfare only in Massachusetts, the interests of farmers and merchants came into conflict in nearly all the states. In the midst of this turmoil, the U.S. Congress under the Articles of Confederation could offer no remedies. In fact, congressional vitality seemed to ebb in these years as the various state governments, not Congress, became the arenas for the resolution of political problems. It was this realization—the sense that the national interest was failing and that a vigorous national government could reverse the direction of American politics—that led nationalists, among them James Madison of Virginia, to press for constitutional reform. Believing that the achievements of the Revolution were in immediate peril, they set out to construct a constitutional mechanism that would harness the vitality of popular republicanism and restrain its vices.

✂ D O C U M E N T S

In 1786 a long smoldering conflict between eastern Massachusetts commercial interests and land-poor farmers burst into flame as the administration of Governor James Bowdoin and the state legislature aggressively pursued procreditor policies. The first two documents, comprising the petition of the Hampshire County farmers (which was one of more than 200 such documents) and the resolutions of the fifty towns that joined in the Hampshire County Convention, show that many people were seriously aggrieved and considered the government at Boston unfair. The Massachusetts legislature responded to such complaints and to the armed crowds that were forcibly closing the courts through the third document, a lecture on majority rule, representative government, and virtuous citizenship. This address was printed in a pamphlet that was sent to every town and every clergyman in the state with the request that it be publicly read in town meetings and from church pulpits. A counterstatement from the Shaysites, the fourth selection here, was printed in reply in one Hampshire County newspaper. Many clergymen read the legislature's address to their congregations, but some also prepared their own sermons on the political unrest—a notable example being the fifth document, a sermon delivered by the Reverend Joseph Lathrop of West Springfield, a town with forty or more Shaysites. After the rebellion was suppressed, Lathrop's nearby colleague, the Reverend Bezaleel Howard of Springfield, wrote a private account of the episode (first made public in 1983) that captures the harsh character of the struggle, as the sixth document reveals.

While this turmoil beset Massachusetts, the U.S. Congress sat in disarray. As Congressman Charles Pinckney's address to the New Jersey legislature, document seven, illustrates, even states that "supported" the Articles of Confederation were undermining it through their inaction on its requisitions. The delegate reports from Congress in 1787 that compose the final selection imply that the national government was languishing and that the most productive action it could take was to issue the call for a constitutional convention.

Hampshire County, Massachusetts, Farmers Call for Help, 1786

Petition from the Town of Greenwich, Massachusetts
16 January 1786

To the Honourable Senate and the House of Representatives in General Court assembled att their next session:

A Petition of the Subscribers humbly sheweth—

That in the time of the late war, being desirous to defend secure and promote the wrights and liberties of the people, we spared no pains but freely granted all that aid and assistance of every kind that our civel fathers required of us.

We are sencable also that a great debt is justly brought upon us by the war and are as willing to pay our shares towards itt as we are to injoy our shars in independancy and constatutional priviledges in the Commonwealth, if itt was in our power. And we beleve that if prudant mesuers ware taken and a moderate quantety of medium to circulate so that our property might sel for the real value we mite in proper time pay said debt.

But with the greatest submittion we beg leave to informe your Honours that unles something takes place more favourable to the people, in a little time att least, one half of our inhabitants in our oppinion will become banckerupt—how can itt be otherwise—the constables are dayly vandering [vendering, i.e., selling] our property both real and personal, our land after itt is prised by the best judges under oath is sold for about one third of the value of itt, our cattle about one half the value, the best inglesh [English] hay thirteen shilings per tone, intervale [native] hay att six shilings per tone, and other things att the same rate. And we beg leave further to informe your honours that sutes att law are very numerous and the atturneys in our oppinion very extravigent and oppressive in their demands. And when we compute the taxes laid upon us the five preceeding years: the state and county, town and class taxes,* the amount is equil to what our farms will rent for. Sirs, in this situation what have we to live on—no money to be had; our estates dayly posted and sold, as above described. What can your honours ask of us unles a paper curancy or some other medium be provided so that we may pay our taxes and debts. Suerly your honours are not strangers to the distresses of the people but doe know that many of our good inhabitants are now confined in gole for det and for taxes: maney have fled, others wishing to flee to the State of New York or some other State; and we believe that for two years past four inhabitants have removed from this State to some other State to one that has come from some other State to settle in this State.

Honoured Sirs, are not these imprisonments and fleeing away of our good inhabitents very injurious to the credit or honour of the Commonwealth? will not the people in the neighbouring States say of this State: altho' the Massachusets bost of their fine constatution, their government is such that itt devours their inhabitants? Notwithstanding all these distresses, we hear of no abatement of sallerys, but his Excellency the Governor must be paid eleven hundred a year out of the moneys collected as before mentoned, and other sallerys and grants to other gentlemen, as your honours very well know. Iff these things are honest, just and rite, we sincearly wish to be convinced of itt: but we honestly confess itt is beyond our skill to reconsile these sallerys and grants with the principles of our Constatution (viz.) piaty, justice, moderation, temperance, etc. . . . .

[Signed by 60 men]

---

* A wartime tax used to pay enlistment bounties to soldiers.

Fifty Hampshire County, Massachusetts, Towns Demand Reform, 1786

At a meeting of delegates from fifty towns in the county of Hampshire, in convention held at Hatfield, in said county, on Tuesday the 22d day of August instant, and continued by adjournments until the twenty fifth, &c. Voted, that this meeting is constitutional.

The convention from a thorough conviction of great uneasiness, subsisting among the people of this county and Commonwealth, then went into an inquiry for the cause; and, upon mature consideration, deliberation and debate, were of opinion, that many grievances and unnecessary burdens now lying upon the people, are the sources of that discontent so evidently discoverable throughout this Commonwealth. Among which the following articles were voted as such, viz.

1st. The existence of the Senate.

2d. The present mode of representation.

3d. The officers of government not being annually dependent on the representatives of the people, in General Court assembled, for their salaries.

4th. All the civil officers of government, not being annually elected by the Representatives of the people, in General Court assembled.

5th. The existence of the Courts of Common Pleas, and General Sessions of the Peace.

6th. The Fee Table as it now stands.

7th. The present mode of appropriating the impost and excise.

8th. The unreasonable grants made to some of the officers of government.

9th. The supplementary aid.

10th. The present mode of paying the governmental securities.

11th. The present mode adopted for the payment and speedy collection of the last tax.

12th. The present mode of taxation as it operates unequally between the polls* and estates, and between landed and mercantile interests.

13th. The present method of practice of the attornies at law.

14th. The want of a sufficient medium of trade, to remedy the mischiefs arising from the scarcity of money.

15th. The General Court sitting in the town of Boston.

16th. The present embarrassments on the press.

17th. The neglect of the settlement of important matters depending between the Commonwealth and Congress, relating to monies and averages.

18th. Voted, This convention recommend to the several towns in this county, that they instruct their Representatives, to use their influence in the next General Court, to have emitted a bank of paper money, subject to a depreciation; making it a tender in all payments, equal to silver and gold, to be issued in order to call in the Commonwealth's securities.

19th. Voted, That whereas several of the above articles of grievances,

---

* Persons 16 years and older.

arise from defects in the constitution; therefore a revision of the same ought to take place.

20th. Voted, That it be recommended by this convention to the several towns in this county, that they petition the Governour to call the General Court immediately together, in order that the other grievances complained of, may by the legislature, be redressed.

21st. Voted, That this convention recommend it to the inhabitants of this county, that they abstain from all mobs and unlawful assemblies, until a constitutional method of redress can be obtained.

22d. Voted, That Mr. Caleb West be desired to transmit a copy of the proceedings of this convention to the convention of the county of Worcester.

23d. Voted, That the chairman of this convention be desired to transmit a copy of the proceedings of this convention to the county of Berkshire.

24th. Voted, That the chairman of this convention be directed to notify a county convention, upon any motion made to him for that purpose, if he judge the reasons offered be sufficient, giving such notice, together with the reasons therefor, in the publick papers of this county.

25th. Voted, That a copy of the proceedings of this convention be sent to the press in Springfield for publication.

The Massachusetts Legislature Advises Thrift, Virtue, and Patience, 1786

An Address from the General Court, to the People of the Commonwealth of Massachusetts

At a period, when grievances are complained of, in divers counties of the State; when the symptoms of discontent are manifest and alarming, and individuals resort to arms, to support their disaffection, and oppose the Courts of Justice; it becomes the duty of the Legislature, to investigate, and, as far as may be, to remove the grounds of complaint; to undeceive those, who are misguided by false representation; and if lenient means are ineffectual, to vindicate by vigorous and decisive measures, the honor of government, and provide for the security of the State. . . .

We have no doubt, that endeavours are used by evil and designing men, to alienate the affections of the people in general, from those who are concerned in the administration of government; but conscious of the rectitude of our intentions, we are convinced, that if the public measures are examined with candour, the confidence you lately reposed in us, will not be lessened. . . .

As we apprehend a great part of the uneasiness in the State, has arisen from misinformation, we shall in the first place subjoin a state of the public debt, as well the particular debt of this Commonwealth, as this State's proportion of the national or Continental debt. . . . [Here follows a detailed accounting of the several kinds of debt.]

Although from the foregoing statement, it appears that a large debt is due, yet when our resources, and the manner in which payment can be made, are considered; we think the inhabitants of the Commonwealth will be satisfied, not only that they are able to pay the debt; but that it may be discharged without greatly distressing them.

The particular debt of this Commonwealth is almost wholly due to its citizens; the payment therefore will not weaken the State by draining it of its property. Considerable sums are expected from the sale of lands in the easterly part of the State, and every measure that prudence will admit, is taken for the speedy sale of those lands. . . .

If an individual is involved in debt, both prudence and honesty require him to be frugal, and pay his debt as soon as may be. By a long and expensive war, we incurred a large public debt, tho' far less than that, which our enemies incurred; but instead of using every effort to pay it, divers persons have employed themselves in devising methods to get rid of it, without payment; many indeed have employed much more time and money to this end, than (if better employed) might have purchased their whole proportion of the public securities; they alledge, that many of the first possessors have been obliged to sell them, for little more than one third of their amount, and therefore that the present holders ought to receive no more; but we should do well to remember, that the public has received the full value of all the notes they have issued; they were made transferable by law, and many of them have been sold; but if we had paid them as we promised, very few would have been sold; and shall we take no measures to pay them now, because we have omitted the payment so long? . . .

The sitting of the General Court in Boston, has occasioned uneasiness; doubtless it would be more convenient for a part of the State, if it was holden at some other place; but the interest and wishes of a part, are not to be considered alone: Boston has long been thought the most convenient place: some of the General Court have supposed otherwise; but the major part were against a removal, and must the minor part therefore rise against the government? Because they could not have every thing as they wished, could they be justified in resorting to force? Such a principle would destroy all society. Attention, however, has been paid to the instruction of many towns respecting the removal of the General Court out of the town of Boston, and a Committee consisting of a member from each county, has been appointed to consider the subject and report.

It never can be the case, that the whole community shall be of the same opinion; in a republican government the major part must govern: if the minor part governs, it becomes an aristocracy: if every one opposes at his pleasure, it is no government, it is anarchy and confusion.

In some parts of the Commonwealth, it is frequently said, if our Representative goes to Court, he will do us no service; for the measures he is in favour of, will not be adopted: but why will they not be adopted? Every measure that is proposed, is attended to, and considered; and if finally rejected, it is because the majority think it inexpedient; and how absurd and contradictory would the proceedings of the Court be, if every proposition should be acceeded to.

The complaints in different parts of the State are repugnant, and petitions from different places, request measures directly opposite; it is impossible therefore, that all should be gratified: what then shall be done? Unless we submit to be controuled by the greater number, the Commonwealth must break in pieces. . . .

It is even said by some, that a new constitution is necessary; and although the sentiments of the persons, who complain, are opposite on this point, the subject may demand some attention. . . .

We have but lately heard that the Senate has been thought by any one to be a grievance; if it has been so considered, we think it must have been owing to inattention; for we are convinced that every judicious man who attends to the nature of our government, will consider that as an important and necessary branch of the Legislature. . . .

The constitution is as free and popular as the preservation of society will admit; and indeed some have feared, it is more so: it has been highly applauded by foreigners and approved by the people: all persons employed in the legislative or executive parts of government, depend annually upon the people for their choice; if the people are dissatisfied with their conduct, they have an opportunity yearly to appoint others, in whom they can more fully confide. Can there be any necessity then, of resorting to irregular, or violent measures, to obtain redress of grievances?

That the people are overburthened with taxes is said to be a grievance: the taxes have indeed been very great; perhaps the General Court have misjudged of the abilities of their constituents, but it may be that those who complain, if they knew the state of the public debt, and the motives of the Legislature, would be satisfied. . . .

Public credit is one of the most important trusts committed to the Legislature; in proportion as that declines, the State is weakened and in danger. It is of the same importance to a community, as a character for truth is to individuals. The want of a paper currency has been complained of as a grievance; but . . . a little attention to the subject, we conceive, must satisfy every intelligent and unprejudiced mind, that the emission of such a currency would be exceedingly prejudicial. If it could be carried into circulation, the solid coin would be exported, the morals of the people would become more depraved, designing men would practice innumerable frauds; and if it should ever afterwards be redeemed, it would plunge the State in deeper distress: If it should not be redeemed, it would cause the ruin of many individuals, and brand the State with infamy. And upon whom would that ruin fall? Not upon the artful and unprincipled, they would gain by the fraud; not upon the prudent and discerning, they would be guarded against it; but the loss would chiefly happen to the widow and the orphan, the simple and unwary; the most innocent and defenceless part of the community; that part, whose interests the Legislature ought to defend with peculiar attention. The widow and orphan are the special charge of the Supreme Being, and all are enjoined to exercise vigilance and tenderness for their welfare. This injunction every man, possessed of natural affections, must feel the force of; for who can tell how soon his wife and his children may fall a prey to sharpers and speculators, if a paper money system shall be adopted. . . .

We feel in common with our neighbours the scarcity of money; but is not this scarcity owing to our own folly? At the close of the war, there was no complaint of it; since that time, our fields have yielded their increase, and heaven has showered its blessings on us, in uncommon abundance; but are we not constrained to allow, that immense sums have been expended, for what is of no value, for the gewgaws imported from Europe, and the more pernicious produce of the West-Indies; and the dread of a paper currency impedes the circulation of what remains: It is said however, that such a currency would give us present relief; but like the pleasure of sin, it would be but for a season; and like that too, it would be a reproach to the community, and would produce calamities without end. . . .

Within a few years the habits of luxury have exceedingly increased, the usual manufactures of the country have been little attended to. That we can buy goods cheaper than we can make them, is often repeated, and is even become a maxim in economy, altho' a most absurd and destructive one. . . .

Without a reformation of manners, we can have little hope to prosper in our public or private concerns. At the close of the war we greedily adopted the luxurious modes of foreign nations. Although our country abounds with all the necessaries of life, the importations from abroad, for our own consumption, have been almost beyond calculation; we have indulged ourselves in fantastical and expensive fashions and intemporate living; by these means our property has been lessened and immense sums in specie have been exported. Government is complained of, as if they had devoured them; and the cry of many persons now is, make us paper money. This request is next in point of imprudence, to that of the Israelites to Aaron, to make them a calf; and a compliance would be but a little more honorable or advantageous, in the one case, than it was in the other.

As the difficulty in paying debts increased, a disregard to honesty, justice and good faith, in public and private transactions become more manifest. That virtue, which is necessary to support a Republic, has declined; and as a people, we are now in the precise channel, in which the liberty of States has generally been swallowed up. But still our case is not desperate; by recurring to the principles of integrity and public spirit, and the practice of industry, sobriety, economy, and fidelity in contracts, and by acquiescing in laws necessary for the public good, the impending ruin may be averted, and we become respectable and happy.—By such means, we may falsify the invidious predictions our enemies, that we should crumble to pieces, and should be too corrupt to maintain republican freedom. In such a cause we may hope, that the God of our fathers, who has defended us hitherto, will prosper the work of his own hands, and save the fair structure of American liberty from falling into ruin. . . .

When the people are distressed with the conduct of any government, it may at least deserve a reflection, whether the difficulty is not with themselves. At the last election in this State, perhaps a greater number of new Members were returned, than at any former period; they came together with a fixed design, to gratify their constituents, in every thing which the interest of the community would permit; and they never lost sight of that object; notwithstanding which, greater dissatisfaction with public measures is expressed at this time, than ever before since the revolution. The Legislature have attended to all the petitions that have been presented, and all the complaints that have been made; so far as justice will allow, they will comply with the requests in those petitions and remove the grounds of those complaints. . . .

The General Court have heard with inexpressible concern, of the insurrections in several counties of the State. The pretence that the Court of Common Pleas, is a grievance, affords but a wretched excuse for such outrageous proceedings; that Court, except a small alteration in the name, has existed time immemorial; no complaints were heard against it in former times; no application has been made to the Legislature before this session to abolish it. . . . But if the Court of Common Pleas has been by any supposed unnecessary, how surprizing then, the idea, that any persons could think themselves justified, in opposing by force, an ancient institution, without taking a single step to obtain redress in a regular method. But not content with obstructing the Courts of Common Pleas, the disaffected have taken arms to prevent the sitting of the Supreme Judicial Court, against which, not a single complaint has been uttered. These proceedings are the more alarming, as they can be accounted for, only on the supposition, that the instigators wish to subvert all order and government, and reduce the Commonwealth, to the most deplorable state of wretchedness and contempt.

In this view, our situation appears exceedingly alarming; sufficiently so, to arrest the most serious attention, and summon the united efforts, of all orders in the State. Some persons have artfully affected to make a distinction between the government and people, as though their interests were different and even opposite; but we presume, the good sense of our constituents will discern the deceit and falsity of those insinuations. Within a few months the authority delegated to us will cease, and all the citizens will be equally candidates in a future election; we are therefore no more interested to preserve the constitution and support the government, than others; but while the authority given us continues, we are bound to exercise it for the benefit of our constituents. And we now call upon persons of all ranks and characters to exert themselves for the public safety. Upon the Ministers of religion, that they inculcate upon the minds of their people, the principles of justice and public virtue; that they earnestly endeavour to impress them with sentiments of reverence to the Deity and benevolence to men, and convince them of the ruinous effects of luxury and licentiousness. Upon the officers of every denomination, that they endeavour to inform the ignorant; and by their examples of economy, to induce others to the practice of the same virtue; and that they use their utmost efforts to suppress the insurrections of such lawless and violent men, as may wish to pull down the fabric of law and government, and level it with the dust. And upon the whole body of the people, that they provide for the instruction of the rising generation; that they practice all those virtues which are the ornament and strength of society, and abstain from those vices and follies, that weaken the State, and have a tendency to its ruin; and especially that they oppose with fortitude and perserverance, all attempts to impede the course of justice and render their own lives and property insecure.

Many who disapprove insurrections against the government, neglect to afford their aid, in suppressing them; but to stand still, inactive spectators in such case, is like a man who when his house is in flames, should stand with folded arms, and console himself with this, that he did not set it on fire.

We persuade ourselves, that the far greater part of those who have been concerned in the late dangerous tumults, have been deluded by the false representations of men who go about to deceive; and we wish them to reflect how fatal such proceedings may prove in the issue, to themselves and their children; that they must increase the public burthens, and embarrass the measures calculated for relief; that it is their own constitution and laws they are endeavouring to overthrow; that this constitution and these laws were formed for the safety of every member of the State; and that the man who attempts to subvert those laws, and that constitution, does in effect make an attempt upon the life, liberty and property of every member of the community; and we conjure them, by all that they hold dear and sacred, forthwith to desist from such ruinous pursuits.

Perhaps there are some, who deaf to the voice of reason, and lost to all sense of justice and virtue, may resolve to continue in their dangerous course; but let them be assured, although they flatter themselves that the considerations of friendship and affinity, may delay the time of recompence; yet the vengeance of an injured community, must one day, pursue and overtake them.

Regulators Call for Popular Support, 1786

To the Printer of the Hampshire Herald

Sir,

It has some how or other fallen to my lot to be employed in a more conspicuous manner than some others of my fellow citizens, in stepping forth in defence of the rights and privileges of the people, more especially of the county of Hampshire.

Therefore, upon the desire of the people now at arms, I take this method to publish to the world of mankind in general, particularly the people of this Commonwealth, some of the principal grievances we complain of, and of which we are now seeking redress, and mean to contend for, until a redress can be obtained, which we hope, will soon take place; and if so, our brethren in this Commonwealth, that do not see with us as yet, shall find we shall be as peaceable as they be.

In the first place, I must refer you to a draught of grievances drawn up by a committee of the people, now at arms, . . . which is heartily approved of; some others also are here added, viz.

1st. The General Court, for certain obvious reasons, must be removed out of the town of Boston.

2d. A revision of the constitution is absolutely necessary,

3d. All kinds of governmental securities, now on interest, that have been bought of the original owners for two shillings, three shillings, four shillings, and the highest for six shillings and eight pence on the pound, and have received more interest than the principal cost the speculator who purchased them—that if justice was done, we verily believe, nay positively know, it would save this Commonwealth thousands of pounds.

4th. Let the lands belonging to this Commonwealth, at the eastward, be sold at the best advantage, to pay the remainder of our domestick debt.

5th. Let the monies arising from impost and excise be appropriated to discharge the foreign debt.

6th. Let that act, passed by the General Court last June, by a small majority of only seven, called the Supplementary Aid, for twenty five years to come, be repealed.

7th. The total abolition of the Inferiour Court of Common Pleas and General Sessions of the Peace.

8th. Deputy Sheriffs totally set aside, as a useless set of officers in the community; and Constables who are really necessary, be empowered to do the duty, by which means a large swarm of lawyers will be banished from their wonted haunts, who have been more damage to the people at large, especially the common farmers, than the savage beasts of prey.

To this I boldly sign my proper name, as a hearty wellwisher to the real rights of the people.

Thomas Grover
Worcester, December 7, 1786.

A Congregational Pastor Counsels Moderation in a Town with Many Shaysites, 1786

Isaiah I. 19, 20   If ye be willing and obedient, ye shall eat the good of the land: but if ye refuse and rebel, ye shall be devoured with the sword; for the mouth of the Lord hath spoken it.

What was spoken by the prophets to the ancient people of God, is written for our use, that we, through the warnings of scripture, might be moved with fear; and, through the comforts of scripture, might have hope. . . .

I. That the land, in which we are placed, is a good land and,

II. That our enjoyment of the good of the land depends on our obedience to God.

I. It may as truly be said of us, as of ancient Israel, that God has given us a good land.

We lately thought it worth defending by our arms: it is still worth securing by our virtue.

It is an extensive land. . . .

It is a pleasant and fruitful land. . . .

This is a healthful land. . . .

It is a land of liberty, and has been so, with little interruption, from the days of our fathers. . . .

No attempts hitherto made, to subvert our liberties, has been successful. They will probably be preserved, until the people themselves, sunk in vice and corruption, destroy them with their own hands. How near we are to this fatal period, Heaven knows! . . .

We are now under a government of our own framing and chusing. There is perhaps scarcely another instance of the kind on earth. It is a privilege, which few nations ever enjoy, and which the same nation probably can never enjoy more than once. . . .

The constitution of these states, and particularly of this, . . . is not, in any sense whatever, a compact between the rulers and the people; but it is a solemn, explicit agreement of the people among themselves. It was constructed by a convention of wise men, whom the people deputed solely for that purpose, and who, at that time, could have no share, and no appearance of a future share in the government they were framing. It was then remitted to the people at large, and competent time allowed for their deliberate examination and discussion; and it was finally adopted and confirmed in consequence of their general approbation. So happily was it adjusted to the views of the people, at a time when the spirit of liberty was at the height, that not a single article was found in the whole, but what met the approbation of more than two thirds of the inhabitants assembled in the several towns to give their voices upon it. It is therefore, in the most absolute sense, The Constitution of the People; and, in this view, it is more sacred than any form of government in Europe. Being framed by the people, it never ought to be changed or altered without their general consent fairly asked, and freely given. There may undoubtedly be defects in it: nothing human is perfect: but still it is our own; not imposed, but chosen. And whatever imperfections attend it, yet it is acknowledged by all, to be formed on the highest principles of liberty. The administration of it is committed to men appointed by, and from among ourselves; to men who are frequently to return to private life; to men who are subject to the same laws and burthens, which they impose on their fellow citizens. The people have it in their power always to influence the measures of government by petition and instructions, and often to change their rulers by new elections. Nations, whose government is absolute, may be under the sad necessity of submitting to oppression, or of repelling it by force. This is a dreadful alternative, and usually terminates in the increase of the evil. We are under no such necessity. Our government is so constituted, that publick oppressions may be soon removed without force, either by remonstrances against the measures of rulers, or by a change of the rulers themselves. . . .

Perhaps it will be asked, "Is there no case in which a people may resist government?" Yes, there is one such case; and that is, when rulers usurp a power oppressive to the people, and continue to support it by military force in contempt of every respectful remonstrance. In this case the body of the people have a natural right to unite their strength for the restoration of their own constitutional government. And, for the same reason, if a part of the people attempt by arms to controul or subvert the government, the rulers, who are the guardians of the constitution, have a right to call in the aid of the people to protect it. . . .

Whatever oppressions we suffer, or seem to suffer, our measures of redress must be only such, as may consist with our internal peace; for being divided against ourselves, we shall become an easy prey to foreign invaders; or rather, shall fall a contemptible prey to one another. . . .

A general distrust is inconsistent with government and subversive of all security. Confidence joined with circumspection tends both to peace and liberty. . . .

Our first obligation to mankind is justice. This is rendering to all their dues, in opposition to every kind of fraud, oppression and violence. The great law, which ought to govern our social conduct, is to do to others, as we would, that they should do to us; to owe no man any thing, but to love one another. . . .

Our next obligation is goodness. The poor we have always with us: and there are times when their number is increased. The late war, as might naturally be expected, has made a considerable change of property. It has reduced many to absolute poverty, and others to an incapacity of sustaining any great share of the common burthen without leaving their families to want. Government, at such a time, ought to adjust their demands to the common ability; and this, we hope, is their aim, for they bear a part of the burthen with others. But it should be considered, that the general rules, by which the measures of government must be directed, will often operate with some inequality. This is an unavoidable imperfection of human society. In such cases, instead of charging government with cruelty, it would be proper for the more strong to assist the weak. Bear ye one another's burthens, says the law of Christ. The law of reason says the same.

No community ought to leave her prudent and industrious members to struggle in vain under an insupportable load. By mutual succour in times of distress we increase the common strength. Reciprocal support and protection is one end of society. . . .

3. The happiness of a people farther depends on industry and frugality.

This, though a good land, will not support us in idleness and profuseness. If it would, it must soon cease to be a good land. In a country, where every man could grow rich with little labour, almost every man would in fact be poor; for there being no spur to industry and few examples of it, the body of the people would sink into idleness, luxury and wretchedness. All the wealth, and all the power would be engrossed by the provident and enterprizing few. The rest would be slaves, or little superiour.

At a time like this, when the expenses, incurred by the late contest for independence, are lying as a burthen on the country, diligence in our callings, and prudence in our manner of living, are of peculiar importance. . . .

4. Our enjoyment of the good of the land will depend on the regular administration of, and a peaceable submission to civil government.

Mankind cannot subsist without society, nor society without government.

If there was no way to controul the selfishness, check the passions and restrain the vices of men, they would soon become intolerable to each other. Government is the combination of the whole community against the vices of each member. The design of it is not meerly to provide for general defence against foreign power, but to exercise a controul over every individual, to restrain him from wrong, and compel him to right, so far as the common safety requires. . . .

That the people are under great burthens, all are agreed. Whether there are grievances, I leave with others to determine. Admitting there are, undoubtedly there may be methods of redress more safe, and more effectual than arms. If any of you have thought this a necessary measure, I only ask, that you would calmly review what I have said on the nature of our government, and seriously consider what may be the consequences of drawing the sword; and possibly you will see reason to alter your sentiments.

The Reverend Bezaleel Howard on Shays's Rebellion and Its Aftermath, 1787

It is an observation almost worn out that Great events proceed from small causes. The stream that was Insignificant at first and Contemptible, Joining Larger rivulets in its progress, by degrees forms itself into large rivers. Thus the formidable Insurrection, Existing in the Commonwealth began with Complaints of Heavy taxes, unequal Distribution of Justice in the Courts of Commonpleas, the unbounded Demands of the Lawyers, the fees of the Executive officers, the multiplicity of Courts, the Governors Salary, the Registers officer, with a Number of other Grievances Either Real or Supposed. For it is to be observed that Every town and almost Every Individual had their particular Grievinces or at least something which they apprehended amiss in Legislative, Executive or Judicial Departments.

These Complaints being Bandied about from one to another and not Losing but rather Increasing the Disaffection, the General talk was County Conventions, one or two members from Each town to Consult the public welfare and point out some Easy and speedy mode of redress. These conventions, However, did little more than to Increase the Clamour of the people and render of our public affairs more Imbarrased; and to Imped the Execution of Law they went so far, either in their Consultation in Convention or in private among the people, to declaim bitterly against the Constitution, more Especially some particular parts of it. The Commonalty now was Grossly Intoxacated with Conventions, and the disaffected finding they could Chuse such, and o[n]ly such, as already had or would readily, upon choice, Imbibe and adopt their seditious sentiments, gave a life[?] to the Infatuation.

The fire being thus Kindled in the County of Hampshire, similar modes of Conduct was begun and pursued by the Counties of Worcester, Bristol, and Berkshire. The Friends of Government soon Illustrated the Banefull

Rev. Bezaleel Howard's account of Shay's Rebellion by Richard D. Brown, *William and Mary Quarterly, 40,* 1983.

consequences of Conventions by many spirited publications, which rather Increased than abated the ardour for Conventioneering, many Gentlemen of the Law pronouncing those Bodies unconstitutional and Illegal and has [sic] having a tendancy to Enflame the minds of the people and to Encourage Cabels [sic], unlawfull assemblies, & etc. However Illigal their Sentiments were who wrote against Conventions, the faction never dare[d] openly to attack, much more to refute, their absurdity and Impropriety. Committees in Convention were Chose[n] to Corrispond with Committees of other Counties and to adopt a uniform plan. The popular odium against Government now ran high. Some was for a State Convention, but as a great number of towns Near the metropolis were averse and highly in favour of the present mode of Government, or the Impractibility of the plan proposed Discouraged them from any further attempt.

The Court of Justice had Hitherto been Held, and the officer[s] discharged their trust as usual upon the plan of the Constitution. The Existence of this Court was now threatened, and private meetings were held accordingly to stop the Court of Commonplease next to [be] holden at Northampton on the third Tuesday of August 1786. The Greatest Obstacle in the way of success was a Leader of those Banditti who should see fit to Embark in this Hazardous undertaking. However, this Impediment was soon surmounted by fixing on a Captain Daniel Shays of Pelham. . . .

Another matter well worthy their serious & Deliberate Consultation was whither [sic] to proceed with or without arms. They upon this occasion signified that they should not be more obnoxious to Government to go with arms than they should with Bludgeons and Clubs, and it would show their Determinate Resolution to have those matters and things Redressed of which they so much and ardently complained, or to overset the Constitution, or at least some part of it, a revision of which they had proposed in Convention. . . .

Government had as yet raised no troops for their defence, and the posse could not be got in any season to Effect any purpose for their Dispersion. The Court, after Considering their present situation, Concluded to the demands of the Insurgents, which was not to proceed to any business whatsoever. This, and some lesser matters, was complyed with. Thus far all things appeared without any opposition on the part of Government, and this was advanced by the mob as an ostensible argument that Government could not raise a force sufficient to disperse 300, and also that three forths of the people was of their sentiment, altho they had not as yet appeared in open Hostilities and Waged war with Government. Their Return Home was in triumph and Joy for their unmolested Expedition. Their numbers Increased in fact on this occasion and took the advantage to represent it very far beyond what it really was.

Those for Government pictured the mob as the Ragmuffins of the Earth, poor Illiterate Rascals who owed more than they were worth and wanted to abolish Government to screen them from paying their honest debts. Others propegated that their ultimate design was to Level al[l] Distinctions of persons and property, that they als[o] had no money to support them in the field should they take it, and no officers to command their forces. These Invectives were freely handed about by the Government party, which rather Exasperated than Consiliated the minds of those disaffected.

Posts were sent to the different parts of the Commonwealth. The Courts of Worcester, Bristol and Berkshire was stopped. Being Elatted with thire success, and Immagining that a full scope might now be given to thire unbounded malpractices, they openly delivered and Declared their Intentions to overset the present Government by their behaviour and resist the Exe-cution of the Laws, tho in their Discourses or talk they professed their Desire of Good laws. Therefore the Inconsistancy of the words & actions, it was concluded, that they did not know themselves what they wanted or what Renovation in Government they would be after or Desire, Especially as none of thire Conventions or themselves had pointed out Remedy for the evils they Complained of.

The Country was alarmed at their Hostile proceedings and proposi[ti]ons made for their Extirpation, but Government did not Interpose in this affair, and the rioters was bold in any Company without fears or dread. . . .

The Governors salary they did complain of, but it could not be remedied untill the Insuing Election. Thire things Evidently Called for amendment and redress, but Guns and Bayonets and Hostile appearances was far from being the proper way to accomplish the design. It was very justly observed that calling town meetings and Instructing the Representative Body might have redressed our Grievances and secured our Liberties more Effectually. It was supported on the other side that they had already petitioned by towns and Counties by the members of Conventions, which was in last June, but the General Court would not nor could ever be so Condescending as to acknowledge any body Legally Existing, and in Consequence Disregarded all such Remonstrances and petitions.

It was also suggested that the Governor was in favour of the British Government and would be glad rather to throw us into Confusion and disorder if he could, and not be known to have to[o] great a hand in it. The Senate was complained of as a useless body which was Expensive to no manner of purpose, and that the House as it now stood was much to[o] large for the easy and ready dispatch of public business which might be done with a Quater of the Number in a much shorter time, to the Great saving of the people, and the like. Their Complaints was freely and without consious propagated and held up to view among the Common people, and tho some were serious in what they proposed as Grievances, yet many were led away with the fals Eloquence of those about them, Like the dogs in a village: if one bark, all bark. . . .

No troops as yet was raised by order of Government for its defence, Except volunteers from Different towns, but as the General [Court] was Called together three months or more Earlier than the prorogation, Great Expectations was raised of what they would do. They met accordingly in October. The first act they made was a riot act to prevent peoples assembling together in public or private to the number of twelve. This was followed by the suspension of the Habeus Corpus act, whereby any person offending might be transported to any Distant County for tryall. The Court also made a list act that all who had been guilty in the late riots, or aided or assisted, by taking the oath of Fidelity by January first 1787 should be Exempt from all further prosecution for their treason.* They also brought in several bills for the more speedy and less Expensive administration of the laws. They Likewise made a tender act. They considered the removal of the Court from sitting in Boston & to remove it to some country town.

But these acts Did not operate to the satisfaction or in any degree to Quiet the minds of the Insurgents or to put a stop to their operations, for soon after they appeared to stop Worcester Court, which they effected. . . . However, after accomplishing [the]ir Design they returned Home.

It was now the month of January. [missing] Government roused from their supiness [missing] Inactivity &c. Gentlemen merchants [missing] in Boston offered Government a sum [of money] on loan sufficient to raise a body of [troops] to put a final period to their Disturbance. General Lincoln was appointed to the Com[mand], who raised in the Counties of Essex [and] Middlesex 2000 men and marched them to Worcester. But before they marched, a party of horse from Boston came up & took one of the Leaders of Worcester County Insurgents, Shadduck, [and] two others Named Parker and Page. Shadduck was badly wounded in the knee in his defence of being taken. However, he was overpowered and with the others took, bound, and carried to Boston and put into prison. The whole Country was all aflame, some approving, others disapproving the taking, wounding, &c., of Shadduck. Orders were Now given to General Shepherd to raise 1200 men in the County of Hampshire and to march to Springfield the 18 of January, and at all Events to defend the public stores on the hill. He accordingly arrived, Quatered a number in the Barracks on the hill, the remainder among the Inhabitants.

Conventions was now no more. It was now a time for action, not for consultation of Grievances. Great was the Anxiety what would be the Issue of this millitary force. The Extremity of the weather, the deebth of the snow from the frequent storms, all which rendered a winter Campain difficult. However, these Inconveniences did not Impede the Resolution of Government or the fources under the Command of the Generals Lincoln & Shepperd. Their men was also in high spirits to put a final period to the futer rising of the mob.

The Insurgents, on the other hand, began to gath[er] in Different places. Shays proceeded from Pelham to Amherst and Greenwich, Palmer, and Wilbraham, where he Collected 1000 or 1200 in one week. Luke Day Collected 7 or 800 and posted himself in West Springfield and kept a guard at the ferry, with orders to let nobody pass and to take up all slays with provision or any other supplys for Government. They now began to take up on both

---

* The "list act" was an act of indemnity offering pardons.

sides Horses, slays, and suspected persons. While thise things were doing, Eli Parsons arrived from Berkshire with 500 men. He took post at Chicopee to prevent all Communication that way. Each occupied their posts without Interfering with the other, Except Shays, who march[ed] with an Intent to form a junction with Day in West Springfield and had advanced for this purpose as far as Wilbraham.

General Shepherd's Situation Grew more and more alarming, being almost surrounded. He pressed on his posts to Lincoln for a Reinforcement. Immediately in the mean time Shays advanced. . . . Shepherd ordered two pieces of artilery to fire over their Heads to Deter or frighten them, but they still pursuing, the commander of the artilery leveled Directly at their front and Discharged a Number of round and grape shot, which Killed four and wounded several. This was on the 25 of January 1787.

Shays retreated with the utmost Disorder. . . .

Notwithstanding the time limited for the taking the oath of allegience was Expired, Yet many Desired and had the oath administered to them, hoping thereby to mitigate their punishment or to alleviate in Some Degree the Criminallity of their offences.

The General Court was Call[ed] Together in this junction of Trouble & Consternation. The first act they passed was an act of Rebellion, Declaring and pronouncing all those rebels and Traitors against Government who had any way assisted, abeted, or any way Given aid and comfort to the Insurgents; also calling on all officers, civil & military, to seize, apprehend and bring to Condign punishment all such. This was followed soon after by the Exclusion act, Defining the punishment, the penalties, the Natural Rights and priviledges those should be deprived of who had, did, or should hereafter any way be Guilty of Treason. It consisted chiefly in this, that if the Insurgents should come in to some magistrate before the 21st day of march next and bring their arms and subscribe the oath of Fidelity, they should have their lives for agreeing, but should not sustain any office, Either Civil or military, for the span of 3 years. Nethir should they vote in any town meeting for the same term, Nor for any military officer; and at the Expiration of said term, upon producing a Certificate from the selectmen of their good behaviour to the General Court, they possibly might receive their arms again. All those who had sustained any offices, Either Civil or military, should not, However, be Benefited by the said act, but be tryed as though no such act had bin promulgated. . . .

What Effect their acts had, more Especially the Exclusion act, will better be seen by the Conduct of those of [the] Government party. . . .

Lincoln Determined to pursue and for this purpose began his movement at Dark. His rout[e] was thro Amherst, Pelham, New Salem, which was a march of 30 miles in one Night. The Night proved so cold and tempestuous that most of his men froze before they reached Petersham, which was Sunday 9 aclock in the morn. By this forced march they came upon Shays unawars and, without firing one Gun, put him and all his troops to a total rout. Every one looked out for himself for a safe Retreat. The Greater part of the men returned by Stealth to their homes, Lurking about and secreting themselves from the Eye of the public. Shays and his principle officers went to the Northward, to New Hampshire, from there to the State of Vermont, skulking about from place to place. . . .

Matter[s] being thus shamefully conducted on the part of the Insurgents, and the forces dayly returning to their respective Homes, the Magistrates, officers, and soldiers of Government took the advantage to Call fourth whom they would, from whatever place they were, and to vent all the spite, malice, and spleen, their jealousies and ill will, in their confinement in the public Goals, taking some under pretense of warrant and Civil authority, taking others by the force of the Bayonet and Military power, some out of spite and malace in them that complained, others upon bare suspicion, many of them Innocent, others more or less Guilty. The Gun and Bayonet was now the only standard of authority. All suspected persons, or those who had not taken an active part on Nither side and perposed to stand witness, were threatened with Imprisonment, should they presume to speak any thing against their present Conduct. Jealousy raging in Every bosom, Envy and malice in Every heart, pride and ostentatious partiality, tyriny and oppresion raging among the magistracy, plainly Discouvering the Byass and Inclination of their mind and the Wickedness of their hearts. Now they had power to punish in what manner they pleased and [missing] military force to strengthen & countenance their proceedings. Their Wills is as law and their Determination Justice. Such a state of anarchy & Confusion, Dispotism and Tyranny succeeded the Dispersion of Shays troops.

Nothing Could be more Injurious to the Liberty and privileges of a peopal than the Conduct of the Justices and the military men. To be a soldier was sufficient to Invest him with power to drag whomsoever they would from their beds at midnight and commit them to Goal untill a partiall Examination could be had and, if Innocent, Dismissed without any recompense for the cruil Behaviour of the Soldiery, some committed to Goal till Bonds were procured for their appearance at the next Supreme Court, but many upon taking the oath, Delivering up their arms, and paying, then went Home. . . .

The General Court Now appointed the Supreme Court to Repair to Great Barrington and sit for the trial of all those Insurgents who had or should [be] taken in that County. . . . In march the court sat, and ten days or a fortnight was Spent in this most Important Enquiry and Examining into the Nature of the Offences and Evidence to support it. [Robert Treat] Paine, the States attorney, Exerted all his Malevolence and Malice on this occasion. And as the Complection of the time now is, but very little Testimony is Necessary towards the Conviction of any one that had in smallest degree assisted or supposed to have assisted or only countenanced. And as Every man more or less has them who are unfriendly about him, who gladly lay hold of such opportunities, witneses were very E[a]sily procured. If the Court, by Information, was as tender as a Court Could be Expected to be on such an occasion, tho was not so Inexorable and unrelenting as many of the prisoners Neighbours. The Evidence was ample and full, and after a full hearing of the parties by themselves or Counsel, six were condemned to die by the Hangman, some to pay Large fines. Among the latter was Judge Whiting of Great Barrington, who was fined £100 and bound for his good behaviour 3 years. The Commissioners was Crowded by people for pardons, for all the Lower and Common sort were within the act, but all Influencial Characters were Debarred from receiving a pardon.

The Supreme Court removed from Barrington to Northhampton to Examine, try, convict, or acquit all who were aiding, assisting, or Comforting the Rebels. Among those Convicted of Treason were John Wheeler of Hardwick, Shays aid de Camp, Henry McCullock of Pelham, Daniel Ludington of Southampton, John White of Coldrain, and Jason Parmeter of Barnardston, who shot Walker. These all received the sentence of Death. Moses Hervey of Montague was tryed and sentenced to pay £50 fine, set on the Gallows with a rope round his Neck one hour, and to be bound to keep the peace five years. Thomas Kellam of Westfield was sentenced to be whipt 20 stripes or pay £20. He performed the latter. Many other[s] was sentenced to Imprisonment and fine.

The Commissioners Sat Every Day, Granting for all those who was well recommended to mercy by two at least Good men of the town to which they belonged. Numbers there were tho, took Shelter and Safety under shadowy wing of these Commissioners, who had such power that whomsoever they pardoned was free Indeed; and the Inveteracy of many of Government party [was such] that Numbers flocked thither who were not Guilty, but was fearfull of the malace of others and took Sanctuary. . . . Shays and the Heads of the faction were fled to Vermont and Canada, where they found protection.

Some time in April [a] Death warrant was made out for those 12 to be Executed on Thursday, the 24 of May, Six at Barington and six at Northampton. Various were the opinions of people with Respect to the propriety of Hanging these men. Bowdoin had (by the Disqualifiing Act and the Suspention of the Habeus Corpus Act and some other proceedings) made himself Quit[e] obnoxious [to] the Majority of the people, and Elections now being come, they left him out, and by a great majority chose John Hancock, Esquire, Governor for the year Insuing. . . .

[The] time of the sitting of the General Court Now Came on, which was 3/4 made up of New members. Bowdoin gave up the Chair to Hancock with sensible Reluctance on the Friends to Governments part, who could not Brook to see the object of their scorn and hate thus Exalted to the Chair of Government. . . . But their Malovolant and spitfull treatment of Hancock, the cruelty of the disqualifiing act, the Suspension of the Habeus Corpus act, and the consequences thence arising, all Conspired to overthrow their favourite plan, and they had in the Conclusion an Entire Contrary Effect from what thos[e] Imps of Hypocrisy and oppresion designed they should have. Who could wonder to see them chop fallen when the news came that Hancock had 3/4 of the votes?

Congressman Charles Pinckney Admonishes the New Jersey Legislature, 1786

Mr. Speaker,

The united states in congress assembled, have been informed, that this house had, on the 20th ultimo, resolved that they could not, consistently with their duty to their constituents, assent to the requisition of September last, for federal supplies. . . .

When these states united, convinced of the inability of each to support a separate system, and that their protection and existence depended on their union—policy, as well as prudence, dictated the necessity of forming one GENERAL and Efficient Government, which, while it protected and secured the whole, left to the several states, those rights of INTERNAL SOVEREIGNTY, it was not necessary to delegate, and which could be exercised without injury to the federal authority. In them were placed all the essential powers which constitute a nation—such are, the exclusive rights of peace and war; of sending and receiving embassies; of forming treaties and alliances; and equipping and raising fleets and armies. To them, also, was delegated the power of obtaining loans on the faith of the united states; and of apportioning to the several members of the union, their quotas of the public expences. . . .

The states having thus by their voluntary act, formed one government as essential to the protection of the whole—and placed in a supreme controuling power the administration of its general concerns, and to which they were to look up for support—each state is bound, according to its abilities, to furnish a proportion of the expences; and the whole are jointly and severally pledged for the public engagements, foreign and domestic. . . . New Jersey has not only assented to the mode by which she is rated, but furnished the returns on which the assessment could be made with exactness: she certainly cannot, therefore, complain of bearing an undue proportion. She will not, I trust, upon reflection, suppose she can, either consistently with her duty to the union, or with safety to its welfare, refuse to comply with the requisition. If she has been over-rated, upon stating the excess in evidence to congress, she will always receive the relief she may be justly entitled to. If, on the other hand, she conceives herself unequally situated, or that she does not participate in those common benefits which the general government was expected to dispense to all its members—if she thinks, with me, that its powers are inadequate to the ends for which it was instituted, and that they should be increased—there can be no doubt of the conduct she ought to pursue. She ought immediately to instruct her delegates in congress, to urge the calling of a general convention of the states, for the purpose of revising and amending the federal system. In this constitutional application, she will meet with all the attention and support she can wish. I have long been of opinion, that it was the only true and radical remedy for our public defects; and shall with pleasure assent to, and support, any measure of that kind, which may be introduced, while I continue a member of that body. . . .

It is certainly more the interest of the small, than it can be of the large states, to preserve the confederation upon its present principles. We are aware of the necessity which compelled the latter to confederate upon terms allowing each state an equal vote in the national councils. Had the system been formed in a time of peace—when no common danger pressed—when deliberation was unaccompanied with apprehension, and the large states preferred conceding the point of proportionable representation, however important, to the greater evil of being again reduced to the power of Great Britain—can it be thought that any union would have been formed upon principles so unequal and oppressive as the present?

Let us for a moment suppose the confederation dissolved, and an assembly of the states convened for the purpose of adopting a system calculated to render the general government firm and energetic—is it not to be reasonably expected, that the large states would contend and insist upon a greater influence than they at present possess? Would they again consent to unite upon principles which should allow states not contributing a twelfth part of their quotas to the public expences, an equal vote with themselves! It is not even to be hoped. It ought, therefore, to appear exceedingly important to the small states to maintain a system so advantageous to their particular interests, when they reflect that in the event of another confederation, they cannot expect to be placed in a situation, to which they are neither entitled by common justice, or an equal attention to the rights of the other members of the union.

Though our present disorders must be attributed, in the first instance, to the weakness and inefficacy of the general government, it must still be confessed they have been precipitated by the refractory and inattentive conduct of the states; most of whom have neglected altogether the performance of their federal duties; and, whenever their state policy or interests prompted, used their retained rights to the injury and disgrace of the federal head.

Delegates Report from a Demoralized Congress, 1787

Stephen Mix Mitchell to Jeremiah Wadsworth

NEW YORK Jany. 24th, 1787

Dear Sir,

Whether I am to tell you we have a Congress or no, I cannot tell.

The Scituation of Congress is truely deplorable. no one seems willing to contribute a Mite to extricate us from the mire into which we are fallen.

Pensylvania in answer to Messrs. King and Monro, have so far declared in favor of dividing the Debt, as to say, they will pay their own Citizens only.

I cannot see there remains any necessity for keeping up a Representation in Congress. in our present Scituation, all we can possibly do, is to recommend, which is an old, stale device and no better than the wish of a few Individuals relative to publick Concerns.

Our Eyes at present are turn'd to Masachusetts and expect by Saturday's post, to hear of feats of Chivalry. We are told that Genl. Lincoln and Mr. Shays are this week to take feild to try the Title for Empire in the feild of Mars; whether Good or ill is to be produced, futurity must discover.

James Madison to George Washington

NEW YORK Feby. 21, 1787

Dear Sir,

Some little time before my arrival here a quorum of the States was made up and Genl. Sinclair put in the Chair. . . . The objects now depending and most immediately in prospect, are 1. The Treaty of peace. . . . 2. a recommendation of the proposed Convention in May. Cong's have been much divided and embarrassed on the question whether their taking an interest in the measure would impede or promote it. . . . Our latest information from Mass'ts gives hopes that the mutiny or as the Legislature there now style it, the Rebellion is nearly extinct. If the measures however on foot for disarming and disfranchising those concerned in it should be carried into effect, a new crisis may be brought on. I have not been here long enough to gather the general sentiments of leading characters touching our affairs and prospects. I am inclined to hope that they will gradually be concentered in the plan of a thorough reform of the existing system. Those who may lean towards a Monarchial Govt. and who I suspect are swayed by very indigested ideas, will of course abandon an unattainable object whenever a prospect opens of rendering the Republican form competent to its purposes. Those who remain attached to the latter form must soon perceive that it can not be preserved at all under any modification which does not redress the ills experienced from our present establishments.

James Madison to Edmund Pendleton

NEW YORK, Feby. 24, 1787

Dear Sir,

. . . The only step of moment taken by Cong's, since my arrival has been a recommendation of the proposed meeting in May for revising the federal articles. Some of the States, considering this measure as an extra constitutional one, had scruples agst. concurring in it without some regular sanction. By others it was thought best that Cong's should remain neutral in the business, as the best antidote for the jealousy of an ambitious desire in them to get more powers into their hands. This suspense was at length removed by an instruction from this State to its delegates to urge a Recommendatory Resolution in congress which accordingly passed a few days ago. . . . In general I find men of reflection much less sanguine as to the new than despondent as to the present System. Indeed the Present System neither has nor deserves advocates; and if some very strong props are not applied will quickly tumble to the ground. No money is paid into the public Treasury; no respect is paid to the federal authority. Not a single State complies with the requisitions, several pass them over in silence, and some positively reject them. The payments ever since the peace have been decreasing, and of late fall short even of the pittance necessary for the Civil list of the Confederacy. It is not possible that a Government can last long under these circumstances. If the approaching convention should not agree on some remedy, I am persuaded that some very different arrangement will ensue. The late turbulent scenes in Mass'ts and infamous ones in Rhode Island, have done inexpressible injury to the republican character in that part of the U. States; and a propensity towards Monarchy is said to have been produced by it in some leading minds. The bulk of the people will probably prefer the lesser evil of a partition of the Union into three more practicable and energetic Governments. The latter idea I find after long confinement to individual speculations and private circles, is beginning to shew itself in the Newspapers. But tho' it is a lesser evil, it is so great a one that I hope the danger of it will rouse all the real friends of the Revolution to exert themselves in favor of such an organization of the confederacy, as will perpetuate the Union, and redeem the honor of the Republican name.

E S S A Y S

J. R. Pole, Rhodes Professor of American History and Institutions at Oxford University, has long been one of the most learned and astute analysts of politics in the Revolutionary era. In the first essay, extracted from his *Political Representation in England and the Origins of the American Republic* (1966), Pole argues that Shays's Rebellion was a consequence of an undeveloped set of expectations and institutions for expressing opposition in Massachusetts. Political-party systems, he suggests, would later provide an alternative to county conventions and other extralegal forms of protest. Gordon S. Wood's prize-winning *Creation of the American Republic, 1776–1787* (1969) is one of the most influential studies of the past generation. In the second selection, Wood, professor of history at Brown University, analyzes the crisis of confidence and the sense of alarm that engulfed nationalists during the mid-1780s.

Shays's Rebellion and the Problem of Opposition Politics

J. R. POLE

A constitutional historian of Massachusetts, after bringing his subject safely through the year 1780, might feel entitled to lay down his pen and contemplate a work well done. Few were disposed to deny that the Constitution had been adopted with the general consent of the governed or that the annually elected legislators conformed to the accepted notion of true representatives. . . .

Within six years, longstanding discontent throughout much of the Commonwealth had been fanned into organised riots, and these in turn were raised, under the hesitant leadership of Captain Daniel Shays, into a minor rebellion. The rebellion, a strangely disjointed, aimless affair, was crushed with slight loss. The State Constitution not only emerged unshaken, but proved itself capable of absorbing the impetus of discontent through the normal elective system; at the ensuing elections, in April 1787, both Governor James Bowdoin and a great majority of representatives lost their seats. Within a few months, and particularly after the ratification of the Federal Constitution, it was easy to believe that the whole episode had been greatly over-rated; but before it was over it had given the legislators and many substantial citizens, in Massachusetts and in other states, a severe fright. If a truly republican government could not hold the allegiance of the people, was the American experiment destined to fail?

The question gave rise to some of the animus against "democracy" expressed in the opening days of the Philadelphia Convention. Shays's Rebellion thus has a peculiar stature, much out of proportion to its local character. The history of Europe is dotted with minor peasant revolts, local, wild, and hopeless, which barely attract the attention of the historian. . . . But the rising of 1786 demonstrated with cruel violence that something had gone wrong with the very institutions of representation which the people of the Bay Colony had fought to defend and had agreed, by conference, to maintain.

The grievances underlying the county conventions of 1786 and the rebellion itself were repeatedly expounded at the time. They may be summarised as economic distresses, arising from the aftermath of war and from legislative policies, administered through, and exacerbated by, the courts, the legal profession, and the county officials. The burden of taxation to meet State debts was compounded by the burden of private debt, and both were made terrifying by the practice, or the threat, of the imprisonment of debtors. The exorbitant expenses of court action often precluded the poorer victims from seeking relief through litigation, even when they had the better case. The petty tyrannies of sheriffs and constables aroused bitter hatred.

No administration could entirely have averted the post-war economic crisis; but the form it took in Massachusetts was in large measure a product of the policies of the General Court, a point firmly grasped by the more articulate and better informed spokesmen of the protest movements.

As early as 1777, the General Court had initiated the hard-money policy which it pursued, with much tacking and veering but with unwavering purpose, right down to the crisis. By Acts of 1780 and 1781, all legal tender except gold and silver was abolished and heavy taxes were imposed. Further measures in the following years constantly proclaimed the dedication of successive legislatures to the principle of redeeming the State's obligations to its creditors at whatever cost to the overburdened and the poor. And the poll tax, the most consistently used means of raising money, being levied at a flat rate, had a most unequal operation.

It seemed by the early spring of 1786 that the hard struggles of the Revolutionary War were to produce, for those who had fought or endured them, nothing better than a dwindling lifetime of debt, poverty, and even imprisonment. What made this intolerable was that every officer of government was engaged as a matter of duty in forcing home the exactions, inflicting the hardships.

The General Court was not unaware of the plight of the country. . . . When every allowance has been made for the imperfections of economic science and the humanity of the legislators, their course on the one hand, and on the other the county conventions and the outbreak of rebellion, raise questions which cannot be answered by examining either economic statistics or the provisions of the Constitution of 1780. The question is why a government consisting solely of duly elected representatives should have pursued a policy capable of alienating a large section of the people and driving the remnant to despair and revolt; the question is also why, under a representative government, the opposition should have been able to find no means of attaining redress, both constitutional and effective.

It is clear that, despite occasional hesitations and tackings, the Assembly majority did not pursue a definable policy. It is also clear that this policy conformed in general to the objectives of the leading economic interest of the seaboard, and that it aroused heated and widespread opposition. . . .

The larger numbers of members from the eastern towns were, of course, within much easier reach of the capital than their colleagues from the interior; their attendance could therefore always be more regular. Their position also gave them the opportunity of seeing each other and conferring in ways denied to the interior. The county conventions so popular in the west, though hotly denounced as unconstitutional and subversive, may reasonably be considered an organised counterpart to this unofficial but immensely useful seaboard advantage. . . .

The Speakers of the House continued to be Representatives either of Boston or of other towns in the seaboard area, right through the war and the Confederation period, with the single and interesting exception of the critical year 1786–7 when the Speaker came from Shrewsbury in Worcester County. For most of the same period the clerk of the House was also a Boston man.

The significance of this unauthorised system was understood by the opposition. Few demands of the protest movement were more insistently repeated than that for the removal of the General Court out of Boston; and Massachusetts was a noteworthy exception to the general tendency to remove the capital in a westerly direction soon after the Revolution. This was frequently linked with demands for a reform in the basis of representation and, significantly, for the abolition of the Senate. These three measures were aimed at the machinery by which the seaboard kept its grip; but it is doubtful whether they would ever have made a permanent difference without the aid of some standing political organisation. . . .

The mere existence of the Senate was a grievance. The conservatism of that body consisted partly in its tendency to reject reforms emanating from the House, partly in the mere presence of a constitutional body based on property rather than persons. The election of James Bowdoin as Governor in 1785, which took place in the General Court owing to the lack of a popular majority for any candidate, was carried with the aid of a senatorial majority of commercial interests. Economic distress and the policies of the General Court had begun to make this principle seem more objectionable than it had seemed in theory in 1780. . . .

The actual distribution of senators on the basis of taxes paid, rather than numbers, did not make a great difference. Suffolk County, with Boston, had six senators instead of the four to which it would have been entitled on a numerical basis; the central and western counties were short by one or two senators; but it is a mistake to assess representation in merely arithmetical terms. All the senators, from whatever counties, were required to be men of substance. . . .

The better informed commentators who contributed essays on economic policy to the newspapers showed much understanding and often a fund of knowledge; but this was brought out only by the crisis and the usual situation in the towns showed little change since the days before the Revolution. Newspapers very seldom reported Assembly debates—the *Hampshire Gazette* was roused to do so as late as November, 1786, and it did not become a habit. The House itself did nothing to inform the people either of its measures or the reason for them; even when it had acted to redress grievances it failed to explain its actions. A contributor sympathetic to the demonstrators pointed out that it would be well if the General Court would inform their constituents more particularly of the state of public affairs; especially of the state's part of the national debt, the amount of the domestic debt, the annual charge for the support of government, and the interest paid annually; the takings of the treasury by imposts, excise, licences and auctions, and taxes; and many other matters of political economy which were later to become the currency of political discussion. Other glimpses of the curiously episodic state of information about public affairs are caught from the instructions of Douglass in May 1787, which remarked to the representative that as he would have better information in that capacity than the town he might make all reasonable alterations; a remark by the chief justice that the representatives were better informed than the towns, and a remark by another town that it "believed" laws had been passed contrary to the peace treaty—plainly admitting to uncertainty about legislative history.

These deficiencies were admitted by the General Court to be part of the reason for the prevailing dissatisfaction—or rather they were proclaimed on the ground that better information would have led to fairer appreciation of the efforts of the legislators. In October 1786 a committee of both branches of the legislature brought in a long report directly designed to answer recent complaints and to provide public information, and several measures of redress were ordained; one of which, the introduction of a new institution to take the place of the unpopular court of Common Pleas, was later rejected by the Senate. Soon afterwards, a formal Address to the People by the General Court gave an account of public revenues, spending, expectations from land sales, and the state of the debt. This was necessary because, it was stated, discontent had arisen largely from misinformation. . . .

In constitutional theory the towns were represented through their right to instruct representatives. Through them the General Court would possess all the information it needed for legislative purposes. The difficulties experienced not only by Massachusetts but by the American economy after the end of the war might have been expected to provide the legislators with all the information they needed. . . .

Why, then, had not the afflicted areas themselves made better use of their constitutional rights to instruct their representatives and to apply for redress? If the instructions and petitions for relief lying in the state archives are grouped together the cries of distress sound insistent and impressive. None speaks clearer than the plea of Ludlow: "We humbly Conceve that your honours are well acquanted with the distresses of the people of this Commonwealth and are possesed of Bowels of pitty and tenderness."

Not all these petitions agreed with each other. Most demanded paper money, and a few denounced it. . . . The other factor of great significance is the chronic non-representation of the smaller towns.

May 1786 began a session at which, in view of the growing discontent, a large delegation might have been expected from the western counties. In fact, of 314 towns entitled to representation no fewer than 145 failed to elect a member. The three western and central counties of Hampshire, Worcester, and Berkshire—entitled between them to 130 representatives—could send only 67. This figure probably represented a strenuous exertion, for it compared favourably with the percentage of the state as a whole. But where Hampshire, Worcester, and Berkshire achieved a representation of about 51 per cent against a state average of about 53, the eastern counties of Suffolk, Essex, and Middlesex sent delegations from 46 of their 78 towns— almost 60 per cent; and if the count is confined to Essex and Suffolk, which between them concentrated most of the seaboard population and mercantile property, the contrast becomes still more striking: 29 out of 40 towns, or 72 per cent. When all the unofficial advantages of the seaboard are weighed in, and the lack of unity, previous consultation, or even uniformity of interest of the interior counties is considered, the political influence of the east becomes almost a tangible thing.

The basic reason for this non-representation was economic. The town records show again and again that when the cost of being assessed for the support of a member throughout the legislative sessions was considered by a community, the gains to be had from representation frequently did not seem worth the price. But the very factors which made representation urgent also made it more burdensome. The harder the times, the more inducement to the towns to cut their costs. That any one town's one or two representatives would be able to make an effective impression on the general policies of the Court or on the condition of the Commonwealth always seemed improbable. It was easier to risk the fine for non-representation and hope for the success of a plea of poverty. The worse the crisis, the worse the representation of the state as a whole at the seat of government; and this was a weakness that applied particularly to the areas of greatest distress. The times thus gave great force to the argument of Greenwich, that all representatives should be paid from the public chest—a view which only some dozen towns had thought worth advancing in their returns on the Constitution of 1780.

But the unwillingness of the dissatisfied towns to make an instrument of reform of the General Court is not fully explained by their poverty. It must be recognised that there occurred a dangerous breakdown of confidence between the General Court and a large body of citizens—a much larger body, to judge by the county conventions, than eventually took part in the disturbances. Against the strangely small number of petitions seeking redress from the legislature, the conventions brought together and gave vent to an impressive volume of indignation.

The link between the county conventions and the Shays disorders is obscure. . . . Whether or not the Convention leaders were possessed with the frenzy of class hatred and the purpose of class war, such motives were freely attributed to them by their enemies.

Much of the frenzy was worked up by the "conservatives," who convinced themselves that a new social revolution was in the making, although there is no evidence of rebel plans against the state government; it was on western ground that the rival forces met, and hardly anyone on either side was hurt. . . .

The conventions were composed of delegates from the towns, regularly elected in town meetings. It was open to each town to decide whether or not to send a delegation, and those in which a majority—or the leading citizens—opposed the whole practice sometimes gave their reasons for declining. Thus Medford, refusing to attend the Worcester Convention of August 1786, declared it an unwarrantable attempt to take the public business out of the hands of those (i.e., the General Court) to whom the Constitution had confided it. The proper procedure was to lay grievances before the General Court through instructions to representatives; but the call did not specify any grievances. The Convention, this statement sharply added, was likely to create more grievances by making parties and counteracting the proceedings of the General Court. Medford believed the state debts to be debts of honour, the price of victory in war. If the states repudiated it, the prediction of their enemies that the Americans were incapable of governing themselves would be completely verified.

The biggest gain from the conventions may well have been that by causing excitement and public debate they attracted attention to the widespread nature of the grievances which called them forth. But as a means of concerting opposition, they were not very effective. The complaints listed in the resolves of the conventions frequently reappeared in the instructions or petitions of the towns which had sent delegations. . . .

It was the general policy of the conventions to correspond with each other on views, grievances, and remedies. Their meetings became more frequent as the crisis developed. It is not surprising that by early in the new year they should have begun to plan for the forthcoming elections. Their whole procedure, indeed their existence, was disagreeably reminiscent, in the opinion of their opponents, of the measures by which the province had been rallied against the Crown. Then, at least from about 1774, there had been a rising degree of unity; it could be argued that the Charter, under attack by the British, was being defended by the people. But once the Constitution of 1780 had gone into force, conventions challenged the legitimacy of the government of the state. It was therefore consistently argued by all their opponents that since the Constitution made no provision for them, but had provided adequate means of representation, they lay outside the Constitution and were illegal. . . .

The charge of illegality can best be understood as an implied counter-assertion that the Constitution, having been established by the consent of the governed, comprehended all possible modes of legitimate political action. That instrument, as Chief Justice [William] Cushing [of Massachusetts] observed, had parcelled out all the power to be exercised under it; no delegated power remained to give to the county conventions, unless it were to counteract the General Court and compel or over-awe them. What then was to be done about real grievances? The answer was plain: follow the ancient usage by applying at regular town meetings to lawful representatives, either by petition or instruction. The Constitution expressly protected the right of instruction and the right of assembly.

This counsel, however, ignored the core of the dissidents' problem. In legislative divisions the instructed members might simply be defeated. It was inherently unlikely that instructions could overturn set legislative policies unless the opposing members had had the opportunity of concerting their own measures. Here and there a specific mistake or grievance might be corrected; but that was not at all the same thing as reversing the entire direction of economic policy. Yet the whole system under which the General Court operated tended to preclude such previous consultation; the country members came together from all over the state; and the very steps by which some co-ordinated policy might have been devised were denounced by all the agents and supporters of central government as unconstitutional. Within the formal constitution of government was an informal but no less powerful system by which the government was carried on. There was no lack of opportunity for concerting policy by the men who were always on the spot and who anyway held most of the strings of power and influence. The county conventions must be understood as the natural—indeed, the normal—response of the discontented elements to the effective exercise of power, through the control of the "system," by their opponents.

The county convention, springing directly from the towns, upon particular occasions and derived from the popular resistance of revolutionary times, seemed to its supporters to be nearer to the people than did the General Court. . . .

The conventions, then, emerged as an old way of meeting new problems. They reflected not so much the power as the lack of effective instruments in the hands of a gravely discontented section of the people. It is this sense of lack which offers us a clearer view of them—though one that was not available to them. The conventions were the only mode of collective protest, of the concerting of policies, which the dissidents could hit on before the rise of the organised political party. Conventions disappeared when parties arose, until in due course the parties revived them for party purposes; but after this they acquired a national, and lost their local, character.

The upheaval of the spring elections of 1787 was all the more remarkable. It was reflected in the sheer scale of participation by the voters. In 1786, some 8,000 of them took part in the election for Governor, being about 11 per cent of the adult white males of the state; this, though slightly low, was not much below the average for such elections since 1780. But 1787 produced a turnout of over 24,000; about 32 per cent and nearly twice as high as any before. The *Worcester Magazine* reported the election of sixteen new senators. The towns made an unprecedented effort to return representatives. No fewer than 228 made elections, leaving only 87 as absentees. (Next year an ebbing of this exertion was already to be noticed, with 108 towns unrepresented.) In Hampshire 41 of 59 towns, in Berkshire 21 of 25, and in Worcester, by a magnificent effort, every one of the 46 towns, returned representatives. Essex also achieved 100 per cent representation of its 18 towns, Suffolk 18 out of 22, and Middlesex 32 out of 38. An extraordinary proportion of the representatives were new; no fewer than 159 out of 253 were counted by the *Worcester Magazine.*

The social composition of the House of Representatives had already begun to change by 1786, if the rank claimed by members can be considered as a guide. The dignity of an "esquire" still told in such matters, but the "esquires" had begun to yield place, particularly to members bearing a military rank dating from the Revolutionary War. In policy, the results of the elections were felt more in relief of distress than in a fundamental change of direction. The former legislature had acted to suspend the collection of debts in specie, and this Act was periodically renewed; and a measure was passed for the relief of poor prisoners committed for debt. Acts were also passed postponing the payment of taxes. The new legislature also showed notable leniency towards the Shaysites, who had been subjected to certain disabilities by the preceding body. To those who had been disfranchised, the suffrage franchise was restored in June 1787 after the disqualification had been in effect for only four months and had applied only to the election of April 1787.

These measures do not disclose a basic reorientation of economic policy. The encouragement and protection of Massachusetts production and commerce, which was already legislative policy under the Confederation, was continued; but the new legislature did not initiate the paper money policy, or the establishment of a "bank of paper money," which were demanded by so many of the stricken towns. It should be recognised that even at the height of discontent, the opposition to these measures was strong and highly articulate, even in the west. The articulateness, the grasp of political language of the economic conservatives, especially when combined with their social position, gave them an advantage that could not easily be outswayed. In the election which turned out the old General Court, even the insurgent county of Berkshire returned two of the staunchest conservatives in America: Henry

Van Schaack and Theodore Sedgwick. The authority of men of their social pre-eminence outweighed adverse political opinions. . . .

The year 1780 established the Constitution of Massachusetts but did not bring any change in the conduct of its politics. The province had long been used to political factions, to the struggle for prominence of energetic men, to the caucus and the manipulation of the town meeting; from about 1774, something like a united front was brought into being against British tyranny, but this front did not hold the government of the Bay Province together. When, soon after the adoption of the new state Constitution, the policy of the legislature began to provoke renewed discontent, the opposition resorted to the use of the county convention, the only form of effective organisation it knew.

Though effective as an expression of grievance, it was less useful for securing redress. The persistent weakness of the opposition was a phenomenon of some complexity. There were real difficulties about the working out of a satisfactory economic policy, and these difficulties were multiplied for those who, being in a permanent minority and not standing at the centre of information and authority, were never in a position to formulate a clear policy of their own. The merchant party did not handle the economic affairs of the state with great success, and were ready to permit modifications and to alleviate undue hardships when the need was pointed out to them: but they did in effect work as a political party. Their strategic position, their opportunities of mutual consultation, and the quorum rule in the House of Representatives gave them all the advantages of a party without the distasteful formality of organisation; nor were they required to face the extremely arduous task, which gave much trouble to later party organisers, of keeping the machinery of a party in existence between elections. . . .

What the opposition needed, instead of a series of county conventions, was a state-wide political party. The need was urgent, a fact which can be seen very clearly in retrospect; but the idea was inchoate, and when it began to take shape it reeked of those signs of conspiracy, of dissent from the agreed will of the sovereign people, of the attempt to interfere with the elemental freedom of the choice made by the voter on the spot at the time of the election, which the managers of the system always found so easy to discern and denounce.

The Crisis of the 1780s

GORDON S. WOOD

The Incongruity of the Crisis

In his commencement address at Harvard College in July 1787, John Quincy Adams spoke of "this critical period," when, it seemed to Adams, the whole

"Vices of the System" by Gordon S. Wood from *The Creation of the Republic*, 1776–1787. Published for the Institute of Early American History and Culture, Williamsburg, Virginia. © 1969 The University of North Carolina Press.

country was "groaning under the intolerable burden of . . . accumulated evils." It was an apt phrase—"critical period"—as John Fiske a century later was to discover. But it was hardly an original one, either with Fiske or with Adams. The belief that the 1780s, the years after the peace with Britain, had become the really critical period of the entire Revolution was prevalent everywhere during the decade. . . .

With the problems of war and reconstruction it is unquestionable that the period was unsettled—a time of financial confusion and social flux, of great expansion and contraction when fortunes were made and lost. New governments had to be erected and made secure; new economic patterns outside of the empire had to be found; and the void left by the emigration of thousands of Tories, many in high political and economic positions, had to be filled—all resulting in political, social, and economic dislocations that have never been adequately measured. On the face of it, however, this dislocation, this unsettlement, hardly seems to warrant the desperate sense of crisis voiced by so many. On the surface at least the American states appeared remarkably stable and prosperous. The political leaders at the uppermost levels remained essentially unchanged throughout the period. Both the Confederation government and the governments of the separate states had done much to stabilize the finances and the economy of the country. The states had already moved to assume payment of the public debt, and the Confederation deficit could not be considered serious. Despite a temporary depression in the middle eighties the commercial outlook was not bleak. As historians have emphasized, the period was marked by extraordinary economic growth. In fact, as contemporaries noticed, it was a decade of very high expectations, clearly reflected in the rapid rate of population growth which despite little immigration was the fastest of any decade in American history. . . .

But the complaints were far from imaginary. They were real, intensely real, rooted, however, not in poverty or in real deprivation but rather in prosperity and in the very unintended promises the Revolution seemed to be offering large numbers of Americans. From the vantage of two hundred years later the Revolution by the 1780s seems to have been a glorious success. The war had been won and independence achieved; the peace with Britain was as much as could have been hoped for in 1775. Yet because the Revolution represented much more than a colonial rebellion, represented in fact a utopian effort to reform the character of American society and to establish truly free governments, men in the 1780s could actually believe that it was failing. Nothing more vividly indicates the intensity of the Americans' Revolutionary expectations than the depth of their disillusionment in the eighties. "What astonishing changes a few years are capable of producing," said Washington in a common exclamation of these years. "Have we fought for this?" was the repeated question. "Was it with these expectations that we launched into a sea of trouble, and have bravely struggled through the most threatening dangers?" All the fervent hopes of 1776 were going awry. Perhaps, as Charles Backus said in 1788, Americans "have had too high expectations from the world." . . .

The Perversion of Republicanism

Almost immediately after the war began the Americans' doubts and anxieties, never far below the surface in 1776, began to emerge with increasing frequency. . . . The British and the Tories had warned in the 1770s that the moment a separation from Britain had taken effect "intestine quarrels will begin," and Americans would "split into parties." Now it seemed that such dire prophesies were being fulfilled. The Revolution, it became more and more obvious, was turning upon itself in ways that had not been foreseen, and men were emphasizing with renewed intensity that "unless a proper education of the rising generation is adopted, a new way of thinking and new principles can be introduced among the People of America, there are little hopes of the present republican Governments or anything like republican Governments being of any duration."

It was ironic but undeniable: by the 1780s the Revolutionary ideals seemed to be breeding the sources of their own miscarriage. "The people," said Fisher Ames in 1787, "have turned against their teachers the doctrines which were inculcated in order to effect the late revolution." All the evils which the Revolution was designed to eliminate were instead being aggravated. "It is a favorite maxim of despotick power, that mankind are not made to govern themselves"—a maxim which the Americans had spurned in 1776. "But alas!" many were now saying, "the experience of ages too highly favours the truth of the maxim; and what renders the reflection still more melancholy is, that the people themselves have, in almost every instance, been the ready instruments of their own ruin." . . .

The republican emphasis on talent and merit in place of connections and favor now seemed perverted, becoming identified simply with the ability to garner votes, thus enabling "the most unfit men to shove themselves into stations of influence, where they soon gave way to the unrestrained inclination of bad habits." . . . Equality was not creating harmony and contentment after all. Indeed, it was noted, equality had become the very cause of the evils it was designed to eliminate. In a free and independent republic "the idea of equality breathes through the whole and every individual feels ambitious, to be in a situation not inferior to his neighbour." . . . Instead of a community of placid yeomen, . . . the society appeared filled with inveterate grumblers. "Every man wants to be a judge, a justice, a sheriff, a deputy, or something else which will bring him a little money, or what is better, a little authority." . . .

The republican aversion to artificial distinctions was being broadened into a general denunciation of all differences, whether economic, social, intellectual, or professional. Writers scoffed at the "academical education" of their aristocratic enemies and boasted that they were "plain, unlettered" men better able to communicate with the people. "Overgrown wealth" itself was attacked: "A certain excess of fortune sets a man above the public opinion, and in equal proportion makes him despise those who are poor." The emergent professionalization of careers became more intensely suspect, and even those fearful of too much leveling satirized the "jargon" and the "peculiarities" of the medical profession as it sought to establish itself by "technical terms" and by prescribing "what is new and uncommon." . . .

Republicanism had not brought the commonwealth consensus that had been anticipated. In fact party strife in all of the states seemed as bitter as before the war. Only now, with the elimination of royal authority and the reduction of magisterial power, the Whig conception of politics could not easily explain or justify the divisiveness. . . .

The Abuses of Legislative Power

Traditional eighteenth-century political theory offered a ready explanation for what was happening. The political pendulum was swinging back: the British rulers had perverted their power; now the people were perverting their liberty. . . . Nevertheless, for some observers, the conventional abuses of the people's liberty, licentiousness and anarchy, no longer seemed to be the only terrors to be feared from the popular end of the political spectrum. By the 1780s some Americans began to perceive a new political phenomenon unfolding in American experience that made nonsense of the traditional conception of politics. True, there were sufficient examples of the people's licentiousness: western Massachusetts was a valley of horrors. But anarchy and the breakdown of government that it connoted no longer seemed an accurate way to describe all of what was happening in the 1780s. An excess of power in the people was leading not simply to licentiousness but to a new kind of tyranny, not by the traditional rulers, but by the people themselves. . . .

The confiscation of property, the paper money schemes, the tender laws, and the various devices suspending the ordinary means for the recovery of debts, despite their "open and outrageous . . . violation of every principle of justice," were not the decrees of a tyrannical and irresponsible magistracy, but laws enacted by legislatures which were probably as equally and fairly representative of the people as any legislatures in history. . . .

The people's will as expressed in their representative legislatures and so much trusted throughout the colonial period suddenly seemed capricious and arbitrary. It was not surprising now for good Whigs to declare that "a popular assembly not governed by fundamental laws, but under the bias of anger, malice, or a thirst for revenge, will commit more excess than an arbitrary monarch." The economic and social instability engendered by the Revolution was finding political expression in the state legislatures at the very time they were larger, more representative, and more powerful than ever before in American history. . . .

Paradoxical as it seemed, it was the very force of the laws of the states, not anarchy or the absence of law, that was vitiating the new republics. All the states with no exceptions were being smothered by a multiplicity of laws, wrote Madison in a comprehensive indictment of the 1780s entitled "Vices of the Political System of the United States," written in 1787 for private circulation and later publicly incorporated into *The Federalist* papers. "The short period of independency has filled as many pages as the century which proceeded it" with laws that were hopelessly mutable. "We daily see laws repealed or suspended, before any trial can have been made of their merits, and even before a knowledge of them can have reached the remoter districts within which they were to operate." Most alarming of all, the laws were repeatedly unjust. . . . Consequently, law was becoming contemptible in the eyes of those from whom it traditionally should have commanded the greatest respect. . . .

But the representative assembly in the several states was not only corrupting the law; it was, as Madison put it in 1788, "drawing all power into its impetuous vortex." All the functions of government, legislative, executive, and judicial, warned Jefferson as early as 1783, were ending up in the legislative body. The diminution of executive authority in the new constitutions, the closing or general breakdown of the courts, the popular fear of magistrates—all reinforced legislative predominance in the governments. . . . "The legislature swallowing up all the other powers," as James Wilson put it, was a widespread practice, the proofs of which in all the states, said Madison in *The Federalist*, "might be multiplied without end."

Democratic Despotism

In the 1780s the Americans' inveterate suspicion and jealousy of political power, once concentrated almost exclusively on the Crown and its agents, was transferred to the various state legislatures. Where once the magistracy had seemed to be the sole source of tyranny, now the legislatures through the Revolutionary state constitutions had become the institutions to be most feared. American "prejudices against the Executive," said James Wilson in 1787, "resulted from a misapplication of the adage that the parliament was the palladium of liberty. Where the Executive was really formidable, King and Tyrant, were naturally associated in the minds of the people." But where the executive was weak, as in the American constitutions, "legislature and tyranny . . . were most properly associated." . . .

Yet there were some Americans who perceived that the problems of the 1780s were not due to the drifting and unrepresentative character of the legislatures, but were rather due to the legislatures' very representativeness. The distresses of the period, in other words, did not arise because the people-at-large had been forsaken by their legislatures, "but because their transient and indigested sentiments have been too implicitly adopted." The evils and vices of state legislation, said James Madison, were not based, as some said, on the temporary deceit of a few designing men who were perverting their representative authority for their own selfish ends. Such vices actually sprang from the emergent nature of American society, and therefore brought "into question the fundamental principle of republican Government, that the majority who rule in such governments are the safest Guardians both of public Good and private rights." "According to Republican Theory," said James Madison, "Right and power being both vested in the majority, are held to be synonimous." But was this truly the case? asked Madison in a brilliant series of letters and essays, describing clearly and cogently what he thought was happening to the traditional assumptions of Whig constitutionalism. "Wherever the real power in a Government lies," he told Jefferson, "there is the danger of oppression. In our Governments the real power lies in the majority of the Community, and the invasion of private rights is chiefly to be apprehended, not from acts of Government contrary to the sense of its constituents, but from acts in which the Government is the mere instrument of the major number of the constituents." The people, it seemed, were as capable of despotism as any prince; public liberty was no guarantee after all of private liberty. . . .

Americans thus experienced in the 1780s not merely a crisis of authority—licentiousness leading to anarchy—which was a comprehensible abuse of republican liberty, but also a serious shattering of older ways of examining politics and a fundamental questioning of majority rule that threatened to shake the foundations of their republican experiments. It was extremely difficult, however, for most Americans to grasp what was happening and fit it into their accepted paradigm of politics. Most commentators were concerned with what they described as the breakdown in governmental authority, the tendency of the people to ignore the government and defy the laws. . . . Yet the pressing constitutional problem was not really the lack of power in the state legislatures but the excess of it—popular despotism. . . .

Shays's Rebellion in western Massachusetts was received with excited consternation mingled with relief by many Americans precisely because it was an anticipated and understandable abuse of republican liberty. Liberty had been carried into anarchy and the throwing off of all government—a more comprehensible phenomenon to most American political thinkers than legislative tyranny. The rebels, announced the town of Boston, must obey the majority. "Let the majority be ever so much in the wrong," it was the only remedy for grievances "compatible with the ideas of society and government!" The insurgents, argued a publicist, must rely on their elected representatives for the redress of wrongs: "Can human wisdom devise a more effectual security to our liberties?" . . .

Many social conservatives did see the rebellion as encouraging the move for constitutional reform. It was both a confirmation of their worst fears—hence their horror, and a vindication of their desires for stronger government—hence their relief. It fitted nicely into the traditional pattern of political thinking and thus cleared the air of much of the confusion which had hung over the 1780s. Yet Shays's Rebellion was irrelevant to the major constitutional difficulty experienced in the Confederation period—the problem of legal tyranny, the usurpation of private rights under constitutional cover. Connecticut had no violence like that of Massachusetts, said Noah Webster, "because the Legislature wear the complexion of the people." . . . Merely subduing the rebels and calling upon them to obey the authority of the legislature did not go to the heart of the Americans' predicament. With "a total change of men" in the legislature, wrote Webster, "there will be, therefore, no further insurrection, because the Legislature will represent the sentiments of the people." Hence some Americans in the 1780s could come to believe that "sedition itself will sometimes make laws."

The classical political spectrum did not make sense to a perceptive and probing mind trying to understand American politics. "It has been remarked," wrote Madison to Jefferson, "that there is a tendency in all Governments to an augmentation of power at the expense of liberty." But for Madison the statement now seemed ill founded. There seemed little danger in the American republics that the tyranny of the rulers would subvert liberty. . . . America had little to fear from the traditional abuse of power by the few over the many. "It is much more to be dreaded that the few will be unnecessarily sacrificed to the many."

Political Pathology

This fear by the few of the power of the many, as crucial as it was in shaping a new understanding of politics and in promoting the desire for a new central government, did not go to the heart of the pervasive sense of anxiety in the 1780s. The crisis was not confined to any one economic or social group. . . . The period was truly critical not solely because members of the social and economic elite felt themselves and their world threatened, but because anyone who knew anything of eighteenth-century political science could not help believing that the American republics were heading for destruction even as they were being created.

The crisis was therefore of the most profound sort, involving no limited political or economic problems but the success of the republican experiment itself. Indeed no more appropriate term than "crisis" could have been used to describe what was happening. Viewing the state as analogous to the human body, Americans saw their country stricken by a serious sickness. The 1780s seemed to mark the point in the life of the young nation where a decisive change had to occur, leading either to recovery or death. It was a "crisis of moral and national reputation." . . .

Throughout all the states orators and writers warned of the vicious effects of wealth and prosperity. "The great body of the people, smote by the charms and blandishments of a life of ease and pleasure, fall easy victims to its fascinations." . . . All men, rich and poor, northerners and southerners, were living "in a manner much more expensive and luxurious, than they have Ability to support," borrowing heavily on the promises of the future, captivated by "an immoderate desire of high and expensive living." . . .

By 1780 Patrick Henry "feared that our Body politic was dangerously sick." The signs of disease spread everywhere. Merchants and farmers were seeking their own selfish ends; hucksters were engrossing products to raise prices. Even government officials, it was charged, were using their public positions to fill their own pockets. The fluctuation in the value of money was making "every kind of commerce and trade precarious, and as every individual is more or less interested in it," was putting a premium on selfishness. Everyone was doing "what was right in his own eyes," and "thus the whole of that care and attention which was given to the public weal is turned to private gain or self preservation." That benevolence among the people had not grown as a result of the Revolution was measured in the frightening increase in litigation, to as many as eight hundred cases in a single New England county court during a year, most of which were actions of debt for only five or six pounds. Vices now seemed more prevalent than before the war. Virtue was being debased by "the visible declension of religion, . . . the rapid progress of licentious manners, and open profanity." Such symptoms of degeneracy threw the clergy especially into confusion. Instead of bringing about the moral reformation they had anticipated from victory, the Revolution had only aggravated America's corruption and sin. . . .

Throughout all the secular and religious jeremiads of the eighties the key term was "luxury," that important social product and symptom of extreme selfishness and pleasure-seeking. . . . "Whenever democratic states degenerate from those noble republican virtues which constitute the chief excellency, spring, and even basis of their government, and instead of industry, frugality, and economy, encourage luxury, dissipation and extravagance," Americans were warned, "we may justly conclude that ruin is near at hand." "No virtue, no Commonwealth." It was that simple. . . .

The Continuance of Hope

For all of the expressions of pessimism in the 1780s, it is clear that not all American intellectuals had lost their confidence in the republican experiment. Jefferson, viewing the new republics while standing amidst the pomp and debauchery of Paris, remained calm and sanguine. America—by contrast—still seemed the land of happy, frugal yeomen. . . . It was absurd, admonished Benjamin Rush in 1787, for Americans to "cry out, after the experience of three or four years, that we are not proper materials for republican government. . . . Let us have patience. Our republican forms of government will in time beget republican opinions and manners. All will end well." Others agreed. Americans were expecting too much too soon. It took time to eliminate ancient prejudices.

The most obvious republican instrument for eliminating these prejudices and inculcating virtue in a people was education. "Wisdom and knowledge, as well as virtue, diffused generally among the body of the people, being necessary for the preservation of their rights and liberties," declared the Massachusetts Constitution of 1780, it was imperative that the government spread "the opportunities and advantages of education in the various parts of the country, and among the different orders of the people." Jefferson was not the only American concerned with erecting a hierarchy of educational institutions from grammar schools to universities. "The spirit and character of a republic," said the Pennsylvania Council of Censors in 1784, "is very different from that of a monarchy, and can only be imbibed by education." It seemed increasingly clear to many, like Benjamin Rush, that if Americans were not naturally virtuous they must be taught to be. "It is possible," said Rush, "to convert men into republican machines." They must be instructed that their lives were not their own. The republican pupil must "be taught that he does not belong to himself, but that he is public property."

The clergy, of course, offered religion as the major instrument of salvation for a corrupted people. Religion was "the source of liberty, the soul of government and the life of a people." Christianity fostered benevolence, a love of one's fellow man and of the community. Religion was the strongest promoter of virtue, the most important ally of a well-constituted republic. . . .

Other Americans, however, were less sure of the efficacy of religion and education in infusing virtue into the American character. Indeed, a long-existing split in the American mind between what has been called the evangelical scheme and the legal scheme was now conspicuously revealed. Although many Americans in 1776 had blended and continued to blend both schemes in an uneasy combination, the events of the 1780s were forcing a separation between those who clung to moral reform and the regeneration of men's hearts as the remedy for viciousness and those who looked to mechanical devices and institutional contrivances as the only lasting solution for America's ills. It was a basic division that separated "unenlightened" from "enlightened," Calvinist from Liberal, and ultimately Antifederalist from Federalist. "No government under heaven," said Benjamin Austin in a bold enunciation of the moral outlook, "could have prevented a people from ruin, or kept their commerce from declining, when they were exhausting their valuable resources in paying for superfluities, and running themselves in debt to foreigners, and to each other for articles of folly and dissipation." As long as men were morally corrupt, "we may contend about forms of government, but no establishment will enrich a people, who wantonly spend beyond their income." But for others, despairing of any such inner regeneration, something more external was necessary. If the people were as corrupt and vicious, as permeated by a commercial spirit as the eighties seemed to indicate, then it was foolish to rely on religion and education alone to curb America's passions and to maintain viable republican societies. "Whenever any disorder happens in any government," declared those committed to a legalistic remedy, "it must be ascribed, to a fault in some of the institutions of it." Only the institutions of government arranged in a certain manner could manage an unvirtuous people. If men's souls could not be redeemed then their governments must be adjusted to their sinfulness. Monarchy, of course, could control a corrupt society, but it was out of the question for most. Only republicanism was "reconcilable with the genius of the people of America" and "with the fundamental principles of the Revolution." The American dilemma was to make "such an arrangement of political power as ensures the existence and security of the government, even in the absence of political virtue," without, however, at the same time destroying republicanism. The task was a formidable and original one: to establish a republican government even though the best social science of the day declared that the people were incapable of sustaining it. Somehow, as Madison put it, Americans must find "a republican remedy for the diseases most incident to republican government."

✕ F U R T H E R   R E A D I N G

Richard Beeman, Stephen Botein, and Edward C. Carter II, eds., *Beyond Confederation: Origins of the Constitution and American National Identity* (1987)

John L. Brooke, *The Heart of the Commonwealth: Society and Political Culture in Worcester County, Massachusetts, 1713–1861* (1989)

——, "To the Quiet of the People: Revolutionary Settlements and Civil Unrest in Western Massachusetts, 1774–1789," *William and Mary Quarterly*, 3d Ser., 46 (1989), 425–462

Jacob Ernest Cooke, *Alexander Hamilton* (1982)

Robert A. Gross, ed., *In Debt to Shays: The Legacy of an Agrarian Rebellion* (1991)

Merrill Jensen, *The New Nation: A History of the United States During the Confederation, 1781–1789* (1950)

Ralph Ketcham, *James Madison: A Biography* (1971)

Leonard W. Levy and Dennis J. Mahoney, eds., *The Framing and Ratification of the Constitution* (1987)

Forrest McDonald, *E Pluribus Unum: The Formation of the American Republic, 1776–1790* (1965)

——, *Novus Ordo Seclorum: The Intellectual Origins of the Constitution* (1985)

[Michael McGiffert, ed.] "The Creation of the American Republic, 1776–1787: A Symposium of Views and Reviews," *William and Mary Quarterly*, 3d Ser., 44 (1987), 549–640

Andrew C. McLaughlin, *The Confederation and the Constitution, 1783–1789* (1905)

Peter S. Onuf, *The Origins of the Federal Republic: Jurisdictional Controversies in the United States, 1775–1787* (1983)

——, "Reflections on the Founding: Constitutional Historiography in Bicentennial Perspective," *William and Mary Quarterly*, 3d. Ser., 46 (1989), 341–375

Jack N. Rakove, *The Beginnings of National Politics: An Interpretive History of the Continental Congress* (1979)

Charles Page Smith, *James Wilson, Founding Father, 1742–1798* (1956)

David P. Szatmary, *Shays' Rebellion: The Making of an Agrarian Insurrection* (1980)

Robert J. Taylor, *Western Massachusetts in the Revolution* (1954)

Gordon S. Wood, *The Creation of the American Republic, 1776–1787* (1969)

The Creation of
the Constitution of 1787

✕

The United States Constitution of 1787 is the oldest operating written constitution in the world. It has been so often and so genuinely celebrated, and for so many generations, that it possesses the stature of a sacred text. In American civic culture, reverence for the Constitution is a fundamental dogma that sustains the document's vitality. For unlike a king or a military dictator, the Constitution commands no armies; it compels obedience to its doctrines only through the force of public allegiance.

Veneration for the men who created the Constitution is a corollary of this positive preconditioning and is expressed in our designation of them as the founding fathers. As with the document itself, it has been difficult to achieve a realistic and balanced assessment of these political leaders. During much of the twentieth century, ever since the publication in 1913 of Charles A. Beard's Economic Interpretation of the Constitution, historians and textbooks have debated the heroic myth and an unheroic antimyth. In the Beardian or Progressive interpretation, as in its neo-Progressive successors, the Constitution has been described as the creation of practical, even selfish, politicians, men bent on forming a government to defend a system of wealth and privilege in which they shared. Although this debate has subsided in the past two decades, it has taught us to recognize—as did the delegates to the convention—that interests, especially those concerning money and power, were ever present forces in politics, then as now. In addition, we have learned that acknowledging the play of interests in the formation of the Constitution does not deny the reality of public spirit and commitment to ideals of liberty. The mingling of interests and idealism was critical to the Constitution's success.

Moreover, we have come to recognize that the design of the Constitution was a contingent event. Not only was it not designed in heaven or by a band of demigods; it was not even the preconceived plan of any one delegate or set of delegates. The Constitution that the framers sent on to Congress in September 1787 resulted from a three-month negotiation and debate in which possibilities were tested, rejected, and then revised and adjusted according to the changing perspectives of various delegates. No one who signed the Constitution saw it as *perfect, but all hoped that it would be good enough to serve the material and political interests of their own state and region, as well as the United States.*

✕ D O C U M E N T S

James Madison was the most important individual in shaping the collective achievement known as the Constitution of 1787. The thirty-six-year-old Virginia delegate made an influential analysis of the defects of the Confederation and its interaction with the state governments in a private memorandum that he circulated among his colleagues and that appears below as the first document. Titling the essay "Vices of the Political System of the United States," Madison offered a view of the problem that supplied the starting point for the Virginia Plan. This plan, which is reproduced here as the second document, was presented to the convention by the more senior John Randolph, the Virginia governor. The plan became the foundation on which, with alterations, the delegates constructed the Constitution.

The Virginia Plan, which called for a national government that linked population and power, was challenged directly by the New Jersey Plan, the third selection. This plan offered a more limited revision of the Articles, one that retained the principle of equality among the states. The delegates debated these two plans (see the fourth document) for a few days before laying aside the New Jersey Plan. Thereafter, they debated a wide range of topics. The selections comprising the fifth document treat democracy and the legislature, sectional interests and legislative apportionment, the qualifications for voters, and slavery and slave imports, and they provide only a sample of what went on. The fact that the debates were closed to the public—secret in fact—enabled the delegates to speak freely on controversial subjects. The final document, the Constitution, is the product of all of the delegates.

James Madison on the Vices of the Political System of the United States, 1787

1.   Failure of the States to Comply with the Constitutional Requisitions

This evil has been so fully experienced both during the war and since the peace, results so naturally from the number and independent authority of the States and has been so uniformly examplified in every similar Confederacy, that it may be considered as not less radically and permanently inherent in, than it is fatal to the object of, the present System.

2.   Encroachments by the States on the Federal Authority

Examples of this are numerous and repetitions may be foreseen in almost every case where any favorite object of a State shall present a temptation. Among these examples are the wars and Treaties of Georgia with the Indians—The unlicensed compacts between Virginia and Maryland, and between Pena. & N. Jersey—the troops raised and to be kept up by Massts.

3. Violations of the Law of Nations and of Treaties

From the number of Legislatures, the sphere of life from which most of their members are taken, and the circumstances under which their legislative business is carried on, irregularities of this kind must frequently happen. Accordingly not a year has passed without instances of them in some one or other of the States. The Treaty of peace—the treaty with France—the treaty with Holland have each been violated. The causes of these irregularities must necessarily produce frequent violations of the law of nations in other respects. . . .

4. Trespasses of the States on the Rights of Each Other

These are alarming symptoms, and may be daily apprehended as we are admonished by daily experience. See the law of Virginia restricting foreign vessels to certain ports—of Maryland in favor of vessels belonging to her own citizens—of N. York in favor of the same.

Paper money, instalments of debts, occlusion of Courts, making property a legal tender, may likewise be deemed aggressions on the rights of other States. As the Citizens of every State aggregately taken stand more or less in the relation of Creditors or debtors, to the Citizens of every other States, Acts of the debtor State in favor of debtors, affect the Creditor State, in the same manner, as they do its own citizens who are relatively creditors towards other citizens. . . .

The practice of many States in restricting the commercial intercourse with other States, and putting their productions and manufactures on the same footing with those of foreign nations, though not contrary to the federal articles, is certainly adverse to the spirit of the Union, and tends to beget retaliating regulations, not less expensive & vexatious in themselves, than they are destructive of the general harmony.

5. Want of Concert in Matters Where Common Interest Requires It

This defect is strongly illustrated in the state of our commercial affairs. How much has the national dignity, interest, and revenue suffered from this cause? Instances of inferior moment are the want of uniformity in the laws concerning naturalization & literary property; of provision for national seminaries, for grants of incorporation for national purposes, for canals and other works of general utility, wch. may at present be defeated by the perverseness of particular States whose concurrence is necessary.

6. Want of Guaranty to the States of Their Constitutions and Laws Against Internal Violence

The confederation is silent on this point and therefore by the second article the hands of the federal authority are tied. According to Republican Theory, Right and power being both vested in the majority, are held to be synonimous. According to fact and experience a minority may in an appeal to force, be an overmatch for the majority. 1. If the minority happen to include all such as possess the skill and habits of military life, & such as possess the great pecuniary resources, one third only may conquer the remaining two thirds. 2. One third of those who participate in the choice of the rulers, may be rendered a majority by the accession of those whose poverty excludes them from a right of suffrage, and who for obvious reasons will be more likely to join the standard of sedition than that of the established Government. 3. Where slavery exists the republican Theory becomes still more fallacious.

7. Want of Sanction to the Laws, and of Coercion in the Government of the Confederacy

A sanction is essential to the idea of law, as coercion is to that of Government. The federal system being destitute of both, wants the great vital principles of a Political Cons[ti]tution. Under the form of such a Constitution, it is in fact nothing more than a treaty of amity of commerce and of alliance, between so many independent and Sovereign States. . . . It is no longer doubted that a unanimous and punctual obedience of 13 independent bodies, to the acts of the federal Government, ought not be calculated on. Even during the war, when external danger supplied in some degree the defect of legal & coercive sanctions, how imperfectly did the States fulfil their obligations to the Union? In time of peace, we see already what is to be expected. . . .

8. Want of Ratification by the People of the Articles of Confederation

In some of the States the Confederation is recognized by, and forms a part of the constitution. In others however it has received no other sanction than that of the Legislative authority. From this defect two evils result: 1. Whenever a law of a State happens to be repugnant to an act of Congress, particularly when the latter is of posterior date to the former, it will be at least questionable whether the latter must not prevail; and as the question must be decided by the Tribunals of the State, they will be most likely to lean on the side of the State.

2. As far as the Union of the States is to be regarded as a league of sovereign powers, and not as a political Constitution by virtue of which they are become one sovereign power, so far it seems to follow from the doctrine of compacts, that a breach of any of the articles of the confederation by any of the parties to it, absolves the other parties from their respective obligations, and gives them a right if they chuse to exert it, of dissolving the Union altogether.

9. Multiplicity of Laws in the Several States

In developing the evils which viciate the political system of the U.S. it is proper to include those which are found within the States individually, as well as those which directly affect the States collectively, since the former class have an indirect influence on the general malady and must not be overlooked in forming a compleat remedy. Among the evils then of our situation may well be ranked the multiplicity of laws from which no State is exempt. As far as laws are necessary, to mark with precision the duties of those who are to obey them, and to take from those who are to administer them a discretion, which might be abused, their number is the price of liberty. As far as the laws exceed this limit, they are a nuisance: a nuisance of the most pestilent kind. Try the Codes of the several States by this test, and what a luxuriancy of legislation do they present. The short period of independency has filled as many pages as the century which preceded it. . . .

10. Mutability of the Laws of the States

This evil is intimately connected with the former yet deserves a distinct notice as it emphatically denotes a vicious legislation. We daily see laws repealed or superseded, before any trial can have been made of their merits; and even before a knowledge of them can have reached the remoter districts within which they were to operate. In the regulations of trade this instability becomes a snare not only to our citizens but to foreigners also.

11. Injustice of the Laws of States

If the multiplicity and mutability of laws prove a want of wisdom, their injustice betrays a defect still more alarming: more alarming not merely because it is a greater evil in itself, but because it brings more into question the fundamental principle of republican Government, that the majority who rule in such Governments, are the safest Guardians both of public Good and of private rights. To what causes is this evil to be ascribed?

These causes lie

1. in the Representative bodies.
2. in the people themselves.

1. Representative appointments are sought from three motives. 1. ambition, 2. personal interest, 3. public good. Unhappily the two first are proved by experience to be most prevalent. Hence the candidates who feel them, particularly, the second, are most industrious, and most successful in pursuing their object: and forming often a majority in the legislative Councils, with interested views, contrary to the interest, and views, of their Constituents, join in a perfidious sacrifice of the latter to the former. A succeeding election it might be supposed, would displace the offenders, and repair the mischief. But how easily are base and selfish measures, masked by pretexts of public good and apparent expediency? How frequently will a repetition of the same arts and industry which succeeded in the first instance, again prevail on the unwary to misplace their confidence?

How frequently too will the honest but unenligh[t]ened representative be the dupe of a favorite leader, veiling his selfish views under the professions of public good, and varnishing his sophistical arguments with the glowing colours of popular eloquence?

2. A still more fatal if not more frequent cause lies among the people themselves. All civilized societies are divided into different interests and factions, as they happen to be creditors or debtors—Rich or poor—husbandmen, merchants or manufacturers—members of different religious sects—followers of different political leaders—inhabitants of different districts—owners of different kinds of property &c &c. In republican Government the majority however composed, ultimately give the law. Whenever therefore an apparent interest or common passion unites a majority what is to restrain them from unjust violations of the rights and interests of the minority, or of individuals? Three motives only 1. a prudent regard to their own good as involved in the general and permanent good of the Community. This consideration although of decisive weight in itself, is found by experience to be too often unheeded. It is too often forgotten, by nations as well as by individuals that honesty is the best policy. 2dly. respect for character. However strong this motive may be in individuals, it is considered as very insufficient to restrain them from injustice. In a multitude its efficacy is diminished in proportion to the number which is to share the praise or the blame. Besides, as it has reference to public opinion, which within a particular Society, is the opinion of the majority, the standard is fixed by those whose conduct is to be measured by it. The public opinion without the Society, will be little respected by the people at large of any Country. Individuals of extended views, and of national pride, may bring the public proceedings to this standard, but the example will never be followed by the multitude. Is it to be imagined that an ordinary citizen or even an assemblyman of R. Island in estimating the policy of paper money, ever considered or cared in what light the measure would be viewed in France or Holland; or even in Massts or Connect.? It was a sufficient temptation to both that it was for their interest: it was a sufficient sanction to the latter that it was popular in the State; to the former that it was so in the neighbourhood. 3dly. will Religion the only remaining motive be a sufficient restraint? It is not pretended to be such on men individually considered. Will its effect be greater on them considered in an aggregate view? quite the reverse. The conduct of every popular assembly acting on oath, the strongest of religious Ties, proves that individuals join without remorse in acts, against which their consciences would revolt if proposed to them under the like sanction, separately in their closets. When indeed Religion is kindled into enthusiasm, its force like that of other passions, is increased by the sympathy of a multitude. But enthusiasm is only a temporary state of religion, and while it lasts will hardly be seen with pleasure at the helm of Government. Besides as religion in its coolest state, is not infallible, it may become a motive to oppression as well as a restraint from injustice. Place three individuals in a situation wherein the interest of each depends on the voice of the others, and give to two of them an interest opposed to the rights of the third? Will the latter be secure? The prudence of every man would shun the danger. The rules & forms of justice suppose & guard against it. Will two thousand

in a like situation be less likely to encroach on the rights of one thousand? The contrary is witnessed by the notorious factions & oppressions which take place in corporate towns limited as the opportunities are, and in little republics when uncontrouled by apprehensions of external danger. If an enlargement of the sphere is found to lessen the insecurity of private rights, it is not because the impulse of a common interest or passion is less predominant in this case with the majority; but because a common interest or passion is less apt to be felt and the requisite combinations less easy to be formed by a great than by a small number. The Society becomes broken into a greater variety of interests, of pursuits, of passions, which check each other, whilst those who may feel a common sentiment have less opportunity of communication and concert. It may be inferred that the inconveniences of popular States contrary to the prevailing Theory, are in proportion not to the extent, but to the narrowness of their limits.

The great desideratum in Government is such a modification of the Sovereignty as will render it sufficiently neutral between the different interests and factions, to controul one part of the Society from invading the rights of another, and at the same time sufficiently controuled itself, from setting up an interest adverse to that of the whole Society. In absolute Monarchies, the prince is sufficiently neutral towards his subjects, but frequently sacrifices their happiness to his ambition or his avarice. In small Republics, the sovereign will is sufficiently controuled from such a Sacrifice of the entire Society, but is not sufficiently neutral towards the parts composing it. As a limited Monarchy tempers the evils of an absolute one; so an extensive Republic meliorates the administration of a small Republic.

An auxiliary desideratum for the melioration of the Republican form is such a process of elections as will most certainly extract from the mass of the Society the purest and noblest characters which it contains; such as will at once feel most strongly the proper motives to pursue the end of their appointment, and be most capable to devise the proper means of attaining it.

12.   Impotence of the Laws of the States

[Madison's memorandum ends here.]

John Randolph Presents the Virginia Plan, 1787*

Mr. Randolph then opened the main business. He expressed his regret, that it should fall to him, rather than those, who were of longer standing in life and political experience, to open the great subject of their mission. But, as the convention had originated from Virginia, and his colleagues supposed that some proposition was expected from them, they had imposed this task on him.

---

* From James Madison's notes.

He then commented on the difficulty of the crisis, and the necessity of preventing the fulfilment of the prophecies of the American downfall.

He observed that in revising the fœderal system we ought to inquire (1) into the properties which such a government ought to possess, (2) the defects of the Confederation, (3) the danger of our situation, and (4) the remedy.

1. The character of such a government ought to secure (1) against foreign invasion; (2) against dissentions between members of the Union, or seditions in particular States; (3) to procure to the several States various blessings, of which an isolated situation was incapable; (4) to be able to defend itself against incroachment; and (5) to be paramount to the State Constitutions.

2. In speaking of the defects of the Confederation he professed a high respect for its authors, and considered them as having done all that patriots could do, in the then infancy of the science of constitutions and of confederacies—when the inefficiency of requisitions was unknown—no commercial discord had arisen among any States—no rebellion had appeared as in Massachusetts—foreign debts had not become urgent—the havoc of paper money had not been foreseen—treaties had not been violated—and perhaps nothing better could be obtained from the jealousy of the States with regard to their sovereignty.

He then proceeded to enumerate the defects: (1) that the Confederation produced no security against foreign invasion; Congress not being permitted to prevent a war nor to support it by their own authority. . . . (2) That the fœderal government could not check the quarrels between States, nor a rebellion in any, not having constitutional power nor means to interpose according to the exigency. (3) That there were many advantages which the United States might acquire, which were not attainable under the Confederation—such as a productive impost, counteraction of the commercial regulations of other nations, pushing of commerce ad libitum, etc., etc. (4) That the fœderal government could not defend itself against incroachments from the States. (5) That it was not even paramount to the State Constitutions, ratified, as it was in many of the States.

3. He next reviewed the danger of our situation, and appealed to the sense of the best friends of the United States—the prospect of anarchy from the laxity of government everywhere; and to other considerations.

4. He then proceeded to the remedy; the basis of which he said must be the republican principle.

He proposed as conformable to his ideas the following resolutions, which he explained one by one.

[Virginia Plan]

1. Resolved, that the Articles of Confederation ought to be so corrected and enlarged as to accomplish the objects proposed by their institution; namely, "common defence, security of liberty and general welfare."

2. Resolved therefore, that the rights of suffrage in the National Legislature ought to be proportioned to the quotas of contribution, or to the

number of free inhabitants, as the one or the other rule may seem best in different cases.

3. Resolved, that the National Legislature ought to consist of two branches.

4. Resolved, that the members of the first branch of the National Legislature ought to be elected by the people of the several States every [blank] for the term of [blank]; to be of the age of [blank] years at least, to receive liberal stipends by which they may be compensated for the devotion of their time to the public service; to be ineligible to any office established by a particular State, or under the authority of the United States, except those peculiarly belonging to the functions of the first branch, during the term of service, and for the space of [blank] after its expiration; to be incapable of re-election for the space of [blank] after the expiration of their term of service, and to be subject to recall.

5. Resolved, that the members of the second branch of the National Legislature ought to be elected by those of the first, out of a proper number of persons nominated by the individual Legislatures, to be of the age of [blank] years at least; to hold their offices for a term sufficient to ensure their independence; to receive liberal stipends, by which they may be compensated for the devotion of their time to the public service; and to be ineligible to any office established by a particular State, or under the authority of the United States, except those peculiarly belonging to the functions of the second branch, during the term of service, and for the space of [blank] after the expiration thereof.

6. Resolved, that each branch ought to possess the right of originating Acts; that the National Legislature ought to be impowered to enjoy the legislative rights vested in Congress by the Confederation, and moreover to legislate in all cases to which the separate States are incompetent, or in which the harmony of the United States may be interrupted by the exercise of individual legislation; to negative all laws passed by the several States, contravening, in the opinion of the National Legislature the articles of Union; and to call forth the force of the Union against any member of the Union failing to fulfil its duty under the articles thereof.

7. Resolved, that a National Executive be instituted; to be chosen by the National Legislature for the term of [blank] years, to receive punctually at stated times, a fixed compensation for the services rendered, in which no increase nor diminution shall be made so as to affect the magistracy, existing at the time of increase or diminution, and to be ineligible a second time; and that besides a general authority to execute the national laws, it ought to enjoy the executive rights vested in Congress by the Confederation.

8. Resolved, that the Executive and a convenient number of the National Judiciary, ought to compose a Council of Revision with authority to examine every Act of the National Legislature before it shall operate, and every Act of a particular Legislature before a negative thereon shall be final; and that the dissent of the said Council shall amount to a rejection, unless the Act of the National Legislature be again passed, or that of a particular Legislature be again negatived by [blank] of the members of each branch.

9. Resolved, that a National Judiciary be established to consist of one or more supreme tribunals, and of inferior tribunals to be chosen by the National Legislature, to hold their offices during good behaviour; and to receive punctually at stated times fixed compensation for their services, in which no increase or diminution shall be made so as to affect the persons actually in office at the time of such increase or diminution. That the jurisdiction of the inferior tribunals shall be to hear and determine in the first instance, and of the supreme tribunal to hear and determine in the dernier resort, all piracies and felonies on the high seas, captures from an enemy, cases in which foreigners or citizens of other States applying to such jurisdictions may be interested, or which respect the collection of the national revenue; impeachments of any National officers, and questions which may involve the national peace and harmony.

10. Resolved, that provision ought to be made for the admission of States lawfully arising within the limits of the United States, whether from a voluntary junction of government and territory or otherwise, with the consent of a number of voices in the National Legislature less than the whole.

11. Resolved, that a republican government and the territory of each State, except in the instance of a voluntary junction of Government and territory, ought to be guarantied by the United States to each State.

12. Resolved, that provision ought to be made for the continuance of Congress and their authorities and privileges, until a given day after the reform of the articles of Union shall be adopted, and for the completion of all their engagements.

13. Resolved, that provision ought to be made for the amendment of the Articles of Union whensoever it shall seem necessary, and that the assent of the National Legislature ought not to be required thereto.

14. Resolved, that the legislative, executive and judiciary powers within the several States ought to be bound by oath to support the articles of Union.

15. Resolved, that the amendments which shall be offered to the Confederation by the Convention, ought at a proper time or times, after the approbation of Congress, to be submitted to an assembly or assemblies of representatives recommended by the several Legislatures to be expressly chosen by the people, to consider and decide thereon.

William Patterson Proposes the New Jersey Plan, 1787

Mr. Patterson, laid before the Convention the plan which he said several of the deputations wished to be substituted in place of that proposed by Mr. Randolph. . . :

1. Resolved, that the articles of Confederation ought to be so revised, corrected & enlarged, as to render the federal Constitution adequate to the exigencies of Government, & the preservation of the Union.

2. Resolved, that in addition to the powers vested in the U. States in Congress, by the present existing articles of Confederation, they be authorized to pass acts for raising a revenue, by levying a duty or duties on

all goods or merchandizes of foreign growth or manufacture, imported into any part of the U. States, by Stamps on paper, vellum or parchment, and by a postage on all letters or packages passing through the general post-office, to be applied to such federal purposes as they shall deem proper & expedient; to make rules & regulations for the collection thereof; and the same from time to time, to alter & amend in such manner as they shall think proper: to pass Acts for the regulation of trade & commerce as well with foreign nations as with each other: provided that all punishments, fines, forfeitures & penalties to be incurred for contravening such acts rules and regulations shall be adjudged by the Common law Judiciaries of the State in which any offence contrary to the true intent & meaning of such Acts rules & regulations shall have been committed or perpetrated, . . . subject nevertheless, for the correction of all errors, both in law & fact in rendering Judgment, to an appeal to the Judiciary of the U. States.

3. Resolved, that whenever requisitions shall be necessary, instead of the rule for making requisitions mentioned in the articles of Confederation, the United States in Congress be authorized to make such requisitions in proportion to the whole number of white & other free citizens & inhabitants of every age sex and condition including those bound to servitude for a term of years & three fifths of all other persons not comprehended in the foregoing description, except Indians not paying taxes; that if such requisitions be not complied with, in the time specified therein, to direct the collection thereof in the non complying States & for that purpose to devise and pass acts directing & authorizing the same; provided that none of the powers hereby vested in the U. States in Congress shall be exercised without the consent of at least [blank] States, and in that proportion if the number of Confederated States should hereafter be increased or diminished.

4. Resolved, that the U. States in Congress be authorized to elect a federal Executive to consist of [blank] persons, to continue in office for the term of [blank] years, to receive punctually at stated times a fixed compensation for their services, in which no increase or diminution shall be made so as to affect the persons composing the Executive at the time of such increase or diminution, to be paid out of the federal treasury; to be incapable of holding any other office or appointment during their time of service and for [blank] years thereafter; to be ineligible a second time, & removeable by Congress on application by a majority of the Executives of the several States; that the Executives besides their general authority to execute the federal acts ought to appoint all federal officers not otherwise provided for, & to direct all military operations; provided that none of the persons composing the federal Executive shall on any occasion take command of any troops, so as personally to conduct any military enterprise as General or in other capacity.

5. Resolved, that a federal Judiciary be established to consist of a supreme Tribunal the Judges of which to be appointed by the Executive, & to hold their offices during good behaviour, to receive punctually at stated times a fixed compensation for their services in which no increase or diminution shall be made, so as to affect the persons actually in office at the

time of such increase or diminution; that the Judiciary so established shall have authority to hear & determine in the first instance on all impeachments of federal officers, & by way of appeal in the dernier resort in all cases touching the rights of Ambassadors, in all cases of captures from an enemy, in all cases of piracies & felonies on the high Seas, in all cases in which foreigners may be interested, in the construction of any treaty or treaties, or which may arise on any of the Acts for regulation of trade, or the collection of the federal Revenue: that none of the Judiciary shall during the time they remain in office be capable of receiving or holding any other office or appointment during their time of service, or for [blank] thereafter.

6. Resolved, that all Acts of the U. States in Congress made by virtue & in pursuance of the powers hereby & by the articles of Confederation vested in them, and all Treaties made & ratified under the authority of the U. States shall be the supreme law of the respective States so far forth as those Acts or Treaties shall relate to the said States or their Citizens, and that the Judiciary of the several States shall be bound thereby in their decisions, any thing in the respective laws of the Individual States to the contrary notwithstanding; and that if any State, or any body of men in any State shall oppose or prevent the carrying into execution such acts or treaties, the federal Executive shall be authorized to call forth the power of the Confederated States, or so much thereof as may be necessary to enforce and compel an obedience to such Acts, or an observance of such Treaties.

7. Resolved, that provision be made for the admission of new States into the Union.

8. Resolved, the rule for naturalization ought to be the same in every State.

9. Resolved, that a Citizen of one State committing an offense in another State of the Union, shall be deemed guilty of the same offense as if it had been committed by a Citizen of the State in which the offense was committed.

Congress Debates the New Jersey and Virginia Plans, 1787

Mr. Lansing called for the reading of the 1st resolution of each plan, which he considered as involving principles directly in contrast; that of Mr. Patterson says he sustains the sovereignty of the respective States, that of Mr. Randolph distroys it: the latter requires a negative on all the laws of the particular States; the former, only certain general powers for the general good. The plan of Mr. R. in short absorbs all power except what may be exercised in the little local matters of the States which are not objects worthy of the supreme cognizance. He grounded his preference of Mr. P.'s plan, chiefly on two objections against that of Mr. R. 1. want of power in the Convention to discuss & propose it. 2. the improbability of its being adopted. 1. He was decidedly of opinion that the power of the Convention was restrained to amendments of a federal nature, and having for their basis the Confederacy in being. The Act of Congress The tenor of the Acts of the States, the Commissions produced by the several deputations all proved this. And this limitation of the power to an amendment of the Confederacy, marked the opinion of the States, that it was unnecessary & improper to go farther. He was sure that this was the case with his State. N. York would never have concurred in sending deputies to the convention, if she had supposed the deliberations were to turn on a consolidation of the States, and a National Government.

2. was it probable that the States would adopt & ratify a scheme, which they had never authorized us to propose? and which so far exceeded what they regarded as sufficient? . . . The States will never feel a sufficient confidence in a general Government to give it a negative on their laws. The Scheme is itself totally novel. There is no parallel to it to be found. The authority of Congress is familiar to the people, and an augmentation of the powers of Congress will be readily approved by them.

Mr. Patterson, said as he had on a former occasion given his sentiments on the plan proposed by Mr. R. he would now avoiding repetition as much as possible give his reasons in favor of that proposed by himself. He preferred it because it accorded 1. with the powers of the Convention, 2. with the sentiments of the people. If the confederacy was radically wrong, let us return to our States, and obtain larger powers, not assume them of ourselves. . . . Our object is not such a Government as may be best in itself, but such a one as our Constituents have authorized us to prepare, and as they will approve. If we argue the matter on the supposition that no Confederacy at present exists, it can not be denied that all the States stand on the footing of equal sovereignty. All therefore must concur before any can be bound. If a proportional representation be right, why do we not vote so here? If we argue on the fact that a federal compact actually exists, and consult the articles of it we still find an equal Sovereignty to be the basis of it. He reads the 5th art: of the Confederation giving each State a vote—& the 13th declaring that no alteration shall be made without unanimous consent. This is the nature of all treaties. . . . It is urged that two branches in the Legislature are necessary. Why? for the purpose of a check. But the reason for the precaution is not applicable to this case. Within a particular State, where party heats prevail, such a check may be necessary. In such a body as Congress it is less necessary, and besides, the delegations of the different States are checks on each other. Do the people at large complain of Congress? No, what they wish is that Congress may have more power. If the power now proposed be not eno', the people hereafter will make additions to it. With proper powers Congress will act with more energy & wisdom than the proposed National Legislature; being fewer in number, and more secreted & refined by the mode of election. The plan of Mr. R will also be enormously expensive. Allowing Georgia & Delaware two representatives each in the popular branch the aggregate number of that branch will be 180. Add to it half as many for the other branch and you have 270. members coming once at least a year from the most distant as well as the most central parts of the republic. In the present deranged state of our finances can so expensive a system be seriously thought of? By enlarging the powers of Congress the greatest part of this expence will be saved, and all purposes will be answered. At least a trial ought to be made.

Mr. [James] Wilson [Pennsylvania] entered into a contrast of the principal points of the two plans so far he said as there had been time to examine the one last proposed. These points were 1. in the Virginia plan there are 2 & in some degree 3 branches in the Legislature: in the plan from N.J. there is to be a single legislature only—2. Representation of the people at large is the basis of the one:—the State Legislatures, the pillars of the other—3. proportional representation prevails in one:—equality of suffrage in the other—4. A single Executive Magistrate is at the head of the one:— a plurality is held out in the other.—5. in the one the majority of the people of the U. S. must prevail:—in the other a minority may prevail. 6. the National Legislature is to make laws in all cases to which the separate States are incompetent &–:—in place of this Congress are to have additional power in a few cases only—7. A negative on the laws of the States:—in place of this coertion to be substituted—8. The Executive to be removeable on impeachment & conviction;—in one plan: in the other to be removeable at the instance of a majority of the Executives of the States—9. Revision of the laws provided for in one:—no such check in the other—10. inferior national tribunals in one:—none such in the other. 11. In the one jurisdiction of National tribunals to extend &c—; an appellate jurisdiction only allowed in the other. 12. Here the jurisdiction is to extend to all cases affecting the National peace & harmony: there, a few cases only are marked out. 13. finally the ratification is in this to be by the people themselves:—in that by the legislative authorities according to the 13 art: of the Confederation.

With regard to the power of the Convention, he conceived himself authorized to conclude nothing, but to be at liberty to propose any thing. In this particular he felt himself perfectly indifferent to the two plans.

With regard to the sentiments of the people, he conceived it difficult to know precisely what they are. Those of the particular circle in which one moved, were commonly mistaken for the general voice. He could not persuade himself that the State Governments & Sovereignties were so much the idols of the people, nor a National Government so obnoxious to them, as some supposed. . . . Where do the people look at present for relief from the evils of which they complain? Is it from an internal reform of their Governments? no, Sir. It is from the National Councils that relief is expected. For these reasons he did not fear, that the people would not follow us into a national Government and it will be a further recommendation of Mr. R.'s plan that it is to be submitted to them, and not to the Legislatures, for ratification.

Proceeding now to the 1st point on which he had contrasted the two plans, he observed that anxious as he was for some augmentation of the federal powers, it would be with extreme reluctance indeed that he could ever consent to give powers to Congress he had two reasons either of which was sufficient. 1. Congress as a Legislative body does not stand on the people. 2. it is a single body. 1. He would not repeat the remarks he had formerly made on the principles of Representation. he would only say that an inequality in it, has ever been a poison contaminating every branch of Government. . . . The Impost, so anxiously wished for by the public was defeated not by any of the larger States in the Union. 2. Congress is a single Legislature. Despotism comes on Mankind in different Shapes, sometimes in an Executive, sometimes in a Military, one. Is there no danger of a Legislative despotism? Theory & practice both proclaim it. If the Legislative authority be not restrained, there can be neither liberty nor stability; and it can only be restrained by dividing it within itself, into distinct and independent branches. In a single House there is no check, but the inadequate one, of the virtue & good sense of those who compose it.

On another great point, the contrast was equally favorable to the plan reported by the Committee of the whole. It vested the Executive powers in a single Magistrate. The plan of N. Jersey, vested them in a plurality. In order to controul the Legislative authority, you must divide it. In order to controul the Executive you must unite it. One man will be more responsible than three. Three will contend among themselves till one becomes the master of his colleagues. In the triumvirates of Rome first Caesar, then Augustus, are witnesses of this truth. The Kings of Sparta, & the Consuls of Rome prove also the factious consequences of dividing the Executive Magistracy. . . .

Mr. [Charles] PINKNEY [South Carolina], the whole comes to this, as he conceived. Give N. Jersey an equal vote, and she will dismiss her scruples, and concur in the National system. He thought the Convention authorized to go any length in recommending, which they found necessary to remedy the evils which produced this Convention. . . .

Congress Debates the Issues, 1787

*Democracy and the Lower House**

In committee of the whole on Mr. Randolph's propositions.

The 3d Resolution "that the National Legislature ought to consist of two branches" was agreed to without debate or dissent, except that of Pennsylvania, given probably from complaisance to Doctor Franklin, who was understood to be partial to a single House of legislation.

Resolution 4, first clause "that the members of the first branch of the National Legislature ought to be elected by the people of the several States" being taken up,

Mr. Sherman [Conn.] opposed the election by the people, insisting that it ought to be by the State Legislatures. The people, he said, immediately should have as little to do as may be about the government. They want information, and are constantly liable to be misled.

Mr. Gerry [Mass.]. The evils we experience flow from the excess of democracy. The people do not want virtue, but are the dupes of pretended patriots. In Massachusetts it had been fully confirmed by experience that they are daily misled into the most baneful measures and opinions by the false reports circulated by designing men, and which no one on the spot can refute. One principal evil arises from the want of due provision for those

---

* Madison's notes for May 31, 1787.

employed in the administration of government. It would seem to be a maxim of democracy to starve the public servants. He mentioned the popular clamour in Massachusetts for the reduction of salaries and the attack made on that of the Governor, though secured by the spirit of the Constitution itself. He had he said been too republican heretofore: he was still however republican, but had been taught by experience the danger of the levilling spirit.

Mr. Mason [Va.] argued strongly for an election of the larger branch by the people. It was to be the grand depository of the democratic principle of the Government. It was, so to speak, to be our House of Commons. It ought to know and sympathise with every part of the community; and ought therefore to be taken not only from different parts of the whole republic, but also from different districts of the larger members of it, which had in several instances, particularly in Virginia, different interests and views arising from difference of produce, of habits, etc., etc. He admitted that we had been too democratic, but was afraid we should incautiously run into the opposite extreme. We ought to attend to the rights of every class of the people. He had often wondered at the indifference of the superior classes of society to this dictate of humanity and policy; considering that however affluent their circumstances, or elevated their situations might be, the course of a few years not only might but certainly would distribute their posterity throughout the lowest classes of society. Every selfish motive, therefore, every family attachment, ought to recommend such a system of policy as would provide no less carefully for the rights and happiness of the lowest than of the highest orders of citizens.

Mr. Wilson [Penn.] contended strenuously for drawing the most numerous branch of the Legislature immediately from the people. He was for raising the federal pyramid to a considerable altitude, and for that reason wished to give it as broad a basis as possible. No government could long subsist without the confidence of the people. In a republican government this confidence was peculiarly essential. . . .

Mr. Madison considered the popular election of one branch of the National Legislature as essential to every plan of free government. He observed that in some of the States one branch of the Legislature was composed of men already removed from the people by an intervening body of electors. That if the first branch of the general legislature should be elected by the State Legislatures, the second branch elected by the first, the Executive by the second together with the first; and other appointments again made for subordinate purposes by the Executive, the people would be lost sight of altogether; and the necessary sympathy between them and their rulers and officers, too little felt. He was an advocate for the policy of refining the popular appointments by successive filtrations, but thought it might be pushed too far. . . .

Mr. Gerry did not like the election by the people. . . . Experience he said had shewn that the State legislatures drawn immediately from the people did not always possess their confidence. . . . He seemed to think the people might nominate a certain number out of which the State legislatures should be bound to choose.

Mr. Butler [S. C.] thought an election by the people an impracticable mode.

On the question for an election of the first branch of the National Legislature by the people:

Mass. ay. Conn. div. N.Y. ay. N.J. no. Penn. ay. Del. div. Va. ay. N.C. ay. S.C. no. Geo. ay.

Sectional Interests and Legislative Apportionment*

Mr. Randolph's motion requiring the Legislature to take a periodical census for the purpose of redressing inequalities in the representation, was resumed.

Mr. Sherman [Conn.] was against shackling the Legislature too much. We ought to choose wise and good men, and then confide in them.

Mr. Mason [Va.] The greater the difficulty we find in fixing a proper rule of representation, the more unwilling ought we to be, to throw the task from ourselves, on the General Legislature. He did not object to the conjectural ratio which was to prevail in the outset; but considered a revision from time to time according to some permanent and precise standard as essential to the fair representation required in the first branch. According to the present population of America, the northern part of it had a right to preponderate, and he could not deny it. But he wished it not to preponderate hereafter when the reason no longer continued. From the nature of man we may be sure that those who have power in their hands will not give it up while they can retain it. On the contrary we know they will always when they can rather increase it. If the southern States therefore should have three-quarters of the people of America within their limits, the Northern will hold fast the majority of representatives. One quarter will govern the three-quarters. The southern States will complain: but they may complain from generation to generation without redress. Unless some principle therefore which will do justice to them hereafter shall be inserted in the Constitution, disagreeable as the declaration was to him, he must declare he could neither vote for the system here, nor support it in his State. . . . He urged that numbers of inhabitants, though not always a precise standard of wealth, was sufficiently so for every substantial purpose.

Mr. Williamson [N.C.] was for making it the duty of the Legislature to do what was right and not leaving it at liberty to do or not do it. He moved that Mr. Randolph's proposition be postponed in order to consider the following: "that in order to ascertain the alterations that may happen in the population and wealth of the several States, a census shall be taken of the free white inhabitants and three-fifths of those of other descriptions on the first year after this Government shall have been adopted, and every [blank] year thereafter; and that the representation be regulated accordingly."

Mr. Randolph agreed that Mr. Williamson's proposition should stand in the place of his. . . .

Mr. Butler [S.C.] and General [C. C.] Pinckney [S.C.] insisted that

---

* Madison's notes for July 11, 1787.

blacks be included in the rule of representation, equally with the whites: and for that purpose moved that the words "three-fifths" be struck out.

Mr. Gerry [Mass.] thought that three-fifths of them was to say the least the full proportion that could be admitted.

Mr. Gorham. [Mass.] This ratio was fixed by Congress as a rule of taxation. Then it was urged by the delegates representing the States having slaves that the blacks were still more inferior to freemen. At present when the ratio of representation is to be established, we are assured that they are equal to freemen. The arguments on the former occasion had convinced him that three-fifths was pretty near the just proportion, and he should vote according to the same opinion now.

Mr. Butler insisted that the labour of a slave in South Carolina was as productive and valuable as that of a freeman in Massachusetts, that as wealth was the great means of defence and utility to the nation they were equally valuable to it with freemen; and that consequently an equal representation ought to be allowed for them in a government which was instituted principally for the protection of property, and was itself to be supported by property.

Mr. Mason could not agree to the motion, notwithstanding it was favorable to Virginia, because he thought it unjust. It was certain that the slaves were valuable, as they raised the value of land, increased the exports and imports, and of course the revenue; would supply the means of feeding and supporting an army, and might in cases of emergency become themselves soldiers. As in these important respects they were useful to the community at large, they ought not to be excluded from the estimate of representation. He could not, however, regard them as equal to freemen, and could not vote for them as such. He added as worthy of remark, that the southern States have this peculiar species of property, over and above the other species of property common to all the States.

Mr. Williamson reminded Mr. Gorham that if the southern States contended for the inferiority of blacks to whites when taxation was in view, the eastern States on the same occasion contended for their equality. He did not, however, either then or now, concur in either extreme, but approved of the ratio of three-fifths.

On Mr. Butler's motion for considering blacks as equal to whites in the apportionment of representation.

Mass. no. Conn. no. [N.Y. not on floor.] N.J. no. Pa. no. Del. ay. Md. no. Va. no. N.C. no. S.C. ay. Geo. ay. . . .

Mr. Rutledge contended for the admission of wealth in the estimate by which representation should be regulated. The western States will not be able to contribute in proportion to their numbers; they should not therefore be represented in that proportion. The Atlantic States will not concur in such a plan. He moved that "at the end of [blank] years after the first meeting of the Legislature, and of every [blank] years thereafter, the Legislature shall proportion the Representation according to the principles of wealth and population." . . .

Mr. Gouverneur Morris. . . . He could not persuade himself that numbers would be a just rule at any time. The remarks of [Mr. Mason] relative to the western country had not changed his opinion on that head. Among other objections, it must be apparent they would not be able to furnish men equally enlightened, to share in the administration of our common interests. The busy haunts of men, not the remote wilderness, was the proper school of political talents. If the western people get the power into their hands, they will ruin the Atlantic interests. The back members are always most averse to the best measures. He mentioned the case of Pennsylvania formerly. The lower part of the State had the power in the first instance. They kept it in their own hands, and the country was the better for it. Another objection with him against admitting the blacks into the census, was that the people of Pennsylvania would revolt at the idea of being put on a footing with slaves. They would reject any plan that was to have such an effect. . . .

Mr. Madison [Va.]. . . . To reconcile the gentleman with himself, it must be imagined that he determined the human character by the points of the compass. The truth was that all men having power ought to be distrusted to a certain degree. The case of Pennsylvania had been mentioned, where it was admitted that those who were possessed of the power in the original settlement, never admitted the new settlements to a due share of it. England was a still more striking example. The power there had long been in the hands of the boroughs, of the minority; who had opposed and defeated every reform which had been attempted. Virginia was in a less degree another example. With regard to the western States, he was clear and firm in opinion that no unfavorable distinctions were admissible either in point of justice or policy. He thought also that the hope of contributions to the Treasury from them had been much underrated. . . . He could not agree that any substantial objection lay against fixing numbers for the perpetual standard of Representation. It was said that Representation and taxation were to go together; that taxation and wealth ought to go together, that population and wealth were not measures of each other. He admitted that in different climates, under different forms of Government, and in different stages of civilization, the inference was perfectly just. He would admit that in no situation numbers of inhabitants were an accurate measure of wealth. He contended however that in the United States it was sufficiently so for the object in contemplation. Altho' their climate varied considerably, yet as the governments, the laws, and the manners of all were nearly the same, and the intercourse between different parts perfectly free, population, industry, arts, and the value of labour, would constantly tend to equalize themselves. . . .

On the question on the first clause of Mr. Williamson's motion as to taking a census of the free inhabitants, it passed in the affirmative. Mass. ay. Cont. ay. N.J. ay. Pa. ay. Del. no. Md. no. Va. ay. N.C. ay. S.C. no. Geo. no.

The next clause as to three-fifths of the negroes being considered,

Mr. King [Mass.], being much opposed to fixing numbers as the rule of representation, was particularly so on account of the blacks. He thought the admission of them along with whites at all, would excite great discontents among the States having no slaves. . . .

Mr. Wilson did not well see on what principle the admission of blacks in the proportion of three-fifths could be explained. Are they admitted as citizens? then why are they not admitted on an equality with white citizens?

are they admitted as property? then why is not other property admitted into the computation? These were difficulties however which he thought must be overruled by the necessity of compromise. He had some apprehensions also from the tendency of the blending of the blacks with the whites, to give disgust to the people of Pennsylvania as had been intimated by his colleague. But he differed from him in thinking numbers of inhabitants so incorrect a measure of wealth. He had seen the western settlements of Pennsylvania, and on a comparison of them with the city of Philadelphia could discover little other difference, than that property was more unequally divided among individuals here than there. Taking the same number in the aggregate in the two situations he believed there would be little difference in their wealth and ability to contribute to the public wants.

Mr. Gouverneur Morris was compelled to declare himself reduced to the dilemma of doing injustice to the southern States or to human nature, and he must therefore do it to the former. For he could never agree to give such encouragement to the slave trade as would be given by allowing them a representation for their negroes, and he did not believe those States would ever confederate on terms that would deprive them of that trade.

On the question for agreeing to include three-fifths of the blacks:

Mass. no. Cont. ay. N.J. no. Pa. no. Del. no. Md. no. Va. ay. N.C. ay. S.C. no. Geo. ay.*

Qualifications for Voters†

Mr. Gouverneur Morris [Pa.] moved to . . . restrain the right of suffrage to freeholders.

Mr. Fitzsimons [Penn.] seconded the motion.

Mr. Williamson [N.C.] was opposed to it.

Mr. Wilson [Pa.] . . . It was difficult to form any uniform rule of qualifications for all the States. Unnecessary innovations he thought too should be avoided. It would be very hard and disagreeable for the same persons at the same time to vote for Representatives in the State Legislature and to be excluded from a vote for those in the National Legislature.

Mr. Gouverneur Morris. Such a hardship would be neither great nor novel. The people are accustomed to it and not dissatisfied with it in several of the States. In some the qualifications are different for the choice of the Governor and of the Representatives; in others for different houses of the Legislature. . . .

Mr. Ellsworth [Conn.] thought the qualifications of the electors stood on the most proper footing. The right of suffrage was a tender point, and strongly guarded by most of the State Constitutions. The people will not readily subscribe to the National Constitution if it should subject them to be disfranchised. The States are the best judges of the circumstances and temper of their own people.

Col. Mason [Va.]. The force of habit is certainly not attended to by those gentlemen who wish for innovations on this point. Eight or nine States

---

* Later this provision was passed.
† Madison's notes for August 7, 1787.

have extended the right of suffrage beyond the freeholders; what will the people there say if they should be disfranchised? A power to alter the qualifications would be a dangerous power in the hands of the Legislature.

Mr. Butler [S.C.]. There is no right of which the people are more jealous than that of suffrage. Abridgments of it tend to the same revolution as in Holland where they have at length thrown all power into the hands of the Senates, who fill up vacancies themselves, and form a rank aristocracy.

Mr. Dickinson [Pa.] had a very different idea of the tendency of vesting the right of suffrage in the freeholders of the country. He considered them as the best guardians of liberty; and the restriction of the right to them as a necessary defence against the dangerous influence of those multitudes without property and without principle with which our country like all others, will in time abound. As to the unpopularity of the innovation, it was in his opinion chimerical. The great mass of our citizens is composed at this time of freeholders, and will be pleased with it.

Mr. Ellsworth. How shall the freehold be defined? Ought not every man who pays a tax, to vote for the representative who is to levy and dispose of his money? Shall the wealthy merchants and manufacturers, who will bear a full share of the public burdens, be not allowed a voice in the imposition of them? Taxation and representation ought to go together.

Mr. Gouverneur Morris. He had long learned not to be the dupe of words. The sound of aristocracy, therefore, had no effect on him. It was the thing, not the name, to which he was opposed, and one of his principal objections to the Constitution as it is now before us, is that it threatens this country with an aristocracy. The aristocracy will grow out of the House of Representatives. Give the votes to people who have no property, and they will sell them to the rich who will be able to buy them. We should not confine our attention to the present moment. The time is not distant when this country will abound with mechanics and manufacturers who will receive their bread from their employers. Will such men be the secure and faithful guardians of liberty? Will they be the impregnable barrier against aristocracy? He was as little duped by the association of the words "taxation and representation." The man who does not give his vote freely is not represented. It is the man who dictates the vote. Children do not vote. Why? because they want prudence, because they have no will of their own. The ignorant and the dependent can be as little trusted with the public interest. He did not conceive the difficulty of defining "freeholders" to be insuperable. Still less, that the restriction could be unpopular. Nine-tenths of the people are at present freeholders, and these will certainly be pleased with it. As to merchants, etc., if they have wealth and value the right, they can acquire it. If not, they don't deserve it.

Col. Mason. We all feel too strongly the remains of antient prejudices, and view things too much through a British medium. A freehold is the qualification in England, and hence it is imagined to be the only proper one. The true idea in his opinion was that every man having evidence of attachment to and permanent common interest with the society ought to share in all its rights and privileges. Was this qualification restrained to freeholders? Does no other kind of property but land evidence a common interest in the proprietor? Does nothing besides property mark a permanent attachment? Ought the merchant, the monied man, the parent of a number of children whose fortunes are to be pursued in his own country, to be viewed as suspicious characters, and unworthy to be trusted with the common rights of their fellow citizens?

Mr. Madison [Va.] The right of suffrage is certainly one of the fundamental articles of republican government, and ought not to be left to be regulated by the Legislature. A gradual abridgment of this right has been the mode in which aristocracies have been built on the ruins of popular forms. Whether the Constitutional qualification ought to be a freehold, would with him depend much on the probable reception such a change would meet with in States where the right was now exercised by every description of people. In several of the States a freehold was now the qualification. Viewing the subject in its merits alone, the freeholders of the country would be the safest depositories of Republican liberty. In future times a great majority of the people will not only be without landed, but any other sort of, property. These will either combine under the influence of their common situation; in which case, the rights of property and the public liberty will not be secure in their hands: or what is more probable, they will become the tools of opulence and ambition, in which case there will be equal danger on another side. . . .

Dr. Franklin [Pa.] It is of great consequence that we should not depress the virtue and public spirit of our common people; of which they displayed a great deal during the war, and which contributed principally to the favorable issue of it. . . . He did not think that the elected had any right in any case to narrow the privileges of the electors. . . . He was persuaded also that such a restriction as was proposed would give great uneasiness in the populous States. The sons of a substantial farmer, not being themselves freeholders, would not be pleased at being disfranchised, and there are a great many persons of that description.

Mr. Mercer [Md.] The Constitution is objectionable in many points, but in none more than the present. He objected to the footing on which the qualification was put, but particularly to the mode of election by the people. The people can not know and judge of the characters of candidates. The worst possible choice will be made. . . .

Mr. Rutledge [Va.] thought the idea of restraining the right of suffrage to the freeholders a very unadvised one. It would create division among the people and make enemies of all those who should be excluded.

Slavery and the Importation of Slaves*

Mr. Sherman [Conn.] . . . disapproved of the slave trade; yet as the States were now possessed of the right to import slaves, as the public good did not require it to be taken from them, and as it was expedient to have as few objections as possible to the proposed scheme of government, he thought it best to leave the matter as we find it. He observed that the abolition of slavery seemed to be going on in the United States, and that the good sense

---

* Madison's notes for August 22, 25, 1787.

of the several States would probably by degrees compleat it. He urged on the Convention the necessity of despatching its business.

Col. Mason [Va.] This infernal trafic originated in the avarice of British merchants. The British Government constantly checked the attempts of Virginia to put a stop to it. The present question concerns not the importing States alone but the whole Union. The evil of having slaves was experienced during the late war. Had slaves been treated as they might have been by the enemy, they would have proved dangerous instruments in their hands. . . . Maryland and Virginia he said had already prohibited the importation of slaves expressly. North Carolina had done the same in substance. All this would be in vain if South Carolina and Georgia be at liberty to import. The western people are already calling out for slaves for their new lands, and will fill that country with slaves if they can be got thro' South Carolina and Georgia. Slavery discourages arts and manufactures. The poor despise labor when performed by slaves. They prevent the immigration of whites, who really enrich and strengthen a country. They produce the most pernicious effect on manners. Every master of slaves is born a petty tyrant. They bring the judgment of Heaven on a country. As nations cannot be rewarded or punished in the next world, they must be in this. By an inevitable chain of causes and effects, Providence punishes national sins, by national calamities. He lamented that some of our eastern brethren had from a lust of gain embarked in this nefarious traffic. As to the States being in possession of the right to import, this was the case with many other rights, now to be properly given up. He held it essential in every point of view that the General Government should have power to prevent the increase of slavery.

Mr. Ellsworth [Conn.] As he had never owned a slave could not judge of the effects of slavery on character: he said, however, that if it was to be considered in a moral light we ought to go farther and free those already in the country. As slaves also multiply so fast in Virginia and Maryland that it is cheaper to raise than import them, whilst in the sickly rice swamps foreign supplies are necessary; if we go no farther than is urged, we shall be unjust towards South Carolina and Georgia. Let us not intermeddle. As population increases, poor laborers will be so plenty as to render slaves useless. Slavery in time will not be a speck in our country. Provision is already made in Connecticut for abolishing it, and the abolition has already taken place in Massachussets. As to the danger of insurrections from foreign influence, that will become a motive to kind treatment of the slaves.

Mr. Pinckney [S.C.] If slavery be wrong, it is justified by the example of all the world. He cited the case of Greece, Rome, and other antient States; the sanction given by France, England, Holland, and other modern States. In all ages one half of mankind have been slaves. If the southern States were let alone they will probably of themselves stop importations. He would himself as a citizen of South Carolina vote for it. An attempt to take away the right as proposed will produce serious objections to the Constitution, which he wished to see adopted.

General Pinckney [S.C.] declared it to be his firm opinion that if himself and all his colleagues were to sign the Constitution and use their personal influence, it would be of no avail towards obtaining the assent of their constituents. South Carolina and Georgia cannot do without slaves. As to Virginia, she will gain by stopping the importations. Her slaves will rise in value, and she has more than she wants. It would be unequal to require South Carolina and Georgia to confederate on such unequal terms. He said the royal assent before the Revolution had never been refused to South Carolina as to Virginia. He contended that the importation of slaves would be for the interest of the whole Union. The more slaves, the more produce to employ the carrying trade, the more consumption also; and the more of this, the more of revenue for the common treasury. . . .

Mr. Dickinson [Pa.] considered it as inadmissible on every principle of honor and safety that the importation of slaves should be authorised to the States by the Constitution. The true question was whether the national happiness would be promoted or impeded by the importation, and this question ought to be left to the National Government, not to the States particularly interested. . . .

Mr. Rutledge [Va.]. If the Convention thinks that North Carolina, South Carolina, and Georgia will ever agree to the plan, unless their right to import slaves be untouched, the expectation is vain. The people of those States will never be such fools as to give up so important an interest. . . .

Mr. Gouverneur Morris wished the whole subject to be committed, including the clauses relating to taxes on exports and to a navigation act. These things may form a bargain among the northern and southern States. . . .

General Pinckney moved to strike out the words "the year eighteen hundred" as the year limiting the importation of slaves, and to insert the words "the year eighteen hundred and eight".

Mr. Gorham seconded the motion.

Mr. Madison. Twenty years will produce all the mischief that can be apprehended from the liberty to import slaves. So long a term will be more dishonorable to the national character, than to say nothing about it in the Constitution.

On the motion; which passed in the affirmative.

N.H. ay. Mass. ay. Conn. ay. N.J. no. Pa. no. Del. no. Md. ay. Va. no. N.C. ay. S.C. ay. Geo. ay. . . .

The first part of the report was then agreed to, amended as follows,

The migration or importation of such persons as the several States now existing shall think proper to admit, shall not be prohibited by the Legislature prior to the year 1808.

N.H. Mass. Conn. Md. N.C. S.C. Geo.: ay
N.J. Pa. Del. Va.   .   .   .   .   no

The Constitution of the United States of America, 1787

We, the people of the United States, in order to form a more perfect union, establish justice, insure domestic tranquillity, provide for the common defense, promote the general welfare, and secure the blessings of liberty to ourselves and our posterity, do ordain and establish this Constitution for the United States of America.

Article One

Section 1. All legislative powers herein granted shall be vested in a Congress of the United States, which shall consist of a Senate and House of Representatives.

Section 2. The House of Representatives shall be composed of members chosen every second year by the people of the several States, and the electors in each State shall have the qualifications requisite for electors of the most numerous branch of the State legislature.

No person shall be a Representative who shall not have attained to the age of twenty five years, and been seven years a citizen of the United States, and who shall not, when elected, be an inhabitant of that State in which he shall be chosen.

Representatives and direct taxes shall be apportioned among the several States which may be included within this Union, according to their respective numbers, which shall be determined by adding to the whole number of free persons, including those bound to service for a term of years, and excluding Indians not taxed, three-fifths of all other persons. The actual enumeration shall be made within three years after the first meeting of the Congress of the United States, and within every subsequent term of ten years, in such manner as they shall by law direct. The number of Representatives shall not exceed one for every thirty thousand, but each State shall have at least one Representative; and until such enumeration shall be made, the State of New Hampshire shall be entitled to choose three, Massachusetts eight, Rhode Island and Providence Plantations one, Connecticut five, New York six, New Jersey four, Pennsylvania eight, Delaware one, Maryland six, Virginia ten, North Carolina five, South Carolina five, and Georgia three.

When vacancies happen in the representation from any State, the executive authority thereof shall issue writs of election to fill such vacancies.

The House of Representatives shall choose their Speaker and other officers, and shall have the sole power of impeachment.

Section 3. The Senate of the United States shall be composed of two Senators from each State, chosen by the legislature thereof, for six years; and each Senator shall have one vote.

Immediately after they shall be assembled in consequence of the first election, they shall be divided as equally as may be into three classes. The seats of the Senators of the first class shall be vacated at the expiration of the second year; of the second class, at the expiration of the fourth year, and of the third class, at the expiration of the sixth year, so that one-third may be chosen every second year; and if vacancies happen by resignation or otherwise during the recess of the legislature of any State, the executive thereof may make temporary appointments until the next meeting of the legislature, which shall then fill such vacancies.

No person shall be a Senator who shall not have attained to the age of thirty years, and been nine years a citizen of the United States, and who shall not, when elected, be an inhabitant of that State for which he shall be chosen.

The Vice-President of the United States shall be President of the Senate, but shall have no vote, unless they be equally divided.

The Senate shall choose their other officers, and also a President pro tempore in the absence of the Vice-President, or when he shall exercise the office of President of the United States.

The Senate shall have the sole power to try all impeachments. When sitting for that purpose, they shall be on oath or affirmation. When the President of the United States is tried, the Chief Justice shall preside: and no person shall be convicted without the concurrence of two-thirds of the members present.

Judgment in cases of impeachment shall not extend further than to removal from office, and disqualification to hold and enjoy any office of honor, trust, or profit under the United States; but the party convicted shall, nevertheless, be liable and subject to indictment, trial, judgment, and punishment, according to law.

Section 4. The times, places, and manner of holding elections for Senators and Representatives shall be prescribed in each State by the legislature thereof; but the Congress may at any time by law make or alter such regulations, except as to the places of choosing Senators.

The Congress shall assemble at least once in every year, and such meeting shall be on the first Monday in December, unless they shall by law appoint a different day.

Section 5. Each house shall be the judge of the elections, returns, and qualifications of its own members, and a majority of each shall constitute a quorum to do business; but a smaller number may adjourn from day to day, and may be authorized to compel the attendance of absent members, in such manner, and under such penalties, as each house may provide.

Each house may determine the rules of its proceedings, punish its members for disorderly behavior, and, with the concurrence of two-thirds, expel a member.

Each house shall keep a journal of its proceedings, and from time to time publish the same, excepting such parts as may in their judgment require secrecy, and the yeas and nays of the members of either house on any question shall, at the desire of one-fifth of those present, be entered on the journal.

Neither house, during the session of Congress, shall, without the consent of the other, adjourn for more than three days, nor to any other place than that in which the two houses shall be sitting.

Section 6. The Senators and Representatives shall receive a compensation for their services, to be ascertained by law and paid out of the Treasury of the United States. They shall, in all cases except treason, felony, and breach of the peace, be privileged from arrest during their attendance at the session of their respective houses, and in going to and returning from the same; and for any speech or debate in either house they shall not be questioned in any other place.

No Senator or Representative shall, during the time for which he was elected, be appointed to any civil office under the authority of the United States, which shall have been created, or the emoluments whereof shall have been increased during such time; and no person holding any office under the United States shall be a member of either house during his continuance in office.

Section 7. All bills for raising revenue shall originate in the House of Representatives; but the Senate may propose or concur with amendments as on other bills.

Every bill which shall have passed the House of Representatives and the Senate shall, before it becomes a law, be presented to the President of the United States; if he approve he shall sign it, but if not he shall return it, with his objections, to that house in which it shall have originated, who shall enter the objections at large on their journal and proceed to reconsider it. If after such reconsideration two-thirds of that house shall agree to pass the bill, it shall be sent, together with the objections, to the other house, by which it shall likewise be reconsidered, and if approved by two-thirds of that house it shall become a law. But in all such cases the votes of both houses shall be determined by yeas and nays, and the names of the persons voting for and against the bill shall be entered on the journal of each house respectively. If any bill shall not be returned by the President within ten days (Sundays excepted) after it shall have been presented to him, the same shall be a law, in like manner as if he had signed it, unless the Congress by their adjournment prevent its return, in which case it shall not be a law.

Every order, resolution, or vote to which the concurrence of the Senate and House of Representatives may be necessary (except on a question of adjournment) shall be presented to the President of the United States; and before the same shall take effect, shall be approved by him, or being dis-approved by him, shall be repassed by two-thirds of the Senate and House of Representatives, according to the rules and limitations prescribed in the case of a bill.

Section 8. The Congress shall have power to lay and collect taxes, duties, imposts, and excises, to pay the debts and provide for the common defense and general welfare of the United States; but all duties, imposts, and excises shall be uniform throughout the United States;

To borrow money on the credit of the United States;

To regulate commerce with foreign nations and among the several States, and with the Indian tribes;

To establish an uniform rule of naturalization, and uniform laws on the subject of bankruptcies throughout the United States;

To coin money, regulate the value thereof, and of foreign coin, and fix the standard of weights and measures;

To provide for the punishment of counterfeiting the securities and current coin of the United States;

To establish post-offices and post-roads;

To promote the progress of science and useful arts by securing for limited times to authors and inventors the exclusive right to their respective writings and discoveries;

To constitute tribunals inferior to the Supreme Court;

To define and punish piracies and felonies committed on the high seas and offenses against the law of nations;

To declare war, grant letters of marque and reprisal, and make rules concerning captures on land and water;

To raise and support armies, but no appropriation of money to that use shall be for a longer term than two years;

To provide and maintain a navy;

To make rules for the government and regulation of the land and naval forces;

To provide for calling forth the militia to execute the laws of the Union, suppress insurrections, and repel invasions;

To provide for organizing, arming, and disciplining the militia, and for governing such part of them as may be employed in the service of the United States, reserving to the States respectively the appointment of the officers, and the authority of training the militia according to the discipline prescribed by Congress;

To exercise exclusive legislation in all cases whatsoever over such district (not exceeding ten miles square) as may, by cession of particular States and the acceptance of Congress, become the seat of the Government of the United States, and to exercise like authority over all places purchased by the consent of the legislature of the State in which the same shall be, for the erection of forts, magazines, arsenals, dockyards, and other needful buildings; and

To make all laws which shall be necessary and proper for carrying into execution the foregoing powers, and all other powers vested by this Constitution in the Government of the United States, or in any department or officer thereof.

Section 9. The migration or importation of such persons as any of the States now existing shall think proper to admit shall not be prohibited by the Congress prior to the year one thousand eight hundred and eight, but a tax or duty may be imposed on such importation, not exceeding ten dollars for each person.

The privilege of the writ of habeas corpus shall not be suspended, unless when in cases of rebellion or invasion the public safety may require it.

No bill of attainder or ex post facto law shall be passed.

No capitation or other direct tax shall be laid, unless in proportion to the census or enumeration hereinbefore directed to be taken.

No tax or duty shall be laid on articles exported from any State.

No preference shall be given by any regulation of commerce or revenue to the ports of one State over those of another; nor shall vessels bound to or from one State be obliged to enter, clear, or pay duties in another.

No money shall be drawn from the Treasury but in consequence of appropriations made by law; and a regular statement and account of the receipts and expenditures of all public money shall be published from time to time.

No title of nobility shall be granted by the United States; and no person holding any office of profit or trust under them shall, without the consent of the Congress, accept of any present, emolument, office, or title, of any kind whatever, from any king, prince, or foreign State.

Section 10. No State shall enter into any treaty, alliance, or confederation; grant letters of marque and reprisal; coin money; emit bills of credit; make anything but gold and silver coin a tender in payment of debts; pass any bill of attainder, ex post facto law, or law impairing the obligation of contracts, or grant any title of nobility.

No State shall, without the consent of Congress, lay any imposts or duties on imports or exports, except what may be absolutely necessary for executing its inspection laws; and the net produce of all duties and imposts, laid by any State on imports or exports, shall be for the use of the Treasury of the United States; and all such laws shall be subject to the revision and control of the Congress.

No State shall, without the consent of Congress, lay any duty of tonnage, keep troops or ships of war in time of peace, enter into any agreement or compact with another State or with a foreign power, or engage in war, unless actually invaded or in such imminent danger as will not admit of delay.

Article Two

Section 1. The executive power shall be vested in a President of the United States of America. He shall hold his office during the term of four years, and together with the Vice-President, chosen for the same term, be elected as follows:

Each State shall appoint, in such manner as the legislature thereof may direct, a number of electors, equal to the whole number of Senators and Representatives to which the State may be entitled in the Congress; but no Senator or Representative, or person holding an office of trust or profit under the United States, shall be appointed an elector.

[The electors shall meet in their respective States and vote by ballot for two persons, of whom one at least shall not be an inhabitant of the same State with themselves. And they shall make a list of all the persons voted for, and of the number of votes for each; which list they shall sign and certify, and transmit sealed to the seat of the government of the United States, directed to the President of the Senate. The President of the Senate shall, in the presence of the Senate and House of Representatives, open all the certificates, and the votes shall then be counted. The person having the greatest number of votes shall be the President, if such number be a majority of the whole number of electors appointed; and if there be more than one who have such majority, and have an equal number of votes, then the House of Representatives shall immediately choose by ballot one of them for President; and if no person have a majority, then from the five highest on the list the said House shall in like manner choose the President. But in choosing the President the votes shall be taken by States, the representation from each State having one vote; a quorum for this purpose shall consist of a member or members from two-thirds of the States, and a majority of all the States shall be necessary to a choice. In every case, after the choice of the President, the person having the greatest number of votes of the electors shall be the Vice-President. But if there should remain two or more who have equal votes, the Senate shall choose from them by ballot the Vice-President.*

The Congress may determine the time of choosing the electors and the day on which they shall give their votes, which day shall be the same throughout the United States.

No person except a natural-born citizen, or a citizen of the United States at the time of the adoption of this Constitution, shall be eligible to the office of President; neither shall any person be eligible to that office who shall not have attained to the age of thirty-five years, and been fourteen years a resident within the United States.

In case of the removal of the President from office, or of his death, resignation, or inability to discharge the powers and duties of the said office, the same shall devolve on the Vice-President, and the Congress may by law provide for the case of removal, death, resignation, or inability, both of the President and Vice-President, declaring what officer shall then act as President, and such officer shall act accordingly until the disability be removed or a President shall be elected.

The President shall, at stated times, receive for his services a compensation, which shall neither be increased nor diminished during the period for which he shall have been elected, and he shall not receive within that period any other emolument from the United States or any of them.

Before he enter on the execution of his office he shall take the following oath or affirmation:

"I do solemnly swear (or affirm) that I will faithfully execute the office of President of the United States, and will to the best of my ability preserve, protect, and defend the Constitution of the United States."

Section 2. The President shall be Commander-in-chief of the Army and Navy of the United States, and of the militia of the several States when called into the actual service of the United States; he may require the opinion, in writing, of the principal officer in each of the executive departments, upon any subject relating to the duties of their respective offices, and he shall have power to grant reprieves and pardons for offenses against the United States, except in cases of impeachment.

He shall have power, by and with the advice and consent of the Senate, to make treaties, provided two-thirds of the Senators present concur; and he shall nominate, and, by and with the advice and consent of the Senate, shall appoint ambassadors, other public ministers and consuls, judges of the Supreme Court, and all other officers of the United States, whose appointments are not herein otherwise provided for, and which shall be established

---

* This procedure was changed by the Twelfth Amendment.

by law; but the Congress may by law vest the appointment of such inferior officers, as they think proper, in the President alone, in the courts of law, or in the heads of departments.

The President shall have power to fill up all vacancies that may happen during the recess of the Senate, by granting commissions which shall expire at the end of their next session.

Section 3. He shall from time to time give to the Congress information of the state of the Union, and recommend to their consideration such measures as he shall judge necessary and expedient; he may, on extraordinary occasions, convene both houses, or either of them, and in case of disagreement between them with respect to the time of adjournment, he may adjourn them to such time as he shall think proper; he shall receive ambassadors and other public ministers; he shall take care that the laws be faithfully executed, and shall commission all the officers of the United States.

Section 4. The President, Vice-President, and all civil officers of the United States shall be removed from office on impeachment for and conviction of treason, bribery, or other high crimes and misdemeanors.

Article Three

Section 1. The judicial power of the United States shall be vested in one Supreme Court, and in such inferior courts as the Congress may from time to time ordain and establish. The judges, both of the supreme and inferior courts, shall hold their offices during good behavior, and shall, at stated times, receive for their services a compensation which shall not be diminished during their continuance in office.

Section 2. The judicial power shall extend to all cases, in law and equity, arising under this Constitution, the laws of the United States, and treaties made, or which shall be made, under their authority; to all cases affecting ambassadors, other public ministers, and consuls; to all cases of admiralty and maritime jurisdiction; to controversies to which the United States shall be a party; to controversies between two or more States; between a State and citizens of another State; between citizens of different States; between citizens of the same State claiming lands under grants of different States, and between a State, or the citizens thereof, and foreign States, citizens, or subjects.

In all cases affecting ambassadors, other public ministers and consuls, and those in which a State shall be a party, the Supreme Court shall have original jurisdiction. In all the other cases before mentioned the Supreme Court shall have appellate jurisdiction, both as to law and fact, with such exceptions and under such regulations as the Congress shall make.

The trial of all crimes, except in cases of impeachment, shall be by jury; and such trial shall be held in the State where the said crimes shall have been committed; but when not committed within any State, the trial shall be at such place or places as the Congress may by law have directed.

Section 3. Treason against the United States shall consist only in levying war against them, or in adhering to their enemies, giving them aid and comfort. No person shall be convicted of treason unless on the testimony of two witnesses to the same overt act, or on confession in open court.

The Congress shall have power to declare the punishment of treason, but no attainder of treason shall work corruption of blood or forfeiture except during the life of the person attainted.

Article Four

Section 1. Full faith and credit shall be given in each State to the public acts, records, and judicial proceedings of every other State. And the Congress may by general laws prescribe the manner in which such acts, records, and proceedings shall be proved, and the effect thereof.

Section 2. The citizens of each State shall be entitled to all privileges and immunities of citizens in the several States.

A person charged in any State with treason, felony, or other crime, who shall flee from justice, and be found in another State, shall, on demand of the executive authority of the State from which he fled, be delivered up, to be removed to the State having jurisdiction of the crime.

No person held to service or labor in one State, under the laws thereof, escaping into another, shall, in consequence of any law or regulation therein, be discharged from such service or labor, but shall be delivered up on claim of the party to whom such service or labor may be due.

Section 3. New States may be admitted by the Congress into this Union; but no new State shall be formed or erected within the jurisdiction of any other State; nor any State be formed by the junction of two or more States or parts of States, without the consent of the legislatures of the States concerned as well as of the Congress.

The Congress shall have power to dispose of and make all needful rules and regulations respecting the territory or other property belonging to the United States; and nothing in this Constitution shall be so construed as to prejudice any claims of the United States or of any particular State.

Section 4. The United States shall guarantee to every State in this Union a republican form of government, and shall protect each of them against invasion, and on application of the legislature, or of the executive (when the legislature cannot be convened), against domestic violence.

Article Five

The Congress, whenever two-thirds of both houses shall deem it necessary, shall propose amendments to this Constitution, or, on the application of the Legislatures of two-thirds of the several States, shall call a convention for proposing amendments, which, in either case, shall be valid to all intents and purposes, as part of this Constitution, when ratified by the Legislatures of three-fourths of the several States, or by conventions in three-fourths thereof, as the one or the other mode of ratification may be proposed by the Congress; provided that no amendment which may be made prior to the Year One thousand eight hundred and eight shall in any manner affect the first and fourth Clauses in the Ninth Section of the first Article; and that no State, without its consent, shall be deprived of its equal suffrage in the Senate.

Article Six

All debts contracted and engagements entered into, before the adoption of this Constitution, shall be as valid against the United States under this Constitution, as under the Confederation.

This Constitution and the laws of the United States which shall be made in pursuance thereof and all treaties made, or which shall be made, under the authority of the United States, shall be the supreme law of the land; and the judges in every State shall be bound thereby, anything in the Constitution or laws of any State to the contrary notwithstanding.

The Senators and Representatives before mentioned, and the members of the several State Legislatures, and all executive and judicial officers, both of the United States and of the several States, shall be bound by oath or affirmation, to support this Constitution; but no religious test shall ever be required as a qualification to any office or public trust under the United States.

Article Seven

The ratification of the Conventions of nine States shall be sufficient for the establishment of this Constitution between the States so ratifying the same.

Done in convention by the unanimous consent of the States present the seventeenth day of September in the year of our Lord one thousand seven hundred and eighty-seven and of the independence of the United States of America the twelfth, in witness whereof we have hereunto subscribed our names.

G. WASHINGTON—President
and deputy from Virginia

✕ *E S S A Y S*

The first essay is by the political scientist and political activist John P. Roche, Olin Distinguished Professor of American Civilization and Foreign Affairs at Tufts University. Although it is a generation old, it remains fresh because of Roche's vivid sense of political problem solving. Grand principles underlie his interpretation, but his focus is on explaining how the delegates, who did not know what they would do in May 1787, ultimately produced the Constitution. Professor Lance G. Banning of the University of Kentucky is a historian who specializes in the early American republic and has written extensively on the ideas and influence of James Madison and Thomas Jefferson. The second selection, his essay on the Constitutional Convention, both underlines the importance of the division between the large and the small states and shows how the compromise solution to that conflict helped to resolve other troublesome issues as well.

The Founding Fathers: A Reform Caucus in Action

JOHN P. ROCHE

The work of the Constitutional Convention and the motives of the Founding Fathers have been analyzed under a number of different ideological auspices. To one generation of historians, the hand of God was moving in the assembly; under a later dispensation, the dialectic (at various levels of philosophical sophistication) replaced the Deity: "relationships of production" moved into the niche previously reserved for Love of Country. . . . The Framers have undergone miraculous metamorphoses: at one time acclaimed as liberals and bold social engineers, today they appear in the guise of sound Burkean conservatives, men who in our time would subscribe to *Fortune*. . . .

The "Fathers" have thus been admitted to our best circles; the revolutionary ferocity which confiscated all Tory property in reach . . . has been converted . . . into a benign dedication to "consensus" and "prescriptive rights." . . . It is not my purpose here to argue that the "Fathers" were, in fact, radical revolutionaries; that proposition has been brilliantly demonstrated. . . . My concern is with the further position that not only were they revolutionaries, but also they were democrats. Indeed, in my view, there is one fundamental truth about the Founding Fathers . . . : they were first and foremost superb democratic politicians. . . . As recent research into the nature of American politics in the 1780s confirms, they were committed (perhaps willy-nilly) to working within the democratic framework, within a universe of public approval. . . . The Philadelphia Convention was not a College of Cardinals or a council of Platonic guardians working within a manipulative, pre-democratic framework; it was a nationalist reform caucus which had to operate with great delicacy and skill in a political cosmos full of enemies to achieve the one definitive goal—popular approbation. . . .

What they did was to hammer out a pragmatic compromise which would both bolster the "National interest" and be acceptable to the people. What inspiration they got came from their collective experience as professional politicians in a democratic society. As John Dickinson put it to his fellow delegates on August 13, "Experience must be our guide. Reason may mislead us."

In this context, let us examine the problems they confronted and the solutions they evolved. The Convention has been described picturesquely as a counter-revolutionary junta and the Constitution as a coup d'état, but this has been accomplished by withdrawing the whole history of the movement for constitutional reform from its true context. No doubt the goals of the constitutional elite were "subversive" to the existing political order, but it

"The Founding Fathers: A Reform Caucus in Action," by John P. Roche, *American Political Science Review*, 55 December 1961. Reprinted by permission of the author and of the publisher.

is overlooked that their subversion could only have succeeded if the people of the United States endorsed it by regularized procedures. . . .

I

When the Constitutionalists went forth to subvert the Confederation, they utilized the mechanisms of political legitimacy. And the roadblocks which confronted them were formidable. At the same time, they were endowed with certain potent political assets. The history of the United States from 1786 to 1790 was largely one of a masterful employment of political expertise by the Constitutionalists as against bumbling, erratic behavior by the opponents of reform. Effectively, the Constitutionalists had to induce the states, by democratic techniques of coercion, to emasculate themselves. . . . And at the risk of becoming boring, it must be reiterated that the only weapon in the Constitutionalist arsenal was an effective mobilization of public opinion.

The group which undertook this struggle was an interesting amalgam of a few dedicated nationalists with the self-interested spokesmen of various parochial bailiwicks. The Georgians, for example, wanted a strong central authority to provide military protection for their huge, underpopulated state against the Creek Confederacy; Jerseymen and Connecticuters wanted to escape from economic bondage to New York; the Virginians hoped to establish a system which would give that great state its rightful place in the councils of the republic. The dominant figures in the politics of these states therefore cooperated in the call for the Convention. In other states, the thrust towards national reform was taken up by opposition groups who added the "national interest" to their weapons system; in Pennsylvania, for instance, the group fighting to revise the Constitution of 1776 came out foursquare behind the Constitutionalists, and in New York, [Alexander] Hamilton and the Schuyler [family] ambiance took the same tack against George Clinton. There was, of course, a large element of personality in the affair: there is reason to suspect that Patrick Henry's opposition to the Convention and the Constitution was founded on his conviction that Jefferson was behind both, and a close study of local politics elsewhere would surely reveal that others supported the Constitution for the simple (and politically quite sufficient) reason that the "wrong" people were against it. . . .

What distinguished the leaders of the Constitutionalist caucus from their enemies was a "Continental" approach to political, economic and military issues. To the extent that they shared an institutional base of operations, it was the Continental Congress (thirty-nine of the delegates to the Federal Convention had served in Congress), and this was hardly a locale which inspired respect for the state governments. . . . Membership in the Congress under the Articles of Confederation worked to establish a continental frame of reference, that a Congressman from Pennsylvania and one from North Carolina would share. . . . This was particularly true with respect to external affairs: the average state legislator was probably about as concerned with foreign policy than as he is today, but Congressmen were constantly forced to take the broad view of American prestige, were compelled to listen to the reports of Secretary John Jay and to the dispatches and pleas from their frustrated envoys in Britain, France and Spain. From considerations such as these, a "Continental" ideology developed which seems to have demanded a revision of our domestic institutions primarily on the ground that only by invigorating our general government could we assume our rightful place in the international arena. . . .

Note that I am not endorsing the "Critical Period" thesis; on the contrary, Merrill Jensen seems to me quite sound in his view that for most Americans, engaged as they were in self-sustaining agriculture, the "Critical Period" was not particularly critical. In fact, the great achievement of the Constitutionalists was their ultimate success in convincing the elected representatives of a majority of the white male population that change was imperative. A small group of political leaders with a Continental vision and essentially a consciousness of the United States' international impotence, provided the matrix of the movement. To their standard other leaders rallied with their own parallel ambitions. Their great assets were (1) the presence in their caucus of the one authentic American "father figure," George Washington, whose prestige was enormous; (2) the energy and talent of their leadership (in which one must include the towering intellectuals of the time, John Adams and Thomas Jefferson, despite their absence abroad), and their communications "network," which was far superior to anything on the opposition side; (3) the preemptive skill which made "their" issue The Issue and kept the locally oriented opposition permanently on the defensive; and (4) the subjective consideration that these men were spokesmen of a new and compelling credo: American nationalism, that ill-defined but nonetheless potent sense of collective purpose that emerged from the American Revolution. . . .

The Constitutionalists got the jump on the "opposition" (a collective noun: oppositions would be more correct) at the outset with the demand for a Convention. Their opponents were caught in an old political trap: they were not being asked to approve any specific program of reform, but only to endorse a meeting to discuss and recommend needed reforms. If they took a hard line at the first stage, they were put in the position of glorifying the status quo and of denying the need for any changes. Moreover, the Constitutionalists could go to the people with a persuasive argument for "fair play"—"How can you condemn reform before you know precisely what is involved?" Since the state legislatures obviously would have the final say on any proposals that might emerge from the Convention, the Constitutionalists were merely reasonable men asking for a chance. Besides, since they did not make any concrete proposals at that stage, they were in a position to capitalize on every sort of generalized discontent with the Confederation.

Perhaps because of their poor intelligence system, perhaps because of over-confidence generated by the failure of all previous efforts to alter the Articles, the opposition awoke too late to the dangers that confronted them in 1787. Not only did the Constitutionalists manage to get every state but

Rhode Island . . . to appoint delegates to Philadelphia, but when the results were in, it appeared that they dominated the delegations. Given the apathy of the opposition, this was a natural phenomenon: in an ideologically non-polarized political atmosphere those who get appointed to a special committee are likely to be the men who supported the movement for its creation. . . . Much has been made of the fact that the delegates to Philadelphia were not elected by the people; some have adduced this fact as evidence of the "undemocratic" character of the gathering. But put in the context of the time, this argument is wholly specious: the central government under the Articles was considered a creature of the component states and in all the states but Rhode Island, Connecticut and New Hampshire, members of the national Congress were chosen by the state legislatures. This was not a consequence of elitism or fear of the mob; it was a logical extension of states'-rights doctrine to guarantee that the national institution did not end-run the state legislatures and make direct contact with the people.

II

With delegations safely named, the focus shifted to Philadelphia. While waiting for a quorum to assemble, James Madison got busy and drafted the so-called Randolph or Virginia Plan with the aid of the Virginia delegation. This was a political master-stroke. Its consequence was that once business got under way, the framework of discussion was established on Madison's terms. There was no interminable argument over agenda; instead the delegates took the Virginia Resolutions—"just for purposes of discussion"—as their point of departure. And along with Madison's proposals, many of which were buried in the course of the summer, went his major premise: a new start on a Constitution rather than piecemeal amendment. . . .

Standard treatments of the Convention divide the delegates into "nationalists" and "states'-righters" with various improvised shadings ("moderate nationalists," etc.), but these are a posteriori categories which obfuscate more than they clarify. What is striking to one who analyzes the Convention as a case-study in democratic politics is the lack of clear-cut ideological divisions in the Convention. Indeed, I submit that the evidence—Madison's Notes, the correspondence of the delegates, and debates on ratification—indicates that this was a remarkably homogeneous body on the ideological level. [Robert] Yates and [John] Lansing [of New York, who favored the New Jersey Plan] . . . left in disgust on July 10. . . . Luther Martin, Maryland's bibulous narcissist, left on September 4 in a huff when he discovered that others did not share his self-esteem; others went home for personal reasons. But the hard core of delegates accepted a grinding regimen throughout the attrition of a Philadelphia summer precisely because they shared the Constitutionalist goal.

Basic differences of opinion emerged, of course, but these were not ideological; they were structural. If the so-called "states'-rights" group had not accepted the fundamental purposes of the Convention, they could simply have pulled out and by doing so have aborted the whole enterprise. Instead of bolting, they returned day after day to argue and to compromise. An interesting symbol of this basic homogeneity was the initial agreement on secrecy: these professional politicians did not want to become prisoners of publicity; they wanted to retain that freedom of maneuver which is only possible when men are not forced to take public stands in the preliminary stages of negotiation. There was no legal means of binding the tongues of the delegates: at any stage in the game a delegate with basic principled objections to the emerging project could have taken the stump (as Luther Martin did after his exit) and denounced the convention to the skies. Yet . . . the delegates generally observed the injunction. Secrecy is certainly uncharacteristic of any assembly marked by strong ideological polarization. . . .

Commentators on the Constitution who have read *The Federalist* in lieu of reading the actual debates have credited the Fathers with the invention of a sublime concept called "Federalism." . . . Federalism, as the theory is generally defined, was an improvisation which was later promoted into a political theory. Experts on "federalism" should take to heart the advice of David Hume, who warned . . . "there is no subject in which we must proceed with more caution than in [history], lest we assign causes which never existed and reduce what is merely contingent to stable and universal principles." In any event, the final balance in the Constitution between the states and the nation must have come as a great disappointment to Madison. . . .

It is indeed astonishing how those who have glibly designated James Madison the "father" of Federalism have overlooked the solid body of fact which indicates that he shared Hamilton's quest for a unitary central government. To be specific, they have avoided examining the clear import of the Madison-Virginia Plan, and have disregarded Madison's dogged inch-by-inch retreat from the bastions of centralization. The Virginia Plan envisioned a unitary national government effectively freed from and dominant over the states. The lower house of the national legislature was to be elected directly by the people of the states with membership proportional to population. The upper house was to be selected by the lower and the two chambers would elect the executive and choose the judges. The national government would be thus cut completely loose from the states. . . . The national legislature was to be empowered to disallow the acts of state legislatures, and the central government was vested, in addition to the powers of the nation under the Articles of Confederation, with plenary authority wherever ". . . the separate States are incompetent or in which the harmony of the United States may be interrupted by the exercise of individual legislation." Finally, just to lock the door against state intrusion, the national Congress was to be given the power to use military force on recalcitrant states. This was Madison's "model" of an ideal national government, though it later received little publicity in *The Federalist*.

The interesting thing was the reaction of the Convention to this militant program for a strong autonomous central government. Some delegates were startled, some obviously leery of so comprehensive a project of reform, but nobody set off any fireworks and nobody walked out. Moreover, in the two weeks that followed, the Virginia Plan received substantial endorsement *en principe*; the initial temper of the gathering can be deduced from the approval "without debate or dissent," on May 31, of the Sixth Resolution which granted Congress the authority to disallow state legislation ". . . contravening in its opinion the Articles of Union." Indeed, an amendment was included to bar states from contravening national treaties.

The Virginia Plan may therefore be considered, in ideological terms, as the delegates' Utopia, but as the discussions continued and became more specific, many of those present began to have second thoughts. . . . They were practical politicians in a democratic society, and no matter what their private dreams might be, they had to take home an acceptable package and defend it—and their own political futures—against predictable attack. On June 14 the breaking point between dream and reality took place. Apparently realizing that under the Virginia Plan, Massachusetts, Virginia and Pennsylvania could virtually dominate the national government—and probably appreciating that to sell this program to "the folks back home" would be impossible—the delegates from the small states dug in their heels and demanded time for a consideration of alternatives. . . .

Now the process of accommodation was put into action smoothly—and wisely, given the character and strength of the doubters. Madison had the votes, but this was one of those situations where the enforcement of mechanical majoritarianism could easily have destroyed the objectives of the majority: the Constitutionalists were in quest of a qualitative as well as a quantitative consensus; . . . it was a political imperative if they were to attain ratification.

III

According to the standard script, at this point the "states'-rights" group intervened in force behind the New Jersey Plan, which has been characteristically portrayed as a revision to the status quo under the Articles of Confederation with but minor modifications. A careful examination of the evidence indicates that only in a marginal sense is this an accurate description. It is true that the New Jersey Plan put the states back into the institutional picture, but one could argue that to do so was a recognition of political reality rather than an affirmation of states'-rights. A serious case can be made that the advocates of the New Jersey Plan, far from being ideological addicts of states'-rights, intended to substitute for the Virginia Plan a system which would both retain strong national power and have a chance of adoption in the states. The leading spokesman for the project asserted quite clearly that his views were based more on counsels of expediency than on principle. . . . In his preliminary speech on June 9, Paterson had stated ". . . to the public mind we must accommodate ourselves," and in his notes for this and his later effort as well, the emphasis is the same. The structure of government under the Articles should be retained:

2. Because it accords with the Sentiments of the People
    [Proof:] 1. Coms. [Commissions from state legislatures defining the ju-
        risdiction of the delegates]
        2. News-papers—Political Barometer. Jersey never would have
            sent Delegates under the first [Virginia] Plan—
    Not here to sport Opinions of my own. Wt. [What] can be done. A little
    practicable Virtue preferrable to Theory.

This was a defense of political acumen, not of states'-rights. . . .

In other words, the advocates of the New Jersey Plan concentrated their
fire on what they held to be the political liabilities of the Virginia Plan—
which were matters of institutional structure—rather than on the proposed
scope of national authority. Indeed, the Supremacy Clause of the Constitution first saw the light of day in Paterson's Sixth Resolution; the New
Jersey Plan contemplated the use of military force to secure compliance with
national law; and finally Paterson made clear his view that under either the
Virginia or the New Jersey systems, the general government would ". . .
act on individuals and not on states." From the states'-rights viewpoint, this
was heresy: the fundament of that doctrine was the proposition that any
central government had as its constituents the states, not the people, and
could only reach the people through the agency of the state government.

Paterson then reopened the agenda of the Convention, but he did so
within a distinctly nationalist framework. Paterson's position was one of
favoring a strong central government in principle, but opposing one which
in fact put the big states in the saddle. . . .

How attached would the Virginians have been to their reform principles
if Virginia were to disappear as a component geographical unit (the largest)
for representational purposes? Up to this point, the Virginians had been in
the happy position of supporting high ideals with that inner confidence born
of knowledge that the "public interest" they endorsed would nourish their
private interest. Worse, they had shown little willingness to compromise.
Now the delegates from the small states announced that they were unprepared to be offered up as sacrificial victims to a "national interest" which
reflected Virginia's parochial ambition. Caustic Charles Pinckney was not
far off when he remarked sardonically that ". . . the whole [conflict] comes
to this": "Give N. Jersey an equal vote, and she will dismiss her scruples,
and concur in the Natil. system." What he rather unfairly did not add was
that the Jersey delegates were not free agents who could adhere to their
private convictions; they had to take back, sponsor and risk their reputations
on the reforms approved by the Convention—and in New Jersey, not in
Virginia. . . .

IV

On Tuesday morning, June 19, . . . James Madison led off with a long,
carefully reasoned speech analyzing the New Jersey Plan which, while intellectually vigorous in its criticisms, was quite conciliatory in mood. "The
great difficulty," he observed, "lies in the affair of Representation; and if

this could be adjusted, all others would be surmountable." (As events were to demonstrate, this diagnosis was correct.) When he finished, a vote was taken on whether to continue with the Virginia Plan as the nucleus for a new constitution: seven states voted "Yes"; New York, New Jersey, and Delaware voted "No"; and Maryland, whose position often depended on which delegates happened to be on the floor, divided. Paterson, it seems, lost decisively; yet in a fundamental sense he and his allies had achieved their purpose: from that day onward, it could never be forgotten that the state governments loomed ominously in the background. . . . Moreover, nobody bolted the convention: Paterson and his colleagues took their defeat in stride and set to work to modify the Virginia Plan, particularly with respect to its provisions on representation in the national legislature. Indeed, they won an immediate rhetorical bonus; when Oliver Ellsworth of Connecticut rose to move that the word "national" be expunged from the Third Virginia Resolution ("Resolved that a national Government ought to be established consisting of a supreme Legislative, Executive and Judiciary"), Randolph agreed and the motion passed unanimously. The process of compromise had begun.

For the next two weeks, the delegates circled around the problem of legislative representation. The Connecticut delegation appears to have evolved a possible compromise quite early in the debates, but the Virginians and particularly Madison (unaware that he would later be acclaimed as the prophet of "federalism") fought obdurately against providing for equal representation of states in the second chamber. . . . On July 2, the ice began to break when through a number of fortuitous events—and one that seems deliberate—the majority against equality of representation was converted into a dead tie. The Convention had reached the stage where it was "ripe" for a solution (presumably all the therapeutic speeches had been made), and the South Carolinians proposed a committee. Madison and James Wilson wanted none of it, but with only Pennsylvania dissenting, the body voted to establish a working party on the problem of representation.

The members of this committee, one from each state, were elected by the delegates—and a very interesting committee it was. Despite the fact that the Virginia Plan had held majority support up to that date, neither Madison nor Randolph was selected (Mason was the Virginian) and Baldwin of Georgia, whose shift in position had resulted in the tie, was chosen. From the composition, it was clear that this was not to be a "fighting" committee: the emphasis in membership was on what might be described as "second-level political entrepreneurs." On the basis of the discussions up to that time, only Luther Martin of Maryland could be described as a "bitter-ender." Admittedly, some divination enters into this sort of analysis, but one does get a sense of the mood of the delegates from these choices—including the interesting selection of Benjamin Franklin, despite his age and intellectual wobbliness, over the brilliant and incisive Wilson or the sharp, polemical Gouverneur Morris, to represent Pennsylvania. His passion for conciliation was more valuable at this juncture than Wilson's logical genius, or Morris' acerbic wit. . . .

It would be tedious to continue a blow-by-blow analysis of the work of the delegates; the critical fight was over representation of the states and once the Connecticut Compromise was adopted on July 17, the Convention was over the hump. Madison, James Wilson, and Gouverneur Morris of New York (who was there representing Pennsylvania!) fought the compromise all the way in a last-ditch effort to get a unitary state with parliamentary supremacy. But their allies deserted them. . . . Moreover, once the compromise had carried (by five states to four, with one state divided), its advocates threw themselves vigorously into the job of strengthening the general government's substantive powers—as might have been predicted, indeed, from Paterson's early statements. It nourishes an increased respect for Madison's devotion to the art of politics, to realize that this dogged fighter could sit down six months later and prepare essays for *The Federalist* in contradiction to his basic convictions about the true course the Convention should have taken.

V

Two tricky issues will serve to illustrate the later process of accommodation. The first was the institutional position of the Executive. Madison argued for an executive chosen by the National Legislature and on May 29 this had been adopted with a provision that after his seven-year term was concluded, the chief magistrate should not be eligible for reelection. In late July this was reopened and for a week the matter was argued from several different points of view. . . . One group felt that the states should have a hand in the process; another small but influential circle urged direct election by the people. There were a number of proposals: election by the people, election by state governors, by electors chosen by state legislatures, by the National Legislature, . . . and there was some resemblance to three-dimensional chess in the dispute because of the presence of two other variables, length of tenure and reeligibility. Finally, after opening, reopening, and re-reopening the debate, the thorny problem was consigned to a committee for resolution.

The Brearley Committee on Postponed Matters was a superb aggregation of talent and its compromise on the Executive was a masterpiece of political improvisation. (The Electoral College, its creation, however, had little in its favor as an institution—as the delegates well appreciated.) The point of departure for all discussion about the presidency in the Convention was that in immediate terms, the problem was non-existent; in other words, everybody present knew that under any system devised, George Washington would be President. Thus they were dealing in the future tense and to a body of working politicians the merits of the Brearley proposal were obvious: everybody got a piece of cake. (Or to put it more academically, each viewpoint could leave the Convention and argue to its constituents that it had really won the day.) First, the state legislatures had the right to determine the mode of selection of the electors; second, the small states received a bonus in the Electoral College in the form of a guaranteed minimum of three votes while the big states got acceptance of the principle of proportional power;

third, if the state legislatures agreed (as six did in the first presidential election), the people could be involved directly in the choice of electors; and finally, if no candidate received a majority in the College, the right of decision passed to the National Legislature with each state exercising equal strength. (In the Brearley recommendation, the election went to the Senate, but a motion from the floor substituted the House; this was accepted on the ground that the Senate already had enough authority over the executive in its treaty and appointment powers.)

This compromise was almost too good to be true, and the Framers snapped it up with little debate or controversy. No one seemed to think well of the College as an institution; indeed, what evidence there is suggests that there was an assumption that once Washington had finished his tenure as President, the electors would cease to produce majorities and the chief executive would usually be chosen in the House. George Mason observed casually that the selection would be made in the House nineteen times in twenty and no one seriously disputed this point. The vital aspect of the Electoral College was that it got the Convention over the hurdle and protected everybody's interests. . . .

In short, the Framers did not in their wisdom endow the United States with a College of Cardinals—the Electoral College was neither an exercise in applied Platonism nor an experiment in indirect government based on elitist distrust of the masses. It was merely a jerry-rigged improvisation which has subsequently been endowed with a high theoretical content. . . .

The second issue on which some substantial practical bargaining took place was slavery. The morality of slavery was, by design, not at issue; but in its other concrete aspects, slavery colored the arguments over taxation, commerce, and representation. The "Three-Fifths Compromise," that three-fifths of the slaves would be counted both for representation and for purposes of direct taxation (which was drawn from the past—it was a formula of Madison's utilized by Congress in 1783 to establish the basis of state contributions to the Confederation treasury) had allayed some Northern fears about Southern over-representation. . . . The Southerners, on the other hand, were afraid that Congressional control over commerce would lead to the exclusion of slaves or to their excessive taxation as imports. Moreover, the Southerners were disturbed over "navigation acts," i.e., tariffs or special legislation providing, for example, that exports be carried only in American ships; as a section depending upon exports, they wanted protection from the potential voracity of their commercial brethren of the Eastern states. To achieve this end, Mason and others urged that the Constitution include a proviso that navigation and commercial laws should require a two-thirds vote in Congress.

These problems came to a head in late August and, as usual were handed to a committee in the hope that, in Gouverneur Morris' words, ". . . these things may form a bargain among the Northern and Southern states." The Committee reported its measures of reconciliation on August 25, and on August 29 the package was wrapped up and delivered. What occurred can best be described in George Mason's dour version (he anticipated Calhoun

in his conviction that permitting navigation acts to pass by majority vote
would put the South in economic bondage to the North—it was mainly on
this ground that he refused to sign the Constitution):

> The Constitution as agreed to till a fortnight before the Convention rose
> was such a one as he would have set his hand and heart to. . . . [Until that
> time] The 3 New England States were constantly with us in all questions
> . . . so that it was these three States with the 5 Southern ones against
> Pennsylvania, Jersey and Delaware. With respect to the importation of
> slaves, [decision-making] was left to Congress. This disturbed the two South-
> ernmost States who knew that Congress would immediately suppress the
> importation of slaves. Those two States therefore struck up a bargain with
> the three New England States. If they would join to admit slaves for some
> years, the two Southern-most States would join in changing the clause which
> required the ⅔ of the Legislature in any vote [on navigation acts]. It was
> done.

On the floor of the Convention there was a virtual love-feast on this
happy occasion. Charles Pinckney of South Carolina attempted to overturn
the committee's decision, when the compromise was reported to the Convention, by insisting that the South needed protection from the imperialism
of the Northern states. But his Southern colleagues were not prepared to
rock the boat and General C. C. Pinckney arose to spread oil on the suddenly
ruffled waters; he admitted that:

> It was in the true interest of the S[outhern] States to have no regulation of
> commerce; but considering the loss brought on the commerce of the Eastern
> States by the Revolution, their liberal conduct towards the views of South
> Carolina [on the regulation of the slave trade] and the interests the weak
> Southn. States had in being united with the strong Eastern states, he thought
> it proper that no fetters should be imposed on the power of making com-
> mercial regulations; and that his constituents, though prejudiced against the
> Eastern States, would be reconciled to this liberality. He had himself prej-
> udices agst the Eastern States before he came here, but would acknowledge
> that he had found them as liberal and candid as any men whatever.

Pierce Butler took the same tack, essentially arguing that he was not too
happy about the possible consequences, but that a deal was a deal. . . .

VI

Drawing on their vast collective political experience, utilizing every weapon
in the politician's arsenal, looking constantly over their shoulders at their
constituents, the delegates put together a Constitution. It was a makeshift
affair; some sticky issues (for example, the qualification of voters) they
ducked entirely; others they mastered with that ancient instrument of political
sagacity, studied ambiguity (for example, citizenship), and some they just
overlooked. In this last category, I suspect, fell the matter of the power of
the federal courts to determine the constitutionality of acts of Congress.
When the judicial article was formulated (Article III of the Constitution),

deliberations were still in the stage where the legislature was endowed with broad power under the Randolph formulation, authority which by its own terms was scarcely amenable to judicial review. In essence, courts could hardly determine when ". . . the separate States are incompetent or . . . the harmony of the United States may be interrupted"; the National Legislature, as critics pointed out, was free to define its own jurisdiction. Later the definition of legislative authority was changed into the form we know, a series of stipulated powers, but the delegates never seriously reexamined the jurisdiction of the judiciary under this new limited formulation. All arguments on the intention of the Framers in this matter are thus deductive and a posteriori, though some obviously make more sense than others.

The Framers were busy and distinguished men, anxious to get back to their families, their positions, and their constituents. . . . They were trying to do an important job, and do it in such a fashion that their handiwork would be acceptable to very diverse constituencies. No one was rhapsodic about the final document, but it was a beginning, a move in the right direction, and one they had reason to believe the people would endorse. In addition, since they had modified the impossible amendment provisions of the Articles . . . to one demanding approval by only three-quarters of the states, they seemed confident that gaps in the fabric which experience would reveal could be rewoven without undue difficulty.

So with a neat phrase introduced by Benjamin Franklin (but devised by Gouverneur Morris) which made their decision sound unanimous, and an inspired benediction by the Old Doctor urging doubters to doubt their own infallibility, the Constitution was accepted and signed. Curiously, Edmund Randolph, who had played so vital a role throughout, refused to sign, as did his fellow Virginian George Mason and Elbridge Gerry of Massachusetts. Randolph's behavior was eccentric; . . . the best explanation seems to be that he was afraid that the Constitution would prove to be a liability in Virginia politics, where Patrick Henry was burning up the countryside with impassioned denunciations. Presumably, Randolph wanted to check the temper of the populace before he risked his reputation, and perhaps his job, in a fight with both Henry and Richard Henry Lee. Events lend some justification to this speculation: after much temporizing . . . Randolph endorsed ratification in Virginia and ended up getting the best of both worlds. . . .

The Constitution, then, was not an apotheosis of "constitutionalism," a triumph of architectonic genius; it was a patch-work sewn together under the pressure of both time and events by a group of extremely talented democratic politicians. They refused to attempt the establishment of a strong, centralized sovereignty on the principle of legislative supremacy for the excellent reason that the people would not accept it. They risked their political fortunes by opposing the established doctrines of state sovereignty because they were convinced that the existing system was leading to national impotence and probably foreign domination. For two years, they worked to get a convention established. For over three months, in what must have seemed to the faithful participants an endless process of give-and-take, they reasoned, cajoled, threatened, and bargained amongst themselves. The result was a Constitution which the people, in fact, by democratic processes, did accept, and a new and far better national government was established. . . .

To conclude, the Constitution was neither a victory for abstract theory nor a great practical success. Well over half a million men had to die on the battlefields of the Civil War before certain constitutional principles could be defined—a baleful consideration which is somehow overlooked in our customary tributes to the farsighted genius of the Framers and to the supposed American talent for "constitutionalism." The Constitution was, however, a vivid demonstration of effective democratic political action, and of the forging of a national elite which literally persuaded its countrymen to hoist themselves by their own boot straps.

What Happened at the Constitutional Convention

LANCE G. BANNING

Meeting at the Pennsylvania State House (Independence Hall), the Constitutional Convention found a quorum on May 25 and sat until September 17. Fifty-five delegates participated in its work, though there were seldom more than forty in the room for any single session. Representing every state except Rhode Island, the delegates comprised a good cross-section of the early national elite. Lawyers (34), merchants (7), farmers (27), public creditors (30), and public servants (10), nearly all were wealthy men, and most had taken generally conservative positions in their states. Yet members came from a variety of local factions and from all the major regions of the several states except the west. The nation might have organized an equally impressive meeting from the ranks of leaders who did not attend. John Adams and Thomas Jefferson were representing the United States abroad in 1787. John Jay and Samuel Adams were passed over. Patrick Henry "smelt a rat" and turned down his election. Still, most states attempted to select their most experienced and best, usually with slight regard to factional considerations, and they succeeded well enough that Jefferson described the roster as a gathering of "demigods." George Washington was present. Inevitably, he was quickly chosen to preside.

Among the delegates as well was young James Madison, Jefferson's close friend, an influential member of the Annapolis Convention, and long a leading advocate of national reforms. Madison had led Virginia, which had led the other states, in organizing the convention and selecting delegates whose talents and distinguished reputations signaled a profound commitment to its work. In the weeks before the meeting, he had taken careful notes on ancient and modern confederacies and prepared a formal memorandum on the "Vices of the Political System of the United States," thinking problems

"The Constitutional Convention" by Lance G. Banning. Abridged with permission of Macmillan Publishing Company from *The Framing and Ratification of the Constitution* edited by Leonard W. Levy and Dennis J. Mahoney. Copyright © 1987 by Macmillan Publishing Company, a Division of Macmillan, Inc.

through to a degree that no one else had done and urging other members of his delegation to arrive in Philadelphia in time to frame some introductory proposals with which the meeting might begin. Virginia's seven delegates assembled daily while they waited for the full convention to obtain a quorum, agreeing on a set of resolutions that might serve as a preliminary basis for discussions. Speaking for the delegation as a whole, Governor Edmund Randolph introduced these resolutions on May 29, as soon as the convention had agreed upon its rules. . . .

A solemn sense of high responsibility and urgent, common purpose was indispensable to the Convention's great achievement, not least because most delegates were only partially prepared for the enormous changes sketched by the Virginia Plan. Seizing the initiative for radical reform, Madison's proposals demonstrated an instinctive grasp of several broad, though hazy, understandings that would limit and direct the course of the proceedings. Leaders of a democratic Revolution, including thirty veterans of the war, the delegates had not forgotten the complaints and hopes that had propelled them into independence. Nearly all of them had come to think that an effective central government would have to have, at minimum, an independent source of revenues, authority to regulate the country's trade, and power to compel obedience to its legitimate commands. Nearly all agreed, as well, that powers that the colonies had stubbornly denied to England would have to be accompanied by careful checks against the possibility of their abuse. Many, nonetheless, were far from willing to consent to the specific kinds of checks proposed by the initial resolutions. The Pennsylvanians and Virginians were prepared from the beginning to insist that powers of this sort could be entrusted only to a well-constructed, fully representative republic. Overawed by the Virginia Plan, accepting many of its goals, and unprepared to offer comprehensive counterresolutions, dissenters were uncertain how to counter its proponents in debate. They nevertheless objected from the start that the convention was empowered only to reform the present federal system, not to overturn it. The framing of the Constitution thus became a complicated story of a fundamental conflict that occurred within the context of a common quest. . . .

Between May 30 and June 13, the Committee of the Whole conducted a complete consideration of the Randolph Plan. During these two weeks, with Madison and James Wilson of Pennsylvania at their head, a brilliant group of delegates from larger states developed a compelling case for radical reform. Distinguishing between a "national" government and one "merely federal," Wilson, Madison, Randolph, George Mason (Virginia), Gouverneur Morris (Pennsylvania), and others argued that the fatal weakness of the old confederation was its unavoidable dependence on the thirteen states for revenues and for a host of intermediary actions necessary to enforce its laws and treaties. Lacking independent means to carry its decisions into action, they explained, Congress had been baffled by the states even when its measures were supported by a huge majority and undeniably were within its proper province. Paper grants of new responsibilities would only add new sources of frustration if the states retained the power to ignore or counteract the central government's decisions; and yet a federal power to compel the states might introduce a constant threat of war between the union and its members. The inescapable necessity, the nationalists maintained, was to abandon the unworkable idea of a government over governments, a sovereignty over sovereignties, and give the central government the courts and other independent means to act directly on the individual members of society. Revolutionary principles required, however, that any government possessing the authority to reach the people's lives and purses would have to represent its citizens immediately and fairly. Given the necessity for larger federal powers, the traditional equality between the states would have to be abandoned in order to preserve equality among the people and majority control. . . .

But as the skeleton of the Virginia Plan acquired some flesh and as it grew increasingly more difficult to settle lesser questions while the great ones went unanswered, the confrontation that had loomed from the beginning could no longer be contained. New Jersey's delegates demanded a decision on apportioning the Congress, insisting on June 9 that proportional representation would destroy the smaller states and place the whole confederation at the mercy of a coalition of its largest members: Massachusetts, Pennsylvania, and Virginia. Ten of thirteen states, warned William Paterson, would certainly reject this scheme. If he could not defeat it in the hall, he would oppose it in his state. New Jersey would "never confederate on the plan before the committee."

. . . James Wilson answered Paterson in kind. "If the small states will not confederate on this plan," he assured them, Pennsylvania and some others "would not confederate on any other." The division that would dominate proceedings for the next five weeks had burst into the open. It would prove the clearest, most dramatic, most persistent argument of the convention—the single conflict over which the gathering repeatedly approached collapse.

For all its threatening potential, nevertheless, the clash between the small states and the large cannot explain developments between May 30 and June 13. It was not the only conflict that emerged, nor can an exclusive emphasis on conflicts and divisions properly illuminate the course of the proceedings. The Constitutional Convention was successful, in the end, because its battles almost always raged in multiple dimensions, because the push-and-pull that marked its course was never simply a result of clashing interests, and because the men involved were more than merely clever brokers for their states. . . .

The first two weeks of the convention seem most helpfully described as an initial exploration during which a complicated pattern of divisions rapidly emerged within a framework of evolving, general understandings. Like Madison, most delegates had come to Philadelphia as worried by conditions in the states as by the problems of the union. They readily agreed with the Virginian that the will of unrestrained majorities was often inconsistent with the rights of the minority or long-term public needs, and that the early Revolutionary constitutions had neglected dangers of this sort by trusting too much power to the lower houses of assembly. . . . Everywhere, as Elbridge Gerry phrased it, the country seemed to suffer from "an excess of democracy." Good government appeared to have been sacrificed to revolutionary fears of unresponsive rulers.

Few members of the Constitutional Convention carried their alarm about majority misrule so far as to suggest nostalgia for aristocrats or kings. Most genuinely shared the people's fierce commitment to a democratic system. Yet nearly all were powerfully determined not to replicate the errors they believed had been committed in the early Revolutionary constitutions. Here, again, the resolutions of May 29 successfully defined the boundaries of disagreement. Sound republics, they suggested, must be built upon two legislative houses: one elected by the people; the other chosen in a manner that would shield its members from the whims of the majority and thus assure continuing protection for the rights of the minority and continuing attention to the nation's long-term needs. The legislature should be counterbalanced by a forceful, separate executive, and the judiciary should be independent of them both. Through almost four months of often bitter quarrels, there was never any serious dispute about these fundamental principles of governmental structure. . . .

The Virginia Plan survived its first examination fundamentally intact. . . . Wilson, Madison, and their lieutenants made it clear that what they wanted was to build a wise and energetic central government upon a broadly popular foundation, blending a responsibility to the majority with multiple securities against an overbearing, popularly elected lower house. Impressed by their analysis of the debilities of the existing system, the convention speedily agreed to substitute a complex and authoritative central government for the present, feeble, unicameral regime. Sharing their dissatisfaction with the constitutions of the states, it worked from the beginning to establish genuinely independent, fully countervailing branches.

Through these early days, Madison and Wilson towered over the convention like a team of titans. . . . Still, the nationalist assault by no means carried everything before it. Although the smallest states seemed relatively isolated in the earliest debates and were severely beaten on the matter of the lower house, the fierce resistance vocalized by Paterson and [George] Read [of Delaware] became increasingly imposing as it coalesced with opposition based on different concerns. Three delegates—no more—were rigidly committed to a "merely federal" system, but [Robert] Yates and [John] Lansing could control New York while Luther Martin often managed to divide the Maryland contingent. For each obstructionist, moreover, there were several others for whom the pervasive fear of popular misrule, which made the resolutions of May 29 a universally attractive model for republican reform, could also reinforce a natural reluctance to surrender local powers to a national majority. Although the delegations from Connecticut and South Carolina were especially inclined to be distrustful of a scheme that would erect a stronger central government on greater popular involvement, almost every delegation was composed of men who differed widely in their judgments of the people's competence as well as in their willingness to shift additional responsibilities to federal hands. As the smaller states discovered partial allies, sometimes here and sometimes there, it seemed increasingly unlikely that a national republic could secure approval both from a majority of states and from the representatives of a majority of the people. Even optimistic nationalists resigned themselves to a campaign that promised to extend throughout the summer.

Confronted with so many overlapping fears, the democratic nationalists encountered rising opposition during the convention's first two weeks and suffered one decisive check. The Virginia Plan provided for election of the senate by the lower house from persons nominated by the states. On June 7, over loud objections from Madison and Wilson, majorities in every delegation disapproved this proposition in favor of election of the senate by the legislatures of the states. . . . Many . . . were forcefully impressed by the insistence of John Dickinson (Delaware) and Roger Sherman (Connecticut) that selection by the local legislatures could collect the sense of states as states, assure a federal harmony, and offer firm securities against potential federal usurpations.

Committed nationalists were deeply disappointed. Fearing that selection of the senate by the states would build into the system exactly the flaw that was destroying the confederation, they also rightly sensed that an insistence on a federal role for states as states would reinforce demands for an equality between them. On June 11, just before the crucial votes, Sherman urged that representation in the lower house might be appointed to free population, while every state might retain an equal vote in the senate. By moving to revive an old confederation formula, which counted a slave as three-fifths of a man, Wilson promptly headed off an argument that might have split the large-state coalition. But the overwhelming vote for proportional representation in the lower house was followed by a very close decision on the senate, where Sherman's motion for equality was narrowly rejected, 6 to 5: Connecticut, New York, New Jersey, Delaware, and Maryland, aye; Massachusetts, Pennsylvania, Virginia, North Carolina, South Carolina, and Georgia, no. A combination of concerns had joined to check the nationalist momentum. Two days later the Committee of the Whole reported its amended resolutions to the House, but the convention then immediately adjourned in order to permit opponents to prepare alternatives to the Virginia Plan.

William Paterson's New Jersey Resolutions, introduced on June 15, were thrown together quickly by the coalition that had voted for an equal senate days before. This coalition was united only by its opposition to the Randolph Plan, and its proposals did not represent the real desires of any of their framers. As Dickinson suggested in a private talk with Madison, many members from the smaller states were not opposed in principle to an effective, "national" system. . . . Under the New Jersey Plan, the general government would still have had the power to impose a stamp tax, postal duties, and an impost, to compel compliance with its requisitions, and to regulate the country's interstate and foreign commerce. Federal laws would still have overridden local legislation. A separate executive and federal courts would still have shared authority with Congress. For Luther Martin and the two New Yorkers, this was clearly rather much. For Dickinson and others, just as clearly, Paterson's proposal that the legislature should remain a single house, in which each state would keep its equal vote, was mainly an attempt to force concessions from the other side. . . .

It soon became apparent that the conflict over representation overshadowed every lesser disagreement. The convention managed, with increasing difficulty, to confirm its preference for a bicameral regime. It voted once again for popular election of the lower house and state election of the upper. It reached agreement on a two-year term for representatives and six years for the senate. At every step, however, members fearful of a wholly national plan attempted to insert provisions that would give the states a larger role in paying or selecting federal officials. Small-state delegates attempted a variety of schemes that might disrupt the large-state coalition. Though Madison and Hamilton insisted that the small states need not fear a combination of the large, because the most important differences within the union were between the North and the South, William Samuel Johnson of Connecticut responded that a general government was being framed for states as well as people and that even Mason had admitted that the states should have some means to guarantee their rights and place within the system.

By the end of June, when the Convention voted 6–4–1 (as usual) for proportional representation in the lower house, the meeting was approaching dissolution. At this point Connecticut again proposed the compromise that Sherman had suggested weeks before, putting the proposal now in the language of an ultimatum. Remarking that the union might be "partly national," but should continue "partly federal" as well, Oliver Ellsworth said that he was not entirely disappointed that the meeting had approved proportional representation in the lower house, which would conform to national ideas and offer safety to the larger states. But he could see no ground for compromise and no alternative to the collapse of the convention and the union if the larger states would not concede an equal senate. . . .

With the meeting at a deadlock and the large-state coalition showing obvious internal stress, Charles C. Pinckney recommended the appointment of a grand committee to devise a compromise. Only Madison and Wilson disapproved, fearing that the tide was turning irreversibly toward an accommodation—as, indeed, it was. Voting for a member from each state, the meeting chose a grand committee that included Ellsworth, Bedford, Paterson, Yates, and Martin, but not a single member from the larger states who had not hinted at a commitment to conciliation. . . .

To Madison and Wilson, the result was not a compromise at all, but a surrender to the smaller states—and one that seriously marred the symmetry of the evolving system. In exchange for equal representation in the upper house, the smaller states accepted proportional representation in the lower and agreed to give the lower house exclusive authority over money bills. This last provision, Madison and Wilson argued, might rob the senate of the power to restrain the lower house on matters where restraint was needed, but it would not prevent minorities from using their position in the senate to defeat the national will. Pleading with the smaller states to give up their demand for a concession plainly incompatible with democratic principles and larger federal powers, the leading nationalists continued to oppose the compromise throughout the next two weeks. They swam against a swelling current.

During these two weeks, the meeting saw a jumble of confusing motions and appointed two additional committees to distribute seats in the first house of representatives. Regional considerations, which had lurked beneath the early 6–4–1 divisions—in which all the southern states had voted with the large-state bloc—now bubbled to the surface. In arguments about a periodic census and admission of new states, as well as in maneuvers over seats in the lower house, members hostile to the three-fifths rule or fearful of the west confronted Southerners who realized that they would be outnumbered 8 to 5 in the projected senate and insisted on provisions that would guarantee their speedy reinforcement from the west, which was a southern section at that time. The smaller northern states proved willing to concede a little on these points in order to secure their more immediate objective. Meanwhile, it became increasingly apparent that several influential members from the larger states were less and less inclined toward a continued confrontation. Not only did they realize that the convention's work would surely be rejected if the smaller states walked out, but some of them conceded that a senate that would represent the states as states might help maintain a federal equilibrium while standing at a proper distance from the lower house. . . . On July 16, the convention voted 5–4–1 for the committee's compromise proposal: Connecticut, New Jersey, Delaware, Maryland, North Carolina, aye; Pennsylvania, Virginia, South Carolina, Georgia, no; Massachusetts divided.

The decision of July 16, as Randolph quickly noted, was not as narrow as the margin might suggest. New York, New Hampshire, and Rhode Island were unrepresented. All would probably have favored equal representation in at least one house. In addition, several moderates from Georgia, Pennsylvania, and Virginia sympathized with those in Massachusetts, Maryland, and North Carolina, who had voted for the Connecticut plan. The large states held a caucus in the aftermath of the decision. Wilson, Madison, and others still preferred to try to face the small states down. The caucus failed to reach agreement. All the members from the larger states returned to the convention, and the smaller states were satisfied from that point forward that opponents of the compromise would make no serious attempt to countermand the vote.

Randolph also said that the decision of July 16 "embarrassed the business extremely." Every previous decision, he explained, had been directly influenced by the supposition that proportional representation would prevail in both branches of the legislature; all would have to be thought through again in light of this new ruling. The implications, for that matter, were even more profound than the Virginian immediately perceived. With the adoption of the Great (or Connecticut) Compromise, every delegate was forced to make new calculations as to how the actions of the central government might touch his state or section. Assured an equal vote in one part of the Congress, the members from the smaller middle states, as Dickinson had predicted, immediately began to favor ample federal powers. Southerners, by contrast, suddenly became more wary, especially of the enormous powers that the gathering had earlier intended for the senate. . . .

Amazingly, on first appearances at least, the members needed only ten more days to reach agreement on the basic features of the Constitution. As Randolph failed to see, however, the decision that the general government would represent both individuals and states prepared the way for resolution of more than just the conflict over representation. Both the large states and the small, the North together with the South, could now anticipate control of one part of the legislature. With every state and section armed with a capacity to counter threats to its essential interests, every delegate felt freer to address the national ills that none of them denied. . . .

Among remaining difficulties, the most perplexing centered on the powers and selection of the chief executive. From July 17 through July 25, the convention literally revolved around these questions. . . . Madison reviewed the options on the 25th. Election by the legislature, he explained, might introduce intrigues and render the executive incapable of acting as a check on legislative usurpations—plainly so if the executive was eligible for reelection. Election by the local legislatures or the state executives, however, might introduce the influence of the very bodies whose "pernicious measures" the convention still intended to control. Two alternatives remained: election by electors chosen by the people, which had been suggested on July 19 by King and Paterson, but handily defeated; or direct election by the people, which he had come to favor but which seemed to put the smaller states, together with the South, at a considerable disadvantage. Hugh Williamson (North Carolina) suggested that the disadvantage to the smaller states could be corrected if the people were required to vote for more than a single candidate. Morris added that the citizens might cast two ballots, one of which would have to be for someone from another state. Yet, reinforced by Gerry, Mason still insisted that the people were least qualified to make a good selection. On the 26th the meeting came full circle to the proposition with which it had started: selection by the national legislature for a single term.

Few were really satisfied with this "solution." . . . Discontent with state equality, fear of legislative domination, and a wish to make it possible for an experienced executive to succeed himself, which seemed impossible to reconcile with legislative choice, were moving Madison and other large-scale nationalists toward popular election and larger executive powers. Yet fear of an elective monarchy, distrust of popular election, and sheer impatience to complete the meeting's tasks still counterbalanced these considerations. On July 24, the House had chosen a Committee of Detail to put its resolutions into order. Now, the members eagerly agreed to an adjournment until Monday, August 6, in order to allow ten days for this committee to report.

. . . John Rutledge (South Carolina), Edmund Randolph, Nathaniel Gorham (Massachusetts), Oliver Ellsworth, and James Wilson assumed responsibility for much more than a careful ordering of the decisions reached in the convention by July 26. In sessions from which only fragmentary records still survive, the Committee of Detail apparently assumed—without objection from their tiring colleagues—that they were free to make significant contributions of their own. Taking note of nearly everything that had transpired in the course of the deliberations, the committee added numerous details to the convention's resolutions and offered several significant additions. Besides providing more elaborate descriptions of executive and judicial powers, their report advanced a new procedure for resolving arguments among the states and recommended that agreement by two-thirds of Congress should be necessary for admission of new states or passage of commercial regulations. It inserted prohibitions of a tax on exports or on interference with the slave trade, which Pinckney had demanded as conditions for his state's agreement. Most significant of all, it offered an enumeration of the powers of the central government, a matter that the full convention had repeatedly postponed, and introduced a range of prohibitions on the sort of local legislation that Madison had planned to counter by a federal veto on state laws, a power that the full convention had decisively refused. . . .

Complicated, often heated arguments concerning these provisions dominated the convention through the second half of August. Though Madison and Wilson joined with King and Morris to condemn the ban on export taxes, protesting that it would deny the government an easy source of revenues and an important weapon in its efforts to compel the Europeans to relax their navigation laws, the planting states were virtually unanimous in their insistence on this prohibition. Georgia and the Carolinas, though opposed by the Virginians as well as by the antislavery members from the North, were equally insistent on prohibiting congressional restrictions on the slave trade, making this an absolute condition of their states' approval of a plan. On August 21 the compromisers from Connecticut and Massachusetts voted with the Southerners to reaffirm the prohibition of a tax on exports, 7 states to 4 (New Hampshire, New Jersey, Pennsylvania, Delaware, no). Sherman, Gerry, Ellsworth, Gorham, and their colleagues indicated, though, that they expected their conciliatory efforts to be met in kind, that they had voted to accept the South's demands in expectation that the Southerners would now prove willing to protect New England's vital interests. On August 22 Morris moved referral of the slave trade, export taxes, and commercial regulation to another grand committee, where these subjects might provide materials for a "bargain" between the North and the South. Several Southerners approved.

The August compromise between the North and the South, Massachusetts and South Carolina, was second in importance only to the bargain of July 16 to the completion of the Constitution. On August 24 the grand committee chaired by William Livingston of New Jersey reported a proposal to prohibit legislative interference with the slave trade until the year 1800, to reaffirm the ban on export taxes, but to strike the clause requiring two-thirds of Congress for the passage of commercial regulations. On August 25, Pinckney moved extension of the prohibition until 1808, Gorham seconded the motion, and the prohibition carried 7 states to 4 (New Jersey,

Pennsylvania, Delaware, Virginia, no). . . . Then, on August 31, on Sherman's motion, the convention voted to refer all postponed questions to still another grand committee. The procedure had become the members' standard strategy for handling issues too complex or too divisive for resolution by the whole.

Chaired by David Brearley of New Jersey, the Committee on Unfinished Business (or on Postponed Parts) untangled the convention's last remaining snarls, the knottiest of which was certainly the long-debated question of a sound executive. . . . Reporting on September 4, . . . the Brearley committee sought to cut this knot by recommending an election for a four-year term by electors chosen in such manner as the local legislatures should direct. Each state would be entitled to as many electors as the total of its seats in Congress, and each elector would cast two ballots, at least one of which would have to be for someone from another state. If a single candidate obtained an absolute majority of the electors' votes, he would be president. If not, the president would be elected by the senate from the five who had the highest totals. (In either case, the person placing second in the voting would become vice-president, an office first suggested and defined by this committee.) Both the cumbersome procedure and the introduction of an officer who was essentially superfluous were carefully contrived to balance the demands of the larger and smaller states. . . .

Some of these details proved problematic. Assuming that the college of electors would seldom show an absolute majority for any single person, most members realized that the committee's plan was meant to give the larger states the largest role in making a preliminary nomination, from which the senate, dominated by the smaller states, would make the final choice. Since the smaller states would have a disproportionate advantage even in the number of electors, several members from the larger states objected. . . . In an excellent example of the way in which the delegates had periodically applied collective wisdom to a common problem, these difficulties were resolved by shifting final choice of the executive from the senate to the house of representatives, which would vote by states on this occasion, and by narrowing to three the individuals from among whom the selection must be made. . . .

September 10 saw final pleas for reconsideration of some features over which several members had become increasingly alarmed. Randolph said that he had introduced "a set of republican propositions" on May 29, but that these resolutions had been so disfigured in the course of the convention that he might "dissent" from the completed plan unless the meeting would provide that state conventions could propose amendments to a second general convention, whose alterations would be final. Sharing Randolph's dread of hazy wording and majority control of commerce, together with his fear that an objectionable senate might combine with a powerful executive to overbalance the people's representatives in the lower house, Mason argued on September 12 that the convention also ought to add a bill of rights. Gerry readily agreed.

Responding partly to these fears, the members did consent to substitute two-thirds of Congress for the three-fourths previously required to override a presidential veto. But with Sherman pointing out that nothing in the Constitution would repeal state declarations or infringe the liberties that they protected, the states unanimously declined to draft a bill of rights. As the convention speedily considered the report of the Committee of Style—obviously eager to adjourn, repeatedly refusing to consider major changes—the final drama was at hand. Mason failed to win insertion of a clause requiring two-thirds of the Congress for the passage of commercial regulations until 1808 (by which date, he may have hoped, the planting states would get their reinforcements from the west). Randolph moved again for a procedure under which the plan would not be ratified until a second general convention could consider changes recommended by the state conventions, warning that he could not sign without some such provision. Concluding that the finished plan "would end either in monarchy or a tyrannical aristocracy," Mason followed with a similar pronouncement, as did Gerry. Randolph's motion was unanimously defeated. Every delegation present voted to approve the finished Constitution and to order it engrossed. . . . Of the forty-two still present on September 17, . . . all but three felt able to subscribe their names to the completed work. Whereupon, as Washington confided to his diary, "the members adjourned to the City Tavern, dined together, and took a cordial leave," nearly all of them agreeing with the venerated Franklin that the emblem on the chair in which the general had presided over their deliberations—testifying by his presence to the gravity of the occasion and the possibility that great executive authority might be entrusted to great virtue—was, indeed, a rising sun.

✕ *F U R T H E R   R E A D I N G*

Terence Ball and J. G. A. Pocock, eds., *Conceptual Change and the Constitution* (1988)

Richard Beeman, Stephen Botein, and Edward C. Carter II, eds., *Beyond Confederation: Origins of the Constitution and American National Identity* (1987)

Herman Belz, Ronald Hoffman, and Peter J. Albert, eds., *To Form a More Perfect Union: The Critical Ideas of the Constitution* (1991)

Richard B. Bernstein and Kym S. Rice, *Are We to Be a Nation? The Making of the Constitution* (1987)

George Athan Billias, *Elbridge Gerry: Founding Father and Republican Statesman* (1976)

Catherine Drinker Bowen, *Miracle at Philadelphia: The Story of the Constitutional Convention, May to September, 1787* (1966)

Christopher Collier and James Lincoln Collier, *Decision in Philadelphia: The Constitutional Convention of 1787* (1986)

Jacob Ernest Cooke, *Alexander Hamilton* (1982)

Max Farrand, *The Framing of the Constitution of the United States* (1913)

———, ed., *The Records of the Federal Convention of 1787* (1937)

James H. Hutson, ed., *Supplement to Max Farrand's "The Records of the Federal Convention of 1787"* (1987)

Ralph Ketcham, *James Madison: A Biography* (1971)

Leonard W. Levy and Dennis J. Mahoney, eds., *The Framing and Ratification of the Constitution* (1987)

Elizabeth P. McCaughey, *Government by Choice: Inventing the United States Constitution* (1987)

Forrest McDonald, *E Pluribus Unum: The Foundation of the American Republic, 1776–1790* (1965)

[Michael McGiffert, ed.], "*The Creation of the American Republic, 1776–1787:* A Symposium of Views and Reviews," *William and Mary Quarterly*, 3d Ser., *44* (1987), 549–640

Andrew C. McLaughlin, *The Confederation and the Constitution, 1783–1789* (1905)
———, *The Foundation of American Constitutionalism* (1932)

Richard B. Morris, *Witnesses at the Creation: Hamilton, Madison, Jay, and the Constitution* (1985)

David E. Narrett and Joyce S. Goldberg, eds., *Essays on Liberty and Federalism: The Shaping of the U.S. Constitution* (1988)

Peter S. Onuf, "Reflections on the Founding: Constitutional Historiography in Bicentennial Perspective," *William and Mary Quarterly*, 3d Ser., *46* (1989), 341–375

Charles Page Smith, *James Wilson, Founding Father, 1742–1798* (1956)

Gordon S. Wood, *The Creation of the American Republic, 1776–1787* (1969)

Neil L. York, ed., *Toward a More Perfect Union: Six Essays on the Constitution* (1988)

Rosemarie Zagarri, *The Politics of Size: Representation in the United States, 1776–1850* (1987)

CHAPTER
13

Ratification Politics
and the Bill of Rights

✕

Part of the mythology that has grown up surrounding the Constitution is that its adoption was inevitable. Today, it is hard to imagine that after all the labors of the constitutional convention, all the shrewdness, wisdom, and insight that went into its debates, the product—our Constitution—might actually have been rejected and thrown on the scrap heap of history. Yet that was a genuine possibility. The procedure written into the Constitution for its adoption, ratification by nine states, supplied its opponents with abundant opportunities to block it. In the four largest states—Massachusetts, New York, Pennsylvania, and Virginia— the Constitution was hotly contested, and in all of these but Pennsylvania, approval came on a close vote after an uphill struggle. Even if ratification could have been achieved without one or more of these large states—and that is doubtful, because of additional opposition in New Hampshire, North Carolina, and Rhode Island—the new nation would scarcely have been viable. Consequently, the ratification struggle, which was not won until June 1788, marked a crucial episode in the creation of the United States of America.

The debates generated by the ratification process have been especially important; not only have they shaped our understanding of the Constitution, but they also led to the adoption of the first ten amendments, the Bill of Rights. The politics of ratification differed from state to state, owing to local circumstances and the allegiances of state leaders, but the arguments employed to attack the Constitution and to defend it were much the same everywhere. They reflected the several strains of ideology that influenced the Revolution, from the liberal, Lockean belief in individual liberty, to the classical republicanism of civic virtue, to the ideal of a strong nation—in addition to the ideology of thrift and industriousness. Nothing less than the future direction of the United States was at stake.

These debates and the Bill of Rights that resulted from the politics of ratification continue to influence American politics and society. Here the classic American political controversies were articulated: over the power of the central government versus the states; the correct relationship between majority rule and minority rights; the proper nature of representation; and the boundaries between executive, legislative, and judicial power. As in 1788, these subjects remain a contested terrain more than 200 years later.

The history of the drafting and ratification of the Constitution teaches us that in most cases it is vain to suppose that we can discover the original intentions of the founding fathers. Indeed, the whole idea that there was some fixed, original intent is misleading. The delegates were rarely unanimous in their thinking at the Philadelphia convention; and once their Constitution entered the ratifying process, it was subject to myriad interpretations by its friends and its foes. Ratification was a political process. Even the Bill of Rights was crafted pragmatically, as a compromise among contending parties. The constitutional achievements of the founders of the United States, while expressing a revolutionary idealism, were ultimately political.

✳ D O C U M E N T S

The four excerpts composing the first documentary selection are taken from *The Federalist Papers,* a series of eighty-five essays explaining and defending the Constitution that were authored by James Madison, Alexander Hamilton, and John Jay. First written between October 1787 and May 1788 to influence voters in New York, and printed in New York City newspapers, they circulated widely and supplied Federalists elsewhere with arguments to defend the Constitution. Since 1788 *The Federalist Papers* have come to be regarded less as a political tract than as the classic textbook for expounding the meaning and intentions of the Constitution.

Opponents of the Constitution, called Antifederalists, also used the press to express their views. Their newspaper access was somewhat limited, however, because more newspapers favored ratification than not. The second selection features three Antifederalist perspectives. Richard Henry Lee of Virginia and James Winthrop of Massachusetts were among the most highly recognized spokespersons for the cause. Mercy Otis Warren of Massachusetts, who concealed her identity under the pseudonym "A Columbian Patriot," published the pamphlet *Observations on the New Constitution,* from which the eighteen reasons are drawn. This work, long believed to have been written by Elbridge Gerry, a Massachusetts delegate who refused to sign the Constitution, illustrates the almost paranoid suspiciousness characteristic of many Antifederalist arguments.

The proceedings in the state ratifying conventions are the focus of the third main documentary selection. These activities reveal the context of Antifederalist criticism within which the movement for a Bill of Rights emerged. Both the Massachusetts proposals and those of Virginia show the nature of Antifederalist concerns. The actual Bill of Rights appears as the final document. Although distinct from the state proposals, it clearly reflects these influences.

The Federalist Expounds the Advantages of the Constitution, 1787–1788

Factions and Their Remedy (James Madison, No. 10)

November 22, 1787

To the People of the State of New York:

Among the numerous advantages promised by a well constructed Union, none deserves to be more accurately developed than its tendency to break and control the violence of faction. The friend of popular governments, never finds himself so much alarmed for their character and fate, as when he contemplates their propensity to this dangerous vice. . . .

By a faction I understand a number of citizens, whether amounting to a majority or minority of the whole, who are united and actuated by some common impulse of passion, or of interest, adverse to the rights of other citizens, or to the permanent and aggregate interests of the community.

There are two methods of curing the mischiefs of faction: the one, by removing its causes; the other, by controling its effects.

There are again two methods of removing the causes of faction: the one by destroying the liberty which is essential to its existence; the other, by giving to every citizen the same opinions, the same passions, and the same interests.

It could never be more truly said than of the first remedy, that it is worse than the disease. Liberty is to faction, what air is to fire, an aliment without which it instantly expires. But it could not be a less folly to abolish liberty, which is essential to political life, because it nourishes faction, than it would be to wish the annihilation of air, which is essential to animal life, because it imparts to fire its destructive agency.

The second expedient is as impracticable, as the first would be unwise. As long as the reason of man continues fallible, and he is at liberty to exercise it, different opinions will be formed. As long as the connection subsists between his reason and his self-love, his opinions and his passions will have a reciprocal influence on each other; and the former will be objects to which the latter will attach themselves. The diversity in the faculties of men from which the rights of property originate, is not less an insuperable obstacle to a uniformity of interests. The protection of these faculties is the first object of Government. From the protection of different and unequal faculties of acquiring property, the possession of different degrees and kinds of property immediately results: and from the influence of these on the sentiments and views of the respective proprietors, ensues a division of the society into different interests and parties.

The latent causes of faction are thus sown in the nature of man; and we see them every where brought into different degrees of activity, according to the different circumstances of civil society. A zeal for different opinions concerning religion, concerning Government and many other points, as well of speculation as of practice; an attachment to different leaders ambitiously contending for pre-eminence and power; or to persons of other descriptions whose fortunes have been interesting to the human passions, have in turn divided mankind into parties, inflamed them with mutual animosity, and rendered them much more disposed to vex and oppress each other, than to co-operate for their common good. So strong is this propensity of mankind to fall into mutual animosities, that where no substantial occasion presents itself, the most frivolous and fanciful distinctions have been sufficient to kindle their unfriendly passions, and excite their most violent conflicts. But the most common and durable source of factions, has been the various and unequal distribution of property. Those who hold, and those who are without property, have ever formed distinct interests in society. Those who are creditors, and those who are debtors, fall under a like discrimination. A landed interest, a manufacturing interest, a mercantile interest, a monied interest, with many lesser interests, grow up of necessity in civilized nations, and divide them into different classes, actuated by different sentiments and views. The regulation of these various and interfering interests forms the principal task of modern Legislation, and involves the spirit of party and faction in the necessary and ordinary operations of Government.

No man is allowed to be a judge in his own cause; because his interest would certainly bias his judgment, and, not improbably, corrupt his integrity. With equal, nay with greater reason, a body of men, are unfit to be both judges and parties, at the same time; yet, what are many of the most important acts of legislation, but so many judicial determinations, not indeed concerning the rights of single persons, but concerning the rights of large bodies of citizens; and what are the different classes of legislators, but advocates and parties to the causes which they determine? . . .

It is in vain to say, that enlightened statesmen will be able to adjust these clashing interests, and render them all subservient to the public good. Enlightened statesmen will not always be at the helm: Nor, in many cases, can such an adjustment be made at all, without taking into view indirect and remote considerations, which will rarely prevail over the immediate interest which one party may find in disregarding the rights of another, or the good of the whole.

The inference to which we are brought, is, that the causes of faction cannot be removed; and that relief is only to be sought in the means of controling its effects.

If a faction consists of less than a majority, relief is supplied by the republican principle, which enables the majority to defeat its sinister views by regular vote: It may clog the administration, it may convulse the society; but it will be unable to execute and mask its violence under the forms of the Constitution. When a majority is included in a faction, the form of popular government on the other hand enables it to sacrifice to its ruling passion or interest, both the public good and the rights of other citizens. To secure the public good, and private rights, against the danger of such a faction, and at the same time to preserve the spirit and the form of popular government, is then the great object to which our enquiries are directed. . . .

By what means is this object attainable? Evidently by one of two only. Either the existence of the same passion or interest in a majority at the same time, must be prevented; or the majority, having such co-existent passion or interest, must be rendered, by their number and local situation, unable to concert and carry into effect schemes of oppression. If the impulse and the opportunity be suffered to coincide, we well know that neither moral nor religious motives can be relied on as an adequate control. . . .

From this view of the subject, it may be concluded, that a pure Democracy, by which I mean, a Society, consisting of a small number of citizens, who assemble and administer the Government in person, can admit of no cure for the mischiefs of faction. A common passion or interest will, in almost every case, be felt by a majority of the whole; a communication and

concert results from the form of Government itself; and there is nothing to
check the inducements to sacrifice the weaker party, or an obnoxious individual. Hence it is, that such Democracies have ever been spectacles of
turbulence and contention; have ever been found incompatible with personal
security, or the rights of property; and have in general been as short in their
lives, as they have been violent in their deaths. Theoretic politicians, who
have patronized this species of Government, have erroneously supposed,
that by reducing mankind to a perfect equality in their political rights, they
would, at the same time, be perfectly equalized and assimilated in their
possessions, their opinions, and their passions.

A Republic, by which I mean a Government in which the scheme of
representation takes place, opens a different prospect, and promises the cure
for which we are seeking. Let us examine the points in which it varies from
pure Democracy, and we shall comprehend both the nature of the cure, and
the efficacy which it must derive from the Union.

The two great points of difference between a Democracy and a Republic
are, first, the delegation of the Government, in the latter, to a small number
of citizens elected by the rest: secondly, the greater number of citizens, and
greater sphere of country, over which the latter may be extended.

The effect of the first difference is, on the one hand to refine and enlarge
the public views, by passing them through the medium of a chosen body of
citizens, whose wisdom may best discern the true interest of their country,
and whose patriotism and love of justice, will be least likely to sacrifice it
to temporary or partial considerations. Under such a regulation, it may well
happen that the public voice pronounced by the representatives of the people,
will be more consonant to the public good, than if pronounced by the people
themselves convened for the purpose. On the other hand, the effect may
be inverted. Men of factious tempers, of local prejudices, or of sinister
designs, may by intrigue, by corruption or by other means, first obtain the
suffrages, and then betray the interests of the people. The question resulting
is, whether small or extensive Republics are most favorable to the election
of proper guardians of the public weal: and it is clearly decided in favor of
the latter by two obvious considerations.

In the first place it is to be remarked that however small the Republic
may be, the Representatives must be raised to a certain number, in order
to guard against the cabals of a few; and that however large it may be, they
must be limited to a certain number, in order to guard against the confusion
of a multitude. Hence the number of Representatives in the two cases, not
being in proportion to that of the Constituents, and being proportionally
greatest in the small Republic, it follows, that if the proportion of fit characters, be not less, in the large than in the small Republic, the former will
present a greater option, and consequently a greater probability of a fit
choice.

In the next place, as each Representative will be chosen by a greater
number of citizens in the large than in the small Republic, it will be more
difficult for unworthy candidates to practise with success the vicious arts, by
which elections are too often carried; and the suffrages of the people being

more free, will be more likely to centre on men who possess the most attractive merit, and the most diffusive and established characters.

It must be confessed, that in this, as in most other cases, there is a mean, on both sides of which inconveniencies will be found to lie. By enlarging too much the number of electors, you render the representative too little acquainted with all their local circumstances and lesser interests; as by reducing it too much, you render him unduly attached to these, and too little fit to comprehend and pursue great and national objects. The Federal Constitution forms a happy combination in this respect; the great and aggregate interests being referred to the national, the local and particular, to the state legislatures.

The other point of difference is, the greater number of citizens and extent of territory which may be brought within the compass of Republican, than of Democratic Government; and it is this circumstance principally which renders factious combinations less to be dreaded in the former, than in the latter. The smaller the society, the fewer probably will be the distinct parties and interests composing it; the fewer the distinct parties and interests, the more frequently will a majority be found of the same party; and the smaller the number of individuals composing a majority, and the smaller the compass within which they are placed, the more easily will they concert and execute their plans of oppression. Extend the sphere, and you take in a greater variety of parties and interests; you make it less probable that a majority of the whole will have a common motive to invade the rights of other citizens; or if such a common motive exists, it will be more difficult for all who feel it to discover their own strength, and to act in unison with each other. Besides other impediments, it may be remarked, that where there is a consciousness of unjust or dishonorable purposes, communication is always checked by distrust, in proportion to the number whose concurrence is necessary.

Hence it clearly appears, that the same advantage, which a Republic has over a Democracy, in controling the effects of faction, is enjoyed by a large over a small Republic—is enjoyed by the Union over the States composing it. Does this advantage consist in the substitution of Representatives, whose enlightened views and virtuous sentiments render them superior to local prejudices, and to schemes of injustice? It will not be denied, that the Representation of the Union will be most likely to possess these requisite endowments. Does it consist in the greater security afforded by a greater variety of parties, against the event of any one party being able to outnumber and oppress the rest? In an equal degree does the encreased variety of parties, comprised within the Union, encrease this security. Does it, in fine, consist in the greater obstacles opposed to the concert and accomplishment of the secret wishes of an unjust and interested majority? Here, again, the extent of the Union gives it the most palpable advantage.

The influence of factious leaders may kindle a flame within their particular States, but will be unable to spread a general conflagration through the other States: a religious sect, may degenerate into a political faction in a part of the Confederacy; but the variety of sects dispersed over the entire face of it, must secure the national Councils against any danger from that source: a rage for paper money, for an abolition of debts, for an equal division of property, or for any other improper or wicked project, will be less apt to pervade the whole body of the Union, than a particular member of it; in the same proportion as such a malady is more likely to taint a particular county or district, than an entire State.

In the extent and proper structure of the Union, therefore, we behold a Republican remedy for the diseases most incident to Republican Government.

The Constitution Is National and Federal
(James Madison, No. 39)

To the People of the State of New York: . . .

The first question that offers itself is, whether the general form and aspect of the government be strictly republican. It is evident that no other form would be reconcilable with the genius of the people of America; with the fundamental principles of the Revolution; or with that honorable determination which animates every votary of freedom, to rest all our political experiments on the capacity of mankind for self-government. If the plan of the convention, therefore, be found to depart from the republican character, its advocates must abandon it as no longer defensible.

What, then, are the distinctive characters of the republican form? . . . We may define a republic to be, or at least may bestow that name on, a government which derives all its powers directly or indirectly from the great body of the people, and is administered by persons holding their offices during pleasure, for a limited period, or during good behavior. It is essential to such a government that it be derived from the great body of the society, not from an inconsiderable proportion, or a favored class of it; otherwise a handful of tyrannical nobles, exercising their oppressions by a delegation of their powers, might aspire to the rank of republicans, and claim for their government the honorable title of republic. It is sufficient for such a government that the persons administering it be appointed, either directly or indirectly, by the people; and that they hold their appointments by either of the tenures just specified; otherwise every government in the United States, as well as every other popular government that has been or can be well organized or well executed, would be degraded from the republican character. . . .

On comparing the Constitution planned by the convention with the standard here fixed, we perceive at once that it is, in the most rigid sense, conformable to it. The House of Representatives, like that of one branch at least of all the State legislatures, is elected immediately by the great body of the people. The Senate, like the present Congress, and the Senate of Maryland, derives its appointment indirectly from the people. The President is indirectly derived from the choice of the people, according to the example in most of the States. Even the judges with all other officers of the Union, will, as in the several States, be the choice, though a remote choice, of the people themselves. The duration of the appointments is equally conformable to the republican standard, and to the model of State constitutions. The House of Representatives is periodically elective, as in all the States; and for the period of two years, as in the State of South Carolina. The Senate is elective, for the period of six years; which is but one year more than the period of the Senate of Maryland, and but two more than that of the Senates of New York and Virginia. The President is to continue in office for the period of four years; as in New York and Delaware the chief magistrate is elected for three years, and in South Carolina for two years. In the other States the election is annual. In several of the States, however, no constitutional provision is made for the impeachment of the chief magistrate. And in Delaware and Virginia he is not impeachable till out of office. The President of the United States is impeachable at any time during his continuance in office. The tenure by which the judges are to hold their places, is, as it unquestionably ought to be, that of good behavior. The tenure of the ministerial offices generally, will be a subject of legal regulation, conformably to the reason of the case and the example of the State constitutions.

Could any further proof be required of the republican complexion of this system, the most decisive one might be found in its absolute prohibition of titles of nobility, both under the federal and the State governments; and in its express guaranty of the republican form to each of the latter.

"But it was not sufficient," say the adversaries of the proposed Constitution, "for the convention to adhere to the republican form. They ought, with equal care, to have preserved the federal form, which regards the Union as a Confederacy of sovereign states; instead of which, they have framed a national government, which regards the Union as a consolidation of the States." And it is asked by what authority this bold and radical innovation was undertaken? The handle which has been made of this objection requires that it should be examined with some precision. . . .

First.—In order to ascertain the real character of the government, it may be considered in relation to the foundation on which it is to be established; to the sources from which its ordinary powers are to be drawn; to the operation of those powers; to the extent of them; and to the authority by which future changes in the government are to be introduced.

On examining the first relation, it appears, on one hand, that the Constitution is to be founded on the assent and ratification of the people of America, given by deputies elected for the special purpose; but, on the other, that this assent and ratification is to be given by the people, not as individuals composing one entire nation, but as composing the distinct and independent States to which they respectively belong. It is to be the assent and ratification of the several States, derived from the supreme authority in each State,—the authority of the people themselves. The act, therefore, establishing the Constitution, will not be a national, but a federal act.

That it will be a federal and not a national act, as these terms are understood by the objectors; the act of the people, as forming so many independent States, not as forming one aggregate nation, is obvious from this single consideration, that it is to result neither from the decision of a majority of the people of the Union, nor from that of a majority of the States. It must result from the unanimous assent of the several States that are parties to it, differing no otherwise from their ordinary assent than in its being expressed, not by the legislative authority, but by that of the people themselves. Were the people regarded in this transaction as forming one nation, the will of the majority of the whole people of the United States would bind the minority, in the same manner as the majority in each State must bind the minority. . . . Each State, in ratifying the Constitution, is considered as a sovereign body, independent of all others, and only to be bound by its own voluntary act. In this relation, then, the new Constitution will, if established, be a federal, and not a national constitution.

The next relation is, to the sources from which the ordinary powers of government are to be derived. The House of Representatives will derive its powers from the people of America; and the people will be represented in the same proportion, and on the same principle, as they are in the legislature of a particular State. So far the government is national, not federal. The Senate, on the other hand, will derive its powers from the States, as political and coequal societies; and these will be represented on the principle of equality in the Senate, as they now are in the existing Congress. So far the government is federal, not national. The executive power will be derived from a very compound source. The immediate election of the President is to be made by the States in their political characters. The votes allotted to them are in a compound ratio, which considers them partly as distinct and coequal societies, partly as unequal members of the same society. The eventual election, again, is to be made by that branch of the legislature which consists of the national representatives; but in this particular act they are to be thrown into the form of individual delegations, from so many distinct and coequal bodies politic. From this aspect of the government, it appears to be of a mixed character, presenting at least as many federal as national features. . . .

The proposed Constitution, therefore, is, in strictness, neither a national nor a federal Constitution, but a composition of both. In its foundation it is federal, not national; in the sources from which the ordinary powers of the government are drawn, it is partly federal and partly national; in the operation of these powers, it is national, not federal; in the extent of them, again, it is federal, not national; and, finally, in the authoritative mode of introducing amendments, it is neither wholly federal nor wholly national.

The System of Checks and Balances (Alexander Hamilton or James Madison, No. 51)

To the People of the State of New York:

To what expedient, then, shall we finally resort, for maintaining in practice the necessary partition of power among the several departments, as laid down in the Constitution? The only answer that can be given is, that as all these exterior provisions are found to be inadequate, the defect must be supplied, by so contriving the interior structure of the government as that its several constituent parts may, by their mutual relations, be the means of keeping each other in their proper places. . . .

In order to lay a due foundation for that separate and distinct exercise of the different powers of government, which to a certain extent is admitted on all hands to be essential to the preservation of liberty, it is evident that each department should have a will of its own; and consequently should be so constituted that the members of each should have as little agency as possible in the appointment of the members of the others. . . .

It is equally evident, that the members of each department should be as little dependent as possible on those of the others, for the emoluments annexed to their offices. Were the executive magistrate, or the judges, not independent of the legislature in this particular, their independence in every other would be merely nominal.

But the great security against a gradual concentration of the several powers in the same department, consists in giving to those who administer each department the necessary constitutional means and personal motives to resist encroachments of the others. The provision for defence must in this, as in all other cases, be made commensurate to the danger of attack. Ambition must be made to counteract ambition. The interest of the man must be connected with the constitutional rights of the place. It may be a reflection on human nature, that such devices should be necessary to control the abuses of government. But what is government itself, but the greatest of all reflections on human nature? If men were angels, no government would be necessary. If angels were to govern men, neither external nor internal controls on government would be necessary. In framing a government which is to be administered by men over men, the great difficulty lies in this: you must first enable the government to control the governed; and in the next place oblige it to control itself. A dependence on the people is, no doubt, the primary control on the government; but experience has taught mankind the necessity of auxiliary precautions. . . .

But it is not possible to give to each department an equal power of self-defence. In republican government, the legislative authority necessarily predominates. The remedy for this inconveniency is to divide the legislature into different branches; and to render them, by different modes of election and different principles of action, as little connected with each other as the nature of their common functions and their common dependence on the society will admit. It may even be necessary to guard against dangerous encroachments by still further precautions. As the weight of the legislative authority requires that it should be thus divided, the weakness of the executive may require, on the other hand, that it should be fortified. An absolute negative on the legislature appears, at first view, to be the natural defence with which the executive magistrate should be armed. But perhaps it would be neither altogether safe nor alone sufficient. On ordinary occasions it might not be exerted with the requisite firmness, and on extraordinary occasions it might be perfidiously abused. . . .

There are, moreover, two considerations particularly applicable to the federal system of America, which place that system in a very interesting point of view.

First. In a single republic, all the power surrendered by the people is submitted to the administration of a single government; and the usurpations are guarded against by a division of the government into distinct and separate departments. In the compound republic of America, the power surrendered by the people is first divided between two distinct governments, and then the portion allotted to each subdivided among distinct and separate departments. Hence a double security arises to the rights of the people. The different governments will control each other, at the same time that each will be controlled by itself.

Second. It is of great importance in a republic not only to guard the society against the oppression of its rulers, but to guard one part of the society against the injustice of the other part. Different interests necessarily exist in different classes of citizens. If a majority be united by a common interest, the rights of the minority will be insecure. . . .

In the extended republic of the United States, and among the great variety of interests, parties, and sects which it embraces, a coalition of a majority of the whole society could seldom take place on any other principles than those of justice and the general good.

No Bill of Rights Is Needed (Alexander Hamilton, No. 84)

To the People of the State of New York:

In the course of the foregoing review of the Constitution, I have taken notice of, and endeavored to answer most of the objections which have appeared against it. . . .

The most considerable of the remaining objections is that the plan of the convention contains no bill of rights. Among other answers given to this, it has been upon different occasions remarked that the constitutions of several of the States are in a similar predicament. I add that New York is of the number. And yet the opposers of the new system, in this State, who profess an unlimited admiration for its constitution, are among the most intemperate partisans of a bill of rights. To justify their zeal in this matter, they allege two things: one is that, though the constitution of New York has no bill of rights prefixed to it, yet it contains, in the body of it, various provisions in favor of particular privileges and rights, which, in substance, amount to the same thing; the other is, that the Constitution adopts, in their full extent, the common and statute law of Great Britain, by which many other rights, not expressed in it, are equally secured.

To the first I answer, that the Constitution proposed by the convention contains, as well as the constitution of this State, a number of such provisions.

Independent of those which relate to the structure of the government, we find the following: Article 1, section 3, clause 7—"Judgment in cases of impeachment shall not extend further than to removal from office, and disqualification to hold and enjoy any office of honor, trust, or profit under the United States; but the party convicted shall, nevertheless, be liable and subject to indictment, trial, judgment, and punishment according to law." Section 9, of the same article, clause 2—"The privilege of the writ of habeas corpus shall not be suspended, unless when in cases of rebellion or invasion the public safety may require it." Clause 3—"No bill of attainder or ex-post-facto law shall be passed." Clause 7—"No title of nobility shall be granted by the United States; and no person holding any office of profit or trust under them, shall, without the consent of the Congress, accept of any present, emolument, office, or title of any kind whatever, from any king, prince, or foreign state." Article 3, section 2, clause 3—"The trial of all crimes, except in cases of impeachment, shall be by jury; and such trial shall be held in the State where the said crimes shall have been committed; but when not committed within any State, the trial shall be at such place or places as the Congress may by law have directed." Section 3, of the same article—"Treason against the United States shall consist only in levying war against them, or in adhering to their enemies, giving them aid and comfort. No person shall be convicted of treason, unless on the testimony of two witnesses to the same overt act, or on confession in open court." And clause 3, of the same section—"The Congress shall have power to declare the punishment of treason; but no attainder of treason shall work corruption of blood, or forfeiture, except during the life of the person attainted."

It may well be a question, whether these are not, upon the whole, of equal importance with any which are to be found in the constitution of this State. The establishment of the writ of habeas corpus, the prohibition of ex-post-facto laws, and of Titles of Nobility, to which we have no corresponding provision in our [New York] Constitution, are perhaps greater securities to liberty and republicanism than any it contains. The creation of crimes after the commission of the fact, or, in other words, the subjecting of men to punishment for things which, when they were done, were breaches of no law, and the practice of arbitrary imprisonments, have been, in all ages, the favorite and most formidable instruments of tyranny. . . .

To the second—that is, to the pretended establishment of the common and statute law by the Constitution, I answer, that they are expressly made subject "to such alterations and provisions as the legislature shall from time to time make concerning the same." They are therefore at any moment liable to repeal by the ordinary legislative power, and of course have no constitutional sanction. The only use of the declaration was to recognize the ancient law, and to remove doubts which might have been occasioned by the Revolution. This consequently can be considered as no part of a declaration of rights, which under our constitutions must be intended as limitations of the power of the government itself.

It has been several times truly remarked that bills of rights are, in their origin, stipulations between kings and their subjects, abridgments of prerogative in favor of privilege, reservations of rights not surrendered to the prince. Such was Magna Charta, obtained by the barons, sword in hand, from King John. Such were the subsequent confirmations of that charter by succeeding princes. Such was the *Petition of Right* assented to by Charles

I., in the beginning of his reign. Such, also, was the Declaration of Right presented by the Lords and Commons to the Prince of Orange in 1688, and afterwards thrown into the form of an act of parliament called the Bill of Rights. It is evident, therefore, that, according to their primitive signification, they have no application to constitutions, professedly founded upon the power of the people, and executed by their immediate representatives and servants. Here, in strictness, the people surrender nothing; and as they retain every thing they have no need of particular reservations. "We, the people of the United States, to secure the blessings of liberty to ourselves and our posterity, do ordain and establish this Constitution for the United States of America." Here is a better recognition of popular rights. . . .

I go further, and affirm that bills of rights, in the sense and to the extent in which they are contended for, are not only unnecessary in the proposed Constitution, but would even be dangerous. They would contain various exceptions to powers not granted; and, on this very account, would afford a colorable pretext to claim more than were granted. For why declare that things shall not be done which there is no power to do? Why, for instance, should it be said that the liberty of the press shall not be restrained, when no power is given by which restrictions may be imposed? I will not contend that such a provision would confer a regulating power; but it is evident that it would furnish, to men disposed to usurp, a plausible pretence for claiming that power. They might urge with a semblance of reason, that the Constitution ought not to be charged with the absurdity of providing against the abuse of an authority which was not given, and that the provision against restraining the liberty of the press afforded a clear implication, that a power to prescribe proper regulations concerning it was intended to be vested in the national government. This may serve as a specimen of the numerous handles which would be given to the doctrine of constructive powers, by the indulgence of an injudicious zeal for bills of rights.

On the subject of the liberty of the press, as much as has been said, I cannot forbear adding a remark or two: in the first place, I observe, that there is not a syllable concerning it in the constitution of this State; in the next, I contend, that whatever has been said about it in that of any other State, amounts to nothing. What signifies a declaration, that "the liberty of the press shall be inviolably preserved"? What is the liberty of the press? Who can give it any definition which would not leave the utmost latitude for evasion? I hold it to be impracticable; and from this I infer, that its security, whatever fine declarations may be inserted in any constitution respecting it, must altogether depend on public opinion, and on the general spirit of the people and of the government. . . .

There remains but one other view of this matter to conclude the point. The truth is, after all the declamations we have heard, that the Constitution is itself, in every rational sense, and to every useful purpose, A BILL OF RIGHTS. The several bills of rights in Great Britain form its Constitution, and conversely the constitution of each State is its bill of rights. And the proposed Constitution, if adopted, will be the bill of rights of the Union. Is it one object of a bill of rights to declare and specify the political privileges of the citizens in the structure and administration of the government? This is done in the most ample and precise manner in the plan of the convention; comprehending various precautions for the public security, which are not to be found in any of the State constitutions. Is another object of a bill of rights to define certain immunities and modes of proceeding, which are relative to personal and private concerns? This we have seen has also been attended to, in a variety of cases, in the same plan. Adverting therefore to the substantial meaning of a bill of rights, it is absurd to allege that it is not to be found in the work of the convention.

Antifederalists Attack the Constitution, 1787–1788

Richard Henry Lee on Why a National Government Will Be Unrepresentative and Despotic

The essential parts of a free and good government are a full and equal representation of the people in the legislature, and the jury trial of the vicinage in the administration of justice—a full and equal representation, is that which possesses the same interests, feelings, opinions, and views the people themselves would were they all assembled—a fair representation, therefore, should be so regulated, that every order of men in the community, according to the common course of elections, can have a share in it—in order to allow professional men, merchants, traders, farmers, mechanics, &c. to bring a just proportion of their best informed men respectively into the legislature, the representation must be considerably numerous—We have about 200 state senators in the United States, and a less number than that of federal representatives cannot, clearly, be a full representation of this people, in the affairs of internal taxation and police, were there but one legislature for the whole union. The representation cannot be equal, or the situation of the people proper for one government only—if the extreme parts of the society cannot be represented as fully as the central—It is apparently impracticable that this should be the case in this extensive country—it would be impossible to collect a representation of the parts of the country five, six, and seven hundred miles from the seat of government. . . .

There are other considerations which tend to prove that the idea of one consolidated whole, on free principles, is ill-founded—the laws of a free government rest on the confidence of the people, and operate gently—and never can extend the influence very far—if they are executed on free principles, about the centre, where the benefits of the government induce the people to support it voluntarily; yet they must be executed on the principles of fear and force in the extremes—This has been the case with every extensive republic of which we have any accurate account.

There are certain unalienable and fundamental rights, which in forming the social compact, ought to be explicitly ascertained and fixed. . . . I do not pay much regard to the reasons given for not bottoming the new constitution on a better bill of rights. I still believe a complete federal bill of rights to be very practicable. . . .

There is no reason to expect the numerous state governments, and their connections, will be very friendly to the execution of federal laws in those internal affairs, which hitherto have been under their own immediate management. There is more reason to believe, that the general government, far removed from the people, and none of its members elected oftener than once in two years, will be forgot or neglected, and its laws in many cases disregarded, unless a multitude of officers and military force be continually kept in view, and employed to enforce the execution of the laws, and to make the government feared and respected. . . . Neglected laws must first lead to anarchy and confusion; and a military execution of laws is only a shorter way to the same point—despotic government.

James Winthrop Explains Why a Large Republic Cannot Work

To the People. . . .

. . . It is the opinion of the ablest writers on the subject, that no extensive empire can be governed upon republican principles, and that such a government will degenerate to a despotism, unless it be made up of a confederacy of smaller states, each having the full powers of internal regulation. This is precisely the principle which has hitherto preserved our freedom. No instance can be found of any free government of considerable extent which has been supported upon any other plan. . . . The reason is obvious. In large states the same principles of legislation will not apply to all the parts. The inhabitants of warmer climates are more dissolute in their manners, and less industrious, than in colder countries. A degree of severity is, therefore, necessary with one which would cramp the spirit of the other. We accordingly find that the very great empires have always been despotick. They have indeed tried to remedy the inconveniences to which the people were exposed by local regulations; but these contrivances have never answered the end. The laws not being made by the people, who felt the inconveniences, did not suit their circumstances. . . . To promote the happiness of the people it is necessary that there should be local laws; and it is necessary that those laws should be made by the representatives of those who are immediately subject to the want of them. By endeavouring to suit both extremes, both are injured.

It is impossible for one code of laws to suit Georgia and Massachusetts. They must, therefore, legislate for themselves. Yet there is, I believe, not one point of legislation that is not surrendered in the proposed plan. . . . The idea of an uncompounded republick, on an average one thousand miles in length, and eight hundred in breadth, and containing six millions of white inhabitants all reduced to the same standard of morals, of habits, and of laws, is in itself an absurdity, and contrary to the whole experience of mankind. The attempt made by Great Britain to introduce such a system, struck us with horrour, and when it was proposed by some theorist that we should be represented in parliament, we uniformly declared that one legislature could not represent so many different interests for the purposes of legislation and taxation. This was the leading principle of the revolution, and makes an essential article in our creed. All that part, therefore, of the new system, which relates to the internal government of the states, ought at once to be rejected.

Mercy Otis Warren Offers Eighteen Reasons to Reject the Constitution

I will first observe . . . the best political writers have supported the principles of annual elections with a precision, that cannot be confuted, though they may be darkned, by the sophistical arguments that have been thrown out with design, to undermine all the barriers of freedom.

2. There is no security in the profered [sic] system, either for the rights of conscience or the liberty of the Press. . . .

3. There are no well defined limits of the Judiciary Powers, they seem to be left as a boundless ocean. . . .

4. The Executive and the Legislative are so dangerously blended as to give just cause of alarm, and every thing relative thereto, is couched in such ambiguous terms—in such vague and indefinite expression, as is a sufficient ground without any objection, for the reprobation of a system, that the authors dare not hazard to a clear investigation.

5. The abolition of trial by jury in civil causes.—This mode of trial the learned Judge Blackstone observes, "has been coeval with the first rudiments of civil government, that property, liberty and life, depend on maintaining in its legal force the constitutional trial by jury." . . .

6. Though it has been said by Mr. Wilson and many others, that a Standing-Army is necessary for the dignity and safety of America, yet freedom revolts at the idea. . . . Standing armies have been the nursery of vice and the bane of liberty from the Roman legions to the . . . planting of the British cohorts in the capitals of America:—By the edicts of an authority vested in the sovereign power by the proposed constitution, the militia of the country, the bulwark of defence, and the security of national liberty . . . may be sent into foreign countries for the fulfilment of treaties, stipulated by the President and two thirds of the Senate.

7. Notwithstanding the delusory promise to guarantee a Republican form of government to every State in the Union—. . . there are no resources left for the support of internal government, or the liquidation of the debts of the State. Every source of revenue is in the monopoly of Congress. . . .

8. As the new Congress are empowered to determine their own salaries, the requisitions for this purpose may not be very moderate, and the drain for public moneys will probably rise past all calculation. . . .

9. There is no provision for a rotation, nor anything to prevent the perpetuity of office in the same hands for life; which by a little well timed bribery, will probably be done, to the exclusion of men of the best abilities from their share in the offices of government. . . .

10. The inhabitants of the United States, are liable to be draged [sic] from the vicinity of their own country, or state, to answer the litigious or

unjust suit of an adversary, on the most distant borders of the Continent: in short the appelate jurisdiction of the Supreme Federal Court, includes an unwarrantable stretch of power over the liberty, life, and property of the subject, through the wide Continent of America.

11. One Representative to thirty thousand inhabitants is a very inadequate representation. . . .

12. If the sovereignty of America is designed to be elective, the circumscribing the votes to only ten electors in this State, and the same proportion in all the others, is nearly tantamount to the exclusion of the voice of the people in the choice of their first magistrate. It is vesting the choice solely in an aristocratic junto, who may easily combine in each State to place at the head of the Union the most convenient instrument for despotic sway.

13. A Senate chosen for six years will, in most instances, be an appointment for life, as the influence of such a body over the minds of the people will be coequal to the extensive powers with which they are vested. . . .

14. There is no provision by a bill of rights to guard against the dangerous encroachments of power in too many instances to be named: . . . The rights of individuals ought to be the primary object of all government, and cannot be too securely guarded by the most explicit declarations in their favor. . . .

15. The difficulty, if not impracticability, of exercising the equal and equitable powers of government by a single legislature over an extent of territory that reaches from the Mississippi to the Western lakes, and from them to the Atlantic Ocean, is an insuperable objection to the adoption of the new system. . . .

16. It is an undisputed fact that not one legislature in the United States had the most distant idea when they first appointed members for a convention, entirely commercial, or when they afterwards authorized them to consider on some amendments of the Federal union, that they would without any warrant from their constituents, presume on so bold and daring a stride, as ultimately to destroy the state governments, and offer a consolidated system, irreversible but on conditions that the smallest degree of penetration must discover to be impracticable.

17. The first appearance of the article which declares the ratification of nine states sufficient for the establishment of the new system, wears the face of dissension, is a subversion of the union of Confederated States. . . .

18. The mode in which this constitution is recommended to the people to judge without either the advice of Congress, or the legislatures of the several states is very reprehensible—it is an attempt to force it upon them before it could be thoroughly understood.

Proceedings in the State Ratifying Conventions, 1788

Massachusetts Proposes Amendments to the Constitution

The Convention, having impartially discussed, and fully considered the constitution for the United States of America, reported to Congress, by the

Convention of delegates from the United States of America, and submitted to us, by a resolution of the General Court . . . Do, in the name, and in behalf of the people of the Commonwealth of Massachusetts, assent to and ratify the said constitution for the United States of America.

And, as it is the opinion of this Convention, that certain amendments and alterations in the said constitution would remove the fears and quiet the apprehensions of many of the good people of this commonwealth, and more effectually guard against an undue administration of the federal government, the Convention do therefore recommend that the following alterations and provisions be introduced into the said constitution.

First, That it be explicitly declared, that all powers not expressly delegated by the aforesaid constitution, are reserved to the several states, to be by them exercised.

Secondly, That there shall be one representative to every thirty thousand persons, according to the census mentioned in the constitution, until the whole number of representatives amounts to two hundred.

Thirdly, That Congress do not exercise the powers vested in them by the 4th section of the first article, but in cases when a state shall neglect or refuse to make the regulations therein mentioned, or shall make regulations subversive of the rights of the people to a free and equal representation in Congress, agreeably to the constitution.

Fourthly, That Congress do not lay direct taxes, but when the monies arising from the impost and excise are insufficient for the publick exigencies, nor then, until Congress shall have first made a requisition upon the states, to assess, levy and pay their respective proportion of such requisition, agreeably to the census fixed in the said constitution, in such way and manner as the legislatures of the states shall think best, and in such case, if any state shall neglect or refuse to pay its proportion, pursuant to such requisition, then Congress may assess and levy such state's proportion, together with interest thereon, at the rate of six per cent per annum, from the time of payment prescribed in such requisition.

Fifthly, That Congress erect no company with exclusive advantages of commerce.

Sixthly, That no person shall be tried for any crime, by which he may incur an infamous punishment, or loss of life, until he be first indicted by a grand jury, except in such cases as may arise in the government and regulation of the land and naval forces.

Seventhly, The Supreme Judicial Federal Court shall have no jurisdiction of causes, between citizens of different states, unless the matter in dispute, whether it concern the realty or personalty, be of the value of three thousand dollars at the least; nor shall the federal judicial powers extend to any action between citizens of different states, where the matter in dispute, whether it concerns the realty or personalty, is not of the value of fifteen hundred dollars at the least.

Eighthly, In civil actions between citizens of different states, every issue of fact, arising in actions at common law, shall be tried by a jury, if the parties or either of them, request it.

Ninthly, Congress shall at no time consent, that any person holding an office of trust or profit, under the United States, shall accept of a title of nobility, or any other title or office, from any king, prince, or foreign state.

Patrick Henry of Virginia Denounces the Constitution

Have they said, We, the states? Have they made a proposal of a compact between states? If they had, this would be a confederation. It is otherwise most clearly a consolidated government. The question turns, sir, on that poor little thing—the expression, We, the people, instead of the states, of America. I need not take much pains to show that the principles of this system are extremely pernicious, impolitic, and dangerous. . . . Here is a resolution as radical as that which separated us from Great Britain. It is radical in this transition; our rights and privileges are endangered, and the sovereignty of the states will be relinquished. . . . The rights of conscience, trial by jury, liberty of the press, all your immunities and franchises, all pretensions to human rights and privileges, are rendered insecure, if not lost, by this change. . . . It is said eight states have adopted this plan. I declare that if twelve states and a half had adopted it, I would, with manly firmness, and in spite of an erring world, reject it. You are not to inquire how your trade may be increased, nor how you are to become a great and powerful people, but how your liberties can be secured; for liberty ought to be the direct end of your government.

. . . Is it necessary for your liberty that you should abandon those great rights by the adoption of this system? Is the relinquishment of the trial by jury and the liberty of the press necessary for your liberty? Will the abandonment of your most sacred rights tend to the security of your liberty? Liberty, the greatest of all earthly blessings—give us that precious jewel, and you may take every thing else! . . . We are come hither to preserve the poor commonwealth of Virginia, if it can be possibly done: something must be done to preserve your liberty and mine. The Confederation, this same despised government, merits, in my opinion, the highest encomium: it carried us through a long and dangerous war; it rendered us victorious in that bloody conflict with a powerful nation; it has secured us a territory greater than any European monarch possesses: and shall a government which has been thus strong and vigorous, be accused of imbecility, and abandoned for want of energy? Consider what you are about to do before you part with the government. . . .

How does your trial by jury stand? In civil cases gone—not sufficiently secured in criminal—this best privilege is gone. But we are told that we need not fear; because those in power, being our representatives, will not abuse the powers we put in their hands. I am not well versed in history, but I will submit to your recollection, whether liberty has been destroyed most often by the licentiousness of the people, or by the tyranny of rulers. I imagine, sir, you will find the balance on the side of tyranny. . . . Most of the human race are now in this deplorable condition. . . .

. . . [It] appears that three fourths of the states must ultimately agree to any amendments that may be necessary. Let us consider the consequence of this. . . . To suppose that so large a number as three fourths of the states will concur, is to suppose that they will possess genius, intelligence, and integrity, approaching to miraculous. . . . A trifling minority may reject the most salutary amendments. Is this an easy mode of securing the public liberty? It is, sir, a most fearful situation, when the most contemptible minority can prevent the alteration of the most oppressive government. . . .

This, sir, is the language of democracy—that a majority of the community have a right to alter government when found to be oppressive. But how different is the genius of your new Constitution from this! How different from the sentiments of freemen, that a contemptible minority can prevent the good of the majority! . . .

A standing army we shall have, also, to execute the execrable commands of tyranny. . . . Your militia is given up to Congress, also, in another part of this plan: they will therefore act as they think proper: all power will be in their own possession. . . .

. . . The distinction between a national government and a confederacy is not sufficiently discerned. Had the delegates, who were sent to Philadelphia, a power to propose a consolidated government instead of a confederacy? Were they not deputed by states, and not by the people? The assent of the people, in their collective capacity, is not necessary to the formation of a federal government. The people have no right to enter into leagues, alliances, or confederations; they are not the proper agents for this purpose. . . . This, therefore, ought to depend on the consent of the legislatures, the people having never sent delegates to make any proposition for changing the government. . . .

Consider our situation, sir: go to the poor man, and ask him what he does. He will inform you that he enjoys the fruits of his labor, under his own fig-tree, with his wife and children around him, in peace and security. Go to every other member of society,—you will find the same tranquil ease and content; you will find no alarms or disturbances. Why, then, tell us of danger, to terrify us into an adoption of this new form of government? And yet who knows the dangers that this new system may produce? They are out of the sight of the common people: they cannot foresee latent consequences. I dread the operation of it on the middling and lower classes of people: it is for them I fear the adoption of this system. . . .

The necessity of amendments is universally admitted. . . . I ask, if amendments be necessary, from whence can they be so properly proposed as from this state? The example of Virginia is a powerful thing, particularly with respect to North Carolina, whose supplies must come through Virginia. Every possible opportunity of procuring amendments is gone, our power and political salvation are gone, if we ratify unconditionally. . . .

We are told that all powers not given are reserved. . . . The English history is frequently referred to by gentlemen. Let us advert to the conduct of the people of that country. The people of England lived without a declaration of rights till the war in the time of Charles I. That king made usurpations upon the rights of the people. . . .

The rights of the people continued to be violated till the Stuart family was banished, in the year 1688. The people of England magnanimously defended their rights, banished the tyrant, and prescribed to William, Prince of Orange, by the bill of rights, on what terms he should reign; and this bill of rights put an end to all construction and implication. Before this, sir, the situation of the public liberty of England was dreadful. For upwards of a century, the nation was involved in every kind of calamity, till the bill of rights put an end to all, by defining the rights of the people, and limiting the king's prerogative. . . . It is alleged that several states, in the formation of their government, omitted a bill of rights. To this I answer, that they had the substance of a bill of rights contained in their constitutions, which is the same thing. . . .

Of what advantage is it to the American Congress to take away this great and general security? . . . Why is the trial by jury taken away? All the learned arguments that have been used on this occasion do not prove that it is secured. Even the advocates for the plan do not all concur in the certainty of its security. Wherefore is religious liberty not secured? . . . This sacred right ought not to depend on constructive, logical reasoning.

When we see men of such talents and learning compelled to use their utmost abilities to convince themselves that there is no danger, is it not sufficient to make us tremble?

Virginia's Declaration of Rights and Proposed Amendments to the Constitution

Mr. Wythe reported, from the committee appointed, such amendments to the proposed Constitution of government for the United States as were by them deemed necessary to be recommended to the consideration of the Congress which shall first assemble under the said Constitution, to be acted upon according to the mode prescribed . . . as follows: —

That there be a declaration or bill of rights asserting, and securing from encroachment, the essential and unalienable rights of the people, in some such manner as the following: —

1st. That there are certain natural rights, of which men, when they form a social compact, cannot deprive or divest their posterity; among which are the enjoyment of life and liberty, with the means of acquiring, possessing, and protecting property, and pursuing and obtaining happiness and safety.

2d. That all power is naturally invested in, and consequently derived from, the people; that magistrates therefore are their trustees and agents, at all times amenable to them.

3d. That government ought to be instituted for the common benefit, protection, and security of the people; and that the doctrine of non-resistance against arbitrary power and oppression is absurd, slavish, and destructive to the good and happiness of mankind.

4th. That no man or set of men are entitled to separate or exclusive public emoluments or privileges from the community, but in consideration of public services, which not being descendible, neither ought the offices of magistrate, legislator, or judge, or any other public office, to be hereditary.

5th. That the legislative, executive, and judicial powers of government should be separate and distinct; and, that the members of the two first may be restrained from oppression by feeling and participating the public burdens, they should, at fixed periods, be reduced to a private station, return into the mass of the people, and the vacancies be supplied by certain and regular elections, in which all or any part of the former members to be eligible or ineligible, as the rules of the Constitution of government, and the laws, shall direct.

6th. That the elections of representatives in the legislature ought to be free and frequent, and all men having sufficient evidence of permanent common interest with, and attachment to, the community, ought to have the right of suffrage; and no aid, charge, tax, or fee, can be set, rated or levied, upon the people without their own consent, or that of their representatives, so elected; nor can they be bound by any law to which they have not, in like manner, assented, for the public good.

7th. That all power of suspending laws, or the execution of laws, by any authority, without the consent of the representatives of the people in the legislature, is injurious to their rights, and ought not to be exercised.

8th. That, in all criminal and capital prosecutions, a man hath a right to demand the cause and nature of his accusation, to be confronted with the accusers and witnesses, to call for evidence, and be allowed counsel in his favor, and to a fair and speedy trial by an impartial jury of his vicinage, without whose unanimous consent he cannot be found guilty, (except in the government of the land and naval forces;) nor can he be compelled to give evidence against himself.

9th. That no freeman ought to be taken, imprisoned, or disseized of his freehold, liberties, privileges, or franchises, or outlawed, or exiled, or in any manner destroyed or deprived of his life, liberty, or property, but by the law of the land.

10th. That every freeman restrained of his liberty is entitled to a remedy, to inquire into the lawfulness thereof, and to remove the same, if unlawful, and that such remedy ought not to be denied nor delayed.

11th. That, in controversies respecting property, and in suits between man and man, the ancient trial by jury is one of the greatest securities to the rights of the people, and to remain sacred and inviolable.

12th. That every freeman ought to find a certain remedy, by recourse to the laws, for all injuries and wrongs he may receive in his person, property, or character. He ought to obtain right and justice freely, without sale, completely and without denial, promptly and without delay; and that all establishments or regulations contravening these rights are oppressive and unjust.

13th. That excessive bail ought not to be required, nor excessive fines imposed, nor cruel and unusual punishments inflicted.

14th. That every freeman has a right to be secure from all unreasonable searches and seizures of his person, his papers, and property; all warrants, therefore, to search suspected places, or seize any freeman, his papers, or property, without information on oath (or affirmation of a person religiously scrupulous of taking an oath) of legal and sufficient cause, are grievous and oppressive; and all general warrants to search suspected places, or to apprehend any suspected person, without specially naming or describing the place or person, are dangerous, and ought not to be granted.

15th. That the people have a right peaceably to assemble together to consult for the common good, or to instruct their representatives; and that every freeman has a right to petition or apply to the legislature for redress of grievances.

16th. That the people have a right to freedom of speech, and of writing and publishing their sentiments; that the freedom of the press is one of the greatest bulwarks of liberty, and ought not to be violated.

17th. That the people have a right to keep and bear arms; that a well-regulated militia, composed of the body of the people trained to arms, is the proper, natural, and safe defence of a free state; that standing armies, in time of peace, are dangerous to liberty, and therefore ought to be avoided, as far as the circumstances and protection of the community will admit; and that, in all cases, the military should be under strict subordination to, and governed by, the civil power.

18th. That no soldier in time of peace ought to be quartered in any house without the consent of the owner, and in time of war in such manner only as the law directs.

19th. That any person religiously scrupulous of bearing arms ought to be exempted, upon payment of an equivalent to employ another to bear arms in his stead.

20th. That religion, or the duty which we owe to our Creator, and the manner of discharging it, can be directed only by reason and conviction, not by force or violence; and therefore all men have an equal, natural, and unalienable right to the free exercise of religion, according to the dictates of conscience, and that no particular religious sect or society ought to be favored or established, by law, in preference to others.

Amendments to the Constitution

1st. That each state in the Union shall respectively retain every power, jurisdiction, and right, which is not by this Constitution delegated to the Congress of the United States, or to the departments of the federal government.

2nd. That there shall be one representative for every thirty thousand according to the enumeration or census mentioned in the Constitution, until the whole number of representatives amounts to two hundred: after which, that number shall be continued or increased, as Congress shall direct, upon the principles fixed in the Constitution, by apportioning the representatives of each state to some greater number of people, from time to time, as population increases.

3d. When the Congress shall lay direct taxes or excises, they shall immediately inform the executive power of each state, of the quota of such state, according to the census herein directed, which is proposed to be thereby raised; and if the legislature of any state shall pass a law which shall be effectual for raising such quota at the time required by Congress, the taxes and excises laid by Congress shall not be collected in such state.

4th. That the members of the Senate and House of Representatives shall be ineligible to and incapable of holding, any civil office under the authority of the United States during the time for which they shall respectively be elected.

5th. That the journals of the proceedings of the Senate and House of Representatives shall be published at least once in every year, except such parts thereof, relating to treaties, alliances, or military operations, as, in their judgment, require secrecy.

6th. That a regular statement and account of the receipts and expenditures of public money shall be published at least once a year.

7th. That no commercial treaty shall be ratified without the concurrence of two thirds of the whole number of the members of the Senate; and no treaty ceding, contracting, restraining, or suspending, the territorial rights or claims of the United States, or any of them, or their, or any of their rights or claims to fishing in the American seas, or navigating the American rivers, shall be made, but in cases of the most urgent and extreme necessity; nor shall any such treaty be ratified without the concurrence of three fourths of the whole number of the members of both houses respectively.

8th. That no navigation law, or law regulating commerce, shall be passed without the consent of two thirds of the members present, in both houses.

9th. That no standing army, or regular troops, shall be raised, or kept up, in time of peace, without the consent of two thirds of the members present, in both houses.

10th. That no soldier shall be enlisted for any longer term than four years, except in time of war, and then for no longer term than the continuance of the war.

11th. That each state respectively shall have the power to provide for organizing, arming, and disciplining its own militia, whensoever Congress shall omit or neglect to provide for the same. That the militia shall not be subject to martial law, except when in actual service, in time of war, invasion, or rebellion; and when not in the actual service of the United States, shall be subject only to such fines, penalties, and punishments, as shall be directed or inflicted by the laws of its own state.

12th. That the exclusive power of legislation given to Congress over the federal town and its adjacent district, and other places, purchased or to be purchased by Congress of any of the states, shall extend only to such regulations as respect the police and good government thereof.

13th. That no person shall be capable of being President of the United States for more than eight years in any term of sixteen years.

14th. That the judicial power of the United States shall be vested in one Supreme Court, and in such courts of admiralty as Congress may from time to time ordain and establish in any of the different states. The judicial power shall extend to all cases in law and equity arising under treaties made, or which shall be made, under the authority of the United States; to all cases affecting ambassadors, other foreign ministers, and consuls; to all cases of admiralty and maritime jurisdiction; to controversies to which the United States shall be a party; to controversies between two or more states, and between parties claiming lands under the grants of different states. In all cases affecting ambassadors, other foreign ministers, and consuls, and those in which a state shall be a party, the Supreme Court shall have original jurisdiction; in all other cases before mentioned, the Supreme Court shall have appellate jurisdiction, as to matters of law only, except in cases of equity, and of admiralty, and maritime jurisdiction, in which the Supreme Court shall have appellate jurisdiction both as to law and fact, with such exceptions and under such regulations as the Congress shall make: but the judicial power of the United States shall extend to no case where the cause of action shall have originated before the ratification of the Constitution, except in disputes between states about their territory, disputes between persons claiming lands under the grants of different states, and suits for debts due to the United States.

15th. That, in criminal prosecutions, no man shall be restrained in the exercise of the usual and accustomed right of challenging or excepting to the jury.

16th. That Congress shall not alter, modify, or interfere in the times, places, or manner of holding elections for senators and representatives, or either of them, except when the legislature of any state shall neglect, refuse, or be disabled, by invasion or rebellion, to prescribe the same.

17th. That those clauses which declare that Congress shall not exercise certain powers, be not interpreted, in any manner whatsoever, to extend the powers of Congress; but that they be construed either as making exceptions to the specified powers where this shall be the case, or otherwise, as inserted merely for greater caution.

18th. That the laws ascertaining the compensation of senators and representatives for their services, be postponed, in their operation, until after the election of representatives immediately succeeding the passing thereof; that excepted which shall first be passed on the subject.

19th. That some tribunal other than the Senate be provided for trying impeachments of senators.

20th. That the salary of a judge shall not be increased or diminished during his continuance in office, otherwise than by general regulations of salary, which may take place on a revision of the subject at stated periods of not less than seven years, to commence from the time such salaries shall be first ascertained by Congress.

And the Convention do, in the name and behalf of the people of this commonwealth, enjoin it upon their representatives in Congress to exert all their influence, and use all reasonable and legal methods, to obtain a ratification of the foregoing alterations and provisions, in the manner provided by the 5th article of the said Constitution; and, in all congressional laws to be passed in the mean time, to conform to the spirit of these amendments, as far as the said Constitution will admit.

The Constitutional Amendments, 1791 (The Bill of Rights)

Article One

Congress shall make no law respecting an establishment of religion, or prohibiting the free exercise thereof; or abridging the freedom of speech, or of the press; or the right of the people peaceably to assemble, and to petition the Government for a redress of grievances.

Article Two

A well-regulated militia being necessary to the security of a free State, the right of the people to keep and bear arms shall not be infringed.

Article Three

No soldier shall, in time of peace, be quartered in any house, without the consent of the owner, nor in time of war but in a manner to be prescribed by law.

Article Four

The right of the people to be secure in their persons, houses, papers, and effects, against unreasonable searches and seizures, shall not be violated, and no warrants shall issue, but upon probable cause, supported by oath or affirmation, and particularly describing the place to be searched, and the persons or things to be seized.

Article Five

No person shall be held to answer for a capital, or otherwise infamous crime, unless on a presentment or indictment of a Grand Jury, except in cases arising in the land or naval forces, or in the militia, when in actual service in time of war or public danger; nor shall any person be subject for the same offense to be twice put in jeopardy of life or limb; nor shall be compelled in any criminal case to be a witness against himself, nor be deprived of life, liberty, or property, without due process of law; nor shall private property be taken for public use, without just compensation.

Article Six

In all criminal prosecutions the accused shall enjoy the right to a speedy and public trial, by an impartial jury of the State and district wherein the crime shall have been committed, which district shall have been previously ascertained by law, and to be informed of the nature and cause of the accusation; to be confronted with the witnesses against him; to have compulsory process for obtaining witnesses in his favor, and to have the assistance of counsel for his defense.

Article Seven

In suits at common law, where the value of controversy shall exceed twenty dollars, the right of trial by jury shall be preserved, and no fact tried by a jury shall be otherwise reexamined in any court of the United States, than according to the rules of the common law.

Article Eight

Excessive bail shall not be required, nor excessive fines imposed, nor cruel and unusual punishments inflicted.

Article Nine

The enumeration in the Constitution of certain rights shall not be construed to deny or disparage others retained by the people.

Article Ten

The powers not delegated to the United States by the Constitution, nor prohibited by it to the States, are reserved to the States respectively or to the people.

✂ *E S S A Y S*

Isaac Kramnick, who holds the Richard J. Schwartz Professorship of Government at Cornell University, specializes in eighteenth-century British and American political theory. In the first essay, he addresses a controversy among historians as to whether Lockean liberalism or classical republicanism was the dominant influence in early national political thought. His analysis reveals that more elements are involved and that the either/or dichotomy is not faithful to the ideas that leaders articulated. In the second essay, Leonard W. Levy, the Andrew W. Mellon Professor and Chairman of the Graduate Faculty of History at Claremont Graduate School, examines the Bill of Rights. Levy shows how closely connected politically the first ten amendments were to James Madison and to the ratification of the Constitution.

The Main Themes of Constitutional Discussion

ISAAC KRAMNICK

Americans, Alexander Hamilton wrote on October 27, 1787, in the New York *Independent Journal,* were "called upon to deliberate on a new Con-

"The 'Great National Discussion:' The Discourse of Politics in 1787" by Isaac Kramnick, *William and Mary Quarterly*, 45, (Jan. 1988). Reprinted by permission of the author.

stitution." His essay, *The Federalist* No. 1, pointed out that in doing this Americans were proving that men could create their own governments "from reflection and choice," instead of forever having to depend on "accident and force." These deliberations on the Constitution would by no means be decorous and genteel. Much too much was at stake, and, as Hamilton predicted, "a torrent of angry and malignant passions" was let loose in the "great national discussion." . . .

How does one read that "great national discussion" two centuries later? Most present-day scholars would follow the methodological guidelines offered by J. G. A. Pocock in this respect. The historian of political thought, Pocock suggests, is engaged in a quest for the "languages," "idioms," and "modes of discourse" that characterize an age. Certain "languages" are accredited at various moments in time "to take part" in the public speech of a country. These "distinguishable idioms" are paradigms that selectively encompass all information about politics and delimit appropriate usage. . . . Pocock cautions that one "cannot get out of a language that which was never in it." People only think "about what they have the means of verbalizing." Anyone studying political texts, then, must use "the languages in which the inhabitants . . . did in fact present their society and cosmos to themselves and to each other."

Problematic in this approach is the assumption that there is but one language—one exclusive or even hegemonic paradigm—that characterizes the political discourse of a particular place or moment in time. This was not the case in 1787. In the "great national discussion" of the Constitution Federalists and Antifederalists, in fact, tapped several languages of politics, the terms of which they could easily verbalize. This [selection] examines four such "distinguishable idioms," which coexisted in the discourse of politics in 1787–1788. None dominated the field, and the use of one was compatible with the use of another by the very same writer or speaker. There was a profusion and confusion of political tongues among the founders. They lived easily with that clatter; it is we two hundred years later who chafe at their inconsistency. Reading the framers and the critics of the Constitution, one discerns the languages of republicanism, of Lockean liberalism, of work-ethic Protestantism, and of state-centered theories of power and sovereignty.

Civic Humanism and Liberalism in the Constitution and Its Critics

Contemporary scholarship seems obsessed with forever ridding the college curriculum of the baleful influence of Louis Hartz. In place of the "Liberal Tradition in America," it posits the omnipresence of neoclassical civic humanism. Dominating eighteenth-century political thought in Britain and America, it is insisted, was the language of republican virtue. Man was a political being who realized his telos only when living in a *vivere civile* with other propertied, arms-bearing citizens, in a republic where they ruled and were ruled in turn. Behind this republican discourse is a tradition of political philosophy with roots in Aristotle's *Politics*, Cicero's *Res Publica,* Machiavelli, Harrington, Bolingbroke, and the nostalgic country's virtuous opposition to Walpole and the commercialization of English life. The pursuit of public good is privileged over private interests, and freedom means participation in civic life rather than the protection of individual rights from interference. Central to the scholarly enterprise of republicanism has been the self-proclaimed "dethronement of the paradigm of liberalism and of the Lockean paradigm associated with it."

In response to these republican imperial claims, a group whom Gordon S. Wood has labeled "neo-Lockeans" has insisted that Locke and liberalism were alive and well in Anglo-American thought in the period of the founding. Individualism, the moral legitimacy of private interest, and market society are privileged in this reading over community, public good, and the virtuous pursuit of civic fulfillment. For these "neo-Lockeans" it is not Machiavelli and Montesquieu who set the textual codes that dominated the "great national discussion," but Hobbes and Locke and the assumptions of possessive individualism.

Can we have it both ways? We certainly can if we take Federalist and Antifederalist views as representing a single text of political discourse at the founding. A persuasive case can be made for the Federalists as liberal modernists and the Antifederalists as nostalgic republican communitarians seeking desperately to hold on to a virtuous moral order threatened by commerce and market society. The Federalist tendency was to depict America in amoral terms as an enlarged nation that transcended local community and moral conviction as the focus of politics. The Federalists seemed to glory in an individualistic and competitive America, which was preoccupied with private rights and personal autonomy. This reading of America is associated with James Madison more than with anyone else, and with his writings in the *Federalist*.

Madison's adulation of heterogeneous factions and interests in an enlarged America, which he introduced into so many of his contributions to the *Federalist,* assumed that the only way to protect the rights of minorities was to enlarge the political sphere and thereby divide the community. . . . In *Federalist* No. 10 Madison described the multiplication of regional, religious, and economic interests, factions, and parties as the guarantor of American freedom and justice. He put his case somewhat differently in a letter to Thomas Jefferson: "Divide et impera, the reprobated axiom of tyranny, is under certain conditions, the only policy, by which a republic can be administered on just principles." Pride of place among "these clashing interests," so essential for a just order, went to the economic interests inevitable in a complex market society. They were described in the often-quoted passage from *Federalist* No. 10:

> The most common and durable source of factions has been the various and unequal distribution of property. Those who hold and those who are without property have ever formed distinct interests in society. . . . creditors . . . debtors. . . . A landed interest, a manufacturing interest, a mercantile interest, a moneyed interest. . . . The regulation of these various and interfering interests forms the principal task of modern legislation.

Government for Madison, much as for Locke, was a neutral arbiter among competing interests. Indeed, in *Federalist* No. 43 Madison described the legislative task as providing "umpires"; and in a letter to George Washington he described government's role as a "disinterested & dispassionate umpire in disputes." . . . As it was for Locke—who wrote that "justice gives every Man a Title to the product of his honest Industry"—so, too, for Madison and the Federalists: justice effectively meant respecting private rights, especially property rights.

The commitment in the preamble to the Constitution to "establish justice" meant for the framers that it would protect private rights, which would help it achieve the next objective—to "insure domestic tranquility." Should there be doubts about this, we have Madison as our guide to what "establish justice" meant. On June 6 he had risen at the convention to answer Roger Sherman's suggestion that the only objects of union were better relations with foreign powers and the prevention of conflicts and disputes among the states. What about justice? was the thrust of Madison's intervention. To Sherman's list of the Constitution's objectives Madison insisted that there be added "the necessity of providing more effectually for the security of private rights, and the steady dispensation of Justice. Interferences with these were evils which had more perhaps than any thing else produced this convention."

The acceptance of modern liberal society in the Federalist camp went beyond a legitimization of the politics of interest and a conviction that government's purpose was to protect the fruits of honest industry. There was also an unabashed appreciation of modern commercial society. . . . Hamilton, for example, in *Federalist* No. 12, insisted that

> the prosperity of commerce is now perceived and acknowledged by all enlightened statesmen to be the most useful as well as the most productive source of national wealth, and has accordingly become a primary object of their political cares. By multiplying the means of gratification, by promoting the introduction and circulation of the precious metals, those darling objects of human avarice and enterprise, it serves to vivify and invigorate the channels of industry and to make them flow with greater activity and copiousness.

Hamilton was perfectly aware that his praise of private gratification, avarice, and gain flew in the face of older ideals of civic virtue and public duty that emphasized the subordination of private interest to the public good. He turned this very rejection of the republican moral ideal into an argument for the need of a federal standing army. This was a further blow to the ideals of civic virtue, which had always seen professional armies as evil incarnate, undermining the citizen's self-sacrificial participation in the defense of the public realm, which was the premise of the militia. America as a market society could not rely on the militia, according to Hamilton. . . .

In *Federalist* No. 8, another defense of standing armies, Hamilton acknowledged the eclipse of older civic ideals of self-sacrifice and participatory citizenship in commercial America: "The industrious habits of the people of the present day, absorbed in the pursuit of gain and devoted to the improvements of agriculture and commerce, are incompatible with the condition of a nation of soldiers, which was the true condition of the people of those [ancient Greek] republics."

Many of the Antifederalists, on the other hand, were still wedded to a republican civic ideal, to the making of America into what Samuel Adams called "a Christian Sparta." The very feature of pluralist diversity in the new constitutional order that Madison saw as its great virtue, the Antifederalists saw as its major defect. . . . A chorus of Antifederalists insisted that virtuous republican government required a small area and a homogeneous population. Patrick Henry noted that a republican form of government extending across the continent "contradicts all the experience of the world." Richard Henry Lee argued that "a free elective government cannot be extended over large territories." . . .

Montesquieu and others had taught Antifederalists "that so extensive a territory as that of the United States, including such a variety of climates, productions, interests, and so great differences of manners, habits, and customs" could never constitute a moral republic. . . . Antifederalists' fears over the absence of homogeneity in the enlarged republic were as important as the issue of size. . . . Most Antifederalists held that a republican system required similarity of religion, manners, sentiments, and interests. They were convinced that no such sense of community could exist in an enlarged republic, that no one set of laws could work within such diversity. "We see plainly that men who come from New England are different from us," wrote Joseph Taylor, a southern Antifederalist. [James Winthrop], on the other hand, declared that "the inhabitants of warmer climates are more dissolute in their manners, and less industrious, than in colder countries. A degree of severity is, therefore, necessary with one which would cramp the spirit of the other. . . . It is impossible for one code of laws to suit Georgia and Massachusetts."

A just society, for many Antifederalists, involved more than simply protecting property rights. Government had more responsibilities than merely to regulate "various and interfering interests." It was expected to promote morality, virtue, and religion. Many Antifederalists, for example, were shocked at the Constitution's totally secular tone and its general disregard of religion and morality. Equally upsetting was the lack of any religious content in Federalist arguments for the Constitution. . . . Antifederalists held that religion was a crucial support of government. . . .

There was, not surprisingly, also a tendency in some Antifederalist circles to see the exchange principles of commercial society, so praised by the Federalists, as threats to civic and moral virtue. Would not the self-seeking activities "of a commercial society beget luxury, the parent of inequality, the foe to virtue, and the enemy to restraint"? The spread of commerce would undermine republican simplicity, for the more a people succumbed to luxury, the more incapable they became of governing themselves. . . .

The problem with the Federalist position for many Antifederalists was the inadequacy of its vision of community based on mere interests and their protection. . . . A proper republican community, for these Antifederalists, required a moral consensus, which, in turn, required similarity, familiarity, and fraternity. . . .

Madison and Hamilton understood full well that this communitarian sentiment lay at the core of much of the Antifederalist critique of the new constitutional order. In *Federalist* No. 35 Hamilton ridiculed the face-to-face politics of those "whose observation does not travel beyond the circle of his neighbors and his acquaintances." Madison in No. 10 described two alternative ways of eliminating the causes of factions and thus the politics of interest: one by "destroying the liberty which is essential to its existence; the other by giving to every citizen the same opinions, the same passions, and the same interests." These were both unacceptable. To do either would cut out the very heart of the liberal polity he championed.

Can one go too far in making the case for the Antifederalists as antiliberal communitarians . . . ? Some were, without doubt, but others responded to the enlargement of the federal government and the enhancement of executive power with a call for the protection of private and individual rights through a bill of rights. Even this, however, may be explained by their communitarian bias. If, after all, government was to be run from some city hundreds of miles away, by people superior, more learned, and more deliberative than they, by people with whom they had little in common, then individual rights needed specific protection. . . .

An equally strong case can be made for the Federalists as republican theorists, and here we see full-blown . . . the overlapping of political languages, in 1787. . . . The crucial move in No. 10 that sets Madison firmly within the republican paradigm is his assumption that the representative function in an enlarged republic would produce officeholders who would sacrifice personal, private, and parochial interest to the public good and the public interest. What made the layers of filtration prescribed by the new constitutional order so welcome was their ultimate purpose—producing enlightened public-spirited men who found fulfillment in the quest for public good. . . . The greater number of citizens choosing representatives in a larger republic would reject "unworthy candidates" and select "men who possess the most attractive merit." A large republic and a national government would lead to "the substitution of representatives whose enlightened views and virtuous sentiments render them superior to local prejudices and to schemes of injustice." . . .

Working out the mechanisms by which this filtration process would "refine" and "enlarge" public views and enhance the quality of the men chosen to express them preoccupied the delegates at Philadelphia. This explains their lengthy deliberations over how governing officials such as the president and senators should be selected. Indirect processes of selection would, Madison wrote in his notes, "extract from the mass of the Society the purest and noblest characters which it contains." . . .

The class focus of the Federalists' republicanism is self-evident. Their vision was of an elite corps of men in whom civic spirit and love of the general good overcame particular and narrow interest. Such men were men of substance, independence, and fame who had the leisure to devote their time to public life and the wisdom to seek the true interests of the country as opposed to the wicked projects of local and particular interests. This republicanism of Madison and the Federalists was, of course, quite consistent with the general aristocratic orientation of classical republicanism, which was, after all, the ideal of the independent, propertied, and therefore leisured citizen. . . .

Filtering out mediocrity for Madison went hand in hand with disinterested pursuit of the public good. Many Antifederalists, for their part, saw legislatures as most representative when their membership mirrored the complexity and diversity of society—when, in fact, each geographical unit and social rank was represented. In offering the mirror, not the filter, as the model for representation, Antifederalists seemed to be calling for the representation of every particular interest and thus appear to resemble interest-centered liberals. . . .

Hamilton repudiated the Antifederalist interest theory in *Federalist* No. 35. "The idea of an actual representation of all classes of the people, by persons of each class," so that the feelings and interests of all would be expressed, "is altogether visionary," he wrote. The national legislature, Hamilton recommended, should be composed only of "landholders, merchants, and men of the learned professions." Ordinary people, however much confidence "they may justly feel in their own good sense," should realize that "their interests can be more effectually promoted" by men from these three stations in life.

The confusion of paradigms is further evident when one analyzes in more detail these Federalist and Antifederalist theories of representation. . . . Antifederalists tended to espouse the traditional republican conviction, dominant in most states under the Articles of Confederation, that representatives should be directly responsible to their constituents and easily removable. This, of course, tapped a rich eighteenth-century republican tradition of demanding frequent elections. Implicit in the Federalist notion of filtration, however, was a denial of the representative as mere delegate or servant of his constituents. . . . Madison's legislators of "refined and enlarged public views," seeking "the true interest of their country," ought not to be subject to yearly review by local farmers and small-town tradesmen.

The Language of Virtuous Republicanism

The meaning of virtue in the language of civic humanism is clear. It is the privileging of the public over the private. Samuel Adams persistently evoked the idioms of Aristotle and Cicero. "A Citizen," he wrote, "owes everything to the Commonwealth." He worried that Americans would so "forget their own generous Feelings for the Publick and for each other, as to set private Interest in Competition with that of the great Community." . . . Republican government required "a positive Passion for the public good, the public Interest. . . . Superiour to all private Passions."

This is not all that virtue meant. . . . The values at risk were apolitical and personal. Madison feared for the sobriety, the prudence, and the industry of Americans. His concern was "the industry and morals of the people." . . . Virtuous republican people could, in fact, be described in noncivic, personal terms by the very same men who used the language of civic humanism. John Adams could see the foundation of virtuous government in men who are "sober, industrious and frugal." . . .

The republican tradition had, to be sure, always privileged economy over luxury. . . . But there is more than the all-pervasive paradigm of republicanism at work here. The inclusion of industry in the litany of virtue directs us to another inheritance, to another language in which Americans in the late eighteenth century conceptualized their personal and political universe. Americans also spoke the language of work-ethic Protestantism derived from Richard Baxter, John Bunyan, and the literature of the calling and of "industry." . . .

Central in work-ethic Protestantism was the vision of a cosmic struggle between the forces of industry and idleness. Its texts vibrated less with the dialectic of civic virtue and self-centered commerce than with the dialectic of productive hardworking energy, on the one hand, and idle unproductive sloth, on the other. Its idiom was more personal and individualistic than public and communal. Work was a test of self-sufficiency and self-reliance, a battleground for personal salvation. All men were "called" to serve God by busying themselves in useful productive work that served both society and the individual. . . .

The Protestant language of work and the calling is, of course, complementary to the liberal language of Locke with its similar voluntaristic and individualistic emphasis. . . . Virtuous man is solitary and private man on his own, realizing himself and his talents through labor and achievement; corrupt man is unproductive, indolent, and in the devil's camp. He fails the test of individual responsibility. Few have captured the compatibility of the liberal and work-ethic Protestant paradigms as well as Tocqueville. . . . Americans, Tocqueville wrote, "owe nothing to any man, they expect nothing from any man; they acquire the habit of always considering themselves as standing alone, and they are apt to imagine that their whole destiny is in their own hands." . . .

In this vocabulary, industry, simplicity, and frugality were the signs not only of a virtuous people but also of a free people. As one Rhode Island writer put it, "the industrious and the frugal only will be free." The Boston *Evening-Post* of November 16, 1767, noted that "by consuming less of what we are not really in want of, and by industriously cultivating and improving the natural advantages of our own country, we might save our substance, even our lands, from becoming the property of others, and we might effectually preserve our virtue and our liberty, to the latest posterity." Three weeks later the *Pennsylvania Journal* proclaimed: "Save Your Money and You Will Save Your Country." . . .

Virtue was becoming privatized in the latter part of the eighteenth century. It was being moved from the realm of public activity to the sphere of personal character. The virtuous man partook less and less of that republican ideal that held sway from Aristotle to Harrington—the man whose landed property gave him the leisure necessary for civic commitment in the public arena, be its manifestations political or martial. Property was still important in the Protestant paradigm—not, however, as grantor of leisure but as the rightful fruit of industrious work.

Gordon Wood has noted that Carter Braxton more than any other in the founding generation of Americans sensed the tension between a republicanism based on public virtue—the "disinterested attachment to the public good, exclusive and independent of all private and selfish interests"—and an American polity where in reality most practiced a private virtue in which each man "acts for himself, and with a view of promoting his own particular welfare." Republican privileging of public over private had never been, according to Braxton, the politics of "the mass of the people in any state." In this observation lay Braxton's real insight. Republican virtue was historically the ideal of a circumscribed, privileged citizenry with an independent propertied base that provided the leisure and time for fulfillment in public life through the moral pursuit of public things. . . . From our perspective, we can credit Braxton with perceiving the decline of republican hegemony in the face of the alternative worlds of Lockean liberalism and the Protestant ethic. . . . Citizenship and the public quest for the common good were for some replaced by economic productivity and industrious work as the criteria of virtue. . . . One's duty was still to contribute to the public good, but this was best done through economic activity, which actually aimed at private gain. Self-centered economic productivity, not public citizenship, would become a badge of the virtuous man. At the heart of this shift from republican to Protestant notions of virtue was also a transvaluation of work and leisure. Many Americans in 1787 would have dissented vigorously from the centuries-old republican paradigm set forth in Aristotle's *Politics*: "In the state with the finest constitution, which possesses just men who are just absolutely and not relatively to the assumed situation, the citizens must not live a mechanical or commercial life. Such a life is not noble, and it militates against virtue. Nor must those who are to be citizens be agricultural workers, for they must have leisure to develop their virtue, and for the activities of a citizen."

The Language of Power and the State

Lost today in the legitimate characterization of the Constitution as bent on setting limits to the power exercised by less than angelic men is the extent to which the Constitution is a grant of power to a centralized nation-state. This loss reflects a persistent privileging of Madison over Hamilton in reading the text. While posterity emphasizes the Constitution's complex web of checks and balances and the many institutionalized separations of powers, the participants in the "great national discussion," on whichever side they stood, agreed with Hamilton that the Constitution intended a victory for power, for the "principle of strength and stability in the organization of our government, and vigor in its operations." . . .

In the political discourse of 1787 there was thus a fourth paradigm at work, the state-centered language of power. It, too, reached back into the classical world, to the great lawgivers and founders Solon and Lycurgus, and to the imperial ideal of Alexander and Julius Caesar. Not republican city states but empire and, much later, the nation-state were its institutional units. . . . This language of politics was focused on the moral, heroic, and self-realizing dimensions of the exercise and use of power. . . .

It was the experience of war that shaped the vision of America's state-builders. The war against Britain provided them with a continental and national experience that replaced the states-centered focus of the pre-1776 generation. A remarkable number of framers of the Constitution either served in the Continental army or were diplomats or administrative officials for the Confederation or members of the Continental Congress. Indeed, thirty-nine of the fifty-five delegates to the Constitutional Convention had sat in the Congress. . . . While most of the Antifederalists were states-centered politicians whose heroics took place before 1776, most of the Federalists were shaped by the need to realize the national interest in an international war. Their common bond was an experience that transcended and dissolved state boundaries.

Madison and Hamilton had sat on the same committee of the Continental Congress in 1782–1783, working on the funding of the war and the maintenance of the French alliance. From experiences like this they and their state-building colleagues came to view the thirteen states collectively as a "country," a country among countries. If their country were going to live in a world of nation-states, it needed to become, like the others, a centralized nation-state with sovereign power to tax, regulate trade, coin money, fund a debt, conduct a foreign policy, and organize a standing army. . . .

Hamilton's preoccupation with money and arms as essential for state-building, and his zeal to push aside any intermediate bodies between the state and individuals, while directly relevant for the case he was making on behalf of the Constitution, were also heavily influenced by his perceptive reading of the pattern of state-building in Europe. . . . Equally evident is his sense that the pattern of European development, with the triumph of coercive centralized nation-states, should be reproduced in America under the Constitution. . . . Hamilton was interested less in the limited liberal state than in the heroic state; heroic state-builders like him cannot fear power, for power is the essence of the state. That power is so often abused does not rule out its creative and useful role. . . .

All of the power-centered paradigm's euphemisms for power—"strength," "vigor," "energy"—come together in Hamilton's conception of the presidential office. The presidency was the heart of the new American state for Hamilton, just as the monarch or chief magistrate was for older European nation-states. . . . The president was the energetic builder of an energetic state. In *Federalist* No. 70 Hamilton argued: "Energy in the executive is a leading character in the definition of good government. . . . A feeble executive implies a feeble execution of the government. A feeble execution is but another phrase for a bad execution; and a government ill executed, whatever it may be in theory, must be in practice, a bad government."

Hamilton saw a close relationship between a state with energy and power at home and a powerful state in the world of states. . . . Hamilton was preoccupied with the interrelationship between commerce, state power, and international politics. . . . But Hamilton did not want to build an American state with all that statehood required—a financial and commercial infrastructure, energetic leadership, and powerful military forces—merely to allow America to hold its own in a world system characterized by conflict, competition, and clashing power. He had a grander vision for the American state, a call to greatness. . . . If Americans would only "concur in erecting one great American system," the American state would be "superior to the control of all transatlantic force or influence, and able to dictate the terms of the connection between the old and the new world." In the face of a vigorous American state Europe would cease to be "mistress of the world." America would become ascendant in the Western Hemisphere.

Hamilton's horizons were dazzling. His internationalism transcended the cosmopolitan vision of his fellow Federalists as it transcended the localism of the Antifederalists. The victory of the state center over the American periphery would in Hamilton's fertile imagination catapult America from the periphery of nations to the center of the world system. . . .

We must not lose sight of the other side in the "great national discussion," however. Hamilton's discourse of power with its vision of an imperial American state attracted the fire of Antifederalists like one of Franklin's lightning rods. It was Patrick Henry who most angrily and most movingly repudiated the Federalist state. Henry's American spirit was Tom Paine's. With the Federalist state America would lose its innocence, and "splendid government" would become its badge, its dress. On the ruins of paradise would be built, if not the palaces of kings, then armies and navies and mighty empires. At the Virginia ratifying convention Henry evoked a different language of politics.

> The American spirit has fled from hence; it has gone to regions where it has never been expected; it has gone to the people of France, in search of a splendid government, a strong, energetic government. Shall we imitate the example of those nations who have gone from a simple to a splendid government? Are those nations more worthy of our imitation? What can make an adequate satisfaction to them for the loss they have suffered in attaining such a government, for the loss of their liberty? If we admit this consolidated government, it will be because we like a great, splendid one. Some way or other we must be a great and mighty empire; we must have an army, and a navy, and a number of things. When the American spirit was in its youth, the language of America was different; liberty, sir, was then the primary object.

What was Madison's relationship to the discourse of power and the Hamiltonian state? Madison was a state-builder, too, but his state was quite different from Hamilton's, and upon these differences a good deal of American politics in the next two decades, as well as to this day, would turn. Madison and Hamilton were in agreement on many things. They agreed on the need to establish an effective unified national government. They agreed on the serious threats to personal property rights posed by the state legislatures and on the role that a central government would play in protecting these rights. They agreed on the need to have the central government run by worthy, enlightened, and deliberative men. They agreed on the Constitution as necessary to provide the essential framework for commercial development through the creation of a national market, public credit, uniform currency, and the protection of contract. To be sure, Madison's vision tilted toward agrarian capitalism and Hamilton's toward manufactures and commerce. Where they markedly disagreed, however, was in giving positive, assertive power, "energy," and "vigor" to the state.

Hamilton held the new American state valuable for its own sake as assertive power. He saw the nation-state with its historic and heroic goals, seeking power in a competitive international system of other power-hungry states. Madison saw the nation-state as necessary only to protect private rights and thus ensure justice. Like Locke he saw the need for a grant of power to the state, but a grant of limited power. Madison saw the central government providing an arena for competitive power, where the private bargaining of free men, groups, and interests would take place, and the state would define no goals of its own other than ensuring the framework for orderly economic life. All the state would do was regulate "the various and interfering interests" or, as Madison put it to Washington in straightforward Lockean terms, be an impartial umpire in disputes. Energy in politics for Madison would come from individuals and groups seeking their own immediate goals, not from an energetic state seeking its own heroic ends. . . .

Madison's limited Federalist state might well appear meek and tame set next to Hamilton's energetic and vigorous state, but it was a matter of perspective. To the Antifederalists, even Madison's state, limited as it was by checks and balances and its cool men resisting the temptations of lawmaking, seemed a monstrous betrayal of the Revolution and its spirit. . . . Like most revolutions, the American began as a repudiation of the state, of power, and of authority in the name of liberty. Like most revolutions, it ended with a stronger state, the revival of authority, and the taming of liberty's excesses. . . .

The Federalists triumphed in the "great national discussion" that was the debate over the ratification of the Constitution. But posterity has not remembered simply the victorious advocates of the Constitution in 1787 and 1788. The Antifederalists have lived on in the American imagination as well. Their worst fears were never realized, which proves the glaring exception in a comparison of the American Revolution with other revolutions. The Antifederalists, while losers in 1788, were neither liquidated nor forced to flee. Nor, more significantly, were their ideas extinguished. Their values lived on in America, as they themselves did, and have been absorbed into the larger pattern of American political culture. . . .

Just as there ultimately was no decisive victor in the political and pamphlet battle, so, too, there was none in the paradigm battle. No one paradigm cleared the field in 1788 and obtained exclusive dominance in the American political discourse. There was no watershed victory of liberalism over republicanism. These languages were heard on both sides during the "great national discussion." So, too, were the two other paradigms available to the framers' generation, the Protestant ethic and the ideals of sovereignty and power. So it has remained. American political discourse to this day tends to be articulated in one or another of these distinguishable idioms.

The Politics of the Bill of Rights

LEONARD W. LEVY

The Bill of Rights consists of the first ten amendments to the Constitution of the United States. Congress submitted those amendments to the states for ratification on September 25, 1789, and the requisite number of state legislatures had ratified them by December 15, 1791. The triumph of individual liberty against government power, as epitomized by the Bill of Rights, is one of our history's noblest and most enduringly important themes. Yet James Madison, justly remembered as the "father" of the Bill of Rights, privately referred on August 19, 1789 to the "nauseous project of amendments." He had proposed the Bill of Rights, in part, because "It will kill the opposition everywhere. . . ." In this attitude lies a suggestion that party politics saturated the making of the first ten amendments. . . .

The omission of a bill of rights was a deliberate act of the Constitutional Convention. . . . On September 12, 1787, George Mason of Virginia remarked that he "wished the plan had been prefaced by a Bill of Rights," because it would "give great quiet" to the people. Mason thought that with the states' bills of rights as models, "a bill might be prepared in a few hours." He made no stirring speech for civil liberties in general or any rights in particular. He did not even argue the need for a bill of rights or move the adoption of one, although he offered to second a motion if one were made. Elbridge Gerry of Massachusetts then moved for a committee to prepare a bill of rights, and Mason seconded the motion. Roger Sherman of Connecticut observed that the rights of the people should be secured if necessary, but because the Constitution did not repeal the bills of rights of the states, the Convention need not do anything. Without further debate the delegates, voting by states, defeated the motion 10–0. Two days later, after the states unanimously defeated a motion by Mason to delete from the Constitution a ban on ex post facto laws by Congress, Charles Pinckney of South Carolina, seconded by Gerry, moved to insert a declaration "that the liberty of the Press should be inviolably observed." Sherman laconically replied, "It is unnecessary. The power of Congress does not extend to the Press," and the motion lost 7–4. Three days later the Convention adjourned.

In the Congress of the Confederation, Richard Henry Lee of Virginia moved that a bill of rights, which he had adapted from his own state's constitution, be added to the federal Constitution. Lee was less interested in the adoption of a bill of rights than in defeating the Constitution. Amendments recommended by Congress required ratification by all the state legislatures, not just nine state ratifying conventions. Lee's motion was defeated, but it showed that, from the start of the ratification controversy, the omission of a bill of rights became an Antifederalist mace with which to smash the Constitution. Its opponents sought to prevent ratification and exaggerated the bill-of-rights issue because it was one with which they could enlist public support. Their prime loyalty belonged to states' rights, not civil rights. . . .

Why did the Constitutional Convention omit a bill of rights? No delegate opposed one in principle. As George Washington informed Lafayette, "there was not a member of the Convention, I believe, who had the least objection to what is contended for by the advocates for a Bill of Rights. . . ." All the framers were civil libertarians as well as experienced politicians who had the confidence of their constituents and the state legislatures that elected them. Even the foremost opponents of ratification praised the make-up of the Convention. . . . How could such an "assembly of demigods," as Jefferson called them, neglect the liberties of the people? . . .

The overwhelming majority of the Convention believed, as Sherman succinctly declared, "It is unnecessary." Why was it unnecessary, given the fact that the Convention recommended a new and powerful national government that could operate directly on individuals? The framers believed that the national government could exercise only enumerated powers or powers necessary to carry out those enumerated, and no provision of the Constitution authorized the government to act on any natural rights. A bill of rights would restrict national powers; but, as Hamilton declared, such a bill would be "dangerous" as well as unnecessary because it "would contain various exceptions to powers not granted and, on this very account, would afford a colorable pretext to claim more than were granted. For why declare that things shall not be done which there is no power to do? Why, for instance, should it be said that the liberty of the press shall not be restrained, when no power is given by which restrictions may be imposed?"

Hamilton expressed a standard Federalist position, echoing other framers and advocates of ratification. Excluding a bill of rights from the Constitution was fundamental to the constitutional theory of the framers. . . .

Civil liberties, the supporters of the Constitution believed, faced real dangers from the possibility of repressive state action, but that was a matter to be guarded against by state bills of rights. They also argued, inconsistently, that some states had no bills of rights but were as free as those with bills of rights. They were as free because personal liberty, to Federalist theoreticians, depended not on "parchment provisions," which Hamilton called inadequate in "a struggle with public necessity," but on public opinion, an extended republic, a pluralistic society of competing interests, and a free and limited government structured to prevent any interest from becoming an overbearing majority.

The fact that six states had no bills of rights, and that none had a comprehensive list of guarantees, provided the supporters of ratification with the argument, made by Wilson among others, that an imperfect bill of rights was worse than none at all because the omission of some rights might justify their infringement by implying an unintended grant of government power. The record was not reassuring; the states had very imperfect bills of rights, which proved to be ineffective when confronted by "public necessity," and the state governments did in fact abridge rights that had not been explicitly reserved.

Virginia's Declaration of Rights, for example, did not ban bills of attainder. In 1778 the Virginia assembly adopted a bill of attainder and outlawry, drafted by Jefferson at the instigation of Governor Patrick Henry, against a reputed cutthroat Tory, one Josiah Philips, and some fifty unnamed "associates." By legislative enactment they were condemned for treason and murder, and on failure to surrender were subject to being killed by anyone. At the Virginia ratifying convention, Edmund Randolph, irked beyond endurance by Henry's assaults on the Constitution as dangerous to personal liberties, recalled with "horror" the "shocking" attainder. When Henry defended the attainder, John Marshall, who supported ratification without a bill of rights, declared, "Can we pretend to the enjoyment of political freedom or security, when we are told that a man has been, by an act of Assembly, struck out of existence without a trial by jury, without examination, without being confronted with his accusers and witnesses, without the benefits of the law of the land?"

The framers of the Constitution tended to be skeptical about the value of "parchment barriers" against "overbearing majorities," as Madison said. He had seen repeated violations of bills of rights in every state. Experience proved the "inefficacy of a bill of rights to those occasions when its control is most needed," he said. In Virginia, for example, despite an explicit protection of the rights of conscience, the legislature had favored an establishment of religion, which was averted only because Madison turned the tide of opinion against the bill. As realists the framers believed that constitutional protections of rights meant little during times of popular hysteria; any member of the Constitutional Convention could have cited examples of gross abridgments of civil liberties in states that had bills of rights.

Virginia's bill was imperfect not just because it lacked a ban on bills of attainder. The much vaunted Declaration of Rights of Virginia also omitted the freedoms of speech, assembly, and petition; the right to the writ of habeas corpus; the right to grand jury proceedings; the right to counsel; separation of church and state; and freedom from double jeopardy and from ex post facto laws. The rights omitted were as numerous and important as those included. Twelve states, including Vermont, had framed constitutions, and the only right secured by all was trial by jury in criminal cases. Although all protected religious liberty, five either permitted or provided for an establishment of religion. Two states passed over a free press guarantee. Four neglected to ban excessive fines, excessive bail, compulsory self-incrimination, and general search warrants. Five ignored protections for the rights of assembly, petition, counsel, and trial by jury in civil cases. Seven omitted a prohibition of ex post facto laws. Nine failed to provide for grand jury proceedings, and nine failed to condemn bills of attainder. Ten said nothing about freedom of speech, while eleven were silent on double jeopardy. Whether omissions implied a power to violate, they seemed, in Federalist minds, to raise dangers that could be prevented by avoiding an unnecessary problem entirely: omit a bill of rights when forming a federal government of limited powers.

That the framers of the Constitution actually believed their own arguments purporting to justify the omission of a bill of rights is difficult to credit. Some of the points they made were patently absurd, like the insistence that the inclusion of a bill of rights would be dangerous and, on historical grounds, unsuitable. The last point most commonly turned up in the claim that bills of rights were appropriate in England but not in America. Magna Carta, the Petition of Right of 1628, and the Bill of Rights of 1689 had been grants wrested from kings to secure royal assent to certain liberties, and therefore had "no application to constitutions . . . founded upon the power of the people" who surrendered nothing and retained everything. That argument, made in *Federalist* number 84 and by leading ratificationists as sophisticated as Wilson and Oliver Ellsworth of Connecticut, was so porous that it could persuade no one. . . .

To imply that bills of rights were un-American or unnecessary merely because in America the people were the source of all power was unhistorical. Over a period of a century and a half America had become accustomed to the idea that government existed by consent of the governed; that people created government; that they created it by written compact; that the compact constituted fundamental law; that the government must be subject to such limitations as are necessary for the security of the rights of the people; and, usually, that the reserved rights of the people were enumerated in bills of rights. Counting Vermont (an independent republic from 1777 until its admission to the Union in 1791), eight states had bills of rights, notwithstanding any opinion that such bills properly belonged only in a compact between a king and his subjects. . . .

Abroad, two wise Americans serving their country in diplomatic missions coolly appraised the proposed Constitution without the obligation of having to support a party line. John Adams, having received a copy of the document in London, wrote a short letter to Jefferson in Paris. The Constitution seemed "admirably calculated to preserve the Union," Adams thought, and he hoped it would be ratified with amendments adopted later. "What think you," he asked, "of a Declaration of Rights? Should not such a Thing have preceded the Model?" Jefferson, in his first letter to Madison on the subject of the Constitution, began with praise but ended with what he did not like: "First the omission of a bill of rights. . . ." After listing rights he thought deserved special protection, starting with freedom of religion and of the press, Jefferson dismissed as campaign rhetoric Wilson's justification for the omission of a bill of rights and concluded, "Let me add that a bill of rights is what the people are entitled to against every government on earth, general or particular, and what no just government should refuse, or rest on inference."

Adams and Jefferson in Europe were much closer to popular opinion than the framers of the Constitution, who had worked secretly for almost four months and, with their supporters, became locked into a position that defied logic and experience. During the ratification controversy, some Federalists argued that the Constitution protected basic rights, exposing them to the reply that they had omitted the liberty of the press, religious freedom, security against general warrants, trial by jury in civil cases, and other basic rights. . . .

If it was unnecessary, Antifederalists asked, why did the Constitution protect some rights? The protection of some opened the Federalists to devastating rebuttal. They claimed that because no bill of rights could be complete, the omission of any particular right might imply a power to abridge it as unworthy of respect by the government. That argument, in effect that to include some would exclude all others, boomeranged. The protection of trial by jury in criminal cases, the bans on religious tests, ex post facto laws, and bills of attainder, the narrow definition of treason, and the provision for the writ of habeas corpus, by the Federalists' own reasoning, were turned against them. . . .

Henry cleverly observed that the "fair implication" of the Federalist argument against a bill of rights was that the government could do anything not forbidden by the Constitution. Because the provision on the writ of habeas corpus allowed its suspension when the public safety required, Henry reasoned, "It results clearly that, if it had not said so, they could suspend it in all cases whatsoever. It reverses the position of the friends of this Constitution, that everything is retained which is not given up; for, instead of this, every thing is given up which is not expressly reserved." . . . [Richard Henry] Lee objected to leaving the rights of the people to "logical inferences," because Federalist principles led to the implication that all the rights not mentioned in the Constitution were intended to be relinquished. . . .

In sum, the usually masterful politicians who had dominated the Convention had blundered by botching constitutional theory and making a serious political error. Their arguments justifying the omission of a bill of rights were impolitic and unconvincing. Mason's point that a bill of rights would quiet the fears of the people was unanswerable. Alienating him and the many who agreed with him was bad politics and handed to the opposition a stirring cause around which they could muster sentiment against ratification. The single issue that united Antifederalists throughout the country was the lack of a bill of rights. No rational argument—and the lack of a bill of rights created an intensely emotional issue because people believed that their liberties were at stake—could possibly allay the fears generated by demagogues like Henry and principled opponents of ratification like Madison. . . . The Antifederalists capitalized on the Federalist blunder, hoping to defeat the Constitution or get a second convention that would revise it in order to hamstring the national government.

In Pennsylvania, the second state to ratify, the minority demanded a comprehensive bill of rights similar to that in their state constitution. Massachusetts, the sixth state to ratify, was the first to do so with recommended amendments. Only two of the recommended amendments, dealing with jury trial in civil suits and grand jury indictment, belonged in a bill of rights. Supporters of the Constitution in Massachusetts had withdrawn a proposed bill of rights on the supposition that Antifederalists would use it as proof that the Constitution endangered liberty. Maryland too would have recommended a bill of rights, but the Federalist majority jettisoned it when the Antifederalists tried to insert curbs on national powers to tax and regulate commerce. Nevertheless, Federalists grudgingly accepted ratification with recommended amendments to ward off conditional ratification or the defeat of the Constitution. New Hampshire, whose approval as the ninth state made ratification an accomplished fact, urged a comprehensive bill of rights for adoption by amendments after the new government went into operation. Virginia and New York, whose ratification was politically indispensable, followed suit. North Carolina was the fourth state to ratify with a model bill of rights among its recommendations. But the states also recommended crippling restrictions on delegated powers.

Thus, the Constitution was ratified only because crucial states, where ratification had been in doubt, were willing to accept the promise of a bill of rights in the form of subsequent amendments to the Constitution. State recommendations for amendments, including those of the Pennsylvania minority, received nationwide publicity, adding to the clamor for a bill of rights. Every right that became part of the first ten amendments was included in state recommendations except the clause in the Fifth Amendment requiring just compensation for private property taken for public use.

James Madison was one of the Federalists who finally realized that statecraft and political expediency dictated a switch in position. At the Virginia ratifying convention in June 1788 Madison had upheld the usual Federalist arguments for the omission of a bill of rights but finally voted to recommend such a bill in order to avoid previous amendments. He later conceded that the Constitution would have been defeated without a pledge from its supporters to back subsequent amendments. In Virginia, Madison's own political position deteriorated because he had opposed a bill of rights. The Antifederalists, who controlled the state legislature, elected two of their own, Richard Henry Lee and William Grayson, as the state's first United States senators. Madison faced a tough contest for election to the House of Representatives, and he feared that the Antifederalists might succeed in their call for a second constitutional convention. He needed to clarify his position on a bill of rights.

Although Madison had periodically apprised Jefferson, in Paris, on ratification developments, he had not answered Jefferson's letter of December 1787 supporting a bill of rights. On October 17, 1788, the eve of his campaign for a House seat, Madison faced the issue. He favored a bill of rights, he wrote, but . . . also worried about the difficulty of adequately protecting the most important rights; experience proved that a bill of rights was a mere parchment barrier when most needed. Government, after all, was the instrument of the majority, which could endanger liberty. "What use then . . . can a bill of rights serve in popular Governments?" Its political truths, he conceded by way of answer, could educate the people, thereby inhibiting majority impulses.

Jefferson's reply of March 15, 1789, had a profound influence on Madison, as Madison's great speech of June 8 would show. An argument for a bill of rights that Madison had omitted, wrote Jefferson, was "the legal check which it puts into the hands of the judiciary." Jefferson believed that an independent court could withstand oppressive majority impulses by holding unconstitutional any acts violating a bill of rights. The point was not new to Madison, for he himself, when defending a ban on ex post facto laws at the Constitutional Convention, had declared that it would "oblige the Judges to declare [retrospective] interferences null and void." As for the point that the delegated powers did not reach the reserved rights of the people, Jefferson answered that because the Constitution protected some rights but ignored others, it raised implications against them, making a bill of rights "necessary by way of supplement." Moreover, he added, the Constitution "forms us into one state as to certain objects," requiring a bill of rights to guard against abuses of power. As for the point that a bill of rights could not be perfect, Jefferson replied with the adage that half a loaf is better than none; even if all rights could not be secured, "let us secure what we can." Madison had also argued that the limited powers of the federal government and the jealousy of the states afforded enough security, to which Jefferson answered that a bill of rights "will be the text whereby to try all the acts of the federal government." The argument that a bill of rights was inconvenient and not always efficacious did not impress Jefferson. Sometimes, he replied, it was effective, and if it inconveniently cramped the government, the effect was short-lived and remediable, whereas the inconveniences of not having a bill of rights could be "permanent, afflicting, and irreparable." Legislative tyranny, Jefferson explained, would be a formidable dread for a long time, and executive tyranny would likely follow.

Jefferson's arguments, however persuasive, would have been unproductive but for the dangerous political situation, which Madison meant to ameliorate. Four states, including his own and New York, had called for a second convention, whose purpose, Madison feared, would be to "mutilate the system," especially as to the power to tax. Omitting it "will be fatal" to the new federal government. Madison correctly believed that many Antifederalists favored an effective Union on condition that a bill of rights bridled the new government. His strategy was to win them over by persuading the first Congress to adopt protections of civil liberties, thereby alleviating the public's anxieties, providing popularity and stability for the government, and isolating those Antifederalists whose foremost objective was "subverting the fabric . . . if not the Union itself."

In the first Congress, Representative Madison sought to fulfill his pledge of subsequent amendments. His accomplishment in the face of opposition and apathy entitles him to be remembered as "father of the Bill of Rights" even more than as "father of the Constitution." Many Federalists thought that the House had more important tasks, like the passage of tonnage duties and a judiciary bill. The opposition party, which had previously exploited the lack of a bill of rights in the Constitution, realized that its adoption would sink the movement for a second convention and make unlikely any additional amendments that would cripple the substantive powers of the government. They had used the bill-of-rights issue as a smokescreen for objections to the Constitution that could not be dramatically popularized, and now they sought to scuttle Madison's proposals. They began by stalling, then tried to annex amendments aggrandizing state powers, and finally depreciated the importance of the very protections of individual liberty that they had formerly demanded as a guarantee against impending tyranny. Madison meant to prove that the new government was a friend of liberty; he also understood that his amendments, if adopted, would thwart the passage of proposals aggrandizing state powers and diminishing national ones. He would not be put off; he was insistent, compelling, unyielding, and, finally, triumphant.

On June 8, 1789, he made his long, memorable speech before an apathetic House, introducing amendments culled mainly from state constitutions and state ratifying convention proposals, especially Virginia's. All power, he argued, is subject to abuse and should be guarded against by constitutionally securing "the great rights of mankind." . . . The great objective he had in mind, Madison declared, was to limit the powers of government, thus preventing legislative as well as executive abuse, and above all preventing abuses of power by "the body of the people, operating by the majority against the minority." Mere "paper barriers" might fail, but they raised a standard that might educate the majority against acts to which they might be inclined.

To the argument that a bill of rights was not necessary because the states constitutionally protected freedom, Madison had two responses. One was that some states had no bills of rights, others "very defective ones," and the states constituted a greater danger to liberty than the new national government. The other was that the Constitution should, therefore, include an amendment that "No State shall violate the equal rights of conscience, or the freedom of the press, or the trial by jury in criminal cases." This, Madison declared, was "the most valuable amendment in the whole list." To the contention that an enumeration of rights would disparage those not protected, Madison replied that the danger could be guarded against by adopting a proposal of his composition that became the Ninth Amendment. If his amendments were "incorporated" into the Constitution, Madison said, using another argument borrowed from Jefferson, "independent tribunals of justice will consider themselves in a peculiar manner the guardians of those rights; they will be an impenetrable bulwark against every assumption of power in the legislative or executive; they will be naturally led to resist every encroachment upon rights expressly stipulated for in the constitution." . . .

Notwithstanding the support of correspondents, Madison's speech stirred no immediate support in Congress. Indeed, every speaker who followed him, regardless of party affiliation, either opposed a bill of rights or believed that the House should attend to far more important duties. Six weeks later Madison "begged" for a consideration of his amendments, but the House assigned them to a special committee instead of debating them. That committee, which included Madison, reported in a week. It added freedom of speech to the rights protected against state abridgement, deleted Madison's reference to no "unreasonable searches and seizures," made some stylistic revisions, but otherwise recommended the amendments substantially as he had proposed them. The committee's report was tabled, impelling Madison on August 3 to implore its consideration.

On August 13 the House finally began to consider the reported amendments, and in the course of debate it made some significant changes. Madison had proposed to "incorporate" the amendments within the text of the Constitution at appropriate points. He did not recommend their adoption as a separate "bill of rights," although he had referred to them collectively by that phrase. Members objected that to incorporate the amendments would give the impression that the framers of the Constitution had signed a document that included provisions not of their composition. Another argument for lumping the amendments together was that the matter of form was so "trifling" that the House should not squander its time debating the placement of the various amendments. Ironically, Roger Sherman, who still believed that the amendments were unnecessary, deserves the credit for insistently arguing that they should be appended as a supplement to the Constitution instead of being interspersed within it. Thus, what became the Bill of Rights achieved its significant collective form over the objections of its foremost proponent, Madison, and because of the desire of its opponents in both parties to downgrade its importance.

The House recast the free exercise of religion clause and its allied clause banning establishments of religion, improving Madison's original language. The House also confined to criminal cases Madison's broad phrasing that no person should be compelled to give evidence against himself. On the other hand the House restored the extremely important principle against unreasonable searches and seizures, dropped by the committee. In another major decision the House decisively defeated Gerry's motion, for the Antifederalists, to consider not just the committee's report but all amendments that the several states had proposed; the Antifederalists thus failed to intrude crippling political amendments. Finally the House added "or to the people" in the recommendation by Madison that the powers not delegated to the United States be reserved to the states. On the whole the House adopted Madison's amendments with few significant alterations during the course of its ten-day debate on the Bill of Rights.

In the midst of that debate Madison wrote a letter to a fellow Federalist explaining why he was so committed to "the nauseous project of amendments" that some of the party supported reluctantly. Protecting essential rights was "not improper," he coolly explained, and could be of some influence for good. He also felt honor-bound to redeem a campaign pledge to his constituents, mindful that the Constitution "would have been certainly rejected" by Virginia without assurances from its supporters to seek subsequent amendments. Politics, moreover, made proposing the amendments a necessity to beat the Antifederalists at their own game. If Federalists did not support the amendments, Antifederalists would claim that they had been right all along and gain support for a second convention. And, Madison wrote, the amendments "will kill the opposition everywhere, and by putting an end to disaffection to the Government itself, enable the administration to venture on measures not otherwise safe."

Madison had, in fact, upstaged and defeated the Antifederalists. That is why Congressman Aedanus Burke of South Carolina cried sour grapes. . . . Later, after the Senate had approved the amendments that became the Bill of Rights, [Virginia senator] Grayson reported, "they are good for nothing, and I believe, as many others do, that they will do more harm than benefit."

The Senate, which kept no record of its debates, had deliberated on seventeen amendments submitted by the House. One the Senate killed, the proposal Madison thought "the most valuable": protection against state infringement of speech, press, religion, or trial by jury. The motion to adopt failed to receive the necessary two-thirds vote, although by what margin is unknown. The Senate also weakened the House's ban on establishments of religion. Otherwise the Senate accepted the House proposals, although the Senate combined several, reducing the total number from seventeen to twelve. The first of the twelve dealt with the relation of population to the number of representatives from each state, and the second would have prevented any law going into effect that would have increased the salaries of members of Congress until after the next election.

The House adamantly refused to accept the Senate's version of its ban on establishments. A conference committee of both houses met to resolve differences. The committee, which included Madison, accepted the House's ban on establishments but otherwise accepted the Senate's version. On September 24, 1789, the House voted for the committee report; on the following day the Senate concurred, and the twelve amendments were submitted to the states for ratification.

Within six months nine states ratified the Bill of Rights, although of the twelve amendments submitted for approval, the first and second were rejected. The four recalcitrant states by mid-1790 were Virginia, Massachusetts, Connecticut, and Georgia. The admission of Vermont to the Union made necessary the ratification by eleven states. Connecticut and Georgia refused to ratify. Georgia's position was that amendments were superfluous until experience under the Constitution proved a need. Connecticut believed that any suggestion that the Constitution was not perfect would add to the strength of Antifederalism.

In Massachusetts, Federalist apathy to the Bill of Rights was grounded on a satisfaction with the Constitution as it was, and the Antifederalists were more interested in amendments that would strengthen the states at the expense of the national government. Nevertheless the Massachusetts lower house adopted all but the first, second, and twelfth amendments, and the upper house adopted all but the first, second, and tenth. Thus both houses of the Massachusetts legislature actually approved what became the First through Seventh Amendments and the Ninth; but a special committee, dominated by Antifederalists, urged that all amendments recommended by Massachusetts should be adopted before the state concurred in any amendments. As a result the two houses never passed a bill promulgating ratification of eight amendments. Jefferson, the secretary of state, believed that Massachusetts, "having been the 10th state which has ratified, makes up the three-fourth [sic] of the legislatures whose ratification was to suffice." He wrote to a Massachusetts official, asking for clarification. The reply was, "It does not appear that the Committee ever reported any bill." In 1939, Massachusetts joined Connecticut and Georgia when they belatedly ratified on the sesquicentennial anniversary of the Constitution.

Ratification of the Bill of Rights by Vermont, in November 1789, left Virginia the last state to act. Its ratification as the eleventh state was indispensable, although the hostility of its Antifederalist leaders presaged a doubtful outcome. . . . The Federalists of Virginia, however, eagerly supported the Bill of Rights in the knowledge that its adoption would appease public fears and stymie the amendments supported by the Antifederalists. Virginia's lower house, controlled by the Federalists, acted quickly, but the opposition dominated the state senate. . . . As a member of the lower house reported to Madison, the senate inclined to reject the Bill of Rights, not because of opposition to its guarantees, but from an apprehension "that the adoption of them at this time will be an obstacle to the chief object of their pursuit, the amendment on the subject of direct taxation." For that reason, Randolph reported to Washington, the Federalists meant to "push" the Bill of Rights; passage would "discountenance any future importunities for amendments."

Virginia's senate at the close of 1789 rejected what became the First, Sixth, Ninth, and Tenth Amendments, at least until the next session, thereby allowing time for the electorate to express itself. The Antifederalists still hoped to drum up support for "radical" amendments, as Lee called them. The senators in the majority also issued a statement grossly misrepresenting the First Amendment (then the third). Madison confidently expected that this Antifederalist tactic would backfire, and it did. For the senators' statement was not only inaccurate on its face; it came from men who with a single exception did not go before the electorate with clean hands. Like Henry and Lee, who planned the senators' statement, the senators had records of having voted against religious liberty and in favor of compulsory taxes for the support of religion. By contrast Madison had led the fight in Virginia against a state establishment of religion and for religious liberty, and his supporters in the Virginia senate had aided him. In the end Madison's confidence proved justified. Jefferson made his influence felt on behalf of the Bill of Rights, and the Antifederalists grudgingly gave ground before public opinion. On December 15, 1791, after two years of procrastination, the senate finally ratified without record vote, thereby completing the process of state ratification and making the Bill of Rights part of the Constitution.

The history of the framing and ratification of the Bill of Rights indicates slight passion on the part of anyone to enshrine personal liberties in the fundamental law of the land. We know almost nothing about what the state legislatures thought concerning the meanings of the various amendments, and the press was perfunctory in its reports, if not altogether silent. But for Madison's persistence the amendments would have died in Congress. Our precious Bill of Rights, at least in its immediate background, resulted from the reluctant necessity of certain Federalists to capitalize on a cause that had been originated, in vain, by the Antifederalists for ulterior purposes. The party that had first opposed the Bill of Rights inadvertently wound up with the responsibility for its framing and ratification, whereas the party that had at first professedly wanted it discovered too late that it was not only embarrassing but disastrous for those ulterior purposes. The Bill of Rights had a great healing effect, however; it did, as Madison originally proposed, "give great quiet" to people. The opposition to the Constitution, Jefferson informed Lafayette, "almost totally disappeared," as Antifederalist leaders lost "almost all their followers." The people of the United States had possessed the good sense, nourished by traditions of freedom, to support the Constitution and the Bill of Rights.

✤ F U R T H E R   R E A D I N G

Richard Beeman, Stephen Botein, and Edward C. Carter II, eds., *Beyond Confederation: Origins of the Constitution and American National Identity* (1987)

Stephen R. Boyd, *The Politics of Opposition: Antifederalists and the Acceptance of the Constitution* (1979)

Robert E. Brown, *Charles Beard and the Constitution: A Critical Analysis of "An Economic Interpretation of the Constitution"* (1956)

Patrick T. Conley and John P. Kaminski, eds., *The Constitution and the States: The Role of the Original Thirteen in the Framing and Adoption of the Federal Constitution* (1988)

Saul Cornell, "Aristocracy Assailed: The Ideology of Backcounty Antifederalism," *Journal of American History,* 76 (March 1990), 1148–1172

Linda Grant De Pauw, *The Eleventh Pillar: New York State and the Federal Constitution* (1966)

David F. Epstein, *The Political Theory of "The Federalist"* (1984)

Alexander Hamilton, John Jay, and James Madison, *The Federalist Papers* (1788)

Merrill Jensen et al., eds., *The Documentary History of the Constitution* (1976)

——, *The New Nation: A History of the United States During the Confederation* (1950)

Michael Kammen, *A Machine That Would Go by Itself: The Constitution in American Culture* (1986)

Cecelia M. Kenyon, ed., *The Antifederalists* (1966)

Charles R. Kesler, ed., *Saving the Revolution: "The Federalist Papers" and the American Founding* (1987)

Leonard W. Levy and Dennis J. Mahoney, eds., *The Framing and Ratification of the Constitution* (1987)

Forrest McDonald, *We the People: The Economic Origins of the Constitution* (1958)

Jackson Turner Main, *The Antifederalists: Critics of the Constitution, 1781–1788* (1961)

Edmund S. Morgan, *Inventing the People: The Rise of Popular Sovereignty in England and America* (1988)

David E. Narrett and Joyce S. Goldberg, eds., *Essays on Liberty and Federalism: The Shaping of the U.S. Constitution* (1988)

Peter S. Onuf, "Reflections on the Founding: Constitutional Historiography in Bicentennial Perspective," *William and Mary Quarterly,* 3d Series, *46* (1989), 341–375

Robert A. Rutland, *The Birth of the Bill of Rights, 1776–1791* (1955)

———, *The Ordeal of the Constitution: The Antifederalists and the Ratification Struggle of 1787–1788* (1966)

Stephen L. Schechter, ed., *The Reluctant Pillar: New York and the Adoption of the Federal Constitution* (1985)

Bernard Schwartz, *The Great Rights of Mankind: A History of the American Bill of Rights* (1987)

Herbert J. Storing, ed., *The Complete Antifederalist* (1981)

———, *What the Antifederalists Were for* (1981)

C H A P T E R
14

Leadership and Heroism
in the Revolutionary Era

⋇

For present-day Americans, the realities of political liberty and nationhood are easy to take for granted. The nation's long-ago colonial status, like living under a monarch and an orthodox, established church, has faded from memory. More than two centuries separate us from the era when these issues were hotly debated, when people had to choose sides—sometimes risking their property, their liberty, their lives. Because we are beneficiaries of a victorious revolution, we are accustomed to a certain complacency: of course, *the right side won the war and organized the nation. It was inevitable, or so it now appears.*

In reality, however, outcomes were usually in doubt, and most endings could have been different. A wide range of forces—economic, political, and social—as well as international relations and historical circumstances, shaped events.

In the end, however, it was people who acted. Individually and collectively, they stepped out of their ordinary paths in the Revolutionary era and started on unfamiliar journeys. Whatever the destination—fame, power, or wealth; or ignominy, exile, or death—personal judgment, motives, and stamina all counted. Leadership and heroism were crucial parts of the Revolutionary experience. And just as one must weigh the role of narrow self-interest in explaining events, so the readiness to sacrifice and to accept risks on behalf of family and community, as well as honor and principle, must be considered.

The question of leadership and heroism in the Revolution is important for another reason. For 200 years Americans have measured themselves against the standards that we believe the Revolutionary generation attained. Romanticism and nationalism have blended with reality to produce an idealized vision of Revolutionary leadership and heroism that has seemed beyond the reach of every succeeding generation. Sometimes this idealization has led to a mournful sense of decline, as if the Revolutionaries were demigods and the present generation mere mortals. Alternatively, skeptics have challenged patriotic mythology by noting the faults of the Revolutionary generation—pointing to human traits of greed, prejudice, and selfish provincialism. This chapter explores both ideals and realities of leadership and heroism in the era of the Revolution and Constitution.

In the first document Abigail Adams briefly sketches her initial impression of
George Washington, the man who would emerge as the hero of the Revolution
and the model leader of the new nation. In the succeeding document John
Adams, working on the Continental Congress's committee in charge of military
preparations, reflects on the ideal attributes of a military leader in a republic. The
heroism demanded of the ordinary citizen is Thomas Paine's theme in the third
selection, his exhortation to the people to support the war in late 1776, after their
first enthusiasm for military activity had waned. The final document, Washington's
famous Farewell Address, although prepared with the assistance of Alexander
Hamilton, evidently reflects the outgoing president's mature reflections on American politics. For more than a century, it was widely read in schools and public
assemblies as a model of statesmanlike leadership.

Abigail Adams on Her First Impressions of George Washington, 1775

I was struck with General Washington. You had prepaired me to entertain
a favorable opinion of him, but I thought the one half was not told me.
Dignity with ease, and complacency, the Gentleman and Soldier look agre-
ably blended in him. Modesty marks every line and feture of his face. Those
lines of Dryden instantly occurd to me

> Mark his Majestick fabrick! he's a temple
> Sacred by birth, and built by hands divine
> His Souls the Deity that lodges there.
> Nor is the pile unworthy of the God.

John Adams on the Qualities Required for Military Leaders, 1776

Let me intreat you, Mr. [William] Tudor, to exert yourself, among the young
Gentlemen of your Acquaintance in the Army, to excite in them, an Ambition to excell: to inspire them, with that Sense of Honour, and Elevation
of sentiment without which they must, and ought to remain undistinguished.
Draw their Attention to those Sciences, and those Branches of Literature,
which are more immediately Subservient to the Art of War. Cant you excite
in them a Thirst for military Knowledge? Make them inquisitive after the
best Writers, curious to know, and ambitious to imitate the Lives and Actions
of great Captains, ancient and modern. An Officer, high in Rank, should
be possessed of very extensive Knowledge of Science, and Literature, Men
and Things. A Citizen of a free Government, he Should be Master of the
Laws and Constitution, least he injure fundamentally those Rights which he
professes to defend. He Should have a keen Penetration and a deep Dis-
cernment of the Tempers, Natures, and Characters of Men. He Should have
an Activity, and Diligence, Superiour to all Fatigue. He should have a
Patience and Self Government, Superiour to all Flights and Transports of

Passion. He Should have a Candour and Moderation, above all Prejudices, and Partialities. His Views should be large enough to comprehend the whole System of the Government and the Army, that he may accommodate his Plans and Measures to the best good, and the essential Movements of those great Machines. His Benevolence and Humanity, his Decency, Politeness and Civility, Should ever predominate in his Breast. He should be possessed of a certain masterly, order, Method, and Decision, Superiour to all Perplexity, and Confusion in Business. There is in Such a Character, whenever and wherever it appears, a decisive Energy, which hurries away before it, all Difficulties, and leaves to the World of Mankind no Leisure, or opportunity to do any Thing towards it, but Admire, it.

There is nothing perhaps upon which the Character of a General So much depends, as the Talent of Writing Letters. The Duty of a constant Correspondence with the Sovereign, whether King or Congress, is inseparable from a Commander in any Department, and the Faculty of placing every Thing, in the happiest Point of Light is as usefull as any, he can possess. I fear this is too much neglected by our young Gentlemen. . . .

Geography is of great Importance to a General. Our Officers should be perfect Masters of American Geography. Nothing is less understood.

Thomas Paine Calls for Sacrifice, 1776

These are the times that try men's souls: The summer soldier and the sunshine patriot will, in this crisis, shrink from the service of his country; but he that stands it NOW, deserves the love and thanks of man and woman. Tyranny, like hell, is not easily conquered; yet we have this consolation with us, that the harder the conflict, the more glorious the triumph. What we obtain too cheap, we esteem too lightly: 'Tis dearness only that gives every thing its value. Heaven knows how to put a proper price upon its goods; and it would be strange indeed, if so celestial an article as FREEDOM should not be highly rated. Britain, with an army to enforce her tyranny, has declared that she has a right (not only to TAX) but "to BIND us in ALL CASES WHATSOEVER," and if being bound in that manner, is not slavery, then is there not such a thing as slavery upon earth. Even the expression is impious, for so unlimited a power can belong only to GOD. . . .

I turn with the warm ardor of a friend to those who have nobly stood, and are yet determined to stand the matter out: I call not upon a few, but upon all; not on THIS state or THAT state, but on EVERY state; up and help us; lay your shoulders to the wheel; better have too much force than too little, when so great an object is at stake. Let it be told to the future world, that in the depth of winter, when nothing but hope and virtue could survive, that the city and the country, alarmed at one common danger, came forth to meet and to repulse it. Say not, that thousands are gone, turn out your tens of thousands; throw not the burden of the day upon Providence, but "shew your faith by your works," that God may bless you. It matters not where you live, or what rank of life you hold, the evil or the blessing will reach you all. The far and the near, the home counties and the back, the rich and the poor, will suffer or rejoice alike. The heart that feels now, is dead: The blood of his children will curse his cowardice, who shrinks back at a time when a little might have saved the whole, and made them happy. I love the man that can smile in trouble, that can gather strength from distress, and grow brave by reflection. 'Tis the business of little minds to shrink; but he whose heart is firm, and whose conscience approves his conduct, will pursue his principles unto death. My own line of reasoning is to myself as strait and clear as a ray of light. Not all the treasures of the world, so far as I believe, could have induced me to support an offensive war, for I think it murder; but if a thief break into my house, burn and destroy my property, and kill or threaten to kill me, or those that are in it, and to "bind me in all cases whatsoever," to his absolute will, am I to suffer it? What signifies it to me, whether he who does it, is a king or a common man; my countryman or not my countryman? whether it is done by an individual villain, or an army of them? If we reason to the root of things we shall find no difference; neither can any just cause be assigned why we should punish in the one case and pardon in the other. Let them call me rebel, and welcome, I feel no concern from it; but I should suffer the misery of devils, were I to make a whore of my soul by swearing allegiance to one whose character is that of a sottish, stupid, stubborn, worthless, brutish man. . . .

I thank GOD that I fear not. I see no real cause for fear. . . . By perseverance and fortitude we have the prospect of a glorious issue; by cowardice and submission, the sad choice of a variety of evils—a ravaged country—a depopulated city—habitations without safety, and slavery without hope—our homes turned into barracks and bawdy-houses for Hessians.

George Washington's Farewell Address to Americans, 1796

United States, September 19, 1796

Friends, and Fellow-Citizens: The period for a new election of a Citizen, to Administer the Executive government of the United States, being not far distant, and the time actually arrived, when your thoughts must be employed in designating the person, who is to be cloathed with that important trust, it appears to me proper, especially as it may conduce to a more distinct expression of the public voice, that I should now apprise you of the resolution I have formed, to decline being considered among the number of those, out of whom a choice is to be made. . . .

The acceptance of, and continuance hitherto in, the office to which your Suffrages have twice called me, have been a uniform sacrifice of inclination to the opinion of duty, and to a deference for what appeared to be your desire. I constantly hoped, that it would have been much earlier in my power, consistently with motives, which I was not at liberty to disregard, to return to that retirement, from which I had been reluctantly drawn. The strength of my inclination to do this, previous to the last Election, had even led to the preparation of an address to declare it to you; but mature reflection on the then perplexed and critical posture of our Affairs with foreign Nations, and the unanimous advice of persons entitled to my confidence, impelled me to abandon the idea.

I rejoice, that the state of your concerns, external as well as internal, no longer renders the pursuit of inclination incompatible with the sentiment of duty, or propriety; and am persuaded whatever partiality may be retained for my services, that in the present circumstances of our country, you will not disapprove my determination to retire.

The impressions, with which I first undertook the arduous trust, were explained on the proper occasion. In the discharge of this trust, I will only say, that I have, with good intentions, contributed towards the Organization and Administration of the government, the best exertions of which a very fallible judgment was capable. Not unconscious, in the outset, of the inferiority of my qualifications, experience in my own eyes, perhaps still more in the eyes of others, has strengthned the motives to diffidence of myself; and every day the encreasing weight of years admonishes me more and more, that the shade of retirement is as necessary to me as it will be welcome. Satisfied that if any circumstances have given peculiar value to my services, they were temporary, I have the consolation to believe, that while choice and prudence invite me to quit the political scene, patriotism does not forbid it.

In looking forward to the moment, which is intended to terminate the career of my public life, my feelings do not permit me to suspend the deep acknowledgment of that debt of gratitude wch. I owe to my beloved country, for the many honors it has conferred upon me; still more for the stedfast confidence with which it has supported me; and for the opportunities I have thence enjoyed of manifesting my inviolable attachment, by services faithful and persevering, though in usefulness unequal to my zeal. If benefits have resulted to our country from these services, let it always be remembered to your praise, and as an instructive example in our annals, that . . . the constancy of your support was the essential prop of the efforts, and a guarantee of the plans by which they were effected. Profoundly penetrated with this idea, I shall carry it with me to my grave, as a strong incitement to unceasing vows that Heaven may continue to you the choicest tokens of its beneficence; that your Union and brotherly affection may be perpetual; that the free constitution, which is the work of your hands, may be sacredly maintained; that its Administration in every department may be stamped with wisdom and Virtue; that, in fine, the happiness of the people of these States, under the auspices of liberty, may be made complete. . . .

Here, perhaps, I ought to stop. But a solicitude for your welfare, which cannot end but with my life, and the apprehension of danger, natural to that solicitude, urge me on an occasion like the present, to offer to your solemn contemplation, and to recommend to your frequent review, some sentiments; which are the result of much reflection, of no inconsiderable observation, and which appear to me all important to the permanency of your felicity as a People. . . .

The Unity of Government which constitutes you one people is also now dear to you. It is justly so; for it is a main Pillar in the Edifice of your real independence, the support of your tranquility at home; your peace abroad; of your safety; of your prosperity; of that very Liberty which you so highly prize. But as it is easy to foresee, that from different causes and from different quarters, much pains will be taken, many artifices employed, to weaken in your minds the conviction of this truth; as this is the point in your political fortress against which the batteries of internal and external enemies will be most constantly and actively (though often covertly and insidiously) directed, it is of infinite moment, that you should properly estimate the immense value of your national Union to your collective and individual happiness; that you should cherish a cordial, habitual and immoveable attachment to it; accustoming yourselves to think and speak of it as of the Palladium [protection] of your political safety and prosperity; watching for its preservation with jealous anxiety; discountenancing whatever may suggest even a suspicion that it can in any event be abandoned, and indignantly frowning upon the first dawning of every attempt to alienate any portion of our Country from the rest, or to enfeeble the sacred ties which now link together the various parts.

For this you have every inducement of sympathy and interest. Citizens by birth or choice, of a common country, that country has a right to concentrate your affections. The name of AMERICAN, which belongs to you, in your national capacity, must always exalt the just pride of Patriotism, more than any appellation derived from local discriminations. With slight shades of difference, you have the same Religeon, Manners, Habits and political Principles. You have in a common cause fought and triumphed together. The independence and liberty you possess are the work of joint councils, and joint efforts; of common dangers, sufferings and successes.

But these considerations, however powerfully they address themselves to your sensibility are greatly outweighed by those which apply more immediately to your Interest. Here every portion of our country finds the most commanding motives for carefully guarding and preserving the Union of the whole.

The North, in an unrestrained intercourse with the South, protected by the equal Laws of a common government, finds in the productions of the latter, great additional resources of Maritime and commercial enterprise and precious materials of manufacturing industry. The South in the same Intercourse, benefitting by the Agency of the North, sees its agriculture grow and its commerce expand. Turning partly into its own channels the seamen of the North, it finds its particular navigation envigorated; and while it contributes, in different ways, to nourish and increase the general mass of the National navigation, it looks forward to the protection of a Maritime strength, to which itself is unequally adapted. The East, in a like intercourse with the West, already finds, and in the progressive improvement of interior communications, by land and water, will more and more find a valuable vent for the commodities which it brings from abroad, or manufactures at home. The West derives from the East supplies requisite to its growth and comfort, and what is perhaps of still greater consequence, it must of necessity owe the secure enjoyment of indispensable outlets for its own productions to the weight, influence, and the future Maritime strength of the Atlantic side of the Union, directed by an indissoluble community of Interest as one Nation. Any other tenure by which the West can hold this essential advantage, whether derived from its own seperate strength, or from an apostate and unnatural connection with any foreign Power, must be intrinsically precarious.

While then every part of our country thus feels an immediate and particular Interest in Union, all the parts combined cannot fail to find in the united mass of means and efforts greater strength, greater resource, proportionably greater security from external danger, a less frequent interruption of their Peace by foreign Nations; and, what is of inestimable value! they must derive from Union an exemption from those broils and Wars between themselves, which so frequently afflict neighbouring countries, not tied together by the same government; which their own rivalships alone would be sufficient to produce, but which opposite foreign alliances, attachments and intriegues would stimulate and imbitter. Hence likewise they will avoid the necessity of those overgrown Military establishments, which under any form of Government are inauspicious to liberty, and which are to be regarded as particularly hostile to Republican Liberty: In this sense it is, that your Union ought to be considered as a main prop of your liberty, and that the love of the one ought to endear to you the preservation of the other.

These considerations speak a persuasive language to every reflecting and virtuous mind, and exhibit the continuance of the Union as a primary object of Patriotic desire. Is there a doubt, whether a common government can embrace so large a sphere? Let experience solve it. To listen to mere speculation in such a case were criminal. We are authorized to hope that a proper organization of the whole, with the auxiliary agency of governments for the respective Sub divisions, will afford a happy issue to the experiment. 'Tis well worth a fair and full experiment With such powerful and obvious motives to Union, affecting all parts of our country, while experience shall not have demonstrated its impracticability, there will always be reason, to distrust the patriotism of those, who in any quarter may endeavor to weaken its bands.

In contemplating the causes wch. may disturb our Union, it occurs as matter of serious concern, that any ground should have been furnished for characterizing parties by Geographical discriminations: Northern and Southern; Atlantic and Western; whence designing men may endeavour to excite a belief that there is a real difference of local interests and views. One of the expedients of Party to acquire influence, within particular districts, is to misrepresent the opinions and aims of other Districts. You cannot shield yourselves too much against the jealousies and heart burnings which spring from these misrepresentations. They tend to render Alien to each other those who ought to be bound together by fraternal affection. . . .

To the efficacy and permanency of Your Union, a Government for the whole is indispensable. . . . Sensible of this momentous truth, you have improved upon your first essay, by the adoption of a Constitution of Government, better calculated than your former for an intimate Union, and for the efficacious management of your common concerns. This government, the offspring of our own choice uninfluenced and unawed, adopted upon full investigation and mature deliberation, completely free in its principles, in the distribution of its powers, uniting security with energy, and containing within itself a provision for its own amendment, has a just claim to your confidence and your support. Respect for its authority, compliance with its Laws, acquiescence in its measures, are duties enjoined by the fundamental maxims of true Liberty. The basis of our political systems is the right of the people to make and to alter their Constitutions of Government. But the Constitution which at any time exists, 'till changed by an explicit and authentic act of the whole People, is sacredly obligatory upon all. The very idea of the power and the right of the People to establish Government presupposes the duty of every Individual to obey the established Government.

All obstructions to the execution of the Laws, all combinations and Associations, under whatever plausible character, with the real design to direct, controul counteract, or awe the regular deliberation and action of the Constituted authorities are distructive of this fundamental principle and of fatal tendency. They serve to organize faction, to give it an artificial and extraordinary force; to put in the place of the delegated will of the Nation, the will of a party; often a small but artful and enterprizing minority of the Community; and, according to the alternate triumphs of different parties, to make the public administration the Mirror of the ill concerted and incongruous projects of faction, rather than the organ of consistent and wholesome plans digested by common councils and modefied by mutual interests. However combinations or Associations of the above description may now and then answer popular ends, they are likely, in the course of time and things, to become potent engines, by which cunning, ambitious and unprincipled men will be enabled to subvert the Power of the People, and to usurp for themselves the reins of Government; destroying afterwards the very engines which have lifted them to unjust dominion.

Towards the preservation of your Government and the permanency of your present happy state, it is requisite, not only that you steadily discountenance irregular oppositions to its acknowledged authority, but also that you resist with care the spirit of innovation upon its principles however specious the pretexts. . . .

I have already intimated to you the danger of Parties in the State, with particular reference to the founding of them on Geographical discriminations. Let me now take a more comprehensive view, and warn you in the most solemn manner against the baneful effects of the Spirit of Party, generally

This spirit, unfortunately, is inseperable from our nature, having its root in the strongest passions of the human Mind. It exists under different shapes in all Governments, more or less stifled, controuled, or repressed; but, in those of the popular form it is seen in its greatest rankness and is truly their worst enemy.

The alternate domination of one faction over another, sharpened by the spirit of revenge natural to party dissention, which in different ages and countries has perpetrated the most horrid enormities, is itself a frightful despotism. But this leads at length to a more formal and permanent despotism. The disorders and miseries, which result, gradually incline the minds of men to seek security and repose in the absolute power of an Individual: and sooner or later the chief of some prevailing faction more able or more fortunate than his competitors, turns this disposition to the purposes of his own elevation, on the ruins of Public Liberty.

Without looking forward to an extremity of this kind (which nevertheless ought not to be entirely out of sight) the common and continual mischiefs of the spirit of Party are sufficient to make it the interest and the duty of a wise People to discourage and restrain it.

It serves always to distract the Public Councils and enfeeble the Public administration. It agitates the Community with ill founded jealousies and false alarms, kindles the animosity of one part against another, foments occasionally riot and insurrection. It opens the door to foreign influence and corruption, which find a facilitated access to the government itself through the channels of party passions. Thus the policy and . . . the will of one country, are subjected to the policy and will of another. . . .

It is important, likewise, that the habits of thinking in a free Country should inspire caution in those entrusted with its administration, to confine themselves within their respective Constitutional spheres; avoiding in the exercise of the Powers of one department to encroach upon another. The spirit of encroachment tends to consolidate the powers of all the departments in one, and thus to create whatever the form of government, a real despotism. A just estimate of that love of power, and proneness to abuse it, which predominates in the human heart is sufficient to satisfy us of the truth of this position. The necessity of reciprocal checks in the exercise of political power; by dividing and distributing it into different depositories, and constituting each the Guardian of the Public Weal against invasions by the others, has been evinced by experiments ancient and modern; some of them in our country and under our own eyes. To preserve them must be as necessary as to institute them. If in the opinion of the People, the distribution or modification of the Constitutional powers be in any particular wrong, let it be corrected by an amendment in the way which the Constitution designates. But let there be no change by usurpation; for though this, in one instance, may be the instrument of good, it is the customary weapon by which free governments are destroyed. The precedent must always greatly overbalance in permanent evil any partial or transient benefit which the use can at any time yield.

Of all the dispositions and habits which lead to political prosperity, Religion and morality are indispensable supports. . . . Reason and experience both forbid us to expect that National morality can prevail in exclusion of religious principle.

'Tis substantially true, that virtue or morality is a necessary spring of popular government. The rule indeed extends with more or less force to every species of free Government. Who that is a sincere friend to it, can look with indifference upon attempts to shake the foundation of the fabric

Promote then as an object of primary importance, Institutions for the general diffusion of knowledge. In proportion as the structure of a government gives force to public opinion, it is essential that public opinion should be enlightened.

As a very important source of strength and security, cherish public credit. One method of preserving it is to use it as sparingly as possible: avoiding occasions of expence by cultivating peace, but remembering also that timely disbursements to prepare for danger frequently prevent much greater disbursements to repel it; avoiding likewise the accumulation of debt, not only by shunning occasions of expence, but by vigorous exertions in time of Peace to discharge the Debts which unavoidable wars may have occasioned, not ungenerously throwing upon posterity the burthen which we ourselves ought to bear. The execution of these maxims belongs to your Representatives, but it is necessary that public opinion should cooperate. To facilitate to them the performance of their duty, it is essential that you should practically bear in mind, that towards the payment of debts there must be Revenue; that to have Revenue there must be taxes; that no taxes can be devised which are not more or less inconvenient and unpleasant. . . .

Observe good faith and justice towds. all Nations. Cultivate peace and harmony with all. Religion and morality enjoin this conduct; and can it be that good policy does not equally enjoin it? It will be worthy of a free, enlightened, and, at no distant period, a great Nation, to give to mankind the magnanimous and too novel example of a People always guided by an exalted justice and benevolence. Who can doubt that in the course of time and things the fruits of such a plan would richly repay any temporary advantages wch. might be lost by a steady adherence to it? Can it be, that Providence has not connected the permanent felicity of a Nation with its virtue? . . .

In the execution of such a plan nothing is more essential than that permanent, inveterate antipathies against particular Nations and passionate attachments for others should be excluded; and that in place of them just and amicable feelings towards all should be cultivated. The Nation, which indulges towards another an habitual hatred, or an habitual fondness, is in some degree a slave. It is a slave to its animosity or to its affection, either of which is sufficient to lead it astray from its duty and its interest. . . . The peace often, sometimes perhaps the Liberty, of Nations has been the victim. . . .

Against the insidious wiles of foreign influence, (I conjure you to believe me fellow citizens) the jealousy of a free people ought to be constantly awake; since history and experience prove that foreign influence is one of the most baneful foes of Republican Government. But that jealousy to be useful must be impartial; else it becomes the instrument of the very influence to be avoided, instead of a defence against it. Excessive partiality for one foreign nation and excessive dislike of another, cause those whom they actuate to see danger only on one side, and serve to veil and even second the arts of influence on the other. . . .

The Great rule of conduct for us, in regard to foreign Nations is in extending our commercial relations to have with them as little political connection as possible. So far as we have already formed engagements let them be fulfilled, with perfect good faith. Here let us stop.

Europe has a set of primary interests, which to us have none, or a very remote relation. Hence she must be engaged in frequent controversies, the causes of which are essentially foreign to our concerns. Hence therefore it must be unwise in us to implicate ourselves, by artificial ties, in the ordinary vicissitudes of her politics, or the ordinary combinations and collisions of her friendships, or enmities:

Our detached and distant situation invites and enables us to pursue a different course. If we remain one People, under an efficient government, the period is not far off, when we may defy material injury from external annoyance; when we may take such an attitude as will cause the neutrality we may at any time resolve upon to be scrupulously respected; when belligerent nations, under the impossibility of making acquisitions upon us, will not lightly hazard the giving us provocation; when we may choose peace or war, as our interest guided by our justice shall Counsel.

Why forego the advantages of so peculiar a situation? Why quit our own to stand upon foreign ground? Why, by interweaving our destiny with that of any part of Europe, entangle our peace and prosperity in the toils of European Ambition, Rivalship, Interest, Humour or Caprice?

'Tis our true policy to steer clear of permanent Alliances, with any portion of the foreign world. So far, I mean, as we are now at liberty to do it, for let me not be understood as capable of patronising infidility to existing engagements (I hold the maxim no less applicable to public than to private affairs, that honesty is always the best policy). . . .

Taking care always to keep ourselves, by suitable establishments, on a respectably defensive posture, we may safely trust to temporary alliances for extraordinary emergencies.

Harmony, liberal intercourse with all Nations, are recommended by policy, humanity and interest. But even our Commercial policy should hold an equal and impartial hand: neither seeking nor granting exclusive favours or preferences; consulting the natural course of things; diffusing and deversifying by gentle means the streams of Commerce, but forcing nothing; establishing with Powers so disposed; in order to give to trade a stable course, to define the rights of our Merchants, and to enable the Government to support them; conventional rules of intercourse, the best that present circumstances and mutual opinion will permit, but temporary, and liable to be from time to time abandoned or varied, as experience and circumstances shall dictate; constantly keeping in view, that 'tis folly in one Nation to look for disinterested favors from another; that it must pay with a portion of its Independence for whatever it may accept under that character; that by such acceptance, it may place itself in the condition of having given equivalents for nominal favours and yet of being reproached with ingratitude for not giving more. There can be no greater error than to expect, or calculate upon real favours from Nation to Nation. 'Tis an illusion which experience must cure, which a just pride ought to discard. . . .

How far in the discharge of my Official duties, I have been guided by the principles which have been delineated, the public Records and other evidences of my conduct must Witness to You and to the world. To myself, the assurance of my own conscience is, that I have at least believed myself to be guided by them. . . .

Though in reviewing the incidents of my Administration, I am unconscious of intentional error, I am nevertheless too sensible of my defects not to think it probable that I may have committed many errors. Whatever they may be I fervently beseech the Almighty to avert or mitigate the evils to which they may tend. I shall also carry with me the hope that my Country will never cease to view them with indulgence; and that after forty five years of my life dedicated to its Service, with an upright zeal, the faults of incompetent abilities will be consigned to oblivion, as myself must soon be to the Mansions of rest.

Relying on its kindness in this as in other things, and actuated by that fervent love towards it, which is so natural to a Man, who views in it the native soil of himself and his progenitors for several Generations; I anticipate with pleasing expectation that retreat, in which I promise myself to realize, without alloy, the sweet enjoyment of partaking, in the midst of my fellow Citizens, the benign influence of good Laws under a free Government, the ever favourite object of my heart, and the happy reward, as I trust, of our mutual cares, labours and dangers.

✳ E S S A Y S

The first essay, by Linda Grant De Pauw, professor of history at George Washington University, analyzes how leadership operated so as to arouse and mobilize ordinary people for political action. The second essay takes up the related subject of how men actually came to enlist and to fight in the war. The author, Robert L. Middlekauff, is professor of history at the University of California at Berkeley and a Korean War veteran of the United States Marine Corps. The third selection, on George Washington, was written by Edmund S. Morgan, Sterling Professor of History Emeritus at Yale University. Morgan seeks to explain the particular attributes Washington possessed that elevated him to his remarkable stature as a leader. The final essay, by the editor of this volume, Richard D. Brown, professor of history at the University of Connecticut, tackles the question of political leadership in the early republic in comparison to present-day American politics.

Politicizing the Politically Inert

LINDA GRANT DE PAUW

Before the battles of Lexington and Concord and for many months—perhaps even for several years afterward—the great majority of the people in British North America did not want war and did not want independence. They did

---

"Politicizing the Politically Inert: The Problem of Leadership in the American Revolution" by Linda Grant De Pauw, from *The American Revolution: Changing Perspectives* edited by William M. Fowler, and Wallace Coyle. Copyright © 1979 by Northeastern University. Reprinted with the permission of Northeastern University Press.

not understand and were not interested in the abstract issues of constitutional law that transformed the sale of cut-rate East India Company tea into a sign of impending tyranny. Nor were they willing to put themselves in danger when the city of Boston got itself into trouble with the English authorities because, for some abstruse reason, a group of political activists decided to dump a load of that tea into the harbor. Like the majority of people in all ages, they found that the personal problems they faced in their daily lives absorbed all of their attention. . . . If they had an opinion on the crisis spreading in New England, it was that they did not want to get involved.

Histories of the American Revolution have never given a clear picture of this large "apathetic majority." . . . During the war they did everything they could to avoid taking sides, believing, to use historian John Shy's words, "that there was nothing at stake that could justify involving themselves and their families in extreme hazard and suffering." Before the war was over, hundreds of thousands of these people had taken a stand in spite of themselves, and after the war they lived as loyal citizens of the United States. Neither they nor their descendants wished to remember the earlier days of political ambivalence, and scholars have concentrated their attention on more interesting minority groups—the prominent leaders, the active Loyalists, the very poor, and the highly articulate. The politically inert, who had been a majority of the population in 1775, disappeared from history.

Because of their great numbers, however, the politically inert were essential to the success of the Revolution, much as they may have wished to remain silent spectators. It is therefore important to ask how they were persuaded to shake off their apathy and become supporters of the Patriot cause. An old-fashioned view of the nature of leadership suggests that the ideas and programs of leading Patriots like Thomas Jefferson and John Adams eventually penetrated to the inert. In fact, the connection between leaders and followers in the Revolution was much less direct and subject to interruptions and even reversals. . . .

In my discussion of the problem of politicizing the inert at the time of the Revolution, I propose to start with a paradigm of public opinion formation developed by the pollster and social science researcher Elmo Roper. He asks us to visualize the population in any age as divided into six concentric circles. The smallest circle contains Great Thinkers. These are the great creative intellects of an age. According to Roper "there probably aren't more than a half a dozen of these in the world at any one time, and usually the perspective of history years later is necessary to give them full recognition and evaluation." As examples of Great Thinkers, Roper cites Adam Smith, Karl Marx, Plato, and Albert Einstein. The second circle contains a group that Roper calls Great Disciples. "They are the people," Roper says, "who do not think out great theories or philosophies, but they have a sufficient understanding and a close enough mental association with those who do to become most effective advocates and protagonists for an idea or philosophy." Great Disciples share "a great power of expression and a forum from which the ideas can be expressed." St. Paul, Spinoza, and Thomas Huxley are examples in this category. The third of Roper's circles contains Great Disseminators. Great Disseminators are those who "have an important forum . . . and . . . are respected and listened to by a number of people." This is a fairly large group because it includes all those who "reach large numbers of people who regularly listen to them—and, to some degree, are impressed with them." Today, members of the United States Congress, national labor leaders, and syndicated columnists would all fall into this category.

The fourth circle contains Lesser Disseminators. These people are also respected as authorities but have a more limited forum. The president of a local union or a local news commentator would be considered a Lesser Disseminator. The occupants of the fifth circle, who are called Participating Citizens, Roper describes thus: "They vote with some regularity, contribute money or work in local and national campaigns, belong to organizations active in civic or public affairs, write letters to Congressmen and public officials, are active in discussions on current affairs and problems. They are members of a multitude of organizations that dot the American scene." The Participating Citizens, according to Roper, are an extremely influential group because each probably has fifty or a hundred neighbors who respect the Participating Citizen as an authority on public affairs and trust him more than they do any Great or Lesser Disseminator. These neighbors are the Politically Inert, the people in the sixth circle, which is the largest of all. "These are people," Roper writes, "who are not very much at home in the world of ideas, at least when ideas are presented to them in raw or undiluted form. They seldom are active in their communities, and they rarely speak out on any subject. They are not vocal about what they believe in. But they are extremely important. For they come to easily the largest number of people in the country . . . and if they are aroused . . . they can determine in a basic sense the political and economic and sociological outlook for some time to come." In other words, they can make a revolution.

Roper advances a hypothesis concerning the method by which ideas pass to the inert, which I propose to apply to the Revolutionary era. Although there is "sometimes a hurdling of one or more groups entirely," Roper suggests that "the Politically Inert come to accept ideas more readily from their Participating Citizen neighbors and that, in turn, the Participating Citizen neighbors are more apt to accept ideas from the Lesser Disseminators, who in turn are swayed by the Greater Disseminators and the Great Disciples." How does this paradigm of six concentric circles look when it is moved to America on the eve of the Revolution?

It seems to me that no one person—certainly no American—occupies the circle reserved for Great Thinkers. The political ideas that stand at the heart of the American Revolution were developed in England during an extraordinarily creative era in the seventeenth century. The great names include Milton, Harrington, Algernon Sidney, and John Locke. . . . The greatest of the Great Disciples were Trenchard and Gordon, the authors of *Cato's Letters*. . . . Their work was not original and it was not long remembered. Nevertheless, as Bernard Bailyn has said, "more than any other single group of writers they shaped the mind of the American Revolutionary generation."

Although there were no American Great Thinkers, there were a few Great Disciples. John Dickinson, Benjamin Franklin, and Thomas Jefferson certainly combined an understanding of the great theories with "great power of expression and a forum from which the ideas [could] be expressed." These men all clearly influenced America's Great Disseminators. A fourth man, however, Thomas Paine, was a Great Disciple of a different kind. He is of special interest because he succeeded in "hurdling," as Roper puts it, and registering direct impact on the Politically Inert. . . .

On the eve of the Revolution the status of Great Disseminator was a function of social class. Those who were "respected and listened to" by large numbers of people and who came to occupy positions that gave them an "important forum" were the people the eighteenth century described as "the better sort" or "the natural aristocrats." . . . Thus, in pre-Revolutionary America the so-called habit of deference led the population as a whole to look to their betters for leadership as a matter of course. Not only royal governors and councilmen came from this socially elite class; members of the popular legislatures, delegates to the Continental Congress, high ranking officers of the Continental army, and the organizers of the first committees of correspondence were all of "the better sort."

Samuel Adams is an interesting specimen of the Great Disseminator class because he, like Tom Paine, demonstrated an ability to "hurdle." He had the predictable influence on Lesser Disseminators but also managed to exert direct influence on Politically Active Citizens. It is often forgotten that Samuel Adams was a man of high social position in Boston. . . . Adams founded the Boston Committee of Correspondence, which became the pattern for similar committees in other parts of the country as well as in the smaller towns outside Boston. The members of the Boston Committee were all men of property with the leisure necessary to indulge their political interests. The committees of correspondence became the instrument through which the Great Disseminators communicated with local Lesser Disseminators. But Samuel Adams did more than serve in conventional Great Disseminator roles. Although he did organize the Boston Committee of Correspondence and filled positions of leadership in the Boston Town Meeting, colonial legislature, and Continental Congress, he also filled positions more appropriate for a Lesser Disseminator. Mercy Otis Warren described Samuel Adams as "social with men of all denominations." He organized a singing society for Boston mechanics, and he organized public celebrations at which middle class citizens were entertained by mimic shows and performances of "Liberty Songs." . . .

During the years 1765 to 1783, the Revolutionary crisis created a need for effective leadership that permitted men of a class below that from which Great Disseminators were usually drawn to move into positions of high influence. John Adams is typical of men of talent who, encouraged by Great Disseminators, managed to rise into positions of prominence. A study done by Jackson Turner Main in 1966 traces the enlargement of the class of Great Disseminators during the war. His detailed examination of the membership of the legislatures in six states showed that while only about 20 percent of men elected to the legislatures before the war had been artisans or yeomen (most had been merchants or lawyers), men with such simple backgrounds more than doubled their strength after independence. In the northern states, they actually came to hold a majority of the seats. An examination of property holdings of the legislators revealed that the men elected to the Southern legislatures after the Revolution owned only about half as much property as the men elected before the war.

Even more conspicuous than the increase in size of the class of Great Disseminators during the Revolution was the expansion of the class of Lesser Disseminators. Lesser Disseminators, remember, are the leaders of the various local groups of which Politically Active Citizens become members. These groups proliferated in the Revolutionary years. Officers and members of the first sons of liberty groups were generally middle-class property owners. But as the number of local leaders grew, social qualifications for leadership at this level became less essential. In 1774 the Continental Congress created the Continental Association to prevent both consumption and importation of British goods and to prevent all exportation to Great Britain. The enforcement of the Association was in the hands of provincial and local committees, all of which necessarily had Lesser Disseminators as leaders. . . . At the same time local "militia" units—often no more than bands of irregulars—began to organize, and the officer of every militia or home guard patrol was a Lesser Disseminator. . . .

Lesser Disseminators are not the stuff of which history is made. It is much easier to study and describe the activities of a small number of presumably "important" individuals than to deal with the complexity of a situation in which the activities of hundreds of undistinguished local leaders had greater influence. A private soldier, present at the Battle of Mud Island in 1777, later reminisced about this fact of life. "I was at the siege and capture of Lord Cornwallis," he wrote, "and the hardships of that were no more to be compared with [those at Mud Island] than the sting of a bee is to the bite of a rattlesnake. But there has been but little notice taken of it, the reason of which is, there was no Washington, Putnam, or Wayne there. Had there been, the affair would have been extolled to the skies. No, it was only a few officers and soldiers who accomplished it in a remote quarter of the army. Such circumstances and such troops generally get but little notice taken of them, do what they will. Great men get great praise; little men, nothing. But it always was so and always will be." . . .

The most promising techniques for studying the Lesser Disseminators are those developed by prosopographers such as Jack Greene and Jackson Turner Main. Using such sources as tax lists, estate inventories, probate records, local histories, and genealogies, for instance, Main was able to trace the increasing democratization of leadership ranks during the Revolution. Recently, a few Lesser Disseminators [such as Alexander McDougall], whom book reviewers often call "secondary leaders," have become subjects of full-length scholarly biographies. Although we cannot be certain that any one of these men was typical, their histories provide a perspective on the Revolution that is lost in biographies of famous Great Disseminators. . . .

Before leaving the circle of Lesser Disseminators, it is worth remembering that most of them were not city men. The needs and attitudes of small farmers, who composed the vast majority of the American population, were not identical with those of city artisans, merchant seamen, and shopkeepers. Nor, as Richard D. Brown has demonstrated, were rural areas content to follow the lead of the cities. We must not be misled into assuming that urban leaders were more important to the Revolution simply because we know more about them. The Samuel Adamses and the Alexander McDougalls of the countryside are often known only as signatures on a petition or names on a muster roll. But for their neighbors they spoke with an authority that could not be equaled by an outsider.

At the beginning of the Revolutionary crisis, the category of Politically Active Citizen was limited to free adult white men, who owned at least some property. The remaining 85 percent of the population was of necessity apolitical. The women, children, servants, slaves, and apprentices who were dependent on male property owners could not vote, hold office or benefit in any direct way from the actions of government. They were unlikely to develop any interest in politics except for strictly local issues, and if they had any opinions contrary to those held by the head of the family it was not to their interest to express them openly. Furthermore, even among the men qualified to become politically active, most preferred to leave politics to "the better sort" and did not participate in the political life of their communities.

The mark of a Politically Active Citizen, as Roper defines the term, is membership in organizations. Those men who first became active in the Revolutionary movement as sons of liberty are distinguished by their social respectability and their tendency to be members of civic groups. The membership of the Charleston Sons of Liberty was described thus: "All that are known were . . . reputably engaged in their maintenance—all in easy circumstances, none rich. At least half of them master mechanics, the very bone and muscle of a thriving community." The Charleston Sons already belonged to so many organizations—including Christopher Gadsden's Artillery Company and the Fellowship Society—that they found it unnecessary to form a new organization to resist the Stamp Act. They carried out their political actions under the title "the Charleston Fire Company"—another group of which they were also already members. In Boston a social club known as the Loyal Nine directed the original actions against the Stamp Act. An analysis of the Boston Committee of Correspondence reveals that "At least eight of the twenty-one members also belonged to the North End Caucus, a private political club which met regularly to discuss and to influence Boston affairs. Members also participated in several Boston congregations, in both of Boston's Masonic lodges, the fire companies of several wards, as well as a variety of private clubs." Elsewhere in the country, civic, religious, or social organizations already in existence enabled Politically Active Citizens to take part in anti-British politics under the leadership of Lesser Disseminators with whom they were already familiar and who had earned their respect and confidence.

The democratizing influence that enabled men like John Adams to become Great Disseminators also acted to expand the category of Politically Active Citizens in the Revolutionary era. Not only did adult white men with some property leave the ranks of the Politically Inert to become active in local committees of safety and militia units, but substantial numbers of slaves and servants ran away from their masters to become politically active as soldiers. Boys who were underage found their personal independence during the war by leaving the farm, sometimes against a father's will, to become part of the American army. Women organized as daughters of liberty to make saltpeter and stockings and to undertake intimidation of Loyalist women through mob actions or committees. Finally, men of "the meaner sort," both in the cities and in the countryside, who usually became active only in support of narrow local or personal interests, began to identify their activities with larger political issues.

Why did these people decide to become involved in the American Revolutionary movement? Roper's hypothesis would suggest that they were aroused by the Patriot ideology as presented to them by Politically Active Citizens in their neighborhoods—members of local committees of safety, militiamen, or members of organizations affiliated with the sons of liberty. Insofar as it can be tested, this hypothesis appears to be sound. It explains the dynamics by which the abstractions of constitutional theorists became a motivating force in the lives of hundreds of thousands of people who ordinarily were indifferent to politics. The key lies in the transformation that the ideas of the Great Thinkers underwent as they passed outward from circle to circle before they were transmitted to the Politically Inert. . . .

Consider, for example, the politicization of the people who ordinarily made up urban mobs of "the meaner sort." They did not necessarily follow the lead of the sons of liberty even when they were clearly anti-British in orientation. Furthermore, they occasionally used methods that the Whig ideology taught were both morally wrong and politically counterproductive. I refer here to such assemblages as that involved in the Golden Hill rioting in New York City in January 1770 and that which provoked the Boston Massacre in March of the same year. These were not "respectable" people of the sort who participated in the demonstrations organized by the sons of liberty or who belonged to formal groups of any sort. They threw up their own leadership, typified by the mulatto Crispus Attucks, and organized—when they did organize—only on the spur of the moment. They, like the sons of liberty, were angered by the presence of an occupying army, but their anger was not derived from an abstract hatred of standing armies. They were angry because soldiers competed for jobs and flirted with local girls. They traded verbal insults and got into fist fights with the off-duty Irish bloody-backs. Although the Whig leaders could explain that such events, such spontaneous risings of "the meaner sort," were an inevitable consequence of the presence of a standing army, the people in the mobs had no need of such explanations to defend their actions. They had specific personal grievances against individual soldiers or groups of soldiers, and they simply got mad as hell.

The Whig ideology predicted that British actions would inevitably lead to attacks on American liberty and American lives. In some measure it was a self-fulfilling prophesy. But most Americans were not drawn into active opposition to Britain by mere predictions, no matter how logically reasoned or how ominous. The Politically Inert were drawn into active support of the Revolution only when the threats to their own lives and liberty were so obvious that there was really no need to draw on ideology of any sort to explain their response. Although these people ultimately embraced as much of the Patriot ideology as they could understand under the tutelage of the sons of liberty and other Politically Active Citizens, the ideology did not provoke their involvement. Rather, the ideology served to justify behavior that would have occurred anyway.

All Americans who fought against Great Britain, and none more so than the formerly inert, believed they fought in self defense. In such cities as New York and Boston, the Politically Inert became politicized even before the battles of Lexington and Concord because of their direct contact with foreign soldiers. For most Americans, however, it was only after April 1775, after there was outright war between Americans and British soldiers, that a real threat to their own lives and liberty became apparent. Then, as British troops began to move against other parts of the country in the following months, large numbers of the Politically Inert were politicized. . . .

It was Tom Paine's understanding of the way events such as these were likely to impress the Politically Inert in all parts of America that made his pamphlet, *Common Sense,* so influential. He expressed their resentment at being forced into a war they did not want and their anger and grief in facing what they considered totally unprovoked attacks. The Politically Inert, after all, had done nothing to injure Great Britain. They were not members of the sons of liberty. Many lived on farms where they were so nearly self-sufficient as to be unconcerned in the economic boycott. Until the summer of 1775 the common people of Virginia apparently believed that the problems with Great Britain only concerned those who could afford to drink tea. But after Lexington and Concord the Politically Inert were made to suffer nonetheless. Paine understood their point of view because he shared it. Unlike other Great Disciples of the Whig ideology, Paine had been indifferent to politics until the exchange of gunfire in April 1775 had shocked him into an appreciation of the threat to American lives as well as freedoms. Before the battle of Lexington, Paine said, "I viewed the dispute as a kind of law-suit, in which I supposed the parties would find a way either to decide or settle it." He had not been a political activist before that time either in his native England or in the America to which he had only recently immigrated. In *Common Sense* he recounted his conversion to activism in passionate language: "No man was a warmer wisher for reconciliation than myself, before the fatal nineteenth of April 1775, but the moment the event of that day was made known, I rejected the hardened, sullen-tempered Pharaoh of England for ever; and disdain the wretch, that with the pretended title of FATHER OF HIS PEOPLE can unfeelingly hear of their slaughter, and composedly sleep with their blood upon his soul."

By the time *Common Sense* was published, on January 9, 1776, there had been sufficient provocation of Politically Inert Americans outside New England to make the threat to life and property credible in all parts of the country without need for any reference to ideological considerations. "Thousands are already ruined by British barbarity," Paine wrote; "(thousands more will probably suffer the same fate.) . . . I make the sufferer's case my own, and I protest, that were I driven from house and home, my property destroyed, and my circumstances ruined, that as man, sensible of injuries, I could never relish the doctrine of reconciliation, or consider myself bound thereby." Thousands of Americans read the pamphlet and accepted Paine's conclusion: the need to repudiate George III and declare independence. But the power of the pamphlet is emotional, not intellectual. Although the pamphlet contains some bits of political theory, most of it lifted entirely from pamphlets given to Paine by his Philadelphia patrons Franklin and Rush, *Common Sense* was successful in spite of, not because of, its theoretical sections. . . . Everyone could understand and relish Paine's arguments urging his readers to trust and follow their instinctive emotional responses to recent events:

> Ye tell us of harmony and reconciliation, can ye restore to us the time that is past? Can ye give to prostitution its former innocence? neither can ye reconcile Britain and America. The last cord now is broken. . . . There are some injuries which nature cannot forgive; she would cease to be nature if she did. As well can the lover forgive the ravisher of his mistress, as the Continent forgive the murders of Britain. . . .

No other pamphlet of the Revolutionary era had such a strong impact in America. *Common Sense* was distributed in great numbers in all parts of the country. . . . In Virginia, Edmund Randolph wrote, "the public sentiment which a few weeks before had shuddered at the tremendous obstacles, with which independence was environed, overleaped every barrier." In Philadelphia it was reported that the pamphlet was ". . . read to all ranks; and as many as read, so many become converted; though perhaps the hour before were most violent against the least idea of independence." Politically Active Citizens, reading to their neighbors in coffee houses and inns, had found a way to reach the Politically Inert. *Common Sense* was even translated into German for the use of that part of the Pennsylvania population that tended toward pacifism for religious reasons and did not understand English. It was said that it "works on the minds of those people amazingly." General Washington, encamped outside of Boston, understood that military events largely explained the impact of Paine's prose: "A few more such flaming arguments, as were exhibited at Falmouth and Norfolk," he wrote, "added to the sound doctrine and unanswerable reasoning contained in the pamphlet *Common Sense,* will not leave numbers at a loss to decide upon the propriety of a separation."

Not everyone who read *Common Sense* or had it read to him immediately became politically active. Paine's argument, after all, required that the reader accept as a threat to his own life and property the destruction of the lives and property of people he did not know personally. For a good many people, an attack on strangers was not a sufficiently immediate threat to cause them to abandon neutrality. But as months and years passed, the proportion of the population wholly untouched by war shrank. The armies of both sides, as well as irregular militia units of both Patriots and Loyalists, brought the threat of violence and property destruction right to the doors of hundreds of thousands of people who were forced, in spite of themselves, to choose sides. Paine, in his *Crisis* papers, continued to appeal to such people, encouraging them to give vent to their feelings. . . .

And so, as the years passed, the class of Politically Inert shrank. Not all of those politicized in the course of the war became Patriots. Many thousands responded to the actions of Patriot committeemen and bands of Patriot militia by embracing the Loyalist cause. But those who did so in hope of protecting their lives and property made the wrong decision. Tens of thousands of Americans who became identified with the Loyalists, even if only because they displayed deficient zeal on the Patriot side, were driven from their homes by their angry neighbors and left the country. Before 1775 perhaps a third of the politically active groups were Loyal. Some changed their minds after the fighting began, many others left the country, and those who remained lost most of their influence. By the end of the war the vast majority of the American people as well as the vast majority of the leadership classes accepted the justice of the Whig cause and the legitimacy of the government established by the committees of correspondence, sons of liberty, and other irregular groups. When the crisis was past, some of the formerly inert had become permanently politicized, but most returned to their formerly indifferent state. Still their participation in the Revolution, however reluctant, had produced a basic political change. America had renounced forever rule by a foreign power and the government of hereditary monarchs.

Why Men Fought in the American Revolution

ROBERT L. MIDDLEKAUFF

Although the statistics are notoriously unreliable, they show that the Revolution killed a higher percentage of those who served on the American side than any war in our history, always excepting the Civil War. Why did these men—those who survived and those who died—fight? Why did they hold their ground, endure the strain of battle, with men dying about them and danger to themselves so obvious? Undoubtedly the reasons varied from battle to battle, but just as undoubtedly there was some experience common to all these battles—and fairly uniform reasons for the actions of the men who fought despite their deepest impulses, which must have been to run from the field in order to escape the danger.

Some men did run, throwing down their muskets and packs in order to speed their flight. American units broke in large actions and small, at Brook-

---

"Why Men Fought in the American Revolution" by Robert L. Middlekauff, *Huntington Library Quarterly, 43,* (Spring 1980). Reprinted with permission of the Henry E. Huntington Library.

lyn, Kip's Bay, White Plains, Brandywine, Germantown, Camden, and Hobkirk's Hill, to cite the most important instances. Yet many men did not break and run even in the disasters to American arms. They held their ground until they were killed, and they fought tenaciously while pulling back.

In most actions the Continentals, the regulars, fought more bravely than the militia. We need to know why these men fought and why the American regulars performed better than the militia. The answers surely will help us to understand the Revolution, especially if we can discover whether what made men fight reflected what they believed—and felt—about the Revolution.

Several explanations of the willingness to fight and die, if necessary, may be dismissed at once. One is that soldiers on both sides fought out of fear of their officers, fearing them more than they did battle. . . . Spirit, bravery, a reliance on the bayonet were all expected of professional soldiers, but professionals acted out of pride—not fear of their officers.

Still, coercion and force were never absent from the life of either army. There were, however, limits on their use and their effectiveness. The fear of flogging might prevent a soldier from deserting from camp, but it could not guarantee that he would remain steady under fire. Fear of ridicule may have aided in keeping some troops in place, however. Eighteenth-century infantry went into combat in fairly close lines and officers could keep an eye on many of their men. If the formation was tight enough officers might strike laggards and even order "skulkers," Washington's term for those who turned tail, shot down. Just before the move to Dorchester Heights in March 1776, the word went out that any American who ran from the action would be "fired down upon the spot." The troops themselves approved of this threat, according to one of the chaplains. . . .

A tactic that surely would have appealed to many soldiers would have been to send them into battle drunk. Undoubtedly some—on both sides— did enter combat with their senses deadened by rum. Both armies commonly issued an additional ration of rum on the eve of some extraordinary action— a long, difficult march, for example, or a battle, were two of the usual reasons. . . . [But] in most actions soldiers went into battle with very little more than themselves and their comrades to lean upon.

Belief in the Holy Spirit surely sustained some in the American army, perhaps more than in the enemy's. There are a good many references to the divine or to Providence in the letters and diaries of ordinary soldiers. Often, however, these expressions are in the form of thanks to the Lord for permitting these soldiers to survive. There is little that suggests soldiers believed that faith rendered them invulnerable to the enemy's bullets. . . .

Others clearly saw more immediate advantages in the fight: the plunder of the enemy's dead. At Monmouth Court House, where Clinton withdrew after dark leaving the field strewn with British corpses, the plundering carried American soldiers into the houses of civilians who had fled to save themselves. The soldiers' actions were so blatant and so unrestrained that Washington ordered their packs searched. And at Eutaw Springs, the Americans virtually gave up victory to the opportunity of ransacking British tents. Some died in their greed, shot down by an enemy given time to regroup while his camp was torn apart by men looking for something to carry off. But even these men probably fought for something besides plunder. When it beckoned they collapsed, but it had not drawn them to the field; nor had it kept them there in a savage struggle.

Inspired leadership helped soldiers face death, but they sometimes fought bravely even when their leaders let them down. Yet officers' courage and the example of officers throwing off wounds to remain in the fight undoubtedly helped their men stick. . . . Cornwallis obviously filled Sergeant Lamb with pride, struggling forward to press into the struggle after his horse was killed. Washington's presence meant much at Princeton, though his exposure to enemy fire may also have made his troops uneasy. His quiet exhortation as he passed among the men who were about to assault Trenton—"Soldiers, keep by your officers"—remained in the mind of a Connecticut soldier until he died fifty years later. There was only one Washington, one Cornwallis, and their influence on men in battle, few of whom could have seen them, was of course slight. Junior and noncommissioned officers carried the burden of tactical direction; they had to show their troops what must be done and somehow persuade, cajole, or force them to do it. The praise ordinary soldiers lavished on sergeants and junior officers suggests that these leaders played important parts in their troops' willingness to fight. Still, important as it was, their part does not really explain why men fought. . . .

The eighteenth-century battlefield was, compared to that of the twentieth, an intimate theater, especially intimate in the engagements of the Revolution, which were usually small even by the standards of the day. The killing range of the musket—eighty to one hundred yards—enforced intimacy, as did the reliance on the bayonet and the general ineffectiveness of artillery. Soldiers had to come to close quarters to kill; this fact reduced the mystery of battle, though perhaps not its terrors. But at least the battlefield lost some of its impersonality. In fact, in contrast to twentieth-century combat, in which the enemy usually remains unseen and the source of incoming fire unknown, in eighteenth-century battles the foe could be seen and sometimes even touched. Seeing one's enemy may have aroused a singular intensity of feeling uncommon in modern battles. The assault with the bayonet—the most desired objective of infantry tactics—seems indeed to have evoked an emotional climax. Before it occurred, tension and anxiety built up as the troops marched from their column into a line of attack. The purpose of their movements was well understood by themselves and their enemies, who must have watched with feelings of dread and fascination. When the order came sending them forward, rage, even madness, replaced the attacker's anxiety, while terror and desperation sometimes filled those receiving the charge. Surely it is revealing that the Americans who ran from battle did so most often at the moment they understood that their enemy had started forward with the bayonet. This happened to several units at Brandywine and to the militia at Camden and Guilford Court House. The loneliness, the sense of isolation reported by modern soldiers, was probably missing at such moments. All was clear—especially that glittering line of advancing steel.

Whether this awful clarity was harder to bear than losing sight of the enemy is problematical. American troops ran at Germantown after grappling with the British and then finding the field of battle covered by fog. At that time groping blindly, they and their enemy struggled over ground resembling a scene of modern combat. The enemy was hidden at a critical moment, and American fears were generated by not knowing what was happening— or about to happen. They could not see the enemy, and they could not see one another, an especially important fact. For, as S. L. A. Marshall, the twentieth-century military historian, has suggested in his book *Men Against Fire,* what sustains men in the extraordinary circumstances of battle may be their relationships with their comrades.

These men found that sustaining such relationships was possible in the intimacy of the American battlefield—and not just because the limited arena robbed battle of some of its mystery. More importantly it permitted the troops to give one another moral or psychological support. The enemy could be seen, but so could one's comrades; they could be seen and communicated with.

Eighteenth-century infantry tactics called for men to move and fire from tight formations which permitted them to talk and to give one another information—and reassurance and comfort. If properly done, marching and firing found infantrymen compressed into files in which their shoulders touched. In battle physical contact with one's comrades on either side must have helped men control their fears. Firing the musket from three compact lines, the English practice, also involved physical contact. The men of the front rank crouched on their right knees; the men of the center rank placed their left feet inside the right feet of the front; the rear rank did the same thing behind the center. This stance was called—in a revealing term— "locking." . . . Men in these dense formations compiled a fine record of holding their ground. And it is worth noting that the inaccuracy of men in the rear rank bespoke their concern for their fellows in front of them.

British and American soldiers in the Revolution often spoke of fighting with "spirit" and "behaving well" under fire. Sometimes these phrases referred to daring exploits under great danger, but more often they seem to have meant holding together, giving one another support, reforming the lines when they were broken or fell into disorder. . . .

Troops in tight lines consciously reassured one another in several ways. British troops usually talked and cheered—"huzzaing" whether standing their ground, running forward, or firing. The Americans may have done less talking and cheering, though there is evidence that they learned to imitate the enemy. Giving a cheer at the end of a successful engagement was standard practice. The British cheered at Lexington and then marched off to be shot down on the road running from Concord. The Americans shouted their joy at Harlem Heights, an understandable action and one which for most of 1776 they rarely had opportunity to perform.

The most deplorable failures to stand and fight usually occurred among the American militia. Yet there were militia companies that performed with great success, remaining whole units under the most deadly volleys. The New England companies at Bunker Hill held out under a fire that veteran British officers compared to the worst they had experienced in Europe. Lord Rawdon remarked on how unusual it was for defenders to stick to their posts even after the assaulting troops had entered the ditch around a redoubt. The New Englanders did it. They also held steady at Princeton—"They were the first who regularly formed" and stood up under the balls "which whistled their thousand different notes around our heads," according to Charles Willson Peale, whose Philadelphia militia also proved their steadiness.

What was different about these companies? Why did they fight when others around them ran? The answer may lie in the relationships among their men. Men in the New England companies, in the Philadelphia militia, and in the other units that held together, were neighbors. They knew one another; they had something to prove to one another; they had their "honor" to protect. Their active service in the Revolution may have been short, but they had been together in one way or another for a fairly long time—for several years, in most cases. Their companies, after all, had been formed from towns and villages. Some clearly had known one another all their lives.

Elsewhere, especially in the thinly settled southern colonies, companies were usually composed of men—farmers, farmers' sons, farm laborers, artisans, and new immigrants—who did not know one another. They were, to use a term much used in a later war, companies of "stragglers" without common attachments, with almost no knowledge of their fellows. For them, even bunched tightly in line, the battlefield was an empty, lonely place. Absence of personal bonds and their own parochialism, coupled to inadequate training and imperfect discipline, often led to disintegration under fire.

According to conventional wisdom, the nearer the American militia were to home the better they fought, fighting for their homes and no one else's. Proximity to home, however, may have been a distraction which weakened resolve; for the irony of going into battle and perhaps to their deaths when home and safety lay close down the road could not have escaped many. Almost every senior American general commented on the propensity of the militia to desert—and if they were not deserting they seemed perpetually in transit between home and camp, usually without authorization.

Paradoxically, of all the Americans who fought, the militiamen best exemplified in themselves and in their behavior the ideals and purposes of the Revolution. They had enjoyed independence, or at least personal liberty, long before it was proclaimed in the Declaration. They instinctively felt their equality with others and in many places insisted upon demonstrating it by choosing their own officers. Their sense of their liberty permitted, even compelled, them to serve only for short enlistments, to leave camp when they liked, to scorn the orders of others—and especially those orders to fight when they preferred to flee. Their integration into their society drove them to resist military discipline; and their ethos of personal freedom stimulated hatred of the machine that served as the model for the army. They were not pieces of machine, and they would serve it only reluctantly and skeptically. At their best—at Cowpens, for example—they fought well; at their worst, at Camden, they fought not at all. There they were, as Greene said, "ungovernable." What was lacking in the militia was a set of professional standards, requirements and rules which might regulate their conduct in battle. What was lacking was professional pride. Coming and going to camp as they liked, shooting their guns for the pleasure of the sound, the militia annoyed the Continentals, who soon learned that most of them could not be trusted. . . .

The Continentals, the American regulars, lacked the polish of their British counterparts but, at least from Monmouth on, they showed a steadiness under fire almost as impressive as their enemy's. And they demonstrated a brave endurance: defeated, they retired, pulled themselves together, and came back to try again. . . .

The Continentals occupied the psychological and moral ground somewhere between the militia and the British professionals. From 1777 on their enlistments were for three years or the duration of the war. This long service allowed them to learn more of their craft and to become seasoned. That does not mean that on the battlefield they lost their fear. Experience in combat almost never leaves one indifferent to danger, unless after prolonged and extreme fatigue one comes to consider oneself already dead. Seasoned troops simply learn to deal with their fear more effectively than raw troops do, in part because they have come to realize that everyone feels it and that they can rely on their fellows.

By winter 1779–1780, the Continentals were beginning to believe that they had no one save themselves to lean on. Their soldierly qualifications so widely admired in America—their "habit of subordination," their patience under fatigue, their ability to stand sufferings and privations of every kind may in fact have led to a bitter resignation that saw them through a good deal of fighting. . . . They would fulfill the ideals of the Revolution and see things through to independence because the civilian population would not.

Thus the Continentals in the last four years of the active war, though less articulate and less independent than the militia, assimilated one part of the "cause" more fully. They had advanced further in making American purposes in the Revolution their own. They had in their sense of isolation and neglect probably come to be more nationalistic than the militia—though surely no more American. . . .

The meaning of these complex attitudes is not what it seems to be. At first sight the performance of militia and Continentals seems to suggest that the great principles of the Revolution made little difference on the battlefield. Or if principles did make a difference, say especially to the militia saturated with natural rights and a deep and persistent distrust of standing armies, they served not to strengthen the will to combat but to disable it. And the Continentals, recruited increasingly from the poor and dispossessed, apparently fought better as they came to resemble their professional and apolitical enemy, the British infantry.

These conclusions are in part askew. To be sure, there is truth—and paradox—in the fact that some Americans' commitments to revolutionary principles made them unreliable on the battlefield. Still, their devotion to their principles helped bring them there. George Washington, their commander-in-chief, never tired of reminding them that their cause arrayed free men against mercenaries. They were fighting for the "blessings of liberty," he told them in 1776, and should they not acquit themselves like men, slavery would replace their freedom. The challenge to behave like men was not an empty one. Courage, honor, gallantry in the service of liberty, all those words calculated to bring a blush of embarrassment to jaded twentieth-century men, defined manhood for the eighteenth century. In battle those words gained an extraordinary resonance as they were embodied in the actions of brave men. Indeed it is likely that many Americans who developed a narrow professional spirit found battle broadly educative, forcing them to consider the purposes of their professional skill.

On one level those purposes had to be understood as having a remarkable importance if men were to fight—and die. For battle forced American soldiers into a situation which nothing in their usual experience had prepared them for. They were to kill other men in the expectation that even if they did they might be killed themselves. However defined, especially by a Revolution in the name of life, liberty, and the pursuit of happiness, this situation was unnatural.

On another level, one which, perhaps, made the strain of battle endurable, the situation of American soldiers, though unusual, was not really foreign to them. For what battle presented in stark form was one of the classic problems free men face: choosing between the rival claims of public responsibility and private wishes, or in eighteenth-century terms choosing between virtue—devotion to the public trust—and personal liberty. In battle, virtue demanded that men give up their liberties and perhaps even their lives for others. Each time they fought they had in effect to weigh the claims of society and liberty. Should they fight or run? They knew that the choice might mean life or death. For those American soldiers who were servants, apprentices, poor men substituting for men with money to hire them, the choice might not have seemed to involve moral decision. After all they had never enjoyed much personal liberty. But not even in that contrivance of eighteenth-century authoritarianism in which they now found themselves, the professional army, could they avoid a moral decision. Compressed into dense formations, they were reminded by their nearness to their comrades that they too had an opportunity to uphold virtue. By standing firm they served their fellows and honor; by running, they served only themselves.

Thus battle tested the inner qualities of men, tried their souls, as Thomas Paine said. Many men died in the test that battle made of their spirits. Some soldiers called this trial cruel; others called it "glorious." Perhaps this difference in perception suggests how difficult it was in the Revolution to be both a soldier and an American. Nor has it ever been easy since.

George Washington's Grasp of Leadership and Power

EDMUND S. MORGAN

When a crowd of American farmers opened fire on the regular troops of the British army some two hundred years ago, the action must have seemed foolhardy to any impartial observer. Such an observer might have been a little surprised at the events that immediately followed, when the farmers put the regulars to rout, chased them from Concord to Boston, and laid siege to that town. But however impressive this performance, it did not alter the fact that the British army was probably the most powerful in the world, having succeeded scarcely a dozen years before in defeating the armies of France, England's only serious rival. For a handful of colonists, unorganized, without any regular source of arms or ammunition, with no army and no navy, to take on the world's greatest power in open war must still have looked like a foolhardy enterprise.   ·

Somehow or other it proved not to be. Yet it remains something of a puzzle that the farmers were able to bring it off. With the benefit of hindsight we can offer a number of explanations. For one thing, the generals whom the British sent to put down the rebels proved to be somewhat less than brilliant in using the immense force at their disposal. For another thing, the colonists got a great deal of assistance from England's old enemy, France. But perhaps most important, the Revolution seems to have elicited from those who participated in it a response that no other event or situation in American history has been able to do.

It was not that extraordinarily large numbers of people were ready to sacrifice their lives or their fortunes for the common good. That has often happened in times of crisis. And the Revolution did not in fact induce this kind of sacrifice very widely. It was always difficult to fill up enlistments in the Continental Army. What was extraordinary about the Revolution was the talent it generated, the number of men of genius who stepped out of farmyards and plantations, out of countinghouses and courtrooms, to play a leading role in winning the war and then in building a national government.

People noticed this from the beginning. Already in the summer of 1775 members of the Continental Congress were observing that "Times like these call up Genius, which slept before, and stimulate it in action to a degree, that eclipses what might before have been fixed as a Standard." . . . And indeed if one were to make a list of the great men of American history, by whatever standards one chooses to measure greatness, an astonishingly large proportion would be found whose careers began or culminated in the Revolution. It would be hard to find in all the rest of American history more than

Text from Edmund S. Morgan, "A Sense of Power" from *The Genius of George Washington*, 1980, pp. 3–25. Reprinted by permission W. W. Norton.

two or three men to rank with Washington, Franklin, Jefferson, Hamilton, Madison, or John Adams.

To say this does not bring us any closer to an explanation of why the Revolution created such an array of talent. . . . I cannot say how George Washington acquired the abilities and the character to achieve what he did, but I would like to try to say where I think his special genius lay, what his genius was and how it operated.

This is not an easy task, for George Washington is and was a hard man to know. Part of the difficulty in approaching him comes from the heroic image in which we have cast him and which already enveloped him in his own lifetime. But it is not simply the plaster image that stands between him and us. We have other national heroes who also became legendary figures in their own lifetimes, a Benjamin Franklin, an Andrew Jackson, an Abraham Lincoln; and yet with them we find no great difficulty in pushing past the image to find the man. In their letters and other writings, in the countless anecdotes they inspired, we can meet them on familiar terms and feel comfortable in their company.

But not George Washington. The familiar anecdotes about Washington tell us to keep our distance. The most arresting one is told about a gathering at the time of the Constitutional Convention in 1787. One evening during the sessions of the Convention a group of Washington's old friends from wartime days were remarking on the extraordinarily reserved and remote manner he maintained, even among his most intimate acquaintances. And the men I am speaking of considered themselves to belong in that category. One of them, Gouverneur Morris, who was always full of boldness and wit, had the nerve to disagree with the rest about Washington's aloofness. He could be as familiar with Washington, he said, as with any of his other friends. Alexander Hamilton called his bluff by offering to provide a dinner with the best of wine for a dozen of them if Morris would, at the next reception Washington gave, simply walk up to him, gently slap him on the shoulder, and say, "My dear General, how happy I am to see you look so well." On the appointed evening a substantial number were already present when Morris arrived, walked up to Washington, bowed, shook hands, and then placed his left hand on Washington's shoulder and said, "My dear General, I am very happy to see you look so well." The response was immediate and icy. Washington reached up and removed the hand, stepped back, and fixed his eyes in silence on Morris, until Morris retreated abashed into the crowd. The company looked on in dismay, and no one ever tried it again.

It seems today a rather extravagant reaction on the part of our national hero, a bit of overkill. It makes us almost as embarrassed for Washington as for poor Morris. Yet it may serve us as an appropriate starting place for our inquiry, because Washington's dignity and reserve, the aloofness that separated him from his contemporaries and still separates him from us, were, I believe, an integral part of the genius that enabled him to defeat the armies of Great Britain and to establish the United States as an independent world power.

Washington's genius lay in his understanding of power, both military power and political power, an understanding unmatched by that of any of his contemporaries. At a time when the United States needed nothing quite so much as military power but had very little, this hitherto obscure Virginia planter knew how to make the best possible use of what there was. And after securing independence, when the United States was trying to establish itself in a war-torn world, he knew how to deal with foreign countries to the maximum advantage of his own. . . .

At the simplest level Washington's understanding of power showed itself in the ability to take command. Some men have the quality; others do not. Washington had it, and in exercising it he nourished the aloofness that became his most conspicuous visible trait. . . . His aloofness had nothing to do with arrogance. It had to do with command.

He explained the matter in a letter to a fledgling colonel in the Continental Army in 1775: "Be easy and condescending in your deportment to your officers," he wrote, "but not too familiar, lest you subject yourself to a want of that respect, which is necessary to support a proper command." . . .

Washington practiced what he preached, and as his talents for command developed there were fewer and fewer persons with whom he could allow himself to be familiar. As commander in chief and later as president, he could scarcely afford it with anyone. The remoteness that still surrounds him was a necessary adjunct of the power he was called upon to exercise.

But Washington's understanding of power went far beyond mere posture. Although he had not had a great deal of military experience before he took charge of the Continental Army in 1775, his participation in the French and Indian War from 1754 to 1758 had exposed him to the geographical conditions of warfare on the American continent and the way in which they must affect the exercise of military power. As commander of the Revolutionary army he was quick to perceive the significance of geographical factors that his opponents seem never to have grasped. At the outset of the war, when the British almost caught him in the Battle of Long Island, he learned the danger of allowing his forces to be bottled up in any location where their retreat might be cut off. Having learned that lesson, he did not make the same mistake again. Though he was not always able to prevent his subordinates from making it, his constant alertness to it enabled him to keep his precarious army in existence. In September, 1777, for example, he sent a letter on the subject to Brigadier General Thomas Nelson in Virginia. In the light of future events it was a remarkable letter. Nelson had proposed to station his forces at Hampton and Yorktown, which lay at the end of the peninsula between the James and the York rivers. Here, of course, they would be in a position to observe the movement of any British troops into the area by sea. But the location, Washington perceived at once, was one where they could be trapped, and he quickly warned Nelson against it. . . . Four years later Lord Cornwallis made the mistake that Washington warned Nelson against, and Washington pounced. . . . For Cornwallis it was the world turned upside down, but for Washington it was a lesson learned long before in the geography of power.

Of course, if the British navy had been on hand in sufficient strength, Cornwallis might have escaped by sea. But Washington did not move until he had the French navy to dominate the seas nearby. He had realized early in the war that without local naval superiority to stand off the British warships, he could not capture a British army at any point on the coast. Washington understood this better than his more experienced French helpers. The Comte de Grasse, in command of the French navy, seems to have missed the whole point of the Yorktown strategy, complaining to Washington that he would prefer to cruise off New York where he might encounter the main British fleet, rather than be an idle spectator in the Chesapeake. Washington knew, however, that even with de Grasse on hand, he was not strong enough to have attacked the main British force in New York. But by picking off Cornwallis at Yorktown he could deal the British a crippling blow.

Washington's appreciation of geographical factors made him not only wary of being trapped like Cornwallis but also averse to defending any particular point, including cities. The British armies were much more powerful than his and capable of taking any place they wanted. It was therefore not worthwhile to erect elaborate stationary defenses. . . . Wars were won by destroying or disarming the enemy, not by trying to spare civilians from occupation. And Washington was bent on winning.

Washington, in other words, was or became a good field general. But his understanding of military power did not stop at the ability to command troops and deploy them effectively. He also understood that the power he could wield in battle depended on the willingness of the civil government to supply him with men and money. He understood the political basis of military power, and he also understood that in the new United States this was a very precarious basis. His army was the creature of a Congress that never quite dared to act like a government. Congress declared independence. It authorized the creation of the army. It even authorized the creation of a navy. But it did not attempt to levy taxes to pay for these things. Instead, it recommended to the states that they make contributions, specifying the amount for each state. Whether a state followed the recommendation depended on how its legislature felt at the time. Ultimately it depended on public opinion. And public opinion was as fickle then as now. Rumors of peace and of British surrender came with every skirmish, and each one produced a debilitating effect on the willingness of taxpayers in the different states to advance money for a war that might soon be over.

Men were almost as hard to get as the money to pay and clothe and feed them. As a result Washington was never able to build an army strong enough to face the British on even terms. At the outset of the war he had hoped to enlist soldiers for the duration. Instead, Congress provided for enlistments of a year only. It took almost that long to collect and build a disciplined fighting force, even from men who already knew how to fire a gun. By the time he had them trained, their terms would be up, and off they would go, frequently taking with them the guns he had issued them. In their place would often come raw militia on even shorter terms, men who were not used to obeying commands and who did not take kindly to them, men who were ready to head for home and tend the crops the moment they were offended by some officer's efforts to bring them in line. In 1780, after the war had dragged on for five years, Washington was still trying to get Congress to place the army on a more lasting basis. . . .

Although Washington's complaints to Congress were fruitless, he never appealed over the heads of Congress to their constituents. He refrained from doing so in part because the very effort to explain the situation to the public would also have explained it to the enemy. He did not dare to advertise the weakness of his force, when the only thing between him and defeat was the fact that the enemy did not realize how weak he was. But his restraint was also based on principle. In spite of the imperious manner with which he bolstered his ability to command, Washington was a republican. He had been fully persuaded that the king of England and the minions surrounding him were conspiring to destroy the liberties of Americans. More than that, he was persuaded that kings in general were a bad lot. He welcomed Thomas Paine's devastating attack not only on George III but on monarchy itself. He never doubted that the United States must be a republic. And the principles of republican liberty as he saw them dictated that the military must be forever subordinate to the civil power. Although he could lament the short-sightedness exhibited by Congress and the state legislatures, he never even suggested that he and his army should be anything but their servants. . . .

Washington was fighting not simply for independence but for an independent republic. He was fighting a people's war, and he knew that he would lose what he was fighting for if he tried to take more power than the people would freely give. One of the difficulties of republican government, as he explained later to uncomprehending foreigners, was that the people have always to feel an evil before they can see it. "This," he admitted, "is productive of errors and temporary evils, but generally these evils are of a nature to work their own cure." In the end, he believed, the people would do the right thing. Washington's patience in waiting for the people to do the right thing is the more remarkable, because he knew that the ineffectiveness of Congress not only prolonged the war needlessly but also exposed the country to needless perils. Because Congress lacked the nerve to vote him the needed men and money, he had to rely on assistance from the French in order to bring the war to a successful conclusion. And reliance on the French could have meant the loss of the very independence Americans were fighting for.

It was perfectly good politics, of course, to seek help against England from England's traditional enemy, and Washington welcomed assistance in the form of arms and ammunition. But he had also to rely on French troops and the French navy. There lay the danger. Once French forces were engaged on the American continent, Washington feared that they would wish to invade and occupy Canada. Ostensibly the United States would be the sole beneficiary of such a move, for the French agreed to forego any territorial claims on the continent in their treaty of alliance with the United States. But Washington had no illusions about the binding power of treaties.

Unfortunately Congress did have illusions. At the beginning of the war Americans had hoped that Canada would join them in rebellion against England, and Washington himself thought it highly desirable to eliminate this bastion of British power. He had sent an expedition to effect the liberation of the province, but the inhabitants had not responded in the manner hoped for, and the expedition was a disaster. With the arrival of French troops, Congressmen developed an enthusiasm for trying again with French forces. The population of Canada was mainly French, and it was plausible to suppose that they would welcome their countrymen more warmly than they had the Americans. But Washington was alarmed. He would not have been in a position to refuse if the French had decided to employ their troops in this way, but he did not want Congress encouraging them to do so. He wrote out all the tactical reasons he could think of against the expedition and sent them in an official communication to Congress. Then he wrote out a private, confidential letter to Henry Laurens, the president of Congress, explaining his real objection. The letter remains one of the more striking examples of the quick perception of political realities that lay behind Washington's understanding of power.

The expedition, he explained to Laurens, would mean "the introduction of a large body of French troops into Canada, and putting them in possession of the capital of that Province, attached to them by all the ties of blood, habits, manners, religion and former connexions of government. I fear this would be too great a temptation to be resisted by any power actuated by the common maxims of national policy." He went on to outline all the economic and political benefits that France would gain by holding on to the province in violation of the treaty. It would not be difficult to find a plausible pretext. The United States had borrowed funds from France on a large scale; and the United States government, if one could dignify Congress by that name, had no power to tax its citizens in order to repay the debt. The United States could scarcely object if France retained Canada as security for the payment. "Resentment, reproaches, and submission" would be the only recourse left to the United States. And Washington went on to read a gentle lecture to the gullible members of Congress: "Men are very apt," he said, "to run into extremes; hatred to England may carry some into an excess of Confidence in France; especially when motives of gratitude are thrown into the scale. Men of this description would be unwilling to suppose France capable of acting so ungenerous a part. I am heartily disposed to entertain the most favourable sentiments of our new ally and to cherish them in others to a reasonable degree; but it is a maxim founded on the universal experience of mankind, that no nation is to be trusted farther than it is bound by its interest; and no prudent statesman or politician will venture to depart from it." . . .

Washington himself never departed from the maxim that he had urged on Henry Laurens, and it served him well when he became President of the

United States. But before looking at his achievements in that position, we may notice one final area of his understanding of military power. As he understood the political basis of military power, so also he understood, far better than Congress did, its economic basis. He looked upon the small troop quotas and short-term enlistments provided by Congress as a squandering of manpower and financial resources. By such timidity, he pointed out, "we have protracted the War, expended Millions and tens of Millions of pounds which might have been saved." What he was saying, in modern terms, was that Congress had paid no attention to the cost-effectiveness of its measures. . . .

As the half-hearted war gradually depleted the country's resources, Washington accepted the reality and called upon Congress to borrow money abroad in order to get the thing over with. He did not worry about the nation's capacity to pay back what it borrowed. The long-range economic potential of the country was enormous. Its population was growing exponentially. But as the war dragged on, he saw that the outcome might hinge on which side could keep paying the bills. He feared it might not be the United States, dependent as it had become, for the short term at least, on the treasury of France. In a shrewd economic comparison of America's enemy and America's ally he concluded that England, with a larger commerce than France, though much smaller in population, had the larger resources. "Though the government is deeply in debt and of course poor, the nation is rich and their riches afford a fund which will not be easily exhausted. Besides, their system of public credit is such that it is capable of greater exertions than that of any other nation. . . . France is in a different position. The abilities of her present Financier have done wonders. By a wise administration of the revenues aided by advantageous loans he has avoided the necessity of additional taxes. But I am well informed, if the war continues another campaign he will be obliged to have recourse to the taxes usual in time of war which are very heavy, and which the people of France are not in a condition to endure for any duration." It was a prescient analysis. The victory at Yorktown came in time to prevent an immediate testing of the economic strength of the two countries, but not in time to prevent the fiscal exhaustion that eight years later required the calling of the French Estates General, the starting point of the French Revolution.

With the victory at Yorktown and the peace that followed, the United States had no further need of the military wisdom of which it had made such poor use. But Washington as a civilian was no less cogent in his understanding of power than he had been as commander in chief. His response to the postwar vicissitudes of the nation matched that of the most constructive political thinkers on the scene, and his influence may have been greater than theirs because of the enormous prestige he now carried.

The ineffectiveness of Congress that had hampered Washington's prosecution of the war continued to threaten the viability of the new republic in peacetime. . . . Congress had no authority to regulate trade for the whole nation. Washington supported every move to give it such authority, but at the same time he despaired of putting power in the hands of men who had demonstrated again and again their timidity in using it. What was the use of giving them more powers, he asked, when "the members seem to be so much afraid of exerting those which they already have, that no opportunity is slipped of surrendering them, or referring the exercise of them, to the States individually?"

Washington had been convinced, long before the war ended, that the national government as it operated under the Articles of Confederation was not adequate to carry out its functions; and he feared it had in effect written its own death warrant by failing to exercise what powers it had. "Extensive powers not exercised," he once observed, ". . . have I believe scarcely ever failed to ruin the possessor." But he hoped against hope that this would not be the case with the United States. When the inhabitants of western Massachusetts rose in arms against their own elected government in Shays' Rebellion, and neither the state nor the national government seemed ready to do anything about it, it looked as though the case was hopeless. Henry Lee urged Washington to use his influence to quiet the troubles, but Washington snapped back, "Influence is no Government. . . . If they have real grievances, redress them. . . . If they have not, employ the force of government against them at once." It was mortifying to see the new American republic exhibiting the weakness that doctrinaire European political philosophers had always attributed to republics. "How melancholy is the reflection," Washington wrote to James Madison, "that in so short a space, we should have made such large strides towards fulfilling the predictions of our transatlantic foe! 'leave them to themselves, and their government will soon dissolve.' . . . What stronger evidence can be given of the want of energy in our governments than these disorders? If there exists not a power to check them, what security has a man for life, liberty, or property?"

But the weakness of the American republic did not diminish Washington's republican ardor. He was outraged by the very idea of rebellion against a republican government, but he was also outraged by the reaction of Americans who talked without horror of substituting a monarch for the ineffective Congress. And after the Massachusetts government finally succeeded in putting down the rebels, he objected to the fact that they had been disfranchised. To deprive them of political rights was as much an abuse of power as the failure to use power effectively against them in the first place. Fortunately a number of other Americans were as disturbed as Washington about the impotence of the national government and the impending dissolution of the union. When they met together in the Constitutional Convention to seek a remedy, it was inevitable that they should choose him to preside; and when the resulting Constitution was adopted it was also inevitable that the people should choose him to preside over the new government it established. He thus gained the opportunity to demonstrate to his countrymen, as well as to the skeptics of the Old World, that a republican government could show as much energy as any other.

Washington brought to the presidency of the United States a determination to establish what he called "a national character," by which he meant something like national reputation. It was essential, in his view, that the country gain a reputation that would oblige other countries to respect it. "We are a young Nation," he had written in 1783, "and have a character to establish. It behoves us therefore to set out right for first impressions will be lasting, indeed are all in all." And in the years that followed the winning of independence, as the power of Congress continued to wane, his great worry had been that the failure of the states to support the union would "destroy our National character, and render us as contemptable in the eyes of Europe as we have it in our power to be respectable." With an effective national government in operation at last, it became possible to establish a proper national character, a reputation that would command respect both at home and abroad. And in his conduct of the presidency Washington bent his every effort toward that end.

He recognized that he was on trial, that the character of the government and the respect accorded it would be measured by the respect that he himself demanded and commanded. As president of a republic he aimed at an elegant simplicity in his style of living, sumptuous enough to escape any imputation of ostentatious poverty, but restrained enough to avoid outright splendor. At the same time he cultivated his characteristic aloofness, even to the point where his critics charged that his condescension smacked of monarchy. And when rebellion broke out against taxes imposed by Congress, he responded with a vigor calculated to demonstrate that the new government would tolerate none of what Daniel Shays had tried in Massachusetts. . . .

In spite of his determination to establish a strong character for the nation, Washington had no yearning for personal power, nor did he want any military adventures of the kind that so often infatuate men who are obsessed with power for its own sake. He did want the United States to grow in strength, for strength must be the ultimate basis of respect. And strength, he was sure, would not come to the United States by going to war. He had had ample experience that war was the way to poverty, and poverty meant impotence. The way for the country to grow strong, he believed, was to eschew internal dissension and steer clear of the quarrels which he saw were about to envelop the nations of Europe. The United States was encumbered with a French alliance, but as Washington read the terms of it, it did not require the United States to become involved in any quarrel that France might have with other countries, including England. And while he was grateful for the assistance received from France in the winning of American independence, he did not think that gratitude had a place in the determination of national policy. As he had pointed out some years earlier to Henry Laurens, the nation, like other nations, should not be counted on to act beyond its own interest. France in helping Americans during the Revolution had acted out of self interest—her interest to have England weakened by loss of the colonies. Now, as Washington saw it, the main interest of the United States was to recover from the economic exhaustion incurred, however needlessly, in the Revolutionary War. The means of recovery, he thought, lay in exploiting the American land to produce as much as possible for sale to nations less fruitfully engaged in quarreling with one another. For this purpose it should welcome immigrants who tired of the heavy taxes that European governments imposed in order to maintain the splendor of their kings and the power of their armies. In America, now that a government existed capable of protecting life, liberty, and property, the industrious and ambitious, the poor, the needy, and the oppressed from all over the world would swell the ranks of American producers, and the United States would grow in power as the oppressive governments of Europe declined.

Washington had no difficulty in persuading the new Congress or the advisers whom he appointed to his cabinet that a policy of neutrality was the way to let the United States develop its powers. But his advisers never understood the operation of the policy as well as Washington did. . . .

Washington realized that the people of the United States would benefit from high prices for their agricultural exports while European farmers were distracted by war. But other than this benefit, he did not propose to take advantage of the distress of any country in order to wring concessions from it, because he was convinced that benefits thus obtained would not last. In 1791, when he was about to appoint Gouverneur Morris (him of the slap on the back) as minister to France, he warned him against seeking to obtain favorable treaties from countries in distress, "for unless," he said, "treaties are mutually beneficial to the Parties, it is in vain to hope for a continuance of them beyond the moment when the one which conceives itself to be over-reached is in a situation to break off the connexion." A treaty had to match the powers and interests of the parties making it. Otherwise it would be indeed a scrap of paper. Washington signed two treaties as president of the United States. The first one, Jay's Treaty with England, was extremely unpopular; and Washington himself did not think well of it. But he signed it because he thought that commercial relations with England would be worse with no treaty than with this one. The popular outcry against it did not move him and indeed struck him as senseless, because he believed that the United States in 1795 was not sufficiently powerful and England was not sufficiently weak to have negotiated a better treaty. . . . It would be foolish to reject Jay's Treaty if it might improve the commercial situation of the United States in any way.

Washington could afford to be equally calm about Pinckney's Treaty with Spain. That treaty was almost as popular with the American people as Jay's had been unpopular, and it has generally been hailed as a triumph because it secured the American right to navigate the Mississippi. Yet it merely obtained what Washington was certain the United States would get anyhow. After the Revolutionary War settlers had poured into the western country in such numbers that by 1795 Spain could not safely have denied them the right to export their produce down the Mississippi. What prompted the concession was not Pinckney's negotiating skill but the expanding American strength in the west and the strong character that Washington had conferred on the national government. Treaties, in Washington's view, were not important. What was important was power.

Washington was not a man of many talents. He had none of the range of the brilliant men around him, the intellectual curiosity of a Jefferson, the fiscal genius of a Hamilton. But in his understanding of power he left them all behind, as he did the British generals who opposed him and the French who assisted him. When he retired from the presidency after eight years, he had placed the United States on the way to achieving the power that he had aspired to for it. In the years that have followed, that power has grown until there are those who wonder whether it has been a good thing for the world. But at the time it looked like a very good thing indeed. And for better or for worse, it was the work of George Washington, the man who still keeps us all at a distance.

Where Have All the Great Men Gone?

RICHARD D. BROWN

There is no clear consensus on what constitutes greatness, nor are there any objective criteria for measuring it—but when we look at holders of high public offices and at the current field of candidates, we know it is missing. Some of our leaders are competent, articulate, engaging, and some are honest and honorable. But greatness is missing.

The leaders of the early republic—George Washington, Thomas Jefferson, John Adams, Benjamin Franklin, Alexander Hamilton, and John Marshall—set the standard for greatness. Since their day only Abraham Lincoln and Franklin D. Roosevelt have attained equivalent stature. Why has mediocrity come to prevail where meritocracy once ruled? Where have all the great men gone?

This question is more complicated than it may first appear, and some will argue that the issues it raises are false and ahistorical, since responses to the question must be subjective. Indeed, some will say that to pose the question is to retreat into romantic mythology where the founders of the republic become the heroic figures of a "golden age." These objections cannot be ignored.

It has been said that a statesman is nothing but a dead politician. From the time we are children we are taught not to speak ill of the dead, and in public rhetoric it is common to elevate them. In our own time admiration for John F. Kennedy exemplifies this phenomenon, and earlier in this century the reputation of the assassinated President William McKinley enjoyed a similar glorification that only gradually ebbed away. Nostalgia distorts historical perceptions, a fact that has nourished revisionist historiography for generations. In fact, revisionism in American historical writing began with the early-twentieth-century discovery that the Founding Fathers were flesh-and-blood politicians, and however obvious that "discovery" now appears, it remains a vital corrective to "golden age" thinking.

Yet even admitting all of this, scholars who have closely scrutinized the major leaders of the early republic continue to be enormously impressed. The array of talented and devoted individuals is awesome. In Massachusetts, for instance, John and Samuel Adams, Elbridge Gerry and John Hancock, Robert Treat Paine and James and Joseph Warren, immediately come to mind, as well as a dozen less exalted figures—a James Bowdoin, a Henry

Knox, a Benjamin Lincoln, a James Sullivan. We need not agree that they all were truly great, but if we compare them with the present incumbents, the sense of loss and deprivation is overwhelming.

At the end of the eighteenth century, as today, political leaders were chiefly drawn from the white male population aged forty to sixty years. Leaving aside questions of wealth and education, Massachusetts in 1790 possessed about thirty thousand such people, the United States as a whole some two-hundred and fifty thousand. Today there are eighty times that number nationwide, twenty million white men aged forty to sixty years. And the total voting population of that age is forty-four million. Considered in light of these figures, the ability of the early republic to generate so many talented officeholders cannot be dismissed as mere patriotic mythology. We are talking about an actual fact.

Biographies cannot provide an explanation. The almost routine emergence of such able leaders was a social phenomenon, and to understand it we must examine the society that produced them. What were the conditions that created this political pattern, and when and why did it recede?

The folklore of politics teaches us that great events produce great men, and we can all think of examples where great events ennobled public figures who had previously, and accurately, been viewed as undistinguished. In 1932 the journalist Walter Lippmann observed that Franklin D. Roosevelt was "an amiable Boy Scout . . . a pleasant man who, without any important qualifications for the office, would very much like to be President." Unquestionably, the crises of the Depression and World War II elevated Roosevelt's leadership. Had he served during the 1920s, there is no reason to believe his Presidency would be memorable.

Yet this phenomenon is not inevitable. Great events and great challenges produce George McClellans and George Wallaces as well as George Washingtons. No natural law requires societies to assign their most talented members to positions of public trust in times of crises. To understand the nature of how we actually do select our leaders, we must begin by examining the systems of recruiting and advancing public officials within a republican government.

I believe that the United States currently operates a peculiar, debased form of meritocracy, which has five major attributes: first, access to high office is extremely competitive; second, keen personal ambition for power and recognition is necessary to propel people into the competition and keep them there; third, the system calls for a record of experience in public or quasi-public affairs; fourth, it requires visibility through media exposure; finally, what these four elements point to is the fifth characteristic of our system of recruitment and advancement—electioneering performance. The ability to perform in election contests, to go out tirelessly day after day in search of support and to win it from people of diverse characteristics—this is the ultimate criterion.

This system of political advancement operates directly through the electorate and indirectly through elites that recognize the ultimate authority of the ballot box. Because the electorate and the elites are so diverse, electioneering on a national scale or in any large state requires tireless campaigning to persuade people from a multitude of different backgrounds, often with directly conflicting interests, to look with hopeful anticipation on a single person. Chameleonlike, the candidate must appeal to boardroom and back room, fans of symphonies and Super Bowls. From the standpoint of electioneering, our current system is meritocratic, but the attributes that lead to success at the ballot box often seem to assure mediocrity in public office.

It was not always thus. At the outset of the republic, recruitment and advancement operated differently. First of all, the electorate was confined to white, male property-holders who had been schooled in the deferential politics of the colonial era. This was an electorate that expected political leaders to be men of wealth and education, not ordinary people like themselves. Moreover, in choosing candidates, voters were accustomed to supporting men whom they knew face-to-face or through local reputation. If they voted for a stranger, it was usually because that stranger carried the endorsement of a trusted member of the local elite. As far as the electorate was concerned, the role of candidates themselves in seeking office was largely passive.

The key process of nominating candidates was dominated by layers of local, state, and national elites. Candidates were selected by their peers, people who had witnessed them in action for years and who knew first-hand their strengths and weaknesses. Whatever the office in question, relatively homogeneous groups of incumbents and their associates selected candidates from among their own number. While the system was open to new men, and choices required approval at the polls, it had a distinctly oligarchic flavor. High esteem among the peer group was a prerequisite for major elective offices.

This brief comparison between the present system, where electoral popularity is the ultimate criterion, and the early republic, where peer-group approval was paramount, helps to focus our analysis, but it does not answer the question of the disappearing great men. Though it might be tempting to offer a simple elitist explanation, this would be worse than inadequate; it would be wrong. Historically the records of elite selection processes are replete with instances of incompetence, corruption, and tyranny—and mediocrity. Whether operated by Byrd in Virginia, Daley in Chicago, or Tweed in New York City, the record of oligarchic rule inside the United States, as elsewhere, is not synonymous with meritocracy. The central question then is not techniques of recruitment and advancement per se; it is the values that animate the process.

During the first generation of the republic there was a clear consensus among leading men in all parts of the nation regarding fundamental political values. This consensus was grounded on the classical models that were central to the curricula at all the colonial colleges, from William and Mary in Virginia to Harvard in Massachusetts. Ideals of citizenship and public office were drawn from the history of the Roman republic. First of all, private, personal virtue was a prerequisite to public virtue and hence a requirement for high office. The object of political leadership was to implement the general public good, and in order to perceive and pursue it, leaders must be men of superior wisdom, energy, initiative, and moral stature. The people were not their guides; they were their charges, to be led along paths selected by the leaders. An aristocracy of merit—Jefferson called it a "natural aristocracy"—should rule.

In practical politics this classical model dictated that the men should never seek the office, the office should seek the man. The historical figure of Cincinnatus, who had been called from his plow to lead his people, was the ideal type. In our Revolutionary days, George Washington and Israel Putnam, among others, were presented in this mold.

Anyone familiar with behind-the-scenes politics from 1776 onward knows that these ideals were commonly violated. The launching of the new state and national governments generated a bonanza in vacant offices, and a wave of office seekers rushed in upon them. In the lower echelons of the civilian and military establishments, place seeking was routine. At higher levels the process of recruitment and advancement was much more complicated, and the influence of the new republican idealism on actual practice was far more evident. Patronage connections remained vital, but the meritocratic possibilities of patronage developed a new importance.

The situation is illustrated by the efforts of the Continental Congress to fill its complement of officers for the Army. British colonial tradition dictated that such offices be filled according to principles of venality—that is, personal influence, tempered by some attention to seniority within the ranks of officers. But the Congress broke with tradition, and on May 10, 1776, it formally adopted a policy of "promoting the officers in the continental service according to their merit." Five months later the Congress even repudiated the principle of seniority in favor of merit, recommending to the states that "all the officers to be hereafter appointed, be men of honor and known abilities, without a particular regard to their having before been in service." This recommendation was political dynamite, and even the normally acquiescent General Washington took issue with it, arguing that unless promotions were compatible with seniority, the officer corps would be demoralized. A compromise was finally proposed in which prior rank and merit both had a part, but with the understanding that Congress might deviate from any of its rules "in favour of merit eminently distinguished and generally acknowledged." In the accompanying debate John Adams vigorously rebutted the arguments of Washington and those who counseled in favor of seniority. "I have no fears from the resignation of Officers if junior Officers are preferred to them," Adams declared. "If they have virtue they will continue with us. If not," he concluded, "their resignation will not hurt us." Adams, a key member of the board of war, had been wrestling with the problem for nearly two years and he was convinced that meritocracy could work.

The difficulty of any merit system is how to measure merit. Early republican leaders sought the judgments of informed gentlemen, relying on their discretion as to whether merit was "eminently distinguished and generally acknowledged." Here personal acquaintance—"connections"—was often crucial, and the meritocratic possibilities of patronage were developed.

At the core of the system trust ruled. Assessments of character and abilities were necessarily subjective, so those who selected candidates for civil and military office had to rely on the testimony of their peers. John Adams's correspondence as a member of the board of war illustrates the system's values and the way it worked. To his old law clerk, Adams wrote in August 1776: "I am . . . determined to pursue this Correspondence, untill I can obtain a perfect Knowledge of the Characters of our Field Officers." Of one man Adams asserted:

> His Genius is equal to any one of his Age. His Education is not inferiour. So far I can Say of my own Knowledge;

but before Adams could recommend promotion, he needed to know more about the candidate's "Morals, his Honour, and his Discretion." On the same day Adams complained in another letter to a colleague that Massachusetts

> continues to act, the most odd Surprizing and unaccountable Part, respecting Officers. They have a most wonderfull Faculty of finding out Persons for Generals and Colonells of whom no Body ever heard before. Let me beg of you, in Confidence to give me your candid and explicit opinion, of the Massachusetts General and Field Officers, and point out such as have any Education, Erudition, Sentiment, Reflection, Address or other Qualification or Accomplishment excepting Honour and Valour for Officers in high Rank. Who and What is General Fellows? Who and What is General Brickett? . . .
>
> If there are any officers, young or old, among the Massachusetts Forces who have Genius, Spirit, Reflection, Science, Literature, and Breeding, do for the Lands sake, and the Armys sake, and the Province sake let me know their Names, Places of Abodes and Characters.

Adams was a part of a national talent search, and he begged for candid assessments of individuals. The reports he received from political acquaint-ances in the Northern states reveal the application of meritocratic principles to the process of advancing people according to known connections. From New York a friend of Adams, a lawyer, now serving as a Continental officer, provided him with these ratings of the Massachusetts colonels:

> Whitcomb: has no Trace of an Officer, his Men under no Government
>
> Reed: A good Officer not of the most extensive Knowledge but far from being low or despicable . . .
>
> Little: A Midling Officer and of tolerable Genius, not great
>
> Serjeant: has a pretty good Character but I have no Acquaintance
>
> Glover: is said to be a good Officer but am not acquainted
>
> Hutchinson: An easy good Man not of great Genius
>
> Baley: is Nothing
>
> Baldwin: a Personable Man but not of the first Character
>
> Learned: Was a good officer, is old, Superanuated and Resigned

Greaton: An excellent Disciplinarian his Courage has been questioned, but
    I dont know with what Justice

Bond: I dont know him

Patterson: A Good Officer of a liberal Education, ingenious and Sensible.

The key qualifications are knowledge, "genius," and judgment in addition to the courage and moral character that were prerequisites.

For the highest positions, such as major general, and later for President, much more was wanted. In August 1776 Adams reflected on the essential qualities for the highest of offices. Such a person, Adams believed:

> should be possessed of a very extensive Knowledge of Science, and Literature, Men and Things. A Citizen of a free Government, he Should be Master of the Laws and Constitution, least he injure fundamentally those Rights which he professes to defend. He Should have a keen Penetration and a deep Discernment of the Tempers, Natures, and Characters of Men. He Should have an Activity, and Diligence, Superiour to all Fatigue. He should have a Patience and Self Government, Superior to all Flights and Transports of Passion. He Should have a Candour and Moderation, above all Prejudices, and Partialities. His Views should be large enough to comprehend the whole System of the Government and the Army. . . . His Benevolence and Humanity, his Decency, Politeness and Civility, Should ever predominate in his Breast. He should be possessed of a certain . . . order, Method, and Decision, Superior to all Perplexity, and Confusion in Business. There is in Such a Character, whenever and wherever it appears, a decisive Energy, which hurries away before it, all Difficulties, and leaves to the World of Mankind no Leisure, or opportunity to do any Thing towards it, but Admire, it.

From the perspective of 1776, Adams's idealism was not idle fantasy. Already the Continental Congress and the republic had found one such individual in George Washington.

In order to discern such qualities one could only resort to known men. Speaking of the selection of officers in October 1775, Adams remarked that "Men of Honour cannot appoint Gentlemen whom they dont know. . . . Nor can they pay a Regard to any Recommendation of Strangers, to the Exclusion of Persons whom they know." Personal knowledge and the recommendations of acquaintances—personal connections—were crucial. Traditionally these were the mechanisms of patronage, where friends and relatives sponsored each other's promotion, with merit no more than a secondary consideration. In the Revolutionary republic at its best, however, the new idealism transformed old, quasi-oligarchic practices into a screen for talent, wisdom, and character.

There was a genuine convergence between the real and the ideal, but it should not be overdrawn. In staffing Massachusetts's officer corps, the champions of meritocracy faced formidable obstacles that were intrinsic to a representative government. The policy of Massachusetts, it was acidly remarked, was "to thrust into Notice Men, whom Nature design'd for Obscurity." Though mediocrity had no defenders, there were real pressures to recruit and advance men of mediocre abilities and, as a corollary, some willingness to discourage the best qualified from public service.

John Adams grasped the problem immediately. In a popular representative government, the elitism that was inseparably connected to the development of a natural aristocracy was suspect:

> Knowledge is among the most essential Foundations of Liberty. But is there not a Jealousy or an Envy taking Place among the Multitude of Men of Learning, and, a wish to exclude them from the public Councils and from military Command? I could mention many Phenomena, in various Parts of these States, which indicate such a growing Disposition. To what Cause Shall I attribute the Surprizing Conduct of the Massachusetts Bay? How has it happened that such an illiterate Group of General and Field Officers, have been thrust into public View, by that Commonwealth which . . . ought to have set an Example to her sisters, by sending into the Field her best Men. Men of the most Genius Learning, Reflection, and Address. Instead of this, every Man you send into the Army as a General or a Collonell exhibits a Character, which nobody ever heard of before, or an aukward, illiterate, ill bred Man . . . there is not a Single Man among all our Collonells that I dare to recommend for a General Officer, except Knox and Porter.

Adams and his peers associated learning and largeness of view with merit, and the fact that these qualities also correlated substantially with wealth and social status seemed natural and appropriate to them.

But ordinary people were not fully in agreement. John Adams wrote in alarm:

> I fear We shall find that popular Elections are not oftener determined, upon pure Principles of Merit, Virtue, and public Spirit, than the Nominations of a Court, if We dont take Care. I fear there is an infinity of Corruption in our Elections already crept in. All Kinds of Favour, Intrigue and Partiality in Elections are as real, Corruption in my Mind, as Treats and Bribes. . . .
> A Sober, conscientious Habit, of electing for the public good alone must be introduced, and every Appearance of Interest, Favour, and Partiality, reprobated, or you will very soon make wise and honest Men wish for Monarchy again, nay you will make them introduce it into America.

Long before the emergence of the Federalist movement, Adams foresaw the tensions between elite political expectations and government based on popular elections.

Actually, Gordon S. Wood, the leading authority on the effort to create the Constitution of 1787, believes that one of its central objectives was to screen out the direct influence of the people from the government, enabling the elites to select from among their own number the people they believed were best qualified to guide the United States. The provisions of the Constitution prescribing the selection of the principal public officials clearly limited the impact of popular elections. The President was to be chosen by an Electoral College, and failing a majority there, by the House of Representatives. The members of the United States Senate were to be elected by the individual state legislatures. The only popularly elected officers would be members of the House of Representatives, but since their constituencies were so large (at least forty thousand people), it was believed that only prominent men of proven abilities would possess the visibility and wide acquaintance necessary for election.

The conviction that men of merit according to upper-class standards must dominate public office was a consistent theme in the Federalist administrations of Washington and Adams, but the election of 1800 and the ensuing party competition between Jeffersonians and Federalists pointed in a new direction. After Jefferson took office, even the majority of Federalists were prepared to give the people what they wanted, tailoring policy to popular wishes instead of to abstract principles of the public good. While it is hard to fix a precise date for the demise of the system of political recruitment and advancement that produced so many great men, it was weakening in the early decades of the new century, and in the presidential election of 1828 its utter defeat is evident.

As President, John Quincy Adams was a political anachronism. His election in 1824 was the only case where the electoral process set up in 1787 to assure the best choice in case of deadlock had actually been employed. When no one commanded a majority in the Electoral College, the selection of the President fell to the House of Representatives. Here his fellow candidate Henry Clay decided that Adams would make a better President than Andrew Jackson, who had won a plurality of popular votes. Whatever Clay's motives, by following this course he directly repudiated the popular vote as well as the instructions of his own Kentucky legislature. The system of elite selection worked, for Adams was indeed superbly qualified for the highest office according to the classical republican canons of education, experience, intelligence, energy, and moral stature. But he lacked popularity and the willingness to seek it. In 1828 he and the meritocratic system he symbolized were defeated.

John Quincy Adams saw clearly what was going on. In his memoirs he confided: "Electioneering for the Presidency has spread its contagion to the President himself. . . . One of the most remarkable peculiarities of the present time is that the principal leaders of the political parties are travelling about the country from State to State, and holding forth, like Methodist preachers, hour after hour, to assembled multitudes, under the broad canopy of heaven." Adams would not lift a finger to pursue reelection. He ignored his own party's pleas for help and even refused to state that he wished to be elected. Like a caricature of the classical ideal, he stood for office in silence.

Meanwhile, professional politicians flocked to Andrew Jackson because his military reputation made him famous and popular. Jackson's career lent itself to magnification, and strategists organized parties, parades, and house-to-house canvassing to turn out the Jackson vote in 1828 on behalf of a common man's crusade. Though Andrew Jackson was a person of unusual ability and genuine achievement, he was elected because he appeared to symbolize popular feelings. In 1840, when the Whigs successfully ran the aged and obscure William Henry Harrison as a Jackson look-alike in the "hard-cider," "log-cabin," "Tippecanoe and Tyler too" campaign, the absolute corruption of the selection process was evident. Mediocrity was more popular than meritocracy, and henceforth it would be qualities associated with electioneering success that would determine recruitment and advancement.

Elites still selected candidates in party caucuses and conventions, but they measured their choices against popular preferences and party loyalty. In an age when sentiment was supplanting reason in religion and the arts, when egalitarianism was destroying the legitimacy of natural as well as hereditary aristocracy, the values embodied in the classical republican ideal lost out in the race for popularity.

During the Civil War the Boston brahmin historian Francis Parkman probed the fundamental issues:

> Our ship is among breakers, and we look about us for a pilot. An endangered nation seeks a leader worthy of itself. . . . In a struggle less momentous it found such leaders. . . . Out of three millions, America found a Washington, an Adams, a Franklin, a Jefferson, a Hamilton; out of twenty millions she now finds none whose stature can compare with these. She is strong in multitudes, swarming with brave men, instinct with eager patriotism. But she fails in that which multitudes cannot supply, those master minds, the lack of which the vastest aggregate of mediocrity can never fill. . . . Where are they? Why is mediocrity in our high places, and the race of our statesmen so dwindled? . . . The people have demanded equality, not superiority, and they have had it: men of the people, that is to say, men in no way raised above the ordinary level of humanity. In degrading its high offices, the nation has weakened and degraded itself.

Ironically, these words were written just as the nation was about to discover the greatness of Abraham Lincoln. Yet the fact of Lincoln's ultimate stature does not diminish the cogency of Parkman's analysis. Lincoln was in fact elected as the common man incarnate. The fact that he subsequently displayed the superior qualities of wisdom, rectitude, and courage was accidental. His immediate predecessors in the highest office, Buchanan, Pierce, Fillmore, and Taylor, like his immediate successors, Johnson, Grant, Hayes, and Garfield, testify that the remarkable qualities Lincoln possessed were not requirements for nomination or election.

Today's political system remains dynamic, and it has departed from that of the nineteenth century in a number of important ways. Senators are now elected directly by the voters. Primary elections for state and national offices have partially supplanted party conventions, and candidates appeal to voters directly through radio and television. Yet these developments represent logical extensions of the popular, egalitarian spirit that animated the nineteenth century.

As a result we elect companionable-seeming people who cannot appear aloof, and who are doomed if they seem arrogant or learned. One observer of the 1976 presidential campaign noted that after Jimmy Carter was criticized for the "lack of a self-deprecating humor, for several days he worked humorous remarks about himself into his public appearances." As a candidate, [Richard] Nixon had labored hard in the same vineyard and even took humor lessons from Bob Hope. For if a candidate possesses qualities that would truly set him off as superior, they must be concealed, since they excite fear and jealousy.

Overall we are more comfortable with people not much different from ourselves. Sen. Roman L. Hruska elevated this observation to a statement of principle in defending President Nixon's nomination of G. Harrold Carswell for the Supreme Court in 1970. Hruska said that he would support Carswell "even if he were mediocre," since "there are a lot of mediocre judges and people and lawyers, and they are entitled to a little representation, aren't they?" Hruska's only error lies in supposing that mediocrity is not already well represented in the high councils of the nation.

Hruska's statement is embarrassing because normally we do not like to admit our suspicion of superiority. In the end, however, we regularly elect plausible, supple politicians who have the patience for endless campaigning and who are appealing rather than admirable.

Still, greatness is not absolutely ruled out. At special historical moments a highest common denominator may be discovered and, as with Lincoln and Roosevelt, greatness may luckily emerge. But greatness, of course, is an exceptional phenomenon; even under the best conditions the odds must always be against it. By selecting leaders as we do, we lengthen those odds dramatically. In order to better our chances, a revolution in our system of recruiting and selecting leaders would be required, as well as a revolution in values. We would have to admit that the people, who glimpse candidates only momentarily from a distance, and through the filters of the media, do not have the capacity to judge who is fit for office. We would have to reject the democratic egalitarian ethos under which our political system has been operating for over a century.

I do not advise revolution. The great men who led in founding our republic would offer the same counsel. After all, they made the Revolution for the sake of liberty through law, and they created the Constitution because history had taught them it was dangerous to rely on the individual merit or virtue of rulers. They placed their faith in constitutional government, arranging power so as to rely on laws, not men. They believed that, in the long run, this gave the best hope for freedom. Their greatest fear was not the mediocrity and inadequacy of leaders, it was the apathy, ignorance, and petty selfishness of the people. When public morals became corrupt, they warned, liberty would languish.

Perhaps their warning is relevant for our own time. Our longing for great men and women to lead us out of the wilderness is, in classical republican terms, a sign of lassitude, of the corruption that encourages demagogues and leads to tyranny. Informed by history, we should understand that the circumstances that led to the sparkling era when personal greatness and high public office coincided were unique, and exceptional. To expect greatness in public office, to anticipate a new meritocracy that can solve our problems, is a fantasy. The public interest and the safety of free government are better served by an alert, informed citizenry seeking to promote the common good. Whether that, too, is fantasy, only time will tell.

✕ *F U R T H E R   R E A D I N G*

John R. Alden, *General Charles Lee: Traitor or Patriot* (1951)
————, *George Washington: A Biography* (1984)
Bernard Bailyn, *The Ordeal of Thomas Hutchinson* (1974)
R. David Edmunds, *Tecumseh and the Quest for Indian Leadership* (1984)
James T. Flexner, *Washington: The Indispensable Man* (1974)
Eric Foner, *Tom Paine and Revolutionary America* (1976)
Douglas Southall Freeman, *George Washington: A Biography* (1948–1957)
Robert A. Gross, *The Minutemen and Their World* (1976)
Isabel Thompson Kelsay, *Joseph Brant, 1743–1807: Man of Two Worlds* (1984)
Pauline Maier, *The Old Revolutionaries: Political Lives in the Age of Samuel Adams* (1980)
Merrill D. Peterson, *Thomas Jefferson and the New Nation* (1970)
Charles Royster, *Light-Horse Harry Lee and the Legacy of the American Revolution* (1981)
————, *A Revolutionary People at War: The Continental Army and American Character, 1775–1783* (1979)
Lynne Withey, *Dearest Friend: A Life of Abigail Adams* (1981)